COLLECTED LETTERS OF

Samuel Taylor Coleridge

Oxford University Press, Amen House, London E.C.4

GLASGOW NEW YORK TORONTO MELBOURNE WELLINGTON
BOMBAY CALCUTTA MADRAS KARACHI CAPE TOWN IBADAN

Geoffrey Cumberlege, Publisher to the University

From a portrait of Coleridge painted in 1798 by W. Shuter; formerly in the possession of the late Miss A. A. King, a grand-niece of Thomas Poole

COLLECTED LETTERS OF

Samuel Taylor Coleridge

———

EDITED BY

EARL LESLIE GRIGGS

VOLUME I

1785–1800

OXFORD

AT THE CLARENDON PRESS

1956

PRINTED IN GREAT BRITAIN

To the Right Honourable

LORD LATYMER

who has so graciously placed at my disposal

his magnificent collection of

Coleridge letters

this work is gratefully dedicated

PREFACE

It is a pleasure to acknowledge my indebtedness and gratitude to the many persons who have helped me.

I must first mention Lord Latymer, to whom these volumes are dedicated. My acquaintance with him goes back many years, and he has at all times shown a spirit of friendly and generous co-operation. Three years ago, after I had given up all hope of locating a large number of important Coleridge holographs, quite unexpectedly I received from him a letter describing a collection of Coleridge manuscripts he had recently inherited. To my great surprise, here at last was almost every letter which I had long sought for in vain. In placing his magnificent collection at my disposal Lord Latymer has immeasurably increased the value of my edition of Coleridge's letters. A debt such as mine to him can only be acknowledged; it can never be repaid. To him and to Lady Latymer I am deeply grateful, too, for their gracious and cordial hospitality.

My present undertaking could not have been initiated without the paternal encouragement of the late Rev. G. H. B. Coleridge. He not only gave me access to his large collection of Coleridge papers, but he and the late Mrs. Coleridge were always the most kind and indulgent of friends. I shall always remember them with deep affection. To their children, too, I must express my affection and indebtedness: to Mr. A. H. B. Coleridge for generously making available to me the Coleridge manuscripts formerly belonging to his father, and for giving me his valuable collection of the E. H. Coleridge transcripts of Coleridge's letters and the correspondence between E. H. Coleridge and J. Dykes Campbell; to Mrs. Phyllis Coleridge Hooper for assistance in my search for Coleridge manuscripts; to the Rev. A. D. Coleridge for loaning me the Thomas Ward copy-book; and to the Rev. Nicholas F. D. Coleridge for the use of his copy of the *Biographia Literaria* containing an important letter from Coleridge to his son Derwent.

Other members of the Coleridge family have been equally helpful: Lord and Lady Coleridge, who gave me permission to use the collection of Coleridge manuscripts formerly in the Chanter's House, Ottery St. Mary, and now in the British Museum; Lady Cave, who graciously placed at my disposal Coleridge's early letters in the 'Salston' collection; and Mr. Paul Coleridge, who made available to me the letters in his possession.

I gratefully acknowledge the courtesy of the librarians and the trustees of the following institutions for granting me permission to publish the Coleridge autograph letters in their collections: Bristol Central Library; British Museum; Coleridge Cottage, Nether Stowey; Cornell University Library; Dove Cottage, Wordsworth Museum; Edinburgh University Library; Guildhall Library, London; Harvard College Library; Highgate Literary and Scientific Institution; Historical Society of Pennsylvania; Huntington Library; Jesus College, Cambridge; John Crerar Library; New York Public Library, the Berg Collection; Pierpont Morgan Library; Redpath Library, McGill University; Royal Institution; Royal Literary Fund; Trinity College, Cambridge; Victoria and Albert Museum; Victoria University Library, Toronto; Washington Allston Trust; Wedgwood Museum; Wellesley College Library; and Yale University Library.

I am likewise deeply grateful to the following persons for their courtesy and generosity in permitting me to publish the Coleridge manuscript letters in their possession: Lord Abinger, Professsor Helen M. Cam, Mr. John B. Chubb, Mr. Basil Cottle, Mr. B. Ifor Evans, Provost of University College, London, Mr. F. H. Harrop, Mr. R. N. Carew Hunt, Miss Joanna Hutchinson, Mr. Nathan Ladden of Maurice Inman Ltd., Mr. W. L. Lewis, Mr. G. W. Michelmore, Professor E. L. McAdam, Jr., Mr. W. Hugh Peal, Mr. Carl H. Pforzheimer, Mr. A. G. B. Randle, the late Mr. Merl F. Renz, Mr. James Shields, Colonel H. G. Sotheby, Mr. Walter T. Spencer, Professor C. B. Tinker, Mr. H. B. Vander Poel, and Mr. G. Whitmore.

In making the acknowledgements above I have mentioned only those institutions and individuals possessing Coleridge holograph letters for the years 1785–1806, and have reserved for subsequent volumes the expression of my indebtedness to the owners of the autograph letters belonging to the middle and later years.

Among the many scholars, librarians, booksellers, and friends who have made liberal contributions to my work, I am especially indebted to Miss Helen Darbishire, who transcribed at Dove Cottage Coleridge manuscripts too fragile for photostating and whose wise and friendly advice has been so helpful to me; to Mr. A. P. Rossiter, Fellow and Tutor of Jesus College, Cambridge, who has brought his scholarship to bear on a number of important questions; to Mr. T. C. Skeat of the British Museum, who has so patiently responded to every query presented to him; to Mr. Robert L. Collison and Mr. P. S. B. Rossiter of the Westminster Public Library, who have solved many bibliographical problems for me; to Dr. Louis B. Wright, Director of the Folger Shakespeare Library and formerly at the Huntington, to whom, in common with scholars all over the world, I owe so much encouragement and practical assistance; to Dr. John D. Gordan, Curator of the Berg Collection, New York Public Library, to Mr. William A. Jackson, Librarian of the Houghton Library, Harvard, and to Mr. Richard Pennington, Librarian of the Redpath Library, McGill University, who have taken a personal interest in my work and rendered me many services; to Miss Kathleen Coburn of Victoria College, who has verified for me certain information in the Coleridge notebooks; to Professor Richard I. Aaron of the University College of Wales, who gave me the benefit of his profound knowledge of Locke; and to Professor Herbert B. Hoffleit of the University of California, who has brought his learning to bear on the Greek and Latin passages in Coleridge's letters.

I must mention, too, the generous assistance of my former associates at the University of Pennsylvania, especially Professors A. C. Baugh, Frederick L. Jones, and George W. McClelland; my colleagues at the University of California, particularly Professors Frederick M. Carey, Carl W. Hagge, and William Matthews, and Dr. Lawrence C. Powell and Mr. Wilbur J. Smith of the University Library; Mr. Philip Long of the Bodeian Library; Mr. W. S. Haugh, Librarian, Bristol Central Library; Mrs. Carma R. Zimmerman of the California State Library; Mr. G. F. Shepherd, Jr., Professor George Harris Healey, and Miss Georgia R. Coffin of the Cornell University Library; Mr. N. S. E. Pugsley, Librarian, Exeter City Library; Mr. W. H. Bond, Mr. Leslie M. Oliver, and Miss Helen Ritchie of the Harvard College Library; Mr. and Mrs. Carey Bliss and Miss Norma Cuthbert of the Huntington Library; Mr. Stephen T. Riley, Librarian, Massachusetts Historical Society; Mr. George K. Boyce, Curator of Manuscripts, Pierpont Morgan Library; Mr. Arthur Wheen, Keeper, Victoria and Albert Museum; Mr. Francis L. Berkeley, Curator of Manuscripts, University of Virginia Library; Mr. E. J. Rudsdale, Curator, Wisbech Museum; Mr. James T. Babb, Librarian, and Miss Marjorie G. Wynne of the Yale University Library; and Mr. T. Lyth, Curator, Wedgwood Museum.

Others I must gratefully acknowledge here: Mr R. E. Abbott, Professor R. C. Bald, Mr. Gordon T. Banks, the late Mr. Oliver R. Barrett, Mr. Morchard Bishop, Mr. R. K. Black, Mr. Basil Blackwell, Mr. Charles S. Boesen, Professor Albert S. Borgman, Mr. Arnold Broadbent, Mr. John Grey Broadbent, Mr. Laidman Browne, Professor John Butt, Professor Francis Christensen, Lady Crewe, Mr. John Crow, Professor Kenneth Curry, Professor Earl Daniels, Mr. Bertram Davis, Professor Bruce Dickins, Miss Emily Driscoll, Mr. Arundell Esdaile, Mr. Payson G. Gates, Dr. J. L. Haney, Mr. David S. Hills, Mr. Henry Hofheimer, Mr. Robert G. Hopkins, Mr. Humphry House, Mr. G. N. S. Hunt, Professor Alfred L. Kellogg,

Mr. Raphael King, the late Mr. William King, Mr. David Kirschen-baum, Dr. Milton Kronovet, Professor John R. Moore, Professor Edith J. Morley, Mr. Percy Muir, Sir John Murray, Miss Winifred A. Myers, Mr. and Mrs. Edmund Nicholls, Professor W. A. Osborne, Mr. Michael Papantonio, Colonel G. A. E. Peyton, O.B.E., Commander of the King's Royal Hussars, Mr. Robert H. Pilling, Captain Frank L. Pleadwell, Mrs. E. F. Rawnsley, the Rev. Dr. M. J. Roberts, Miss Janetta G. Scurfield, Professor Cecil C. Seronsy, Mr. Charles A. Stonehill, Mr. Arthur Swann, Mr. John C. C. Taylor, Mr. Donald C. Thompson, Mr. W. T. Trimble, Mr. Justin G. Turner, Mr. D. H. Varley, Miss Vera Watson, Mr. Ralph L. Wedgwood, Professor Virgil K. Whitaker, Mr. Antony Whitehouse, and Mr. Frederick T. Wood.

To the late Sir E. K. Chambers, the late Prof. R. D. Havens, and the late Prof. Newman I. White, I am much indebted for invaluable assistance.

It is a pleasure to acknowledge the faithful and painstaking work of my research assistant, Miss Harriet Carey.

I am most grateful to the Trustees of the University of Pennsylvania for financial assistance in assembling photostats and microfilms; to the Trustees of the Huntington Library for a Fellowship during the year 1945–6; to the American Philosophical Society for two grants for travel and research in England; and to the Regents of the University of California for liberal research funds. Without such support, my present undertaking could not have been carried forward.

Most of all I am indebted to my wife, my co-worker throughout this long task.

E. L. G.

University of California
Los Angeles

CONTENTS

ILLUSTRATIONS

LIST OF LETTERS

LETTER	DATE	RECIPIENT	PAGE
		1804 *(cont.)*	
559	17 February	Robert Southey	1066
560	18 February	John Rickman	1067
561	19 February	Mrs. S. T. Coleridge	1068
562	20 February	Robert Southey	1071
563	28 February	John Rickman	1074
564	5 March	Lady Beaumont	1075
565	6 March	Humphry Davy	1077
566	8 March	Sir George Beaumont	1078
567	10 March	Sara Hutchinson	1080
568	12 March	Robert Southey	1083
569	13 March	William Sotheby	1086
570	13 March	John Rickman	1087
571	13 March	George Bellas Greenough	1089
572	14 March	John Rickman	1090
573	15 March	George Dyer	1091
574	17 March	William Sotheby	1093
575	17 March	John Rickman	1094
576	18 March	John Rickman	1096
577	20 March	Robert Southey	1097
578	23 March	J. G. Ridout	1098
579	24 March	William Sotheby	1099
580	24 March	Thomas Wedgwood	1100
581	25 March	Humphry Davy	1101
581a	26 March	Lady Beaumont	1104
582	26 March	John Rickman	1104
583	26 March	William Sotheby	1106
584	27 March	Sir George and Lady Beaumont	1106
585	27 March	George Bellas Greenough	1107
586	27 March	Richard Sharp	1108
587	27 March	Thomas Poole	1108
588	27 March	Mrs. S. T. Coleridge	1109
589	28 March	Robert Southey	1110
590	29 March	Daniel Stuart	1112
591	1 April	Mrs. S. T. Coleridge	1114
592	4 April	The Wordsworths	1115
593	5 April	Daniel Stuart	1119
594	6 April	John Rickman	1120
595	6 April	Sir George Beaumont	1121
596	7 April	Robert Southey	1123
597	16 April	Robert Southey	1125
598	19 April	James Webbe Tobin	1130
599	21 April	Daniel Stuart	1131
600	5 June	Mrs. S. T. Coleridge	1135
601	5 July	William Sotheby	1140
602	5 July	Mrs. S. T. Coleridge	1142
603	6 July	Robert Southey	1144

ABBREVIATIONS AND PRINCIPAL REFERENCES

Abbreviations

Biog. Lit.	Coleridge, S. T.: *Biographia Literaria*, . . . 2 vols., 1817; ed. by H. N. Coleridge, 2 vols., 1847; ed. by J. Shawcross, 2 vols., 1907. (When necessary the edition is indicated.)
Campbell, *Life*	Campbell, J. D.: *Samuel Taylor Coleridge, a Narrative of the Events of His Life*, 1894
Campbell, *Poetical Works*	Campbell, J. D., ed.: *The Poetical Works of Samuel Taylor Coleridge*, 1893
Chambers, *Life*	Chambers, E. K.: *Samuel Taylor Coleridge: A Biographical Study*, 1938
Charles Lamb and the Lloyds	Lucas, E. V.: *Charles Lamb and the Lloyds*, 1898
Coleridge	Blunden, E., and Griggs, E. L., editors: *Coleridge: Studies by Several Hands* . . ., 1934
E. L. G.	Griggs, E. L., ed.: *Unpublished Letters of Samuel Taylor Coleridge*, . . . 2 vols., 1932
Early Letters	De Selincourt, E., ed.: *The Early Letters of William and Dorothy Wordsworth (1787–1805)*, 1935
Early Rec.	Cottle, Joseph: *Early Recollections; chiefly relating to the late Samuel Taylor Coleridge*, . . . 2 vols., 1837
Essays on His Own Times	Coleridge, Sara, ed.: *Essays on His Own Times*, . . . *By S. T. Coleridge*, 3 vols., 1850
Frag. Remains	Davy, John: *Fragmentary Remains, Literary and Scientific, of Sir Humphry Davy*, . . . 1858
John Rickman	Williams, Orlo: *Life and Letters of John Rickman*, 1912
Journals	De Selincourt, E., ed.: *Journals of Dorothy Wordsworth*, 2 vols., 1952
Lamb Letters	Lucas, E. V., ed.: *The Letters of Charles Lamb, to which are added those of his sister, Mary Lamb*, 3 vols., 1935
Later Years	De Selincourt, E., ed.: *The Letters of William and Dorothy Wordsworth: the Later Years*, 3 vols., 1939
Letters	Coleridge, E. H., ed.: *Letters of Samuel Taylor Coleridge*, 2 vols., 1895
Letters from the Lake Poets	[Coleridge, E. H., ed.] *Letters from the Lake Poets* . . . *to Daniel Stuart*, 1889
Letters to Estlin	Bright, H. A., ed.: *Unpublished Letters from Samuel Taylor Coleridge to the Rev. John Prior Estlin* (Philobiblon Society, *Miscellanies*, xv, 1877–84)
Life and Corres.	Southey, C. C., ed.: *The Life and Correspondence of the late Robert Southey*, 6 vols., 1849–50

Abbreviations and Principal References

Abbreviations

Memoir of William Taylor	Robberds, J. W., ed.: *A Memoir of the Life and Writings of the late William Taylor of Norwich,*. . . 2 vols., 1843
Memoirs of Wordsworth	Wordsworth, Christopher: *Memoirs of William Wordsworth*, 2 vols., 1851
Memorials of Coleorton	Knight, Wm., ed.: *Memorials of Coleorton, being Letters . . . to Sir George and Lady Beaumont,* . . . 2 vols., 1887
Middle Years	De Selincourt, E., ed.: *The Letters of William and Dorothy Wordsworth: the Middle Years*, 2 vols., 1937
Poems	Coleridge, E. H., ed.: *The Complete Poetical Works of Samuel Taylor Coleridge,* . . . 2 vols., 1912
Rem.	Cottle, Joseph: *Reminiscences of Samuel Taylor Coleridge and Robert Southey*, 1847
Southey Letters	Warter, J. W., ed.: *Selections from the Letters of Robert Southey*, 4 vols., 1856
Southey's Poet. Works	*The Poetical Works of Robert Southey*, 10 vols., 1838. (The engraved title-pages of vols. i–iii are dated 1837.)
Thomas Poole	Sandford, Mrs. Henry: *Thomas Poole and His Friends*, 2 vols., 1888
Tom Wedgwood	Litchfield, R. B.: *Tom Wedgwood the First Photographer,* . . . 1903
William Godwin	Paul, C. Kegan: *William Godwin: His Friends and Contemporaries*, 2 vols., 1876
Wise, *Bibliography*	Wise, T. J., *A Bibliography of.* . . *Samuel Taylor Coleridge*, 1913
Wordsworth	Dunklin, G. T., ed.: *Wordsworth: Centenary Studies,* . . . 1951
Wordsworth and Coleridge	Griggs, E. L., ed.: *Wordsworth and Coleridge: Studies in Honor of George McLean Harper*, 1939
Wordsworth, *Poet. Works*	De Selincourt, E., and Darbishire, Helen, editors: *The Poetical Works of William Wordsworth*, 5 vols., 1940–9

INTRODUCTION

I

THE living Coleridge fascinated his contemporaries, and almost without exception they paid tribute to his genius. Wordsworth called him 'the most *wonderful* man that he had ever known'; Southey spoke of his mind as 'infinitely and ten thousand-thousand-fold the mightiest of his generation'; and Hazlitt wrote that 'hardly a speculation has been left on record from the earliest time, but it is loosely folded up in Mr. Coleridge's memory, like a rich, but somewhat tattered piece of tapestry'. He was a fount of inspiration to his friends and communicated far more than his literary productions represent; for his published works, seminal and stimulating as they are, but fragmentarily reveal his unrivalled capacities. Ever a prey to the multitudinous ideas which crowded in upon him, he could conceive where he could not execute, and it is to his letters, which opened the flood-gates of his mind, that we must turn to form an estimate of the comprehensiveness of his intellectual activity and the magnificence as well as the weakness of his character.

Read in consecutive order, the letters tell the story of his life. Every mood, every thought, everything he ever did, perhaps, is mirrored in the letters, and they bring us as close to a realization of what he actually was as we shall ever come. Here is revealed, in the words of Henry James, Coleridge's 'rare, anomalous, magnificent, interesting, curious, tremendously suggestive character, vices and all, with all its imperfections on its head'. Coleridge, indeed, draws his own self-portrait. The incomparable autobiographical letters, for example, not only supply the best information concerning his earliest years but also present an unforgettable character sketch.

An insatiable intellectual curiosity, a restless and inquiring mind, led Coleridge to range over almost the whole of man's knowledge, and his letters reflect his preoccupation with a wide variety of subjects—poetry, philosophy, science, politics, criticism, theology. His 'Idea-pot' bubbled over with literary plans, and scattered through the letters are the titles and grandiose schemes for books, essays, poems, and dramas, conceived and promised, but never executed. He recognized the weakness of 'wavering' about many works. 'That is the disease of my mind,' he wrote to Poole; 'it is comprehensive in it's conceptions & wastes itself in the contemplations of the many things which it might do.' So vast were many of the ambitious projects he outlined and so determined was he to track everything to its source, that accomplishment lay beyond him. 'I should not think of devoting less than 20 years to an Epic Poem,' he wrote to Cottle; 'ten to collect materials and warm my mind with universal science. I would be a tolerable Mathematician, I would thoroughly know Mechanics, Hydrostatics, Optics, and Astronomy, Botany, Metallurgy, Fossilism, Chemistry, Geology, Anatomy, Medicine—then the *mind of man*—then the *minds of men*—in all Travels, Voyages and Histories. So I would spend ten years—the next five to the composition of the poem—and the five last to the correction of it.'

As the letters trace his intellectual development, so they portray his gregarious nature. Craving human sympathy, Coleridge made friends in every walk of life, and under the stimulus of friendship his letters often take on a buoyant tone, his 'Heart at a full Gallop adown Hill'. Letter-writing to him was a means of disburdening himself. 'My whole heart shall be laid open like any sheep's heart,' he wrote to Mrs. Evans; 'my Virtues, if I have any, shall not be more exposed to your view than my weaknesses.' Sometimes we seem to be overhearing a confessional, so intimate are the outpourings of conscience. 'I have in this one dirty business of Laudanum an hundred times deceived, tricked, nay, actually & consciously LIED.' Always we are in the company of a man disarmingly frank in the way he speaks of his hopes and aspirations, his health and personal afflictions. Conscious of his own failings and gifted with brilliant psychological insight, Coleridge, the 'subtle-souled psychologist', was ever ready with explanations, apologies, and regrets, and he never hesitated to share his introspective questings with others. As a result, his letters are overflowing with impassioned self-analysis.

The letters are as many-sided as Coleridge himself—a veritable potpourri of personal, literary, and philosophical ingredients. 'Anything', Virginia Woolf once remarked, 'may tumble out of that great maw; the subtlest criticism, the wildest jest, the exact condition of his intestines.' At times Coleridge is a suffering and tormented man caught in a quagmire of debts, domestic woes, and ill health, and his letters, filled with frustration and despair, become wearisome outpourings of excuses, resolves, self-condemnation, and morbid introspection; at other times, as 'undisturbed as a Toad in a Rock', he can write of the abstruse subjects so dear to his heart. The poetic or the reflective Coleridge is never far to seek; even when he is most vexatious in practical affairs, he yet retains his greatness in contemplative studies. Nothing escapes his attention, and the lofty and the mundane jostle each other for ascendancy. Surely, no letter writer ever served up a stranger mixture of earth and heaven, of grim desperation and hilarious good humour.

Although the letters may at times contain too much of ill health, too much of life's petty detail, too much of remorse and self-justification, Coleridge was capable of redeeming the most tedious matter with flashes of singular beauty or profound insight. Among the most important of these are the critical comments, often brilliant and suggestive, sprinkled here and there throughout the letters. The observation may be only a phrase—'the divine Chit chat of Cowper'; it may be a pithy sentence—'I *think* too much for a *Poet*; [Southey] too little for a *great* Poet'; it may be an explanation of the allegorical significance of the word 'Haemony' as used in *Comus*; or it may be a letter entirely devoted to literary criticism, as the remarkable appreciation of Sir Thomas Browne written for Sara Hutchinson in 1804. No one, perhaps, has ever dealt with the *Hydriotaphia* and *The Garden of Cyrus* with greater sympathetic insight; indeed, the letter reveals as much of Coleridge as of the 'whimsical Knight' of Norwich. There are a number of discerning criticisms of Wordsworth, for from the beginning of their association Coleridge recognized the genius of his friend. It is significant to note, however, that he soon came to suspect a '*radical* Difference' between his own opinions concerning poetry and those of Wordsworth. Twice during the summer of 1802 he expressed disagreement with parts of the Preface, and he found himself disturbed by 'a daring Humbleness of Language & Versification, and a strict adherence to matter of fact, even to prolixity', in certain of Wordsworth's poems, thereby anticipating the superb criticism of the *Biographia Literaria*. The famous distinction between imagination and fancy is likewise foreshadowed. In 1802, in illustrating the superiority of Hebrew to Greek poetry, he speaks of the 'Fancy, or the aggregating Faculty of the mind', as opposed to the '*Imagination*, or the *modifying*, and *co-adunating* Faculty'; and in 1804, in an appreciation of Wordsworth, he employs almost the same phrases. The letters, therefore, not only include many examples of excellent literary criticism but afford evidence of Coleridge's early maturity and development as a critic.

While Coleridge could write pointedly, even epigrammatically, often he is profuse and his style undisciplined. 'An idea starts up in my head,' he explained to Godwin; 'away I follow it thro' thick & thin, Wood & Marsh, Brake and Briar.' On another occasion he protested to Southey: 'My mind is so full, that my thoughts stifle & jam each other / & I have presented them as shapeless Jellies.' His defence of his use of parentheses is, indeed, a further com-

mentary on his habits of mind: 'Of Parentheses I may be too fond
—and will be on my guard in this respect—. But I am certain
that no work of empassioned and eloquent reasoning ever did or
could subsist without them—They are the *drama* of Reason—
and present the thought growing, instead of a mere Hortus siccus.'
At his best, nevertheless, Coleridge touched his letters with
magical expression. Consider the memorable description of
Hazlitt: 'brow-hanging, shoe-contemplative, *strange*/. . . He sends
well-headed & well-feathered Thoughts straight forwards to the
mark with a Twang of the Bow-string.' Or note the comment on
Dorothy Wordsworth: 'her eye watchful in minutest observation
of nature—and her taste a perfect electrometer—it bends, pro-
trudes, and draws in, at subtlest beauties & most recondite faults.'
Or turn to the tender descriptions of his infant Sara, who 'smiles,
as if she were basking in a sunshine, as mild as moonlight, of her
own quiet Happiness'; and of his son Hartley, 'a Spirit dancing
on an aspen Leaf'. Alive with poetic imagery and sparkling phrase,
yet frequently burdened with laborious detail and pedantic ex-
pression, Coleridge's style alternately soars and droops. Virginia
Woolf in her inimitable way sums it up most effectively: 'The great
sentences pocketed with parentheses, expanded with dash after
dash, break their walls under the strain of including and qualifying
and suggesting all that Coleridge feels, fears and glimpses. Often
he is prolix to the verge of incoherence, and his meaning dwindles
and fades to a wisp on the mind's horizon. Yet in our tongue-tied
age there is a joy in this reckless abandonment to the glory of
words. Cajoled, caressed, tossed up in handfuls, words yield those
flashing phrases that hang like ripe fruit in the many-leaved tree
of his immense volubility.'

Although Coleridge has left some remarkable and beautiful letters,
he is not among the best of English letter-writers. His critical
acumen and psychological insight, however, as well as the brilliance
of individual passages, give an unusual quality to the letters. They
present an invaluable record of Coleridge's mind and heart and an
extraordinary portrait of a wayward but consummate genius—the
greatest thinker of his age.

II

This edition, numbering nearly 1,800 letters and drawn mainly
from original manuscripts, is the first attempt to bring together in
a single work all the known letters of Samuel Taylor Coleridge.
The present volumes contain the correspondence from 1785 to the
end of the year 1806—641 letters (Letters 499*a* and 581*a* and a

fragment of a letter printed in a note on page 208 having been
added while this work was in the press). The text of 83 per cent.
of the letters in these two volumes is drawn from holographs,
6 per cent. from transcripts, and 11 per cent. from printed sources.
Subsequent volumes will contain the letters written during the
years 1807–34. This work has been long overdue. My delay must
be attributed in part to the War, in part to the difficulty of tracing
the numerous holographs dispersed in 150 collections in England,
Scotland, Switzerland, France, Australia, New Zealand, Canada,
Hawaii, and the United States. It is through the co-operation of
many persons, therefore, that so large a percentage of Coleridge's
letters can now be printed from the original manuscripts.

During his lifetime Coleridge himself printed a handful of his
letters, and soon after his death in 1834, Thomas Allsop (*Letters,
Conversations and Recollections of S. T. Coleridge*, 1836) and
Joseph Cottle (*Early Recollections*, 1837, and *Reminiscences*, 1847)
each published, in part and with omissions, the correspondence
mainly addressed to himself. Later Mrs. Henry Sandford published,
often fragmentarily, a number of Coleridge's letters to Thomas
Poole (*Thomas Poole and His Friends*, 1888), and the letters to
Daniel Stuart were published with omissions in the privately
printed *Letters from the Lake Poets*, 1889. During the nineteenth
century and on down to the present day, a long succession of
miscellaneous publications—memoirs, biographies, magazines, and
newspapers—have continued to print small groups of Coleridge's
letters. The first representative collection did not appear, however,
until 1895, when E. H. Coleridge published the *Letters of Samuel
Taylor Coleridge*, an edition containing 260 letters of his grandfather.
Many of these were printed with omissions. Arthur Turnbull's
Biographia Epistolaris, 1911, need be mentioned only in passing,
since it is far from complete and merely reprints 219 letters drawn
from earlier publications. In 1932 I printed 400 letters as a supplement
to the work of E. H. Coleridge. In my edition the text of a
large number of the letters was drawn from transcripts made by
E. H. Coleridge rather than from the originals. At that time the
holographs were believed by the late Rev. G. H. B. Coleridge to
have been lost through the theft of a box of manuscripts and
papers belonging to E. H. Coleridge. My recent discovery of most
of these originals, however, would make it appear that few, if any,
manuscript letters were among the stolen papers. A third of
Coleridge's correspondence still remains unpublished; and in addition,
since the holographs of most of the published letters have
come to light, it is now possible to restore to the text the numerous
passages omitted by previous editors.

No edition of the letters can hope to be definitive and it is likely that certain holographs have eluded my prolonged search. The letters which have been preserved, moreover, do not represent the whole of Coleridge's voluminous correspondence. Only a few of the letters to Lamb have survived; and according to her grand-daughter, Mrs. Wordsworth burned all but a few of the letters to Sara Hutchinson. Most of the letters to the Wordsworth family, including many of those used by Christopher Wordsworth and William Knight in their studies of Wordsworth, have disappeared. Surviving fragments and letters with passages inked out or cut away make it certain, too, that Mrs. Coleridge and other members of the family, shocked by the publication of the intimate correspondence with Allsop and Cottle, went carefully through the Coleridge letters in their possesssion and destroyed a number of them.

The Text. Every effort has been made to reproduce the manuscripts exactly as they were written. To this practice there are some slight exceptions, but Coleridge's capricious use of capital letters, unorthodox spellings, abbreviations, except for the expansion of 'wch', and punctuation, save in rare instances in which the sense demanded alteration, have been retained; and on the assumption that such characteristic misspellings as 'Edingburgh', 'Condilliac', and 'knowlege', as well as other idiosyncrasies in the text, will be recognized as Coleridge's own, *sic* has been sparingly employed. Obviously slips of the pen, such as the repetition of a word, however, have been silently corrected; Greek accents, which Coleridge usually omitted, have been added; and cancelled words in the manuscripts have been ignored, unless, as in a few cases, they supply pertinent information. Although the elevation of the final letter or letters in such words as 'Mr', 'Esqre', and 20th' is characteristic of Coleridge, all superior letters have been uniformly lowered. Words singly underscored in the manuscript have been printed in italics, those doubly underscored in small capitals, and those underscored three or more times in large capitals.

Coleridge had very definite ideas about the use of capital letters: 'I greatly approve of the German Rule of distinguishing all Noun-Substantives by a Capital.' In his epistolary practice, however, he deviated from this 'Rule' and sprinkled capitals at random. It is sometimes difficult to determine whether an initial capital letter was intended, and the decision becomes a matter of individual judgement likely to change with successive examinations of the manuscript.

Square brackets enclose the following items: (*a*) conjectural or corrected dates; (*b*) decipherable words inked out in the holographs; (*c*) words supplied to complete the sense, but through mere oversight omitted from the manuscript; (*d*) any additions to the text rendered necessary by defects in the holographs, such as holes, tears, frayed edges, and faded ink; and (*e*) doubtful readings of the manuscript; these are followed by a question mark within the brackets.

Three dots (. . .) placed at the beginning or the end of a letter indicate its fragmentary nature; if used within the text itself, they point to a lacuna in the manuscript.

For the sake of uniformity, the following editorial policy has been adopted: (*a*) the *date* and the *place*, if given, are printed at the beginning of the letter; (*b*) the *conclusion*, which Coleridge often 'displayed' over several lines, is telescoped for economy of space, such telescoping being indicated by vertical lines; (*c*) any *postscript* written at the top or along the side of a manuscript is moved to its normal position after the signature.

The *headnotes* indicate: (*a*) the *address*, if it appears in the holograph; (*b*) the source of the text—whether from a manuscript, transcript, or printed text; (*c*) the ownership of the manuscript; (*d*) whether the letter is unpublished; (*e*) the previous publication and omissions, if any (the bibliographical reference is limited either to the first or to the most significant publication, since nothing would be gained by listing all previous printings of each letter); and (*f*) the *postmark* and *place stamp*, if given.

The *footnotes* are mainly biographical or bibliographical, but include justification of conjectural dates, comment on the text, and cross references. Likewise, since Coleridge quotes a number of his own poems in the letters, variant readings are preserved in the footnotes.

1. *To his Mother*

Pub. Letters, *i. 21.* This letter, the earliest of Coleridge's letters of which there is any record, was written from Christ's Hospital, which Coleridge attended 1782 to 1791. It is the only surviving letter to his mother.

February 4, 1785 [London, Christ's Hospital]

Dear Mother,—I received your letter with pleasure on the second instant, and should have had it sooner, but that we had not a holiday before last Tuesday, when my brother delivered it me. I also with gratitude received the two handkerchiefs and the half-a-crown from Mr. Badcock, to whom I would be glad if you would give my thanks. I shall be more careful of the somme, as I now consider that were it not for my kind friends I should be as destitute of many little necessaries as some of my schoolfellows are; and Thank God and my relations for them! My brother Luke[1] saw Mr. James Sorrel, who gave my brother a half-a-crown from Mrs. Smerdon, but mentioned not a word of the plumb cake, and said he would call again. Return my most respectful thanks to Mrs. Smerdon for her kind favour. My aunt was so kind as to accommodate me with a box. I suppose my sister Anna's[2] beauty has many admirers. My brother Luke says that Burke's Art of Speaking[3] would be of great use to me. If Master Sam and Harry Badcock are not gone out of (Ottery), give my kindest love to them. Give my compliments to Mr. Blake and Miss Atkinson, Mr. and Mrs. Smerdon,[4] Mr. and Mrs. Clapp, and all other friends in the country. My uncle, aunt, and cousins join with myself and Brother in love to my sisters, and hope they are well, as I, your dutiful son,

S. Coleridge, am at present.

P.S. Give my kind love to Molly.

2. *To Luke Coleridge*

MS. the Rev. A. D. Coleridge. *Pub. with omis.* Ill. London News, *1 April 1893, p. 397.* While this letter is not addressed, internal evidence indicates that it was written to Luke and delivered by George.

Dear Brother   [12 May 1787]

To begin a letter I esteem the hardest part: therefore pardon me if I use the hackneyed strain of, 'I take the opportunity of my

---

[1] Luke Herman Coleridge, 1765–90.   [2] Ann Coleridge, 1767–91.
[3] Coleridge probably refers to James Burgh, *The Art of Speaking*, 1761.
[4] The Rev. Fulwood Smerdon became Vicar of Ottery St. Mary on the death of Coleridge's father, the Rev. John Coleridge, on 4 Oct. 1781.

brother's departure from town &c. &c.['] I pray you pardon my
not writing before. Five times have I set down with a fix'd resolu-
tion to write you; and five times have I torn it before I have writ
Half of it. Nothing in it pleased me. All was STUFF, as Mr Boyer[1]
phrases it. But now can I write with much better will, if only to
rejoice with you at your success.[2] I am apt to think, that for you
Fortune will take of[f] her bandage, and reward merit for once.
But I have forgot. My Aunt desired me in the beginning of this
epistle to assure you 'of her kindest love to you: she never felt so
much pleasure in her life, as at your success.['] Old Bishop is some-
what better than an Atheist. He seldom fails of exerting his
oratorical . . . [homiletical?] abilities on the subject of our Saviour;
the immortality of the soul. His arguments are very strong. As,
Any wise man may see, *as how* it cant be so. Heaven would not be
large enough to hold all the souls of all men, who have ever liv'd.
It is remarkable how zealous all these infidels are to persuade you
to embrace their fantastical doctrines. Addison finely says: 'They
play for nothing:[3] if they win, they win nothing; but if they
lose ——. *We* are safe on both sides.['] Well: but to return (a good
way to apologize for a digression) I shall acquaint you, how my
affairs stand in our little world. Legrice,[4] and I, are very polite,
very civil, and very cold. So that I doubly lament your absence,
as I have now no one, to whom I can open my heart in full con-
fidence. I wish you would *remedy* that evil by keeping up an
epistolary correspondence with me. It would in some measure
supply the place of conversation. I suppose, I shall be Graecian
in about a year. Mr Boyer says, that if I take particular care of my
exercises etc. I may find myself rewarded sooner than I expected.
I know not exactly what he means; but I believe, it is something
concerning putting me in the first form. I have sent you a couple
of my English Verses, which my Brother thinks pretty good. I
should of all things wish to see you, before I am Graecian. Alia alio.
You wished to make me a present of Burke's art of Speaking. I am

[1] The Rev. James Boyer was the Master of the Upper Grammar School at
Christ's Hospital. For Coleridge's well-known tribute to him see *Biographia
Literaria*, ch. i.

[2] The records in the London Hospital show that Luke Coleridge was
admitted there on 5 Oct. 1784, and continued his studies for twelve months.
His 'success' may have been the initiation of his medical practice at Thorver-
ton, near Exeter.

[3] Cf. *Spectator*, No. 185: 'They are a sort of Gamesters who are eternally
upon the Fret, though they play for nothing.'

[4] Charles Valentine Le Grice (1773–1858), a fellow student of Coleridge's
at Christ's Hospital. He became a sizar of Trinity College, Cambridge, in June
1792, and took his degree in 1796.

much obliged to you, but do not want it. One of the boys lent it
me the other day. He is often injudicious in his directions on
laying the emphasis; and as for action, if you were to follow his
rules, your hands and arms would be comfortably tired, before you
got to the end of a speech. If you could send me a Young's night
thoughts, I should be much obliged to you. Miss Cabrier[1] and my
Cousin Bowdon behave more kindly to me, than I can express.
I dine there every Saturday. But above all, I can never sufficiently
express my gratitude to my Brother George.[2] *He* is father, brother,
and every thing to me. If you see Mr Blake, present my compli-
ments to him. Ought I to write him a letter?

Here I shall make an end of this epistle by assuring you

That I shall ever remain | Your unalterable friend, and |
Affectionate Brother,

S. T. Coleridge

P.S. In your next, tell me how to direct to you.

Easter Holidays[3]

Verse 1st

Hail! festal Easter, that dost bring
Approach of sweetly smiling spring,
    When Nature's clad in green:
When feather'd songsters through the grove
With beasts confess the power of love,
    And brighten all the scene.

Verse 2d

Now Youths the breaking stages load,
That swiftly rattling o'er the road
    To Greenwich haste away;
While some with sounding oars divide
Of smoothly flowing Thames the tide;
    All sing the festive lay.

---

[1] Miss Cabriere, 'an old Maid of great sensibilities & a taste for Literature',
with whom Betsy Bowdon lived.

[2] George Coleridge (1764–1828) took his degree at Pembroke College, Ox-
ford, in 1784 and soon afterwards became a master in Newcome's Academy,
Hackney. In 1794 he was appointed Schoolmaster and Chaplain Priest at
Ottery St. Mary.

[3] *Poems*, i. 1.

Verse 3d

With mirthful dance they beat the ground,
Their shouts of joy the hills resound
   And catch the jocund noise;
Without a tear, without a sigh,
Their moments all in transport fly
   Till evening ends their joys.

Verse 4th

But little think their joyous hearts
Of dire Misfortune's varied smarts,
   Which youthful years conceal;
Thoughtless of bitter smiling woe,
Which all mankind are born to know,
   And they themselves must feel.

Verse 5th

Yet he, who wisdom's paths shall keep,
And virtue firm, that scorns to weep
   At ills in fortune's power;
Through this life's variegated scene,
In raging storms—or calms serene,
   Shall chearful spend the hour.

Verse 6th

While steady virtue guides his mind,
Heav'n born content he still shall find,
   That never sheds a tear;
Without respect to any tide,
His hours away in bliss shall glide,
   Like Easter all the year.

Nil pejus est caelibe vitâ[1]

Verse 1st

What pleasures shall he ever find?
What joys shall ever glad his heart?
Or who shall heal his wounded mind,
If tortur'd by misfortune's smart?
Who Hymaeneal bliss will never prove,
That more than friendship, friendship mix'd with love.

[1] *Poems*, i. 4.

(4)

Verse 2d

Then without child or tender wife
To soothe each care, each woeborn sigh
[Lonel]y he treads the paths of life
A stranger to Affection's tye;
And when from death he meets his final doom,
No mourning wife with tears of love shall wet his tomb.

Verse 3d

Tho' Fortune, riches, honours, pow'r
Had giv'n, with every other toy;
Those gilded trifles of the hour,
Those painted nothings sure to cloy:
He dies forgot, his name no son shall bear,
To shew, the man so blest once breath'd the vital air.

May 12th 1787

3. *To George Coleridge*

Address: Revd G. Coleridge | Mr Neweome's | Hackney.
MS. Lady Cave. Pub. Letters, *i. 22.*
Stamped: Tuesday.

[Christ's Hospital, 26 May 1789][1]

Dear Brother

You will excuse me for reminding you that, as our Holidays commence next week, and I shall go out a good deal, a good pair of breeches will be no inconsiderable accession to my appearance. For though my present pair are excellent for the purposes of drawing Mathematical Figures on them—and though a walking thought, Sonnet or Epigram would appear on them in very *splendid* type—yet they are not altogether so well adapted for a female eye. Not to mention that I should have the charge of Vanity brought against me for wearing a Looking Glass. I hope, you have got rid of your Cold—and

am Your affection: Brother
Samuel Taylor Coleridge

P.S. Can you let me have them time enough for readaptation before Whitmond[a]y? I mean, that they may be made up for me before that time?

[1] References in this letter, which bears a Tuesday stamp, indicate that it was probably written on the Tuesday preceding Whit Sunday. Since Coleridge first became acquainted with the Evans sisters in his sixteenth year, through their brother Tom, who entered Christ's Hospital on 7 May 1784, this letter probably belongs to the year 1789.

4. *To George Coleridge*

Address: Revd G. Coleridge | Mr Newcome's | Hackney
MS. Lady Cave. Hitherto unpublished.
Stamped: Thursday.

[February–March 1791]

Dear Brother

I have inclosed the Ποιημάτιον,[1] which I should have sent before, had not business prevented—I have inclosed with it a Latin Ode upon the occasion of Trollope's Honour[2]—of which I want your opinion.

Your's
S T Coleridge

Honos alit artes.

Cernis, volucris, quae regit alites,
Inane vastum scandit ut altior,
    Scanditque fixis viva Solis
        Lumina suspiciens ocellis?

Sic, sic, honoris munera splendida,
Victoriae et qui suspiciet decus,
    Sub pectus illi Musa fervet,
        Spes fovet, et Timor urget anceps.

Propono nobis vos imitabiles,
Quos tollit Isis, Camus et aemulus,
    Ornatque Musarum Triumphus,
        Vos, quibus *hae* patuere sedes!

Fraterno ovantûm pectora gaudio
Trollope, nostrûm fervida palpitant!
    Nobismet olim, Spes susurrat,
        Par decus alma dies ministret.

---

[1] No such 'little poem' has come to light.

[2] A. W. Trollope (1768–1827) went from Christ's Hospital to Pembroke College, Cambridge, in 1787, and the College Register records that he was given leave to proceed to his degree on 14 Jan. 1791. The college authorities suggest that he probably took his degree during the Lent term. The 'honour' must have been the second Chancellor's Classical Medal. Trollope probably received it and his degree at the same time.

[6]

5. *To George Coleridge*

Address: Revd G. Coleridge | Mr Newcome's | Hackney
MS. New York Public Lib. Pub. Poems, *i. 21.*

March 31st 1791

Prospectus and Specimen of a Translation of Euclid in a series of
Pindaric Odes.

> If Pegasus will let *thee* only ride him
> Spurning my clumsy efforts to o'erstride him,
> Some fresh expedient the Muse will try,
> And walk on stilts, although she cannot fly.

Dear Brother—

I have often been surprized, that Mathematics. the Quintessence
of Truth, should have found admirers so few and so languid—
Frequent consideration and minute scrutiny have at length un-
ravelled the cause—Viz—That, though Reason is feasted, Imagina-
tion is starved: whilst Reason is luxuriating in it's proper Paradise,
Imagination is wearily travelling over a dreary desart. To assist
Reason by the stimulus of *Imagination* is the *Design* of the following
Production. In the *execution* of it much may be objectionable. The
verse (particularly in the introduction of the Ode) may be accused
of unwarrantable liberties; but they are liberties equally homo-
geneal with the exactness of Mathemat: disquisition and the bold-
ness of *Pindaric* Daring. I have three strong champions to defend
me against the attacks of Criticism: the Novelty, the Difficulty,
and the Utility of the Work. I may justly plume myself, that I
first have drawn the Nymph Mathesis from the visionary caves of
Abstracted Idea, and caused her to unite with Harmony. The first-
born of this union I now present to you: with interested motives
indeed, as I expect to receive in return the more valuable offsprings
of your Muse—

Thine ever
S T Coleridge—

This is now—This was erst
Proposition the first and Problem the first.

1

> On a given finite Line,
> Which must no way incline,
> To describe an equi =
> = lateral TRI
> A EN GEE EL E*

* Poetice for Angle. [S. T. C.]

(7)

Now let A B
Be the given Line,
Which must no way incline,
The great Mathematician
Makes this Requisition,
That we describe an equi=
=lateral Tri=
=angle on it.
Aid us, Reason! Aid us, Wit!

2

From the centre A. at the distance A B
Describe the circle B C D.
At the distance B A from B, the centre
The round A C E to describe *boldly venture*.*
(Third Postulate see)
And from the point C,
In which the Circles make a pother
Cutting and slashing one another
Bid the straight lines a journeying go,
C A, C B those lines will show
To the points, which by A B are reckon'd;
And Postulate the second
For authority ye know.
A B C
Triumphant shall be
An Equilateral Triangle—
Not Peter Pindar carp, not Zoilus can wrangle.

* delendus fere — [S .T. C.]

3rd

Because the point A is the centre
Of the circular B C D;
And Because the point B is the centre
Of the circular A C E,
A C to C B and C B to C A
Harmoniously equal for ever must stay.
Then C A and B C
Both extend the kind hand
To the Basis A B,
Unambitiously join'd in Equality's band.
But to the same power when two powers are equal—
My Mind forebodes the sequel,

My mind does some celestial impulse teach,
And equalizes each to each.
Thus C A with B C strikes the same sure alliance,
Which C A and B C had with A B before:
And in mutual reliance,
None attempting to soar
  Above another
The unanimous Three,
C A and B C and A B—
All are equal, each to his Brother.
Preserving the balance of Power so true:
Ah! the like would the proud *Autocratorix do!
At taxes impending not Britain would tremble,
Nor Prussia struggle her fear to dissemble,
  Nor the Mah'met-sprung Wight,
  The Great Musselman
  Would stain his Divan,
With Urine, the soft-flowing Daughter of Fright.

   * Th[e Empress of] the [Russians.] Note by S. T. C.

4th

But rein your stallion in, too daring Nine!
Should Empires bloat the scientific line?
Or with dishevell'd hair all madly do ye run
For Transport, that your task is done?
  For done it is—the cause is try'd!
  And Proposition, gentle maid,
Who soothly ask'd stern Demonstration's aid,
  Has prov'd her right: and A B C
  Of angles three
  Is shewn to be of equal side.
And now our weary steed to rest in fine,
'Tis rais'd upon A B, the straight, the given line.

6. *To George Coleridge*

MS. Lady Cave. Pub. Ill. London News, *1 April 1893, p. 397.* This letter is
written in a copperplate hand.

May 17th 1791

My dear Brother

  Indeed I should have written you before, but that a bad sore
throat and still worse cough prevented me from mustering Spirits
adequate to the undertaking. The sore-throat gargarization and

(9)

attention have removed: my cough remains—and is indeed in it's zenith: not Cerberus ever bark'd louder: every act of tussitation seems to divorce my bowells and belly—indeed if the said parties had not had a particular attachment to one another, they must have been long ago separated. Well—

> from catarrhs may Heaven preserve
> The lungs Of all my Tribe!

I hope, the country has had it's wonted success in recruiting you[r] Health and Spirits for the approaching School-campaign. My Mother, I trust, is well—my Brother James[1] too, Mrs J— and Mrs L. Coleridge. I intended to have written to my Brother James —but Mr Pitt and I have the honor of resembling one another in one particular—he in his *bellatory*, and I in my *epistolary* depart- ment—we are both men of *Preparations*. I availed myself of your note to draw upon my Aunt for half a guinea. My Aunt and Mrs Parker are well, I *believe*—for I have not been out lately— indeed, I believe, but *once* since your absence—and that was the time, when at a Lady's House I met Mr Tomkins,[2] who is con- fessedly the FINEST WRITER IN EUROPE. He is likewise a Literary Character, having published an elegant collection of Poems selected from the works of the best English Poets. One or two of the poems (by no means bad ones) are his own productions. We had a long conversation together, in the close of which *he* declared, that he thought me a very clever young man—and *I* declared that I thought his Collection of Poems one of the best Collections, I had ever seen. Whereupon he insisted on my going with him to Mack- lin's, to whose Gallery he can introduce whom he pleases; and here he shewed me the Title-page of Macklin's famous Bible, written by himself. It was, without hyperbole, most astonishingly beautiful. I could not help *delicately* insinuating that I conceived such writing not more the production of a fine-formed Hand, than the emanation of an elegant Soul; and I ended with lamenting my own most shameful deficiency in this respect. He desired to see my writing— I shewed him some—he might have read it by the light of my Blushes. He however humanely endeavor'd to recover me from

---

[1] James Coleridge (1759–1836) was the eldest of the surviving sons of the Rev. John Coleridge. Joining the army in 1775 he rose to the rank of captain but left the army on his marriage in 1788. Later he 'took a leading part in the Volunteer movement'. In 1796 he bought the Chanter's House close by the church in Ottery St. Mary, and lived there until his death. See Lord Coleridge, *The Story of a Devonshire House*, 1905, pp. 62–65.

[2] Thomas Tomkins (1743–1816), the calligrapher. He produced ornamental titles to a number of valuable books, particularly T. Macklin's Bible. For many years he kept a writing-school in Foster Lane, London.

my confusion by observing, that though it fell short of perfection in the articles of Neatness, Straightness of Direction, and Similitude of Dimension, it contained never the less the seeds of a good hand, which Time and Attention alone were wanting to mature. He has given me a very pressing invitation, which I mean to accept, hoping to profit by his Instructions and Example.

I could not avoid being thus particular in the relation of these circumstances, since I regard *them* as the causes, and *that time* as the Æra of my surprizing conversion—a conversion to be paralleled by none since the Conversion of St. Paul. And now, my dear Brother, Duty as well as affection prompts me to conclude the narration of this event by admonishing you to pursue the same course of reformation: as your hand-writing, though sufficiently gentlemanlike, is most hieroglyphically obscure. . . . [Remainder of manuscript missing.]

7. *To George Coleridge*

Address: Rev'd G. Coleridge | Mr Newcome's | Hackney.
MS. Lady Cave. Hitherto unpublished.

June 22nd 1791

Dear Brother

This is the Poem,[1] you wished to see—I have likewise sent you a Sonnet, which I accidentally found in looking over my papers, and by the date of it see that I wrote it just after my return from the country. Three Letters yesterday coming upon me had so impoverish'd me, that I was obliged to draw upon my Aunt for a Shilling on your account—Will you be so kind, as to bring in town with you that little Ode or Hymn, which, you told me, you had interwoven in your Fall of Man—I think, it is Mercy, that speaks it—?

Your affect—obliged Broth.
S T Coleridge

On wide or narrow scale shall Man
Most happily describe Life's plan?
Say, shall he bloom and wither there,
Where first his infant buds appear?
Or upwards dart with soaring force,
And dare some more ambitious course?

Obedient now to Hope's command
I bid each humble wish expand—

[1] *Poems*, i. 30.

(11)

And fair and bright Life's prospects seem,
When Hope displays her cheering beam,
And Fancy's vivid colourings stream.
How pants my breast, before my eyes
While Honour waves her radiant prize,
And Emulation stands me nigh,
The Goddess of the eager eye!

With foot advanc'd and anxious heart
Now for the fancied goal I start—
Ah! why will Reason intervene
Me and my promis'd joys between?
She stops my course, she chains my speed,
While thus her forceful words proceed.
Ah! listen, Youth, ere yet too late,
What evils on thy course may wait—
To bend the head, to bow the knee,
A minion of Servility;
At low Pride's frequent frown to sigh,
And watch the glance in Folly's eye—
To toil intense—yet toil in vain!
And feel, with what an hollow pain
Pale Disappointment hangs her head
O'er darling Expectation dead.

The scene is chang'd—& Fortune's gale
Shall belly out each prosp'rous sail!
Yet sudden Wealth, full well I know,
Did never Happiness bestow—
That wealth, to which we were not born,
Dooms us to Sorrow or to Scorn—
Behold yon flock, which long had trod
O'er the short Grass of Devon's sod,
To Lincoln's rank rich meads transferr'd—
And in their Fate thy own be fear'd.
Thro' every limb Contagions fly;
Deformed, choak'd—they burst and die.

When Luxury opens wide her arms,
And smiling wooes thee to those charms,
Whose fascination thousands own—
Shall *thy* brow wear the Stoic frown?
And when her goblet she extends,
Which mad'ning myriads press around,

What pow'r divine thy soul befriends,
That *Thou* should'st dash it to the ground?
No—*Thou* shalt drink, and *thou* shalt know
Her transient bliss, her lasting woe—
Her maniac joys, that know no measure,
With Riot rude and painted Pleasure:
Till (sad reverse!) th' Enchantress vile
To frowns converts her wonted smile—
Her train impatient to destroy
Observe the frown with gloomy joy—
On thee with harpy fangs they seize—
The hideous offspring of Disease—
Swoln Dropsy ignorant of Rest;
And Fever garb'd in scarlet vest;
Consumption driving the quick hearse;
And Gout, that howls the frequent curse;
With Apoplex of heavy head,
That surely aims his dart of Lead.

But say—Life's Joys unmix'd were given
To Thee, some favourite of Heaven
Without, within—tho' all were Health—
Yet what e'en thus are Fame, Pow'r, Wealth,
But sounds, that variously express
What's thine already—Happiness.
'Tis thine the converse deep to hold
With all the famous Sons of old—
And thine the happy waking dream,
While Hope pursues some favorite theme,
As oft, when Night o'er heaven has spread,
Round this maternal seat you tread,
Where far from Splendor, far from Riot,
In Silence wrapt sleeps careless Quiet.
'Tis thine with Fancy oft to talk;
And thine the peaceful Evening Walk;
And what to thee the sweetest are,
The setting sun, the evening star,
The tints that live along the sky,
And moon, that meets thy 'raptur'd eye,
Where oft the tear does grateful start—
Dear silent Pleasures of the Heart!
Ah! being blest! for Heaven shall lend
To share thy simple joys—a friend.
Ah! doubly blest! if Love supply

(13)

Lustre to this now heavy eye,
And with unwonted Spirit grace
That fat vacuity of face.
Or if e'en Love, the mighty Love
Shall find this change his power above,
Some lovely maid perchance thou'lt find
To read thy visage in thy mind.

One blessing more demands thy care:
Once more to Heaven address the prayer.
For humble Independence pray,
The Guardian Genius of thy way;
Whom (sages say) in days of yore
Meek Competence to Wisdom bore.
So shall thy little vessel glide
With a fair breeze adown Life's tide,
And Hope, if e'er thou 'gin'st to sorrow,
Remind thee of some fair to-morrow,
Till Death shall close thy tranquil eye,
While Faith proclaims, 'Thou shalt not die.'

Sonnet[1]

As late I journey'd o'er th' extensive plain,
Where native Otter sports his scanty stream,
Musing in torpid Woe a Sister's pain—
The glorious prospect woke me from the dream.
At every step it widen'd to my sight—
Woods, meadows, verdant hills, and barren steep
Following in quick succession of Delight—
Till all—at once my ravish'd eye did sweep!
May this (I cried) my course thro' life pourtray!
New scenes of Wisdom may each step display,
And Knowlege open, as my days advance:
Till, when Death pours at length th' undarken'd ray,
My eye shall dart thro' infinite expanse,
While Thought suspended lies in Transport's blissful trance!

Sept: 1789.

[1] *Poems*, i. 11.

8. *To George Coleridge*

Address: Revd G. Coleridge | Mr Newcome's | Hackney
MS. Lady Cave. Pub. with omis. Letters, *i. 22.*

October 16th [1791]

Dear Brother

Here I am—videlicet—Jesus College.[1] I had a tolerable Journey
—went by a night-coach packed up with five more—one of whom
had a long, broad, red, hot face—four feet by three. I very luckily
found Middleton[2] at Pembroke—who (after Breakfast &c) con-
ducted me to Jesus. Dr Pearce[3] is in Cornwall and not expected
to return to Cambridge till the Summer: and what is still more
extraordinary—(and (n. b.) rather shameful) neither of the Tutors
are here. I *keep* (as the phrase is) in an absent member's rooms, till
one of the aforesaid duetto return to appoint me my own. The
Letter, which Mr Corp wrote directed to the Bursar (n.b. Mr Corp
behaved very civil) attains or attaches, as you would say, no more
to the Bursar, than the Bed maker. The Tutor is the Letteree in
this case. I accordingly did not deliver it—but reserve it for the
proper man. Neither Lectures, or Chapel—or any thing—is begun.
The College very thin—and Middleton has not the least acquain-
tance with any of Jesus, except a very blackguardly fellow, whose
phisiog: I did not like. So I sit down to dinner in the Hall in silence
—except the noise of suction, which accompanies my eating—and
rise-up ditto. I then walk off to Pembroke and sit with my friend
Middleton.

I am very disagreeably situated on account of Mr B's plan of
suspending the ten pound. I might daily by means of Middleton
and his friends buy furniture, which will be necessary, at half
the price, which I can have it when the bills are sent in to [the]
College Tutor. If I had that money I could save near ten pound
of the twenty allowed by the Hospital. Besides one feels cold and
naked and shivering, and gelid, and chilly and such like synonimes
—without a little money in one's pocket. N.B. I am the first, on
whom Boyer has ventured to try this famous experiment—and if
you do not think, *you* can let me have it consistently with your
trust—I shall write a nasty letter to him. The burthen of it will
be—Mr Boyer, you have no order from Committee or Court for

---

[1] Coleridge was admitted to Jesus College, Cambridge, as a sizar on 5 Feb.
1791, began his residence in October, and matriculated 31 Mar. 1792.

[2] Thomas Fanshaw Middleton (1769–1822) became Bishop of Calcutta in
1814. Coleridge had known him at Christ's Hospital and never ceased to revere
him.

[3] Dr. William Pearce, the Master of Jesus College.

this plan—and if you had, they have no right to issue such an order. The money was hardly and dearly earned by that igno- minious custom of begging—and even though the donors had a power of retracting their gift, I received nothing but sixpences from [the] Governors. This may be strange language to [a] man, who like Boyer is so used to admire the influence of Committees and contemplate with awe the omnipotence of general courts—it is true though—and therefore I shall write it at him, only in more energetic language.

Pray let me hear from you—Le Grice will send a parcel in two or three days—By these parcels my letters to and from you will be [conveyed]—My respects to Mr and Mrs Sparrow[1]—I shall write to Mr Sparrow, after my examination &c—N.B. I am queerly off about the Rustat Scholarship[2]—Believe me,

with sincere affection and | gratitude | Your's ever
S T Coleridge

9. *To George Coleridge*

Address: Revd G. Coleridge | Mr Newcome's | Hackney
MS. Lady Cave. Pub. E.L.G. i. 1.

[Early November 1791][3]

Dear Brother

As I am now settled in my rooms, and as College Business is commenced, I shall be able to give you some little account of matters. We go to Chapel twice a day—every time we miss, we pay twopence, and fourpence on Surplice days—id est, Sundays, Saints' days, and the eves of Saints' Days. I am remarkably religious upon an economical plan.

We have Mathematical Lectures, once a day—Euclid and Algebra alternately. I read Mathematics three hours a day—by which means I am always considerably before the Lectures, which are very good ones. Classical Lectures we have had none yet—nor shall I be often *bored* with them. They are seldom given, and when given, very thinly attended.

After Tea—(N. b / Sugar is very dear) I read Classics till I go to bed—viz—eleven o'clock. If I were to read on as I do now— there is not the least doubt, that I should be Classical Medallist, and a very high Wrangler—but *Freshmen* always *begin* very

[1] Mr. Sparrow was the Headmaster of Newcome's Academy.

[2] Coleridge was admitted to the Rustat Scholarship in Nov. 1791. Cf. Arthur Gray, *History of Jesus College*, 1902, p. 181.

[3] Since this letter refers to a violent cold and attributes it to the 'dampness of my rooms', a phrase exactly repeated in the next letter, postmarked 28 Nov. 1791, it probably belongs to early November.

furiously. I am reading Pindar, and composing Greek verse, like a mad dog. I am very fond of Greek verse, and shall try hard for the Brown's Prize ode. At my Leisure hours I translate Anacreon—I *have* translated the first, the second, the 28th, the 32nd, the 43rd, and the 46th—Middleton thinks I have translated the 32nd (Ἄγε, ζωγραφῶν ἄριστε) very well—I think between us both, we might translate him entirely—You *have* translated 6 or 7, have you not?

Dr Pierce is not come up to College—The Rustat Scholarship will be worth to me 27 pound a year—There is a new regulation at our College, they tell me—that without any exception the man, who takes the highest honour in his year of the candidates, is to be elected Fellow—This will be a bit of a stimulus to my exertions.

There is no such thing as *discipline* at our college—There was once, they say—but so long ago, that no one remembers it. Dr Pierce, if I am not very much misinformed, will introduce it with a vengeance this year. We have had so very large an admittance, that it will be absolutely necessary.

We do one declamation every term[1]—two are spoken in a week, one English, one Latin. Consequently when the college was very thin, the men were pestered with two or three in a term. Themes and verses are in disuse at our College—whether the doctor intends to [restore] them [or] no, I cannot tell.

I have a most vio[lent] cold in my head—a favour, which I owe to the dampness of my rooms.

The Rustat Scholarship depends in some measure upon residence—otherwise it would be worth 30£ a year to me. But I should lose by this gain—while in the country, I can be at no expence: but unnecessary residence is a very *costly* thing.

Le Grice will send me a parcel in a few days—pray, let me hear from you.

My compliments to Mr and Mrs Sparrow—and believe me with love and gratitude | Your's
S T Coleridge

10. *To George Coleridge*

Address: Revd G. Coleridge | Mr Newcome's | Hackney | near | London
MS. Lady Cave. Pub. E.L.G. i. 3.
Postmark: 28 November 1791. *Stamped*: Cambridge.

My dear Brother

I am very much distrest on account of your illness: I can form some idea of your sufferings from what I have seen my brother

---

[1] Cf. Letter 12.

James suffer, when spasmodically affected. I hope to God, the spitting of blood has ceased. You should not take much animal food, nor any violent exercise. I should have written you on the receipt of your letter, had it not found me nailed to my bed with a fit of the Rheumatism. Yesterday I exhibited my first resurrexit. I am very weak, and have a disagreeable *tearing* pain in my head, when I move. I was very unwell, when I wrote last to you; but the day after I grew so much worse, that I was obliged to take to my bed. Cambridge is a damp place—the very palace of winds: so without very great care one is sure to have a violent cold. I am not however certain, that I do not owe my Rheumatism to the dampness of my rooms. Opium never used to have any disagreeable effects on me—but it has upon many.[1]

After I had last written you, there were one or two sentences in Ned's[2] letter, which then hurt me so much, that this cooperating with my feverish state of body and mind produced a letter 'paulo iracundior.['] I was afterwards so sensible of my folly in this, that I should have written him again to have begged his pardon for it, but I was unable. I received a very kind answer from Ned—in the former part of it he writes in a violent style, and then very good-naturedly desires me to observe, what Anti-graces a letter written in the first *impulse* of passion possesses. Yesterday, not without much effort, I wrote him such a letter, as will, I hope, utterly erase from his memory my late effusions of petulance and passion.

My dear Brother, I assure you, I am an Œconomist. I keep no company—that is, I neither give or receive invitations to wine parties; because in our college there are no end to them. I eat no suppers. Middleton acts to me with great friendship. While I was confined to my bed, though he was reading for an act, and could ill spare his time, he yet came, and sat with me often. After he has taken his degree, he has promised to read Mathematics with me, which will be of infinite service to me. As I had *got* before my lectures, my illness has not thrown me behind them. We have not had a classical lecture yet. Dr Pierce is not come to College yet.

I have by me two original little odes of G[ray;][3] they are very elegant, and will please you. They were never published. My compliments to Mr and Mrs Sparrow. As I know Mr Sparrow likes a good thing, you will communicate to him this epigram made

---

[1] This is the first reference to opium in Coleridge's correspondence.

[2] Coleridge's brother, Edward Coleridge (1760–1843).

[3] Coleridge must have obtained copies of these odes from the manuscripts of Thomas Gray in Pembroke College. For Coleridge's early interest in Gray see Letter 13.

lately by a man of Trinity upon a little garden belonging to
Dr Joett [Jowett], a man of small stature.

> This little garden little Joett made,
> And fenc'd it with a little palisade.
> A little taste hath little Dr Joett,
> This little garden doth a little shew it.[1]

An Epitaph on Mr More.

> Here lies More—no more is he:
> More and no more! how can that be?

We have had a dreadful circumstance at Cambridge. Two men
of Pembroke quarrelled, went to Newmarket, and the challenger
was killed. A fellow of our college made a very just observation,
that formerly students of Colleges were censur'd for being pedants
—but that now they were too much men of the world.—

I hope, when I next hear from you, to find your health perfectly
reestablished—in the mean time believe me with love & gratitude

Your affec: broth.
S T Coleridge

11. *To George Coleridge*

Address: To | The Revernd G. Coleridge | Mr Newcome's | Hackney | near |
London
MS. Lady Cave. Pub. Letters, *i. 23.*
Postmark: ⟨25⟩ January 1792.   *Stamped*: Cambridge.

Jan: 24th 92

Dear Brother

Happy am I, that the country air and exercise have operated
with due effect on your Health and Spirits—and happy too, that
I can inform you, that my own corporealities are in a state of better
Health, than I ever recollect them to be. This indeed I owe in
great measure to the care of Mrs Evans,[2] with whom I spent a
fortnight at Christmas: the relaxation from Study, cooperating
with the chearfulness and attention, which I met there, proved
very potently medicinal. I have indeed experienced from her a

---

[1] These lines were probably written by Francis Wrangham and are said to
have cost him a fellowship at Trinity Hall. Cf. Letter 62.

[2] Mrs. Evans was the widowed mother of Tom Evans, whom Coleridge
befriended at Christ's Hospital. 'She had three daughters, [Mary, Anne, and
Elizabeth,] and of course I fell in love with [Mary,] the eldest.' James Gillman,
The Life of Coleridge, 1838, p. 28.

tenderness scarcely inferior to the solicitude of maternal affection. I wish, my dear Brother, that sometime, when you walk into town, you would call at Villers' street—and take a dinner or dish of tea there. Mrs Evans has repeatedly expressed her wish, and I *too* have made a half promise, that you would. I assure you, you will find them not only a very amiable, but a very sensible family.

I send a parcel to Le Grice on Friday Morning, which (*you may depend on it as a certainty*) will contain your sermon.[1] I hope, you will like it.

I am sincerely concerned at the state of Mr Sparrow's Health.— Are his complaints consum[p]tive?—Present my respects to him and Mrs Sparrow.

When the Scholarship falls, I do not know. It *must be* in the course of two or three months. I do not relax in my exertions— neither do I find it any impediment to my mental acquirements, that prudence has obliged me to relinquish the 'mediae pallescere nocti.[']

We are examined as Rustats, on the Thursday in Easter Week. The examination for *my* year is 'the last book of Homer and Horace's [De] Arte poetica[']—The Master (i e Dr Pierce) told me, that he would do me a service by pushing my examination as deep as he possibly could. If ever hogs-lard is pleasing, it is, when our *superiors* trowel it on.

Mr Frend's company is by no means invidious.[2] On the contrary, Pierce himself is very intimate with him. No! Tho' I am not an *Alderman*, I have yet *prudence* enough to *respect* that *gluttony of Faith* waggishly yclept Orthodoxy.

Philanthropy generally keeps pace with Health—my acquaintance becomes more general. I am intimate with an undergraduate

---

[1] Among the MSS. in the Coleridge family there is a transcript of a sermon 'written when the Author was but 17 years old'. The sermon uses Psalm xcv. 10 as its text. Apparently Coleridge was in the habit of preparing sermons for his brother. See Letters 17 and 293.

[2] William Frend (1757–1841), at this time a Fellow of Jesus College but in ill repute for his religious views, had been removed from the office of tutor in 1788. On 3 Apr. 1793, in consequence of his recent pamphlet, *Peace and Union recommended to the Associated Bodies of Republicans and Anti-republicans*, the Master and Fellows of Jesus College decided that he should not be permitted to reside in the college until he had cleared himself, a decision confirmed by the Visitor. On 28 May 1793, after a stormy trial before the Vice-Chancellor, Frend was found guilty of having violated the statutes of the university by his pamphlet, and when he refused to retract and confess his error, as ordered, he was 'banished from the university'. It is said that the undergraduates, among whom Coleridge was conspicuous, were unanimously in Frend's favour.

of our College, his name Caldwell,[1] who is pursuing the same line of Study (nearly) as myself. Though a man of fortune, he is prudent: no[r] does he lay claim to that right, which wealth confers on it's possessor, of being a fool.

Middleton is fourth Senior Optimate—an honourable place, but by no means so high as the whole University expected, or (I believe) his merits deserved. He desires his love to Stevens:[2] to which you will add mine.

At what time am I to receive my pecuniary assistances?— Quarterly or half yearly? The Hospital issue their money half yearly, and we receive the products of our Scholarship—at once— a little after Easter. Whatever additional supply you and my Brothers may have thought necessary would be therefore more conducive to my comfort, if I received it quarterly—as there are a number of little things, which require us to have some ready money in our pockets—particularly, if we happen to be unwell. But this as well as every thing of the pecuniary kind I leave entirely ad arbitrium tuum. I have written my Mother, of whose health I am rejoiced to hear. God send, that she may long continue to recede from old age, while she advances towards it! Pray, write me very soon—Your's with gratitude & affection

S T Coleridge

12. *To Mrs. Evans*

MS. Mr. Carl H. Pforzheimer. Pub. with omis. Letters, *i. 26.*

Feb: 13th 1792

My very dear—

What word shall I add sufficiently expressive of the warmth which I feel? You covet to be near my heart. Believe me, that You and my Sisters have the very first row in the front box of my Heart's little theatre—and—God knows! *you are not crowded.* There, my dear Spectators! you shall see what you shall see— Farce, Comedy, & Tragedy—my Laughter, my Chearfulness, and my Melancholy. A thousand figures pass before you, shifting in perpetual succession—these are my Joys and my Sorrows, my Hopes and my Fears, my Good tempers, and my Peevishnesses: you will however observe two, that remain unalterably fixed—and these are Love and Gratitude. In short, my dear Mrs Evans! my whole heart shall be laid open like any sheep's heart: my Virtues, if I have any, shall not be more exposed to your view than my

---

[1] George Caldwell, afterwards Fellow and Tutor of Jesus College.
[2] L. P. Stevens, at this time Senior Assistant-Master at Newcome's Academy.

Weaknesses. Indeed I am of opinion, that Foibles are the cement of Affection, and that, however we may *admire* a perfect character, we are seldom inclined to love or praise those, whom we cannot sometimes blame.—Come Ladies! will you take your seats in this play house? Fool that I am! Are you not already there? Believe me, You are.——

I am extremely anxious to be informed concerning your Health. Have you not felt the kindly influence of this more than vernal weather, as well as the good effects of your own recommenced regularity? I would, I could transmit you a little of my superfluous Good health! I am indeed at present most wonderfully well—and if I continue so, I may soon be mistaken for one of your *very* children: at least, in clearness of complexion, and rosiness of cheek I am no contemptible likeness of them, tho' that ugly arrangement of features, with which Nature has distinguished me, will, I fear, long stand in the way of such honorable assimilation.

You accuse me of evading the bet—and imagine that my silence proceeded from a consciousness of the charge—But you are mistaken—I not only read *your* letter first, but, on my sincerity! I felt no inclination to do otherwise: and I am confident, that if Mary had happened to have stood by me, and had seen me take up *her* letter in preference to her *Mother's,*—with all that ease and energy, which she can so gracefully exert upon proper occasions, she would have lifted up her beautiful little leg, and kicked me round the room. Had *Anne* indeed favor'd me with a few lines, I confess, I should have seized hold of them before either of your letters—but then this would have arisen from my love of NOVELTY, and not from any deficiency in filial respect.—So much for your bet!—

You can scarcely conceive, what uneasiness poor Tom's accident has occasioned me—in every thing, that relates to him, I feel a solicitude truly fraternal. Be particular concerning him in your next. I was going to write him an half-angry letter for the long intermission of his correspondence; but I must change it to a consolatory one.—You mention not a word of Bessy—Think you, I do not love her?—

And so, my very dear Mrs Evans, you are to take your Welch journey in May?—Now may the very Goddess of Health, the rosy cheeked Goddess that blows the breeze from the Cambrian Mountains, renovate that dear old Lady, and make her young again! I always loved that old Lady's looks. Yet do not flatter yourselves, that you shall take this journey tête à tête. You will have an unseen companion at your side, one, who will attend you in your jaunt, who will be present at your arrival, one, whose heart will melt with unutterable tenderness at your maternal transports, who will climb

the Welch hills with you, who will feel himself happy in knowing
you to be so!—In short, as St Paul says, tho' absent in body, I
shall be present in mind. Disappointment! You must not, you shall
not be disappointed—and if a poetical invocation can help you to
drive off that ugly foe to Happiness, here it is for you—

To Disappointment.[1]

Hence! thou fiend of gloomy sway,
That lov'st on withering blast to ride
O'er fond Illusion's air-built pride,
    Sullen Spirit! Hence! Away!

Where Avarice lurks in sordid cell,
Or mad Ambition builds the dream,
Or Pleasure plots th' unholy scheme,
    There with Guilt and Folly dwell!

But oh! when Hope on Wisdom's wing
Prophetic whispers pure delight,
Be distant far thy cank'rous blight,
    Daemon of envenom'd sting!

Then haste thee, Nymph of balmy gales!
Thy poet's prayer, sweet May! attend!
Oh! place my Parent and my Friend
    'Mid her lovely native vales.

Peace, that lists the woodlark's strains,
Health, that breathes divinest treasures,
Laughing Hours, and social Pleasures,
    Wait my friend in Cambria's plains.

Affection there with mingled ray
Shall pour at once the raptures high
Of Filial and Maternal Joy—
    Haste thee then, Delightful May!

And oh! may Spring's fair flowrets fade,
May Summer cease her limbs to lave
In cooling stream, may Autumn grave
    Yellow o'er the corn-cloath'd glade,

Ere from sweet retirement torn
She seek again the ‡crowded mart!
Nor thou, my selfish selfish heart,
    Dare her slow return to mourn!

[1] *Poems*, i. 34.   ‡ London [S. T. C.]

In what part of the country is my dear Anne to be—Mary must and shall be with you—I want to know all your summer residences, that I may be on that very spot with all of you. It is not improbable, that I may steal down from Cambridge about the beginning of April just to look at you, that when I see you again in Autumn I may know, how many years younger the Welch air has made you. I shall go into Devonshire on the 21st of May, unless my good fortune in a particular affair should detain me till the 4th of June—. I lately received the thanks of the College for a declamation,[1] I spoke in public—indeed I meet with the most pointed marks of respect, which, as I neither flatter or fiddle, I suppose to be sincere—I write these things not from Vanity, but because I know, they will please you.

I intend to leave off suppers and two or three other little unnecessaries, and in conjunction with Caldwell hire a Garden for the summer—It will be nice exercise. Your Advice. La! it will be so charming to walk out in one's own *garding*, and sit and drink Tea in an arbour, and pick pretty nosegays—To plant and transplant—and be dirty and amused!——Then to look with contempt on you Londoners with your mock gardens at your smoky windows —making a beggarly shew of withered flowers stuck in pint pots, and quart pots, and chamber pots—menacing the heads of the passengers below. Foh! Oh! 'twill be very *praty* to make water—I meant to say—to water the *garding* morn and eve—O La! give me your advice.

How is Mr Tomkyns? Present my compliments to him. Now suppose I conclude something in the manner, with which Mary concludes all her Letters to me—'*Believe me your sincere friend*, and dutiful humble servant to command['']——

Now I do hate that way of concluding a letter—'Tis as dry as a stick, as stiff as a poker, and as cold as a cucumber. It is not half so good as my old God bless you

and | Your affectionately grateful
S T Coleridge

13. *To Mary Evans*

MS. Mr. Carl H. Pforzheimer. Pub. Letters, *i. 30.*

13th Feb: [1792]

Ten of the most talkative young ladies now in London—!!!!!

Now by the most accurate calculation of the specific quantities of sounds a female tongue, *when it exerts itself to the utmost*, equals

---

[1] 'A Latin essay on *Posthumous Fame*, described as a declamation and stated to have been composed by S. T. Coleridge, March, 1792, is preserved at Jesus College, Cambridge. Some extracts were printed in the college magazine, *The Chanticleer*, Lent Term, 1886.' *Letters*, i. 29 n.

the noise of 18 sign posts, which the wind swings backwards and forwards in full creak. If then 1 equals 18, 10 must equal 180——consequently the circle at Jermyn street unitedly must have produced a noise equal to that of 180 old crazy sign posts inharmoniously agitated, as aforesaid. Well! to be sure there are few disagreeables, for which the pleasure of Mary and Anne Evans' company would not amply compensate—but faith! I feel myself half-inclined to thank God, that I was 52 miles off during this *clattering clapperation* of tongues. Do you keep Ale at Jermyn Street?—if so, I hope, it is not *soured*.

Such, my dear Mary, were the reflections that instantly suggested themselves to me on reading the former part of your letter—believe me however, that my gratitude keeps pace with my sense of your exertions—as I can most feelingly conceive the difficulty of writing amid that second edition of Babel with additions. That your Health is restored gives me sincere delight. May the giver of all pleasure and pain preserve it so!—I am likewise glad to hear, that your *hand* is *rewhiten'd*, though I cannot help smiling at a certain young Lady's *effrontery* in having boxed a young Gentleman's ears, till her own hand became *black and blue*, and then attributing those unseemly marks to the poor unfortunate object of her resentment. *You are at liberty certainly to say what you please.*

It has been confidently affirmed by most excellent judges (tho' the best may be mistaken) that I have grown very handsome lately.—Pray—that I may have grace not to be vain.—Yet ah! who can read the stories of Pamela, or Joseph Andrews, or Susannah and the three elders—and not perceive what a dangerous snare Beauty is—. Beauty is like the grass, that groweth up in the Morning, and is withered before night. Mary! Anne!

Do not be vain of your beauty!!!!!——

I keep a Cat. Amid the strange collection of strange animals, with which I am surrounded, I think it necessary to have some meek well-looking being, that I may keep my social affections alive. Puss like her master is a very gentle brute, and I behave to her with all possible politeness.—Indeed—a Cat is a very worthy animal—To be sure, I have known some very malicious Cats in my life time—but then they were old—and besides, they had not nearly so many legs as you, my sweet Pussy. I wish, Puss! I could break you of that indecorous habit of turning your back front to the fire—It is not frosty Weather now.

N.B. If ever, Mary, you should feel yourself inclined to visit me at Cambridge, pray do not suffer the consideration of my having a Cat to deter you. *Indeed* I will keep her *chained up* all the while, you stay.

I was in company the other day with a very dashing literary Lady. After my departure a friend of mine asked her her opinion of me. She answered—'The best I can say of him is, that He is a very gentle Bear.['] What think you of this character?

What a lovely anticipation of Spring the last three or four days have afforded! Nature has not been very profuse of her ornaments to the country about Cambridge—yet the clear rivulet, that runs thro' the grove adjacent to our College, and the numberless little birds (particularly Robins) that are singing away,—and above all—the little Lambs, each by the side of it's Mother—recall the most pleasing ideas of pastoral simplicity, and almost sooth one's soul into congenial innocence. Amid these delightful scenes, of which the uncommon flow of Health, I at present possess, permits me the full enjoyment, I should not deign to think of London, were it not for a little family whom, I trust, I need not name. What bird of the Air whispers me, that You too will soon enjoy the same and more delightful pleasures in a much more delightful country? What we strongly wish, we are very apt to believe—at present my presentiments on that head amount to Confidence.

Last Sunday Middleton and I set off at one [o']clock on a ramble —We sauntered on, chatting and contemplating, till to our great surprize we came to a Village seven miles from Cambridge—And here at a farm house we drank Tea—the rusticity of the habitation and the inhabitants was charming—we had cream to our Tea, which tho' not brought in *a lordly dish*, Sisera would have jumped at. Being here informed that we could return to Cambridge another way, over a common, for the sake of diversifying our walk we chose this road—'if road it might be call'd, where road was none'—tho' —we were not unapprized of it's difficulties. The fine Weather deceived us. We forgot, that it was a summer day in warmth only, and not in length—but we were soon reminded of it. For on the pathless solitude of this common the night overtook us: we must have been four miles distant from Cambridge. The night, tho' calm, was as dark as the place was dreary—here steering our course by our imperfect conceptions of the point, in which *we conjectured* Cambridge to lie, we wandered on 'with cautious steps and slow.['] We feared the bog, the stump, and the fen: we feared the Ghosts of the night—at least, those material and knock me down Ghosts, the apprehension of which causes you, Mary (valorous girl, that you are!) always to peep under your bed of a night. As we were thus creeping forwards like the two children in the wood, we spy'd something white moving across the common—This we made up to—tho' contrary to our *supposed* destination.—It proved to be a man with a white bundle. We enquired our Way, and luckily he

was going to Cambridge—he informed us, that we had gone half
a mile out of our way, and that in five minutes more we must have
arrived at a deep quagmire grassed over. What an escape! The
Man was as glad of our company as we of his—for, it seemed, the
poor fellow was afraid of Jack o' lantherns—the superstition of
this county attributing a kind of fascination to those wandering
vapours, so that whoever fixes his eyes on them is forced by some
irresistable impulse to follow them. He entertained us with many
a dreadful tale—. By nine o'clock we arrived at Cambridge—
betired, and bemudded. I never recollect to have been so much
fatigued.

Do you spell the word—*scarsely*? When Momus, the fault-
finding God, endeavoured to discover some imperfection in Venus,
he could only censure the creaking of her Slipper. I too, Momuslike,
can only fall foul on a single s. Yet will not my dear Mary be angry
with me, or think the remark trivial, when she considers, that half
a grain is of consequence in the weight of a diamond.

I had entertained hopes, that you would *really* have sent me a
piece of sticking plaister—which would have been very con-
venient at that time, I having cut my finger. I hate to *buy* sticking
plaister, etc. What is the use of a man's knowing you Girls, if he
cannot *chouse* you out of such little things, as that? Do not your
fingers, Mary, feel an odd kind of titillation to be about my ears
for my impudence?

On Saturday night as I was sitting by myself all alone I heard
a creaking sound, something like the noise which a crazy chair
would make, if pressed by the tremendous weight of Mrs Barlow's
extremities. I cast my eyes around—and what should I behold,
but a *Ghost* rising out of the floor! A deadly paleness instantly
overspread my body, which retained no other symptom of Life,
but it's violent trembling: my hair (as is usual in frights of this
nature) stood upright by many degrees stiffer than the Oaks of the
Mountains, yea, stiffer than Mr ——; yet was it rendered *oily
pl[ian]t* by the profuse perspiration, that burst from every pore.
The Spirit advanced with a book in his hand, and having first
dissipated my terrors, said as follows: I am the Ghost of Gray—
there lives a young Lady (then he mentioned *your* name) of whose
judgment I entertain so high an opinion, that *her* approbation of
my Works would make the turf lie lighter on me: present her with
this book—and transmit it to her as soon as possible—adding my
Love to her. And as for you, O Young Man (*now* he addressed
himself to me) write no more verses—in the first place, your poetry
is vile stuff; and secondly (here he sighed almost to bursting) all
Poets go to —ll, we are so intolerably addicted to the Vice of

Lying!—He vanished—and convinced me of the truth of his last dismal account by the sulphureous stink, which he left behind him.

His first mandate I have obeyed, and, I hope, you will receive *safe* your ghostly admirer's present—but so far have I been from obeying his second injunction, that I never had the scribblo-mania stronger on me, than for these last three or four days—nay, not content with suffering it myself, I must pester those, I love best, with the blessed effects of my disorder. Besides two *things*, which you will find in the next sheet, I cannot forbear filling the remainder of *this* sheet with an Odeling—tho' I know and approve your aversion to *mere prettiness*, and tho' my tiny love ode possesses no other property in the world. Let then it's *shortness* recommend it to your perusal—*by the by*, the *only* thing, in which it resembles you: for Wit, Sense, Elegance, or Beauty it has none.

An Ode in the manner of Anacreon.[1]

As late in wreaths gay flowers I bound,
Beneath some roses LOVE I found,
And by his little frolic pinion
As quick as thought I seiz'd the minion,
Then in my Cup the prisoner threw,
And drank him in it's sparkling dew:
And sure I feel my angry Guest
Flutt'ring his Wings within my breast!

Are you quite asleep, dear Mary? Sleep on—but when you awake, read the following productions—and then, I'll be bound, you will sleep again sounder than ever.

A Wish written in Jesus Wood Feb: 10th 1792[2]

Lo! thro' the dusky silence of the groves,
Thro' vales irriguous, and thro' green retreats,
With languid murmur creeps the placid stream,
    And works it's secret way!

Awhile meand'ring round it's native fields
It rolls the playful wave, and winds it's flight:
Then downward flowing with awaken'd speed
    Embosoms in the Deep!

Thus thro' it's silent tenor may my Life
Smooth it's meek stream, by sordid Wealth unclogg'd,
Alike unconscious of forensic storms,
    And Glory's blood stain'd palm!

[1] *Poems*, i. 33.   [2] Ibid.

And when dark Age shall close Life's little day,
Satiate of sport, and weary of it's toils,
E'en thus may slumbrous Death my decent limbs
    Compose with icy hand!

A lover's complaint to his Mistress, who deserted him in quest of
a more wealthy Husband in the East Indies.[1]

The dubious light sad glimmers o'er the sky:
'Tis Silence all. By lonely anguish torn
With wandering feet to gloomy groves I fly,
And wakeful Love still tracks my course forlorn.

Ah! will you, cruel Julia! will you go?
And trust you to the Ocean's dark dismay?
Shall the wide wat'ry world between us flow?
And Winds unpitying snatch my Hopes away?

Thus could you sport with my too easy heart?
Yet tremble, lest not unavenged I grieve!
The Winds may learn your own delusive art,
And faithless Ocean smile—but to deceive.

If I have written too long a letter, give me an hint—& I will
avoid a repetition of the offence.

As a compensation for the above written rhymes (which if you
ever condescend to read a second time, pray, let it be by the light
of their own flames) in my next letter I will send some delicious
poetry lately published by the exquisite Bowles.[2]

To morrow morning I fill the rest of this sheet with a letter to
Anne—and now, Good Night, dear Sister! and peaceful slumbers
await us both!

                         S T Coleridge—11 o'clock.

14. *To Anne Evans*

MS. Mr. Carl H. Pforzheimer. Pub. Letters, *i. 37.*

                                February 14th 1792

Dear Anne

To be sure, I felt myself rather disappointed at my not receiving
a few lines from you; but I am nevertheless greatly rejoiced at
your amicable dispositions towards me. Please to accept two kisses,
as the seals of reconciliation: you will find them on the word

---

[1] Ibid. 36.
[2] William Lisle Bowles (1762–1850), whose *Sonnets*, first published in 1789,
excited the enthusiasm of Coleridge at Christ's Hospital. Cf. *Biog. Lit.* ch. i.

'Anne' at the beginning of the letter—at least, there I left them. I must however give you warning, that the next time you are affronted with Brother Coly, and shew your resentment by that most cruel of all punishments, Silence—I shall address a letter to you as long and as sorrowful as Jeremiah's Lamentations, and somewhat in the style of your Sister's favorite Lover, beginning with—

To the Irascible Miss.

Dear Miss—&c—

My dear Anne, you are my VALENTINE. I dreamt of you this morning, and I have seen no female in the whole course of the day, except an old bedmaker belonging to the College—and I don't count her one, as the bristle of her beard makes me suspect her to be of the masculine gender. Some one of the Genii must have conveyed your image to me so opportunely—nor will you think this impossible, if you will read the little volumes, which contain their exploits, and crave the honor of your acceptance.

If I could draw, I would have sent a pretty heart stuck thro' with arrows, with some such sweet posy underneath it as this—

The rose is red, the Violet blue,
The Pink is sweet—and so are You.

But as the Gods have not made me a drawer (of any thing but corks) you must accept the will for the deed.

You never wrote or desired your Sister to write, concerning the bodily health of the Barlowites, tho' you know my Affection for that family. Do not forget this in your next.

Is Mr Caleb Barlow recovered of the Rheumatism?

The quiet ugliness of Cambridge supplies me with very few communicables in the news way. The most important is, that Mr Tim. Grubskin, of this town Citizen, is dead. Poor Man! he loved fish too well. A violent commotion in his bowells carried him off. They say, he made a very good end. This is his Epitaph.

A loving friend and tender parent dear,
Just in all his actions, and He the Lord did fear,
Ho*pe*ing, that, when the day of Resurrection comes,
He shall arise in Glory like the Sun.

It was composed by a Mr Thistlethwait, the town cryer—and is much admired.—We are all mortal.—!—! His Wife carries on the business—it is whispered about the town, that a match between her and Mr Coe, the shoemaker, is not improbable—he certainly appears very assiduous in consoling her—but as to any thing matrimonial, I do not write it as a well authenticated fact.

I went the other evening to the concert, and spent the time there much to my heart's content in cursing Mr Hague, who played on the Violin most piggishly, and a Miss (I forget her name) Miss Humstrum, who sung most sowishly! O the Billington! That I should be absent during the Oratorios!—The Prince unable to conceal his pain—Oh! Oh! Oh! Oh! Oh! Oh! Oh! Oh! Oh!—To which House is Mrs B. engaged this Season?——

The Mutton and winter cabbage are confoundedly tough here, tho' very venerable for their old age. Were you ever at Cambridge, Anne? The River Cam is a handsome stream of a muddy complexion, somewhat like Miss Yates, to whom you will present my Love—(if you like.) In Cambridge there are 16 Colleges, that look like work-houses, and 14 Churches, that look like little houses. The Town is very fertile in alleys, and mud, and cats, and dogs, besides men, women, ravens, clergy, proctors, Tutors, Owls, and other two legged cattle. It likewise—but here I must interrupt my description to hurry to Mr. Costivebody's lectures on Euclid, who is as mathematical an Author, my dear Anne, as you would wish to read on a long summer's day.

Addio! God bless you, Ma chère Soeur, and your affectionate Frère,

S T Coleridge.

P.S. I add a postscript on purpose to communicate a joke to you. A party of us had been drinking wine together, and three or four freshmen were most deplorably intoxicated—(I have too great a respect for delicacy to say Drunk). As we were returning homewards two of them fell into the gutter (or kennel.) We ran to assist one of them—who very generously stuttered out, as he lay sprawling in the mud—Nnn no nn no!—ssave my ffrfrfriend there—nnever mind me—*I* can swim.

Won't you write me a long letter now, Anne?

P.S. Give my respectful compliments to Betty, and say, that I enquired after her health with the most emphatic energy of impassioned avidity.

15. *To Mary Evans*

MS. Mr. Carl H. Pforzheimer. Pub. Letters, *i. 41.*

Feb: 22nd [1792.] Jesus College. Cambridge—
Dear Mary

Writing long letters is not the fault, into whi[ch] I am most apt to fall—but whenever I do, by some inexplic[ab]le ill luck, my prolixity is always directed to those, whom I would yet least of all wish to torment. You think, and think rightly, that I had no occasion to *increase* the preceding accumulations of wearisomeness—but I wished to inform you, that I have sent the poem of Bowles, which I mentioned in a former sheet—tho', I dare say, you would have discovered this without my information—. If the pleasure, which you receive from the perusal of it, prove equal to that, which I have received, it will make you some small return for the exertions of friendship, which you must have found necessary in order to travel through my long long long letter.

Though it may be a little affronting to point out beauties, which would be obvious to a far less sensible heart than your's—yet I cannot forbear the self-indulgence of remarking to you the exquisite description of HOPE in the third page, and of Fortitude in the sixth—but the poem on leaving a place of residence appears to me to be almost superior to any of Bowles' compositions.

I hope, that the Jermyn Street Ledgers are well—How can they be otherwise in such lovely keeping?

Your Jessamine Pomatum, I trust, is as strong and as odorous as ever—and the roasted Turkies at Villar's street, honoured, as usual, with a thick crust of your Millè (what do you call it?) powder.

I had a variety of other interesting enquiries to make—but Time and Memory fail me.

Without a swanskin Waistcoat what is Man? I have got a swanskin waistcoat—a most attractive external.

Your's with sincerity of friendship
Samuel Taylor C

16. *To Mrs. Evans*

Address: Mrs Evans | York House, | Villar's Street | Strand | London   Single Sheet.
MS. Mr. Carl H. Pforzheimer. Pub. Letters, *i. 39.*

Feb: 22nd [1792]

Dear Madam

The incongruity of the dates in these letters you will immediately perceive. The truth is, that I had written the foregoing heap of nothingnesses 6 or 7 days ago,[1] but I was prevented from sending it by a variety of disagreeable little impediments—

Mr Massy must be arrived in Cambridge by this time—but to call on an utter stranger just arrived with so trivial a message as your's and his Uncle's Love to him, when I myself had been in

---

[1] Letters 12–15 were enclosed in this letter.

Cambridge 5 or 6 weeks, would appear rather awkward—not to say, ludicrous. If however I meet him at any Wine party (which is by no means improbable) I shall take the opportunity of mentioning it en passant. As to Mr M's debts—the most intimate friends in College are perfect strangers to each other's private affairs—consequently it is little likely, that I should procure any information of this kind.

I hope, and trust, that neither yourself or my sisters have experienced any ill-effects from this wonderful change of Weather—A very slight cold is the only favour, with which it has honoured *me*. I feel myself apprehensive for all of you—but more particularly for Anne, whose frame I think most susceptible of cold.

Yesterday a Frenchman came dancing into my room, of which he made but three steps, and presented me with a card—I had scarcely collected, by glancing my eye over it, that he was a Tooth monger, before he seized hold of my muzzle, and baring my teeth (as they do a Horse's in order to know his age) he exclaimed as if in violent agitation—Mon Dieu! Monsieur—all your teeth will fall out in a day or two, unless you permit me the honour of *scaling* them!—This ineffable piece of Assurance discovered such a Genius for Impudence, that I could not suffer it to go unrewarded—so after a hearty laugh I sat down, and let the rascal *chouse* me out of half a guinea by scraping my grinders—the more readily indeed, as I recollected the great penchant, which all your family have for delicate teeth.

So (I hear) Allen[1] will be most precipitately emancipated—Good Luck have thou of thy emancipation, Bobbee! Tell him from me, that if he does not kick Richards'[2] fame out of doors by the superiority of his own, I will never forgive him.

If you will send me a box of Mr Stringer's tooth powder—Mama!—We will accept of it.

And now, Right Reverend Mother in God, let me claim your permission to subscribe myself

with all observance & gratitude | Your most obedient | humble Servant, | and | lowly Slave—

SAMUEL TAYLOR COLERIDGE

Reverend in the future tense, and Scholar of Jesus College in the present tense.

[1] 'Robert Allen, Coleridge's earliest friend, and almost his exact contemporary (born October 18, 1772), was admitted to University College, Oxford, as an exhibitioner, in the spring of 1792.' *Letters*, i. 41 n.

[2] George Richards (1767–1837), a former student at Christ's Hospital, gained the Chancellor's Prize in 1787 and in 1789, and he won a prize for a poem on the *Aboriginal Britons* in 1791.

17. To George Coleridge

MS. Lady Cave. Pub. with omis. Letters, i. 42.

Monday Night   April [2, 1792]

Dear Brother

You would have heard from me long since, had I not been entangled in such various businesses as have occupied my whole time—Besides my ordinary business which, as I look forward to a smart contest some time this year, is not an indolent one, I have been writing for *all* the prizes—namely—the Greek Ode, the Latin Ode, and the Epigrams. I have little or no expectation of success—as a Mr Smith, a man of immense Genius, author of some Papers in the Microcosm, is among my numerous competitors.[1] The prize medals will be adjudged about the beginning of June. If you can think of a good thought for the beginning of a Latin Ode upon the miseries of the W. India Slaves, communicate—My Greek Ode is, I think, my chef d'œuvre in poetical composition.[2]

I have sent you a sermon metamorphosed from an obscure publication by vamping, transposition, &c—if you like it, I can send you two more of the same kidney.

Our examination as Rustats comes on the Thursday in Easter Week. After it is over, a man of our College has offered to take me to town in his Gig, and if he can, bring me back. I think, I shall accept his offer, as the expence at all events will not be more than 12 Shillings, and my very commons, and Tea, &cc would amount to more than that in the week which I intend to stay in town. Almost all the men are out of College—and I am most villainously vapoured. I wrote the following the other day under the Title of a Fragment found in a Lecture Room.[3]

> Where deep in mud Cam rolls his slumbrous stream,
> And Bog and Desolation reign supreme,
> Where all Boe[o]tia clouds the misty brain,
> The Owl Mathesis pipes her loathsome strain.
> Far far aloof the frighted Muses fly,
> Indignant Genius scowls and passes by:

[1] Robert Percy Smith (1770–1845). At Eton College he became intimate with George Canning and John Hookham Frere and with them started a school magazine, the *Microcosm*. In 1791 he won the Browne Medal for a Latin ode.

[2] For the text of Coleridge's *Greek Prize Ode on the Slave Trade*, which won the Browne Gold Medal in 1792, see J. D. Campbell, *The Poetical Works of Coleridge*, 1893, p. 476. Coleridge sent an autograph copy of the ode to his brother George. It is dated 16 June 1792, and is now among Lady Cave's MSS.

[3] *Poems*, i. 35.

The frolic Pleasures start amid their dance,
And Wit congealed stands fix'd in Wintry trance.
But to the sounds with duteous haste repair
Cold Industry, and wary-footed Care,
And Dullness dosing on a couch of Lead
Pleas'd with the song uplifts her heavy head,
The sympathetic numbers lists awhile,
Then yawns propitiously a frosty smile. . . . . . .
                                                          Cetera desunt.

This morning I went for the first time with a party on the River.
The clumsy Dog, to whom we had entrusted the sail, was fool
enough to fasten it. A Gust of Wind embraced the opportunity of
turning over the Boat, and baptizing all that were in it. We swam
to shore, and walked dripping home, like so many River Gods.
Thank God! I do not feel as if I should be the worse for it.

I hope, Mr and Mrs Sparrow are well—present my compliments
to them.

I was matriculated on Saturday—Oath taking is very healthy
in Spring, I should suppose.

I am grown very fat. We have two men at our college, great
cronies, their names Head and Bones, the first an unlicked cub
of a Yorkshireman, the second a very fierce Buck—I call them
Raw Head, and *Bloody* Bones.

As soon as you can make it convenient, I should be thankful, if
you would transmit me ten or five pounds, as I am at present
cashless.

Pray, was the Bible Clerk's place accounted a disreputable one
at Oxford in your time? Poor Allen, who is just settled there,
complains of the great distance with which the Men treat him—
'Tis a childish University—Thank God! I am at Cambridge.

Pray let me hear from you soon, and whether your Health has
held you out this long campaign—. I hope however soon to see
you—till when believe me

                                with gratitude and affection | Your's ever
                                                          S T Coleridge.

An Epitaph for Howard's tomb on the Banks of the Dnieper.[1]
N.B. I have got great credit by this.

> Οὐαρδοῦ τόδε σῆμ’, ὃς ἀνέστιον ἤλασεν ἴχνος
>   Τοῖς ἀβοηθήτοις ὄφρα βοηθὸς ἔοι.
> Πᾶσι ταλαιπώροις σωτήριον ἄστρον ἔλαμψε
>   Τὸ πρὶν ἀελπίστοις δαπτομένοις τε κέαρ.

[1] Coleridge's *Epitaph* was probably prompted by Bowles's poem, *The Grave of Howard.*

'Αμφεπόλη δ' ἄφοβος θαλάμους ἀπέλαστα νοσούντων,
Δεσμωτῶν τε φρεσὶν κλέψεν ἄγρυπνον ἄχος.
Νυνὶ ἀπανθρώποις κοιμᾶται ταῖσι παρ' ὄχθαις
Καὶ μακρῶν "Ελεος παῦσιν ἔχει καμάτων.

[Translation by Mr. Sparrow of Newcome's Academy.]

Here Howard rests. Grief's woe-worn sons to raise
Mark where unhous'd the holy pilgrim strays.
Health's beaming ray each child of Anguish cheers;
Care dies and hope revives when he appears.
Fearless he trod where death's pale victims lie,
And charm'd to rest the pris'ners unclos'd eye.
Now a lone shade fast by these banks he sleeps,
And Mercy from long toils Eternal Sabbath keeps.

18. *To George Coleridge*

Address: Revd G. Coleridge | Mr Newcome's | Clapton near Hackney | London
MS. Lady Cave. Pub. E.L.G. i. 5.
Postmark: 14 July 1792. *Stamped*: Salisbury.

July 13th 1792

Dear George

Here I am—videlicet—Salisbury, arrived on Wednesday
Night, and am in good health and Spirits—. My Brother Edward
is well—if you except a Punnomania, with which he at present
foams—his puns are very bad—of this he is conscious and there-
fore unwilling to allow Merit to those of others. I hope, that the
cold-sprung luminary has ceased to irradiate your left cheek—.
Mrs E. Coleridge made particular enquiries after your health—
she calls you her FRIEND.[1] I sate down to write you with a whole
Ocean of communicables in my head, but alas! for the Evapora-
tion—And I find the Muse as coy in her visitations as the Episto-
lary Spirit—. I shall be with my Brother James on Monday—
My reasons for leaving Salisbury are—that if I do not visit my
Brother James now, I shall not be able to do it at any future
period—on account of his Sidmouthianism—so my plan or rather
Edward's is, that I am to return to Salisbury when YOU return
from Devon, from which place I shall write you more copiously.
I anticipate your arrival at Ottery—your presence, like the Sun,
will relax the frost of my genius, and, like a cathartic, purify it of
all obstructions, so that I expect to flow away in a bloody flux of

---

[1] Edward Coleridge was settled as Assistant Master in Dr. Skinner's school
at Salisbury. His 'first marriage to a woman twenty years older than his
mother, was the source of many family jests'. Lord Coleridge, *The Story of
a Devonshire House*, 56.

poetry—. N.B. Ned never *reasons*—but he argumentates thro' the Medium of similies. By the by, I compared the carbuncle on your cheek to the star of Venus passing over the disk of the Sun.

In Devonshire, I shall write Mr Sparrow—

God love you— | Your's ever

S T Coleridge

P.S. Edward's love—N.B. Ned has proposed an in melius to my similie by comparing your carbuncle to an ignis fatuus passing over a Dunghill.

19. *To George Coleridge*

Address: Rev'd G. Coleridge | Mr Newcome's | Clapton, near Hackney | London.
MS. Lady Cave. Pub. with omis. E.L.G. i. 6.
Postmark: 9 August 1792. *Stamped*: Exeter.

Monday Morn—[6 August 1792]

Had I not entered into a most bloody cutthroat resolution to write you, my dear Brother, I could find two very good excuses for omitting it—the having nothing to say—and a Pen so execrably bad, as to discompose most grievously the epistolary part of my nervous system.—I left Tiverton on Wednesday, and migrated from Ottery to Exeter on Saturday—and there I am, at present very happy, and (exceptis Cloacinae templis infaustissimis) very comfortable—. All are well and all desire their Love to you. Mother I left well—and Mrs Hodge &c &c—I rather wonder at my not having heard from you—this will be the third Letter, which you will have received from me—But I complain not—knowing the multiplicity of your avocations. James is at Sidmouth—Little Betsey looks like Hebe after her Marriage with Hercules—seriously speaking, the little maid looks charmingly—. I hope, you will be quite well, when you come into Devonshire—for I have promised myself a vast deal of snug comfortability with you—I have nothing more to say—so shall fill up the Letter with a Simile, which I wrote after an Evening Walk before Supper—I had met Smerdon and Spouse.[1]

Tho' much averse at folk to flicker,
To find a Simile for Vicar
I've made thro' Earth, and Air, and Sea
A Voyage of Discovery—
And let me add (to ward off strife)
For Vicar & for Vicar's Wife.

[1] *Poems*, i. 37.

(37)

She, gross & round beyond belief,
A Superfluity of Beef:
Her mind and body of a piece
And both compos'd of Kitchen Grease—
In short, Dame Truth might safely dub her
'Vulgarity enclos'd in Blubber.[']
HE, meagre Bit of Littleness,
All Snuff, and Musk, and Politesse,
So thin, that strip him of his cloathing
He'd totter on the Edge of Nothing—*
In case of Foe he well might hide
Snug in the Collops of *her* side.
Ah then—what simile can suit?
Spind[l]e Leg in great Jack Boot?
Pismire crawling in a Rutt?
Or a Spiggot in a Butt?
[So?] I Ha'd and Hem'd awhile,
When Mrs Memory with a smile
Thus twitch'd my Ear—'Why sure, I ween
In London Streets thou oft hast seen
The very image of this Pair,
A Little Ape with large she bear
Tied by hapless chain together,
An unlick'd mass the One—the other
An Antic lean with nimble crupper—[']
But stop, my Muse! for here comes Supper.

* a good Line [S.T.C.]

Love to Mr & Mrs Sparrow.—God love you & your S T C.

20. *To George Coleridge*

Address: Revd G. Coleridge | Mr Newcome's | Clapton near | Hackney | London
MS. Lady Cave. Hitherto unpublished.
Postmark: 27 August 1792. *Stamped*: Honiton.

S. T. C. Georgio, suo fratri carissimo S.D.

Vos in Londinum salvos venisse, gaudemus. Jacobo autem
subirascitur mater nostra, quod de ungue suo lacerato nos certiores
non fecit: ipsa autem de valetudine sua plus solito conqueritur, et
digitos pedis quam ignitissimos habet. Laterali dolore laborat
Hodgaea—Hodgaeus autem est ipse animo perturbatiore, quam ut
alienos dolores respiciat, et magis ipse videtur aliorum consolatione
indigere, quam aliis posse suum officium praestare. Rerum enim
Gallicanarum βουλιμίᾳ quâdam macrescit: quae autem de iis

(38)

deferuntur, maestissima: nam neque Lutetienses, urbe capta, vivi cremati sunt, neque Paynius Duroverni trucidatus fuit, quo tempore in Galliam decedebat. Edvardus in Saresberiam hesterno die (10 Kal: Sep) abiit, et me Muni atque Silentio tradidit.

Ast Hunc Otteriae Juvenes flerunt abeuntem,
Crassaque spurcities Hobbî, Smerdonque pusillus,
Quem male morigeri tenuat petulantia cunni,
Et longo voces gaudens producere tractu,
Atque 'hem' congeminans media inter verba, Kesellus,
Atque gravis Payno Hodgaeus, Tuckerque Baconque
Pingues ingenio, ventrisque abdomine pingues.
Hunc Nymphae flerunt—veteres venerata furores
Deflevit Sarah, procerae fratria formae,
Singultimque 'Vale' declivis in oscula dixit.
Quin, Hodgaea! tuis ah! diae lucis ocellis
Cara! tuis maeror nubes induxit aquosas,
Cui moritura Venus sua dicitur ossa dedisse.
Quin *Dorothea bovina, oculis et Vaughnia lippis,
Quin †Porcina dolet, cui pustula crebra vagatur
Per nasum atque genas pituitâ marcida pingui.
Et frustra optatos heu! suspirans hymenaeos
Regali insignita malo Bissonia collum
Horsaei maestis tonsoria questibus implet.

* Scilicet, Smerdonia [S.T.C.] † Baconia. [S.T.C.]

Procul dubio homo facetus est Edvardus iste, et sale Plautino conditus: quin et amabilis, si istam fucatae munificentiae ostentationem deponat, et esse quam videri mallet. Plebeculae oculos minus perstringeret, sibi autem magis placeret. Minuitur enim quodam modo se probantis conscientiae delectatio, quoties ostentando quis factum pretium famae acceperit.—Scripsi ad Franciscum[1] nostrum—et epistolam Kesello commisi: nam uxor illius Shorii, qui Indiae provinciam jam nunc est sortitus, Dominae Cornish Glos est.[2] Hac autem gloriolâ suâ usque ad insaniam perfruitur Kesellus. Deambulanti in coemeterio se mihi obvium nuper dedit—et—Heus! Domine Samuel! Salve!—Scis forsitan, quod Dominus ille Shorius, (hem!) ille, inquam, quem toti Indiae proconsulari potestate (hem!) rex praefecit, sororis mei generi

---

[1] Francis Syndercombe Coleridge (1770–92) was wounded at the fall of Seringapatam on 6 Feb. 1792, and died shortly afterwards. Coleridge did not learn of his brother's death until early in 1793. Cf. Letter 26.

[2] Charlotte Cornish was the wife of John Shore and the sister of George Cornish, who was married to John Kestell's daughter Sarah. George Cornish later befriended Coleridge. Cf. Letters 40 and 41.

(hem) mei, inquam, generi sororis est maritus. Tu autem velim ad Franciscum scribas (litterae nunquam non tutissime perferentur) ego autem ipse (hem) illum proconsuli vehementer commendabo, nec dubito quin fratris tui res ita tractabit proconsul, ut intelligatur meam commendationem (hem) non vulgarem fuisse.—Ohe! quam risum nostrum desideravi! Melius autem visum est ridere in Stomacho, et assentatiunculâ quâdam non, ut opinor, prorsus reprehendendâ hominis stultitiam alere et titillare. Tumidissimum Animal! ὡς σοβεῖ! Mater autem nostra verba ejus ventosissima auribus esurienter haurit, et splendidissima quaeque somniat.— Ciceroni me penitus deditum velim credas, et operam daturum, ut quam expectationem concitavi, eam sustinere et tueri possim, vel si perire necesse sit,

$$Μὴ \ μὰν \ ἀσπουδεί \ γε \ καὶ \ ἀκλειῶς \ ἀπολοίμην!^1$$

Omnes te jubent salvere plurimum. Fac ut valeas, et ad me rescribas, neque tantâ brevitatis ostentatione. Otteriae. IX Kal: Septembres.—Anne ad Layardum scripsisti de re *Sacello-clericanâ?* —Stephanum meo nomine salutabis, et amicum meum optimum— Walthamstowensem—*Passer ille quidem, rara tamen Avis.* Vale.

Vini nobis ne 'gutta quidem[']—Caecubum vestrum depromere non licet—sic matris stat sententia, et tantae molis est tibi et Edvardo displicere.—

[Translation.]

Ottery, 24 August

S. T. C. to his dear brother George, greeting.

I am glad you have arrived safely in London. Our mother is rather annoyed with James, because he did not inform us about his torn nail; she laments her poor health more than usual, and her toes are absolutely on fire. Mrs. Hodge is suffering from pain in the side. Mr. Hodge however is too worried himself to pay attention to other people's troubles, and seems to need consolation from others, rather than being able to offer proper attention to them. He is made quite low by a sort of ravenous hunger for news from France. The reports of these matters that we receive are very sad: the people of Paris were not burned alive when the city was captured, and Payne was not cut to pieces at Canterbury when he was making his way to France. Edward went off to Salisbury yesterday (23 August) and has left me to . . . and silence.

The flower of Ottery's manhood bewailed his departure: fat dirty Hobbs; and little weakly Smerdon, who is reduced to a shadow by the impudence of a disobedient wanton, and Kesell, who loves to draw out his words to extreme length, and multiply his 'ahems' in the middle of his sentences; and Hodge, who hates Tom Payne; and Tucker and

---

¹ *Iliad*, xxii. 304.

Bacon, stout of heart, and stout of fleshy belly. The maidens mourned him too; Sarah, respected of old for her temper, like her sister-in-law in her tall beauty, sobbed 'Goodbye', as she leaned down to kiss him. Nay, but your divinely shining eyes, dear Mrs. Hodge, were hidden in a watery cloud by grief—you to whom Venus is said to have given her bones before she died. Yes, even bovine Dorothy, even Miss Vaughan of the bleary eyes, even Miss Bacon mourns, on whose nose and cheeks many a pimple pastures, foul with oozing matter. And Miss Bisson, too, with the scrofulous neck, sighing over a marriage, alas, hoped for in vain, fills Horsey's barber's shop with her sad laments.

There is not the least doubt that Edward is a wit, seasoned with Plautine salt; and he will be likeable too, if he gives up that display of sham generosity, and would prefer reality to show. He would not attract the eyes of the rabble so much, but he would be more at harmony in himself. The satisfaction we gain from a quiet conscience is somehow lessened, when we accept as the reward of renown that which is got by mere ostentation.—I have written to our brother Francis—and entrusted the letter to Kesell: for the wife of Shore, who has just been appointed Governor-General of India, is the sister-in-law of Mrs. Cornish. Kesell is absolutely beside himself with the enjoyment of this little bit of glory. He has just come to meet me as I was walking down through the church-yard: 'Hallo! Mr. Samuel, how d'ye do! You know, I suppose, that Lord Shore, ahem! Lord Shore, you know, whom the King has just made Governor-General of all India, is the husband of my son-in-law's sister; ahem, I say my son-in-law's sister's husband! I should be glad, if you would write to Francis yourself (the post is always perfectly reliable); but I myself, ahem, will recommend him to the Governor-General very strongly, and I have no doubt but the Governor-General will deal with your brother's affairs in such a way that my recommendation, ahem, will be understood to be no ordinary one!'—Oh, how I missed the way we used to laugh! But I thought it better to suppress my amusement, and to feed and stimulate the man's folly by mildly agreeing with him, which I hope was not altogether blameworthy. What a puffed-up creature! What pomposity! Our mother positively drinks in his long-winded speeches, and dreams of the most wonderful prospects.—I should like you to believe that I have been spending all my time with Cicero, and that I shall take care, when I have created an expectation, to sustain and preserve it, or if I must come to grief 'God forbid that I should perish without effort and without renown!'

Everyone sends you warmest greetings. Look after yourself, and write back to me, and not with such self-conscious brevity next time! Have you written to Layard about the *chapel-clerkship*?—You will give my regards to Stephens, won't you?—and to my very good friend from Walthamstow—*He is indeed a Sparrow, and yet a rare bird*. Best wishes to you.

As to wine, not 'a single drop'—I must not get out your Caecuban—that is mother's fixed ruling, and what a grief it is to displease you and Edward.

21. *To George Coleridge*

Address: Revd G. Coleridge | Mr Newcome's | Clapton near Hackney | London.
MS. Lady Cave. Hitherto unpublished.
Postmark: 12 November 1792.

Mi frater,

Descensurus sum in certationem quatuordecem dies ex hac subscripta.[1]—Vix existimare potes, quám me hujus negotii taedeat—piget, mî carissime, piget palpitantibus praecordiis vivere. Spes autem mihi pertenuis ostenditur—imo, nulla. Nam sudorum meorum, quantumvis maximi, numquam me paenituisset, si feliciter sudati fuissent.—

Stipendium de anno ex *Marsdonia* exhibitione £20 aestimandum est—sed minus a veritate rei abhorrerem, si £10 dicerem. Quomodo autem se res habet, eâ exhibitione nunc utitur *homo recens, ὡς κατὰ τέχνην εἰπεῖν.* Quód ad me de rationibus meis scripsisti, tuam amicitiam et amorem erga me recognovi—tui scilicet, quam semper suavitate fratrem, consilio parentem expertus fui. Sed animo sum perturbatiori, et defatigato magis, quam ut iis respondeam. Tu autem velim credas me citò responsurum esse, et copiosissime responsurum. Iacobum nostrum filio auctum esse, salvâ uxore ejus, gaudeo.—

Tuckettus[2] tibi plurimam salutem dicit. Vale, mi suavissime, et charissime frater, Vale!—

Cam: Jes: Coll:—Die Novembris undecimâ.—

[Translation.]

Jesus Coll: Camb.   11 November

My dear brother

A fortnight from the date hereof I shall be entering the fray. You can scarcely imagine how weary I am of this business, how I abhor, my dear George, living under this strain. My prospects are almost hopeless—in fact quite hopeless. However weary my labours, I should not have regretted them, if only they had not been labours in vain.

The *Marsdon* Exhibition is supposed to be worth £20 a year—but I should be less wide of the truth if I said £10. However that may be, this exhibition is now held by a *freshman*—to use the college jargon. As to what you wrote to me about my accounts, I do realize your friendliness and love towards me—for you have always been a brother to me in kindness and a father in wisdom, as I well know. But I am

---

[1] Coleridge refers to the University Craven Scholarship. Cf. Letter 23.
[2] G. L. Tuckett, a Cambridge acquaintance. See Letter 32 for Tuckett's activities during Coleridge's army experience.

too worried and tired out to reply; please believe me, though, that I will reply soon—and reply very fully. I am glad that our brother James has a son and that his wife is doing well.

Tuckett sends you his warmest greetings. Ever yours, my kindest and dearest brother.

22. *To George Coleridge*

Address: Revd G. Coleridge | Mr Newcome's | Clapton near Hackney | London.
MS. Lady Cave. Pub. with omis. E.L.G. i. 7.
Postmark: 19 November 1792.

Sunday Evening   Novembr 18th 1792
My dear Brother

I have sent for your minutest examination the Latin letter which I am to send to each of my examiners. If there be the least in-accuracy in it, let it not escape your microscopic eye, for I should be sorry to offend in the vestibule of my examination. So, my dear Brother, whet the knife of criticism upon the sole of affection, and sit down *at* it with anticipative grin, like a monthly reviewer preparing to cut up a limb of Orthodoxy.

I am sorry to add, that my health is considerably impaired— and my face, a soil at all times more favorable to the crocus than the rose, looks at present peculiarly sepulchral.—If possible, answer my letter by return of post—and believe me
with affection and gratitude | Your's most sincerely
S T Coleridge

Respects to Mr & Mrs Sparrow—Remember me to Stephens.—

Vir Spectatissime

Etsi angustioribus terminis continentur hujusce Academiae dignitates, quam quae ob quotidianam frequentiam parvi habendae essent, tamen nullo modo eâ sunt paucitate, ut omnia desperent ii, quibus summorum praemiorum spes pertenuis ostenditur.

Is autem, qui nobis ad certationem nunc jam proponitur, qualis quantusque sit honor, neutiquam me latet; neque sum de magnitudine petitionis admonendus. Quód igitur hoc praesertim campo mihi collibitum est decurrere, si Verecundiae fines transiero, cupiditati meae paullo forsan ambitiosiori ignoscas velim—θεῖον γὰρ ἀγαθὸν ἡ τιμή. Complures profectò, quibuscum neque aetate, neque ingenio, neque artium disciplinis sim comparandus, sui diffidentiâ impeditos mihi videre videor. Quae quoties mihi in mentem venirent, ac simul illos suspicerem, qui hunc honorem,

quo usi sunt, suo* splendore et famâ affecêre, ipse meam parvi-
tatem recognovi, parumque abfuit, quin spe infracta, et langue-
scente industriâ id experiri nollem, quod me assequi posse
desperem. Atqui verebar, ne difficultatis patrocinium pigritiae
meae viderer quaesivisse: et porrò, (quod initio summonui)
sperabam, fore ut hâc contentione memet ad alia certamina
acuerem. Ergo, victori sint sua praemia! Mihi palmae erit aliquid
generosius ausisse! Tantùm hoc liceat mihi de me praedicare,
omnibus nervis contendisse, ut primorum exspes primis quae sint
proxima assequar, et quamvis me superatum iri haud obscure
praeviderim, Μὴ μὰν ἀσπουδεί γε καὶ ἀκλειῶς ἀπολοίμην. Verum
enimvero qualemcunque sors tulerit casum, hâc persuasione
recreatus dolorem meum abstergebo, ibi non inhonestum esse
vinci, ubi victoria est honestissima. Sum tibi, Vir spect:
mori cultu et observantia | devinctissimus &c—

* *Porson* examines for this scholarship, which he himself vacated.—[Note
by S.T.C.] Richard Porson (1759–1808), the illustrious Greek scholar, had won
the Craven Scholarship in 1781; after vacating it in 1792 he was elected
Regius Professor of Greek at Cambridge.

[Translation.]

Most Respected Sir,

Although the positions of honour in this University are confined
within too narrow limits, to be cheapened in estimation by the frequency
of daily intercourse, yet they are by no means so few, as to give cause
for utter despair to those, whose hope of the highest prizes appears
extremely slight.

Of the nature and magnitude of the distinction, which is now offered for
competition among us, I am by no means unaware, nor do I need to be
admonished of the importance of the honour I am seeking. If, in having
determined to become a contestant in this particular arena, I should
seem to overstep the bounds of modesty, I hope that my perhaps somewhat
immoderate ambition may obtain your pardon—'for honour is a bounty
wondrous fair'. I seem to observe a number of those, with whose years,
ability, and learning I cannot compare, who are restrained by distrust
of their own powers. When I considered this, and at the same time
observed those past holders of this Exhibition, who have shed lustre
upon it by the brilliance of their reputations, I recognized my own
insignificance, and it almost came about that, with confidence sapped
and diligence failing, I no longer wished to put myself to that test, in
which I despaired of success. Nevertheless I feared that I might seem
to have sought to make the difficulty of the task a cloak for my own
laziness; and moreover, (as I have hinted in my opening) I hoped that by
this competition I should train myself up for other contests. So, to the
victor be the prizes! It will be prize enough for me if I have but made a
gallant effort. Only may I be able to say this of myself, that though

without hope of the first rank I strove nevertheless with all my might,
to attain to the second, and, though I clearly envisage my defeat, yet
'let me not perish without effort and without renown'. And indeed what-
ever be the issue that fate brings, I shall assuage my disappointment by
the restorative power of this conviction, that where victory brings the
highest honour, 'tis no dishonour to be beaten. I am, most respected
Sir, morally, academically, and personally, your most obliged &c.

23. *To George Coleridge*

Address: Revd G. Coleridge | Ottery St Mary | Devon
MS. Lady Cave. Pub. E.L.G. i. 10.
Postmark: 14 January 1793.   *Stamped*: Cambridge.

Sunday 13th [January, 1793]

Dear Brother

Our Fate is at last decided—and I, as I expected, in the number
of the unsuccessful. After an examination of six days' continuance
our number was reduced from 17 to 4—the survivors were Bethel
and Keate of King's, Butler of St John's,[1] and myself.—We then
underwent a different process of examination—after which the
Vice chancellor sent for Butler, and informed him, that between
those, who had been dismissed, and the 4, who had been retained,
the distinction was wide and marked—; but that we had proved
so very equal that the examiners were long undecided—but had
at last determined in his favor, because from his Age he deserved it
the most (he is the youngest of us), and because they thought him
the *most proper* to receive it[2]—I believe, he is a Sizar.

[1] Christopher Bethell (1773–1859), later Bishop of Bangor; John Keate
(1773–1852), later Headmaster of Eton; and Samuel Butler (1774–1839), later
Bishop of Lichfield.
[2] Writing in the *Analyst* in 1834, Samuel Butler protested against a recent
biographical memoir of Coleridge in that paper and went on to defend Cole-
ridge's industry:
'As I was his contemporary at the University, & enjoyed his youthful
friendship (the kindly remembrance of which continued between us till his
death, though we had few opportunities of personal intercourse) I beg to
state that his Biographer has under-valued both his struggles & his success.
'In the summer of 1792 he gained the Browne Medal for his Ode on the
slave trade, which contains some highly spirited & poetical passages, tinged
with melancholy & moral pathos; in the months of December & January
following, he was a competitor for the University Scholarship then vacant
by the election of the illustrious Richard Porson to the Greek Professorship,
Porson himself being the principal examiner. Although he was not successful
he was so far distinguished as to be one of the four who at a certain period
of the examination were selected from the general body of candidates, &
formed into a separate class for a second more severe and decisive trial.
'I believe no other opportunity occurred for his exertion during his stay

—As to myself I am perfectly satisfied both with the mode of the examination and the event of it—; but our Master, Dr Pierce, who conceives the most hyperbolic ideas of my abilities, & had entertained the most sanguine expectations of my success, is sadly chagrined—nay, he went so far, as to tell me in confidence, that I had not had fair play—'no composition in Greek Prose, none in Greek Verse, no original English composition—you would have beat them hollow—I know, you would' &c. But I have no reason to complain—as, if you except the above mentioned articles, I verily believe, we circumnavigated the Encyclopaedia—so very severe an examination was never remembered.——I have this oil to pour into the wound of my vanity, my information is certain and authentic that the most elegant Scholar among the examiners gave a decided Vote in my Favor.——Dr Pierce has given me the Librarian and Chapel clerk's Place—it is worth 33 pound a year; but then I cannot be absent from chapel above 3 or 4 times in a week, and I must get up to chapel almost every morning—; but all good things have their contingencies of evil.—.—

I am now employing myself omni Marte in translating the best Lyric Poems from the Greek, and the modern Latin Writers—which I mean in about half a year's time to publish by Subscription.[1] By means of Caldwell, Tucket, & Middleton I can ensure more than two hundred Subscribers—so that this and frugality will enable me to pay of[f] my debts, which have corroded my Spirits greatly for some time Past.—I owe about 50£ to my Tutor—and about 8£ elsewhere. The debt to my Tutor is entirely the arrears of my two first Quarters—and I have owed it to him ever since!—My income from the School is 40£—from the Rustat Scholarship this year it will be about 23£—or perhaps a little more—from the Chapel clerkship 33£.——And as I eat no Supper, or Tea, and keep little company my expences this year *excluding* Travelling into Devonshire will be about 50£—so that I shall be nearly 26£ plus.—My commons I have for nothing—they being included in the Chapelclerkship—so that it is little expence to be resident.—I think therefore of staying all the Summer in Cambridge—which will increase my Rustat Scholarship to 30£.—Such are my accounts.—I have been lesson'd by the wholesome discipline of Experience,

at College; he may therefore be fairly said to have distinguished himself on every occasion of competition for first rate honours while at the University, and I feel happy in this opportunity of testifying my regard, & doing justice to the memory of a man whom we cannot but admire for his talents & high attainments, pity for his severe & protracted sufferings, and reverence for the patience & Christian resignation with which he endured them.'

[1] This proposed work, though it occupied Coleridge's mind for some time, was never carried out. Cf. Letters 43, 65, p. 116, and 81.

that Nemo felix qui debet—: and I hope, I shall be the happier man for it.——

—I trust, that your indisposition has been compleatly removed by the peace and quiet of Ottery—My anxiety concerning [the] Scholarship did not so insulate me, but that my Fancy frequently wandered there—the state of your health indeed, when you quitted Hackney, was such as demanded solicitude. Pray let me hear from you as soon as possible—Give my Duty to my Mother, whom I will write in a few days—and my Love to my Sister—my Comp's to Mrs Hodge—&c &c—and believe me with affection

Your grateful & obliged
S T Coleridge

24. *To Mrs. Evans*

MS. New York Public Lib. Pub. with omis. Letters, *i. 45.*

Feb: 5th [1793]

My dear Mrs Evans

This is the third day of my resurrection from the Couch, or rather, the Sofa of Sickness. About a fortnight ago a quantity of matter took it into it's head to form in my left gum, and was attended with such violent pain, inflammation, and swelling, that it threw me into a fever—however—God be praised—my gum has at last been opened, a villainous tooth extracted, and all is well. I am still very weak—as well I may, since for 7 days together I was incapable of swallowing anything but Spoon meat—so that in point of Spirits I am but the Dregs of my former self—a decaying flame agonizing in the Snuff of a tallow Candle—a kind of hob-goblin, clouted and bagged up in the most contemptible Shreds, Rags, and yellow Relics of threadbare Mortality. The event of our examination was such, as surpassed my expectations, and per-fectly accorded with my wishes. After a very severe trial of 6 days' continuance the Number of the Competitors was reduced from 17 to 4—and after a further process of ordeal we, the Survivors, were declared equal—each to the other—and the Scholarship according to the will of it's founder awarded to the Youngest of us—who was found to be a Mr Butler of St John's College.—I am just two months older than he is[1]—& tho' I would doubtless have rather had it myself, I am yet not at all sorry at his success—for he is sensible, and unassuming—and besides—from his circumstances such an accession to his annual income must have been very acceptable to him. So much for myself.—

---

[1] Actually Coleridge was 15 months Butler's senior.

I am greatly rejoiced at your Brother's recovery—in proportion indeed to the anxiety and fears, I felt, on your account during his illness.—I recollected, my most dear Mrs Evans, that you are frequently troubled with a strange forgetfulness of yourself, and too too apt to go far beyond your strength, if by any means you may alleviate the Sufferings of others—ah! how different from the majority of those, whom we courteously dignify with the Name of human:—a vile herd, who sit still in the severest distresses of their *Friends,* and cry out, There is a Lion in the way!—animals, who walk with leaden sandals in the paths of Charity, yet to gratify their own inclinations will run a mile in a breath. Oh!—I do know a set of little, dirty, pimping, petyfogging, ambi-dextrous fellows, who would set your house on fire, tho' it were but to roast an egg for themselves! Yet surely—considering it even in a selfish view, the pleasures that arise from whispering peace to those who are in trouble, and healing the broken in heart are far superior to all, the unfeeling can enjoy.

—I need not say how concerned I am for my poor Anne, whose frame is a system of such sweet tones and modulations, that I am perfectly enraged with any Sickness, that untunes so harmoniously attuned an instrument. I hope, that my Condolances will come too late, and should rather have been exchanged for Congratulations. I have enclosed a little work of that great and good man, Arch-deacon Paley—it is entitled motives of Contentment—addressed to the poorer part of our fellow Men—the 12th page I particularly admire—& the 20th. The Reasoning has been of some Service to *me*—who am of the Race of the Grumbletonians.—My dear friend, Allen, has a resource against most misfortunes in the natural gaiety of his temper—whereas my hypochondriac gloomy Spirit *amid blessings* too frequently warbles out the hoarse gruntings of discontent—!—Nor have all the lectures, that Divines and Philo-sophers have given us for these 3000 years past, on the vanity of Riches, and the Cares of greatness, &c—prevented me from sincerely regretting, that Nature had not put it into the head of some *Rich* Man to beget *me* for his *first born*—whereas now I am likely to get bread, just when I shall have no teeth left to chew it.— Cheer up, my little one! (thus I answers I) *better late than never.* Hath Literature been thy choice—and hast thou food and rai-ment—? Be thankful, be *amazed* at thy good fortune! Art thou dissatisfied and desirous of other things? Go, and make twelve votes at an election: it shall do thee more service, and procure thee greater preferment, than to have made twelve commentaries on the twelve Prophets.—

My dear Mrs Evans! excuse the wanderings of my castle building Imagination—I have not a thought, which I conceal from you—I *write* to others, but my Pen talks to you.—Convey my softest Affections to Betty, and believe me,

Your grateful & affectionate Boy
S T Coleridge.

25. *To Mary Evans*

MS. Mr. Carl H. Pforzheimer. Pub. with omis. Letters, i. 47.

Jes: Coll:—Cam:—Feb: 7th 1793

I would to Heaven, my dear Miss Evans, that the God of Wit, or News, or Politics, would whisper in my ear something, that might be worth sending fifty four miles—; but—alas! I am so closely blocked up by an army of Misfortunes, that really there is no passage left open for Mirth or any thing else—Now just to give you a few articles in the large Inventory of my Calamities.— Imprimis—A gloomy uncomfortable Morning. Item—My head akes—Item—The Dean has set me a swinging Imposition for missing Chapel—Item—of the two only coats, which I am worth in the world, both have holes in the elbows—Item—Mr Newton, our Mathematical Lecturer, has recovered from an Illness.—But the story is rather a laughable one—so I must tell it you.—Mr Newton (a very tall thin man, with a little tiny blushing Face) is a great Botanist—Last Sunday as he was strolling out with a friend of his, some curious plant suddenly caught his eye—he turned round his head with great eagerness to call his companion to a participation of the discovery——and unfortunately continuing to walk forward he fell into a pool—deep—muddy—and full of Chick Weed.—I was lucky enough to meet him, as he was entering the College Gates on his return (a sight I would not have lost for the Indies!) His best black cloaths all green with duck weed—he shivering and dripping—in short, a perfect River God.—I went up to him (you must understand, we hate each other most cordially) and sympathized with him in all the tenderness of Condolance.—The consequence of his misadventure was a violent Cold attended with fever, which confined him to his room—prevented him from giving Lectures, and freed me from the necessity of attending them—but this misfortune I supported with truly Christian Fortitude—however I constantly asked after his health with filial anxiety—and this morning making my usual enquiries, I was informed to my infinite astonishment and vexation, that he was perfectly recovered and intended to give Lectures this very day!!!—Verily I swear, that six of his duteous pupils, myself as their General, sallied forth to the Apothecary's house with a fixed determination to thrash him for having performed so speedy a cure—but luckily for himself the Rascal was not at home.——But here comes my fidling Master—for—(but this is a secret—) I am learning to play on the Violin.—Twit twat—twat twit—pray, Mr De la peuche, do you think, I shall ever make any thing of this Violin?—do you think, I have an ear for Music?—'Un Magnifique! Un superbe! / Par honeur, Sir, you be a ver great Genius in de music.——Good morning, Monsieur!'—This Mr De la peuche is a better judge, than I thought for.——

This new whim of mine is partly a scheme of self defence—three neighbours have run Music-mad lately—two of them fiddle-scrapers, the third a flute-tooter—and are perpetually annoying me with their vile performances, compared with which the gruntings of a whole herd of Sows would be seraphic Melody. Now I hope by frequently playing myself—to render my ear callous—as a lady of quality, being reprimanded by her husband for having eat onions, (or garlick) answered him—Why don't you eat onions yourself, my Dove, and then you would not smell them!—Besides—the evils of Life are crowding upon me—and Music is 'the sweetest assu[a]ger of Cares.'—It helps to relieve and sooth the mind, and is a sort of refuge from Calamity—from slights and neglects and censures and insults and disappointments; from the warmth of real enemies and the coldness of pretended friends; from your *well wishers* (as they are justly called, in opposition, I suppose, to *well doers*) men, whose inclinations to serve you always decrease, in a most mathematical proportion, as their opportunities to do it increase; from the

> 'proud man's contumely, and the spurns,
> Which patient Merit of th' unworthy takes'[1]

from grievances, that are the growth of all times and places and not peculiar to *this age*—which Authors call—this *critical* age, and Divines, *this sinful age*, and Politicians, this *age of Revolutions*.— An acquaintance of mine calls it this *learned age*, in due reverence to his own abilities, and like Monsieur Whatd'ye call him, who used to pull off his Hat, when he spoke of himself.—The poet Laureat calls it—*this golden age*—and with good reason—

> For *him* the fountains with Canary flow,
> And, best of fruit, spontaneous guineas grow.—

Pope in his Dunciad makes it *this leaden age*; but I chuse to call it without an epithet—*this Age*. Many things we must expect to

---

[1] *Hamlet*, III. i. 71–74.

meet with, which it would be hard to bear, if a compensation were not found in honest endeavors to do well; in virtuous affections and connections; and in harmless and reasonable amusements. And why should *not* a man amuse himself sometimes? Vive la bagatelle!—

I received a letter this morning from my friend Allen—he is up to his ears in business, and I sincerely congratulate him upon it—occupation, I am convinced, being the great secret of happiness. 'Nothing makes the temper so fretful as Indolence' said a young Lady, who beneath the soft surface of feminine delicacy possesses a mind acute by Nature, and strengthened by habits of Reflection.—'pon my word, Miss Evans, I beg your pardon a thousand times for bepraising you to your Face—but really I have written so long, that I had forgot, to whom I was writing.—

Have you read Mr Fox's letter to the Westminster Electors? It is quite the *political Go* at Cambridge, and has converted many souls to the Foxite Faith.—

Poor Le Grice has lost half his exhibition—on Christmas Day he dined with the *Grecians* at Christ's Hospital—where, while a little elevé with wine, he met the Steward, with whom he had been in a state of perpetual warfare:—a quarrel ensued—and indeed almost a battle: and in the conclusion, which is the most tragical part of the Story, the Committee have deprived him of 20£ a year.——

Have you seen the Siddons this season? or the Jordan? An acquaintance of mine has a tragedy coming out early in the next Season—the principal character of which Mrs Siddons will act.— He has importuned me to write the Prologue and Epilogue—but conscious of my inability I have excused myself with a jest—and told him—I was too good a Christian to be accessory to the damnation of any thing.—

I hope, Mrs Barlow is well—I have dreamt about her so often lately, that tho' not much inclined to superstition, I am afraid that something must have been the matter with her.—She is really a most charming woman—and no doubt, in Holland, where they proportion *Beauty* to the *Weight*, she would have been the *Toast* of the whole country—how many Ton does she weigh—in her cloaths?——

——There is an old proverb—of—a river of words, and a spoonful of sense—and I think, this letter has been a pretty good proof of it—: but as Nonsense is better than blank paper, I will fill this side with a song, I wrote lately—my friend, Charles Hague,[1] the

[1] Charles Hague (1769–1821), violinist and later Professor of Music at Cambridge.

composer, will set it to wild music, I shall sing it, and accompany myself on my Violin.—Ca ira!—

Cathlóma, who reigned in the Highlands of Scotland about 200 years after the birth of our Saviour, was defeated and killed in a war with a neighbouring Prince—and Nina-thoma, his Daughter (according [to] the custom of those times and that country) was imprisoned in a cave by the Sea Side: this is supposed to be her Complaint.——¹

> How long will ye round me be swelling,
> O ye blue-tumbling waves of the Sea?
> Not always in caves was my dwelling,
> Nor beneath the cold blast of the Tree.
>
> Thro' the high-sounding Hall of Cathlóma
> In the steps of my Beauty I stray'd:
> The Warriors beheld Nina thoma,
> And they blessed the dark-tressed Maid.
>
> By my Friends, by my Lovers discarded
> Like the Flower of the Rock now I waste,
> That lifts it's fair head unregarded,
> And scatters it's leaves on the blast.
>
> A Ghost! by my cavern it darted!
> In moon-beams the Spirit was drest—
> For lovely appear the departed,
> When they visit the dreams of my Rest.
>
> But dispers'd by the tempest's commotion
> Fleet the shadowy forms of Delight:
> Ah! cease, thou shrill Blast of the Ocean!
> To howl thro' my Cavern by night.

Are you asleep, my dear Mary?—I have administered rather a strong Dose of Opium—: however, if in the course of your Nap you should chance to dream, that

I am with the ardour | of fraternal friendship | Your affec-
tionate S. T. Coleridge,

you will never have dreamt a truer dream in all *your born days*.

¹ *Poems*, i. 39.

26. *To George Coleridge*

Address: Revd G. Coleridge | Mr Newcome's | Hackney | London
MS. Lady Cave. Pub. E.L.G. i. 7.
Postmark: 9 February 1793. *Stamped*: Cambridge.

My dear Brother

A little more than a fortnight ago a quantity of matter chose to form in the socket of a decayed tooth, & brought with [it] such violent swelling, inflammation, & other parapharnalia [*sic*] of Pain, as threw me into a fever; but, God be praised! my Gum has at last been opened, my tooth drawn, and this is the fifth day of my convalescence.

I have been very faulty in omitting to write Dr Layard: this Post shall rectify the error, as far as it can be rectified. Dr Pearce, as if fearful lest I should *transfer* my gratitude, took infinite pains to convince me, that Dr L's recommendation had not at all influenced him: nay, he seemed almost offended at my having applied to any but himself. This, as you may suppose, I mean to be inter nos.—Dr L. has every possible claim on my thanks.

—Poor Francis![1] I have shed the tear of natural affection over him.—He was the only one of my Family, whom similarity of Ages made more peculiarly my Brother—he was the hero of all the little tales, that make the remembrance of my earliest days interesting!—Yet his Death filled me rather with Melancholy than Anguish.—I quitted Ottery, when I was so young, that most of those endearing circumstances, that are wont to render the scenes and companions of our childhood delightful in the recollection, I have associated with the place of my education—and when at last I revisited Devon, the manners of the Inhabitants annihilated whatever tender ideas of pleasure my Fancy rather than my Memory had pictured to my Expectation. I found them (almost universally) to be gross without openness, and cunning without refinement.—

But of the state of my feelings with regard to my Brothers, James and Edward, how shall I speak with Truth, yet Delicacy?— I will open my whole heart to you.—Fraternal Affection is the offspring of long Habit, and of Reflection.—But when I first went into the country, I had scarcely seen either James or Edward— they had neither been the companions or the guardians of my Childhood.—To love them therefore was a sensation yet to be learnt—: to be learnt at an age, when my best affections had been forestalled; and when long wont to admire and esteem the few, I

[1] See Letter 20, p. 39, n. 1, concerning Francis Coleridge's death in 1792.

loved—I deemed admiration and esteem necessary parts in the constitution of affection.—I soon perceived, that Edward never thought—that all his finer feelings were the children of accident—and that even these capricious sensibilities were too often swallowed in the vanity of appearing great to little people.—In my brother James I recognized a man of reflection, and *therefore* of virtue—but as the object of that reflection was from his peculiar situation necessarily himself, I saw or thought, I saw, an interested somewhat—a too great attention to external appearances—a warmth in his own concerns, a coldness in those, that related to others, which seemed to render him unapt to be beloved.—Add to this—that both the one and the other exacted a deference, which conscious of few obligations to *them*, aware of no *real* inferiority, and laughing at the artificial claims of primogeniture, I felt myself little inclined to pay.—However, I will write to them—I will assume the semblance of Affection—perhaps, by persevering in appearing, I at last shall learn to be, a Brother.

—I have taken your advice with regard to the mourning—when perfectly convenient to you, I shall accept your offer of the note with gratitude.—Believe your most affectionate

S T Coleridge

27. *To Anne Evans*

MS. Mr. Carl H. Pforzheimer. Pub. Letters, *i. 52.*

Feb: 10th—1793—   Jes: Coll:—Cambridge

My dear Anne

A little before I had received your Mamma's letter, a bird of the air had informed me of your illness—and sure never did owl or night-raven ('those mournful messengers of heavy things') pipe a more loathsome Song. But I flatter myself that ere you have received this scrawl of mine, by care & attention you will have lured back the rosy-lipped Fugitive, Health.—I know of no misfortune so little susceptible of consolation, as Sickness: it is indeed easy to offer comfort, when we ourselves are well; *then* we can be full of grave saws upon the duty of resignation, &c; but alas! when the sore Visitations of Pain come *home*, all our Philosophy vanishes—and nothing remains to be seen—I speak of myself—but a mere sensitive animal, with little wisdom and no patience.—Yet if any thing can throw a melancholy smile over the pale wan Face of Illness, it must be the sight and attentions of those, we love. There are one or two Beings, in this planet of our's,

whom God has formed in so kindly a mould, that I could almost
consent to be ill in order to be nursed by them.

O Turtle-eyed Affection!—
If thou be present—who can be distrest?
Pain seems to smile, and Sorrow is at rest:
No more the Thoughts in wild repinings roll,
And tender murmurs hush the soften'd soul.

But I will not proceed at this rate:—for I am writing and thinking
myself fast into the Spleen, and feel very obligingly disposed to
communicate the same doleful Fit to you, my dear Sister.—Yet
permit me to say, it is almost your own fault—you were half-angry
at my writing *laughing Nonsense* to you—and see what you have
got in exchange—pale-faced, solemn, stiff-starched Stupidity.—I
must confess indeed, that the latter is rather more in unison with
my present feelings—which from one untoward freak of fortune
or other are not of the most comfortable kind——within this last
month I have lost a Brother and a Friend! But I struggle for
chearfulness—and sometimes, when the Sun shines out, I succeed
in the effort.—This at least I endeavor—not to infect the chearful-
ness of others, and not to write my vexations upon my forehead.
I read a story lately of an old Greek Philosopher, who once
harangued so movingly on the miseries of Life, that his Audience
went home, & hanged themselves—but he himself (my Author
adds) lived many years afterwards in very sleek condition.—
  God love you, my dear Anne!—and receive, as from a Brother,
the warmest affections

of your

S. T. Coleridge

28. *To George Coleridge*

Address: Revd G. Coleridge | Mr Newcome's | Clapton near Hackney | London
MS. Lady Cave. Hitherto unpublished.
Postmark: 18 February 1793. *Stamped*: Cambridge.

Pecuniam chartaceam, mî frater, accepi: de quâ amo te, ut
debeo, plurimum.—Castra aestiva me Cantabrigii positurum scito,
et Musis severioribus sacrificia praestaturum. Studia literarum
quotidie magis et magis amo: in eis me oblector, in eis omnia et
seria et joca colloco.—Sensi, sensi, voluptatem, quae ex turpioribus
capitur, celeriter transire: dolorem autem diuturnum relinquere.
At Labor in rebus honestis collocatus, ipse quidem effugit; memo-
riam autem sui in animo relinquit plenam solidissimae voluptatis.

Thesis nobis Odaica Laus Astronomiae[1]—nisi aut animi aut
corporis invaletudine impediar, poeticis quadrigis iterum vehar.

> Ite mordaces, procul ite, Curae!
> Me vocat notis Helicon viretis,
> Me sacrum lauri nemus, et canorum
>   Phocidos antrum.
> O ubi molles Heliconis umbrae!
> O ubi Cydnus, violisque pictum
> Cynthiae rupis caput! O sonori
>   Flumina Pindi!
> Me quis ad vestros Aquilo recessus,
> Aut quis alatâ Zephyrus quadrigâ
> Deferat fessum, gelidosque Cyrrhae
>   Sistat ad amnes?
> Pieris, Graiae fidicen Camaenae,
> Dic, ubi molli resupina somno
> Foeta rumorum cubet eruditis
>   Fama sub antris?

Vale, mi frater—frater animo et voluntate erga me plane
paternâ.—Invitus finem facio, ita mihi videor, dum haec scribo,
jucunde tecum fabulari.—Mi Frater, etiam atque etiam vale.——

[Translation.]

My dear brother,

I have received the banknotes: for this business I send you my
warmest love—as indeed I ought. I have decided to take up my station
for the summer at Cambridge, and to offer sacrifice to the more austere
Muses. I love classical studies more every day: they are my delight, and
in them I find both my serious and my lighter occupations. I know—
how well I know—that the pleasure obtained from lower pursuits rapidly
vanishes; but the regret they leave behind is long-lasting. But labour
expended on worth-while subjects is quickly past, yet the memory which
it leaves in the mind is a source of most enduring pleasure.

The subject given us for an Ode is The Praise of Astronomy—unless
I am hindered by indisposition of body or mind, I shall again launch
into poetry.

Begone afar, ye gnawing Cares! I hear the call of Helicon's familiar
swards, the call of the sacred laurel grove, and Phocis' cave of melody.

O spot where are found the soft shadows of Helicon, where is Cydnus,
and the crest of Cynthia's rock, bright with violets! O music of the
streams of Pindus!

[1] Coleridge submitted a *Greek Ode on Astronomy* for the Browne Medal in
1793, but he was *proxime accessit* to John Keate. The original of the ode is
no longer extant, but Southey published a translation of it, dated 1802, in his
Poet. Works, 10 vols., 1838, ii. 170.

What South wind will bear me, or what Zephyr will carry me in my weariness on winged chariot, to your secret nooks, and set me beside the cool waters of Cyrrha?

Pieris, lyrist of the Grecian Muse, tell me where are those caves of learning in which Fame lies resting in gentle sleep, mother of reputations yet unborn.

Best wishes, my dear brother—a brother whose love and care towards me are truly paternal. I do not want to conclude, so much do I seem to be happily chatting with you as I write this. Best wishes to you, my dear brother, all the very best!

29. *To George Coleridge*

Transcript Coleridge family. Pub. Letters, *i. 53.*

Wednesday Morning   July 28th [24?,] 1793[1]

My dear Brother

I left Salisbury on Tuesday Morning—should have stayed there longer but that Ned ignorant of my coming had preengaged himself on a journey to Portsmouth with Skinner. I left Ned well & merry, as likewise his wife, who by all the Cupids! is a very worthy old Lady. Monday afternoon Ned, Tatum & myself sat from four till ten drinking—and then arose as cool as three undressed Cucumbers. Edward and I—(O! the wonders of this Life) disputed with great coolness & forbearance the whole time——we neither of us were *convinced*, tho' now & then Ned was *convicted*. Tatum Umpire sat, and by decision more embroiled the fray.

I found all well in Exeter—to which place I proceeded directly as my Mother might have been unprepared from the supposition I meant to stay longer at Salisbury.—I shall dine with James today at Brother Phillips![2]

My ideas are so discomposed by the jolting of the coach, that I can write no more at present.

A piece of Gallantry. I presented a moss rose to a Lady[3]—Dick Hart[4] asked her if she was not afraid to put it in her bosom as perhaps there might be Love in it. I immediately wrote the

---

[1] This letter and Letter 30 show that Coleridge left Salisbury on Tuesday 23 July, and proceeded directly to Exeter. Very shortly he went on to Tiverton, where he stayed 'about 10 days'. He arrived at Ottery on or about 3 Aug., having been at Sidmouth the day before.

[2] The husband of Coleridge's half-sister, Elizabeth.

[3] Another manuscript version of this poem was written in pencil on the blank pages of a copy of Langhorne's *Collins*, and is there entitled 'On presenting a Moss Rose to Miss F. Nesbitt'. *Poems of S. T. Coleridge*, ed. by Derwent and Sara Coleridge, 1852, p. 380.

[4] Richard Hart of Exeter, whose sister was the widow of Luke Coleridge.

following little ode or song or what you please to call it. It is of the namby pamby Genus.[1]

> As late each Flower that sweetest blows
>   I pluck'd, the Garden's pride;
> Within the petals of a Rose
>   A sleeping Love I 'spy'd.
>
> Around his brows a lucid wreath
>   Of many a mingled hue:
> And purple glow'd his cheek beneath
>   Inebriate with Dew.
>
> I softly seized th' unguarded Power
>   Nor scar'd his balmy rest,
> And plac'd him caged within the Flower
>   On Angelina's Breast.
>
> But when all reckless of the Guile
>   Awoke the Slumberer sweet,
> He struggled to escape awhile,
>   And stamp'd his angry feet.
>
> Ah! soon the soul entrancing Sight
>   Subdued the impatient Boy:
> He gaz'd, he thrill'd with deep delight
>   Then clapt his Wings for Joy.
>
> And—Oh! he cried—what Charms refin'd
>   This magic Throne endear:
> Another Love may Venus find,
>   I'll fix my Empire here!

An Extempore. Ned during the dispute thinking he had got me down, said, Oh Sam! you blush. Sir, answered I,

> Ten thousand Blushes
> Flutter round me drest like little Loves
> And veil my visage with their crimson wings.

There is no meaning in the Lines but we both agreed they were very pretty. If you see Mr Hussy, you will not forget to present my respects to him—and to his accomplished Daughter, who certes is a very sweet young Lady.

God bless you. Your grateful & affectionate
                                    S. T. Coleridge.

[1] *Poems*, i. 45.

30. *To George Coleridge*

Address: The reverend G. Coleridge at | Mr Newcome's Esq. | Clapton near Hackney | London
MS. Lady Cave. Pub. with omis. Letters, *i. 55.*
Postmark: 5 August 1793. *Stamped*: Honiton.

[Ottery St. Mary]
My dear Brother

Since my arrival in the Country, I have been anxiously expecting a Letter from you—nor can I divine the reason of your Silence.— From the Letter to my Brother James, a few Lines of which he read to me, I am fearful, that your Silence proceeds from Displeasure—If so, what is left for me to do—but to grieve? The Past is not in my Power—for the follies, of which I may have been guilty, I have been greatly disquieted—and I trust, the Memory of them will operate to future consistency of Conduct.——[1]

My Mother is very well—indeed better for her illness—her complexion and eye—the truest indications of Health—are much clearer.——Little William[2] and his Mother are well. My Brother James is at Sidmouth—I was there yesterday—He, his Wife, & Children are well—Frederick is a charming Child—little James[3] had a most providential escape the Day before Yesterday.—As my Brother was in the Field, contiguous to his House, he heard two men scream—and turning round saw a horse leap over little James, and then kick at him—he ran up, found him unhurt—the men said that the Horse was feeding with his tail toward the child, and looking round ran at him open mouthed, pushed him down, and leaped over him, and then kicked back at him—their screaming,

---

[1] From the onset of his Cambridge residence Coleridge was plagued over the lack of money, and in Jan. 1793, after reporting his failure to win a Craven Scholarship, he sent his brother a résumé of his situation and of his plans to liquidate the debts, 'which have corroded my Spirits greatly for some time Past'. At the same time he noted that his debt to his tutor was 'entirely the arrears of my two first Quarters—and I have owed it to him ever since'. By the summer of 1793, when the present letter was written, his financial affairs had reached a crisis and he was awaiting with trepidation a discussion of his debts, which had grown to £148. 17*s*. 1¼*d*. His brothers, apparently after censuring him, provided him with a sum of money; but he frittered away part of it on his way to Cambridge, and on his arrival at college he was confronted with a host of petty bills he had either forgotten or neglected to mention— indeed, he dared not mock his tutor with the small amount which remained. Desperate over his plight and afraid to face his family, he seems to have contemplated suicide. See letter 36, p. 68.

[2] William Hart Coleridge (1789–1849), later Bishop of Barbados, was the son of Luke Coleridge, who died in 1790.

[3] James and Frederick were sons of Coleridge's brother James.

my Brother supposes, prevented the Horse from repeating the
Blow. Brother was greatly agitated, as you may suppose.

I stayed at Tiverton about 10 days, and got no small κῦδος
among the young Belles by complimentary effusions in the poetic
Way—

A Specimen—

Cupid turned Chymist.———[1]

Cupid, if storying Legends tell aright,
Once fram'd a rich Elixir of Delight.
A cauldron o'er love-kindled flames he fix'd,
And in it Nectar and Ambrosia mix'd:
With these the magic Dews, which Evening brings,
Brush'd from th' Idalian* Star by fairy wings:
Each tender Pledge of sacred faith he join'd,
Each gentler Pleasure of th' unspotted mind;
Gay Dreams, whose tints with beamy brightness glow,
And Hope, the blameless Parasite of woe.
With joy he view'd his chymic process rise,
The steaming Cauldron bubbled up in Sighs,
Sweet Sounds transpir'd, as when th' enamour'd Dove
Pours the soft Murmurs of responsive Love.
The finish'd Work not Envy's self could blame—
And 'Kisses' was the precious Compound's name.
With part the God his Cyprian mother blest,
And breath'd on Nesbitt's lovely lips the rest.[2]

* The planet Venus, the Evening Star. [S. T. C.]

Do you know Fanny Nesbitt? She was my fellow-traveller in the
Tiverton diligence from Exeter.—I think a very pretty Girl.—
The orders for Tea are—Imprimis—5£b of 10s Green. Item—4£b
of 8s Green—in all—9£b of Tea.—
Poor Mrs King is dead—and Mr King is almost heart broken—
He has left Ottery for about a Month—I very much wished to
have been in orders, that I might have done the Duty in his
absence for him—Mrs Smerdon is very ill, and has left Ottery
for a while—Smerdon as melancholy as an old cat.—My Sister
Betsey too is unwell—We wish to persuade her to come over to us,
& stay a week at Ottery [for] the benefit of the Air.—

---

[1] *Poems*, i. 46.

[2] A note included in the 1852 edition of Coleridge's *Poems*, p. 380, errone-
ously states that this poem and the one in Letter 29 'were originally addressed
to a Miss F. Nesbitt, at Plymouth'. Actually the poem in Letter 29 was
written at Exeter; the one in this letter at Tiverton. The autograph of *Cupid
turned Chymist*, pencilled in a copy of Langhorne's *Collins*, is signed S. T.
Coleridge, and is dated 'Friday evening, [26 July] 1793'.

(60)

There has been a sad piece of work about Miss Bacon and Charlotte Cosserat—they went to a Fortune-teller—who choused them out of a two guinea piece, & three pounds' worth of cloaths— Mr Bacon very foolishly had the Woman thrown into Prison—she was tried at the assizes, & acquitted. If she can get friends, I apprehend, she means to prosecute the Justice of Peace for false Imprisonment.—Mother desires love—and Sister Sally—and little Will.—The dear Boy looks pale—from eating so much Fruit, I suppose.—God bless you & your obliged

S T Coleridge——

31. *To the Editor of the 'Morning Chronicle'*

Pub. Morning Chronicle, 7 *November 1793.*

In early November Coleridge purchased a ticket in the Irish Lottery, an act immortalized by his lines, *To Fortune,* which appeared with this letter in the *Morning Chronicle.* He failed to win a prize at the drawings, which were concluded about 26 November, but 'an accident of a very singular kind' turned him from 'the dernier resort of misery', and he enlisted in the army a few days later.

[Early November 1793]
Sir,

The following Poem[1] you may perhaps deem admissible into your journal—if not, you will commit it εἰς ἱερὸν μένος Ἡφαίστοιο. I am,

With more respect and gratitude than I ordinarily feel for Editors of Papers, your obliged, &c.,

Cantab.—S. T. C.

32. *To G. L. Tuckett*

Address: G. L. Tuckett Esq | No. 2 | Hare Court | Temple | London
MS. Lady Cave. Pub. with omis. Letters, *i. 57.*

Enlisting in the 15th or King's Light Dragoons on 2 December 1793, and sworn in at Reading two days later, Coleridge adopted the *nom de guerre* of Silas Tomkyn Comberbache, thereby effectually concealing his identity from the army authorities and his whereabouts from his family. His love for Mary Evans may have been a contributing cause of his enlistment—'I never durst even in a whisper avow my passion, though I knew she loved me—Where were my Fortunes?'—but it was his college debts which precipitated his action. Tuckett, as this letter shows, learned of Coleridge's predicament

[1] The title of the enclosed poem was *To Fortune, On buying a Ticket in the Irish Lottery. Composed during a walk to and from the Queen's Head, Gray's Inn Lane, Holborn, and Hornsby's and Co., Cornhill.* Cf. *Poems,* i. 55.

from 'the young men at Christ's Hospital' and not only passed on the informa-
tion to George Coleridge but also consulted with Coleridge's commanding
officer.
Postmark: 7 February 1794. *Stamped*: Henley.

Thursday night—Feb: 6th.—[1794]
Dear Tuckett—

I have this moment received your long Letter!—The Tuesday
before last—on account of the Reading Fair—our Regiment was
dispersed for the week in and about the towns within ten miles of
Reading—and as it was not known before we set off, to what places
who of us would go, my letters were kept at the Reading Post
Office till our return—I was conveyed to Henly upon Thames—
which place our Regiment left last Tuesday—but I was ordered
to remain—on account of those dreadfully troublesome eruptions,
which so grimly constellated my Posteriors—and that I might
nurse my Comrade, who last Friday sickened of the confluent small
Pox.—So Here I am—videlicet—the Pest house of the Henly work
house.——It is a little house of one apartment situated in the
midst of a large garden—about a hundred yards from the house—
it is four strides in length, and three in breadth—has four windows,
which look towards all the winds.—The almost total want of Sleep,
the putrid smell and the fatiguing Struggles with my poor Comrade
during his delirium are nearly too much for me in my present
state—In return, I enjoy external Peace, & kind & respectful
behaviour from the People of the Work house. Tuckett! Your
motives must have been excellent ones—how could they be other-
wise? As an *agent* therefore, you are not only blameless, but your
efforts in my behalf demand my gratitude—*that* my heart will pay
you, into whatever depth of Horror your mistaken activity may
eventually have precipitated me—. As an *agent*, you stand
acquitted—but the action was *morally* base.—In an hour of
extreme anguish under the most solemn Imposition of secrecy I
entrusted my place & residence to the young men at Christ's
Hospital—the intelligence, which you extorted from their Im-
becillity, should have remained sacred with you—it lost not the
obligation of secrecy by the transfer.—But your *motives* justify
you—to the eye of your friendship the divulging might have
appeared *necessary*—but what shadow of *necessity* is there to excuse
you in shewing my letters—to stab the very heart of confidence!—.
You have acted, Tuckett! so uniformly well, that reproof must be
new to you—I doubtless shall have offended you—I would to God,
that I too possessed the tender irritableness of unhandled Sensi-
bility—mine is a sensibility gangrened with inward corruption,
and the keen searching of the air from without! Your gossip with

the commanding officer seems so totally useless and unmotived, that I almost find a difficulty in believing it[1]——

—A letter from my Brother George! I feel a kind of pleasure that it is not directed[2]—it lies unopened—am I not already sufficiently miserable? The anguish of those who love me—of him, beneath the shade of whose protection I grew up—does it not plant my pillow with thorns, and make my dreams full of terrors?—Yet I dare not burn the letter—it seems, as if there were an horror in the action—. —One pang—however acute—is better than long continued sollicitude—My Brother George possesses the cheering consolations of Conscience——but I am talking I know not what / yet there is a pleasure doubtless an exquisite pleasure mingled up in the most painful of our virtuous Emotions——

Alas! my poor Mother! What an intolerable weight of guilt is suspended over my head by a hair on one hand—and if I endure to live—the look ever downward—insult—pity—and hell.—

God or chaos preserve me! What but infinite Wisdom or infinite Confusion can do it!

[No signature in manuscript]

33. *To George Coleridge*

Address: Revd G. Coleridge | Mr Newcome's | Hackney | near | London
MS. Lady Cave. Pub. Letters, *i. 59.*
Postmark: 8 February ⟨1794.⟩ *Stamped*: Henley.

My more than Brother What shall I say—what shall [I] write to you? Shall I profess an abhorrence of my past conduct? Ah me— too well do I know it's Iniquity—but to abhor! this feeble & exhausted heart supplies not so strong an Emotion. O my wayward Soul! I have been a fool even to madness. What shall I dare to promise? My mind is illegible to myself—I am lost in the labyrinth, the trackless wilderness of my own bosom. Truly may I say—I am wearied of being saved. My frame is chill and torpid— the Ebb and Flow of my hopes & fears has stagnated into recklessness—one wish only can I read distinctly in my heart—that it were possible for me to be forgotten as tho' I never had been! The shame and sorrow of those who loved me—the anguish of him, who protected me from my childhood upwards—the sore travail of her who bore me—intolerable Images of horror! They haunt my sleep—they enfever my Dreams! O that the shadow of Death

---

[1] Undeterred by this rebuke Tuckett apparently revealed Coleridge's whereabouts at Cambridge. See Letter 38. For his sneering attitude towards Coleridge two years later see note to Letter 112, p. 192 n. 1.

[2] Undoubtedly Tuckett had forwarded George Coleridge's letter to Coleridge.

were on my Eyelids! That I were like the loathsome form, by which
I now sit! O that without guilt I might ask of my Maker Annihila-
tion! My Brother—my Brother—pray for me—comfort me, my
Brother![1] I am very wretched—and tho' my complaint be bitter,
my stroke is heavier than my groaning.—

S T Coleridge

34. *To George Coleridge*

Address: The reverend G. Coleridge | Mr Newcome's | Hackney | near
London.—
MS. Lady Cave. Pub. with omis. Letters, i. 60.
Postmark: ⟨12⟩ February ⟨1794⟩.   *Stamped*: Henley.

Tuesday Night [11 February 1794]

I am indeed oppressed—oppressed with the greatness of your
Love.—Mine eyes gush out with tears—my heart is sick and
languid with this weight of unmerited kindness. I had intended to
have given you a minute history of my thoughts, and actions for
the last two years of my Life—A most severe and faithful history
of the heart would it have been—the Omniscient knows it.—But
I am so universally unwell—and the hour so late—that I must
defer it till to morrow. To night I shall have a bed in a separate
room from my comrade—and, I trust, shall have repaired my
strength by Sleep ere the morning—For eight days and nights I

---

[1] George Coleridge lost no time in replying. 'I was comforted', he wrote,
'by the Sight of your own hand-writing/ . . . Knowing your Situation, I only
wish to hear from you, what your views are, whether directed to a particular
object; or to *any* that I can point out suited to your abilities—This should
be settled previous to your emancipation being negotiated—When you have
given me your opinion: that matter shall be transacted as agreeably as possible
to your feelings—Some leading Ideas on the Subject from you might facilitate
our endeavors. . . . Your Brother James I am assured *will* if necessary stand
forward in the business—'

A day or two later he wrote again: 'Mr. Plampin [Coleridge's tutor at Jesus
College] sent me this morning [10 February] the sense of the College respecting
you and your affairs—He expresses from them a hope of your early return—
continues your name on the boards, and says that such steps if agreeable to
yourself may still secure to you your Christ's Hospital allowance & Rustat
Scholarship, full now 70£ per annum. In such case your decision should be
certainly to return for every reason in the world. . . . A handsome Sum shall
be gotten ready for the liquidation of your College debts, if either my interest
or person can procure it—and the business of your discharge commenc'd
immediately—Write me as swift as wind—that I may take every step for
restoring you to happiness & myself—Mr. Bowyer (I hear) insinuates that you
[had] leave of him to leave College—God bless him—for a man of his disposi-
tion to descend to so amiable a fraud demands no trifling respect from us—
I saw Tuckett yesterday—We talk'd, regretted & hop'd—'

Facsimile of a Letter from Samuel Taylor Coleridge to James Coleridge, dated Feb: 20th 1794

have not had my Cloaths off—My Comrade is not dead—there is every hope of his escaping Death—Closely has he been pursued by the mighty Hunter!

Undoubtedly—my Brother! I would wish to return to College— I know, what I *must suffer* there—but deeply do I feel, what I *ought* to suffer.—Is my Brother James still at Salisbury? I will write to him—to all!

Concerning my emancipation, it appears to me, that my discharge may be easily procured by *Interest*—with great difficulty by NEGOCIATION—but of this is not my Brother James a more competent Judge?

What my future Life may produce, I dare not anticipate.—Pray for me my Brother.—I will pray nightly to the Almighty Dispenser of good and evil, that his Chastisements may not have harrowed up my heart in vain!—Scepticism had mildewed my hope in the Saviour—I was far from disbelieving the Truth of revealed Religion, but still farther from a steady Faith.—True and active Faith, the 'Comforter that should have relieved my Soul,['] was far from me—

Farewell—to morrow I will resume my Pen.——Mr Bowyer!— indeed—indeed—my heart thanks him! how often in the petulance of Satire, how ungratefully have I injured that man!

S. T. Colerid[ge.]

35. *To James Coleridge*

Address: Captn James Coleridge | Tiverton | Devonshire
MS. British Museum. Pub. Letters, *i. 61.* A photograph of this manuscript hangs in the Officers' Mess of the Regiment, now the 15th King's Royal Hussars.
Stamped: Henley.

Feb: 20th 1794

In a mind, which Vice has not utterly divested of sensibility, few occurrences can inflict a more acute pang, than the receiving proofs of tenderness, and love where only resentment and reproach were expected and deserved. The gentle Voice of Conscience, which had incessantly murmured within the soul, then raises it's tone, and speaks with the tongue of thunder. My conduct towards you and towards my other Brothers has displayed a strange Combination of Madness, Ingratitude, & Dishonesty—But you forgive me—May my Maker forgive me! May the Time arrive, when I shall have forgiven myself!——

With regard to my Emancipation, every enquiry I have made, every piece of Intelligence, I could collect, alike tends to assure me, that it may be done by *Interest*, but not by negociation without an Expence, which I should tremble to write.—Forty guineas were offered for a discharge the day after the young man was sworn in— and were refused—His friends made Interest—and his discharge came down from the War Office—If however negociation *must* be first attempted, it will be expedient to write to our Colonel—his Name is Gwynne[1]—he holds the rank of General in the Army—his address—General Gwynne K.L.D. | King's Mews | London. | My assumed Name is Silas Tomkyn Comberbache[2] 15th or King's Reg. of Light Dragoons—G. Troop—My *Number* I do not know— it is of no Import.

The Bounty, I received, was 6 guineas and a half—but a light horseman's bounty is a mere Lure—it is expended for him in things which he must have had without a Bounty—Gaiters, a pair of Leather Breeches, Stable Jacket and Shell, Horse Cloth, Surcingle, Watering Bridle, Brushes, and the long et cetera of military accoutrement. I *enlisted* the 2nd of Decemb[er,] 1793, was attested and sworn in the 4th—

I am at present nurse to a sick man, and shall I believe stay at Henly another week—there will be a large draught from our Regiment to complete our Troops abroad—the men were picked out to day—I suppose, I am not one—being a very indocile Equestrian—Farewell!

—S. T. Coleridge

Our Regiment are at Reading, and Hounslow, and Maidenhead, and Kensington—Our head quarters—Reading, Berks.—The commanding Officer there—Lieutenant Hopkinson, our adjutant.—

36. *To George Coleridge*

Address: Revd G. Coleridge | Mr Newcome's | Hackney | near | London Single.
MS. Lady Cave. Pub. E.L.G. i. 12.
Postmark: 24 February 1794. *Stamped*: Henley.

—Sunday night. Feb. [23,] 1794
My Brother would have heard from me long ere this, had I not been unwell—unwell indeed—I verily thought, that I was hasten-

[1] Soon after receiving this letter James Coleridge wrote to General Gwyn, and the subsequent difficulties encountered in obtaining a discharge by 'negociation' bear out the wisdom of Coleridge's advice. See headnote to Letter 43.

[2] Coleridge's assumed name has been consistently misspelled (Allsop, Cottle, Gillman, Campbell, E. H. Coleridge, and Chambers). Here the manuscript reads Comberbache.

ing to that quiet Bourne, Where grief is hush'd—And when my recovered Strength would have enabled me to have written to you, so utterly dejected were my Spirits, that my letter would have displayed such a hopelessness of all future Comfort, as would have approached to Ingratitude—

Pardon me, my more than brother—! if it be the sickly jealousy of a mind sore with 'self-contracted miseries'—but was your last letter written in the same tone of tenderness with your former! Ah me! what awaits me from within and without, after the first tumult of Pity shall have subsided—Well were it, if the consciousness of having merited it could arm my Heart for the patient endurance of it—.

Sweet in the sight of God and celestial Spirits are the tears of Penitence—the pearls of heaven—the Wine of Angels!—Such has been the Language of Divines—but Divines have exaggerated.— Repentance may bestow that tranquillity, which will enable man to pursue a course of undeviating harmlessness, but it can not restore to the mind that inward sense of Dignity, which is the parent of every kindling Energy!—I am not, what I was:—*Disgust*—I *feel*, as if it had—jaundiced all my Faculties.

I laugh almost like an insane person when I cast my eye backward on the prospect of my past two years—What a gloomy *Huddle* of eccentric Actions, and dim-discovered motives! To real Happiness I bade adieu from the moment, I received my first Tutor's Bill—since that time since that period my Mind has been irradiated by Bursts only of Sunshine—at all other times gloomy with clouds, or turbulent with tempests. Instead of manfully disclosing the disease, I concealed it with a shameful Cowardice of sensibility, till it cankered my very Heart.—I became a proverb to the University for Idleness—the time, which I should have bestowed on the academic studies, I employed in dreaming out wild Schemes of impossible extrication. It had been better for me, if my Imagination had been less vivid—I could not with such facility have shoved aside Reflection! How many and how many hours have I stolen from the bitterness of Truth in these soul-enervating Reveries—in building magnificent Edifices of Happiness on some fleeting Shadow of Reality! My Affairs became more and more involved—I fled to Debauchery—fled from silent and solitary Anguish to all the uproar of senseless Mirth! Having, or imagining that I had, no *stock* of Happiness, to which I could look forwards, I seized the empty gratifications of the moment, and snatched at the Foam, as the Wave passed by me.——I feel a painful blush on my cheek, while I write it—but even for the Un. Scholarship, for which I affected to have read so severely, I did not read three days uninterruptedly—for the whole six weeks, that preceded the examination, I was almost constantly intoxicated! My Brother, you shudder as you read——

When the state of my affairs became known to you, and by your exertions, and my Brothers' generous Confidence a fair Road seemed open to extrication—Almighty God! What a sequel!——

I loitered away more money on the road, and in town than it was possible for me to justify to my Conscience—and when I returned to Cambridge a multitude of petty Embarrassments buzzed round me, like a Nest of Hornets—Embarrassments, which in my wild carelessness I had forgotten, and many of which I had contracted almost without knowing it—So small a sum remained, that I could not mock my Tutor with it—My Agitations were delirium—I formed a Party, dashed to London at eleven o'clock at night, and for three days lived in all the tempest of Pleasure— resolved on my return—but I will not shock your religious feelings —I again returned to Cambridge—staid a week—such a week! Where Vice has not annihilated Sensibility, there is little need of a Hell! On Sunday night I packed up a few things,—went off in the mail—staid about a week in a strange way, still looking forwards with a kind of recklessness to the dernier resort of misery—An accident of a very singular kind prevented me—and led me to adopt my present situation—where what I have suffered —but enough—may he, who in mercy dispenseth Anguish, be gracious to me!

> Ulcera possessis alte suffusa medullis
> Non leviore manu, ferro sanantur et igni,
> Ne coeat frustra mox eruptura cicatrix—
> Ad vivum penetrant flammae, quò funditus humor
> Defluat, et vacuis corrupto sanguine venis
> Exundet fons ille mali. Claud.[1]——

I received a letter from Tiverton on Thursday full of wisdom, and tenderness, and consolation—I answered it immediately—Let me have the comfort of hearing from you—I will write again to morrow night—

S. T. C.—

---

[1] Claudianus, *In Eutropium*, ii. 13. Coleridge reads *coeat* for *noceat*, *exundet* for *arescat*, and *ille* for *ipse*.

37. To George Coleridge

Address: Revd G. Coleridge | Mr Newcome's | Hackney | near | London
MS. Lady Cave. Pub. E.L.G. i. 15.
Postmark: 28 February 1794. *Stamped*: Henley.

Thursday Night——[27 February 1794]
My dear Brother

Your letter rekindled my hopes of myself—With every motive, that dear bought experience, that overwhelmed Gratitude, can suggest, I must be indeed a very monster of Imbecillity to relapse, or be stationary in the road of well doing! Let me build Confidence on Humility——

—I owe my Shoemaker at Cambridge 3£—and I owe my Taylor a Bill—of what amount, I am not positively accurate—but to the best of my remembrance it is about 10£. Besides these, I owe nothing.

—Rather a disagreeable circumstance has happened to me here— When I first became resident near the poor house as attendant on the Sick man, for a few days I procured and dressed my own food— But my going backwards and forwards to the Town being offensive and dangerous to the uninfected, the Mistress of the Workhouse continued to send me down my dinner—I begg'd leave to pay her regularly as for my board—She would not hear of it—and told me, I was extremely welcome—it was a trifle that made no perceivable difference in her large Family—I accepted her offer, and spent my weekly stipend in the additional comforts, I so much wanted—At the end of the month—being to day—a Bill is prepared on the army accounts for my Board—the Governors of the Workhouse having heard, that I had received my Food constantly—& the Mistress of the House being dangerously sick in bed.—This bill I must prevent from being presented—for board and washing they have charged me for the Month 23 Shillings—and this I must apply to you for—I must settle it on Saturday, as on that day I quit Henly for High Wickham in Oxfordshire.—

I have received a letter from my Brother James with an account of the Steps, which are taken for my Liberation—God bless him!

I did not think, it was so late—I conclude hastily, that I may perform my Resolution of writing my honored Parent, and my Brother Edward—

God preserve you | & your obliged & grateful Brother
S. T. Coleridge

38. *To George Coleridge*

Address: Revd G. Coleridge | Mr Newcome's | Hackney | London
MS. Lady Cave. Pub. E.L.G. i. 16.
Postmark: 3 March 179⟨4⟩.   *Stamped*: High Wycombe.

My dear Brother

By the advice of the Cornet, to whom on not receiving a letter from you on Saturday I applied, I have suffered the Bill to go in to the Adjutant—the Cornet advises me to explain the matter to the Adjutant—but to have the money ready for discharging the Bill—I moved from Henly on Saturday—on the Baggage Cart—it rained a mizzley rain the whole Journey, which tho' but 12 miles took us four hours—so that I feel all over me a violent cold, and a feverette—but it will soon go off, I trust. My present address is— | the Compasses | High Wycomb | Bucks— | Your direction tho' corruptly spelt &c answered——You may with perfect assurance of safety inclose the money in a letter to me—unless you have an opportunity of sending me a parcel by any of the numerous Coaches passing thro' Wycomb—but none pass your way—and a letter is equally a safe vehicle.

My present situation is indeed fatiguing, and involves a long et cetera of disagreeables—but to me, who have suffered so acutely from the diseases of the inward man, externals have lost much of the formidable.—I hear from Allen, that Le Grice has discovered my present situation (from Tuckett, I suppose) and was then on his journey to Henly—I am sorry [for] this on many accounts.—

The moments I can abstract from more interesting and more intrusive thoughts I am dedicating to the Cambridge Odes—whatever be my lot with respect to College this can do me no harm, and by amusing me certainly does some good—Whate'er betides, some Solace have I won—Farewell—my dear Brother—I pray, that I may be sometime in kind as well as kin

Your Brother
S. T. Coleridge

39. *To George Coleridge*

Address: Revd G. Coleridge | Mr Newcome's | Hackney | London
MS. Lady Cave. Pub. with omis. Letters, i. 62.
Postmark: 5 March 1794.   *Stamped*: High Wycombe.

Tuesday Evening—[4 March 1794]

My dear Brother

Accept my poor thanks for the day's Inclosed, which I received safely—I explained the whole matter to the Adjutant, who

(70)

laughed—and said, I had been used scurvily—he deferred settling the bill till Thursday Morning.—A Captain Ogle of our Regiment, who is just returned from abroad (where if report may be trusted he behaved not the most heroically)[1] has taken great notice of me—when he visits the stables of a night, he always enters into Conversation with me—and to day finding from the Corporal's Report that I was unwell, he sent me a couple of bottles of Wine—these Things demand my gratitude—[2]

I wrote last week—currente calamo—a declamation for my dear Friend, Allen—on the comparative good and Evil of Novels—the credit, which A. got by it, I should almost blush to tell you—All the Fellows have got copies—and they meditate having it printed, and dispersing it thro' the University—The best part of it I built on a sentence in a late Letter of your's—and indeed I wrote most part of it *feelingly.*

I met yesterday—smoking in a recess—a chimney corner of the pot-house, at which I am quartered, a man of the greatest information and most original Genius, I ever lit upon. His Philosophical Theories of Heaven & Hell would have both amused you, and given you hints for much speculation—he solemnly assured me, that he believed himself divinely inspired—he slept in the same room with me, and kept me awake till 3 in the morning with his Ontological Disquisitions. Some of the Ideas would have made you shudder from their daring Impiety—others would have astounded you with their sublimity—My Memory tenacious & systematizing would enable [me] to write an Octavo from his Conversation—'I find (says he) from the intellectual Atmosphere, that emanes from, and envelopes you, that you are in a state of Recipiency'—He was deceived—I have little *Faith,* yet am wonderfully fond of speculating on mystical schemes—Wisdom may be gathered from the maddest flights of Imagination, as medicines were stumbled upon in the wild processes of Alchemy—

God bless you & | Your ever grateful

S. T. Coleridge

I leave this place on Thursday—10 o'clock—for Reading—A letter will arrive in time before I go.—

[1] This parenthetical statement was omitted by E. H. Coleridge.

[2] This is the only reference to Captain Nathaniel Ogle in Coleridge's army letters. He may have exerted himself in a private capacity; but since he had just returned from abroad and since his name is nowhere mentioned in the correspondence between George Coleridge and the military authorities, it would seem that his services were of the nature of those mentioned in this letter. The statements made after Coleridge's death by Mary Russell Mitford and W. L. Bowles were apparently based on misinformation concerning Ogle's part in the negotiations for Coleridge's release.

40. *To George Cornish*[1]

Address: G. Cornish Esq. | Great George Street | Westminster
Transcript Coleridge family. Pub. E.L.G. i. 17.
Postmark: 13 March 1794.

Reading. Wed. March 12th, 1794

My heart thanks you, dear Sir! for the kindness and delicacy of your attention towards me[2]—the tenderness of those, whom I love and esteem, has increased in an inverse proportion to my well-doing—a reflection, which gives me pleasure, while it humiliates me. My assumed name, and my address are— | Mr Comberbache | 15th K. L. D. White Hart | Reading Berks.— | What steps my Brothers are taking towards my emancipation, I know not—not having heard from my Brother G. for this last week—: but I apprehend that Mr Rider has been solicited to employ his interest with our Colonel—whether or when this is to take place, I am ignorant. Our Colonel's name is Gwynne—he has, I believe, the rank of General in the army—his residence in town is at the King's Mews—

My situation has, I find, been disclosed within these few days to my Cambridge friends—I have received several Letters written in the tenderest tone of Friendship and Consolation. I am assured

---

[1] George Cornish of Ottery St. Mary.

[2] In a letter to his wife George Cornish describes his meeting with Coleridge on Sunday, 9 Mar. 1794: 'At Reading it occurred to me that I might probably find out Sam Colridge—say not a word about it as the family may think me meddling, but I felt a sort of attachment for him and therefore endeavoured to find him out—for which purpose I spoke to many of the Dragoons who knew of no such name. At last a well-spoken man described to me Sam Colridge conceiving him to be the man I meant—but says he, Sir, if I tell him there is a gentleman wants to see him he will not come. I will make some excuse to bring him this way in five minutes. I saw the man with another coming towards me, when to my infinite surprise I saw Sam Colridge full accoutred as a Dragoon. The moment he saw me he turned away. I called to him; he then stopped. We walked together along the street, but it was some minutes before he spoke to me; he seemed much agitated. After a little time he discovered I did not mean to insult his misfortunes but to alleviate them if I could; he gave me a little detail of his sufferings, but he says they are not half enough to expiate his follies—The soldier told me he received half a guinea a week and a newspaper daily, but he told me he had refused any assistance—Whether his brothers mean to punish him or whether they have not sufficient interest to procure his discharge I know not, but he is not discharged yet and goes through all the drudgery of a Dragoon recruit. I need not say how I felt; he has never been from my thoughts since. I offered him some money—which he refused, but not in a way but what I saw it would be acceptable to him. I therefore gave him a guinea, which was all I had except a few shillings and fortunately I had no more, for as I then felt he would have had it all. Don't say a word about it.'

that 'with undiminished esteem and increased affection they look forward to my arrival among them, as of a lost Brother.' I have been, deeply do I feel that I have been, the dupe of my Imagination, the slave of Impulse, the child of Error and Imbecillity—yet when I look back on the number and character of those, who have honored me with their Regard, I am almost reconciled to myself, and half-listen to the whispers of self-adulation.

Adieu, dear Sir! Accept the poor esteem and gratitude of your obliged

S. T. Coleridge.

41. *To George Coleridge*

Address: Reverend George Coleridge | —Mr Newcome's | Hackney | London
MS. Lady Cave. Pub. Letters, *i. 66.*
Stamped: Reading.

Friday Night.—[14 March 1794]

My dear Brother

I have been rather uneasy, that I have not heard from you since my departure from High Wycombe—your letters are a comfort to me in the comfortless Hour—they are Manna in the Wilderness. I should have written you long ere this, but in truth I have been blockaded by an whole army of petty Vexations—bad quarters &c—and within this week I have been thrown three times from my Horse, and run away with to the no small pertubation of my nervous system almost every day.—I ride an horse young, and as undisciplined as myself. After tumult and agitation of any kind the mind and all it's affections seem to *dose* for a while—and we sit shivering with chilly feverishness wrapped up in the ragged and threadbare cloak of mere animal enjoyment.

On Sunday last, I was surprized, or rather confounded with a visit from Mr Cornish—*so* confounded, that for more than a minute I could not speak to him. He behaved with great delicacy, and much apparent solicitude of Friendship. He passed thro' Reading with his Sister, Lady Shore. I have received several Letters from my friends at Cambridge—of most soothing Contents. They write me, that 'with undiminish[ed] esteem, and increased affection the *Jesuites* look forward to my return, as to that of a lost Brother.[']—

My present address is | the White Hart | Reading | Berks.—
Adieu, most dear Brother!

S. T. Coleridge

42. *To George Coleridge*

Address: Revd G. Coleridge | Mr Newcome's | Hackney | London
MS. Lady Cave. Pub. Letters, *i. 64.*
Postmark: 25 March 1794. *Stamped*: Reading.

Sunday Night—[23 March 1794]

I have endeavoured to feel what I ought to feel—affiliated to you from my childhood what must be my present sensations? but I know you, my dear Brother! and I entertain an humble confidence, that my efforts in well-doing shall in some measure repay you.—There is a vis inertiae in the human mind—I am convinced that a man once corrupted will ever remain so, unless some sudden revolution, some unexpected change of Place or Station shall have utterly altered his connection. When these Shocks of adversity have electrified his moral frame, he feels a convalescence of soul, and becomes like a being recently formed from the hands of Nature.

—The last letter I received from you at High Wycomb was that almost blank letter, which inclosed the guinea—I have written to the Post-master.—I have breeches, and waistcoats at Cambridge—three or four Shirts, and some neck cloths, and a few pair of Stockings—the clothes which rather from the order of the Regiment than the impulse of my necessities I parted with in Reading on my first arrival at the Regiment, I disposed of for a mere trifle comparatively, and at a small expence can recover them—all but my Coat and Hat—they are gone irrevocably—My Shirts which I have with me are all but one worn to rags, mere rags—their texture was ill adapted to the Labor of the Stables.

Shall I confess to you my weakness, my more than Brother! I am afraid to meet you—. When I call to mind the toil and wearisomeness of your avocations, and think how you sacrifice your amusements, and your health—when I recollect your habitual and self-forgetting Economy, how generously severe—my soul sickens at it's own guilt—A thousand Reflections crowd on my Mind—they are almost too much for me. Yet you, my Brother, would comfort me—not reproach me—and extend the hand of forgiveness to one, whose purposes were virtuous tho' infirm, and whose energies vigorous, tho' desultory.—Indeed I long to see you, altho' I cannot help dreading it.——

I mean to write Dr Pearce—the letter I will inclose to you—perhaps it may not be proper to write—perhaps it may be necessary—you will best judge. The discharge should, I think, be sent down to the Adjutant—yet I don't know—it would be more comfortable to me to receive my dismission in London were it not for the appearing in these Cloaths.

By to morrow I shall be enabled to tell the exact expences of equipping &c.

—I must conclude abruptly—

God bless you | Your grateful | S T Coleridge

43. *To George Coleridge*

Address: Revd G. Coleridge | Mr Newcome's | Hackney | London
MS. Lady Cave. Pub. Letters, *i. 66*

Postmark: 27 March 1794.   *Stamped*: Reading.

Although in late February James Coleridge had made an application to General Gwyn for the release of his brother from the army, no reply had been forthcoming by the middle of March, thus leaving the family wholly without information concerning the intention of the army authorities. During this interval George Coleridge had given his attention to Coleridge's college indebtedness and the possibility of liquidating it by instalments. Knowing, too, that Coleridge could retain his Rustat Scholarship only by appearing at the examination in Easter week, he was fearful of the consequences of any further delay and appealed himself to General Gwyn:

'About a fortnight since a letter was committed to your Servant's hand for you from Captn. Coleridge, in behalf of an unfortunate Brother, who has, incautious of the consequences, enlisted in the Regnt. under your Command—His discharge was therein requested, and as his peculiar situation at College made dispatch necessary, we are alarm'd at your silence—If you will gratify me with an interview on any day, but on a Sunday, I shall be happy to wait on you—'

Captain Hopkinson, now in command of the King's Light Dragoons, replied on 20 March 1794:

'General Gwyn sent me your Letter this Morning desiring me to make his excuse to you for not answering it himself—caused by the whole of his Time being taken up in raising a new Regiment of Cavalry His Majesty has honored him with the Command of.

'I . . . shall be exceedingly happy to contribute to the relief of your anxiety for your Brother and will, if in my power, obtain you his Discharge. If you can make it convenient to call here any Morning about Ten o'clock, I shall with pleasure inform you of the only mode I can think of to indemnify the Regiment for the loss of a Recruit, should Mr Coleridge be discharged.'

Captain Hopkinson obviously requested a substitute recruit, for on 26 Mar., an intermediary, C. Pell, wrote to George Coleridge:

'After parting with you I made the enquiry relative to procuring a Man; but am sorry to say that the *Gentlemen Crimps* (who are the only people to be resorted to on such an occasion) will not undertake it under 25 Guineas; however if you wish it, I will certainly call on Captn. Hopkinson and use every influence I shall find myself Master of to induce him to lower his demand.'

What next transpired is unknown, but on 8 April, Captain Hopkinson wrote to George Coleridge:

'Yesterday I returned the Discharge to the Adjutant with directions to deliver it to Mr Coleridge and to tell him he was at liberty to return to his Friends whenever he pleased.'

Apparently the demand for a substitute recruit was abandoned, and the commanding officer, 'whose responsibility it was to forward recommendations to the War Office', offered insanity as the grounds for Coleridge's release, the Regulations permitting the granting of a discharge by such a method. The muster roll of the regiment reads: 'discharged S. T. Comberbach / Insane / 10 Apl.', and the regimental monthly return for May 1794, signed by Captain Nathaniel Ogle, reiterates: 'the other Man was dischd. being Insane.' Cf. Vera Watson, 'Coleridge's Army Service', *Times Literary Supplement*, 7 July 1950, p. 428. There is no evidence that either Coleridge or his family knew of the means adopted for his release. See E. L. Griggs, 'Coleridge's Army Experience', *English*, Summer 1953, pp. 171–5.

[26 March 1794]

My dear Brother

I find, that I was too sanguine in my expectations of recovering all my Clothes—My Coat, which I had supposed gone, and all the Stockings—viz—4 pair of almost new silk stockings, and 2 pair of new silk & cotton I can get again—for 23 Shillings—I have ordered therefore a pair of Breeches, which will be 19 Shillings, a Waistcoat at 12 Shillings, a pair of Shoes at 7s—4d. Besides these I must have an Hat, which will be 18 Shillings, and two Neck-cloths which will be 5 or 6 Shill.—These things I have ordered—— My travelling expences will be about half a guinea—Have I done wrong in ordering these things? Or did you not mean me to do it by desiring me to arrange what was necessary for my personal appearance at Cambridge? I have so seldom acted right, that in every step I take of my own accord I tremble lest I should be wrong.—I forgot in the above account to mention a flannel Waistcoat—it will be 6 Shillings—The military dress is almost oppressively warm—and so very ill as I am at present, I think it imprudent to hazard cold——.

I will see you at London—or rather at Hackney.—

There will be two or three trifling Expences on my leaving the Army—I know not their exact amount.——

The Adjutant dismissed me from all Duty yesterday.——

My head throbs so, and I am so sick at Stomach that [it] is with difficulty I can write—

—One thing more I wished to mention—There are three Books, which I parted with at Reading—the Bookseller, whom I have occasionally obliged by composing Advertisements for his News-paper, has offered them me at the same price, he bought them— They are—a very valuable Edition of Casimir by Barbou, a Synesius by Canterus, and Bentley's F[irst] Quarto Edition[1]—

---

[1] *Mathiae Casimiri Sarbievii, . . . Carmina. Nova editio, prioribus longe*

They are worth 30 [Shilli]ngs at least—and I sold them for 14.—
The two first I mean to translate—I have finished two or three
Odes of Casimir—and shall on my return to College send them to
Dodsley as a specimen of an intended Translation[1]—Barbou's
Edition is the only one, that contains all the works of Casimir—
God bless you—Your grateful

S. T. C.

44. *To George Coleridge*

Address: Reverend G. Coleridge | Mr Newcome's | Hackney | London
MS. Lady Cave. Pub. Letters, *i. 68.*
Postmark: 31 ⟨March⟩ 1794.

March 30th 1794—Sunday Night

My dear Brother

I received your enclosed—I am fearful, that as you advise me
to go immediately to Cambridge after my discharge,[2] that the
utmost contrivances of Economy will not enable [me] to make it
adequate to all the expences of my Cloaths, and Travelling—I shall
go across the Country on many accounts—the expence (I have
examined) will be as nearly equal as well can be—The *fare* from
Reading to High Wycomb on the outside is four Shillings—from
High Wycomb to Cambridge (for *there is* a Coach that passes thro'
Cambridge from Wycomb) I suppose about 12 Shillings—perhaps
a little more—I shall be two days and a half on the road—two
nights—Can I calculate the expence at less than half a guinea,
including all things? An additional guinea would perhaps be
sufficient—Surely my Brother I am not so utterly abandoned as
not to feel the *meaning* and *duty* of *Economy*—O me! I wish to God
I were happy—but it would be strange indeed, if I were so.

---

auctior et emendatior, Parisiis, typ. J. Barbou, 1759; *Synesius*, ed. with Greek
and Latin text, by G. Canterus, 1567; and probably Richard Bentley's *Horace*,
the quarto edition appearing in 1711.
  [1] In the *Cambridge Intelligencer* for 14 June and 26 July 1794, Coleridge
inserted an advertisement: 'Proposals for publishing by Subscription *Imitations from the Modern Latin Poets*, with a critical and biographical Essay on
the Restoration of Literature.... In the Course of the Work will be introduced
a copious Selection from the Lyrics of Casimir, and a new Translation of the
Basia of Secundus.' Except for the translation of a single ode of Casimir
(cf. *Poems*, i. 59) this plan came to nothing.
  [2] Possibly George Coleridge feared that his brother might linger in London
if he saw Mary Evans, though Tuckett offered assurance that a meeting was
unlikely: 'He must, I am conscious, feel too much shame to entertain even
a wish of having an interview with Mrs. Evans' family.'

I long ago theoretically and in a less degree experimentally knew the necessity of Faith in order to regular Virtues—nor did I ever seriously disbelieve the existence of a future State—In short, my religious Creed bore and perhaps bears a correspondence with my mind and heart—I had too much Vanity to be altogether a Christian—too much tenderness of Nature to be utterly an Infidel. Fond of the dazzle of Wit, fond of subtlety of Argument, I could not read without some degree of pleasure the levities of Voltaire, or the reasonings of Helvetius—but tremblingly alive to the feelings of humanity, and su[s]ceptible of the charms of Truth my Heart forced me to admire the beauty of Holiness in the Gospel, forced me to *love* the Jesus, whom my Reason (or perhaps my *reasonings*) would not permit me to *worship*—My Faith therefore was made up of the Evangelists and the Deistic Philosophy—a kind of *religious Twilight*—I said—*perhaps bears*—Yes! my Brother—for who can say—*Now* I'll be a Christian—Faith is neither altogether voluntary, or involuntary—We cannot believe what we choose—but we can certainly cultivate such habits of thinking and acting, as will give force and effective Energy to the Arguments on either side—.

If I receive my discharge by Thursday, I will be—God pleased— in Cambridge on Sunday—Farewell! my Brother—believe me your severities only wound me as they awake the *Voice within* to speak ah! how more harshly! I feel gratitude and love towards you, even when I shrink and shiver——

Your Affectionate
S. T. Coleridge

45. *To George Coleridge*

Address: Revd G. Coleridge | Hackney | London
MS. Lady Cave. Pub. with omis. Letters, *i. 69.*
Postmark: 7 April 1794. *Stamped*: Reading.

My dear Brother

The last three days I have spent at Bray, near Maidenhead at the House of a Gentleman who has behaved with particular attention to me—I accepted his invitation, as it was in my power in some measure to repay his kindness by the revisal of a Performance, he is about to publish—and by writing him a dedication & preface. At my return I found two Letters from you, the one containing the two guineas, which will be perfectly adequate to my expences—O my Brother—what some part of your letter made me feel, I am ill able to express—but of this at another time—I have signed the certificate of my Expences, but not my discharge—The moment I receive it I shall set off for Cambridge immediately— most probably through London—as the Gentleman, whose house I was at at Bray, has pressed me to take his horse, and accompany him on Wednesday Morning, as he himself intends to ride to town that day—If my discharge comes down on Tuesday morning, I shall embrace his offer—particularly as I shall be introduced to his Bookseller, a thing of some consequence to my present views.—

Clagget has set four songs of mine most divinely—for two violins and a piano forte——

I have done him some services—and he wishes me to write a serious Opera, which he will set—and have introduced—it is to be a joint work—I think of it—the rules for *adaptable* composition which he has given me are excellent—and I feel my powers greatly strengthened—owing, I believe, to my having read little or nothing for these last four months—

God bless you, my Brother
I am | with affectionate | Gratitude | Your
S T Coleridge

46. *To George Coleridge*

Address: The Reverend G. Coleridge | Mr Newcome's | Hackney | London
MS. Lady Cave. Pub. E.L.G. i. 19.
Postmark: 12 April 1794. *Stamped*: Cambridge.

[11 April 1794]

My dear Brother

On Wednesday night I arrived from Reading—I took my place immediately in the Cambridge Fly—went there half past 7, found the Horses not put to—so walked on before—saw another Coach go up a different road—pursued it under a false supposition—in the mean time the Fly passed by—I missed it—so went to Cambridge on the outside of the Mail—and have arrived safe. I have not yet seen Dr Pearce—he is gone out to Dinner—I wrote to him as soon as I got up this morning—From violent pain in my Limbs, I am not able to write distinctly what I would wish to say—only that I am with excess of warmest gratitude & affection

Your Brother
S. T. Coleridge

47. *To George Coleridge*

Address: Revd G. Coleridge | Mr Newcome's | Hackney | London
MS. Lady Cave. Pub. Letters, *i. 70.*
Postmark: 1 May 1794. *Stamped*: Cambridge.

My dear Brother

I have been convened before the fellows[1]—Dr Pearce behaved
with great asperity, Mr Plampin with exceeding and most delicate
kindness—My Sentence is, a Reprimand (not a public one, but
implied in the sentence), a month's confinement to the precincts
of the College, and to translate the works of Demetrius Phalareus
[*sic*] into English—It is a thin quarto of about 90 Greek Pages.
All the fellows tried to persuade the Master to greater Lenity, but
in vain—without the least affectation I applaud his conduct—and
think nothing of it—The confinement is nothing—I have the fields
and Grove of the college to walk in—and what can I wish more?
What do I wish more? Nothing. The Demetrius is dry, and utterly
intransferable to *modern* use—and yet from the Dr's words I
suspect that he wishes it to be a publication—as he has more than
once sent to know how I go on, and pressed me to exert erudition
in some notes—and to write a preface. Besides this, I have had a
Declamation to write in the routine of College Business—and the
Rustat Examination—at which I got credit—. I get up every
morning at 6 o clock.—

Every one of my acquaintance I have dropped solemnly and
for ever except those of my College with whom before my departure
I had been least of all connected—who had always remonstrated
against my Imprudences—yet have treated me with almost
fraternal affection—Mr Caldwell, particularly.—I thought, the
most *decent* way of dropping acquaintances, was to express my
intention openly and irrevocably.

—I find, that I must either go out at a By term or degrade to
the Christmas after next—but more of this to morrow—I have
been engaged in finishing a Greek Ode—I mean to write for all the
Prizes—I have had no time upon my ha[nds.] I shall aim at
correctness & perspicu[ity], not *genius*—My last ode was so
sublime that nobody could understand it——*if* I should be so *very
lucky* as to win one of the Prizes, I could *comfortably* ask the Dr's
Advice concerning the *time* of my degree—I will write to morrow—
God bless you—my Brother—my Father!

S. T. Coleridge

[1] 'The entry in the College Register of Jesus College is brief and to the
point: "1794 Apr.: *Coleridge admonitus est per magistrum in praesentiâ socio-
rum.*"' Letters, i. 70 n.

48. *To George Coleridge*

Address: Revd G. Coleridge | Mr Newcome's | Hackney | London;
readdressed in another hand: Ottery St. Mary | Devon.
MS. Lady Cave. Pub. E.L.G. i. 19.
Postmark: 6 May 1794.   *Stamped*: Cambridge.

Sund. Evening.   May 4th—[1794]

My dear Brother

I have been very solicitous to write you particularly concerning my affairs—but Mr Plampin has been absent from College for this last week. This only can I inform you of, that exclusive of my Tutor's Bills[1] my other Debts are mere trifles, which without the smallest deviation from decency or custom I need not pay for this year at least. I pray earnestly to God, that he will continue my health and abilities—with his blessing, I doubt not that I shall be able by my exertions to repay my benefactors, gradually yet certainly. Every enjoyment—except of *necessary* comforts—I look upon as criminal. To *have* practised a severe Economy might perhaps have been a merit in me—to practise it now is only—not to be a monster.—

I pray, my Brother! that your stay in the country will have repaired those breaches in your Health, which anxiety and my Guilt must have made—You shall not have arrived long there, before you shall hear from me—

Your grateful
S. T. Coleridge

[1] The tutor's bills amounted to £132. 6s. 2¼d. at Lady Day, 1794, the income from the Rustat, the Christ's Hospital Exhibition, &c., having somewhat reduced the total arrears of midsummer 1793. (Cf. Letter 30, p. 59, n. 1) On 16 Apr. Plampin sent George Coleridge the conditions of Coleridge's reinstatement, noting that 'at least one half of the sum due for his college bills is to be immediately discharged'; and shortly afterwards, George Coleridge replied:
'I have deposited at your Banker's sixty Pounds, a Sum which our utmost present exertions had collected for a supposed Moiety of the debt—It grieves me that the exact demand was not complied with: but the Christ's Hospital allowance at this time, as also the Rustat Scholarship at the Easter Quarter, may possibly, besides paying of the quarterly Account, compensate for the deficiency— . . . I cannot in a few words explain to you the difficulties of so large a pecuniary contribution in our family. . . . Whatever Sum I can be master of by Midsummer I will deposit with your Banker.

49. *To Samuel Butler*

Transcript British Museum. Pub. E.L.G. i. 20.

[*Circa* 14 June 1794][1]

My dear Sir,

I assure you I received pleasure almost to tears from your letter. There are hours in which I am inclined to think very meanly of myself, but when I call to memory the number & character of those who have honoured me with their esteem, I am almost reconciled to my follies, and again listen to the whispers of self-adulation.

That I felt pain on my return to Cambridge from the circumstance of your not having called upon me, it would be vain to deny. Misfortune is a 'Jealous God'. I attribute it however to the sickly peevishness of a mind sore with recent calamity.

Tomorrow morning early I set out on a pedestrian scheme for Oxford—from whence after a stay of three or four days I proceed to Wales,[2] make a tour of the Northern part & return to Cambridge. The whole of my peregrination will take about six weeks.

If you are disengaged will you take your bread & cheese with me this evening?

Believe me with great esteem your | Sincere
S. T. Coleridge.

Permit me to thank you for having noticed my literary efforts.

50. *To Robert Southey*

Address: Robert Southey | No 8 | Westcott Buildings | Bath;
readdressed in another hand: Miss Tyler's | Bristol.
MS. Lord Latymer. Pub. with omis. Letters, *i. 72.*
Coleridge and Southey were introduced by Robert Allen on Coleridge's

---

[1] On 19 June (his letter was begun on 12 June) Southey wrote to Grosvenor Bedford concerning Coleridge's visit to Oxford: 'Allen is with us daily, and his friend from Cambridge, Coleridge, whose poems [*Imitations*] you will oblige me by subscribing to, either at Hookham's or Edwards's. . . . My friend he already is and must hereafter be yours.' (MS. letter, Bodleian Library.) By 19 June, therefore, Coleridge had been in Oxford several days. Furthermore, Southey's reference to the *Imitations* and to the booksellers, Hookham and Edwards, suggests that Coleridge had brought with him copies of his *Proposals for publishing by Subscription Imitations from the Modern Latin Poets*, in which both booksellers are mentioned. Since the advertisement is dated 10 June and was published in the *Cambridge Intelligencer* on 14 June, Coleridge probably did not leave Cambridge until 15 June. This letter to Butler, then, must have been written the day before.

[2] Coleridge and his travelling companion, Joseph Hucks, actually lingered about three weeks in Oxford before setting off for Wales on 5 July.

arrival at Oxford in June 1794. For a study of the Coleridge–Southey relationship see E. L. Griggs, 'Robert Southey's Estimate of Samuel Taylor Coleridge', *Huntington Lib. Quar.*, Nov. 1945, pp. 61–94.
Stamped: Gloucester.

July 6th—[1794.] Sunday Morn. Gloucester

S. T. Coleridge to R. Southey—Health & Republicanism!

When you write, direct to me to be left at the Post Office, Wrexham, Denbighshire N. Wales. I mention this circumstance *now*, lest carried away by a flood of confluent ideas I should forget it.— You are averse to Gratitudinarian Flourishes—else would I talk about hospitality, attentions &c &c—however as I must not thank you, I will thank my Stars. Verily, Southey—I like not Oxford nor the inhabitants of it—I would say, thou art a Nightingale among Owls—but thou art so songless and heavy towards night, that I will rather liken thee to the Matin Lark—thy *Nest* is in a blighted Cornfield, where the sleepy Poppy nods it's red-cowled head, and the weak-eyed Mole plies his dark work—but thy soaring is even unto heaven.—Or let me add (for my Appetite for Similies is truly canine at this moment) that as the Italian Nobles their new-fashioned Doors, so thou dost make the adamantine Gate of Democracy turn on it's golden Hinges to most sweet Music.

Our Journeying has been intolerably fatiguing from the heat and whiteness of the Roads—and the un*hedged* country presents nothing but *stone*-fences dreary to the Eye and scorching to the touch—But we shall soon be in Wales.

Gloucester is a nothing-to-be-said-about Town—the Women have almost all of them sharp Noses. As we walked last night on the Severn Banks, a most lovely Girl glided along in a Boat—there were at least 30 naked men bathing—she seemed mighty unconcerned—and they addressing her with not the most courtly gallantry, she snatched the Task of Repartee from her Brother who was in the Boat with her, and abused them with great perseverance & elocution. I stared—for she was elegantly dressed— and not a Prostitute. Doubtless, the citadel of her chastity is so impregnably strong, that it needs not the ornamental Out-works of Modesty.

It is *wrong*, Southey! for a little Girl with a half-famished sickly Baby in her arms to put her head in at the window of an Inn— 'Pray give me a bit of Bread and Meat'! from a Party dining on Lamb, Green Pease, & Sallad—Why ? ? Because it is *impertinent* & *obtrusive*!—I am a Gentleman!—and wherefore should the clamorous Voice of Woe *intrude* upon mine Ear! ?

My companion is a Man of cultivated, tho' not vigorous, under-

standing—his feelings are all on the side of humanity——yet such
are the unfeeling Remarks, which the lingering Remains of Aristo-
cracy occasionally prompt. When the pure System of Pantocracy[1]
shall have aspheterized the Bounties of Nature, these things will
not be so—! I trust, you admire the word 'aspheterized' from α
non, σφέτερος proprius! We really *wanted* such a word—instead of
travelling along the circuitous, dusty, beaten high-Road of Diction
you thus cut across the soft, green pathless Field of Novelty!—
Similies forever! Hurra! I have bought a little Blank Book, and
portable Ink horn—as I journey onward, I ever and anon pluck
the wild Flowers of Poesy—'inhale their odours awhile'—then
throw them away and think no more of them—I will not do so!—
Two lines of mine—

> And o'er the Sky's unclouded blue
> The sultry Heat suffus'd a *brassy* hue.

—The Cockatrice is a foul Dragon with a *crown* on it's head.
The Eastern Nations believe it to be hatched by a Viper on a
Cock's Egg. Southey.—Dost thou not see Wisdom in her *Coan* Vest
of Allegory? The Cockatrice is emblematic of Monarchy—a
monster generated by *Ingratitude* on *Absurdity*. When Serpents
sting, the only Remedy is—to *kill* the *Serpent*, and *besmear* the
Wound with the *Fat*. Would you desire better *Sympathy?*—

Description of Heat from a Poem I am manufacturing—the
Title 'Perspiration, a Travelling Eclogue[']—[2]

> The Dust flies smothering, as on clatt'ring Wheels
> Loath'd Aristocracy careers along.
> The distant Track quick vibrates to the Eye,
> And white and dazzling undulates with heat.
> Where scorching to th' unwary Traveller's touch
> The stone-fence flings it's narrow Slip of Shade,
> Or where the worn sides of the chalky Road
> Yield their scant excavations (sultry Grots!)
> Emblem[3] of languid Patience, we behold
> The fleecy Files faint-ruminating lie.—

Farewell, sturdy Republican! Write me concerning Burnet[4] &
thyself and concerning &c &c—My next shall be a more sober &
chastised Epistle—but you see I was in the humour for Metaphors
—and to tell thee the Truth, I have so often serious reasons to

---

[1] Later Pantisocracy.
[2] *Poems*, i. 56.
[3] Image. [Cancelled word in line above.]
[4] George Burnett (1776?–1811) was a fellow student of Southey's at Balliol
College, Oxford.

quarrel with my Inclination, that I do not chuse to contradict it for Trifles.—To Lovell,[1] Fraternity & civic Remembrances. Hucks' Compliments!

S. T. Coleridge

51. *To Robert Southey*

Address: Robert Southey | No 8 | Westcott Buildings | Bath
MS. Lord Latymer. Pub. with omis. Letters, *i. 74.*
Stamped: Denbigh.

Wrexham. Sunday July 13th [1794]

Your Letter, Southey! made me melancholy. Man is a bundle of Habits: but of all Habits the Habit of Despondence is the most pernicious to Virtue & Happiness. I once shipwrecked my frail bark on that rock—a friendly plank was vouchsafed me. Be you wise by my experience—and receive unhurt the Flower, which I have climbed Precipices to pluck. Consider the high advantages, which you possess in so eminent a degree—Health, Strength of Mind, and confirmed *Habits* of strict Morality. Beyond all doubt, by the creative powers of your Genius you might supply whatever the stern Simplicity of Republican Wants could require—Is there no possibility of procuring the office of Clerk in a Compting House? A month's application would qualify you for it. For God's sake, Southey! enter not into the church. Concerning Allen I say little— but I feel anguish at times.—This earnestness of remonstrance— I will not offend you by asking your Pardon for it! The following is a *Fact*—A Friend of Hucks's after long struggles between Principle and *Interest* (as it is improperly called) accepted a place under Government—he took the Oaths—shuddered—went home and threw himself in an Agony out of a two pair of stairs' Window! These *dreams* of Despair are most soothing to the Imagination—I well know it. We shroud ourselves 'in the mantle of Distress, And tell our poor Hearts, This is *Happiness*!['] There is a *dignity* in all these solitary emotions, that flatters the pride of our Nature. Enough of sermonizing. As I was meditating on the capabilities of Pleasure in a mind like your's I unwarily fell into Poetry[2]—

> 'Tis thine with faery forms to talk,
> And thine the philosophic walk,
> And (what to thee the sweetest are)
> The setting Sun, the Evening Star,

[1] Cf. Letter 53.
[2] The following lines are an adapted version of lines 80–105 of the poem *Happiness*. See *Poems*, i. 32, and Letter 7.

The tints, that live along the Sky,
And Moon, that meets thy raptur'd eye,
Where grateful oft the big drops start—
Dear silent Pleasures of the Heart!
But if thou pour one votive Lay,
For humble Independence pray,
Whom (sages say) in days of yore
Meek Competence to Wisdom bore.
So shall thy little Vessel glide
With a fair Breeze adown the Tide—
Till Death shall close thy tranquil eye
While Faith exclaims 'Thou shalt not die![']

'The heart-smile glowing on his aged Cheek   Mild as decaying Light of Summer's eve'—are lines eminently beautiful. The whole is pleasing—. For a motto! Surely my Memory has suffered an epileptic fit. A Greek Motto would be pedantic—These Lines will perhaps do.

All mournful to the pensive Sage's eye
The Monuments of human Glory lie:
Fall'n Palaces crushed by the ruthless haste
Of Time, and many an Empire's silent waste
But where a Sight shall shuddering Sorrow find
Sad as the ruins of the human mind?[1]

Bowles

A Better will soon occur to me—

Poor Poland! They go on sadly there.

Warmth of particular Friendship does not imply absorption. The nearer you approach the Sun, the more intense are his Rays— yet what distant corner of the System do they not cheer and vivify? The ardour of private Attachments makes Philanthropy a necessary *habit* of the Soul. I love my *Friend*—such as *he* is, all mankind are or *might be*! The deduction is evident—. Philanthropy (and indeed every other Virtue) is a thing of *Concretion*— Some home-born Feeling is the *center* of the Ball, that, rolling on thro' Life collects and assimilates every congenial Affection. These thoughts the latter part of your letter suggested.

What did you mean by *H*. has '*my understanding*[']? I have puzzled myself in vain to discover the import of the sentence. The only sense it *seemed* to bear was so like *mock-humility*, that I scolded myself for the momentary supposition.—

My heart is so heavy at present, that I will defer the finishing of

[1] These lines are from Bowles's poem, *The Philanthropic Society*. The last two lines form the motto of Southey's *Botany-Bay Eclogues*.

this letter till to morrow——I saw a face at Wrexham Church this morning, which recalled 'thoughts full of bitterness' and images too dearly loved!—'Now past and but remembered like sweet sounds of Yesterday![']—At Ross (16 miles from Gloucester) we took up our quarters at the King's Arms, once the House of Kyrle, the M. of R. I gave the window-shutter the following Effusion.[1]

> Richer than Misers o'er their countless hoards,
> Nobler than Kings or king-polluted Lords,
> Here dwelt the man of Ross! O Trav'ler, hear!
> Departed Merit claims the glistening Tear.
> Friend to the friendless, to the sick Man Health
> With gen'rous joy he view'd his modest wealth.
> He heard the Widow's heav'n-breath'd prayer of Praise,
> He mark'd the shelter'd Orphan's tearful gaze—
> And o'er the dowried Maiden's glowing cheek
> Bade bridal love suffuse it's blushes meek
> If 'neath this roof thy wine-cheer'd moments pass,
> Fill to the good man's name one grateful glass!
> To higher zest shall Memory wake thy Soul,
> And Virtue mingle in the sparkling Bowl.
> But if, like me, thro' Life's distressful Scene
> Lonely and sad thy Pilgrimage hath been;
> And if, thy breast with heartsick anguish fraught
> Thou journeyest onward tempest-tost in thought—
> Here cheat thy cares—in generous Visions melt—
> And *dream* of Goodness, thou hast never felt.

I will resume the pen to morrow.—

Monday 11 o clock. Well—praised be God! here I am—videlicet—Ruthin, 16 miles from Wrexham.—At Wrexham Church I glanced upon the face of a Miss E. Evans, a young Lady with [whom] I had been in habits of fraternal correspondence—She turned excessively pale—she thought it my Ghost, I suppose—I retreated with all possible speed to our Inn—there as I was standing at the window passed by Eliza Evans, and with her to my utter surprize her Sister, Mary Evans—quam efflictim et perdite amabam. I apprehend, she is come from London on a visit to her Grandmother, with whom Eliza lives. I turned sick, and all but fainted away!—The two Sisters, as H. informs me, passed by the window anxiously, several times afterwards—but I had retired—

> Vivit sed mihi non vivit—nova forte marita
> Ah dolor! alterius carâ a cervice pependit.

[1] *Poems*, i. 57.

Vos, malefida valete accensae Insomnia mentis,
Littora amata, valete! Vale ah! formosa Maria![1]

My fortitude would not have supported me, had I recognized
her—I mean, *appeared* to do it!—I neither eat, or slept yesterday—
but Love is a local Anguish—I am 16 miles distant, and am not
half so miserable.—I must endeavor to forget it amid the terrible
Graces of the wildwood scenery that surrounds me—I never durst
even in a whisper avow my passion, though I knew she loved me—
Where were my Fortunes? And why should I make her miserable?
Almighty God bless her—! her Image is in the sanctuary of my
Heart, and never can it be torn away but with the strings that
grapple it to Life.——Southey! There are few men of whose
delicacy I think so highly as to have written all this—I am glad,
I have so deemed of you—We are soothed by communication—

Denbigh—8 miles from Ruthin.

And now to give you some little account of our journey—From
Oxford to Gloucester, to Ross, to Hereford, to Leominster, to
Bishop's castle, to Welsh Pool, to Llanvillin nothing occurred
worthy notice except that at the last place I preached Pantisocracy
and Aspheterism with so much success that two great huge
Fellows, of Butcher like appearance, danced about the room in
enthusiastic agitation—And one of them of his own accord called
for a large Glass of Brandy, and drank it off to this, his own Toast—
God save the King. And may he be the Last—Southey! Such men
may be of use—they would *fell* the Golden Calf secundum Artem.
From Llanvilling we penetrated into the interior [of] the Country
to Llangunnog, a Village most roman[tica]lly situated—We dined
there on hash'd Mutton, Cucumber, Bread & Cheese and Butter,
and had two pots of Ale—The sum total of the expence 16 pence
for both of us! From Llanvunnog we walked over the mountains to
Bala—most sublimely terrible! It was scorchingly hot—I applied
my mouth ever and anon to the side of the Rocks and sucked in
draughts of Water cold as Ice, and clear as infant Diamonds in
their embryo Dew! The rugged and stony Clefts are stupendous—
and in winter must form Cataracts most astonishing—At this time
of the year there is just water enough dashed down over them to
'soothe not disturb the pensive Traveller's Ear.['] I slept by the
side of one an hour & more. As we descended down the Mountain
the Sun was reflected in the River that winded thro' the valley

[1] *Poems*, i. 56. [Translation: She lives, but lives not for me: as a loving
bride perhaps—ah, sadness!—she has thrown her arms around another man's
neck. Farewell, ye deceitful dreams of a love-lorn mind; ye beloved shores,
farewell; farewell, ah, beautiful Mary!]

with insufferable Brightness—it rivalled the Sky. At Bala is
nothing remarkable except a Lake of 11 miles in circumference.
At the Inn I was sore afraid, that I had caught the Itch from a
Welch Democrat, who was charmed with my sentiments: he
grasped my hand with flesh-bruising Ardour—and I trembled, lest
some discontented Citizens of the *animalcular* Republic should have
emigrated. Shortly after, into the same room a well drest clergy-
man, and four others—among whom (the Landlady whispers me)
was a Justice of Peace and the Doctor of the Parish—I was asked
for a Gentleman—I gave General Washington[1]—The parson said
in a low voice—(Republicans!)—After which the medical man
said—damn Toasts! I gives a sentiment—May all Republicans be
gulloteen'd!—Up starts the Welch Democrat—May all *Fools* be
gulloteen'd—and then you will be the first! Thereon Rogue,
Villain, Traitor flew thick in each other's faces as a hailstorm—
This is nothing in Wales—they *make calling one another Liars* &c—
necessary vent-holes to the sulphureous Fumes of the Temper!
At last, I endeavored to arbitrate by observing that whatever
might be our opinions in politics, the appearance of a Clergyman
in the Company assured me, we were all *Christians*—tho' (con-
tinued I) it is rather difficult to reconcile the last Sentiment with
the Spirit of Christianity. Pho!—quoth the Parson—Christianity!
Why, we an't at Church now? Are we?—The Gemman's Sentiment
was a very good one—'it shewed, he was *sincere* in his principles![']
——Welch Politics could not prevail over Welch Hospitality—
they all except the Parson shook me by the hand, and said I was
an open hearted honest-speaking Fellow, tho' I was a bit of a
Democrat.

From Bala we travelled onward to Llanvollin, a most beautiful
Village in a most beautiful situation. On the Road we met the
Cantabs of my College, Brooke[s] & Berdmore—these rival
pedestrians, perfect *Powells,* were vigorously pursuing their tour—
in a *post chaise!* We laughed famously—their only excuse was, that
Berdmore had got *clapped*—or else &c—From Llangollen to
Wrexham, from Wrexham to Ruthin—to Denbigh. At Denbigh is
a ruined Castle—it surpasses every thing I could have conceived—
I wandered there an hour and a half last evening (this is Tuesday
Morning). Two well drest young men were walking there—
Come—says one—I'll play my flute—'twill be romantic! Bless
thee for the thought, Man of Genius & Sensibility! I exclaimed—
and pre-attuned my heartstring to tremulous emotion. He sat
adown (the moon just peering) amid the most awful part of the

[1] In retelling this anecdote in the next letter Coleridge substituted the name
Dr. Priestley.

Ruins—and—romantic Youth! struck up the affecting Tune of
Mrs Casey!—'Tis fact upon my Honor!

God bless you—Southey! We shall be at Aberistwith this day
week—when will you come out to meet us—there you must direct
your letter. Hucks' compliments—I anticipate much accession of
Republicanism from Lovell! I have positively done nothing but
dream of the System of no Property every step of the Way since
I left you—till last Sunday.

Heigho!——

[No signature in manuscript.]

52. *To Henry Martin*[1]

Address: [Henry] Martin Es[q.] | Silton (or Sirton) | near Mere | Wilts.
MS. Mr. W. Hugh Peal. Fird ¡*sub. with omis.*, Gentleman's Magazine, *March
1836, p. 242, from a copy transmitted by W. L. Bowles*. This transcript, now in
the Guildhall Library, London, is in an unknown handwriting and contains
neither the *Lines written at Ross* nor *The faded Flower*. In 1847 H. N. Coleridge
reprinted the letter from the *Gentleman's Magazine*, but erroneously gave the
addressee as 'Mr. Masters of Jesus College' (*Biog. Lit.* ii. 338.)

The letter, including the two poems, was first published, with omissions,
from the original manuscript in the *New Monthly Magazine*, in August 1836,
p. 420; along with it there appeared a fragmentary essay of Coleridge's, 'The
study of History is preferable to the study of Natural Philosophy'. The holo-
graph of Coleridge's letter and the manuscript of the essay have been kept
together since their first publication in 1836 and are now in the collection of
Mr. W. Hugh Peal.
Postmark: 25 July 1794.   *Stamped*: Caernarvon.

July 22nd 1794

Dear Martin

From Oxford to Gloucester ×, to Ross ×, to Hereford, to
Leominster ×, to Bishop's castle ×, to Montgomery, to Welchpool,
Llanvilling ×, Llangunnog, Bala ×, Druid House ×, Llangollin,
Wrexham × ×, Ruthin, Denbigh ×, St Asaph, Holywell ×, Rudland
[Rhuddlan], Abergeley ×, Aberconway ×, Abber × over a ferry to
Beaumaris (Anglesea) × Amlock [Amlwch] ×, Copper mines,
Gwindu, Moel don over a ferry to Caernarvon have I journeyed, now
philosophizing with Hucks, now melancholizing by myself, or else
indulging those day-dreams of Fancy, that make realities more
gloomy. To whatever place I have affixed the mark ×, there we
slept. The first part of our Tour was intensely hot—the roads white
and dazzling seemed to undulate with heat—and the country bare
and unhedged presented nothing but stone-fences dreary to the

---

[1] Henry Martin of Jesus College, to whom Coleridge dedicated *The Fall of
Robespierre*. See Letter 61.

Eye and scorching to the Touch—At Ross we took up our Quarters
at the King's Arms, once the House of Mr Kyrle, the celebrated
Man of Ross—I gave the Window shutter a few Verses, which I
shall add to the end of the letter—The walk from Llangunnog to
Bala over the mountains was most wild and romantic—there are
immense and rugged Clefts in the mountains; which in winter must
form Cataracts most tremendous—now there is just enough sun-
glittering water dashed down over them to soothe, not disturb the
Ear. I climbed up a precipice, on which was a large Thorn-tree, and
slept by the side of one of them near two hours. At Bala I was
apprehensive, that I had caught the Itch from a Welch Democrat,
who was charmed with my Sentiments—he bruised my hand with
a grasp of ardor, and I trembled, lest some discontented Citizens of
the *Animalcular* Republic might have emigrated. Shortly after,
in came a Clergyman well drest, and with him 4 other Gentlemen—
I was asked for a public Character—I gave, Dr Priestley[1]—the
Clergyman whispered his Neighbour who it seems, is the Apothe-
cary of the Parish—(Republicans!)—Accordingly when the *Doctor*
(as they call apothecaries) was to have given a name, 'I gives a
sentiment, Gemmen! May all Republicans be *gul*loteen'd!['] Up
starts the Democrat 'May all Fools be gulloteen'd—and then
you will be first![']—Fool, Rogue, Traitor, Liar &c flew in each
other's faces in hailstorms of Vociferation. This is nothing in Wales
—they *make* it—: necessary vent-holes for the sulphureous Fumes
of their Temper! I endeavoured to calm the Tempest by observing
—'that however different our Political Opinions might be, the
appearance of a Clergyman in the Company assured me, that we
were all *Christians*—though I found it rather difficult to reconcile
the last sentiment with the spirit of Christianity.' 'Pho.' quoth the
Clergyman! 'Christianity! Why an't at *Church* now—are we? The
Gemman's Sentiment was a very good one, because it shews him
to be *sincere* in his principles.'—Welch Politics could not however
prevail over Welch Hospitality—they all shook hands with me,
(except the Parson) and said, I was an open-speaking, honest-
hearted Fellow, tho' I was a *bit* of a Democrat.—On our Road from
Bala to Druid House we met Brookes and Berdmore—our rival
Pedestrians, a Gemini of *Powells*, were vigorously marching on-
ward—in a post-chaise! Berdmore had been *ill*. We were not a little
glad to see each other. Llangollin is a village most romantically
situated—but the Weather was so intensely hot, that we saw only
what was to be admired—we could not admire.—At Wrexham the

---

[1] Joseph Priestley (1733–1804), theologian and scientist, embarked for the
United States in Apr. 1794. Coleridge paid him tribute in a sonnet (*Poems*,
i. 81) and in lines 371–6 of *Religious Musings*.

Tower is most magnificent—and in the Church is a white marble monument of Lady Middleton superior meâ quidem sententiâ to any thing in Westminster Abbey. It had entirely escaped my Memory, that Wrexham was the residence of a Miss E. Evans, a young Lady with whom in happier days I had been in habits of fraternal correspondence—she lives with her Grandmother—As I was standing at the Window of the Inn she passed by, and with her to my utter Astonishment her Sister, Mary Evans—quam efflictim et perdite amabam—yea, even to Anguish—. They both started—and gave a short cry—almost a faint shriek—I sickened and well nigh fainted—but instantly retired. Had I appeared to recognize her, my Fortitude would not have supported me

> Vivit, sed mihi non vivit—nova forte marita
> Ah dolor! alterius carâ a cervice pependit.
> Vos, malefida valete accensae insomnia Mentis,
> Littora amata, valete! Vale ah! formosa Maria!—

Hucks informed me, that the two Sisters walked by the Window 4 or 5 times, as if anxiously—Doubtless, they think themselves deceived by some Face strikingly like me—God bless her! Her Image is in the Sanctuary of my Bosom—and never can it be torn from thence but with the strings that grapple my heart to Life.— This circumstance made me quite ill—I had been wandering among the wild-wood scenery and terrible graces of the Welch mountains to wear away, not to revive, the Images of the Past! But Love is a local Anguish—I am 50 miles distant, and am not half so miserable.—At Denbigh is the finest ruined Castle in the Kingdom—it surpassed every thing, I could have conceived. I wandered there two hours in a still Evening, feeding upon melancholy.—Two well drest young Men were roaming there—'I will play my Flute here'—said the first—'it will have a *romantic* effect.' Bless thee, Man of Genius and Sensibility! I silently exclaimed. He sate down amid the most awful part of the Ruins—the Moon just began to make her Rays predominant over the lingering Daylight—I preattuned my feelings to Emotion—and the Romantic Youth instantly *struck up* the sadly-pleasing Tune of Mrs Casey!

> The British Lion is my Sign—
> A Roaring Trade I drive on &c.—

Three miles from Denbigh on the Road to St Asaph is a fine Bridge with *one Arch*—of great grandeur—stand at a little distance, and *through* it you see the woods waving on the *Hill-bank* of the River in a most lovely point of view. A *beautiful* prospect is always more picturesque, when seen at some little distance thro' an Arch.

I have frequently thought of Mich. Taylor's[1] way of viewing a Landscape by putting his head between his Thighs.—Under the arch was the most perfect Echo, I ever heard. Hucks sung, 'Sweet Echo' with great effect. At Holywell I bathed in the famous St Winifred's Well—it is an excellent cold Bath—at Rudland is a fine ruined Castle—Abergeley is a large Village on the Sea Coast—Walking on the sea sands—I was surprized to see a number of fine Women bathing promiscuously with men and boys—*perfectly* naked! Doubtless, the citadels of their Chastity are so impregnably strong, that they need not the ornamental Outworks of Modesty. But seriously speaking, where sexual Distinctions are least observed, Men & women live together in the greatest purity. Concealment sets the Imagination a working, and, as it were, *cantharidizes* our desires.

Just before I quitted Cambridge I met a countryman with a strange Walking Stick, 5 feet in length—I eagerly bought it—and a most faithful servant it has proved to me. My sudden affection for it has mellowed into settled Friendship. On the morning of our leaving Abergeley just before our final departure I looked for my Stick, in the place where I had left it over night—It was gone—! I alarumed the House—No one knew anything of it—In the flurry of anxiety I sent for the cryer of the Town—and gave him the following to cry about the town and on the beach—which he did with a gravity for which I am indebted to his stupidity.

Missing from the Bee Inn, Abergeley—A curious Walking-Stick. On one side it displays the head of an Eagle, the Eyes of which represent rising Suns, and the Ears Turkish Crescents. On the other side is the portrait of the Owner in Wood-work. Beneath the head of the Eagle is a Welch Wig—and around the neck of the Stick is a Queen Elizabeth's Ruff in Tin. All adown it waves the Line of Beauty in very ugly Carving. If any Gentleman (or Lady) has fallen in love with the above-described Stick & secretly carried off the same, he (or she) is hereby earnestly admonished to conquer a Passion, the continuance of which must prove fatal to his (or her) Honesty; and if the said Stick has slipped into such Gentleman's (or Lady's) hand thro' Inadvertence, he (or she) is required to rectify the mistake with all convenient Speed.—God save the King.

Abergeley is a fashionable Welch Watering Place—and so singular a proclamation excited no small crowd on the Beach—among the rest a lame old Gentleman, in whose hands was descried

---

[1] Probably Michael Angelo Taylor (1757–1834), frequently caricatured by James Gillray.

my dear Stick. The old Gent. who lodged at our Inn, felt great
confusion, and walked homewards, the solemn Cryer before him,
and a various Cavalcade behind him. I kept the Muscles of my Face
in tolerable Subjection. He made his lameness an apology for
borrowing my Stick, supposed he should have returned before I
had wanted it &c—Thus it ended except that a very handsome
young Lady put her head out of a Coach Window, and begged my
permission to have the Bill, which I had delivered to the Cryer. I
acceded to the request with a compliment, that lighted up a blush
on her Cheek, and a Smile on her Lip.

We passed over a ferry and landed at Aberconway—We had
scarcely left the Boat ere we descried Brookes & Berdmore, with
whom we have joined Parties, nor do we mean to separate.—Our
Tour thro' Anglesea to Caernarvon has been repaid by scarcely one
object worth seeing. To morrow we visit Snowdon—&c—Brookes,
Berdmore and myself at the imminent hazard of our Lives scaled
the very Summit of Penmaenmawr—it was a most dreadful
expedition! I will give you the account in some future Letter.

I sent for Bowles's Works, while at Oxford—how was I
shocked—Every Omission and every alteration disgusts Taste &
mangles Sensibility. Surely some Oxford Toad has been squatting
at the Poet's Ear, and spitting into it the cold Venom of Dullness.
It is not Bowles—He is still the same (the added Poems prove it)—
descriptive, dignified, tender, sublime. The Sonnets added are
exquisite—Abbe Thule has marked Beauties—and the Little Poem
at Southampton is a Diamond—in whatever light you place it, it
reflects beauty and splendor. The 'Shakespeare' is sadly unequal
to the rest—yet in whose Poems, except in those of Bowles, would
it not have been excellent?[1]

Direct to me, my dear Fellow!—to be left at the Post Office,
Bristol—and tell me every thing about yourself, how you have
spent the Vacation &c—

believe me, with gratitude and fraternal friendship

> Your obliged
> S. T. Coleridge

[1] On the Guildhall Library transcript of this letter, Bowles wrote the fol-
lowing note to the editor of the *Gentleman's Magazine*: 'My dear Sir I send
you an original letter of poor Coleridge. . . . You can say, if you print this
letter, & I think many parts most interesting—with regard to his criticism on
me, that it is suppos'd he alludes to some negligent comp's . . . in [the] 2d
volume—but Mr. Pickering is about to publish in two volumes, the selected
& best works—.' Bowles was obviously pleased with Coleridge's praise and
wished to explain the adverse comments. Accordingly the editor, in printing
Coleridge's letter in the *Gentleman's Magazine* in Mar. 1836, incorporated
Bowles's explanation.

Lines written at Ross, at the King's Arms—once the House of Mr Kyrle.

Richer than Misers o'er their countless hoards,
Nobler than Kings or king-polluted Lords,
Here dwelt the Man of Ross! O Stranger,[1] hear!
Departed Merit claims the glistening tear.
If 'neath this Roof thy wine-cheer'd moments pass,
Fill to the good man's name, one grateful glass.
To higher Zest shall Memory wake thy soul,
And Virtue mingle in th' ennobled Bowl.
But if, like me, thro' Life's distressful Sc[ene]
Lonely and sad thy Pilgrimage hath be[en;]
And if, thy Breast with heart-sick angu[ish fraught,]
Thou journeyest onward tempest-tost in [thought;]
Here cheat thy cares; in generous Visio[ns melt,]
And *dream* of Goodness, thou hast never *felt.*

The faded Flower.[2]

Ungrateful He, who pluck'd thee from thy stalk,
Poor faded Flowret! on his careless way;
Inhaled awhile thy odours on his walk,
Then onward pass'd and left thee to decay.
Ah melancholy Emblem! had *I* seen
Thy modest Beauties dew'd with evening's Ge[m,]
I had not rudely cropt thy parent stem;
But left thee blushing 'mid the enliven'd Green.
And now I bend me o'er thy wither'd Bloom,
And drop the tear—as Fancy at my Side
Deep-sighing points the fair frail Abra's Tomb,[3]—
'Like thine, sad Flower! was that poor Wanderer's pride!
'O lost to Love & Truth! whose selfish Joy
'Tasted her vernal sweets—but tasted to destroy![']

Of course B and B desire their kind remembrances.

[1] The reading, 'O Stranger,' is not noted by E. H. Coleridge. Cf. *Poems*, i. 57.

[2] Another version of this sonnet was first published in 1795 in *Poems* by Robert Lovell and Robert Southey, p. 68. Neither Coleridge nor Southey included the poem in later editions of his poetical works. On the basis of its appearance in the *New Monthly Magazine*, J. D. Campbell first published it as Coleridge's in 1893, and E. H. Coleridge included it in *Poems*, i. 70. An undated entry in the Gutch notebook seems to be related to the subject-matter of this sonnet. 'Little Daisy—very late Spring. March—Quid si vivat? Do all things in Faith. Never pluck a flower again!—Mem.'

[3] In the Southey (1795) version read 'Emma's' for 'Abra's'. A transcript of this sonnet bearing the initials S. T. C. and written in an unknown hand is in the Pierpont Morgan Library. It is dated 10 July 1794, and in line 11 reads 'Emma's' rather than 'Abra's'.

53. *To Robert Lovell*[1]

Address: Mr Robert Lovell | College Green
MS. Lord Latymer. Hitherto unpublished.

Bush Inn [Bristol]
Tuesday Morning. [5 August 1794][2]

To Mr. Robert Lovell

I must request you to inform me, whether Southey be at Bristol
or Bath—if at Bristol—where?[3]

I am, Sir, | with great respect | Your fellow Citizen
S. T. Coleridge

54. *To Charles Heath*[4]

Address: Mr. Charles Heath | Monmouth.
Pub. Monthly Repository, *viii, 1834, p. 740.*

Jesus College, Cambridge.[5] 29th August, 1794
Sir,

Your brother has introduced my name to you; I shall therefore
offer no apology for this letter. A small but liberalized party have
formed a scheme of emigration on the principles of an abolition of
individual property. Of their political creed, and the arguments
by which they support and elucidate it, they are preparing a few
copies—not as meaning to publish them, but for private distribu-
tion. In this work they will have endeavoured to prove the exclu-
sive justice of the system and its practicability; nor will they have
omitted to sketch out the code of contracts necessary for the
internal regulation of the society; all of which will of course be
submitted to the improvements and approbation of each com-

[1] Robert Lovell, whom Coleridge met in Bristol soon after his return from
his Welsh tour, was married to Mary Fricker. He was early converted to
Pantisocracy.

[2] The formal tone of this note to Lovell and the term, 'Your fellow Citizen',
suggest that the letter was written in early August, shortly after Coleridge
arrived in Bristol from Wales.

[3] In a letter to Cottle, dated 6 Mar. 1836, Southey wrote: 'After some weeks,
Coleridge returning from his tour, came to Bristol on his way, and stopped
there.' (MS. New York Public Lib.) To this sentence Cottle added the phrase,
'(I being there.),' thus creating an erroneous impression of Southey's where-
abouts. Cf. *Rem.* 404.

[4] Charles Heath was probably the topographer (1761–1831), who was twice
mayor of Monmouth. His brother, an apothecary in Bristol, was a convert to
Pantisocracy.

[5] Writing from London, Coleridge probably so headed his letter in anticipa-
tion of his early return to Cambridge. Cf. Letter 60.

ponent member. As soon as the work is printed, one or more copies shall be transmitted to you.[1] Of the characters of the individuals who compose the party, I find it embarrassing to speak; yet, vanity apart, I may assert with truth, that they have each a sufficient strength of head to make the virtues of the heart respectable; and that they are all highly charged with that enthusiasm which results from strong perceptions of moral rectitude, called into life and action by ardent feelings. With regard to pecuniary matters it is found necessary, if twelve men with their families emigrate on this system, that 2000£ should be the aggregate of their contributions; but infer not from hence that each man's quota is to be settled with the littleness of arithmetical accuracy. No; *all* will strain *every* nerve, and then I trust the surplus money of some will supply the deficiencies of others. The minutiae of topographical information we are daily endeavouring to acquire; at present our plan is, to settle at a distance, but at a convenient distance, from Cooper's Town on the banks of the Susquehannah. This, however, will be the object of future investigation. For the time of emigration we have fixed on next March. In the course of the winter those of us whose bodies, from habits of sedentary study or academic indolence, have not acquired their full tone and strength, intend to learn the theory and practice of agriculture and carpentry, according as situation and circumstances make one or the other convenient.

Your fellow Citizen,
S. T. Coleridge.

55. *To Robert Southey*

Address: Robert Southey | Miss Tyler's | College Green | Bristol   Single
MS. British Museum. Pub. E. L. G. i. 21.
Postmark: 6 September 1794.

Monday Morning. [1 September 1794]

Southey! my dear Fellow! I sit down in melancholy mood—So if you find me gloomy, be not disappointed. I arrived safe after a most unpleasant Journey—I lost my Casimir on the Road.

The day after my arrival I finished the first act—I transcribed it.—The next Morning Franklin (of Pembroke, Cam.—a ci devant *Grecian* of our School—so we call the first Boys) called on me and persuaded me to go with him & Breakfast with Dyer, Author of

---

[1] This work was never printed, but a fuller account of the pantisocratic scheme will be found in a letter from Thomas Poole to a Mr. Haskins. See *Thomas Poole*, i. 97–98.

the Complaints of the Poor,[1]—on Subscription, & &c——I went—explained our System—he was enraptured—pronounced it impregnable—He is intimate with Dr Priestley—and doubts not, that the Doctor will join us.—He shewed me some Poetry, and I shewed him part of the first Act,[2] which I happed to have about me—He liked it hugely—it was a 'Nail, that would drive'—offered to speak to Robinson, his Bookseller——In short, he went—Rob. was in the country—he went to Johnson's & to Kearsley's—the former objected, because Dyer (who is a Reviewer) had confessedly only read the first act—/ So on Saturday he called on me, and I gave him the whole to look over—and to morrow morning I breakfast with him. Hactenus de Tragoediâ.——

The same morning, that I breakfasted with Dyer, after many struggles between the *pride vestiarian* and the wish to see Grovesnor [*sic*] C. Bedford, I carried your letter—He came down—I stayed with him only five minutes—during which time he alluded to America—in these words—'I am sorry, very sorry. I will not say, that Southey will leave *all* his friends behind him. A very numerous Body I am sure he will—and *one*, certainly, who will feel a pang he cannot easily express.'—The tear started into his Eye—On my going he begged to take my Address—Now my Vestiture was so very anti-genteel, that I was ashamed on my arrival in London to go to my own Coffee-house (the Hungerford)—For this Reason, and because that I had not a Potosi Mountain in my Purse, I slept at the Angel Inn, near Christ's Hospital—and lived with the *Grecians,* in one of whose *Studies* I am now writing—Conceive the inward Astonishment of G. C. Bedford when with a very grave face—I told him

The Angel Inn
Angel Street
Butcher Hall Lane
Newgate Street!

Nil admirari is the quintessence
of Politeness as well as of Wisdom—

Grovesnor did not stare—and I thought highly of his civility—So, you see—Southey—your new Cambridge Friend has not done you much Honor—

---

[1] George Dyer (1755–1841) was educated at Christ's Hospital and Emmanuel College, Cambridge. His *Complaints of the Poor People of England* was published in 1793.

[2] *The Fall of Robespierre. An Historic Drama,* of which Coleridge wrote the first act and Southey the remaining two, was published in Coleridge's name by Benjamin Flower in 1794. See Letter 60, where Coleridge explains why it was published in his name alone.

Every night since my arrival I have spent at an Ale-house by courtesy called 'a Coffee House'—The 'Salutation & Cat,' in Newgate Street—We have a comfortable Room to ourselves—& drink Porter & *Punch* round a good Fire.—My motive for all this is that every night I meet a most intelligent young Man who has spent the last 5 years of his Life in America—and is lately come from thence as An Agent to sell Land. He was of our School—I had been kind to him—he remembers it—& comes regularly every Evening to 'benefit by conversation' he says—He says, two thousand Pound will do—that he doubts not, we can contract for our Passage under 400£.—that we shall buy the Land a great deal cheaper when we arrive at America—than we could do in England— or why (adds he) am I sent over here? That 12 men may *easily* clear *three hundred* Acres in 4 or 5 months—and that for 600 hundred Dollars a Thousand Acres may be cleared, and houses built upon them—He recommends the Susqusannah [*sic*] from it's excessive Beauty, & it's security from hostile Indians—Every possible assistance will be given us—We may get credit for the Land for 10 years or more as we settle upon it—That literary Characters make *money* there—that &c &c—He never saw a *Byson* in his Life—but has heard of them—They are quite backwards.— The Musquitos are not so bad as our Gnats—and after you have been there a little while, they don't trouble you much. He says, the Women's *teeth are* bad there—but not the men's—at least—not nearly so much—attributes it to neglect—to particular foods—is by no means convinced, it is the necessary Effect of Climate.—

Remember me to your Mother—to our Mother—am I not affiliated? I will write her when I arrive at Cambridge—To Lovell and Mrs Lovell my *fraternal* Love—to Miss F *more*.[1] To all remember me—tell Edith[2] and Martha and Eliza[3] that I even *now* see all their faces and that they are my very dear Sisters.

The younger Le Grice (a sweet-tempered Fellow—he goes with me to Cambridge) and Favell,[4] who goes to Cambridge next October twelve month—have intreated that they may be allowed to come over after us when they quit College—This morning Favell put this Sonnet into my hand—

---

[1] Referring to Sara Fricker, to whom Coleridge had became engaged a fortnight earlier, mistaking, as he said three months afterwards, 'the ebullience of *schematism* for affection'.

[2] Edith Fricker and Robert Southey were married on 14 Nov. 1795.

[3] Martha and Eliza Fricker; the latter came to be Coleridge's favourite sister-in-law.

[4] Samuel Le Grice and Samuel Favell, Coleridge's former schoolfellows at Christ's Hospital.

Sonnet

Flashes of Hope, that lighten o'er my Soul!
Shapings of Fancy, than all Earth possess'd
More lovely, more extatic! o'er my Breast
What glittering Waves of vision'd Rapture roll.

With silent sweet survey of tearful Joy
I gaze the Vale, where bloom in fadeless Youth
Love, Beauty, Friendship, Poesy, and Truth.
My Brethren! O my Brethren! then I cry——

And you, Ye mild-eyed Forms! a Brother's Kiss
Give me! that I may drink of your love-bowl
And mix in every draught the high-wrought Soul,
And pluck from every Bank the Rose of Bliss!——
Mock me not, Phantoms! lest my poor fond Heart
Outcast for ever into madness start!——

Both Le Grice & Favell have all the generous ardent Feelings that
characterize Genius—they are 19 years old—and beg their fraternal
Remembrances to you—

To Doctor Heath remember me kindly—to Mr & Mrs Harwood
for whom I retain high esteem & respect—as to Mr Wade[1]—

—Do not forget to give my respects to Shad.[2]—Kiss little
Edward for me—Let me hear from you—I quit London on
Wednesday morning.

S. T. Coleridge

Taggart is a sensible fellow—remember me to him. You see I
conclude my Epistles like the Apostle Paul—

56. *To George Dyer*

Address: George Dyer | No 45 | Carey Street.
MS. Mr. E. L. McAdam, Jr. Hitherto unpublished.

Thursday Morning—[11 September 1794]
Dear Sir,

I shall go to Cam. tonight in the Mail.[3] If you will please to send
the Books by this little Boy, I will take care to have them safely

---

[1] Josiah Wade, a Bristol tradesman who was to become one of Coleridge's
most intimate friends.

[2] Shadrach Weekes, the servant of Southey's aunt, Miss Tyler.

[3] Coleridge did not arrive in Cambridge until 17 Sept.

delivered—I am rather unwell—i.e. heavy of head & turbulent of Bowells,—or I should have called on you—

> I am | with great respect | Your fellow-Citizen
> S. T. Coleridge

57. *To Robert Southey*

Address: Robert Southey | No 8 | Westcott Buildings | Bath
MS. Lord Latymer. Hitherto unpublished.
Postmark: 11 September 1794.

> Thursday—[11 September 1794]

My dear Southey

Robinson, the Bookseller, is still from town—and the other Booksellers have declined it, or offered too little. I will immediately have it printed at Cambridge—Dyer will dispose of 50 in London—Mr Field another 50, at Cambridge I can dispose of at least 50—perhaps more—some at Exeter—at Bristol you can certainly get rid of 50—It will repay us amply—the two last acts want a few alterations—which Dyer pointed out—of course I have your permission to be plenipo-emendator. Shall I send down—what number of Copies of the Tragedy to Bristol ? We will print 500.

I have been seriously unwell for these last two days, which is the Reason that I deferred my departure to Cam. till tomorrow—I am rather better—but still heavy of head, turbulent of Bowell, and inappetent.

In my list of *Subscribers*,[1] I hear, there are the names of Parr,[2] Disney, Lindsay,[3] Wakefield,[4] and Bowles:—two Bishops, and 4 Lords!!—

Allen & Bloxam, after we quitted Oxford, took the Tour of the Isle of White [*sic*]—I have not heard from Bobbee.

I long to be at Cambridge—detesting this vile City.

My head begins to throb painfully—I must conclude—. Tell Mrs Southey, I had the Night Mair last night—I dreamt (vision of terrors!) that she refused to go to America! God bless her!——

To Lovell, and Mary, the wife of Lovell, and to &c &c say all the *friendly* things for me—to &c—all the *tender* things.—

> Your's
> S. T. Coleridge

[1] Referring to the proposed *Imitations from the Modern Latin Poets*.
[2] Samuel Parr (1747–1825), scholar and pedagogue.
[3] John Disney (1746–1816) and Theophilus Lindsey (1723–1808), prominent Unitarians.
[4] Gilbert Wakefield (1756–1801), controversial writer, was imprisoned in 1799 for a seditious publication.

My fraternal or rather cousin-german remembrances to Citizen Robert Rover.—

The young Le Grice has got into a Scrape for concluding his *Speech* of *Thanks* to the *Governors* [of Christ's Hospital] with this Sentence

Laudes vestras efferre, gratias vobis quam cumulatissimas agere, nobis prope in morem abiit: mihi autem nobilius aliquid traditum est, quippe qui *gratuler* vobis; Justitiae, Deae optimae Maximae, vos aliquantulum obtemperasse——

Godwin *thinks* himself *inclined* to *Atheism*[1]—acknowleges there are arguments *for* Deity, he cannot answer—but not so many, as *against* his Existence—He is writing a book about it. I set him at Defiance—tho' if he convinces me, I will acknowlege it in a letter in the Newspapers—I am to be introduced to him sometime or other.—

Horsley,[2] the Bishop, is believed in the higher Circles and by all the World of Authors to be—a determined *Deist*.—What a villain, if it is true!—

58. *To Edith Fricker*

MS. Mr. H. B. Vander Poel. Hitherto unpublished.

Jes. Coll.   Wednesday Night—Sept. 17.—94
Dear Miss Edith

I *had* a Sister—an only Sister. Most tenderly did I love her! Yea, I have woke at midnight, and wept—because *she was not.*

There is no attachment under heaven so pure, so endearing. The Brother, who is blest with it I have envied him! Let whatsoever discompose him, he has still a gentle Friend, in whose soft Bosom he may repose his Sorrows, and receive for every wound of affliction the Balm of a Sigh.[3]

My Sister, like you, was beautiful and accomplished—like you, she was lowly of Heart. Her Eye beamed with meekest Sensibility. I know, and *feel*, that I am *your Brother*—I would, that you would say to me—'I *will* be your Sister—your *favorite* Sister in the Family of Soul.[']

S. T. Coleridge

---

[1] William Godwin (1756–1836), author of *Enquiry concerning Political Justice and Its Influence on Morals and Happiness*, 1793. Godwin later said that he was led to theism by Coleridge. Cf. C. Kegan Paul, *William Godwin*, 2 vols., 1876, i. 357–8.

[2] Samuel Horsley (1733–1806), at this time Bishop of Rochester.

[3] For a poetical expression of these sentiments see the poem, *To C. Lamb*, 11 f. in Letter 77.

59. To Robert Southey

Address: Robert Southey | Miss Tyler's | Bristol
MS. Lord Latymer. Pub. Letters, i. 81.
Stamped: Bath.

Sept—18th—[1794]   10 o clock Thursday Morning

Well, my dear Southey! I am at last arrived at Jesus. My God! how tumultuous are the movements of my Heart—Since I quitted this room what and how important Events have been evolved! America! Southey! Miss Fricker!—Yes—Southey—you are right—Even Love is the creature of strong Motive—I certainly love her. I think of her incessantly & with unspeakable tenderness—with that inward melting away of Soul that symptomatizes it.

Pantisocracy—O I shall have such a scheme of it! My head, my heart are all alive—I have drawn up my arguments in battle array—they shall have the *Tactician* Excellence of the Mathematician with the Enthusiasm of the Poet—The Head shall be the Mass—the Heart the fiery Spirit, that fills, informs, and agitates the whole—Harwood!—Pish! I say nothing of him——

SHAD GOES WITH US. HE IS MY BROTHER!

I am longing to be with you—Make Edith my Sister—Surely, Southey! we shall be frendotatoi meta frendous. Most friendly where all are friends. She must therefore be more emphatically my Sister.

Brookes & Berdmore, as I suspected, have spread my Opinions in mangled forms at Cambridge—Caldwell the most excellent, the most pantisocratic of Aristocrats, has been laughing at me—Up I arose terrible in Reasoning—he fled from me—because 'he could not answer for his own Sanity sitting so near a madman of Genius!' He told me, that the Strength of my Imagination had intoxicated my Reason—and that the acuteness of my Reason had given a directing Influence to my Imagination.—Four months ago the Remark would not have been more elegant than Just—. Now it is Nothing.—

I like your Sonnets exceedingly—the best of any I have yet seen.—tho' to the eye Fair is the extended Vale—should be   To the Eye   Tho' fair the extended Vale[1]—I by no means disapprove of Discord introduced to produce *effect*—nor is my Ear so fastidious as to be angry with it where it could not have been avoided without weakening the Sense—But Discord for Discord's sake is rather too licentious.—

'Wild wind' has no other but alliterative beauty—it applies to

---

[1] See Sonnet VI, Southey, *Poet. Works*, ii. 93. See note to Letter 76 concerning the sonnet, *On Bala Hill*.

a storm, not to the Autumnal Breeze that makes the trees rustle mournfully—Alter it to

That rustle to the sad wind moaning by.

'''Twas a long way & tedious'—& the three last lines are marked Beauties—unlaboured Strains poured soothingly along from the feeling Simplicity of Heart.—The next Sonnet[1] is altogether exquisite—the circumstance common yet new to Poetry—the moral accurate & full of Soul. '*I never saw*['] &c is most exquisite——I am almost ashamed to write the following—it is so inferior—Ashamed! No—Southey—God knows my heart—I am *delighted* to feel you superior to me in Genius as in Virtue.[2]

> No more my Visionary Soul shall dwell
> On Joys, that were! No more endure to weigh
> The Shame and Anguish of the evil Day,
> Wisely forgetful! O'er the Ocean swell
> Sublime of Hope I seek the cottag'd Dell,
> Where Virtue calm with careless step may stray,
> And dancing to the moonlight Roundelay
> The Wizard Passions weave an holy Spell.
> Eyes that have ach'd with Sorrow! ye shall weep
> Tears of doubt-mingled Joy, like their's who start
> From Precipices of distemper'd Sleep,
> On which the fierce-eyed Fiends their Revels k[eep,]
> And see the rising Sun, & feel it dart
> New Rays of Pleasance trembling to the Heart.

I have heard from Allen—and write the *third* Letter to him. Your's is the *second*.—Perhaps you would like two Sonnets I have written to my Sally.——

When I have received an answer from Allen, I will tell you the contents of his first Letter.—

My Comp— to Heath——

I will write you a huge big Letter next week—at present I have to transact the Tragedy Business, to wait on the Master, to write to Mrs Southey, Lovell, &c &c—

God love you— &

S. T. Coleridge

---

[1] See Sonnet VIII, ibid. ii. 94.

[2] *Poems*, i. 68. This sonnet first appeared in Southey's *Life and Corres.* i. 224, where it is erroneously attributed to S. Favell, but there is no reason to doubt Coleridge's authorship, especially since the octave was incorporated into the *Monody on the Death of Chatterton*, lines 140–7. See also Letter 74, in which Coleridge says of this sonnet, 'I wrote the whole but the second & third Line'.

60. *To Robert Southey*

Address: Robert Southey | Miss Tyler's, Bristol.[1]
MS. Lord Latymer. Pub. with omis. Letters, i. 84.
Stamped: Bath.

Friday Morning—Sept. 19. 1794.

My fire was blazing chearfully—the Tea-kettle even now boiled over on it—how sudden-sad it looks! but see—it blazes up again as cheerily as ever!—Such, dear Southey! was the effect of your this morning's letter on my heart. Angry! no, I esteem & confide in you the more—: but it *did* make me sorrowful.—I was blameless—it was therefore only

a passing Cloud empictur'd on the Breast.

Surely had I written to *you* the *first* letter you directed to *me* at Cambridge, I *would* not have believed that you *could* have received it without immediately answering it. Still less that you *could* have given a momentary pain to her that loved you. If I could have imagined no *rational* Excuse for you, I would have peopled the Vacancy with Events of Impossibility!——

On Wednesday—Sept. 17—I arrived in Cambridge—perhaps the very hour, you were writing in the severity of offended Friendship, was I pouring forth the Heart to Sarah Fricker—I did not call on Caldwell—I saw no one—on the moment of my Arrival I shut my door, and wrote to her. But why not before?—

In the first Place Miss F. did not authorize me to direct immediately to her—It was *settled*, that through *you* in our weekly *Parcels* were the Letters to be conveyed.—The moment I arrived at Cambridge—and all yesterday—was I writing Letters to you, to your Mother—to Lovell &c—to complete a Parcel.—

In London I wrote twice to you—intending daily to go to Cambridge, of course, I deferred the *Parcel* till then—I was taken ill—very ill.—I exhausted my Finances—and ill as I was I sat down and scrawled a two guineas' Worth of Nonsense for the Booksellers—which Dyer disposed of for me—Languid, sick at heart—in the back Room of an Inn—happy conjunction of circumstances for me to write to Miss F.—! Besides, I told her, I should write the moment I arrived at Cambridge—I have fullfilled the Promise——Recollect, Southey! that when you mean to go to a place—to morrow—and to morrow—and to morrow—the time that intervenes is lost—Had I meant at first to stay in London a fortnight, a fortnight should not have elapsed without my writing to her—If you are satisfied, tell Miss F. that *you* are *so*—but assign no Reasons. I ought not to have been *suspected*.

[1] On the address sheet Coleridge wrote, 'Read this letter *first*'.

The Tragedy will be printed in less than a week—I shall put my
Name—because it will sell at least an hundred Copies at Cam-
bridge—. It would appear ridiculous to put two names to *such* a
Work—But if you choose it, mention it—and it shall be done—
To every man, who *praises* it, of course I give the *true* biography of
it—to those, who laugh at it, I laugh again—and I am too well
known at Cambridge to be thought the less of—even tho' I had
published James Jennings' Satire.[1]

Watt was a villain—and became a Traitor, that when matters
were to a head, he might have the Merit of being an *Informer*—.
I am pleased with Zephariah Fry——.

Southey—! Precipitance is wrong. There may be too high a state
of *Health*—perhaps even *Virtue* is liable to a *Plethora*! I have been
the Slave of Impulse, the Child of Imbecillity—But my incon-
sistencies have given me a tarditude & reluctance to think ill of
any one—having been often suspected of wrong, when I was
altogether right, from *fellow-feeling* I judge not too hastily from
appearances. Your undeviating Simplicity of Rectitude has made
you too rapid in decision—having never erred, you feel more
indignation at Error, than *Pity* for it. There is *Phlogiston* in your
heart. Yet am I grateful for it—you would not have written so
angrily—but for the greatness of your esteem & affection. The
more highly we have been wont to think of a Character, the more
pain & irritation we suffer from the discovery of it's Imperfec-
tions.—

My heart is very heavy—much more so, than when I began to
write—

Your's most fraternally
S. T. Coleridge

61. *To Henry Martin*

Pub. The Fall of Robespierre, *1794.* This dedicatory letter bears the heading
'To H. Martin, Esq. of Jesus College, Cambridge'.

Jesus College, September 22, 1794

Dear Sir,

Accept, as a small testimony of my grateful attachment, the
following Dramatic Poem, in which I have endeavoured to detail,
in an interesting form, the fall of a man, whose great bad actions

---

[1] James Jennings (1772–1833), a native of Huntspill, Somerset, and an
acquaintance of Southey's. His satire, *The Times*, was published in 1794. It
is in very lame anapaestic verse and censures the corruptions of the age. Its
total sale was said to have been less than a dozen copies. [Note contributed
by Mr. Geoffrey Carnall.]

have cast a disastrous lustre on his name. In the execution of the work, as intricacy of plot could not have been attempted without a gross violation of recent facts, it has been my sole aim to imitate the empassioned and highly figurative language of the French Orators, and to develope the characters of the chief actors on a vast stage of horrors.

Yours fraternally,
S. T. Coleridge.

62. *To Francis Wrangham*[1]

Address: The reverend F. Wrangham | Cobham | Surry   Single
MS. Mr. W. Hugh Peal. Hitherto unpublished.
Postmark: 27 September 1794.   *Stamped*: Cambridge.

Jes. Coll. Camb.   Sept. 26th 1794

Dear Wrangham

I was somewhat disappointed by your abrupt departure—yet you acted wisely—I trust, we shall soon see you again—.—

I finished the translation—or rather Imitation—of your exquisite Brutoniad[2]—I am afraid, the thoughts in my language will appear like the armour of Saul on David. However you have both the Esse & the Posse of my poor Muse—I am labouring under a waking Night-mair of Spirits—so farewell.

Your's *fraternally* in the | family of Soul—
S. T. Coleridge.

P.S. I inclosed it according to your desire in a note to Eliza Brunton.

To Miss Brunton (now Mrs Merry)

on her departure from Cambridge—Oct. 1790

(Imitated from the Latin of the reverend F. Wrangham)[3]

> Maid of unboastful Charms! whom white-rob'd Truth
> Right onwards guiding thro' the Maze of Youth
> Forbade the Circe Praise to witch thy Soul,
> And dash'd to Earth th' intoxicating Bowl—

[1] Francis Wrangham (1769–1842), classical scholar, attended Trinity Hall, Cambridge, and after failing to win a fellowship in his college he became a curate in Cobham, Surrey, about this time.

[2] Wrangham's *Hendecasyllabi ad Bruntonam e Granta Exituram* was addressed to the actress, Elizabeth Brunton, who had won great acclaim as Euphrasia. Her father was John Brunton, an actor of provincial fame and manager of the Norwich company.

[3] *Poems*, i. 66. First published in Wrangham's *Poems*, 1795. The holograph contains minor corrections in Wrangham's hand, the most significant alteration being the substitution of 'fragrant' for 'starry' in line 33.

Thee meek-Ey'd Pity eloquently fair
Clasp'd to her Bosom with a Mother's care—
And, as she lov'd thy kindred form to trace,
The slow Smile wander'd o'er her pallid face.

For never yet did mortal Voice impart
Tones more congenial to the sadden'd heart;
Whether to rouse the sympathetic glow
Thou pourest lone Monimia's tale of Woe
Or haply cloathest with funereal Vest
The bridal Loves, that wept in Juliet's Breast.

O'er our chill limbs the thrilling Terrors creep,
Th' entranced Passions their still vigil keep—
While the deep Sighs responsive to the song
Sound thro' the Silence of the trembling throng.

But purer Raptures lighten'd from thy face
And spread o'er all thy form an holier grace,
When from the Daughter's Breasts the Father drew
The Life he gave, and mix'd the big Tear's dew.
Nor was it thine th' heroic strain to roll
With mimic feelings foreign from the soul—
Bright in thy Parent's Eye we mark'd the tear—
Methought he said, 'Thou art no *Actress* here!
A semblance of thyself the Grecian Dame
And Brunton & Euphrasia still the same!'

O soon to seek the City's busier scene,
Pause thee awhile, thou chaste-ey'd Maid serene!
Till Granta's Sons from all her sacred bowers
With grateful hand shall weave Pierian flowers
To 'twine a *starry* Chaplet round thy Brow,
Enchanting Ministress of virtuous Woe!

I prefixed to it the following poemation—which is very pretty,
but rather silly or so.[1]

That Darling of the Tragic Muse—
    When Wrangham sung her praise,
Thalia lost her rosy hues
    And sicken'd at his Lays.

[1] *Poems*, i. 67. First published in Wrangham's *Poems*, 1795. This manuscript
also contains minor corrections by Wrangham.

But transient was th' unwonted Sigh,
    For soon the Goddess 'spied
A Sister Form of mirthful Eye—
    And danc'd for Joy—and cried:

'Meek Pity's sweetest Child, proud Dame!
    The fates have giv'n to you!
Still bid your Poet boast her *Name*—
    I have my Brunton too.'[1]

63. *To Robert Southey*

Address: Robert Southey | Miss Tyler's | College Green | Bristol
MS. Lord Latymer. Pub. with omis. Letters, *i. 86.*
Postmark: 27 September 1794.   *Stamped*: Cambridge.

Friday Night.   [26 September 1794]

My dear dear Southey

I am beyond measure distressed & agitated by your letter to
Favell—On the evening of the Wednesday before last I arrived in
Cambridge—that night & the next day I dedicated to writing to
you, to Miss F— & &c &c &c. On the Friday Morning as I was
about to send off the Parcel I received your letter of phlogistic
Rebuke—I answered it immediately—wrote a second letter to
Miss F.—inclosed them in the aforesaid Parcel—& sent them off
by the Mail directed to Mrs Southey—No 8—Westcott Buildings
—Bath—They should have arrived on Sunday Morning. Perhaps
you have not heard from Bath—perhaps—damn perhapses—My
God! my God! what a deal of pain you must have suffered—before
you wrote that Letter to Favell.——

It is our St[o]urbritch Fair[2] time and the Norwich Company are
theatricalizing. They are the first provincial Actors in the King-
dom—Much against my Will I am engaged to drink Tea and go
to the Play with Miss Brunton (Mrs Merry's Sister.) The young
Lady and indeed the whole Family have taken it into their heads to
be very much attached to me—tho' I have known them only 6
days. The Father (who is the Manager & Proprietor of the Theatre)
inclosed in a very polite note a free Ticket for the Season—The
young Lady is said to be the most literary of the beautiful, and the
most beautiful of the literatae—It may be so—my faculties &
discernments are so compleatly jaundiced by vexation, that the

---

[1] According to an unpublished note by J. D. Campbell these lines were
probably addressed to Ann Brunton.
[2] Coleridge refers to the famous Stourbridge Fair. E. H. Coleridge misread
this passage as 'an Ipswich Fair time', which is meaningless.

Virgin Mary & Mary Flanders—alias Moll, would appear in the same hues.——

All last night was I obliged to listen to the damned chatter of Mortlock, our Mayor—a fellow, that would certainly be a Pantisocrat, were his head & heart as highly illuminated as his Face. At present he is a High Church man & a Pittite—and is guilty (with a very large fortune) of so many Rascalities in his public Character, that he is obliged to drink three bottles of Claret a day in order to acquire a stationary rubor and prevent him from the trouble of running backwards & forwards for a blush once every five minutes. In the tropical Latitudes of this fellow's Nose was I obliged to fry—I wish, you would write a lampoon upon him —in me it would be unchristian Revenge!

Our Tragedy is printed all but the Title page—it will be complete by Saturday Night.

God love you—I am in the queerest humour in the world—and am out of love with every body——

S. T. Coleridge

64. *To Francis Wrangham*

Address: The reverend F. Wrangham | Cobham | Surry.
MS. Huntington Lib. Pub. E. L. G. i. 25.
Postmark: 10 October 1794.   *Stamped*: Cambridge.

Thursday—Oct. 9th 1794

The Scriptures tell me, dear Wrangham! that Ingratitude is worse than the Sin of Witchcraft: that I may not therefore be condemned of the former, I must plead guilty to the latter—with this distinction, that instead of being the Wizard, I am the Bewitched. I have indeed incautiously drank too deeply from the bowl of the blameless Circe—the sweet intoxication, that makes the Heart forget it's duties & it's cares. I give you however but little credit for your conjecture—as, if I mistake not, you drew the Truth from the Well of your own Experience. The Brunton left us yesterday morning—since which time Caldwell & I have chaunted a love-lorn Duet most pathetically.——

Now would my Heart impell me to pour forth a declamation of praises on her character—but I will not do it for two Reasons— Firstly, because it would have too much *Truth* to possess any *Novelty* to *you*—& secondly, because if I once fairly got into the Subject—

> An Host of Elephants were atomies
> To tug me from the Strain—— as

Mr Greathead says[1]——but if you ask, who was the rather a favorite—Caldwell, of course. Had she not deemed more highly of him than of me, I should have deemed less highly of her. There is a Hue of Elegance suffused over his Virtues & Abilities, that gives them a decided preference to the same Qualities in other men——

Whether he has performed your commission, he will himself inform you—I have not asked him—as on the receipt of your letter to *me*, he said, he would write you himself.

Your plan of the Quadragesimal Imitations I like quoad se rather than quoad te—I think you superior to it. There are other objections—The merit of those little Poems consists almost entirely in the neatness of the Latinity—in English Poetry, we want a greater *body of mind*, than they possess.—Nor are they in general Originals—the Thoughts are found elsewhere—To give Imitations of Imitations & *retranslate*—would it answer? Your Cinna is an illustrious exception—I like it much—the penultimate Line is however weak—*facundia* ought not to have been lost:—A Perry *might* have written Lies—*eloquent* Lies—not. In the easy verse, which you have with great judgment [a]dopted, a trochee in the fourth foot may be tolerated—in general, it has an unpleasant effect on the ear—it is slovenly—I allude to the 'vulgăr tŏ beguile.'

Your Love Ode is beautiful—it is almost too good for Flower— Were it not so beautiful, I should not remark so small a fault as the falling off the sense in the 'in his Side.' The word 'Swain' in the antecedent Line is (perhaps I have an irrational antipathy to it) but to my ideas it conveys too much of the Cant of Pastoral— Would it not be better thus—

> Fly, fatal Shaft! (with cruel zeal
> The conscious Murd'ress cried)
> Go teach this Stoic Heart to feel
> The Vengeance* due to Pride—
>
> * or Anguish [S. T. C.]

It cannot be inserted *this* week—and before next Wednesday I shall hear from you—(rather impudent or so!) but my epistolary expectations are in inverse proportion to my deserts.—

If you mean to continue your Imitations—you must procure the *second* Volume of the Quadragesimalia——you may procure it from Oxford—Christ Church meditates a third Volume—but not

[1] Cf. Bertie Greatheed, *The Regent: A Tragedy*, 1788, iv. ii. 29–31:

> Despair with damning hold
> Clings on so fast, a wild of elephants
> Were atomies to tear it from this trunk.

for some years—if you have any friend at Christ Church he can easily get the Manuscript from the Tutor—& transcribe one most elegant thing of Canning's—the subject is—The cursing of Crassus on his de[parture] from the City on the Parthian Expedition—It is really a fine little Poem—

Shortly after new Year's day I shall pay a Visit to Norwich—*Middleton* resides there—& Mr & Mrs Brunton have given me an invitation too pressing to be refused——I hope however to see *Cobham* at Christmas—and to go from thence to Norwich—

God bless you | &

S. T. Coleridge

65. *To Robert Southey*

Address: Robert Southey[1]
MS. Lord Latymer. Pub. with omis. Letters, i. 87.

Jes. Coll. Cambridge. Oct. 21st [1794]

To *you alone*, Southey! I write the first part of this letter—to yourself confine it—

'Is this handwriting altogether erased from your Memory? To whom am I addressing myself? For whom am I now violating the Rules of female Delicacy? Is it for the same Coleridge, whom I once regarded as a Sister her best-beloved Brother? Or for one who will RIDICULE that advice from me, which he has *rejected* as offered by his family? I will hazard the attempt. I have no right—nor do I feel myself inclined, to reproach you for the Past. God forbid! You have already suffered too much from self-accusation. But I conjure you, Coleridge! earnestly and solemnly conjure you, to consider long and deeply, before you enter into any rash Schemes. There is an Eagerness in your Nature, which is ever hurrying you into the sad Extreme. I have heard that you mean to leave England: and on a Plan so absurd and extravagant, that were I for a moment to imagine it *true*, I should be obliged to listen with a more patient Ear to Suggestions, which I have rejected a thousand Times with scorn and anger—yes! whatever Pain I might suffer I should be forced to exclaim—"O what a noble Mind is here *o'erthrown*. Blasted with Exstacy"!—You have a Country. Does it demand nothing of You? You have doting Friends. Will you break their Hearts? There is a God—Coleridge! Though I have been told (*indeed* I do not believe it) that you doubt of his Existence

---

[1] On the address sheet Coleridge wrote: 'The large Sheet is the first Letter—this your second—What is become, of the Niemi Spirits?'

and disbelieve a hereafter.—No! you have too much Sensibility to
be an Infidel. You know I never was rigid in my opinions concern-
ing Religion—and have always thought *Faith* to be only Reason
applied to a particular Subject—In short, I am the same Being,
as when you used to say—We thought in all things alike. I often
reflect on the happy hours we spent together, and regret the Loss
of your Society. I cannot easily forget those whom I once loved—
nor can I easily form new Friendships. I find Women in general
vain—all of the same Trifle: and therefore little and envious—and
(I am afraid) without sincerity—: and of the other sex those, who
are offered and held up to my esteem, are very prudent and very
worldly.—If you value my peace of mind, you must *on no account*
answer this Letter, or take the least Notice of it. I *would* not for
the World *any part* of my Family should suspect, that I have
written to you. My mind is sadly harassed by being perpetually
obliged to resist the solicitations of those whom I love. I need not
explain myself——Farewell—Coleridge—! I shall always feel that
I have been your *Sister*.[']——

No name was signed;—it was from Mary Evans.[1]—I received it
about three weeks ago. I loved her, Southey! almost to madness.
Her Image was never absent from me for three Years—for *more*
than three Years.—My Resolution has not faltered—but I want
a Comforter.—I have done nothing—I have gone into Company—
I was constantly at the Theatre here till they left us—I endeavored
to be perpetually with Miss Brunton—I even hoped, that her
Exquisite Beauty and uncommon Accomplishments might have
cured one Passion by another. The latter I could easily have
dissipated in her absence—and so have restored my affections to
her, whom I do not love—but whom by every tie of Reason and
Honor I ought to love. I am resolved—but wretched!—But Time
shall do much—you will easily believe that with such feelings I
should have found it no easy Task to write to ——.[2] I should have
detested myself, if after my first Letter I had written coldly—how
could I write *as warmly*?—I was vexed too and alarmed by your

---

[1] In an unpublished letter J. D. Campbell suggests that Mary Evans's
appeal was probably made at the express request of George Coleridge. Such
an assumption seems reasonable. Deeply distressed by Coleridge's unorthodox
behaviour and unable to effect any change of opinion by his own letters of
'remonstrance, and Anguish, & suggestions', George Coleridge quite under-
standably may have turned to the one person likely to influence his brother.
Mary Evans's letter, to be sure, produced noticeable effects. On the one hand,
Coleridge reveals in his letters a growing dissatisfaction with Pantisocracy,
which included, of course, marriage to Sara Fricker; on the other hand, he
was awakened from the resignation with which he had accepted the loss of
Mary Evans and caught at the vain hope of winning her love. Cf. Letter 71.
[2] Sara Fricker.

letter concerning Mr & Mrs Roberts, Shad & little Sally—*I* was
wrong, very wrong in the affair of Shad—& have given you
Reason to suppose, that I should assent to this Innovation—I will
most assuredly go with you to America on *this* Plan—but re-
member, Southey! *this* is *not our* Plan—nor can I defend it. 'Shad's
children will be educated as our's—and the Education we shall
give them will be such as to render them incapable of blushing at
the want of it in their Parents.'—PERHAPS! With this one Word
would every Lilliputian Reasoner demolish the System. Wherever
Men *can* be vicious, some *will* be. The leading Idea of Pantisocracy
is to make men *necessarily* virtuous by removing all Motives to
Evil—all possible Temptations. 'Let them dine with us and be
treated with as much equality as they would wish—but perform
that part of Labor for which their Education has fitted them.'—
Southey should not have written this Sentence—my Friend, my
noble and high-souled Friend should have said—to his Dependents
—Be my Slaves—and ye shall be my Equals—to his Wife &
Sisters—Resign the *Name* of Ladyship and ye shall retain the
thing.—Again—Is every Family to possess one of these Unequal
Equals—these Helot Egalité-s? Or are the few, you have men-
tioned—'with more toil than the Peasantry of England undergo'—
to do for all of us 'that part of Labor which their Education has
fitted them for'? If your remarks on the other side are just, the
Inference is, that the Scheme of Pantisocracy is impracticable—
but I hope & believe, that it is not a *necessary* Inference. Your
remark of the Physical Evil in the long Infancy of men would
indeed puzzle a Pangloss—puzzle him to account for the wish of
a benevolent heart like your's to discover malignancy in it's
Creator. Surely every Eye but an Eye jaundiced by habit of peevish
Scepticism must have seen, that the Mother's cares are repaid even
to rapture by the Mother's endearments—and that the long help-
lessness of the Babe is the *means* of our superiority in the filial &
maternal Affection & Duties to the same feelings in the Brute
Creation—it is likewise among other causes the *means* of Society—
that thing which makes Man a little lower than the Angels.—If
Mrs S. & Mrs F. go with us—they can at least prepare the Food of
Simplicity for us—Let the married Women do only what is abso-
lutely convenient and customary for pregnant Women or nurses—
Let the Husbands do *all* the Rest—and what will that all be—?
Washing with a Machine and cleaning the House. One Hour's
addition to our daily Labor—and *Pantisocracy* in it's most perfect
Sense is practicable.—That the greater part of our Female Com-
panions should have the task of Maternal exertion at the same time,
is very *improbable*—but tho' it were to happen, An Infant is almost

always sleeping—and during it's Slumbers the Mother may in the same Room perform the little offices of ironing Cloaths or making Shirts.—But the Hearts of the Women are not *all* with us.—I do believe that Edith & Sarah are exceptions—but do even they know the bill of fare for the Day—every duty that will be incumbent on them—?—

All necessary knowlege in the Branch of Ethics is comprised in the Word Justice—that the Good of the whole is the Good of each Indiv[id]ual. Of course it is each Indiv[id]ual's *duty* to be Just, *because* it is his *Interest*. To perceive this and to assent to it as an abstract proposition—is easy—but it requires the most wakeful attentions of the most reflective minds in all moments to bring it into practice—It is not enough, that we have once swallowed it—The *Heart* should have *fed* upon the *truth*, as Insects on a Leaf—till it be tinged with the colour, and shew it's food in every the minutest fibre. In the book of Pantisocracy I hope to have comprised all that is good in Godwin—of whom and of whose book I will write more fully in my next letter. (I think not so highly of him as you do—and I have read him with the greatest attention—) This will be an advantage to the *minds* of our Women——

What have been your feelings concerning the War with America, which is now inevitable? To go from Hamburgh will not only be an heavy additional expence—but dangerous & uncertain—as Nations at War are in the habit of examining Neutral Vessels to prevent the Importation of Arms and seize subjects of the hostile Governments—— It is said, that one cause of the Ministers' being so cool on this business is that it will prevent Emigration, which it seems would be treasonable, to an hostile Country—Tell me all you think on these subjects.—

What think you of the difference in the Prices of Land as stated by Cowper from those given by the American Agents? By all means read & ponder on Cowper[1]—and when I hear your thoughts, I will give you the Result of my own.——

Sonnet[2]

Thou bleedest, my poor Heart! & thy Distress
Doth Reason ponder with an anguish'd smile
Probing thy sore wound sternly, tho' the while

---

[1] Cf. Thomas Cooper, *Some Information respecting America*, 1794. Cooper matriculated at University College, Oxford, in 1779, three years before Coleridge entered Christ's Hospital, and was not the 'intelligent young Man of our School', whom Coleridge had befriended, and who reported on the Susquehanna at the Salutation and Cat. See Letter 55.

[2] *Poems*, i. 72.

Her Eye be swoln and dim with heaviness.[1]
Why didst thou *listen* to Hope's whisper bland ?
Or, listening, why *forget* it's healing Tale,
When Jealousy with feverish Fancies pale
Jarr'd thy fine fibres with a Maniac's hand ?
Faint was that Hope and rayless: yet 'twas fair
And sooth'd with many a dream the Hour of Rest!
Thou should'st have lov'd it most when most opprest,
And nurs'd it with an Agony of Care,
Ev'n as a Mother her sweet infant heir
That pale and sickly droops upon her Breast.

When a Man is unhappy, he writes damned bad Poetry, I find.
——My Imitations too depress my Spirits—the task is arduous
and grows upon me—instead of two Octavo Volumes—to do all I
hoped to do—two Quartos would hardly be sufficient——

Of your Poetry I will send you a minute critique, when I send
you my proposed alterations.—The Sonnets are exquisite—
Banquo[2] is not what it deserves to be—Towards the end it grows
very flat—wants variety of Imagery—you dwell too long on
Mary, yet have made less of her than I expected—the other
Figures are not sufficiently distinct—indeed the Plan of the Ode
(after the first 40 lines, which are most truly sublime) is so evident
an Imitation of Gray's Descent of Odin, that I would rather adopt
Shakespere's mode of introducing the figures themselves—and
making the description now the Witch's and now Fleance's—
Banquo is scarcely dead—(behind I hear my Father cry &c)—I
detest Monodramas—but I never wished to establish my Judgement
on the throne of Critical Despotism. Send me up the Elegy on the
exiled Patriots and the Scripture Sonnets—I have promised them
to Flower[3]—the first will do *good*—and more good in a Paper than
in any other Vehicle.

My thoughts are floating about in a most Chaotic State—I had
almost determined to go down to Bath and stay two days—that
I might say every thing I wished—You mean to acquaint your
Aunt with the Scheme—As she knows it, and knows, that you
know that she knows it—*Justice* cannot require it—but if your
own Comfort makes it necessary, by all means do it—with all

[1] My Heart! thou bleedest—And thy distress
   I ponder with a faint and anguish'd Smile
   Probing thy sore wound sternly; though the while
   Mine Eye be swoln and dim with heaviness.
[Cancelled version of the first four lines.]
   [2] *The Race of Banquo*, Southey's *Poet. Works*, ii. 155.
   [3] Editor of the *Cambridge Intelligencer*.

possible Gentleness—She has loved you tenderly—be firm therefore
as a Rock—mild as the Lamb.—I sent 100 Robespierres to Bath
10 days ago and more.—500 Copies of Robespierre were printed—
100 to Bath—100 to Kearsley in London—25 to March at Norwich
—30 I have sold privately (25 of these 30 to Dyer, who found it
inconvenient to take 50) the rest are dispersed among the Cam-
bridge Booksellers—the delicacies of academic Gentlemanship
prevented me from disposing of more than the 5 propriâ personâ—
of course we only get 9 pence for each Copy from the Booksellers.
I expected that Mr Field would have sent for 50; but have heard
nothing of it. I sent a copy to him with my respects—and have
made presents of 6 more. How they sell in London, I know not—
all that are in Cambridge will sell—a great many are sold—I have
been blamed for publishing it considering the more important
work, I have offered to the Public—N'importe—'Tis thought a
very *Aristocratic* Performance—you may suppose how hyper-
democratic my character must have been—. The Expences of
Paper, Printing, and Advertisements—are nearly 9 pound—We
ought to have charged 1s—6d a copy.—

I presented a Copy to Miss Brunton with these Verses in the
blank Leaf.[1]—

> Much on my early Youth I love to dwell
> Ere yet I bade that guardian Dome farewell,
> Where first beneath the echoing Cloysters pale
> I heard of Guilt, and wonder'd at the tale!
> Yet, tho' the hours flew by on careless wing,
> Full heavily of Sorrow would I sing.
> Aye as the Star of Evening flung it's beam
> In broken Radiance on the wavy stream,
> My pensive Soul amid the *twilight** gloom
> Mourn'd with the Breeze, O Leé Bo! o'er thy tomb.
> Where'er I wander'd, Pity still was near,
> Breath'd from the Heart, and glitter'd in the tear:
> No knell, that toll'd, but fill'd my anguish'd Eye,
> 'And suffering Nature wept that *one* should die'!
>
> Thus to sad Sympathies I sooth'd my breast
> Calm,† as the Rainbow in the weeping West;
> When slumb'ring Freedom rous'd by high Disdain
> With giant fury burst her triple chain.
> Fierce on her Front the blasting Dog star glow'd;
> Her banners, like a midnight meteor, flow'd;

---

[1] *Poems*, i. 64. * *shadowy* [S. T. C.] † (Bright?) [S. T. C.]

Amid the yelling of the storm-rent Skies
She came, and scatter'd Battles from her Eyes!
Then Exultation woke the patriot fire
And swept with wilder hand th' empassion'd Lyre.
Red from the Tyrant's wounds I shook the Lance,
And strode in Joy the reeking plains of France!

In ghastly horror lie th' Oppressors low——
And my Heart akes tho' Mercy struck the Blow!
With wearied thought I seek the Amaranth Shade
Where peaceful Virtue weaves her *myrtle* Braid.
And O! if Eyes, whose holy Glances roll
The eloquent Messengers of the pure Soul;
If Smiles more winning and a gentler Mien,
Than the love-wilder'd Maniac's brain hath seen
Shaping celestial forms in vacant air;
If *these* demand the wond'ring Poet's care——
If Mirth and soften'd Sense, and Wit refin'd,
The blameless Features of a lovely Mind;
Then haply shall my trembling Hand assign
No *fading* Flowers to Beauty's saintly Shrine.
Nor, BRYNTON! thou the blushing Wreath refuse;
Though harsh her Notes, yet guileless is my Muse.
Unwont at Flattery's Voice to plume her wings,
A Child of Nature, as she feels, she sings.

S. T. C.

—Till I dated this Letter, I never recollected that Yesterday was my Birth Day[1]—22 years old.——

I have heard from my Brothers—from him particularly, who has been Friend, Brother, Father—'Twas all remonstrance, and Anguish, & suggestions, that I am deranged!!—

Let me receive from you a letter of Consolation—for believe me! I am most compleatly wretched—

Your's most affectionately
S. T. Coleridge

66. *To Robert Southey*

MS. Lord Latymer. Pub. with omis. Letters, *i. 101.*

[*Circa* 23 October 1794]

Last night, dear Southey! I received a special Invitation from Dr Edwards (the great Grecian of Cambridge and heterodox

---

[1] A lifelong error; Coleridge was born 21 Oct. 1772.

Divine)[1] to drink Tea and spend the Evening—I there met a counsellor whose name is Lushington—a Dημocrat—and a man of the most powerful and Briaréan Intellect—I was challenged on the subject of Pantisocracy, which is indeed the universal Topic at this University—A Discussion began and continued for *six* hours. In conclusion, Lushington & Edwards declared the System impregnable, supposing the assigned Quantum of Virtue and Genius in the first Individuals. I came home at one o'clock this morning exulting in the honest Consciousness of having exhibited closer argument in more elegant and appropriate Language, than I had ever conceived myself capable of. Then my heart smote me— for I saw your Letter on the propriety of taking Servants with us.—I had answered that Letter—and feel conviction that you will perceive the error, into which the Tenderness of your Nature had led you. But other Queries obtruded themselves on my Understanding—The more perfect our System is—supposing the necessary Premises—the more eager in anxiety am I—that the necessary Premises should exist.

O for that Lyncéan Eye, that can discover in the Acorn of Error the rooted and widely spreading Oak of Misery!—

Quere. Should not all, who mean to become members of our Community, be incessantly meliorating their Tempers and elevating their Understandings? Qu: Whether a very respectable Quantity of *acquired* knowlege (History, Politics, above all, *Metaphysics*, without which no man *can* reason but with women & children) be not a prerequisite to the improvement of the Head and Heart? Qu. Whether our Women have not been taught by us habitually to contemplate the littlenesses of indiv[id]ual Comforts, and a passion for the *Novelty* of the Scheme, rather than the generous enthusiasm of Benevolence? Are they saturated with the Divinity of Truth sufficiently to be always wakeful? In the present state of their minds whether it is not probable, that the *Mothers* will tinge the Mind of the Infants with prejudications?——

These Questions are meant *merely* as motives to you, Southey! to be strengthening the minds of the Women and stimulating them to literary Acquirements.—But, Southey!—there are *Children* going with us. Why did I never dare in my disputations with the Unconvinced to *hint* at this circumstance? Was it not, because I knew even to certainty of conviction, that it is subversive of *rational* Hopes of a permanent System? These children—the little Fricker for instance and *your* Brothers—Are they not already *deeply* tinged with the prejudices and errors of Society? Have they not

---

[1] Dr. Thomas Edwards had published *A Discourse on the Limits and Importance of Free Inquiry in Matters of Religion* in 1792.

learnt from their Schoolfellows *Fear* and *Selfishness*—of which the
necessary offspring are Deceit, and desultory Hatred? *How* are
we to prevent them from infecting the minds of *our* Children? By
reforming their Judgments?—At so early age *can* they have *felt*
the ill consequences of their Errors in a manner sufficiently vivid
to make this reformation practicable? Reasoning is but *Words*
unless where it derives force from the repeated experience of the
person, to whom it is addressed.—*How* can we ensure their silence
concerning *God* &c—? Is it possible, *they* should enter into our
motives for this silence? If not we must produce their *obedience* by
Terror. Obedience? Terror? The Repetition is sufficient——I need
not inform you, that they are as inadequate as inapplicable—I
have told you, Southey! that I will accompany you on an *im-
perfect* System. But *must* our System be thus necessarily imperfect?
I ask the Question that I may know whether or not I should write
the Book of Pantisocracy——I can not describe our System in
circumstances *not* true:—nor can I *omit* any circumstances that
are true. Can I *defend* all that are *now* true? Is it not a pity, that a
System so impregnable in itself should be thus blasted? Have you
forgot the word 'Justice[']?—Or have the *Feelings* prevailed over
the Dea optima maxima? They have not:—yet, Southey! be on
your Guard against them!—What would I not give for a Day's
conversation with you? So much, that I seriously think of Mail
coaching it to Bath—altho' but for a Day.

I received your letter of OYez—it brought a smile on a counten-
ance, that for these three weeks has been ever cloudy & stern, in
it's solitary Hours—In company, Wit and Laughter are Duties.
Slovenly? I could mention a Lady of fashionable rank and *most*
fashionable Ideas who declared to Caldwell—that *I* (S. T. Coleridge)
was a man of the most *courtly* & polished manners, of the most
gentlemanly address—she had ever met with.

But I will not *crow* / Slovenly indeed!——

[No signature in manuscript]

67. *To Francis Wrangham*

Address: The reverend F. Wrangham | Cobham | Surry.
MS. Harvard College Lib. Pub. E. L. G. i. 27.

Octob. 24, 1794

Dear Wrangham

I am so unwell, that I should have deferred the gratification, I
feel in writing to you—but that I could not send Musgrove to you
empty handed—

I wished to write you particularly concerning your Imitation

Scheme—my first advice is, that you should drop it altogether and apply your abilities to original compositions—perhaps, to genteel Comedy—as a department of literature most lucrative—& may I not add, peculiarly adapted to your cast of Genius?—If however you adhere to your former Plan—would it not be a more entertaining Work—to select the eminently beautiful Poematia from Brunck's Analects[1]—print them with notes—and add or connex Imitations? I could engage to mark out *30* to you most exquisite in their kind, yet little noticed. My assistance such as it is would of course be at your service, in whatever manner you found it convenient to employ it.

I have sent you the Tragedy of Robespierre—, 'libellus, qui mihi subito calore et quâdam festinandi voluptate fluxit. *Biduo* effusus est—quamvis metuo, ne verum istuc versus quoque ipsi de se probent.'

My head throbs so violently and my Spirits are so low, that I shall just add a Sonnet[2] & conclude—It was occasioned by a letter (which I lately received from a young Lady, whom for five years I loved—almost to madness) dissuasive from my American Scheme—; but where Justice leads, I will follow—though her Path be through thorns & roughness—The Scotts desire their compliments. *Compliments!* Cold aristocratic Inanities—! I abjure their nothingness. If there be any whom I deem worthy of remembrance—I am their Brother. I call even my Cat Sister in the Fraternity of universal Nature. Owls I respect & Jack Asses I love: for Aldermen & Hogs, Bishops & Royston Crows I have not particular partiality—; they are my Cousins however, at least by Courtesy. But Kings, Wolves, Tygers, Generals, Ministers, and Hyaenas, I renounce them all— or if they *must* be my kinsmen, it shall be in the 50th Remove— May the Almighty Pantisocratizer of Souls pantisocratize the Earth, and bless you and

S. T. Coleridge!—

68. *To Robert Southey*

Address: Robert Southey | No 8 | West gate Buildings | Bath   *Single*
MS. Lord Latymer. Pub. Letters, *i.* 95.
Postmark: 6 November 1794. *Stamped*: Cambridge.

[3 November 1794][3]

My feeble and exhausted Heart regards with a criminal indifference the Introduction of Servitude into our Society—; but my

---

[1] R. F. P. Brunck, *Analecta Veterum Poetarum Graecorum*, 3 vols., 1772–6.
[2] After his signature Coleridge added the sonnet, 'Thou bleedest, my poor Heart', as given in Letter 65.
[3] This letter was begun on Monday, 3 Nov., and completed the next day.

Judgement is not asleep: nor can I suffer your Reason, Southey!
to be entangled in the web, which your feelings have woven. Oxen
and Horses possess not intellectual Appetites—nor the powers of
acquiring them. We are therefore Justified in employing their
Labor to our own Benefit—Mind hath a divine Right of Sover-
eignty over Body—But who shall dare to transfer this Reasoning
from 'from Man to Brute' to 'from Man to Man[']! To be employed in
the Toil of the Field while *We* are pursuing philosophical Studies—
can Earldoms or Emperorships boast so huge an Inequality? Is
there a human Being of so torpid a Nature, as that placed in our
Society he would not feel it?—A *willing* Slave is the worst of
Slaves—His *Soul* is a Slave.—Besides, I must own myself in-
capable of perceiving even the temporary *convenience* of the pro-
posed Innovation—The *Men* do not want assistance—at least,
none that *Shad* can particularly give—And to the Women what
assistance can little Sally, the *wife* of Shad, give—more than any
other of our married women? Is she to have no domestic Cares of
her own? No house? No husband to provide for? No Children?
——*Because* Mr & Mrs Roberts are not likely to have Children, I
see, *less* objection to their accompanying us.—Indeed—indeed—
Southey! I am fearful that Lushington's prophecy may not be
altogether vain—'Your System, Coleridge! appears strong to the
head and lovely to the Heart—but depend upon it you will never
give your *women* sufficient strength of mind, liberality of heart,
or vigilance of Attention—*They* will spoil it!'

I am extremely unwell—have run a nail into my Heel—and
before me stand 'Embrocation for the throbbing of the Head'—
'To be shaked up well that the Ether may mix.'—'A Wine-glass
full to be taken when faint'—'Sdeath! how I hate the Labels of
Apothecary's Bottles.——Ill as I am I must go out to Supper—
Farewell for a few Hours.

'Tis past one o clock in the morning—I sate down at twelve
o'clock to read the 'Robbers' of Schiller—I had read chill and
trembling until I came to the part where Moor fires a pistol over
the Robbers who are asleep—I could read no more—My God!
Southey! Who is this Schiller? This Convulser of the Heart? Did
he write his Tragedy amid the yelling of Fiends?—I should not
like to [be] able to describe such Characters—I tremble like an
Aspen Leaf—Upon my Soul, I write to you because I am frightened
—I had better go to Bed. Why have we ever called Milton sublime?
That Count de Moor—horrible Wielder of heart-withering
Virtues—! Satan is scarcely qualified to attend his Execution as
Gallows Chaplain[1]——

[1] Cf. Coleridge's sonnet, *To the Author of 'The Robbers'*, Poems, i. 72.

Tuesday Morning.

I have received your Letter—Potter—of Emanuel—drives me up to Town in his Phaeton on Saturday Morning—I hope to be with you by Wednesday Week. Potter is a 'Son of Soul'—a Poet—of liberal sentiments in politics—yet (would you believe it?) possesses six thousand a year independent.—

I feel grateful to you for your Sympathy—There is a feverish distemperature of Brain, during which some horrible phantom threatens our Eyes in every corner, until emboldened by Terror we rush on it—and then—why then we return, the Heart indignant at it's own palpitation! Even so will the greater part of our mental Miseries vanish before an Effort. Whatever of mind we *will* to do, we *can* do! What then palsies the Will? The Joy of Grief! A mysterious Pleasure broods with dusky Wing over the tumultuous Mind—'and the Spirit of God moveth on the darkness of the Waters'! She WAS VERY lovely, Southey! We formed each other's minds—our ideas were blended—Heaven bless her! I cannot forget her—every day her Memory sinks deeper into my heart—

> Nutrito vulnere tabens
> Impatiensque mei, feror undique, solus, et excors,
> Et desideriis pascor!——

I wish, Southey! in the stern severity of Judgment, that the two Mothers were *not* to go and that the children stayed with them—Are you wounded by my want of feeling? No! how highly must I think of your rectitude of Soul, that I should dare to say this to so affectionate a Son! *That* Mrs Fricker—we shall have her teaching the Infants *Christianity*,—I mean—that mongrel whelp that goes under it's name—teaching them by stealth in some ague-fit of Superstition!—

There is little danger of my being *confined*—*Advice* offered with *respect* from a *Brother*—*affected coldness*, an *assumed alienation*—mixed with involuntary bursts of ANGUISH and disappointed *Affection*—questions concerning the mode in which I would have it mentioned to my aged Mother—these are the daggers, which are plunged into *my* Peace!—Enough! I should rather be offering consolation to your sorrows, than be wasting my feelings in egotistic complaints! 'Verily my Complaint is bitter—yet my Stroke is heavier than my Groaning'.——

God love you—my dear Southey!

S. T. Coleridge——

A Friend of mine hath lately departed this Life in a frenzy fever induced by Anxiety![1] poor fellow—a child of frailty like me: yet

---

[1] The Rev. Fulwood Smerdon, vicar of Ottery St. Mary, died in Aug. 1794.

he was amiable—! I poured forth these incondite Lines in a moment of melancholy dissatisfaction: . . .[1]

Song[2]

1

When Youth his faery reign began,
Ere Sorrow had proclaim'd me—Man;
While Peace the *present* Hour beguil'd,
And all the lovely *Prospect* smil'd;
Then, Mary! 'mid my lightsome glee
I heav'd the painless sigh for thee!

2

And when along the wilds of Woe
My harrass'd Heart was doom'd to know
The frantic burst of Outrage keen,
And the slow Pang that gnaws unseen;
Then shipwreck'd on Life's stormy Sea
I heav'd an anguish'd Sigh for thee!

3

But soon Reflection's hand imprest
A stiller sadness on my breast;
And sickly Hope with waning Eye
Was well content to droop and die!
I yielded to the stern Decree,
Yet heav'd the languid Sigh for thee!

4

And though in distant climes to roam
A Wanderer from my native home
I fain would woo a gentle Fair
To soothe the aching sense of Care,
Thy Image may not banish'd be—
Still, Mary! still I sigh for thee!

S. T. C.

God love you——

---

[1] Here follow the *Lines on a Friend*, as given in Letter 69. Cf. *Poems*, i. 76.
[2] Ibid. 62.

69. *To George Coleridge*

Address: Reverend George Coleridge | Mr Newcome's | Clapton | near Hackney | London   *Single*
MS. Lady Cave. *Pub. with omis.* Letters, *i. 103.*
Postmark: 7 November 1794.   *Stamped*: Cambridge.

Thursday Nov. 6th 1794.

My dear Brother

Your letter of this morning gave me inexpressible Consolation—I thought, that I perceived in your last the cold and freezing features of alienated affection—Surely—said I—I have trifled with the Spirit of Love, and it has passed away from me!

There is a Vice of such powerful Venom, that one Grain of it will poison the overflowing Goblet of a thousand Virtues. This Vice Constitution seems to have implanted in me, and Habit has made it almost omnipotent. It is INDOLENCE! Hence whatever Web of Friendship my Presence may have woven, my Absence has seldom failed to unravel. Anxieties that stimulate others, infuse an additional narcotic into my mind. The appeal of Duty to my Judgement, and the pleadings of affection at my Heart—have been heard indeed—and heard with deep regard—Ah! that they had been as constantly obeyed—But so it has been—Like some poor Labourer, whose Night's sleep has but imperfectly refreshed his overwearied frame, I have sate in drowsy uneasiness—and doing nothing have thought, what a deal I had to do! But I trust, that the Kingdom of Reason is at hand and even now cometh!—

How often and how unkindlily are the ebullitions of youthful disputatiousness mistaken for the result of fixed Principles! People have resolved, that I am a Dǐmocrat—and accordingly look at every thing I do through the Spectacles of Prejudication. In the feverish Distemperature of a *bigotted* Aristocrat's Brain some phantom of Dǐmocracy threatens him in every Corner of my Writings.—

> And Hebert's atheist Crew, whose maddening hand
> Hurl'd down the altars of the living God
> With all the Infidel's Intolerance[1]——

'Are these Lines in *character*['] (observed a sensible *friend* of mine) —'in a speech on the Death of the Man, whom it just became the Fashion to style the ambitious *Theocrat*?'—I fear, *not*—was my answer—I gave way to my own Feelings.—The first speech of Adelaide[2]—*Whose Automaton* is this Character! Who spoke thro'

[1] *The Fall of Robespierre*, Act III, lines 189–91, *Poems*, ii. 516.
[2] Ibid., Act I, lines 197 f.

Le Gendre's mouth, when he says—[']O what a precious name is Liberty—To scare or cheat the simple into Slaves![']¹ But in several parts I have, it seems, in the strongest language boasted the impossibility of subduing France—. Is not this Sentiment highly characteristic? Is it *forced* into the Mouths of the Speakers? Could I have even omitted it without evident Absurdity—. But granted, that it is my own opinion—Is it an *anti-pacific* one—*I* should have classed it among the *Anti-polemics.*—Again—Are *all* who entertain and express this opinion Dŕmocrats? God forbid! They would be a formidable party indeed! I know many violent Anti-reformists, who are as violent against the *War* on the ground that it may introduce that reform, which they (perhaps not unwisely) imagine, would chaunt the Dirge of our Constitution.——

Solemnly, my Brother! I tell you—I am *not* a Dŕmocrat. I see evidently, that the present is *not* the *highest* state of Society, of which we are *capable*—And after a diligent, I *may* say, an intense study of Locke, Hartley and others who have written most wisely on the Nature of Man—I appear to myself to see the point of *possible* perfection at which the World may perhaps be destined to arrive—But how to lead Mankind from one point to the other is a process of such infinite Complexity, that in deep-felt humility I resign it to that Being—'Who shaketh the Earth out of her place and the pillars thereof tremble'—[']Who purifieth with Whirlwinds and maketh the Pestilence his Besom'—Who hath said—that [']Violence shall no more be heard of'—'the people shall not build and another inhabit—they shall not plant and another eat[']— [']The Wolf and the Lamb shall feed together!'—

I have been asked what is the best conceivable mode of meliorating Society—My Answer has been uniformly this—'Slavery is an Abomination to every feeling of the Head and the Heart—Did Jesus teach the *Abolition* of it? No! He taught those principles, of which the necessary *effect* was—to abolish all Slavery. He prepared the *mind* for the reception before he poured the Blessing—.['] You ask me, what the friend of universal Equality *should* do—I answer—[']Talk not of Politics—*Preach the Gospel!*'—Yea! my Brother! I have at all times in all places exerted my powers in the defence of the Holy One of Nazareth against the Learning of the Historian, the *Libertinism* of the Wit, and (his worst Enemy!) the Mystery of the Bigot!—But I am an Infidel, because I cannot thrust my head into a *mud guttar* and say—'How *deep* I am!—for [I am *drunk*'!]²—And I am a Dŕmocrat, because I will not join in the maledictions of the Despotist—because I will *bless all* men and

¹ *The Fall of Robespierre*, Act i, lines 40–41.
² Passage in brackets inked out in manuscript.

curse no one!—I have been a fool even to madness—and I am therefore an excellent hit for Calumny to aim her poisoned *probabilities* at! As the poor Flutterer, who by hard struggling has escaped from the birdlimed thorn-bush, still bears the clammy Incumbrance on his feet and wings, so am I doomed to carry about with me the sad mementos of past Imprudence and Anguish from which I have been imperfectly released.—

Mr Potter, of Emanuel, drives me up to Town in his Phaeton on Saturday Morning—of course I shall see you on Sunday——

Poor Smerdon! the reports concerning His literary plagiarism (as far as concerns *my* assistance) are *falsehoods*. I have felt much for him—and on the morning I received your Letter, poured forth these incondite Rhymes—of course, they are meant for a *Brother's* Eye![1]—

> Smerdon! thy Grave with aching Eye I scan,
> And inly groan for Heaven's poor Outcast, Man!
> 'Tis Tempest all—or Gloom!—in earliest Youth
> If gifted with th' Ithuriel Lance of Truth
> He force to start amid her feign'd Caress
> Vice, Siren Hag! in native Ugliness,
> A Brother's Fate shall haply rouse the Tear—
> And on he goes in heaviness and fear!
> But if his fond Heart call to Pleasure's Bower
> Some pigmy Folly in a careless Hour,
> The faithless Guest quick stamps th' inchanted ground
> And mingled Forms of Misery threaten round;
> Heart-fretting Fear with pallid Look aghast
> That courts the future Woe to hide the past;
> Remorse, the poison'd Arrow in his side;
> And loud lewd Mirth to Anguish close allied:
> Till Frenzy, frantic Child of moping Pain,
> Darts her hot lightning Flash athwart the Brain!
>
> Rest, injur'd Shade! shall Slander couching near
> Spit her cold Venom in a dead man's Ear?
> 'Twas thine to feel the sympathetic glow
> In Merit's Joy, and Poverty's meek Woe,
> Thine all that cheer the moment as it flies,
> The zoneless Cares and smiling Courtesies!
> Nurs'd in thy Heart the generous Virtues grew—
> And in thy Heart they wither'd!—such chill dew
> Wan Indolence on each young blossom shed,

[1] *Poems*, i. 76.

And Vanity her filmy network spread
With Eye, that prowl'd around in asking gaze
And Tongue, that traffick'd in the Trade of Praise!
Thy follies such! the hard World mark'd them well—
Were they *more* wise, the Proud who never fell?
Rest, injur'd Shade! the poor Man's grateful Prayer
On heaven-ward wing thy wound[ed] Soul shall bear!
As oft in Fancy's thought thy Grave I pass,
And sit me down upon it's recent Grass—
With introverted Eye I contemplate
Similitude of Soul—perhaps of Fate!
To me hath Heaven with liberal hand assign'd
Energic Reason & a shaping Mind,
The daring ken of Truth, the patriot's part,
And Pity's Sigh, that breathes the gentle heart
Sloth-jaundic'd all! and from my graspless hand
Drop Friendship's precious Pearls, like hour glass sand.
I weep—yet stoop not! the faint Anguish flows,
A dreamy Pang in Morning's fev'rish Doze!
Is that pil'd Earth our Being's passless Moun[d?]
Tell me, cold Grave! is Death with Poppies crown'd[?]
Tir'd Centinel, with fitful starts I [nod,]
And fain would sleep, [though pillowed on a clod!]

God love you, d[ear] | Brother | & your affectionately |
grateful
S. T. Coleridge

70. *To Unknown Correspondent*

MS. New York Public Lib. Hitherto unpublished.

Thursday Morning. [6 November 1794][1]

Dear Sir

I have this moment received your Letter—A Gentleman who
is going to London will put this in the penny post—I will take an
opportunity to write fully on the indifferent matters—I hasten to
the coincidences and supposed Imitations—I regard it a[s] a
fortunate circumstance for my feelings that these parralelisms occur
in the two poems of 'Absence' and 'Genevieve.' The f[irs]t I wrote

[1] Since *Genevieve* was published in the *Cambridge Intelligencer* on 1 Nov.
1794; and since in this letter Coleridge says that *Absence* was written '*three
years ago*' (i.e. 1791), and that he gave a copy of the poem to Lovell '*three
months* ago' (i.e. Aug. 1794), this letter was probably written on 6 Nov. 1794,
before his departure for London.

about this time *three* years a[go], exactly as it now is with the exception of ['I] haste to woo' instead of 'Once more I woo'[1]— Mr Love[ll] has a copy of it which I gave him three *m[on]ths* ago.— Genevieve I wrote two years before [I] quitted School—It has been set to Music mor[e] than once—and was published without m[y] knowlege in the *Morning* Chronicle (of London) in the summer months *two Years* ago.[2]—Some[b]ody told me at that time that the [Ma]gazines had transferred it into their poetical [de]partment—I saw it only in the Chroni[cle].

I will write you soon by means of a Friend fully upon a variety of Subjects—and believe I feel obliged to you for communicating your suspicions so openly—whether or no the passages could fairly have given rise to them, I cannot say—as [I] have lent your Poems to a friend—Concerning those Poems depend upon it I will not be inactive an hour.

[S.] T. Coleridge

I have an obscure Recollec[tion] that the poem of 'Absence' was publis[hed] without my knowlege about the same time with 'Genevieve'—but of this I am not certain as the said Poem was never a favourite eit[her] with myself or my friends—.

71. *To Mary Evans*

Address: Miss Evans | No 17 | Sackville Street | Piccadilly
MS. Mr. Carl H. Pforzheimer. Pub. Letters, *i. 122.* From late September, when he received Mary Evans's letter dissuasive of the pantisocratic scheme, Coleridge was living under 'a waking Night-mair of Spirits', and his sonnet ('Thou bleedest, my poor Heart') was occasioned by that letter. In writing the following appeal, he did not anticipate a favourable response, but he wrote with no other expectation than that of 'arming my fortitude by total hopelessness'.

[London.]   [Early November 1794][3]

Too long has my Heart been the torture house of Suspense. After infinite struggles of Irresolution I will at last dare to request of

---

[1] In 1796 and thereafter line 3 of *Absence* reads: 'I haste to urge the learned toil.'

[2] By '*two Years* ago' Coleridge probably meant two summers ago, since *Genevieve* was published in the *Morning Chronicle* on 15 July 1793, over the signature 'C.—Ætatis 14'. Heretofore bibliographers have identified *To Fortune*, published on 7 Nov. 1793, in the *Morning Chronicle*, as Coleridge's first appearance in print.

[3] Letters 68 and 69 show that Coleridge probably arrived in London on 8 Nov.; Letter 72 suggests that he was back in Cambridge before 1 Dec. The present letter was written between these dates; and since in the third paragraph it so clearly echoes the sonnet ('Thou bleedest, my poor Heart') which Coleridge quoted on 21 Oct. (Letter 65) and again on the 24th (Letter 67), it probably belongs to early November.

you, Mary! that you will communicate to me whether or no you
are engaged to Mr ———.[1] I conjure you not to consider this request
as presumptuous Indelicacy. Upon mine Honor, I have made it
with no other Design or Expectation than that of arming my
fortitude by total hopelessness. Read this Letter with benevolence
—and consign it to Oblivion.

For four years I have *endeavored* to smother a very ardent
attachment—in what degree I have succeeded, you must know
better than I can. With quick perceptions of moral Beauty it was
impossible for me not to admire in you your sensibility regulated
by Judgment, your Gaiety proceeding from a cheerful Heart
acting on the stores of a strong Understanding. At first I volun-
tarily invited the recollection of these qualities into my mind—I
made them the perpetual Object of my Reveries—yet I enter-
tained no one Sentiment beyond that of the immediate Pleasure
annexed to the thinking of You. At length it became an Habit.
I awoke from the Delusion, and found that I had unwittingly
harboured a Passion which I felt neither the power or the courage
to subdue. My associations were irrevocably formed, and your
Image was blended with every idea. I thought of you incessantly:
yet that Spirit (if Spirit there be that condescends to record the
lonely Beatings of my heart) that Spirit knows, that I thought of
you with the purity of a Brother. Happy were I, had it been with
no more than a Brother's ardor!

The Man of dependent fortunes while he fosters an attachment
commits an act of Suicide on his happiness. I possessed no Estab-
blishment—my views were very distant—I saw, that you regarded
me merely with the kindness of a Sister——What expectations
could I form? I formed no expectations—I was ever resolving to
subdue the disquieting Passion: still some inexplicable Suggestion
palsied my Efforts, and I clung with desperate fondness to this
Phantom of Love, it's mysterious Attractions and hopeless
Prospects. It was a faint and rayless Hope! Yet It soothed my
Solitude with many a delightful day-dream. It was a faint and
rayless Hope! Yet I nursed it in my Bosom with an Agony of
Affection, even as a Mother her sickly Infant.——

But these are the poisoned Luxuries of a diseased Fancy! In-
dulge, Mary! this my first, my last request—and restore me to
Reality, however gloomy. Sad and full of heaviness will the
Intelligence be—my heart will die within me—I shall receive it
however with steadier resignation from yourself, than were it
announced to me (haply on your marriage Day!) by a Stranger!

[1] Fryer Todd, a man of 'good fortune', whom Mary Evans married on
13 Oct. 1795.

Indulge my request—I will not disturb your Peace by even a *Look* of Discontent—still less will I offend your Ear by the Whine of selfish Sensibility. In a few months I shall enter at the Temple[1]— and there seek forgetful Calmness—where only it can be found—in incessant and useful Activity.

Were you not possessed of a Mind and of a Heart above the usual Lot of Women I should not have written you sentiments, that would be unintelligible to three fourths of your Sex. But our Feelings are congenial, though your [our?] attachment is doomed not to be reciprocal. You will not deem so meanly of me as to believe hat I shall regard Mr——with the jaundiced Eye of disappointed Passion. God forbid! He, whom you honor with your Affections, becomes sacred to me. I shall love him for *your* Sake—the time may perhaps come, when I shall be Philosopher enough—not to envy him for *his own*!

S. T. Coleridge.

I return to Cambridge tomorrow Morning.

72. *To the Editor of the 'Morning Chronicle'*

Pub. Morning Chronicle, *1 December 1794.*

Jesus College, Cambridge. [Late November 1794]

Mr. Editor,

If, Sir, the following Poems will not disgrace your poetical department, I will transmit you a series of *Sonnets* (as it is the fashion to call them), addressed, like these, to eminent Contemporaries.[2]

S. T. C.

---

[1] This is the sole reference to the study of law in Coleridge's letters. George Coleridge, who certainly saw his brother at this time, probably made some such proposal.

[2] To Coleridge's sonnet, *To the Honourable Mr. Erskine,* which was published along with this letter in the *Morning Chronicle,* the editor added the following comment: 'Our elegant Correspondent will highly gratify every reader of taste by the continuance of his exquisitely beautiful productions. No. II. [*To Burke*] shall appear on an early day.' In all, eleven *Sonnets on Eminent Characters* were printed in the *Morning Chronicle* between 1 Dec. 1794 and 29 Jan. 1795. Seven of these sonnets are included in Letters 74 and 75.

73. *To Robert Southey*

Address: Robert Southey | No 8 | West gate Buildings | Bath
MS. Lord Latymer. Hitherto unpublished.
Postmark: 9 December 1794.

[London.]   Tuesday Evening—[9 December 1794]
My dear Southey

My very Virtues are of the slothful order—God forbid, my Vices should be otherwise—. I never feel anger—still less retain resentment—but I should be a monster, if there had risen in my heart even a *propensity* to either towards you, whose conduct has been regulated by *affection*——. I wish my heart was more worthy of your *esteem*.

I received your poetry, which will be of no pecuniary service to me; but, I hope, to receive a remittance from Cambridge within a day or two—and then I will set off for Bristol—though I find, they are making a row about me at Jesus—.[1]

As to the Welsh scheme—pardon me—it is nonsense—We must go to America, if we can get Money enough.

With regard to neglect respecting ——,[2] do you accuse me justly? I have written 5 or 4 letters since my absence—received one. I am not conscious of having injured her otherwise, than by having mistaken the ebullience of *schematism* for affection, which a moment's reflection might have told me, is not a plant of so mushroom a growth—had it ever not been counteracted by a prior attachment / but my whole Life has been a series of Blunders! God have mercy upon me—for I am a most miserable Dog—

The most criminal action of my Life was the 'first letter I wrote to ——.['] I had worked myself to such a pitch, that I scarcely knew I was writing like an hypocrite—

However it still remains for me to be externally Just though my Heart is withered within me—and Life seems now to give me disgust rather than pain—

My Love to your Mother and to Edith—and to whomever it is right or convenient.

God almighty bless you | and (a forlorn wish!)
S. T. Coleridge.

---

[1] Although Coleridge did not go back to Jesus College again, the college authorities waited until 6 Apr. 1795 before ordering his name to be removed from the boards on 14 June 1795, unless he returned before that date. Likewise, on 22 Apr. 1795, the Christ's Hospital Committee 'unanimously agreed . . . that his [Coleridge's] Exhibitions which have been paid to the 5th inst. be from that time withheld until the Committee may see cause to make a further Report to the Court upon this subject'. Lawrence Hanson, *The Life of S. T. Coleridge*, 1938, p. 439.   [2] Sara Fricker.

74. *To Robert Southey*

Address: Robert Southey | No 8 | Westgate Buildings | Bath   *Single*
MS. Lord Latymer. Pub. Letters, *i. 106.*
Postmark: 11 December 1794.

My dear Southey

I sit down to write you, not that I have any thing particular
to say—but it is a relief, and forms a very respectable part in my
Theory of Escapes from the Folly of Melancholy. I am so habituated
to philosophizing, that I cannot divest myself of it even when my
own Wretchedness is the subject. I appear to myself like a sick
Physician, feeling the pang acutely, yet deriving a wonted pleasure
from examining it's progress and developing it's causes.

Your Poems[1] & Bowles are my only morning Companions—.
The Retrospect—! quod qui non prorsus amat et deperit, illum
omnes et Virtutes et Veneres odere! It is a most lovely Poem—and
in the next edition of your Works shall be a perfect one. The Ode
to Romance is the best of the Odes. I dislike that to Lycon except-
ing the last stanza, which is superlatively fine— The phrase of, let
honest Truth be *vain*—is obscure.—Of your blank Verse Odes the
Death of Mattathias is by far the best—that you should ever write
another

Pulcher Apollo, veta! Musae, prohibete, venustae!

They are to Poetry what dumb bells are to Music—they can be
read only for *exercise*—or to make a man tired that he may be
sleepy.—The Sonnets are wonderfully inferior to those which I
possess of your's—of which that to Valentine (if long and
lingering seem one little Day The motley Crew of Travellers
among—) that on the Fire (not your last which is a very so so
one)—on the Rainbow / particularly the four last Lines—& two or
three others are all divine and fully equal to *Bowles*—. Some parts
of Miss Rosamund are beautiful—the *working* scene—and that line
with which the Poem ought to have concluded—And think who
lies so cold & pale below. Of the pauper's funeral that part in which
you have done me the honor to imitate me is by far the worst—the
thought has been so much better expressed by Gray—On the whole
(like many of yours) it wants compactness and totality—the same
thought is repeated too frequently in different words—That all

---

[1] While writing this letter Coleridge obviously had before him the Lovell–
Southey *Poems*, dated 1795 on the title-page but actually published in the
autumn of 1794. Cf. Southey's *Poet. Works*, ii, Preface, xi. Coleridge's com-
ments, however, extend to four poems, *To Valentine, The Rainbow, The
Pauper's Funeral*, and *The Chapel Bell*, which first appeared in Southey's
Poems of 1797.

these faults may be remedied by compression, my Editio purgata
of the Poem shall shew you.[1]

> What? and not *one* to heave the pious Sigh?
> Not one whose sorrow-swoln and aching Eye
> For social Scenes, for Life's endearments fled
> Shall drop a tear, and dwell upon the Dead?
> Poor wretched Outcast! I will sigh for thee
> And sorrow for forlorn Humanity!
> Yes, I will sigh! but not that thou art come
> To the stern Sabbath of the silent Tomb:
> For squalid Want and the black Scorpion, Care
> (Heart-withering Fiends!) shall never enter there!
> I sorrow for the ills, thy Life has known
> As thro' the World's long Pilgrimage alone
> Haunted by Poverty and woe begone
> Unlov'd, unfriended thou didst journey on—
> Thy Youth in Ignorance and Labor past,
> And thy Old Age all Barrenness and Blast!
> Hard was thy Fate, which, while it doom'd to Woe,
> Denied thee Wisdom to support the Blow;
> And robb'd of all it's Energy thy Mind
> Ere yet it cast thee on thy Fellow kind,
> Abject of Thought, the Victim of Distress,
> To wander in the World's wide wilderness.
>
> Poor Outcast! sleep in peace. The Winter's storm
> Blows bleak no more on thy unshelter'd Form!
> Thy Woes are past—thou restest in the Tomb!
> I pause—& ponder on the Days to come.

Now—is it not a beautiful Poem?—
Of the Sonnet 'No more the visionary Soul shall dwell'[2]—I
wrote the whole but the second & third Line—Of the 'Old Man in
the snow'[3] / I wrote the ten last Lines *entirely*—and part of the
four first.—Those ten Lines are perhaps the best I ever did write.

Lovell has no *taste*—or *simplicity* of feeling—. I remarked that
when a man read Lovell's poems he 'Mus Cus['] (i.e. a rapid way
of pronouncing Must curse.) but when he thought of Southey's—

---

[1] In publishing *The Pauper's Funeral* in 1797, Southey followed, with a few
exceptions, Coleridge's 'Editio purgata'. Cf. Southey, *Poems*, 1797, p. 47.

[2] *Poems*, i. 68.

[3] See *Pity*, ibid. 93. In the Preface to his *Poems* of 1796 Coleridge said he
was indebted to Samuel Favell for a rough sketch of this sonnet. For a later
estimate of these lines see Letter 153.

He'd Buy on![1] For God's sake let us have no more Bions or Grac-
chuses—I abominate them—Southey is a name much more proper
& handsome—and I venture to prophesy, *will* be more *famous.*

Your Chapel Bell I *love*—and have made it by a *few* alterations
and the *omission* of one Stanza (which, though beautiful quoad se,
interrupted the *run* of the thought / I love to see the aged Spirit
soar /) a perfect poem. As it followed the exiled Patriots—I altered
the second [and fourth] Line[s] to (So Freedom taught) in high-voic'd
Minstrel's weed—For cap & gown to leave the Patriot's meed—[2]
The last Verse *now* runs thus—

But thou, Memorial of monastic Gall!
What Fancy sad or lightsome hast *thou* given?
Thy vision-scaring sounds alone recall
The Prayer, that *trembles* on a *Yawn* to Heaven.—
And *this* Dean's Gape, and *that* Dean's nasal Tone,[3] And &c——

Would not this be a fine subject for a *wild* Ode—

St Withold footed thrice the Oulds—
He met the Night Mare & her nine Foals—
He bade her alight and her troth plight—
And 'aroynt thee, Witch[']—he said![4]—

I shall set about one, when I am in a Humour to *abandon* myself to
all the Diableries, that ever met the Eye of a Fuseli![5]

Le Grice has jumbled together all the quaint stupidity, he ever
wrote—amounting to about *30* pages—and published it in a book
about the size & dimensions of Children's twopenny Books—. The
Dedication is *pretty*—He calls the Publication 'Tineum.['] For what
reason or with what meaning would give Madam Sphinx a compleat
Victory over Œdipus.

A Wag has handed about, I hear, an obtuse acute angle of Wit—
under the name of 'an Epigram[']—'Tis almost as bad as the
subject.—

[1] In the 1795 volume Southey's poems were signed 'Bion', Lovell's
'Moschus'.

[2] In 1797 the first four lines of *The Chapel Bell* read:
Lo I, the man who erst the Muse did ask
    Her deepest notes to swell the Patriot's meeds,
Am now enforced, a far unfitter task,
    For cap and gown to leave my minstrel weeds;

[3] In 1797 Southey printed the last verse of *The Chapel Bell* as here, but in
1838 he altered the line 'And *this* Dean's Gape, and *that* Dean's nasal Tone',
to 'The snuffling, snaffling Fellow's nasal tone'. *Poet. Works*, ii. 143.

[4] Adapted from *King Lear*, III. iv. 125–9.

[5] Henry Fuseli, 1741–1825, the artist.

A Tiny Man of tiny Wit
A Tiny book has publish'd—
But not—alas! one tiny Bit
His tiny Fame establish'd.—

To Bowles.[1]

My heart has thank'd thee, Bowles! for those soft Strains
That on the still air floating tremblingly
Woke in me Fancy, Love & Sympathy.
For hence not callous to a Brother's pains
Thro' Youth's gay prime and thornless Paths I went
And when the *darker* Day of Life began
And I did roam, a thought-bewilder'd Man!
Thy kindred Lays an healing Solace lent,
Each lonely Pang with dreamy Joys combin'd
And stole from vain Regret her Scorpion stings;
While shadowy Pleasure with mysterious wings
Brooded the wavy and tumultuous Mind,
Like that great Spirit, who with plastic Sweep
Mov'd on the darkness of the formless Deep!

Of the following Sonnet the four *last* Lines were written by Lamb—a man of uncommon Genius—Have you seen his divine Sonnet of—O! I could *laugh* to hear the winter winds[2] &c?

Sonnet.[3]

O gentle Look, that didst my Soul beguile,
Why hast thou left me? Still in some fond Dream
Revisit my sad Heart, auspicious Smile!
As falls on closing Flowers the lunar Beam—.

What time in sickly Mood at parting Day
I lay me down and think of happier Years—
Of Joys, that glimmer'd in Hope's twilight Ray,
Then left me darkling in a vale of Tears.

O pleasant Days of Hope, for ever flown!
Could I recall you—!—But that thought is vain.
Availeth not Persuasion's sweetest Tone
To lure the fleet-wing'd Travellers back again—
On on they haste to everlasting Night,
Nor can a Giant's arm arrest them in their Flight!

[1] *Poems*, i. 84; first pub. by Coleridge in the *Morn. Chron.* 26 Dec. 1794.
[2] First published in Coleridge's *Poems*, 1796, p. 57.
[3] *Poems*, i. 47.

The four last lines are beautiful—but they have no particular meaning, which 'that Thought is *vain!*' does not convey[1]—And I cannot write without a *body* of *thought*—hence my *Poetry* is crowded and sweats beneath a heavy burthen of Ideas and Imagery! It has seldom Ease—The little Song ending with 'I heav'd the ——sigh for thee'![2] is an exception—and accordingly I like it the best of all, I ever wrote.

My Sonnets to eminent Contemporaries are among the better Things, I have written.—That to Erskine is a bad Specimen—I have written 10—and mean to write 6 more.—In 'Fayette' I *unwittingly* (for I did not know it at the Time) borrowed a *thought* from You.

I will conclude with a little Song of mine, which has no other Merit than a pretty simplicity of silliness.[3]—

> If, while my Passion I impart,
>   You deem my words untrue,
> O place your Hand upon my Heart—
>   Feel, how it throbs for *You.*
>
> Ah no!—reject the thoughtless Claim
>   In pity to your Lover!
> That thrilling Touch would aid the flame
>   It wishes to discover!

I am a compleat Necessitarian—and understand the subject as well almost as Hartley himself—but I go farther than Hartley and believe the corporeality of *thought*—namely, that it is motion—. Boyer thrashed Favell most cruelly the day before yesterday—I sent him the following Note of consolation.

'I condole with you on the unpleasant motions, to which a certain Uncouth Automaton has been mechanized; and am anxious to know the motives, that impinged on it's optic or auditory nerves, so as to be communicated in such rude vibrations through the medullary substance of It's Brain, thence rolling their stormy Surges into the capillaments of it's Tongue, and the muscles of it's arm. The diseased Violence of It's thinking corporealities will, depend upon it, cure itself by exhaustion—In the mean time, I trust, that you have not been assimilated in degradation by losing

---

[1] In publishing this sonnet in 1796 Coleridge retained lines 11 and 12 as written by Lamb, but altered lines 13 and 14 to read:
> Yet fair, though faint, their images shall gleam
> Like the bright Rainbow on a willowy stream.

[2] Cf. Letter 68, p. 124.

[3] *Poems*, i. 58.

the ataraxy of your Temper, and that the Necessity which dignified you by a Sentience of the Pain, has not lowered you by the accession of Anger or Resentment.'——

—God love you, Southey! / My Love to your Mother!

S. T. Coleridge

75. *To Robert Southey*

Address: Robert Southey | No 8 | Westgate Buildings | Bath
MS. Lord Latymer. Pub. with omis. Letters, *i. 114.*
Postmark, 18 December 1794.

Wednesday—Dec. 17th 94

When I am unhappy, a sigh or a groan does not feel sufficient to relieve the oppression of my Heart—I give a long *whistle*—/ This by way of a detached Truth.——

How infinitely more to be valued is Integrity of Heart than Effulgence of Intellect—A noble sentiment and would have *come home* to me, if for 'Integrity' you had substituted 'Energy'.— The Skirmishers of Sensibility are indeed contemptible when compared with the well-disciplined Phalanx of right onward Feelings. O ye invincible Soldiers of Virtue, who arrange yourselves under the Generalship of Fixed Principles—that you would throw up your Fortifications around my Heart!——I pronounce this a very sensible, apostrophical, metaphorical Rant.

I dined yesterday with Perry, and Grey (the proprietors & Editors of the Morning Chronicle) at their House—and met Holcroft[1]—He either misunderstood Lovell, or Lovell misunderstood him, I know not which—but it is very clear to me, that neither of them understand or enter into the *views* of our System. Holcroft *opposes* it violently—& thinks it not *virtuous*. His arguments were such as Nugent and twenty others have used to us before him—they were *nothing*.

There is a fierceness and *dogmatism* of conversation in Holcroft, for which you receive little compensation either from the variety of his information, the closeness of his Reasoning, or the splendor of his Language. He talks incessantly of Metaphysics, of which he appears to me to *know nothing*—to have *read nothing*—/ He is ignorant as a Scholar—and neglectful of the smaller Humanities, as a Man—/ Compare him with Porson! My God! to hear Porson *crush* Godwin, Holcroft &c—They absolutely tremble before him! I had the honor of *working* H. a little—and by my great *coolness*

---

[1] Thomas Holcroft (1745–1809), whose *Road to Ruin* was first presented in early 1792. He was indicted for high treason and imprisoned in Oct. 1794, but was released without a trial the following December.

and command of impressive Language certainly *did him over*—/
Sir! (said he) I never knew so much real wisdom—& so much rank
Error meet in one mind before! Which (answered I) means, I
suppose—that in some things, Sir! I agree with you and in others
I do not.—

He absolutely infests you with *Atheism*—and his arguments are
such, that the nonentities of Nugent consolidate into Oak or Iron
wood by the comparison!—As to his taste in Poetry—he thinks
lightly or rather contemptuously of Bowles' Sonnets—'the
language flat & prosaic and inharmonious—& the sentiments fit
only for Girls!['] Come—come—Mr Holcroft—as much unintelli-
gible Metaphysics and as much bad Criticism as you please—but
no *Blasphemy* against the divinity of *a Bowles*!—/ *Porson* idolizes
the Sonnets. However it happened, I am higher in *his* good Graces
than he in mine—If I am in town I dine with him and Godwin[1]
&c at his house on Sunday.

I am astonished at your preference of the 'Elegy'! I think it the
worst thing, you ever wrote—

Qui *Gratio* non odit, amat tua carmina, *Avaro*![2]

Why—'tis almost as bad as Lovell's Farm house—and that would
be at least a thousand Fathoms deep in the Dead Sea of Pessimism.

> The hard World scoff'd my Woes—the chaste one's Pride
> Mimic of Virtue mock'd my keen distress
> *Her little Boon with cruel taunts denied,[3]
> And Vice alone would shelter wretchedness.
> Even Life is loathsome now &c—

> * *Implied in the second Line* [S. T. C.].

These two Stanzas are exquisite—but the lovely thought of 'the
hot Sun &c as pityless as proud Prosperity[']—loses part of it's
Beauty by the Time being Night. It is among the chief excellencies
of Bowles, that his Imagery appears almost always prompted by
the surrounding Scenery.

Before you write a Poem, you should say to yourself—What do
I intend to be the *Character* of this Poem—Which *Feature* is to be
predominant in it?—So you may make it a Unique. But in this
Poem now *Charlotte* speaks & now the Poet—Assuredly the Stanzas

---

[1] Godwin says, 'It was in the close of this year [1794] that I first met with
Samuel Taylor Coleridge'. *William Godwin*, i. 119.

[2] A parody of 'Qui Bavium non odit, amet tua carmina, Maevi'. Virgil,
Ecl. iii. 90. Gratio was the name of the occupant of Lovell's *The Decayed Farm-
House*; Avaro, the name of the tenant in Southey's *The Miser's Mansion*.

[3] This line struck out in the MS.

of Memory, thou worst of Fiends! &c 'and Gay Fancy fond &
frolic' &c are altogether *poetical*—/ You have repeated the same
Rhymes ungracefully & the thought on which you harp so long
recalls too forcibly the Εὕδεις, βρέφος—of Simonides—Unfortun-
ately the 'Adventurer' has made this sweet Fragment an object
of popular admiration—On the whole I think it unworthy of your
other Botany Bay Eclogues—yet deem the two Stanzas above
selected superior—almost to any thing you ever wrote—Quod est
magna res dicere—a great thing to say /—

Sonnet[1]

Tho' king-bred Rage with lawless Tumult rude
Have driv'n our PRIESTLEY o'er the Ocean swell;
Tho' Superstition & her wolfish Brood
Bay his mild Radiance, impotent & fell;
Calm in his Halls of Brightness he shall dwell!
For lo! RELIGION at his strong behest
Disdainful rouses from the papal spell
And flings to Earth her tinsel-glitt'ring Vest,
Her mitred State & cumbrous Pomp unholy;
And JUSTICE wakes to bid th' Oppressor wail,
That ground th' ensnared Soul of patient Folly;
And from her dark retreat by Wisdom won
Meek NATURE slowly lifts her matron Veil,
To smile with fondness on her gazing Son!

Sonnet[2]

O what a loud and fearful Shriek was there,
As tho' a thousand Souls one Death groan pour'd!
Great KOSCIUSKO 'neath an hireling's sword
The Warriors view'd!—Hark! thro' the list'ning Air
When pauses the tir'd Cossack's barbarous Yell
Of Triumph, on the chill & midnight Gale
Rises with frantic burst or sadder swell
The 'Dirge of murder'd Hope'!—while Freedom pale
Bends in *such* Anguish o'er her destin'd Bier,
As if from eldest Time some Spirit meek
Had gather'd in a mystic Urn each Tear
That ever furrow'd a sad Patriot's cheek,
And She had drench'd the Sorrows of the Bowl
Ev'n till she reel'd, intoxicate of Soul!—

Tell me which you like the best of the above two—

[1] *Poems*, i. 81; first pub. *Morn. Chron.* 11 Dec. 1794.
[2] *Poems*, i. 82; first pub. *Morn. Chron.* 16 Dec. 1794.

I have written one to Godwin—but the mediocrity of the eight first Lines is *most miserably magazinish*! I have plucked therefore these scentless Road flowers from the Chaplet—and intreat thee, thou River God of Pieria, to weave into it the gorgeous Water Lily from thy stream, or the far smelling Violets on thy Bank——the six last lines are these[1]

> Nor will I not thy holy guidance bless
> And hymn thee, GODWIN! with an ardent lay,
> For that thy Voice, in Passion's stormy Day,
> When wild I roam'd the bleak Heath of Distress,
> Bade the bright Form of JUSTICE meet my Way,
> And told me, that her name was HAPPINESS![2]

Give me your minutest opinion concerning the following Sonnet —whether or no I shall admit it into the number—The mode of bepraising a man by enumerating the beauties of his *Polygraph* is at least an original one—so much so that I fear it will be somewhat unintelligible to those, whose Brains are not τοῦ ἀμείνονος πηλοῦ.— (You have read S's poetry—and know that the Fancy displayed in them [it] is sweet and *delicate* to the highest degree.)

To R. B. Sheridan Esq.—[3]

> Some winged Genius, Sheridan! imbreath'd
> His *various* Influence on thy natal hour:
> My Fancy bodies forth the Guardian Power,
> His temples with Hymettian Flowrets wreath'd;
> And sweet his Voice, as when o'er Laura's bier
> Sad Music trembled thro' Vauclusa's Glade,
> Sweet as at Dawn the love-lorn Serenade
> That bears soft Dreams to Slumber's list'ning Ear!
> Now patriot Zeal and Indignation high
> Swell the full Tones! And now his Eye beams dance
> Meanings of Scorn and Wit's quaint Revelry!

[1] *Poems*, i. 86; first pub. *Morn. Chron.* 10 Jan. 1795.

[2] Southey penned the following lines on the manuscript of Coleridge's letter. If they were sent to Coleridge, he made no use of them.

> What tho' Oppression's blood-cemented fane
>   Stands proudly threat'ning arrogant in state,
>   Not thine his savage priests to immolate
> Or hurl the fabric on the encumber'd plain
> As with a whirlwind's fury. It is thine
>   When dark Revenge mask'd in the form ador'd
>   Of Justice, lifts on high the murderous sword
> To save the erring victim from her shrine.
> To Godwin.

[3] *Poems*, i. 87; first pub. *Morn. Chron.* 29 Jan. 1795.

Th' Apostate by the brainless Rout ador'd
Writhes inly from the bosom-probing Glance,
As erst that nobler Fiend beneath great Michael's Sword!

I will give the second Number as deeming that it possesses
Mind[1]——

As late as I roam'd thro' Fancy's shadowy Vale,
With wetted Cheek and in a Mourner's Guise,
I saw the sainted Form of Freedom rise:
She spake!—not sadder moans th' Autumnal Gale.
'Great Son of Genius! sweet to me thy Name,
'Ere in an evil Hour with alter'd Voice
'Thou bad'st oppression's hireling Crew rejoice
'Blasting with wizard Spell my laurell'd fame.
'Yet never, BURKE! thou drank'st Corruption's Bowl!
'Thee stormy Pity and the cherish'd Lure
'Of Pomp, and proud Precipitance of Soul,
'Urg'd on with wild'ring Fires.—Ah—Spirit pure!
'That Error's mist had left thy purged Eye—
'So might I clasp thee with a Mother's Joy.[']

Address to a young Jack Ass & it's *tethered* Mother[2]

Poor little Foal of an oppressed Race,
I love the languid Patience of thy Face!
And oft with friendly hand I give thee Bread,
And clap thy ragged Coat & pat thy Head.
But what thy dulled Spirit hath dismay'd,
That never thou dost sport upon the Glade,
And (most unlike the Nature of Things Young)
That still to Earth thy moping Head is hung?
Do thy prophetic Fears anticipate,
Meek child of Misery! thy future Fate,
The starving Meal & all the thousand Aches,
That 'patient Merit of the unworthy takes'?
Or is thy sad heart thrill'd with filial pain
To see thy wretched Mother's lengthen'd Chain?
And truly very piteous is *her* Lot
Chain'd to a Log upon a narrow Spot
Where the close-eaten Grass is scarcely seen,
While sweet around her waves the tempting Green.
Poor Ass! thy Master should have learnt to shew
Pity—best taught by Fellowship of Woe:

---

[1] *Poems*, i. 80; first pub. *Morn. Chron.* 9 Dec. 1794.
[2] *Poems*, i. 74.

For much I fear, that *he* lives, like thee
Half-famish'd in a Land of Luxury!
How *askingly* it's steps toward me bend—
It seems to say—'And have I then *one* Friend?[']—
Innocent Foal! thou poor despis'd Forlorn!—
I hail thee Brother, spite of the Fool's Scorn!
And fain I'd take thee with me in the Dell
Of high-soul'd Pantisocracy to dwell;
Where Toil shall call the charmer Health his Bride,
And Laughter tickle Plenty's *ribless* side!
How thou would'st toss thy Heels in gamesome Play
And frisk about, as Lamb or Kitten, gay—
Yea—and more musically sweet to me
Thy dissonant harsh Bray of Joy would be
Than *Banti's* warbled airs, that sooth to rest
The Tumult of a scoundrel Monarch's Breast!—

How do you like it?—
I took the Liberty—Gracious God! pardon me for the aristo-
cratic frigidity of that expression——I indulged my Feelings by
sending this among my *Contemporary* Sonnets.[1]

Southey! thy Melodies steal o'er mine Ear
Like far off Joyance or the Murmuring
Of wild Bees in the sunny Showers of Spring—
Sounds of such mingled Import as may cheer
The lonely Breast, yet rouse a mindful Tear.
Wak'd by the Song doth hope-born Fancy fling
Rich Showers of dewy Fragrance from her wing,
Till sickly Passion's drooping Myrtles sear
Blossom anew! But O! more thrill'd I prize
Thy sadder strains, that bid in Mem'ry's dream
The faded forms of past Delight arise—
Then soft on Love's pale Cheek the tearful Gleam
Of Pleasure smiles, as faint yet beauteous lies
The imag'd Rainbow on a willowy stream.

God love you & your Mother & Edith & Sara & Mary & little
Eliza & & & & & S. T. Coleridge—

---

[1] *Poems*, i. 87; first pub. *Morn. Chron.* 14 Jan. 1795.

76. *To Mary Evans*

MS. Mr. Carl H. Pforzheimer. Pub. Letters, *i. 124.* This letter brings to a close
the love affair with Mary Evans, but Coleridge was to see her again in 1808.
Two additional letters to her, one belonging to that year, the other to 1820,
have survived.

24th December 1794

I have this moment received your Letter, Mary Evans! It's
firmness does honor to your understanding, it's gentleness to your
humanity. You condescend to accuse yourself—most unjustly!
You have been altogether blameless. In my wildest day-dream of
Vanity I never supposed that you entertained for me any other
than a common friendship.

To love you Habit has made unalterable. This passion however,
divested, as it now is, of all Shadow of Hope, will lose it's dis-
quieting power. Far distant from you I shall journey thro' the vale
of Men in calmness. He cannot long be wretched, who dares be
actively virtuous.

I have burnt your Letters—forget mine[1]—and that I have
pained you, forgive me!

May God infinitely love you!

S. T. Coleridge—

[1] Although the Evans family 'always understood' that Mary Evans 'on her
marriage destroyed a number of Coleridge's letters to her', she did preserve
those printed in the present edition; and among her papers, now in Mr. Carl
H. Pforzheimer's Library, there are three poems in Coleridge's handwriting
and another in that of Mary Evans. Of the three poems, two are by Coleridge—
Written at the King's Arms, Ross, and *Song* ('When Youth his faery Reign
began'); the third, *On Bala Hill,* is certainly not Coleridge's, since Coleridge
refers to it as Southey's in Letter 59 and since it appeared, in a slightly different
version, in Southey's *Poems,* 1797, p. 114. (See Coleridge's *Poems,* i. 56 and
note.) The fact that Mary Evans possessed copies made by Coleridge of these
three poems, all composed in the summer and autumn of 1794, suggests
further correspondence between them.

A fourth poem among the Evans papers, *Stanzas written after a long absence,*
is in Mary Evans's handwriting. It was published anonymously with this title
in the *Morning Post* on 20 Oct. 1803. Southey later included it in his *Poetical
Works,* ii. 198, under the title *To Mary,* with the date 1802, and it is un-
doubtedly his composition. Apparently Mary Evans saw the poem in the
Morning Post, erroneously assumed that it was Coleridge's, and copied it. Her
copy, it is worth noting, follows exactly the text in the *Morning Post,* except
for the omission of the last three stanzas.

77. *To Robert Southey*

Address: Robert Southey | No/ 8 | West gate Buildings | Bath   Single
MS. Lord Latymer, *Pub. with omis.* Letters, *i. 125.*
Postmark: 29 December 1794.

I am calm, dear Southey! as an Autumnal Day, when the Sky
is covered with grey moveless Clouds. To *love her* Habit has made
unalterable: I had placed her in the sanctuary of my Heart, nor
can she be torn from thence but with the Strings that grapple it
to Life. This Passion however, divested as it now is of all Shadow
of Hope, seems to lose it's disquieting Power. Far distant, and
never more to behold or hear of her, I shall sojourn in the Vale of
Men sad and in loneliness, yet not unhappy. He cannot be long
wretched who dares be actively virtuous. I am well assured, that
she loves me as a favorite Brother. When she was present, she was
to me only as a very dear Sister: it was in absence, that I felt those
gnawings of Suspense, and that Dreaminess of Mind, which
evidence an affection more restless, yet scarcely less pure, than the
fraternal. The Struggle has been well nigh too much for me—but,
praised be the All-merciful! the feebleness of exhausted Feelings
has produced a Calm, and my Heart stagnates into Peace.

Southey! my ideal Standard of female Excellence rises not above
that Woman. But all Things work together for Good. Had I been
united to her, the Excess of my Affection would have effeminated
my Intellect. I should have fed on her Looks as she entered into
the Room—I should have gazed on her Footsteps when she went
out from me.

To lose her!—I can rise above that selfish Pang. But to marry
another—O Southey! bear with my weakness. Love makes all
things pure and heavenly like itself:—but to marry a woman whom
I do *not* love—to degrade her, whom I call my Wife, by making her
the Instrument of low Desire—and on the removal of a desultory
Appetite, to be perhaps not displeased with her Absence!—
Enough!—These Refinements are the wildering Fires, that lead
me into Vice.

Mark you, Southey!—*I will do my Duty.*

I have this moment received your Letter. My Friend—you want
but one Quality of Mind to be a—perfect character—. Your
Sensibilities are tempestuous—you feel *Indignation* at Weakness—
Now Indignation is the handsome Brother of Anger & Hatred—
His looks are 'lovely in Terror'—yet still remember, *who* are his
Relations. I would ardently, that you were a Necessitarian—and
(believing in an all-loving Omnipotence) an Optimist. That puny Imp
of Darkness yclept Scepticism—how could it dare to approach

the hallowed Fires, that burn so brightly on the Altar of your Heart?

Think you, I wish to stay in Town? I am all eagerness to leave it—and am resolved, whatever be the consequence, to be at Bath by Saturday—I thought of walking down.

I have written to Bristol—and said, I could not assign a particular Time for my leaving Town—I spoke indefinitely that I might not disappoint.

I am not, I presume, to attribute some verses addressed to S. T. C. in the M. Chronicle to you—. To whom?——

My dear Allen!—wherein has he offended? He did never promise to form one of our Party—But of all this when we meet.

Would a Pistol preserve Integrity?—To concentrate Guilt—no very philosophical mode of preventing it.——

I will write of indifferent Subjects.—

Your Sonnet 'Hold your Mad hands![']¹—is a noble Burst of Poetry—/ But my Mind is weakened—and I turn with selfishness of Thought to those milder Songs, that develope my lonely Feelings. Sonnets are scarcely fit for the hard Gaze of the Public— Manly yet gentle Egotism is perhaps the only conversation which pleases from these melancholy Children of the Muse.—I read with heart and *taste* equally delighted your Prefatory Sonnet / I transcribe not so much to give you my corrections as for the pleasure it gives me.²

> With wayworn Feet a Pilgrim woe-begone
> Life's upland Steep I journeyed many a day,
> And hymning many a sad yet soothing Lay
> Beguil'd my wand'ring with the Charms of Song.
> Lonely my Heart and rugged was my Way—
> Yet often pluck'd I as I past along
> The wild and simple Flowers of Poesy:
> And as beseem'd the wayward Fancy's child
> Entwin'd each random weed that pleas'd mine Eye.
> Accept the wreath, Beloved! it is wild
> And rudely-garlanded—yet scorn not thou
> The humble Offering, where the sad Rue weaves
> With gayer Flowers it's intermingled Leaves—
> And I have twin'd the Myrtle for thy Brow!

It is a lovely Sonnet—Lamb likes it with tears in his Eyes.—

¹ This was the first of Southey's six sonnets on the Slave Trade. *Poet. Works*, ii. 55.

² Ibid. p. xix. The sonnet as printed in 1838 differs considerably from Coleridge's version.

His Sister has lately been very unwell—confined to her Bed
dangerously—She is all his Comfort—he her's. They dote on each
other. Her mind is elegantly stored—her Heart feeling—Her
illness preyed a good deal on his Spirits—though he bore it with
an apparent equanimity, as beseemed him who like me is a Uni-
tarian Christian and an Advocate for the Automatism of Man.—

I was writing a poem which when finished you shall see—and
wished him to describe the Character & Doctrines of Jesus Christ
for me—but his low Spirits prevented him—The Poem is in blank
Verse on the Nativity[1]——

I sent him these careless Lines which flowed from my Pen ex-
temporaneously——

To C. Lamb.[2]

Thus far my sterile Brain hath fram'd the Song
Elaborate & swelling—but the Heart
Not owns it. From thy spirit-breathing powers
I ask not now, my Friend! the aiding Verse
Tedious to thee, and from thy anxious thought
Of dissonant Mood. In Fancy, well I know,
Thou creepest round a dear-lov'd Sister's Bed
With noiseless step, and watchest the faint Look
Soothing each Pang with fond Solicitudes
And tenderest Tones medicinal of Love.
I too a Sister *had*—an only Sister—
She loved me dearly—and I doted on her—
On her soft Bosom I repos'd my Cares
And gain'd for every wound an healing Tear.
To her I pour'd forth all my puny Sorrows,
(As a sick Patient in his Nurse's arms)
And of the Heart those hidden Maladies
That shrink asham'd from even Friendship's Eye.
O! I have woke at midnight, and have wept
Because she was not!—Cheerily, dear Charles!
Thou thy best Friend shalt cherish many a year—
Such high presages feel I of warm Hope!
For not uninterested the dear Maid
I've view'd, her Soul affectionate yet wise,
Her polish'd Wit as mild as lambent Glories
That play around an holy Infant's head.
He knows (the Spirit who in secret sees,
Of whose omniscient & all-spreading Love

---

[1] This is Coleridge's first reference to *Religious Musings*.
[2] *Poems*, i. 78.

Aught to implore were Impotence of Mind)
That my mute Thoughts are sad before his Throne,
Prepar'd, when he his healing Ray vouchsafes,
To pour forth Thanksgiving with lifted heart
And praise him gracious with a Brother's Joy!

Wynne[1] is indeed a noble Fellow—more when we meet—

Your's

S. T. Coleridge

78. *To Robert Southey*

Address: Robert Southey | No 8 | West gate Buildings | Bath
MS. Lord Latymer. Hitherto unpublished. This appears to be a fragment, of
which the first part is no longer extant.
Postmark: 2 January 1795.

The roads are dangerous—the horses soon knock'd up—The
outside to a Man who like me has no great Coat, is cold and
rheumatismferous—the Inside of a Coach to a man, who like me
has very little money, is apt to produce *a sickness on the Stomach*—
Shall I walk? I have a sore throat—and am not well.—

I will dash through the Towns and helter skelter it into Bath
in the

Flying Waggon!

Two Miles an hour! That's your Sort—! I shall be supplied with
Bread and Cheese from Christ's Hospital and shall take a bottle of
Gin for myself and Tuom, the Waggoner!—Plenty of Oronoko
Tobacco—Smoke all the Way—that's your Sort!

Wrapped up in Hay—so warm! There are four or five Calves
Inside—Passengers like myself—I shall fraternize with them! The
folly & vanity of young men who go in Stage Coaches!—!—!——!—

The Waggon does not set off before Sunday Night—I shall be
with you by Wednesday,[2] I suppose.—

S. T. Coleridge.

[1] C. W. W. Wynn (1775–1850), Southey's school fellow at Westminster and
lifelong friend.
[2] On receiving this letter Southey and Lovell walked to Marlborough to
meet the wagon, 'but *no S. T. Coleridge was therein*!' J. Cottle, *Rem.* 405;
and on 9 Jan. 1795 Southey wrote pointedly to Sara Fricker: 'Friday night—
no Coleridge! . . . This state of expectation totally unfits me for any thing.
When I attempt to employ myself the first knock at the door wakes all my
hopes again & again disappoints them. . . . I am kept in exercise by walking
to meet the coaches—Did he say Wednesday [January 7] positively to you?
I told you about the middle of the week. Why will he ever fix a day if he
cannot abide **by it**?' (Unpublished letter.)

79. *To Robert Southey*

Address: Robert Southey | to be delivered to him on his | coming out of the Bath Coach.[1]
MS. Lord Latymer. Hitherto unpublished. Southey has been justifiably condemned for interfering with Coleridge's life. As the preceding letters show, Coleridge, grieving over Mary Evans, had no wish to return to Bristol and Sara Fricker. 'Coleridge', wrote Southey later, 'did not come back to Bristol till January 1795, *nor would he, I believe, have come back at all*, if I had not gone to London to look for him. For having got there from Cambridge at the beginning of winter, there he remained without writing to Miss F. or to me.' Campbell, *Life*, 42.

[Mid-January 1795][2]

My dearest Southey

Come to me at the Angel Inn, Angel Street, St Martin's le grand, Newgate Street—

I am not glad that you are come to town—and yet I am glad.—

It was total Want of Cash that prevented my Expedition—

Coleridge

80. *To Robert Southey*

Address: Robert Southey | No 8 | West gate Buildings | Bath
MS. Lord Latymer. Pub. with omis. Letters, *i. 121.*
Stamped: Bristol.

Monday Morning. [19 January 1795][3]

My dear Southey

I will not say that you treat me coolly or mysteriously—yet assuredly you seem to look upon me as a man whom vanity or some other inexplicable Cause have alienated from the System— On what could you build so injurious a suspicion?—Wherein when roused to the recollection of my Duty have I shrunk from the performance of it?—I hold my Life & my feebler feelings as ready sacrifices to Justice—καυχάω ὑπορᾷς [ὑφορᾷς?] γάρ. I dismiss a subject so painful to me as self-vindication—painful to me only as addressing it to *you* on whose esteem and affection I have rested with the whole weight of my Soul.

[1] It is obvious from this address that Southey sent Coleridge a blunt announcement of his sudden determination to come to London 'to reclaim his stray'.

[2] Since Southey wrote to Sara Fricker from Bath on Friday 9 Jan. and hoped to hear from her two days later, he probably did not go to London until the week of 11 Jan.; and since Coleridge had been in Bristol 'two or three days', when he wrote to Southey from there on 19 Jan., this letter was written in mid-January, somewhere between 11 and 19 Jan. See Letter 93, p. 164.

[3] Since the Lovells were married on 20 Jan. 1794 (see postscript) this letter was written on 19 Jan.

Southey! I must tell you, that you appear to me to write as a man who is aweary of a world, because it accords not with his ideas of perfection—your sentiments look like the sickly offspring of disgusted Pride. *Love* is an active and humble Principle—It flies not away from the Couches of Imperfection, because the Patients are fretful or loathsome.

Why, my dear very dear Southey! do you wrap yourself up in the Mantle of self-centering *Resolve*—and refuse to us your bounden Quota of Intellect? Why do you say, I—I—I—will do so and so— instead of saying as you were wont to do—It is all *our Duty* to do so and so—for such & such Reasons—

For God'[s] sake—my dear Fellow—tell me what we are to gain by taking a Welch Farm? Remember the principles & proposed Consequences of Pantisocracy—and reflect in what degree they are attainable by Coleridge, Southey, Lovell, Burnet & Co—some 5 men *going partners* together? In the next place—supposing that we had proved the preponderating Utility of our aspheterizing in Wales—let us by our speedy & united enquiries discover the sum of money necessary—whether such a farm with so very large a house is to be procured without launching our frail & unpiloted Bark on a rough Sea of Anxieties?—How much money will be necessary for *furnishing* so large a house? How much necessary for the main- tenance of so large a family—18 people—for a year at least?——

I have read my Objections to Lovell—if he has not answered them altogether to my fullest conviction—he has however shewn me the wretchedness, that would fall on the majority of our party from any delay, in so forcible a Light—that if 300 pound be adequate to the commencement of the System which I very much doubt—I am most willing to give up all my other views / and embark immediately with you—/

If it be determined that we shall go to Wales—for which I now give my Vote—in what time? Mrs Lovell thinks it impossible that we should go in less than three months—If this be the Case, I will accept the Reporter's place to the $T\eta$legraph—live upon a guinea a week—and transmit the [rest]—finishing in the mean time my Imitations——

However I will walk to Bath tomorrow Morning & return in the Evening—

Mr & Mrs Lovell, Sarah, Edith—all desire their best loves to you and are anxious concerning your Health—

　　　　　　　　　May God love you & your affectionate
　　　　　　　　　　　　　　　　　S. T. Coleridge

P.S. Tomorrow is the Anniversary of Robert's Wedding—God almighty love them!——My filial respects to your Mother.

81. *To George Dyer*

Address: George Dyer | No 45 | Carey Street | Lincoln's Inn Fields | London
Single.
MS. Historical Society of Pennsylvania. Pub. E. L. G. i. 29.
Stamped: Bristol.

No 25 College Street, Bristol.
[Late February 1795]

My dear Sir

Intending to return from day to day I postponed writing to you—I will however delay it no longer.—I am anxious and per- turbed beyond measure concerning my proposed expedition to Scotland—I will pour out my heart before you as water.—In the Autumn of last year, you know, we formed our American Plan, and with precipitance that did credit to our hearts rather than heads, fixed on the coming April as the time of our embarkation. *This* following circumstances have rendered impracticable—but there are other engagements not so dissoluble. In expectation of emigrating on the Pantisocratic Plan I payed my addresses to a young Lady, whom 'οὐτ' αἰνεῖν[1] ἐστι κακοῖσι θέμις!'—Independ- ently of the Love and Esteem which her Person, and polished understanding may be supposed to have inspired into a young man, I consider myself as under particular Ties of Gratitude to her—since in confidence of my Affection she has rejected the Addresses of two men, one of them of large Fortune—and by her perseverant attachment to me disobliged her Relations in a very uncomfortable Degree.—Perpetually obliged to resist the entreaties and to endure the reproachful admonitions of her Uncle &c, she vainly endeavors to conceal from me how heavy her heart is with anxiety, how disquieted by Suspense—To leave her for two or three years would, I fear, be sacrificing her health and happiness— In short, why should I write circuitously to you? So commanding are the requests of her Relations, that a short Time must decide whether she marries me whom she loves with an affection to the ardor of which my Deserts bear no proportion—or a man whom she strongly dislikes, in spite of his fortune and solicitous atten- tions to her. These peculiar circumstances she had with her usual Delicacy concealed from me till my arrival at Bristol.——What am I to do with regard to the Earl of Buchan? Am I to live in the house with the Erskines? Is this a necessary accompaniment of Tutorage?—Or could I take Lodgings in Edingburgh or where ever else the young Gentlemen are situated?—If, as I suppose, these questions must be answered in the Negative, do you not

---

[1] Underlined once in MS.

think it my Duty to decline the offer? Southey is exerting his
Influence to procure a situation in London[1]—I am now about to
write to Scott at the Telegraph Office to know if I can get a
Reporter's Place, and on this wait till I can call forth the Exertions
of my Friends.—My Subscription Work I shall be able to bring out
by the Close of the year— I shall clear more than an 100 pound by
it—Besides, Southey & I have one or two schemes of literary co-
operation which we will impart to you in London—

My dear Sir! believe me, my heart beats high with gratitude to
you— / I know you will write to me as to a Brother!—

Since I have been in Bristol I have endeavored to disseminate
Truth by three political Lectures[2]—I believe, I shall give a
fourth— / But the opposition of the Aristocrats is so furious and
determined, that I begin to fear, that the Good I do is not pro-
portionate to the Evil I occasion—Mobs and Mayors, Blockheads
and Brickbats, Placards and Press gangs have leagued in horrible
Conspiracy against me—The Democrats are as sturdy in the sup-
port of me—but their number is comparatively small— / Two or
three uncouth and unbrained Automata have threatened my
Life—and in the last Lecture the Genus infimum were scarcely
restrained from attacking the house in which the 'damn'd Jacobine
was jawing away.'

The first Lecture I was *obliged* to publish, it having been con-
fidently asserted that there was Treason in it. Written at one
sitting between the hours of twelve at night and the Breakfast
Time of the day, on which it was delivered, believe me that no
literary Vanity prompted me to the printing of it—The reasons
which compelled me to publish it forbad me to correct it——Scott
will beg your acceptance of as many Copies as you may choose to
give away——

I am glad to see your Book advertised—I have [pla]ced orders
for Ten—Cottle, the Bookseller here has sent for them—

Southey speaks of you with high esteem & nascent *friendship*—
You will esteem and love him—His Genius and acquirements are
uncommonly great—yet they bear no proportion to his moral
Excellence—He is truly a man of *perpendicular Virtue*—a *down-*

---

[1] On 8 Feb. 1795 Southey wrote to Grosvenor Bedford that he was 'in
treaty with The Telegraph, and . . . [hoped] to be their correspondent'. *Life
and Corres.* i. 232.

[2] These three lectures were: *A Moral and Political Lecture, On the Present
War*, and *The Plot Discovered; Or an Address to the People, against Ministerial
Treason*. The first appeared as a separate publication in late February or early
March 1795; in November it was republished with the second lecture as *Con-
ciones ad Populum. The Plot Discovered* was published separately in Nov. 1795.
See *Essays on His Own Times*, 3 vols., 1850, i. 1–98.

right upright Republican! He is *Christianizing* apace—I doubt not, that I shall present him to you right orthodox in the heterodoxy of Unitarianism.

To Mr Friend present my most grateful respect—God almighty bless him!——

To Gilbert Wakefield mention my name as of one who remembers him respectfully—/

A Pompous Dissenter here says that though he disapproves of the *Socinian* Rebellion against the divinity of Christ, he must allow that Dr Disney is an uncommon Character in these days when the advocate for Liberty and Deist are almost synonimous—'He is at once, Sir, Theophilus and Phileleutheros![']——

God bless you & your | grateful
S. T. Coleridge

82. *To Joseph Cottle*

Pub. Early Rec. *i. 16.* Joseph Cottle (1770–1853), the Bristol bookseller and publisher of Coleridge's *Poems* of 1796 and 1797, as well as of *Lyrical Ballads*, 1798, issued in 1837 his *Early Recollections; chiefly relating to the late Samuel Taylor Coleridge*, a work containing nearly a hundred letters or fragments of letters from Coleridge to Cottle, Wade, and others. In 1847 Cottle published his *Reminiscences of Samuel Taylor Coleridge and Robert Southey*, which reprints, sometimes with changes, the earlier work, but to which was added a series of letters from Coleridge to the Wedgwoods. The manuscripts of about half of the Coleridge letters printed by Cottle have come to light, and a collation of the holographs with the printed text reveals an irresponsible editorial policy. Cottle's tampering with the text of Coleridge's letters falls into three main categories: the misdating of letters and the garbling of the text by interpolations or omissions, in such a way as to distort or alter the meaning; the transference of passages from one letter to another; and the printing of a single manuscript as two or more letters. (*Ex. gr.* Letters 89, 92, 118, 172, 180, 181, 184, 187, 188, and 195.)

To Southey must go a share of the responsibility for the publication of *Early Recollections* and for the inclusion of the opium letters, despite the objections of the Coleridge family; and yet his opinion of the work, as expressed after its appearance, anticipates the judgement of subsequent scholars: 'Never surely was there any book that would so completely mislead any one who should use it as materials either for Coleridge's biography or mine, the confusion of dates & circumstances being such as I never saw elsewhere.' It is, therefore, particularly to be deplored that the originals of all the Coleridge letters printed by Cottle cannot be traced. Cf. E. L. Griggs, 'Southey's Estimate of Coleridge', *Huntington Lib. Quar.* Nov. 1945, pp. 89–93.

[*Circa* 7 March 1795][1]

My dear Sir,

Can you conveniently lend me five pounds, as we want a little

[1] On or about 7 Mar. Coleridge had been in Bristol seven weeks.

more than four pounds to make up our lodging bill, which is indeed much higher than we expected; seven weeks, and Burnet's lodging for twelve weeks, amounting to eleven pounds?

Yours affectionately,
S. T. Coleridge.

83. *To George Dyer*

Address: George Dyer | No 45 | Carey Street | Lincoln's Inn Fields | London [On the address sheet the following notation appears in another hand.] Wm Wordsworth | No 15 | Chalton Street | Sommers Town
MS. Mr. James Shields. Pub. E. L. G. i. 32.
Postmark: 10 March 1795.

My dear Sir

I received your second Letter last Night—your first—which required an immediate answer—should not have remained unanswered so long voluntarily—but I have been very ill with a rheumatic fever—thank God, I am recovered.—

In a late Letter you tell me not to be too sanguine in my expectations of the profits of the Latin Poets—I rated those profits at one hundred pounds—and I have now 450 Subscribers—300 Copies pay all the Expences—. However, I assure you, I speculate not on that work.

There is one sentence in your last letter which affected me greatly—'I feel a degree of languor &c &c and by seeing & frequently feeling much illiberality acquire something of misanthropy'—! —It is melancholy to think, that the best of us are liable to be shaped & coloured by surrounding Objects—and a demonstrative proof, that Man was not made to live in Great Cities! Almost all the physical Evil in the World depends on the existence of moral Evil—and the long-continued contemplation of the latter does not tend to meliorate the human heart.—The pleasures, which we receive from rural beauties, are of little Consequence compared with the Moral Effect of these pleasures—beholding constantly the Best possible we at last become ourselves the best possible. In the country, all around us smile Good and Beauty—and the Images of this divine καλοκάγαθόν are miniatured on the mind of the beholder, as a Landscape on a Convex Mirror. Thompson in that most lovely Poem, the Castle of Indolence, says—

> [']I care not, Fortune! what you me deny—
> You cannot rob me of free Nature's Grace!

You cannot shut the Windows of the Sky,
Through which the Morning shews her dewy face—
You cannot bar my constant feet to rove
Through Wood and Vale by living Stream at Eve'—/[1]

Alas! alas! she *can* deny us all this—and can force us fettered and handcuffed by our Dependencies & Wants to *wish* and *wish* away the bitter Little of Life in the felon-crowded Dungeon of a great City!——

God love you, my very dear Sir! I would that we could form a Pantisocracy in England, and that you could be one of us!—The finely-fibred Heart, that like the statue of Memnon, trembles into melody on the sun-beam touch of Benevolence, is most easily jarred into the dissonance of Misanthropy. But you will never suffer your feelings to be benumbed by the torpedo Touch of that Fiend— / I know you—and know that you will drink of every Mourner's sorrows, even while your own Cup is trembling over it's Brink!—

We certainly shall not come to London without a certainty of Employment—but what I most ardently wish, is to be employed in some department of Literature which does not require my Residence in Town. Is it possible that I could gain an employment in this new Work, the Citizen?—'Where the Fame is nothing, & the Profits sure'—with one sentence you have incompassed the whole extent of my Wishes. My Hopes, when most highly-plumed by my Fancy, soar not more sublimely, than to labor and live—to be useful & to be happy— / Not to be poor—would make me very rich!—If by any means I could procure a salary of a guinea a week, I would be well content to work like a Russian— / In short, we wish and mean to live (in all the severity of Economy) in Wales—near some Town, where there is a speedy Communication with London— / Can any Thing be procured, which may employ us there?—

I did not expect, that you would have thought so well of my political Lecture—the second & third are far superior to it in point of Composition— / but I had no *necessity* for publishing them—and therefore no Temptation— / I was soon obliged by the persecutions of Darkness to discontinue them—Southey is now about to give a course of Historical Lectures—unconnected with—at least not *immediately* relative to—the politics of the Day / ——Southey desires his remembrances to you in warmth of esteem / .

A Friend of our's is soon coming to London—who will convey to you a little Pacquet from me—I shall soon transmit to the Morning

---

[1] *Castle of Indolence*, ii. iii.

Chronicle 5 more Sonnets to Eminent characters[1]—among the rest, one to Lord Stanhope!—[2]

I receive great pleasure from your Letters—write soon.

To Dr Gregory[3] present my respects—to Gilbert Wakefield. Is Mr Frend in Town?

> God love you & | your obliged & grateful
> S. T. Coleridge

Poor *Brothers*![4] They'll make him know the *Law* as well as the *Prophets*!

84. *To Joseph Cottle*

Pub. Rem. *38, where the text is more complete than in* Early Rec. *i. 55.*

[Spring 1795]

Dear Cottle,

Shall I trouble you (I being over the mouth and nose, in doing something of importance, at Lovell's) to send your servant into the market, and buy a pound of bacon, and two quarts of broad beans; and when he carries it down to College St. to desire the maid to dress it for dinner, and tell her I shall be home by three o'clock? Will you come and drink tea with me, and I will endeavour to get the etc. ready for you?

> Yours affectionately,
> S. T. C.

[1] Despite Coleridge's reiterated intention (see Letter 74), only eleven *Sonnets on Eminent Characters* were published in the *Morning Chronicle*, the last on 29 Jan. 1795.

[2] This statement proves conclusively that the sonnet *To Lord Stanhope*, which appeared five weeks earlier (31 Jan. 1795) in the *Morning Chronicle*, over the signature, 'One of the People', and erroneously attributed to Coleridge by J. D. Campbell, could not have been his. The sonnet *To Earl Stanhope* written by Coleridge never appeared in the *Morning Chronicle* and was first published against his wishes in his *Poems* of 1796. See Campbell, *Poetical Works*, 43 and 575, *Poems*, i. 89, Letter 145, and E. L. Griggs, 'Notes concerning Certain Poems by Samuel Taylor Coleridge,' *Modern Language Notes*, Jan. 1954, pp. 28–29.

[3] George Gregory (1754–1808), divine and man of letters, published a *Life of Chatterton* in 1789.

[4] Richard Brothers (1757–1824), a religious enthusiast, was arrested on 4 Mar. 1795 for treasonable practices and confined as a criminal lunatic.

85. *To Joseph Cottle*

Pub. Early Rec. *i. 52.*

[*Circa* 29 July 1795][1]

My dear friend,

The printer may depend on copy[2] on Monday morning, and if he can work a sheet a day, he shall have it.

S. T. C.

86. *To Joseph Cottle*

July 31st, 1795

Pub. Early Rec. *i. 52.*

Dear Cottle.

By the thick smokes that precede the volcanic eruptions of Etna, Vesuvius, and Hecla, I feel an impulse to fumigate, at 25, College-Street, one pair of stairs' room; yea, with our Oronoco, and if thou wilt send me by the bearer, four pipes, I will write a panegyrical epic poem upon thee, with as many books as there are letters in thy name. Moreover, if thou wilt send me 'the copy book,' I hereby bind myself, by to-morrow morning, to write out enough copy for a sheet and a half.

God bless you!
S. T. C.

87. *To Robert Southey*

Address: Robert Southey.
MS. Lord Latymer. Pub. Letters, *i. 134.*

[Early August 1795][3]

My dear Southey

It would argue imbecillity and a latent wickedness in myself, if for a moment I doubted concerning your purposes and final

---

[1] According to Cottle this note was written 'a day or two' before Letter 86.

[2] Coleridge apparently refers to copy for his *Poems on Various Subjects*, which appeared on 16 Apr. 1796.

[3] In August Southey received a letter from his uncle, Herbert Hill, urging him to take Orders, and he immediately communicated its contents to Coleridge. Since Southey seemed undecided, Coleridge wrote this letter to him that same night. (See letter 93, p. 165, for Coleridge's review of the circumstances.) It was not, however, until 22 Aug. that Southey reported in a letter to Bedford his decision not to enter the church but to study law instead. (*Life and Corres.* i. 245.) Coleridge's letter, therefore, must belong to early August.

determination. I write, because it is possible, that I may suggest
some idea to you which should find a place in your Answer to your
Uncle—and I *write*, because in a letter I can express myself more
connectedly than in conversation.

The former part of Mr Hill's reasonings is reducible to this—It
may not be vicious to entertain pure and virtuous sentiments—
their criminality is confined to the promulgation (If we believe
Democracy to be pure and virtuous, to us it is so.)—Southey!
Pantisocracy is not the Question—it's realization is distant—
perhaps a miraculous Millenium—What you have seen, or think,
that you have seen of the human heart, may render the formation
even of a pantisocratic *seminary* improbable to you—but this is not
the question—Were 300£ a year offered to you as a man of the
world, as one indifferent to absolute Equality, but still on the
supposition that you were commonly honest, I suppose it possible
that doubts might arise—Your mother, your brothers, your Edith
would all crowd upon you—and certain Misery might be weighed
against distant & perhaps unattainable happiness—But the point
is, whether or no you can *perjure* yourself[1]—.— There are Men,
who hold the necessity and moral optimism of our religious
Establishment—it's peculiar dogmas they may disapprove—but
of innovation they see dreadful and unhealable Consequences—
and they will not quit the Church for a few follies, or absurdities,
any more than for the same reason they would desert a valued
friend—. Such men I do not condemn—whatever I may deem of
their reasonings, their hearts and consciences I include not in the
Anathema—But you disapprove of an Establishment altogether—
you believe it iniquitous—a mother of Crimes!—It is impossible
that *you* could uphold it by assuming the badge of Affiliation!

Our prospects are not bright—but to the eye of reason as bright
as when we first formed our Plan—nor is there any opposite
Inducement offered, of which you were not then apprized, or had
cause to expect. Domestic Happiness is the greatest of things
sublunary—and of things celestial it is perhaps impossible for
unassisted Man to believe any thing greater—: but it is not strange
that those things, which in a pure form of Society will constitute
our first blessings, should in it's present morbid state, be our most
perilous Temptations—!—'He that doth not love Mother & Wife
less than me, is not worthy of me!'

This have I written, Southey! altogether disinterestedly. Your
desertion or adhaesion will in no wise affect my feelings, opinions,
or conduct—and in a very inconsiderable degree, my fortunes!

---

[1] Southey echoed this idea in his letter of 22 Aug.: 'My uncle urges me to
enter the church; but the gate is perjury. . . .' *Life and Corres.* i. 245.

That Being, who is 'in will, in deed, Impulse of all to all' whichever
be your determination, will make it ultimately the best——
God love you, my dear Southey!

——S. T. Coleridge

88. *To Joseph Cottle*

MS. Victoria and Albert Museum. Pub. Walter Savage Landor, *John Forster,*
2 vols., 1869, i. 353 n.

[*Circa* 22 August 1795][1]

Dear Cottle

I congratulate Virtue & her Friends, that Robert Southey has
relinquished all intentions of taking Orders—he leaves our Party
however, and means, he thinks, to study the Law.

Your's
S. T. Coleridge

89. *To Joseph Cottle*

Address: Mr. Joseph Cottle.
Transcript Coleridge family. Pub. Collection of Alfred Morrison, *1895, ii. 248.*

Wednesday Night.   September 30th, [1795]

My dear Sir,

I am returned—I shall do myself the pleasure of sleeping at
your House to-morrow evening—if I be no inconvenient Visitor—
but (of course) I shall see you to-morrow morning.

There are some old *Prints,* I believe—belonging to us in the
room above the shop / if you would be so kind as to put one above
the other and send them to Miss Fricker's, Red Cliff Hill, before
9 to-morrow morning I shall deem myself obliged to you as by that
time the cart will be setting off with our goods.[2] My respect to your
good Mother & to your Father—and believe me to have toward
you the inward and spiritual gratitude & affection though I am
not *always* an adept in the outward & visible signs.[3]

God bless you
S. T. Coleridge.

---

[1] This letter was probably written about the same time, 22 Aug., that
Southey announced his intention to study law. *Life and Corres.* i. 245.

[2] In anticipation of his forthcoming marriage on 4 Oct. 1795, Coleridge had
leased a cottage at Clevedon, Somerset, on the Bristol Channel.

[3] Cottle extracted the last sentence of this manuscript and added it to his
version of Letter 181 of this edition. See *Early Rec.* i. 198.

90. *To Joseph Cottle*

Pub. Early Rec. *i. 59.* 'Two days after his marriage', Cottle remarks, 'I received a letter from Mr. Coleridge (which now lies before me) requesting the kindness of me, to send him down, with all dispatch, the following little articles. . . . The next day [October 7] I rode down to pay my respects to the newly-married couple.'

[5 October 1795]

A riddle slice; a candle box; two ventilators; two glasses for the wash-hand stand; one tin dust pan; one small tin tea kettle; one pair of candlesticks; one carpet brush; one flower dredge; three tin extinguishers; two mats; a pair of slippers; a cheese toaster; two large tin spoons; a bible;[1] a keg of porter; coffee; raisins; currants; catsup; nutmegs; allspice; cinnamon; rice; ginger; and mace.

91. *To Thomas Poole*

Address: Mr Thomas Poole | Stowey | near Bridgewater | Somerset
MS. British Museum. Pub. with omis. Letters, *i. 136.* Thomas Poole (1765–1837) was a tanner at Nether Stowey and one of Coleridge's most intimate friends.
Stamped: Bristol.

Wednesday Evening.   [7 October 1795]

My dear Sir—God bless you!—or rather, God be praised for that he *has* blessed you—!——

On Sunday Morning I was *married*—at St Mary's, Red Cliff—poor Chatterton's Church— / The thought gave me a tinge of melancholy to the solemn Joy, which I felt—united to the woman, whom I love best of all created Beings.—We are settled—nay—quite domesticated at Clevedon—Our comfortable Cot!—!—

Mrs Coleridge—Mrs COLERIDGE!!—I like to *write* the name—well—as I was saying—Mrs Coleridge desires her affectionate regards to you—I talked of you on my wedding night——God bless you!—I hope that some ten years hence you will believe and know of my affection towards you what I will not now profess.

The prospect around us is perhaps more *various* than any in the kingdom—Mine Eye gluttonizes.——The Sea—the distant Islands!—the opposite Coasts!—I shall assuredly write Rhymes—let the nine Muses prevent it, if they can—/.

---

[1] This Bible bears the inscription, 'Given to me by Joseph Cottle after my marriage—S. T. Coleridge', and on the first fly-leaf Coleridge wrote: 'Married at St Mary Red Cliff to Sara Fricker on the fourth day of October, 1795—I being 23 years old the twentieth day following of the same month.' Later entries record the births of Coleridge's four children.

Cruickshanks,[1] I find, is married to Miss Buclé—. I am happy to hear it—he will surely, I hope, make a good husband to a woman, to whom *he* would be a villain who should make a bad one——.

I have given up all thoughts of the Magazine[2]—for various Reason[s]. Imprimis—I must be connected with R. Southey in it, which I could not be with comfort to my feelings.[3] Secundò—It is a thing of monthly *Anxiety* & quotidian Bustle—Tertiò—It would cost Cottle an 100 pounds in buying Paper &c all on an uncertainty—Quartò—To publish a Magazine for *one* year would be nonsense—and if I pursue what I mean to pursue—my school plan—I could not publish it for more than one year—. Quintò—Cottle has entered into an engagement to give me a guinea & a half for every hundred Lines of Poetry, I write—which will be perfectly sufficient for my maintenance, I only amusing myself on Mornings—and all my prose works he is eager to purchase. Sextò—In the course of half-a year I mean to return to Cambridge (having previously taken my name off from the university controll) and taking Lodgings there for myself and wife finish my great work of Imitations in 2 vols—My former works may, I hope, prove somewhat of genius and erudition—this will be better—it will shew great Industry, and manly consistency—at the end of it I shall publish proposals for School &c— / .

[Cottle] has spent a day with me—and takes this letter to Bristol—my next will be long and full of SOMETHING—this is inanity & egotism. Pray, let me hear from you—directing the letter to Mr Cottle's—who will forward it—My respectful & grateful remembrance to your Mother[4]—& believe me, dear Poole! your affectionate & mindful—*Friend*—shall I so soon dare to say?—Believe me, my *heart* prompts it—.

S. T. Coleridge

---

[1] The Cruikshanks (Coleridge spelled the name in various ways) were residents of Nether Stowey, John Cruikshank being Lord Egmont's agent there.

[2] Coleridge refers to his and Southey's unrealized venture, which was to be called the *Provincial Magazine*. Cf. *Life and Corres.* i. 231.

[3] For the details of Coleridge's open break with Southey, see Letter 93.

[4] 'S. T. C. used to say there were three kinds of old women—i.e., "That old woman—That old Witch—and that dee-ar old Soul." This saying I had from Mama. Old Mrs. Poole—T. Poole's mother was "that *dear* old soul" and some other Ottery person, that old woman.' [MS. note by Coleridge's daughter.]

92. *To Joseph Cottle*

Address: Mr Joseph Cottle
MS. Harvard College Lib. Pub. E. L. G. i. 35. Cottle took his usual liberties
with this manuscript, publishing it only in part and making two separate
letters of it. See *Early Rec.* i. 138, 139, and 285.

[October 1795][1]

My dear Sir

There must be *four* Sheets / I find—all of which are all finished—
yea—polish'd—in addition to these *now sent* there are two more
Epistles & the Nativity & the notes / but I have left at Stowey the
six Sheets already printed—I do not want them—only let George
Burnet look over them and write down—to what Poems and to
what parts of what Poems there are references to Notes—he can
do it in ten Minutes—and you shall have them & the remaining
Poems on Saturday morning by nine o'clock—it is impossible, that
they can finish what I have now sent before that time.—There is
a beautiful little poetic Epistle of Sara's, which I mean to print
here[2]—What if the first part of her letter to you—viz—down to—
'And you, dear Sir! the arch-magician![']³—were likewise printed—
so as to have two of her Poems?—It is remarkably elegant and
would do honor to *any* Volume of *any Poems*.

As I mean to have none but large Poems in the second Volume[4]—
none under three hundred Lines, therefore I have crowded all my
little pieces into this.

My Sara, I believe, is indebted to her Mother a guinea and an
half—if it prove convenient to you, will you inclose it to her, and
put it to my account?

The Nativity is not quite three hundred Lines—it has cost me
much labor in polishing, more than any poem I ever wrote—and
I believe, deserves it more—Before it be sent to the press, if you
would desire Mr Estlin[5] to peruse it, and to correct anything he
particularly dislikes, I should thank you— / and let it be printed

---

[1] Since Coleridge quotes a line from Sara's poem, *The Silver Thimble*, a
poetic acknowledgement of a gift sent by Cottle immediately after his visit
to Clevedon on 7 Oct., this letter seems to belong to Oct. 1795. Likewise, the
fact that *Religious Musings* is here called by its earlier title, *Nativity*; the
reference to the 'six Sheets' of printed poems left behind at Stowey when
Coleridge visited Poole in September; and the mention of sea-bathing, all
suggest Clevedon and the early days of marriage.

[2] Cottle says, 'The first epistle I never received'. *Early Rec.* i. 285.

[3] This is line 16 of *The Silver Thimble*, attributed to 'a Young Lady' in the
1796 *Poems*. Mrs. Coleridge later told her daughter that she wrote but little
of the poem. Cf. *Poems*, i. 104.

[4] Only one volume appeared in 1796.

[5] John Prior Estlin (1747–1817), a Unitarian minister in Bristol.

as he returns it—for I have an implicit confidence in the soundness
of his Taste in compositions of the higher cast.

The Epistle to Tom Poole[1] which will come with the Nativity, is,
I think, one of my most *pleasing* compositions.——

God bless you—

S. T. Coleridge

I smoked yesterday afternoon—and then imprudently went into
the Sea—the Consequence was that on my return I was taken
sick—and my triumphant Tripes cataracted most Niagara-ishly—

N.B. On Wednesday Morning by nine o'clock the Preface shall
be sent[2]—they cannot want it before—or if they do, they shall
have it on Monday by some conveyance or other—.

93. *To Robert Southey*

MS. Lord Latymer. Pub. Letters, *i. 137.*

Friday Morning   November [13], 1795

Southey! I *have* 'lost Friends'—Friends who still cherish for
me Sentiments of high Esteem and unextinguished Tenderness.
For the Sum Total of my Misbehaviour, the Alpha and Omega of
their Accusations, is Epistolary Neglect. I never spake of them
without affection, I never think of them without Reverence. Not
'to this Catalogue', Southey! have I 'added *your* name'. You are
lost to *me*, because you are lost to Virtue.

As this will probably be the last time I shall have occasion to
address you, I will glance thro' the History of our connection, and
regularly retrace your Conduct and my own. In the month of June,
1794, I first became acquainted with your person and character.
Before I quitted Oxford, we had struck out the leading features
of a Pantisocracy: while on my Journey thro' Wales, you invited
me to Bristol with the full hopes of realizing it—: during my abode
at Bristol, the Plan was matured: and I returned to Cambridge hot
in the anticipation of that happy Season, when we should remove
the *selfish* Principle from ourselves, and prevent it in our children,
by an *Abolition* of Property: or in whatever respects this might be
impracticable, by such similarity of Property, as would amount
to a *moral Sameness,* and answer all the purposes of *Abolition.*
Nor were you less zealous: and thought, and expressed your
opinion, that if any man embraced our System, he must com-

[1] Coleridge never published such an epistle. A few lines addressed to Poole
were included in a letter to Thelwall, dated 31 Dec. 1796. See Letter 170.

[2] Coleridge was still writing 'the first rude Sheet of my Preface' several
months later. Cf. Letter 105.

paratively disregard 'his father and mother and wife and children and brethren and sisters, yea, and his own Life also': or he could 'not be our disciple'. In one of your Letters alluding to your Mother's low Spirits and situation—you tell me, that I 'cannot suppose any *individual* feelings will have an undue weight with you[']—and in the same letter you observe (alas! your recent conduct has made it a prophecy!) 'God forbid! that the *Ebullience* of *Schematism*[1] should be over. It is the Promethean Fire that animates my soul—and when *that* is gone, all *will be Darkness*!'——
'I have DEVOTED myself!'——

Previously to my departure from Jesus College, and during my melancholy detention in London, what convulsive Struggles of Feeling I underwent, and what sacrifices I made, you know. The liberal Proposal from my Family affected me no farther than as it pained me to wound a revered Brother by the positive and immediate Refusal, which Duty compelled me to return.—But there was a—I need not be particular—You remember what a Fetter I burst, and that it snapt, as if it had been a Sinew of my Heart. However I returned to Bristol, and my addresses to Sara, which I at first payed from Principle not Feeling, from Feeling & from Principle I renewed: and I met a reward more than proportionate to the greatness of the Effort. I love and I am beloved, and I am happy!——

Your Letter to Lovell, (two or three days after my arrival at Bristol) in answer to some objections of mine to the Welsh Scheme, was the first Thing that alarmed me. Instead of—'It is our duty' 'such and such are the reasons'—it was 'I and I' and 'will and will'—sentences of gloomy and self-centering Resolve.[2] I wrote you a friendly Reproof, and in my own mind attributed this unwonted Stile to your earnest desires of realizing our Plan, and the angry Pain which you felt when any appeared to oppose or defer it's execution. However, I came over to your opinion, of the utility and in course the duty of rehearsing our Scheme in Wales—and so rejected the Offer of being established in the Earl of Buchan's Family. To this period of our connection I call your more particular attention and remembrance, as I shall revert to it at the close of my Letter.

 We commenced lecturing. Shortly after, you began to recede in your conversation from those broad Principles, in which Pantisocracy originated. I opposed you with vehemence: for I well knew that no Notion on morality or it's motives could be without consequences. And once (it was just before we went in to Bed) you confessed to me that you had acted wrong. But you relapsed: your

---

[1] Cf. Letter 73.   [2] Cf. Letter 80.

manners became cold and gloomy: and pleaded with increased
pertinacity for the Wisdom of making Self an undiverging Center.
At Mr Jardine's[1] your language was *strong indeed*—recollect it—
You had left the Table and we were standing at the Window. Then
darted into my mind the Dread, that you were meditating a
Separation. At *Chepstow* your Conduct renewed my Suspicion:
and I was greatly agitated even to many Tears. But in Percefield
Walks you assured me that my Suspicions were altogether un-
founded, that our differences were merely speculative, and that
you would certainly go into Wales. I was glad and satisfied. For
my Heart was never bent from you but by violent strength—and
heaven knows, how it leapt back to esteem and love you. But alas!
a short time passed, ere your departure from our first principles
became too flagrant. Remember when we went to Ashton on the
Strawberry Party. Your conversation with George Burnet on the
day following he detailed to me. It scorched my throat. Your
private resources were to remain your individual property, and
every thing to be separate except on five or six acres. In short, we
were to commence Partners in a petty Farming Trade. This was
the Mouse of which the Mountain Pantisocracy was at last safely
delivered! I received the account with Indignation & Loathings of
unutterable Contempt. Such opinions were indeed unassailable—
the Javelin of Argument and the arrows of Ridicule would have
been equally misapplied—a Straw would have wounded them
mortally. I did not condescend to waste my Intellect upon them;
but in the most express terms I declared to George Burnet my
opinion (and, Southey! next to my own Existence there is scarce
any Fact of which at this moment I entertain less doubt) to Burnet
I declared it to be my opinion, '*That you had long laid a Plot* of
Separation, and were now developing it—by proposing such a vile
mutilation of our Scheme, as you must have been conscious, I
should reject decisively & with scorn.['] George Burnet was your
most affectionate Friend: I knew his unbounded veneration for you,
his personal attachment. I knew likewise his gentle Dislike of *me*.
Yet him I bade be the Judge. I bade him choose his associate. I
would adopt the full System or depart. George, I presume, detailed
of this my conversation what part he chose: from him however I
received your sentiments—viz—that you would go into Wales on
what plan I liked.—Thus your System of Prudentials and your
Apostacy were not sudden: these constant Nibblings had sloped
your descent from Virtue.

You received your Uncle's Letter. I said—What Answer have
you returned. [(]For to think with almost superstitious Veneration

[1] The Rev. David Jardine, Unitarian minister at Bath.

of you had been such a deep-rooted Habit of my Soul, that even then I did not dream, you could hesitate concerning so infamous a Proposal.) 'None.' (you replied) 'Nor do I know what Answer I shall return.' You went to Bed. George sat half-petrified—gaping at the pigmy Virtue of his supposed Giant. I performed the Office of still-struggling Friendship by writing you my free Sentiments concerning the enormous Guilt of that which your Uncle's doughty Sophistry recommended.[1]

On the next morning I walked with you towards Bath—again I insisted on it's criminality. You told me, that you had 'little notion of Guilt', and that 'you had a pretty Sort of lullaby Faith of your own'. Finding you invulnerable in conscience, for the sake of mankind I did not however quit the Field; but prest you on the difficulties of your System. Your Uncle's Intimacy with the Bishop, and the Hush, in which you would lie for the two years previous to your Ordination, were the arguments (variously urged in a long and desultory Conversation) by which you solved those difficulties.— 'But your Joan of Arc—the sentiments in it are of the boldest Order. What if the Suspicions of the Bishop be raised, and he particularly questions you concerning your opinions of the Trinity, and the Redemption?' O (you replied) I am pretty well up to their Jargon and shall answer them accordingly. In fine, you left me fully persuaded, that you would enter into holy Orders. And after a week's Interval or more you desired George Burnet to act independently of you, & *gave him an invitation to Oxford.*—Of course, we both concluded that the matter was now absolutely determined. Southey! I am not besotted, that I should not know nor hypocrite enough not to tell you, that you were diverted from being a Priest—only by the weight of Infamy which you perceived coming towards you, like a Rush of Waters!

Thus with good Reason I considered [you] as one who had *fallen back into the Ranks*; as a man admirable for his abilities only, strict indeed in the lesser Honesties, but like the majority of men unable to resist a strong Temptation—FRIEND is a very sacred appellation—You were become an Acquaintance, yet one for whom I felt no common tenderness. I could not forget what you had been. Your Sun was set: your Sky was clouded: but those Clouds and that Sky were yet tinged with the recent Sun. As I considered you, so I treated you. I studiously avoided all particular Subjects, I acquainted you with nothing relative to myself—literary Topics engrossed our Conversation. You were too quicksighted not to perceive it. I received a letter from you. 'You have withdrawn your confidence from me, Coleridge! Preserving still the face of

[1] Cf. Letter 87.

friendship when we meet, you yet avoid me and carry on your plans in secrecy'! If by 'the face of Friendship' you meant that kindliness which I shew to all because I feel it for all, your statement was perfectly accurate. If you meant more, you contradict yourself, for you evidently perceived from my manners, that you were 'a weight upon' me 'in company, an intruder unwish'd and unwelcome.['] I pained you by 'cold Civility, the shadow which Friendship leaves behind him.[']—Since that Letter I altered my conduct no otherways than by avoiding you more—. I still generaliz'd, and spoke not [of myself excepting my proposed literary works. In short, I spoke to you as I should have done to any other man of Genius who had happened to be my *acquaintance*— Without the farce & tumult of a Rupture I wish you to sink into that Class.—'Face to face you never changed your manners to me'— And yet I pained you by 'cold civility[']—Egregious contradiction——Doubtless, I always treated you with urbanity and meant so to do—but I *locked up* my heart from you, and you perceived it and I intended you to perceive it. 'I planned works in conjunction with you'—Most certainly—the *magazine,* which long before this you had planned equally with me, and if it had been carried into execution, would of course have retained your third Share of the Profits.—What had you done that should make you an unfit literary associate to me?—Nothing.—My opinion of you as a *man* was altered—not as a Writer. Our Muses had not quarrelled. I should have read your Poetry with equal Delight and corrected it with equal Zeal, if correction it needed.—I received you on my return from Shurton with 'my usual Shake of the Hand.' You gave me your hand—and dreadful must have been my feelings, if I had refused to take it. Indeed, so long had I known you, so highly venerated, so dearly loved you, that my Hand would have taken your's *mechanically.*—But is shaking the Hand a mark of Friendship?—Heaven forbid! I should then be a Hypocrite many days in the week—It is assuredly the *pledge of Acquaintance, and nothing more.* But after this did I not with most scrupulous care avoid you?—You know, I did.

In your former Letter you say that I made use of these words to you—[']You will be retrograde that you may spring the farther forward'—You have misquoted, Southey!—You had talked of rejoining Pantisocracy in about 14 years—I exploded the probability—but as I saw you determined to leave it, hoped and wished it might be so—*hoped* that you might run backwards only to leap the farther forward.—Not to mention, that during that *conversation,* I had taken the weight and pressing Urgency of your motives as truths granted—but when on examination I found them a shew

& mockery of unreal things, doubtless my opinion of you must have become far less respectful.—You quoted likewise the last sentence of my Letter to you, as a proof that I approved of your design—you *knew* that sentence to imply no more than the pious confidence of Optimism—However wickedly you might act, God would make it ultimately the best[1]—. You *knew*, this was the meaning of it. I could find twenty Parallel passages in the Lectures —indeed such expressions applied to bad actions had become a habit of my Conversation—you had named, not unwittily, Dr Pangloss. And Heaven forbid, that I should not now have faith, that however foul your Stream may run here, yet that it will filtrate & become pure in it's subterraneous Passage to the Ocean of Universal Redemption.

Thus far had I written when the necessities of literary Occupation crowded upon me—and I met you in Red Cliff, and unsaluted and unsaluting pass'd by the man to whom for almost a year I had told my last thoughts when I closed my eyes, and the first when I awoke! But 'Ere this I have felt Sorrow![']——I shall proceed to answer your Letters—and first excriminate myself, and then examine your conduct. You charge me with having industriously trumpeted your Uncle's Letter. When I mentioned my intended journey to Clevedon with Burnet, and was asked by my immediate friends why *you* were not with us, should I have been silent and implied something mysterious, or have told an open untruth and made myself your accomplice? I could do neither. I answered that you were quite undetermined: but had some thoughts of returning to Oxford. To Danvers indeed and to Cottle I spoke more particularly—for I knew their prudence, and their love for you—: and my Heart was very full. But to Mrs Morgan I did not mention it. She met me in the streets, and said— So! Southey is going into the Church—'tis all concluded—'tis in vain to deny it!—I answered—you are mistaken—you must contradict. Southey has received a splendid offer—but he has not determined—This, I have some faint recollection, was my answer— but of this particular conversation my recollection is very faint. By what means she received the Intelligence, I know not—probably from Mrs Richardson, who might have been told it by Mr Wade. A considerable Time after, the Subject was renewed at Mrs Morgan's, Burnet and my Sara being present. Mrs M. told me, that you had asserted to her, that with regard to the Church you had but barely hesitated, that you might consider your Uncle's Arguments—that you had not given up one Principle—and that *I* was more your Friend, than ever.——I own, I was roused to an agony of Passion;

[1] Cf. Letter 87.

nor was George Burnet undisturbed. Whatever I said that after-
noon (and since that Time I have but repeated what I then said,
in gentler Language) George Burnet did give his *decided Amen* to.
And I said, Southey!—that you had given up every Principle—
that confessedly you were going into the Law, more opposite to
your avowed principles, if possible, than even the Church—and
that I had in my pocket a letter, in which you charged me with
having withdrawn my friendship; and as to your barely hesitating
about your Uncle's Proposal, I was obliged in my own defence to
relate all that past between us, all on which I had founded a con-
viction so directly opposite.

I have, you say, distorted your conversation by 'gross mis-
representation and wicked and calumnious falsehoods. It has been
told me by Mrs Morgan, that I said, I have seen my Error! I have
been drunk with principle!'——Just over the Bridge, at the
bottom of High Street, returning one night from Red Cliff Hill, in
answer to my pressing contrast of your then opinions of the selfish
kind with what you had formerly professed, you said—I was
intoxicated with the novelty of a System! That you said, 'I have
seen my error', I never asserted. It is doubtless implied in the
sentence which you did say—but I never charged it to you as your
expression. As to your reserving Bank Bills &c to yourself, the
Charge would have been so palpable a Lie, that I must have been
madman as well as villain to have been guilty of it—if I had,
George Burnet & Sara would have contradicted it. I said, that your
conduct in little things had appeared to me tinged with selfishness,
and George Burnet attributed, and still does attribute your defec-
tion to your unwillingness to share your expected Annuity with
us.[1] As to the long Catalogue of other Lies, they not being particu-
larized, I of course can say nothing about them—Tales may have
been fetched & carried with embellishments calculated to improve
them in every thing but the Truth. I spoke 'the plain & simple
Truth' alone.

And now for your Conduct & Motives. My Hand trembles when
I think what a series of falsehood & duplicity I am about to bring
before the Conscience of a Man, who has dared to write me, that
'his Conduct has been uniformly open.[']

I must revert to your first Letter, and here you say—
'The Plan you are going upon is not of sufficient Importance to
justify me to myself in abandoning a family, who have none to
support them but me.' The Plan, *you* are going upon! What Plan

---

[1] In the summer of 1795 C. W. W. Wynn 'offered Southey an annuity of
£160, to begin as soon as he [Wynn] came of age in October, 1796'. Jack
Simmons, *Southey*, 1945, p. 55.

was *I* meditating save to retire into the Country with George Burnet & yourself, and taking by degrees a small farm there be *learning* to get my own bread by my bodily Labor—and there to have all things in common—thus disciplining my body & mind for the successful Practice of the same thing in America with more numerous Associates—? And even if this should never be the Case, ourselves & our children would form a society sufficiently large. And was not this your own Plan? The Plan, for the realizing of which you invited me to Bristol—the plan, for which I abandoned my friends, and every prospect & every certainty, and the Woman whom I loved to an excess which you in your warmest dream of fancy could never shadow out?—When I returned from London, when you deemed Pantisocracy a DUTY—a duty unaltered by numbers—when you said, that if others left it, you and George Burnet and your Brother would stand firm to the post of Virtue— what then were our circumstances? Saving Lovell, our number was the same—yourself & Burnet & I—Our *Prospects* were only an uncertain Hope of getting 30 Shillings a week between us by writing for some London Paper—for the remainder we were to rely on our agricultural Exertions—And as to your family you stood precisely in the same situation as you now stand. You meant to take your Mother with you and your Brother—And where indeed would have been the Difficulty? She would have earned her maintenance by her management & savings—considering the matter even in this cold-hearted Way. But when you broke from us, our Prospects were brightening—by the magazine or by Poetry we might and should have got 10 guineas a month.—

But if you are acting right, I should be acting right in imitating you—What then would George Burnet do—He, 'whom you seduc'd

> With other promises & other vaunts
> Than to repent, boasting *you* could subdue
> Temptation!'——[1]

He cannot go into the Church—for you did 'give him Principles'! And I wish that you had indeed 'learnt from him, how infinitely more to be valued is Integrity of Heart than effulgence of Intellect'. Nor can he go into the Law—for the same Principles declare against it—and he is not calculated for it. And his Father will not support any expence of consequence relative to his further education—for Law or Physic he could not take his degrees in or be called to, without a sinking of many hundred pounds.—What, Southey! was George Burnet to do??——

[1] *Paradise Lost*, iv. 83–86.

Thus even if you had persisted in your design of taking Orders, your motives would have been weak & shadowy and vile: but when you changed your ground for the Law, they were annihilated. No man dreams of getting Bread in the Law till six or eight years after his first entrance at the Temple? And how very few even then?—Before this Time your Brothers would have been put out—and the money which you must of necessity have sunk in a wicked Profession would have given your Brother an education, and provided a premium fit for the first Compting House in the world.

But I hear, that you have again changed your Ground. You do not now mean to study the Law—but to maintain yourself by your writings and on your promis'd Annuity, which, you told Mrs Morgan, would be more than 100£ a year. Could you not have done the same with *us*? I neither have or could deign to have an hundred a year—Yet by my own exertions I will struggle hard to maintain myself, and my Wife, and my Wife's Mother, and my associate. Or what if you dedicated this hundred a year to your family? Would you not be precisely as I am? Is not George Burnet accurate, when he undoubtingly ascribes your conduct to an unparticipating Propensity—to a total want of the boasted *flocci-nauci-nihili-pilificating* Sense? O Selfish, money-loving Man! what Principle have you not given up?—Tho' Death had been the consequence, I would have spit in that man's Face & called him Liar, who should have spoken that last Sentence concerning *you*, 9 months ago. For blindly did I esteem you. O God! that *such a mind* should fall in love with that low, dirty, gutter-grubbing Trull, WORLDLY PRUDENCE!!

Curse on all *Pride*! 'Tis a Harlot that buckrams herself up in Virtue only that she may fetch a higher Price—'Tis a *Rock*, where Virtue may be planted but cannot strike Root.

Last of all, perceiving that your Motives vanished at the first ray of examination, and that those accounts of your Mother & Family, which had—drawn easy tears down wrinkled Cheeks—had no effect on keener minds, your last resource has been—to calumniate me—If there be in nature a Situation perilous to Honesty, it is this—when a man has not heart to *be*, yet lusts to *seem*, virtuous. My INDOLENCE you assigned to Lovell as the Reason for your quitting Pantisocracy. Supposing it true, it might indeed be a Reason for rejecting *me* from the System? But how does this affect Pantisocracy, that you should reject *it*? And what has Burnet done, that He should not be a worthy Associate! He who leaned on you with all his head and his heart? He who gave his all for Pantisocracy & expected that Pantisocracy would be at least Bread & Cheese to Him?——But neither is the charge a true

one. My own lectures[1] I wrote for myself—eleven in number—
excepting a very few pages, which most reluctantly you eked out
for me—And such Pages! I would not have suffered them to have
stood in a Lecture of your's. To your Lectures I dedicated my
whole mind & heart—and wrote one half in *Quantity*—; but in
Quality, you must be conscious, that all the *Tug* of Brain was mine:
and that your Share was little more than Transcription. I wrote
with vast exertion of all my Intellect the parts in the Joan of Arc,[2]
and I corrected that and other Poems with greater interest, than I
should have felt for my own. Then my own Poems—and the re-
composing of my Lectures—besides a Sermon—and the correction
of some Poems for a friend—I could have written them in half the
Time and with less expence of Thought.—I write not these things
boastfully—but to excriminate myself. The Truth is—You sate
down and wrote—I used to saunter about and think what I should
write. And we ought to appreciate our comparative Industry by
the quantum of mental exertion, not the particular mode of it:
By the number of Thoughts collected, not by the number of Lines,
thro' which these Thoughts are diffused.

But I will suppose myself guilty of the Charge. How would an
honest Man have reasoned in your Case, and how acted? Thus.
'Here is a Man who has abandoned all for what I believe to be
Virtue—But he professed himself an imperfect Being when he
offered himself an associate to me. He confessed that all his
valuable Qualities were "sloth-jaundiced["]—and in his Letters is
a bitter self-accuser. This man did not deceive me—I accepted of
him in the hopes of curing him—but I half despair of it. How shall
I act? I will tell him fully & firmly, that much as I love Him, I love
Pantisocracy more: and if in a certain time I do not see this dis-
qualifying propensity subdued, I must and will reject him.' Such
would have been an honest man's reasonings—Such his conduct.
Did You act so? Did you ever mention to me 'face to face' my
indolence as a motive for your recent Conduct? Did you even
mention it in Percefield Walks? And some time after, that night
when you scattered some most heart-chilling sentiments, and in
great agitation I did ask you *solemnly*, whether you disapproved of
any thing in *my* Conduct. And you answered—Nothing. I like
you better now than at the commencement of our Friendship!—
An Answer which so startled Sara, that she affronted you into
angry Silence by exclaiming, What a Story!—George Burnet, I
believe, was present. This happened after all our Lectures—after

---

[1] See *Early Rec.* i. 20 and 25–28 for the prospectuses of Coleridge's lectures.
[2] Coleridge contributed 255 lines to Book II of Southey's *Joan of Arc*, first
published in 1796. Cf. *Poems*, i. 131.

every one of those Proofs of Indolence on which you must found
your Charge—A charge which with what Indignation did you
receive when brought against me by Lovell! Yet *then* there was
some Shew for it—I *had* been criminally indolent! But since then
I have exerted myself more than I could have supposed myself
capable. Enough.

I heard for the first Time on Thursday that you were to set off
for Lisbon on Saturday Morning. It gave me great Pain on many
accounts—but principally, that those moments which should be
sacred to your Affections, may be disturbed by this long Letter.

Southey! as far as Happiness will be conducive to your Virtue,
which alone is final Happiness, may you possess it! You have left
a large Void in my Heart—I know no man big enough to fill it.
Others I may love equally & esteem equally: and some perhaps I
may admire as much. But never do I expect to meet another man,
who will make me unite attachment for his person with reverence
for his heart and admiration of his Genius! I did not only venerate
you for your own Virtues, I prized you as the Sheet Anchor of
mine! And even [as] a Poet, my Vanity knew no keener gratifica-
tion than your Praise—But these Things are past by, like as when
an hungry man dreams, and lo! he feasteth—but he awakes, and
his Soul is empty!——

May God Almighty bless & preserve you! And may you live to
know, and feel, and acknowlege that unless we accustom ourselves
to meditate adoringly on him, the Source of all Virtue, no Virtue
can be permanent.

Be assured that G. Burnet still loves you better than he can love
any other man—and Sara would have you accept her Love &
Blessing, accept it, as the future Husband of her best-loved Sister!

Farewell!

S. T. Coleridge.

94. *To Joseph Cottle*

Pub. Early Rec. *i. 54.*

[December 1795]

My dear Friend,
   The Printer may depend on copy by to-morrow.

S. T. C.

95. *To Joseph Cottle*

Pub. Early Rec. *i. 150.*

[Late December 1795]

My dear friend,

I am fearful that you felt hurt at my not mentioning to you the proposed 'Watchman', and from my not requesting you to attend the meeting.[1] My dear friend, my reasons were these. All who met were expected to become subscribers to a fund;[2] I knew there would be enough without you, and I knew, and felt, how much money had been drawn away from you lately.

God Almighty love you!
S. T. C.

96. *To Joseph Cottle*

Address: Mr Cottle | Brunswick Square
MS. New York Public Lib. Pub. with omis. Early Rec. *i. 184.*

[1 January 1796]

My dear Cottle

I have been forced to disappoint not only you, but Dr Beddoes[3] on an affair of some importance—Last night I was induced by strong & joint solicitation to go to a Card-club, to which Mr M. belongs, after the Playing was over—to sup & spend the remainder of the night—having made a previous compact, that I should not drink. However, just on the verge of 12, I was desired to drink only one wine glass of Punch in honor of the departing Year—& after 12, one other in honor of the new year. Tho' the glasses were very small wine glasses, yet such was the effect produced during my sleep, that I awoke unwell—& in about 20 minutes after, had a relapse of bilious vomiting with pains in the biliary Ducts.—I am now just now out of my bedroom—and recovered—& with care, I doubt not, I shall be as well as ever tomorrow—be *assured*, if I do not see you then, it will be from some relapse, which I have no reason, thank Heaven! to anticipate——

Your's affectionately
S. T. Coleridge

---

[1] Late in 1795 Coleridge determined to publish a periodical, to be known as the *Watchman*. The first number appeared on 1 Mar. 1796. See J. D. Campbell, *Life*, 285–8, for the Prospectus.

[2] Chief among the subscribers was Josiah Wade. See Letter 101.

[3] Dr. Thomas Beddoes (1760–1808), father of the poet, was a Bristol physician of considerable repute.

97. *To Josiah Wade*

Address: Mr Wade | No 5 Wine Street Bristol
Transcript Coleridge family. Pub. E. L. G. i. 37.
On 9 January 1796, Coleridge set off on a tour to procure subscribers for the
Watchman, and according to Chambers, *Life*, 51, he returned to Bristol on
13 February. For Coleridge's later account of this tour see J. Shawcross,
Biographia Literaria, 2 vols., 1907, i. 114–19.

Sunday Morning [10 January 1796]
My dear Wade

We were five in number, and twenty five in quantity—The
moment I entered the Coach I stumbled on a huge projection,
which might be called a Belly with the same propriety that you
might name Mount Atlas a Molehill—Heavens! that a man should
be unconscionable enough to enter a stage-coach, who would want
elbow-room if he were walking on Salisbury Plain!!! This said
Citizen Squelch-gut was a most violent Aristocrat, but a pleasant
humorous Fellow in other respects, and remarkably well informed
in agricultural Science—so that the time passed pleasantly enough—
We arrived at Worcester half past two—I of course dined at the
Inn, where I met Mr Stevens—After dinner I christianized myself
—i.e. washed and changed—and marched in finery and cleanliness
to High Street. Mr Barr[1] received me most kindly—his Wife is
indeed a charming Matron. A more matronly and more pleasing
Woman I do not recollect to have seen. We had much and very
various conversation in which Mr Barr appeared to me a deep
thinking Man. With regard to BUSINESS, there is no chance of doing
any thing in Worcester—the Aristocrats are so numerous and the
influence of the Clergy so extensive, that Mr Barr thinks that no
Bookseller will venture to publish THE work. I dine with him to
day—and this evening I shall see Mr Sandford—To my lasting
regret Mr Osborn is out of town—I am anxious about this printing
dilemma, and should be *very* anxious, were not you and Charles
Danvers my Proxies—Proxies more valuable than their Principal.
An excellent Man is Charles Danvers—Sincere and earnest in the
investigation of Truth, exemplary in domestic duty, and an active
Philanthropist. With great generosity of character he unites a
proper circumspectness; and without coldness he is always calm.
When I regarded Southey's as a *colossal* Virtue, even then I thought
Charles Danvers the spirit of Southey made perfect. He had his
Sanctity without his Severity—his fortitude without his Frown.

Tomorrow I shall go through the Manufactory with Mr Barr—
and on Tuesday morning set off for Birmingham—Worcester is a

[1] The porcelain manufacturer of the firm of Flight and Barr.

beautiful Town—but of all the neat houses give me the Houses of Kemsay [Kempsey]—I never saw so neat a Village—At Birmingham I shall of course write you again.—I did not sleep at Mr Barr's—Mr Flight the partner having arrived from London that very evening.

Dear Wade! There are Topics, on which the Voice falters and hesitates, but the Pen flows with particular rapidity—but I will not even *write* of my obligations to you—you know I *feel* them! and they are not painful to me, because, independent of gratitude, I should have loved and esteemed you—Remember me kindly to Mrs Wade and believe me to be what you believe me

S. T. Coleridge[1]

98. *To Josiah Wade*

Pub. Early Rec. *i. 165.*

Birmingham, Jan. [18,] 1796

My dear friend,

. . . My exertions here have been incessant, for in whatever company I go, I am obliged to be the figurante of the circle. Yesterday I preached twice, and, indeed, performed the whole service, morning and afternoon. There were about fourteen hundred persons present, and my sermons, (great part extempore) were *preciously peppered with Politics.* I have here, at least, double the number of subscribers, I had expected. . . .

99. *To Josiah Wade*

Pub. Letters, *i. 151.*

Nottingham, Wednesday morning, January 27, 1796

My dear Friend,—You will perceive by this letter that I have changed my route. From Birmingham, which I quitted on Friday last (four o'clock in the morning), I proceeded to Derby, stayed there till Monday morning, and am now at Nottingham. From Nottingham I go to Sheffield; from Sheffield to Manchester; from Manchester to Liverpool; from Liverpool to London; from London to Bristol. Ah, what a weary way! My poor crazy ark has been tossed to and fro on an ocean of business, and I long for the Mount Ararat on which it is to rest. At Birmingham I was extremely

---

[1] In printing this letter Cottle added the following postscript, which does not appear in the transcript of the letter: 'P.S. I hope and trust that the young citizeness is well, and also Mrs. Wade. Give my love to the latter, and a kiss for me to little Miss Bratinella.' *Early Rec.* i. 165.

unwell; a violent cold in my head and limbs confined me for two days.[1] Business succeeded very well there; about an hundred subscribers, I think. At Derby tolerably well. Mr. Strutt[2] (the successor to Sir Richard Arkwright) tells me I may count on forty or fifty in Derby and round about.

Derby is full of curiosities, the cotton, the silk mills, Wright,[3] the painter, and Dr. Darwin,[4] the everything, except the Christian! Dr. Darwin possesses, perhaps, a greater range of knowledge than any other man in Europe, and is the most inventive of philosophical men. He thinks in a *new* train on all subjects except religion. He bantered me on the subject of religion. I heard all his arguments, and told him that it was infinitely consoling to me, to find that the arguments which so great a man adduced against the existence of a God and the evidences of revealed religion were such as had startled me at fifteen, but had become the objects of my smile at twenty. Not one new objection—not even an ingenious one. He boasted that he had never read one book in defence of *such stuff*, but he had read all the works of infidels! What should you think, Mr. Wade, of a man, who, having abused and ridiculed you, should openly declare that he had heard all that your *enemies* had to say against you, but had scorned to enquire the truth from any of your own friends? Would you think him an honest man? I am sure you would not. Yet of such are all the infidels with whom I have met. They talk of a subject infinitely important, yet are proud to confess themselves profoundly ignorant of it. Dr. Darwin would have been ashamed to have rejected Hutton's[5] theory of the earth without having minutely examined it; yet what is it to us *how* the earth was made, a thing impossible to be known, and useless if known? This system the doctor did not reject without having severely studied it; but *all at once he makes up his mind* on such important subjects, as whether we be the outcasts of a blind idiot called Nature, or the children of an all-wise and infinitely good God; whether we spend a few miserable years on this earth, and then sink into a clod of the valley, or only endure the anxieties of mortal life in order to fit us for the enjoyment of immortal happiness. These subjects are unworthy a philosopher's investigation. He deems that there is a certain *self-evidence* in infidelity, and becomes an atheist by intuition. Well did St. Paul say: 'Ye have an evil *heart* of unbelief.' I had an introductory letter from

[1] This clause, which E. H. Coleridge omitted, is drawn from *Early Rec.* i. 166.
[2] Jedediah Strutt (1726–97), cotton spinner.
[3] Joseph Wright (1734–97).
[4] Erasmus Darwin (1731–1802), physician and author of *The Botanic Garden*.
[5] James Hutton (1726–97) published his *Theory of the Earth* in 1795.

Mr. Strutt to a Mr. Fellowes[1] of Nottingham. On Monday evening
when I arrived I found there was a public dinner in honour of
Mr. Fox's birthday, and that Mr. Fellowes was present. It was a
piece of famous good luck, and I seized it, waited on Mr. Fellowes,
and was introduced to the company. On the right hand of the
president whom should I see but an old College acquaintance?
He hallooed out: '*Coleridge, by God!*' Mr. Wright, the president of
the day, was his relation—a man of immense fortune. I dined at
his house yesterday, and underwent the intolerable slavery of a
dinner of three courses. We sat down at four o'clock, and it was
six before the cloth was removed.

What lovely children Mr. Barr at Worcester has! After church,
in the evening, they sat round and sang hymns so sweetly that they
overwhelmed me. It was with great difficulty I abstained from
weeping aloud—and the infant in Mrs. Barr's arms leaned forwards,
and stretched his little arms, and stared and smiled. It seemed a
picture of Heaven, where the different orders of the blessed join
different voices in one melodious allelujah; and the baby looked
like a young spirit just that moment arrived in Heaven, startling
at the seraphic songs, and seized at once with wonder and rapture.

My kindest remembrances to Mrs. Wade, and believe me, with
gratitude and unfeigned friendship, your

S. T. Coleridge.

100. *To the Rev. John Edwards*[2]

Address: Revd J. Edwards | No. 26 | opposite St Philip's Church | Birmingham
MS. Trinity College Library, Cambridge. Pub. E. L. G. i. 39.
Stamped: Nottingham.

Friday Morning—[29 January 1796]

My dear Sir.

Among my numerous obligations to Mr Estlin I hold his intro-
ductory letter to you not one of the least—but 'let that pass,
Hal!'——I am an awkward hand at thanking people.—

Dr Darwin is an extraordinary man, and received me very
courteously—He had heard, that I was a Unitarian, and bantered
incessantly on the subject of Religion—on which subject he con-
fessed that he had never read a single page. He is an Atheist—but
has no new arguments and does not seem acquainted with many

---

[1] John Fellows (1756–1823), a silk merchant and father of the archaeologist,
Sir Charles Fellows, was a prominent member of the High Pavement Chapel,
Nottingham.

[2] The Rev. John Edwards was the Unitarian minister of the New Meeting
at Birmingham.

ingenious old ones.—When he talks on any other subject, he is a
wonderfully entertaining & instructive old man. Dr Crompton[1]
unluckily was not in Derby—I left your Letter & a prospectus—
Business succeeded tolerably there.—From Derby I proceeded to
Nottingham, where I now am—Mr Strutt of Derby, the successor
of Sir Richard Arkwright, gave me a letter to Mr Fellowes——and
I am likely to do a good deal of Business here. On Sunday I preach
a Charity Sermon—if they could have procured any one to have
gone to Birmingham to supply your place, they meant to have
dispatched a precatory letter to you—for, I find, your name is *up*,
as we used to say at Cambridge, so in lieu of a better they have
fixed on me—in one sense, I was not sorry for the application—as
the *Sacred* may eventually help off the *profane*—and my *Sermons*
spread a sort of sanctity over my *Sedition*.

Did the Advertisement appear in the Birmingham Paper? Has
Belsher received any accession to the number of Subscribers?—Be
so kind as to desire him at the conclusion of a fortnight to write
me word how many I may send—directing to me—S. T. Coleridge,
Mr Wade's, No. 5, Wine Street, Bristol.—The Work will not be
published till Tuesday, the first of March.

I never received my breeches & Shoes—did Mr Harwood send
them? Where directed?—If he have not sent them, desire him to
send them on Monday Morning by the Sheffield Coach, directed to
me at 'the Tontine, Sheffield'.—The parcel had better be delivered
on the Sunday Evening.

I have got among all the first families in Nottingham, and am
marvellously caressed—: but to tell you the truth I am quite
home-sick—aweary of this long long absence from Bristol.—I was
at the *Ball*, last night—and saw the most numerous collection of
handsome men & Women, that I ever did in one place—but alas!
the faces of Strangers are but moving Portraits—and far from
my comfortable little cottage I feel as if I were in the long damp
Gallery of some Nobleman's House, amused with the beauty or
variety of the Paintings, but shivering with cold, and melancholy
from loneliness.

Mr Fellowes (to whom I was introduced by a letter from Mr
Strutt) gave one of my Prospectuses to an Aristocrat—He glanced
his eye on the motto 'That All may know the Truth, and that the
Truth may make us free'—A *Seditious* beginning! quoth he—.
Sir! said Mr Fellowes—the motto is quoted from another Author—
Poo! quoth the Aristocrat—what Odds is it whether he wrote it
himself or quoted it from any *other seditious Dog*? Please (replied

---

[1] Dr. Peter Crompton of Derby, who later settled at Eton House, near
Liverpool.

Mr F.) to look into the 32nd [Verse of the 8th] Chapter of John, and you will find, Sir! that that *seditious Dog* was—JESUS CHRIST! —This is literally & accurately fact. The Gentleman's name was Needham.—Fellowes came grinning to me—you never saw a man grin more luxuriously.—This is one proof among thousands that Aristocrats do not read their Bible.—I leave Nottingham on Monday Morning.—I shall expect to be favored with a line from you addressed to me 'to be left at the Post-Office, Sheffield.['] ——
Present my respects to the Reverend Mr Coates—

believe me | your's sincerely
S. T. Coleridge

101. *To Josiah Wade*

Address: Mr Wade | No 5 Wine Street, Bristol
Transcript Coleridge family, Pub. with omis. Early Rec. *i. 169.*

Sheffield, Tuesday Morning [2 February 1796]
My very dear Friend

I arrived at this place late last night by the Mail from Nottingham, where I had been treated with kindness & friendship, of which I can give you but a faint idea. I preached a charity Sermon there last Sunday—I preached in *coloured Cloths*. With regard to the *gown* at Birmingham I suffered myself to be *overpersuaded*— first of all, my Sermon being of so political a tendency had I worn my blue Cloaths, it would have injured *Edwards*—they would have said, he had stuck a political Lecturer in his pulpit—secondly, the Society is of *all* sorts—Arians, Trinitarians &c—I must have shocked a multitude of prejudices—& thirdly, there is a difference between *an Inn* and a *place of Residence.* In the first your example is of little consequence; in *a single instance* only, it indeed ceases to operate as example, and would be imputed to a vicious affectation or an unaccommodating Spirit—assuredly I would not do it in a place where I intended to preach often—and even in the vestry at Birmingham when they at last persuaded me—I told them, that I was acting against my better knowledge and should possibly feel uneasy after—so this account of the matter you must consider as reasons, & palliations concluding with 'I plead guilty, my Lord'! Indeed I want firmness, I perceive, I do.—I have that within me which makes it difficult for me to say, No! repeatedly to a number of persons who seem uneasy & anxious.

I am distressed & sorely agitated about Mrs Coleridge's state of Health—I shall quit this place on Thursday—Manchester on the

Monday following, Liverpool on the twelfth day[1]—so that I fear
I shall not be able to meet you in London—

I acknowlege the receipt of the 5 Guinea Note. I did not
enquire concerning the number of Subscribers to the Loan—but of
those who seem likely to take in the work in Bristol—

I shall merely pass *thro'* London—leaving Letters for all my
Literary friends—

My next letter I will direct for you at 139 Cheapside—sending
you the advertisements &c, I would wish inserted in the mean
time. When you arrive at London[2] will you call on Mr Robinson,
intreating him to negociate a publisher—Ridgway, I think, the
best—but I will write to Robinson—

My kind remembrance to Mrs Wade. God bless her and you and
like a bad Shilling slipt in between two Guineas your

faithful & affectionate friend
S. T. Coleridge

I would write more but the Mail is going off—

102. *To the Rev. John Edwards*

Address: Revd J. Edwards | No. 26 | oppose St Philip's Church | Birmingham
MS. Trinity College Library, Cambridge. Pub. E. L. G. i. 41.
Stamped: Sheffield.

Thursday—Febr. 4th. 1795 [1796]

Your spells, my dear Sir! might have been *Prosper-like*; but they
are not like to prosper—so that both orthographically & hetero-

---

[1] Despite this plan, Coleridge did not go either to Liverpool or London,
but after a short stay in Manchester hastened home by way of Lichfield. See
Letters 104 and 126.

[2] Since Coleridge was not able to include London on his *Watchman* tour, he
left to Wade the task of obtaining subscribers there. While in London Wade
met Coleridge's friend, Robert Allen, who wrote on 25 Feb. concerning both
the *Watchman* and Wade:

My dear fellow

It is wasting time to say how sincerely interested I am in the success of
your present undertaking. I went round to all my friends yesterday dis-
tributing your Bills, and hope I have been successful in getting you a few
Purchasers. . . .

I enjoy'd enough of the company of your friend Mr. Wade to wish for
a renewal of that pleasure, whenever opportunity may occur. While I was
with him, his whole soul seem'd to be absorb'd in your affairs. I never saw
a man more warmly interested in another's welfare than he is in yours. It
was highly gratifying to me, to find that your merit was so fully discovered
by strangers. . . .

I shall not be able to write often—but whenever I can, you may depend
on hearing from

Your affectionate Friend
R. Allen.

(181)

graphically, like Ashur, I must abide in these *Breaches*. As Harwood's form possesses such lubric & fugacious qualities, I presume you must *thumb him*, before you can safely exclaim, '*You're him*!['] Great Goddess of *Grinnosity*! what infernal nonsense will not your *true** *Carthagian* squ[i]tter, rather than not *let* a *pun*!

I preached on Sunday—to very good purpose, as far as the plate went. Indeed, (altogether) my Sermon was the best composition, I have been ever guilty of. I can give you but faint ideas of the kindness & hospitality, with which I was treated at Nottingham. I arrived at Sheffield Monday night—on Tuesday Morning called on Mr Kirkby with the letter from Bristol / the only letter I had from Bristol for Sheffield. Mr Kirkby is journeying. I then called on Mr Naylor.[1] He too was absent. But finding that he was on a visit at a friend's house only four miles off, I trudged thither over hill & dale, thro' a worse Road than ever Flitertigibbet [*sic*] led poor Tom.—This friend proved to be Mr Meanly[2]—that tobacco-toothed Parson with a majestic periphery of guts, whom we met (together with Scofield) at Mr Coates's.[3] Mr Naylor received me politely—Mrs Naylor with kindliness. (N.B. She is an engaging little Girl.) Naylor declined interesting himself in my 'Watchman,' or even procuring me a Publisher—his motives were such as I could not but enter into & approve. He had formerly been joint-proprietor (with poor Montgomery)[4] of the Iris: and now that poor Montgomery is in prison, of course could not without great indelicacy promote a work which might injure the Sale of his Paper. However he recommended me to call on Mr Smith,[5] a bookseller—and gave me a letter to a Mr Shore, a man of fortune who lives at Mearsbrook, two miles from Sheffield.—I left him—it was now dark—: and into pits & out of pits, and against stones & over stones I contrived to stumble some mile & a half out of my way—/ I enquired my road at a Cottage—and on lifting up the latch beheld a tall old Hag, whose soul-gelding Ugliness would chill to eternal chastity a cantharidized Satyr——However an Angel of Light could not have been more civil—& she sent her Son to conduct me home.—Yesterday Morning I called on Mr Shore—who

---

* Homo Pun-icus. [Note by S. T. C.]

[1] The Rev. Benjamin Naylor, assistant minister at the Upper Chapel, Sheffield.

[2] The Rev. Astley Meanley, minister at the Underbank Chapel, Stannington, near Sheffield.

[3] The Rev. Radcliffe Scholefield, Unitarian minister of the Old Meeting at Birmingham. The Rev. John Coates was his assistant.

[4] James Montgomery (1771–1854), the poet, was imprisoned in Jan. 1796 for libellous statements respecting Colonel Athorpe, a magistrate.

[5] John Smith of Sheffield. Cf. Letter 115.

behaved civilly to me & promised to recommend my work as far
as he was able—& offered me 3 guineas—towards it's expences,
which (of course) I declined. (N.B. The Governors of the Charity
at Nottingham offered me three guineas for my Charity, which I
positively declined; but this morning I have received by Notting-
ham Coach a parcel (without letter or name) containing eight
pair of silk stockings, ribbed, striped, & plain—and a sealed parcel
for Mrs Coleridge, containing I know not what—it being sealed.—)
On my return from Mr Shore's, I called on Smith, the Bookseller—
I opened my business, left my prospectus, and called on him a
second time to receive his answer an hour after.—'Sir! (said he)
I have frequently heard of you; and the very motives, why I ought
to publish & promote your work, are the motives that make me
hesitate to do it—: I am afraid that from the superiority of it's
plan and your known abilities it will interfere with, & perhaps
greatly lessen, the sale of poor Montgomery's paper—which I edit
during his confinement—: without pay or profit, I assure you, but
he is my particular friend.'

I answered him—'I hope, you do me the justice to believe, that I
entirely enter into your feelings & approve of them; and if it
cannot be published without injuring Montgomery, I will apply to
no other Bookseller, but give it up altogether.—[']He thanked me
for my &c in the name of Montgomery & said, he would advise
with a few friends. This morning he returned me a final answer—
that to advertise & publickly disperse the work here would certainly
injure Montgomery; but that he thought that 20 or 30 might be
disposed of among friends—& so the matter rests.—To morrow
morning I set off for Manchester at six o'clock—it is only 48 miles
distant—and the Coach will not arrive there till 10 o'clock at night.
By heavens! a tortoise would out-gallop us! My dear Edwards!
do conjure up some dozen Ariels, & bid them hover round me
whispering pleasant day-dreams.

God bless you & S. T. Coleridge.

P.S. I have opened my letter again to tell you, I have just received
my Breeches &c from Harwood. Pray, let me hear from you—
directed to be left at the Post-office, Liverpool. I will write again
from Manchester.

P.S. You promised to order a Joan of Arc for each of the
Libraries—do not order them from a London Bookseller, because
with my first parcel I can send them from Bristol, which will be
a great saving to Cottle.

103. *To Josiah Wade*

Pub. Early Rec. *i. 172.*

Manchester, [6 February 1796]

My dear friend,

I arrived at Manchester, last night, from Sheffield, to which place I shall only send about thirty numbers. I might have succeeded there, at least, equally well with the former towns, but I should injure the sale of the Iris, the editor of which Paper (a very amiable and ingenious young man, of the name of James Montgomery) is now in prison, for a libel on a bloody-minded magistrate there. Of course, I declined publickly advertizing or disposing of the Watchman in that town.

This morning I called on Mr. —— with H's letter. Mr. —— received me as a rider, and treated me with insolence that was really amusing from its novelty. 'Over-stocked with these Articles.' 'People always setting up some new thing or other.' 'I read the Star and another Paper: what can I want with this paper, which is nothing more?' 'Well, well, I'll consider of it.' To these entertaining bon mots, I returned the following repartee,—'Good morning, Sir.' . . .

God bless you,
S. T. C.

104. *To Josiah Wade*

Pub. Early Rec. *i. 171.*

[Lichfield, *circa* 10 February 1796][1]

My dear friend,

. . . I succeeded very well here at Lichfield. Belsher, Bookseller, Birmingham; Sutton, Nottingham; Pritchard, Derby; and Thomson, Manchester, are the publishers. In every number of the Watchman, there will be printed these words, 'Published in Bristol, by the Author, S. T. Coleridge, and sold &c. &c.'

I verily believe no poor fellow's idea-pot ever bubbled up so vehemently with fears, doubts and difficulties, as mine does at present. Heaven grant it may not boil over, and put out the fire! I am almost heartless! My past life seems to me like a dream, a feverish dream! all one gloomy huddle of strange actions, and dim-discovered motives! Friendships lost by indolence, and happiness murdered by mismanaged sensibility! The present hour I seem in a quickset hedge of embarrassments! For shame! I ought not

---

[1] On hearing of Mrs. Coleridge's illness, Coleridge cut short his tour and arrived in Bristol on 13 Feb. Cf. Chambers, *Life*, 51.

to mistrust God! but indeed, to hope is far more difficult than to
fear. Bulls have horns, Lions have talons.

> The Fox, and Statesman subtile wiles ensure,[1]
> The Cit, and Polecat stink and are secure;
> Toads with their venom, Doctors with their drug,
> The Priest, and Hedgehog, in their robes are snug!
> Oh, Nature! cruel step-mother, and hard,
> To thy poor, naked, fenceless child the Bard!
> No Horns but those by luckless Hymen worn,
> And those, (alas! alas!) not Plenty's Horn!
> With naked feelings, and with aching pride,
> He bears th' unbroken blast on every side!
> Vampire Booksellers drain him to the heart,
> And Scorpion Critics cureless venom dart!
>
> S. T. C.

105. *To Joseph Cottle*

Address: Mr Cottle | Bookseller
MS. Havard College Lib. Pub. with omis. Letters *i. 154.*

Red Cliff Hill[2]   Feby 22 1796

My dear Sir

It is my business & duty to thank God for all his dispensations,
and to believe them the best possible—but indeed I think I should
have been more thankful, if he had made me a journeyman Shoe-
maker, instead of an 'Author by Trade'!——I have left my
friends, I have left plenty—I have left that ease which would have
enabled me to secure a literary immortality at the price of pleasure,
and to have given the public works conceived in moments of
inspiration, and polished with leisurely solicitude: and alas! for
what have left them—for a specious rascal who deserted me in the
hour of distress, and for a scheme of Virtue impracticable &
romantic.—So I am forced to write for bread—write the high
flights of poetic enthusiasm, when every minute I am hearing a
groan of pain from my Wife—groans, and complaints & sickness!—
The present hour, I am in a quickset hedge of embarrassments,
and whichever way I turn, a thorn runs into me—. The Future is
cloud & thick darkness—Poverty perhaps, and the thin faces of
them that want bread looking up to me!—Nor is this all—my
happiest moments for composition are broken in on by the reflec-

---

[1] *Poems*, ii. 1089.
[2] When Coleridge returned from the *Watchman* tour, he rejoined Mrs. Cole-
ridge at her mother's on Redcliffe Hill in Bristol.

tion of—I *must* make haste—I am too late—I am already months
behind! I have received my *pay* before hand!——O way-ward and
desultory Spirit of Genius! ill canst thou brook a task-master!
The tenderest touch from the hand of *Obligation* wounds thee, like
a scourge of Scorpions!—

I have been composing in the fields this morning, and came home
to write down the first rude Sheet of my Preface—when I heard
that your brother had been with a note for me from you—I have
not seen it; but I guess it's contents——[1] I am writing as fast as
I can—depend on it, you shall not be out of pocket for me! I feel
what I owe you—& independently of this I love you as a friend—
Indeed so much that I regret, seriously regret that *you* have been
my Copy-holder—— / If I have written petulantly forgive me—
God knows, I am sore all over——God bless you & believe me, that
setting gratitude aside I love and esteem you & have your interest
at heart full as much as my own—

S. T. Coleridge

106. *To Joseph Cottle*

Address: Mr Joseph Cottle
MS. Harvard College Lib. Pub. E. L. G. i. 36.

[Late February 1796]

My dear Friend

I meant to have been with you on Saturday—but Mrs Coleridge's
Spirits would not permit me, George Burnet being absent. I shall
come in tomorrow to dine with W. Coates—The poem addressed
to you[2] print with your name or with the title already prefixed, as
you like—but thus let it be concluded

> So Nature mourn'd, when sunk the First Day's Light,
> With Stars unseen before spangling her robe of night.
> Still soar, my FRIEND! those richer views among,
> Strong, rapid, fervent, flashing Fancy's beam!
> Virtue and Faith shall love your gentler song;
> But Poesy demands th' impassion'd theme.

---

[1] On the manuscript of this letter Cottle wrote: 'A Friendly Note to ask
STC to a good dinner! J. C.', and in printing the letter added an elaborate
explanation. Not wishing to appear in the light of an overbearing taskmaster,
he attributed Coleridge's outburst to a misunderstanding. It seems obvious,
however, that Cottle had importuned Coleridge on more than one occasion, thus
prompting him to 'guess' at the contents of the unread note. *Early Rec.* i. 141.

[2] *Poems*, i. 102.

Wak'd by Heaven's silent dews at Eve's mild gleam
What balmy sweets POMONA breathes around!
But if the vext air rush, a stormy stream,
Or Autumn's shrill Gust moan in plaintive sound,
With Fruits and Flowers she loads the tempest-honor'd ground.

The poem to begin thus—Unboastful Bard! whose verse &c—

Epistle V.

The production of a young Lady addressed to the author of the Poems alluded to in the preceding Epistle. She had lost her thimble —and her complaints being accidentally overheard by him, her friend, he immediately sent her four silver thimbles, to take her choice of.—[1]

the two [four] last Lines to be thus printed—

Yes, Bard polite! you but obeyed the Laws
Of Justice, when the Thimble you had sent:
What wounds, your thought-bewild'ring Muse might cause,
'Tis well, your finger-shielding Gifts prevent!

Sara
God bless you, my dear Sir, | and
S. T. Coleridge

107. *To Joseph Cottle*

Pub. Early Rec. *i. 54.*

[Early March 1796][2]

My dear Cottle,
    The Religious Musings are finished, and you shall have them on Thursday.

S. T. C.

[1] *Poems*, i. 104.
[2] Since Coleridge 'wrote and rewrote' *Religious Musings*, the last poem printed in the 1796 volume, it seems safe to assume that he could not have called the poem 'finished' before early March 1796. Likewise, Cottle's statement offers confirmation: 'A part of the poem was even written after all before in the volume was printed; the press being suspended till he had progressively completed it.' See Chambers, *Life*, 48; *Early Rec.* ii. 52; and Campbell, *Poetical Works*, 579.

108. *To the Rev. John Edwards*

Address: The reverend Mr Edwards | No. 26 | opposite St Philip's Church |
Birmingham

MS. Trinity College Library, Cambridge. Pub. E. L. G. i. 45.
Stamped: Bristol.

Saturday, March 12th, 1795 [1796]

Dear Edwards

Since I last wrote you, I have been tottering on the edge of
madness—my mind overbalanced on the e contra side of Happi-
ness / the repeated blunders of the printer, the forgetfulness &
blunders of my associate &c &c abroad, and at home Mrs Coleridge
dangerously ill, and expected hourly to miscarry. Such has been
my situation for this last fortnight— I have been obliged to take
Laudanum almost every night.[1] Blessed be God! the prospect
begins to clear up—Mrs Coleridge is considerably better, tho' she
still keeps her bed. My printing promises to go on with clockwork
regularity—and you will have Thursday's 'Watchman' on
Thursday[2]—if you will be so kind as to inform Mr Clark that to a
certainty it will arrive on Thursday Morning by the Bristol Mail.—
And always for the future *you* will have the Number the same hour
on which it is *published* in Bristol—. With regard to the carriage,
concerning which Mr Clark has written to me, would it be too
heavy a tax on his profits, if for every forty numbers he sold, he
paid sixpence towards the Carriage—thus—the Carriage to
Birmingham of all the parcels included in one wrapper will be
3*s*-6*d*—Now supposing Mr Clark sells 120 numbers in Birmingham
he should charge *me* two Shillings for carriage—if 160, eighteen
pence—if 220, one shilling & so on— ?——Now supposing he should
sell 160 numbers, this would *leave* him a profit of eleven shillings
and four pence every eight days—. If I had said sixpence in every
thirty instead of 40, surely I had not been unreasonable—.

I received last week a song of some tolerable merit entitled
'Supposition' dated 'the Museum, Birmingham[']—& subscribed
J. B****t—in the former part of the Letter he speaks of you
familiarly—This Song in my last number I promised to insert in
the next—but looking into Wednesday's Courier I read the follow-
ing note—To Correspondents—J. B.'s Song shall be inserted with

---

[1] This is the first indication that Coleridge was using drugs to relieve mental
distress. The earlier reference to opium (cf. Letter 10) points to an occasional
use for medicinal purposes, not as here, to a daily recourse to it. See also
Letters 150 and 151.

[2] The *Watchman* was published at eight-day intervals to avoid the stamp
tax. It ran for ten issues, from Tuesday, 1 Mar., to Friday, 13 May 1796.
Number III, to which Coleridge here refers, appeared on Thursday, 17 Mar.

some trifling alterations which Prudence has dictated—This alarms me—I have displaced the type (for the Song *is* set) and have been waiting anxiously to see whether or no it be [the] same or different—. If it be [the] same & should come out in the Courier before Thursday, it will injure my work—if *not* the same, and I should, which [I] fear, I must do—omit it in this next Number, I may perhaps affront a friend both by the omission and by the suspicion which caused it. For if it be the *same* song, 'tis a paultry mode & &c—[1]

My dear Edwards! I wished much to hear [from] you, how you like the Watchman, or rather what you dislike in it—And if Friendship & Genius should inspire a crotchet or two, to favor me with them.——In the course of a fortnight I get into my new house in Oxford Street, Bristol—& in the Spring, I shall make a point of compelling you 'by my so potent spells' to spend a fortnight or so with me—you might surely get your meeting served for one sunday—My Essay on Fasting[2] has given *great* offence to the *Slang-men* of Calvin's *Superstition-Shops* and even Mr Estlin does not altogether relish it, and as to *Hort*,[3] he *sighs* more than he *says*—. Concerning these Things what sayeth the Reverend Mr Coates?—God bless you—Mrs Coleridge in languid but not unaffectionate tones desires me to give her love to you.

S. T. Coleridge

109. *To Joseph Cottle*

Pub. Early Rec. *i. 157.*

[*Circa* 12 March 1796][4]

My dear Cottle,

My eye is so inflamed that I cannot stir out. It is alarmingly inflamed. In addition to this, the Debates which Burnet undertook to abridge for me, he has abridged in such a careless, slovenly manner, that I was obliged to throw them into the fire, and am now doing them myself! . . .

S. T. C.

[1] *Supposition.—a New Song*, appeared in the third number of the *Watchman*, on 17 Mar. It is signed 'J. B —. from Museum, Birmingham'. Cf. Letter 112, p. 193 n. 2.

[2] The Essay on Fasts, with the motto from Isaiah xvi. 11, 'Wherefore my bowels shall sound like an harp', appeared on Wednesday, 9 Mar. 1796, in the second number of the *Watchman*.

[3] See Coleridge's lines, *To the Rev. W. J. Hort while teaching a young lady some song-tunes on his flute, Poems*, i. 92.

[4] Although Cottle dates this letter 'April, 1796', the dissatisfaction with Burnett expressed in it suggests that it was written about the same time as

110. *To Josiah Wade*

Transcript Coleridge family. Pub. E. L. G. i. 74.

Monday Morning. [*Circa* 14 March 1796][1]

My very dear Friend—You have disabled yourself from *surprising* me. I have been lately too much in the habit of receiving from you fresh instances of zealous friendship and delicate generosity—I know how to *feel*—there is that within me which passeth all verbal professions. I decline your liberal offer for many reasons—first, Mr Cottle has ever conducted himself towards me with unbounded Kindness: and *one* unkind Act, no, nor twenty, can obliterate the grateful remembrance of it. Secondly, by indolence and frequent breach of promise I had deserved a severe reproof from him, altho' my present brain-crazing circumstances made this an improper time for it. Thirdly, this morning I have received an *apologetic* letter from him—in which he entreats me to forgive him and to attribute his last letter to an infirmity of temper which we are all subject to at times.—But while I decline one act of Kindness from you, I must solicit another—namely that you would enable me to settle the enclosed Bill. This morning I received the Letter from Mr Biggs[2]—you will see the amount to [be] about 10£.—In the course of a Month or 5 weeks I shall settle with my Booksellers when I will begin to repay you my long, long bill by instalments——

I hope to God you are better today—I will call in on you in the afternoon, if I possibly can—but am afraid, I shall not be able— Mrs Coleridge is rather better & desires her best love & compliments.

Your affectionate friend
S. T. Coleridge

111. *To Joseph Cottle*

Pub. Collection of Alfred Morrison, *1895, ii. 249.*

[*Circa* 19 March 1796][3]

My dear Cottle,—I have finished all the copy for the *Watchman* which I need supply till Monday. Of course I have this night and

Letter 108, in which there is a similar complaint. Burnett was Coleridge's assistant in the *Watchman* venture.

[1] It is clear that Cottle's '*one* unkind Act' was a demand for copy for the *Poems* (see Letter 105); the reference to Mrs. Coleridge's improved health points to March (see Letter 108); and Coleridge's plan to settle his account with the booksellers in 'the course of a Month or 5 weeks' indicates that this letter to Wade was written not long after the launching of the *Watchman*.

[2] Nathaniel Biggs, Bristol printer.

[3] The comment that 'I . . . shall continue in stirrups' in this letter closely

to-morrow for you—Mrs. Southey is with her sister—and I have the evening alone and in peace, and my spirits calm. I shall consult my poetic honour and of course your interest more by staying at home than by drinking tea with you. I should be happy to see my poems out by the conclusion of next week, and shall continue in stirrups, that is, shall not dismount my Pegasus, till Monday morning, at which time you will be able to thank God for having done with your affectionate friend always, but author evanescent.

112. *To the Rev. John Edwards*

Address: Revd Mr Edwards | No. 26 | opposite St Philip's Church | Birmingham
MS. Trinity College Library, Cambridge. Pub. E. L. G. i. 47.
Stamped: Bristol.

Sunday Morning   March 20th 1796

Dear Edwards

Believe me grateful for your communications which appear this week. Erskine's speech was excellent—the quotation happy beyond any thing I ever read.—I see by the STAR that Binns[1] is taken up by an order from the Secretary of state: if there be any particulars which have not appeared in the Star, I beseech you, be so kind as *immediately* to transmit them.

The Essay on Fasting has not promoted my work—indeed altogether I am sorry that I wrote it. What so many men wiser and better than myself think a solemn subject ought not to have been treated ludicrously. But it is one of the disadvantages attendant on my undertaking, that I am obliged to *publish* extempore as well as compose.—My last Number pleased beyond those which preceded it.—

From Birmingham I received an invocation to *Liberty*, far above mediocrity; but I do not understand the word 'Evanid': as there used.—You will see the Verses in the next Watchman.[2]—The letters from Liverpool I have received—poor Meanly! His mountain shall melt beneath the fervent heat—! I have received several *trimming* letters from anonymous correspondents—one of them written with great elegance. It begins thus—.—'Alas! alas! COLERIDGE, the digito-monstratus of Cambridge, commenced

parallels what Coleridge wrote to Edwards on 20 Mar.: 'but now I am in stirrups all day, yea, and sleep in my Spurs.' The two letters were probably written about the same time.

[1] Successive numbers of the *Watchman* carried notices about John Binns (1772–1860). Binns was imprisoned on charges of treason in 1798, and after his release in 1801, he immigrated to America.

[2] The *Invocation to Liberty* appeared in the *Watchman*, IV, 25 Mar. 1796. Line 8 contains the word Evanid.

Polit[ical] Newsmonger, Newspaper-paragraph-thief, Re-retailer of retailed Scurrility, keeper of [an] Asylum for old, poor, and decayed Jokes' &c—then follow friendly Admonitions, heart-felt Condolances, and other *exacerbating Sugar-comfits*—all that oil of Vitriol, which these Pseudo-samaritans pour into the Wounds of Misery.[1]—But I am perfectly callous except where Disapprobation tends to diminish Profit—there indeed I am all one Tremble of sensibility, Marriage having taught me the wonderful uses of that vulgar article, yclept BREAD——. My wife, my wife's Mother, & little Brother, & George Burnet—five mouths opening & shutting as I pull the string! Dear Edwards! I know you do not altogether approve of direct Petitions to Deity—but in case there *should* be any efficacy in them, out of pity to the Guts of others pray for the Brains of your Friend.—Formerly I could select a fine morning, chuse my road, and take an airing upon my Pegasus right leisurely —but now I am in stirrups all day, yea, and sleep in my Spurs. But so the World wags—and where is the use of complaining? Misery is an article, which every Market is so glutted with, that it can no where be encouraged as an Import.

Yesterday Mrs Coleridge miscarried[2]—but without danger and with little pain. From the first fortnight of Pregnancy she has been so very ill with the Fever, that she could afford no nourishment to the Thing which might have been a Newton or an Hartley—it had wasted & melted away.—I think the subject of Pregnancy the most obscure of all God's dispensations—it seems coercive against Immaterialism—it starts uneasy doubts respecting Immortality, & the pangs which the Woman suffers, seem inexplicable in the system of optimism—Other pains are only friendly admonitions that we are not acting as Nature requires—but here are pains most horrible in consequence of having obeyed Nature. Quere—How is it that Dr Priestley is not an atheist?—He asserts in three different Places, that God not only *does*, but *is*, every thing.—But if God *be* every Thing, every Thing is God—: which is all, the Atheists assert—. An eating, drinking, lustful *God*—with no *unity* of

[1] One of Coleridge's 'Pseudo-samaritans' may have been G. L. Tuckett, who in 1794 ferreted out Coleridge's army identity and revealed it to his commanding officer, family, and Cambridge friends. (See Letters 32 and 38.) Even before the first *Watchman* appeared, Tuckett had this prophecy to make to Robert Allen: 'You know how subject Coleridge is to fits of idleness. Now, I'll lay any wager, Allen, that after three or four numbers the sheets will contain nothing but Parliamentary Debates, and Coleridge will add a note at the bottom of the page: "I should think myself deficient in my duty to the Public if I did not give these *interesting* Debates at *full* length."' *Ill. London News*, 15 Apr. 1893, p. 463.

[2] Coleridge later says he was mistaken about his wife's miscarriage. See Letter 119. Hartley Coleridge was born on 19 Sept. 1796.

Consciousness——these appear to me the unavoidable Inferences from his philosophy—Has not Dr Priestly forgotten that *Incomprehensibility* is as necessary an attribute of the First Cause, as Love, or Power, or Intelligence?——

The Bishop of Llandaff has answered Payne[1]—I mean to arrange all Payne's Arguments in one Column, and Watson's Answers in another—it will do good.——Estlin's Sermon has some good Points in it; but Estlin hath not the catenating Faculty—he wants the silk thread that ought to run through the Pearl-chain of Ratiocination.—

Who & what is Bisset?[2]—and do you know who E.N. is? The Birminghamites are my best Friends.—

God bless you & believe me | gratefully & affectionately
Your's, S. T. Coleridge

P.S. In the last watchman instead of 'Now life & joy' read 'New Life & Joy th' expanding Flowret feels'[3]—did you like the Verses?——

113. *To Joseph Cottle*

Address: Mr Cottle
MS. Harvard College Lib. Pub. with omis. Early Rec. i. 56.

[Late March 1796][4]

My dear very dear Cottle

I will be at your Shop at half past six—if you will give me a dish of Tea—and between that time & eleven o'clock at night I will write out the whole of the notes & the preface—As I give you leave to turn the lock & key on me—I have this morning received so many North-country letters that imperiously demand immediate answers —and some of them—from literati—not trivial or mere matter of

---

[1] Richard Watson (1737–1816) became Bishop of Llandaff in 1782. Coleridge refers to Watson's *An Apology for the Bible; in a series of letters addressed to T. Paine, Author of the Age of Reason, Part the Second, being an investigation of true and fabulous theology.* 1796.

[2] James Bisset (1762?–1832), artist, publisher, and poet, 'secured himself an honourable place in the annals both of Birmingham and Leamington'. *D.N.B.* Bisset is probably the J. B. whom Coleridge mentions in Letter 108.

[3] See *Poems*, i. 96.

[4] Although this letter is endorsed by Cottle, Apr. 1797, it must have been written in 1796. On 30 Mar. Coleridge told Poole, 'My poems are finished' (Letter 114). The promise here to 'write out the whole of the notes & the preface' suggests a date in late March. Likewise the 'North-country letters that imperiously demand immediate answers' obviously refer to correspondence concerning the *Watchman*. See Letter 112.

Business-answers—that I cannot come before—especially as I am
engaged at three o'clock to dine with Michael Castle——You may
depend on it, I will not be a minute past my time—if I am, I permit
you to send a note to Michael Castle requesting him to send me
home to fulfil engagements, like an honest man—

S. T. Coleridge

114. *To Thomas Poole*

Address: Mr Thomas Poole | Stowey | near | Bridgewater | Somerset.   *Single*
MS. British Museum. Pub. Letters, *i. 155.*
Stamped: Bristol.

March 30th 1796

My dear Poole

For the neglect in the transmission of 'the Watchman' you must
blame George Burnet, who undertook the business.—I however
will myself see it sent this week with the preceding numbers. I am
greatly obliged to you for your communication[1]—it appears in this
number.—I am anxious to receive more from you, and likewise to
know what you *dislike* in the Watchman, and what you like; but
particularly the former.—You have not given me your opinion of
'the plot discovered'——

Since you last saw me, I have been well-nigh distracted—The
repeated & most injurious Blunders of my Printer out of doors,
and Mrs Coleridge's increasing danger at home added to the gloomy
prospect of so many mouths to open & shut, like puppets, as I
move the string—in the eating & drinking way—but why complain
to you? Misery is an article with which every market is so glutted,
that it can answer no one's purpose to export it.—Alas! alas!—
Oh! Ah! Ah! Oh!—&c. I have received many abusive letters—
post-paid, thanks to the friendly Malignants—but I am perfectly
callous to disapprobation, except where it tends to lessen profit.—
There indeed I am all one Tremble of Sensibility, Marriage having
taught me the wonderful uses of that vulgar commodity, yclept
Bread.—The Watchman succeeds so as to yield a *bread-and-
cheesish* profit.—Mrs Coleridge is recovering apace, and deeply
regrets that she was deprived of seeing [you]—We are in our new
house,[2] where there is a bed at your service whenever you will
please to delight us with a visit—Surely in spring you might force
a few days into a sojourning with me——

[1] See the *Watchman*, No. V, for Poole's comments on the slave trade. See
No. IV for Coleridge's essay on the same subject.

[2] Late in March Coleridge and his wife settled in Oxford Street, Kingsdown,
Bristol.

Dear Poole! you have borne yourself towards me most kindlily with respect to my epistolary ingratitude—but I know, that you forbad yourself to feel resentment towards me, because you had previously made my neglect ingratitude. A generous temper endures a great deal from one whom it has obliged deeply.

My poems are finished[1]—I will send you two copies the moment they are published—In the third number of the Watchman there are a few lines entitled 'The Hour when we shall meet again['] which I think you will like. I have received two or three letters from different Anonymi requesting me to give more Poetry—. One of them writes—'Sir! I detest your principles, your prose I think very so so—; but your poetry is so exquisitely beautiful, so gorgeously sublime, that I take in your Watchman solely on account of it—In Justice therefore to me & some others of my stamp I intreat you to give us more Verse & less democratic scurrility—

Your admirer not
Esteemer.'

Have you read over Dr Lardner on the Logos?[2] It is, I think, scarcely possible to read it, and not be convinced—

I find, that the Watchman comes more easy to me—so that I shall begin about my Christian Lectures——I will immediately order for you unless you immediately countermand it Count Rumford's Essays[3]—in Number V of the Watchman[4] you will see why—I have inclosed Dr Beddoes' late pamphlets—neither of them as yet published—The Doctor sent them to me.—I can get no one but the Doctor to agree with me, in my opinion that Burke's Letter to a Noble Lord[5] is as contemptible in style as in matter—it is sad stuff—

My dutiful Love to your excellent Mother, whom, believe me, I think of frequently & with a pang of Affection—God bless you—I'll try & contrive to scribble a line & a half every time the man goes with the Watchman to you.

---

[1] The following receipt is still extant:

Stamp Four Pence Received the 28th of March 1796 the sum of thirty guineas for the copy right of my Poems beginning with the Monody on Chatterton and ending with 'Religious Musings'.

S. T. Coleridge

[2] Coleridge refers to Nathaniel Lardner's *A Letter concerning the Logos*, 1759.

[3] Benjamin Thompson (1753–1814), Count von Rumford began publishing his *Essays, Political, Economical, and Philosophical* in 1796, the fourth and last volume appearing in 1802.

[4] Coleridge reviewed Count Rumford's *Essays* in the *Watchman*, No. V.

[5] Edmund Burke's *Letter to a Noble Lord*, 24 Feb. 1796, was reviewed in the first number of the *Watchman*. See *Essays on His Own Times*, i. 107–19.

N.B. The Essay on Fasting I am ashamed of—but it is [one] of my misfortunes that I am obliged to publish extempore as well as compose—

God bless you | &
S. T. Coleridge

115. *To John Smith*

Address: Mr Smith Junr | Sheffield
MS. Highgate Institution. Hitherto unpublished.

April 1st [1796]

Dear Sir

I have [been] in daily expectation of a letter from you in answer to my last—I have inclosed 25 of No. V. of the Watchman. I should be happy to hear from you whether or no you would permit me to send you on sale or return a few copies of my Conciones ad Populum, & of the Plot Discovered—as in my next Watchman I shall inclose a Bill signifying that such Pamphlets of *mine* are to be had of all the Publishers of the *Watchman*.

Your's sincerely
S. T. Coleridge

116. *To Benjamin Flower*[1]

Pub. Monthly Repository, *vol. viii, 1834, p. 653.*

April 1, 1796

Dear Sir,

I transmitted you by Mr. B——, a copy of my 'Conciones ad Populum,' and an address against the Bills.[2] I have taken the liberty of enclosing ten of each, carriage paid, which you may perhaps have an opportunity of disposing of for me—if not, *give* them away. The one is an eighteen-penny affair—the other 9*d*. I have likewise enclosed the numbers that have been hitherto published of the 'Watchman,'—some of the *Poetry* may perhaps be serviceable to you in your paper. That sonnet on the rejection of Mr. Wilberforce's Bill in your Chronicle the week before last, was written by Southey, author of 'Joan of Arc,' a year and a half ago, and sent to me per letter—how it appeared with the late signature, let the Plagiarist answer. . . . I have sent a copy of my

---

[1] Benjamin Flower (1755–1829), a Cambridge friend and editor of the *Cambridge Intelligencer*. In 1799 he was imprisoned for a libel against Bishop Watson.
[2] The outer wrapper of *The Plot Discovered*, 1795, bore the title, *A Protest against Certain Bills*. Coleridge sometimes refers to his lecture under this name.

poems; [there is a preface to be added, and a sheet of additional notes.]¹ Will you send them to Lunn and Deighton, and ask of them whether they would choose to have their names on the title-page as publishers? and would you permit me to have yours? Robinson, and I believe, Cadell, will be the London publishers. Be so kind as to send an *immediate* answer.

Please to present one of each of my pamphlets to Mr. Hall.² I wish that I could reach the perfection of *his* style. I think his style the best in the English language—if he have a rival, it is Mrs. Barbauld.

You have, of course, seen Bishop Watson's 'Apology for the Bible;' it is a complete confutation of Paine—but that was no difficult matter. The most formidable infidel is Lessing, the author of 'Emilia Galotti.' I ought to have written, *was*, for he is dead.³ His book is not yet translated, and is entitled, in German, 'Fragments of an Anonymous Author.'⁴ It unites the wit of Voltaire with the subtlety of Hume, and the profound erudition of *our* Lardner. I had some thoughts of translating it with an answer, but gave it up, lest men, whose tempers and hearts incline them to disbelief, should get hold of it; and, though the answers are satisfactory to my own mind, they may not be equally so to the minds of others.

I suppose you have heard that I am married. I was married on the 4th of October.

I rest for all my poetical credit on the *Religious Musings*.

Farewell; with high esteem, yours sincerely,

S. T. Coleridge.

117. *To Caius Gracchus*

Pub. Watchman, *No. V.*

Coleridge's letter is a reply to a communication signed Caius Gracchus and published in the *Bristol Gazette* on 24 March 1796. Coleridge reprinted Gracchus's letter and answered the attack in the *Watchman* on 2 April. The Gracchus letter reads in part: 'The "WATCHMAN" having within these few weeks attracted the Notice of the Citizens of Bristol, through the Channel of your Paper I presume to make a few Comments on the Execution of that Work. In the first Number we observe the *Debut* of this Publication upon the political Theatre made with "professions of Meekness". The Author's bias

---

¹ 'These words [in brackets] struck through.' Note in the *Monthly Repository*.
² Robert Hall (1764–1831), Baptist divine. Coleridge's praise of Hall's style rivals his enthusiastic and exaggerated eulogies of Bowles.
³ Lessing's *Emilia Galotti* was published in 1772. Lessing died in 1781.
⁴ Cf. *Zur Geschichte und Litteratur. Dritter Beitrag*, 1774, *Vierter Beitrag*,1777 ; and G. E. Lessing, *Sämtliche Schriften*, ed. by Karl Lachmann and Franz Muncker, 21 vols., 1886 f., vol. xii.

being towards principles not men, will lead him to write in the "Spirit of Meekness". The first effects of this Spirit, are, an abuse of every existing Review, implicating them with party and calumniating opinions—fully convinced of the little prejudice he possesses, he becomes Reviewer, declaring that he will execute the Trust "without Compliment or Resentment". The first specimen of his Critical Abilities is exhibited on the brilliant Pamphlet of *Mr. Burke.*—His "Spirit of Meekness" is evident when he says "when men of low and creeping faculties wish to depreciate Works of Genius, it is their fashion to sneer at them as mere Declamation ;—this mode has been practised by some low-minded Sophisters with respect to the Work in Question", and passing immediately from these characters to himself and his opinions of Mr. Burke, he becomes the herald of his own fame ; and with his "ere I begin the task of blame" adds to the many Trophies he already enjoys in his own ideas. . . .

'Inconsistency in the character of this Philosopher, seems a prominent feature. Thus in p. 19. does he say "how vile must that system be, which can reckon by anticipation among its certain enemies the Metaphysician, who employs the strength and subtlety of his Reason to investigate by what causes being acted upon, the human mind acts most worthily". The "Enquiry concerning Political Justice" by *Mr. Godwin*, except by the prejudiced, will be allowed to be a deep Metaphysical Work though abstruse, yet to those who are earnest enquirers after Truth sufficiently clear in its deductions from every argument. It is a Work, which, if many of the ideas are not new has concentered the whole mass of argument in a manner unequalled in the English Language—Therefore, do we class it among those productions who seek by their discussions to meliorate the condition of Man. In p. 73, we find a chapter entitled "Modern Patriotism" "sententious and prejudiced";—in this *Mr. Godwin's* Enquiry is considered as vicious, and improper in its tendency. The Philosopher has mentioned the Arguments of *Mr. Godwin* without giving the Reasons of, or the Deductions drawn from them by that acute writer;—should he find himself competent let him take up the Gauntlet and defend in a regular train of Argument supported by Reason, the system which he conceives to be injured by the Work.—But the Difference would be too great—the one a cool Reasoner supporting his Doctrine with propriety, and waiting for the human mind to be more enlightened to prepare it for his theory,—the other an Enthusiast supporting his Arguments by lofty Metaphors and high-toned Declamation.

'Wishing that the "WATCHMAN" in future, may be conducted with less prejudice and greater liberality,

I remain, yours &c.
Caius Gracchus.'

[2 April 1796]

You have attacked me because I ventured to disapprove of Mr. Godwin's Works: I notice your attack because it affords me an opportunity of expressing more fully my sentiments respecting those principles.—I must not however wholly pass over the former part of your letter. The sentence 'implicating them with party and calumniating opinions,' is so inaccurately worded, that I must *guess* at your meaning. In my first Essay I stated that literary works were generally reviewed by personal friends or private

enemies of the Authors. This I *know* to be fact; and does the spirit
of Meekness forbid us to tell the Truth? The passage in my Review
of Mr. Burke's late pamphlet, you have wilfully misquoted: 'with
respect to the work in question,' is an addition of your own. That
work in question I myself considered as mere declamation; and
therefore deemed it woefully inferior to the former production of the
venerable Fanatic.—In what manner I could add to my numerous
ideal trophies by quoting a beautiful passage from the pages which
I was reviewing, I am ignorant. Perhaps the spirit of vanity lurked
in the use of the word '*I*'—'ere *I* begin the task of blame.' It is
pleasant to observe with what absurd anxiety this little mono-
syllable is avoided. Sometimes 'the present Writer' appears as its
substitute: sometimes the modest Author adopts the style of
Royalty, swelling and multiplying himself into 'We'; and some-
times to escape the egotistic phrases of 'in my opinion,' or, as I
think, he utters dogmas, and positively asserts—exempli gratia:
'*It is* a work, which, &c.' You deem me inconsistent, because,
having written in praise of the Metaphysician, I afterwards appear
to condemn the Essay on political Justice. Would an eulogist of
medical men be inconsistent if he should write against vendors of
(what he deemed) poisons? Without even the formality of a 'since'
or a 'for' or a 'because,' you make an unqualified assertion, that
this Essay will be allowed by all, except the prejudiced, to be a
deep, metaphysical work, though abstruse, &c. &c. Caius Gracchus
must have been little accustomed to abstruse disquisitions, if he
deem Mr. Godwin's work abstruse:—A chief (and certainly not a
small) merit is its perspicuous and *popular* language. My chapter
on modern patriotism[1] is that which has irritated you. You con-
demn me as prejudiced—O this enlightened age! when it can be
seriously charged against an Essayist, that he is prejudiced in
favour of gratitude, conjugal fidelity, filial affection, and the
belief of God and a hereafter!!

Of smart pretty Fellows in Bristol are numbers, some
Who so modish are grown, that they think plain sense cumbersome;
And lest they should seem to be queer or ridiculous,
They affect to believe neither God nor *old Nicholas*![2]

I do consider Mr. Godwin's Principles as vicious; and his book as
a Pander to Sensuality. Once I thought otherwise—nay, even

---

[1] Cf. *Watchman*, III, 17 Mar. 1796.
[2] *Poems*, ii. 952. These lines, according to Professor Lewis Patton, 'were
borrowed, with some slight changes from the *Anthologia Hibernica*, I (Dublin,
1793), 142', and were in their 'original form the second stanza of a "Song by
a Dr. McDonnell"'. Cf. *Times Literary Supplement*, 3 Sept. 1938, p. 570.

addressed a complimentary sonnet to the Author, in the Morning Chronicle,[1] of which I confess with much moral and poetical contrition, that the lines and the subject were equally bad. I have since *studied* his work; and long before you had sent me your contemptuous challenge, had been preparing an examination of it, which will shortly appear in 'the Watchman' in a series of Essays. You deem me an *Enthusiast*—an Enthusiast, I presume, because I am not quite convinced with yourself and Mr. Godwin that mind will be omnipotent over matter, that a plough will go into the field and perform its labour without the presence of the Agriculturist, that man may be immortal in this life, and that Death is an act of the Will!!!—You conclude with wishing that the Watchman 'for the future may be conducted with less prejudice and greater liberality:'—I ought to be considered in two characters—as the Editor of the Miscellany, and as a frequent Contributor. In the latter I contribute what I believe to be truth; let him who thinks it error, contribute likewise, that where the poison is, there the antidote may be. In my former, that is, as the Editor, I leave to the Public the business of canvassing the nature of the principles, and assume to myself the power of admitting or rejecting any communications according to my best judgment of their style and ingenuity. The Miscellany is open to all *ingenious* men whatever their opinions may be, whether they be the Disciples of Filmer, of Locke, of Paley, or of Godwin. One word more of 'the spirit of meekness.' I meant by this profession to declare my intention of attacking things without expressing malignity to persons. I am young; and may occasionally write with the intemperance of a young man's zeal. Let me borrow an apology from the great and excellent Dr. Hartley, who of all men least needed it. 'I can truly say, that my free and unreserved manner of speaking, has flowed from the sincerity and earnestness of my heart.' But I will not undertake to justify all that I have said. Some things may be too hasty and censorious; or however, be unbecoming my age and station. I heartily wish that I could have observed the true medium. For want of candour is not less an offence against the Gospel of Christ, than false shame and want of courage in his Cause.

S. T. Coleridge.

---

[1] *Poems*, i. 86.

118. *To Joseph Cottle*

Address: Mr Cottle

MS. Harvard College Lib. Pub. E. L. G. i. 44.

In printing this letter Cottle omitted the clause, 'I will not give away *one* at your expence except for your interest'; he changed 'I will send you a Sheet full of Sonnets' to 'I will give away a sheet full of Sonnets'; and he took the names of C. Lamb, Wordsworth, and Dr. Parr from another letter (No. 195) and added them to the list of persons for whom Coleridge requested complimentary copies of his *Poems*. See *Early Rec.* i. 159–61.

[Early April 1796][1]

My ever dear Cottle

I will wait on you this Evening by nine o'clock, till which hour I am *on Watch*.—Your Wednesday's Invitation, of course, I accept; but I am rather sorry, that you should add *this* expence to former liberalities. Two Editions would but barely repay you——
Is it not possible to get 25 or 30 of the Poems ready by to morrow— as Parsons of paternoster row has written to me pressingly about them——'People are perpetually asking after them—*all* admire the Poetry in the Watchman.'—I shall send them with 100 of the first number—which he has written for.—I think if you were to send half a dozen Joans of Arc on sale or return, it would not be amiss——To all the places in the North we will send my Poems, my Conciones &c, & the Joans of Arc together per waggon—you shall pay the Carriage for the London, & the Birmingham parcel— *I* for the Sheffield, Derby, Nottingham, Manchester, & Liverpool.— With regard to the Poems, I mean to give away, I wish to make it a common interest——that is, I will not give away *one* at your expence except for your interest—I will send you a Sheet full of Sonnets—1 to Mrs Barbauld, one to Wakefield, one to Dr Beddoes, one to Wrangham (a reviewer in the British Critic, & a college acquaintance of mine, an admirer of me & a *pitier* of my principles) & one to George Augustus Pollen Esq. Mrs Barbauld's brother, Dr Aikin, was the person who reviewed Joan of Arc in the Analytical Review—& you *owe* that Review to Estlin's praises of the Poem at Mrs Barbauld's.—Beside these, I should only wish two copies—one for myself & one for my Brother.——The Sonnets I mean to write in the blank Leaf.[2]——

[1] The holograph of this letter bears three endorsements: May 4, corrected to Mch. 4, and April 1796. The fact that Coleridge asks whether 25 or 30 copies of his *Poems* can be ready by tomorrow indicates that this letter was written just before the volume appeared. On 11 Apr. and again on 15 Apr., Coleridge inscribed copies of the *Poems*; the volume was published on 16 Apr. See Letters 120 and 121, and T. J. Wise, *A Bibliography of Samuel Taylor Coleridge*, 1913, p. 27.

[2] There is no evidence that Coleridge inscribed sonnets in the blank leaves of his *Poems*, as he intended.

Concerning the Paper for the Watchman——I was vexed to hear your proposals of trusting it to Biggs, or Reid who if they under-took it at all, would have a profit, which—heaven knows—I cannot afford—My plan was—either that you should write to your paper-maker, saying—that you had recommended him to ME & ordering for *me* 20 or 40 Reams at a half-year's Credit—or else in your own name—in which case—I would transfer to you Reid's *weekly* account amounting to 120 three-pence half-pennys (i.e. 35 Shillings) and the Birmingham *monthly* account amounting to 560 three pences (i.e.) 7£.–14£ a Month.—

For the books I thank you—

God bless you | &
S. T. Coleridge

at your own house in the Barton, or at the Shop-house this Evening?

119. *To Thomas Poole*

Address: Mr T. Poole | Stowy
MS. *British Museum Pub. with omis*. Biog. Lit., *ed. H. N. Coleridge, 2 vols., 1847, ii. 360.*

April 11th, 1796

My dear, very dear Friend! I have sent the fifth, sixth, & *part* of the seventh number—all as yet printed. Your censures are all right—I wish, your praises were equally so. The Essay on Fasts I am ashamed of: it was conceived in the spirit, & clothed in the harsh scoffing, of an Infidel.—You wish to have one long Essay—so should I wish—; but so do not my Subscribers wish. I feel the perplexities of my undertaking increase daily—In London, & Bristol the Watchman is read for it's original matter, & the News & Debates barely tolerated: the people [at] Liverpool, Man-chester, Birmingham, &c take [it only] as a Newspaper, & regard the Essays & Poems [as int]ruders unwished for & unwelcome. In short, a Subscriber instead of regarding himself as a point in the circumference entitled to some one diverging ray, considers me as the circumference & himself as the Centre to which *all* the rays ought to converge.—To tell you the truth, I do not think the Watchman will succeed—hitherto I have scarcely sold enough to pay the expences—no wonder when I tell you, that on two hundred which Parsons in Paternoster Row sells weekly, he gains eight shillings more than I do—Nay, I am convinced, that at the end of the half year he will have cleared considerably more by his 200 than I by the proprietary-ship of the whole Work.——

Colson has been indefatigable in my service, & writes with such

Zeal for my interests and such warmth of sorrow for my sufferings, as if he wrote with fire & tears.—God bless him! I wish above all things to realize a school—I could be well content to plod from Morning to night, if only I could secure a severe competence—but to toil incessantly for uncertain bread weighs me down to Earth.—

Your Night-dream has been greatly admired—Dr Beddoes spoke in high commendation of it. Your thoughts on Election I will insert whenever Parliament is dissolved—I will insert them as the opinions of a sensible correspondent, entering my individual protest against giving a vote in any way or for any person——If you ha[d] an estate in the swamps of Essex, you could n[ot] send an aguish man there to be your manag[er—] he would be unfit for it—You could not honestly send an hale hearty man there—for the situation would to a moral certainty give him the ague. So with Parliament—I will not send a Rogue there— & I would not send an honest man—for it is 20 to one, that he will become a Rogue.—

Count Rumford's Essays you shall have by next parcel—I thank you for your kind permission with respect to Books.—I have sent down to you Elegiac stanzas by Bowles—they were given me—they are altogether unworthy Bowles. I have sent you Beddoes Essay on the merits of William Pitt[1]—you may either keep it and I will get another for myself on your account, or if you see nothing in it to library-ize it, send it me back next Thursday—or whenever you have read [it]. My own Poems you will welcome—I pin all my poetical credit on the Religious Musings.

In the poem you so much admired in the Watchman for 'Now Life & Joy[']—read 'New Life & Joy[']—Chatterton shall appear modernized.—Dr Beddoes intends, I believe, to give a course of Chemistry in a most *elementary* manner—the price, two guineas. I wish, ardently wish, that you could possibly attend them—live with me. My house is most beautifully situated—an excellent room & bed are at your service—if you had any scruple about putting me to additional expence, you should pay me 7 shillings a week—& I should gain by you.—

Mrs Coleridge is remarkably well—& sends her kind Love. I thought, she had miscarried—but it is not so—she is very big.—Pray, my dear dear Poole! do not neglect to write me every week—your critique on Joan of Arc & the Religious Musings I expect—

Your dear Mother I long to see—tell her, I love her with filial respectfulness. Excellent woman!——

Farewell.—God bless you | & | Your grateful & affectionate
S. T. Coleridge—

[1] In the *Watchman*, IX, 5 May 1796, there appeared an *Analysis* of an 'Essay on the Public Merits of Mr. Pitt, by Thomas Beddoes, M.D.'

120. *To Thomas Poole*

Transcript British Museum. Pub. with omis. Thomas Poole, *i. 202.* The transcript bears the following heading: 'Written April 11th, 1796 in the first Page of Mr S. T. Coleridge's Poems on various Subjects.'

April 11th 1796

To T. Poole

My very dear Friend! I send these poems to you with better heart than I should to most others, because I know that you will read them with affection however little you may admire them. I love to shut my eyes, and bring up before my imagination that Arbour, in which I have repeated so many of these compositions to you—. Dear Arbour! an Elysium to which I have so often passed by your Cerberus, & Tartarean tan-pits!

God bless you my dear Poole! | & your grateful & affectionate
Friend
S. T. Coleridge

121. *To Joseph Cottle*

Pub. Early Rec. *i. 144.*

Bristol, April 15, 1796

Dear Cottle.

On the blank leaf of my poems, I can most appropriately write my acknowledgments to you, for your too disinterested conduct in the purchase of them. Indeed, if ever they should acquire a name and character, it might be truly said, the world owed them to you. Had it not been for you, none perhaps of them would have been published, and some not written.

Your obliged and affectionate friend,
S. T. Coleridge.

122. *To John Thelwall*[1]

Address: John Thelwall
MS. Pierpont Morgan Lib. Pub. E. L. G. i. 50.

[Late April 1796][2]

Dear Thelwall

Pursuing the same end by the same means we ought not to be strangers to each other.—I have heard that you were offended by

---

[1] John Thelwall (1764–1834) was imprisoned in the Tower in May 1794; later tried for treason he was finally acquitted in December. Shortly after his release he published *Poems written in Close Confinement in the Tower and Newgate*, 1795.

[2] This letter, probably written shortly after Coleridge's *Poems* appeared on 16 Apr. 1796, repeats in slightly different terms Coleridge's own high estimate

the manner in which I mentioned your name in the Protest against the Bills—I have looked over the passage again, and cannot discover the objectionable sentence.[1] The words 'unsupported Malcontent' are caught up from the well-known contemptuous pages of Aristocratic Writers & turned upon them: they evidently could not be spoken in my own person, when 5 or 6 lines below, I affirm that you are the 'Voice of Tens of Thousands'—certainly therefore not 'an unsupported Malcontent.'—I meant the passage—(not as complimentary: for I detest the vile traffic of literary adulation) but as a Tribute of deserved praise.—When I recited the Protest, the passage was 'unsupported Malcontents' meaning myself & you—but I afterwards was seized with a fit of modesty & omitted myself—[2]

I beg your acceptance of my Poems[3]——you will find much to blame in them——much effeminacy of sentiment, much faulty glitter of expression. I build all my poetic pretentions on the Religious Musings—which you will read with a POET's Eye, with the same unprejudicedness, I wish, I could add, the same pleasure, with which the atheistic Poem of Lucretius. A Necessitarian, I cannot possibly disesteem a man for his religious or anti-religious Opinions—and as an *Optimist*, I feel diminished concern.——I have studied the subject deeply & widely—I cannot say, without prejudice: for when I commenced the Examination, I was an Infidel.

I am obliged to conclude abruptly—I should be happy to hear from you, & if you ever visit Bristol, have a Bed at your service—
With esteem | I am | Your's &c
S. T. Coleridge

123. *To Joseph Cottle*

Address: Mr Cottle | Bookseller
MS. Harvard College Lib. Pub. with omis. Early Rec. i. 145. Concerning the publication proposed in this letter Chambers writes: 'Something in Count Rumford's *Essays*, when he [Coleridge] read them for the *Watchman* in April,

of *Religious Musings*, as expressed in a letter to Flower of 1 Apr and in another to Poole of 11 Apr.
[1] Cf. *Essays on His Own Times*, i. 70.
[2] This explanation drew from Thelwall what must have been a fiery reply. It was designed to reassure Coleridge that no offence had been taken, but we may judge of its tenor by Coleridge's answer of 13 May.
[3] Thelwall waited until he had read Coleridge's poems before submitting a detailed criticism of them on 10 May. For his letter see *Modern Language Review*, Jan. 1930, pp. 85–90.

had struck him. It is not quite clear what it was; probably a plan for garden cities, with which Rumford had already experimented in Bavaria.' *Life*, 54.

Saturday April 30th 1796—

Dear Cottle

Since I last conversed with you on the subject, I have been thinking over again the plan I suggested to you concerning the application of Count Rumford's Plan to the City of Bristol——I have arranged in my mind the manner & matter of the Pamphlet, which would be three Sheets, & might be priced at one Shilling—the title

Considerations addressed to the
Inhabitants of Bristol
on a subject of importance
unconnected with
Politics.—

Now I have by me the History of Birmingham, & the History of Manchester——by observing the names, revenues, & expenditures of their charities I could easily alter the calculations of the Bristol address, & at a trifling expence & few variations the same Work might be sent to Manchester & Birmingham——Considerations addressed to the Inhabitants of Birmingham &c—Considerations addressed to the Inhabitants of Manchester &c. I could so order it by writing to a particular friend at both places, that the pamphlet should be thought to have been written *at* each place——as it certainly would be *for* each place.——I think therefore that 750 might be printed in all——

Now will you undertake this—either to print it & divide the profits with me—or (which indeed I should prefer) would you give me three guineas for the Copy-right[1]—?——I would give you the first sheet on Thursday next—the second on the Monday following —the third on the Thursday following—which you of course would transcribe—and to each Sheet I would annex the alterations to be made, when the Press was stopped at each 250.——

Your's
S. T. Coleridge

---

[1] Cottle says he 'presented Mr. C. with the three guineas, but forbore the publication'. *Early Rec.* i. 146 n.

124. *To Thomas Poole*

Address: Mr Thomas Poole | Stowey | Near Bridgewater | Somerset
MS. British Museum. Pub. with omis. Biog. Lit., *ed. H. N. Coleridge, 1847, ii.*
363. The manuscript contains emendations by Poole.
Stamped: Bristol.

May 5th 1796

My very dear Friend

The Heart is a little relieved, when vexation converts itself into anger. But from this privelege I am utterly precluded by my own epistolary 'sins & negligences.'—Yet in very truth thou must be an hard-hearted fellow to let me trot for four weeks together every Thursday to the Bear Inn—to receive *no* letter. I have sometimes thought that Milton did not deliver my last parcel—; but he assures me he did.——

This morning I received a truly fraternal letter from Richard Poole of Sherbourne—containing good & acceptable advice.—He deems my religious Musings too *metaphysical for common readers.* I answer—the Poem was not written for common Readers. In so miscellaneous a collection as I have presented to the Public, Singula cuique should be the Motto.—There are however instances of vicious affectation in the phraseology of that poem—'Unshudder'd, unaghasted'[1] for instance.——Good Writing is produced more effectually by rapidly glancing thro' language as it already exists, than by an hasty recourse to the *Mint* of Invention. The 'Religious Musings' has more *mind* than the Introduction of B. IId of *Joan* of *Arc,* but it's versification is not equally rich: it has more passages of sublimity, but it has not that diffused air of severe Dignity which characterizes *my Epic Slice.* Have I estimated my own performances rightly?——

My house is at present a house of Mourning. My Wife's Mother has *lived dying* these last six weeks, and she is not yet dead—& the Husband of my Wife's Sister, Robert Lovell, (author of the two Sonnets in No. 5) died on Tuesday Morning of a putrid fever, & has left an Infant & a Widow.[2] All Monday Night I sate up *with*

---

[1] The passage in *Religious Musings* containing these words was later revised. Cf. *Poems,* i. 112 n.

[2] Lovell's last letter to his wife is preserved in the Huntington Library.

South'ton   Saturday April 23: 96

Dear Love

As I do not find that I get better & as it is very uncomfortable to be ill in an Inn—I have taken my Place in the Bristol Coach for Monday morning —sets out at Six. & you may expect to see me same Evening about eight— adieu, am very weak. hope you are all well.

truly yours
Lovell

her—she was removed to the Kitchen, the furthest room in the House from her Husband's Bed-chamber—there being a Court-yard between the two.—It was, you know, a very windy night—but his loud, deep, unintermitted groans mingled audibly with the wind, & whenever the wind dropt, they were very horrible to hear, & drove my poor young Sister-in law frantic. I prayed by her with fervor & very frequently—it soothed her with almost miraculous consolation—At one o'clock the Clock in the Kitchen went down—'Ah!' (said She) 'it is stopt—Now it clicked & told the hour & did all it's Maker willed it to do—and now it is stopped.'—(A long pause) 'O God! O God! my poor Love will stop'—.—Here her agonies became wild—I hastened out, knocked up a Chairman, & had her conveyed to my House——He died ten o'clock that morning——She is quite calm, & perpetually questions me concerning the Resurrection.—Her Husband when I first knew him was an Atheist—he became a Deist—& a month before he fell ill publickly professed himself a convert to Christianity.[1] I look back on my conversations with him with great & solacing Pleasure.—She will, I believe, be protected by her father-in-law, who is a wealthy Quaker—

With regard to my own affairs they are as bad, as the most Trinitarian Anathemizer, or rampant Philo-despot could wish in the moment of cursing—After No. 12, I shall cease to cry the state of the political atmosphere—It is not pleasant, Thomas Poole! to have worked 14 weeks for nothing—*for nothing*—nay—to have given the Public in addition to that toil five & 40 pounds!—When I began the Watchman, I had forty pounds worth of paper *given me*—yet *with this* I shall not have received a farthing at the end of the Quarter of the Year—To be sure, I have been somewhat fleeced & overreached by my London Publisher——In short, my tradesmen's Bill[s] for the Watchman, including what Paper I have bought since the seventh number, the Printing, &c—amount to exactly five pounds more than the whole amount of my receipts——Meantime Mrs Coleridge asks about baby-linen & anticipates the funeral expences of her poor Mother——

---

[1] While these volumes were in the press, the following fragment to an unknown correspondent came to light and is now in the editor's possession:

May 3rd 1796 Oxford Street, Bristol

. . . agonies are heart-rending:—she is removed to my House—

About a month ago R. Lovell openly professed himself a convert to Christianity.——

Southey has spent the last half year in Spain with his uncle—he is expected home weekly.—

God bless you, my dear Sir! & S. T. Coleridge

O Watch Man! thou hast watched in vain—said the Prophet Ezekiel, when, I suppose, he was taking a prophetic glimpse of my sorrow-sallowed Cheeks.—

My Plans are reduced to two—. The first impracticable—the second not likely to succeed—

Plan the first is as follows.

Plan 1st.—I am studying German, & in about six weeks shall be able to read that language with tolerable fluency. Now I have some thoughts of making a proposal to Robinson, the great London Bookseller, of translating all the works [of] Schiller, which would make a portly Quarto, on the conditions that he should pay my Journey & wife's to & from Jena, a cheap German University where Schiller resides—& allow me two guineas each Quarto Sheet —which would maintain me—. If I could realize this scheme, I should there study Chemistry & Anatomy, [and] bring over with me all the works of Semler & Michaelis, the German Theologians, & of Kant, the great german Metaphysician. On my return I would commence a School for 8 young men at 100 guineas each— proposing to *perfect* them in the following studies in order as follows——

I. Man as Animal: including the complete knowlege of Anatomy, Chemistry, Mechanics & Optics.—

2. Man as an *Intellectual* Being: including the ancient Metaphysics, the systems of Locke & Hartley,—of the Scotch Philosophers—& the new Kantian S[ystem—]

3. Man as a Religious Being: including an historic summary of all Religions & the arguments for and against Natural & Revealed Religion. Then proceeding from the individual to the aggregate of Individuals & disregarding all chronology except that of mind I should perfect them 1. in the History of Savage Tribes. 2. of semi-barbarous nations. 3 of nations emerging from semi-barbarism. 4. of civilized states. 5 of luxurious states. 6 of revolutionary states.—7.—of Colonies.—During these studies I should intermix the knowlege of languages and instruct my scholars in Belles Lettres & the principles of composition.—Now seriously—do you think that one of my Scholars thus perfected would make a better Senator than perhaps any one Member in either of our Houses?——

Bright Bubbles of the aye-ebullient brain!

Gracious Heaven! that a scheme so big with advantage to this Kingdom, therefore to Europe, therefore to the World should be demolishable by one monosyllable from a Bookseller's Mouth! No!——Genii &c—

My second Plan is to become a Dissenting Parson & abjure Politics & carnal literature. Preaching for Hire is not right; because it must prove a strong temptation to continue to profess what I had ceased to believe, *if ever* maturer Judgment with wider & deeper reading should lessen or destroy my faith in Christianity. But tho' not right in itself, it may become right by the greater wrongness of the only Alternative—the remaining in neediness & Uncertainty. That in the one case I should [be e]xposed to temptation, is a mere *contingency*: that under necessitous circ[umstances] I am exposed to great & frequent temptatio[ns is] a melancholy certainty.—

Write, my dear Poole! or I will crib all the rampant Billingsgate of Burke to abuse you—

Count Rumford is being reprinted——

God bless you &

S. T. Coleridge—

P.S.—I open the parcel which was to have gone for you—& which Milton promised to call for at Mr Cottle's—but did not—A rascal! So I must send this Letter by post—& defer the Watchmen till next Thursday.—Pray, write me by Milton—pray do—May 6th.

125. *To Thomas Poole*

Address: [Mr] T. Poole.
MS. British Museum. Pub. with omis. Letters, *i. 158.*

In this letter Coleridge acknowledges a communication from Poole concerning a plan for financial assistance. Seven or eight friends pledged themselves to contribute 5 guineas annually 'as a trifling mark of their esteem, gratitude, and admiration'. John Cruikshank was chosen treasurer but the office later fell to the Rev. J. P. Estlin. Payments of £35 or £40 were made in 1796 and 1797, but were discontinued when Coleridge received an annuity from the Wedgwoods in 1798. See *Thomas Poole*, i. 142–4, and Letter 191.

[13 May 1796]

Poole! the Spirit, who counts the throbbings of the solitary heart,[1] knows that what my feelings ought to be, such they are. If it were in my power to give you any thing which I have not already given, I should be oppressed by the letter now before me— but no! I feel myself rich in being poor; and because I have nothing to bestow, I know how much I have bestowed. Perhaps I shall not

[1] Cf. lines 48–50 of the poem, *To the Rev. George Coleridge*, dated 26 May 1797, *Poems*, i. 175:

> He who counts alone
> The beatings of the solitary heart,
> That Being knows . . .

make myself intelligible—but the *strong, and unmixed Affection,* which I bear to you, seems to exclude all Emotions of *Gratitude,* and renders even the principle of *Esteem* latent and inert: it's Presence is not perceptible, tho' it's absence could not be endured.—

Concerning the scheme itself I am undetermined—not that I am ashamed to receive—God forbid! I will make every possible Exertion: my Industry shall be at least commensurate with my Learning & Talents: if these do not procure me and mine the necessary Comforts of Life, I can receive as I would bestow, & in either case, receiving or bestowing, be *equally* grateful to my Almighty Benefactor. I am undetermined therefore, not because I receive with pain & reluctance, but because I suspect that you attribute to others your own enthusiasm of Benevolence, as if the Sun should say—With how rich a purple those opposite Windows are burning! But with God's permission I shall *talk* with you on this Subject—. By the last page of No. X you will perceive that I have this day dropped The Watchman.[1] On Monday Morning I will go per Caravan to Bridgewater where, if you have a horse of tolerable meekness unemployed, you will let him meet me.—

I should blame you for the exaggerated terms in which you have spoken of me in the proposal—did I not perceive the motive.—You wished to make it appear an *offering* not a *favor*—& in excess of delicacy have, I fear, fallen into some grossness of flattery.—

God bless you—my dear, very dear Friend.—The Widow is calm—& amused with her beautiful Infant. She is likewise become religious—indeed we are all more so than we were!—God be ever praised for all things.—

Mrs Coleridge loves you—& says, she would fall on your Neck & kiss you.—. . .[2]

126. *To John Fellows*

Address: J. Fellowes Esq. | Nottingham
MS. Cornell University Lib. Hitherto unpublished.

May 13th 1796

My dear Sir

A few days ago I received thro' George Dyer a small note which you were so kind as to address to me while you were in London—I

---

[1] The last number of the *Watchman* appeared on 13 May 1796. 'The reason', Coleridge notified his readers, 'is short and satisfactory—the Work does not pay its expenses.'

[2] The conclusion and signature, about one-third of a page, are missing from the manuscript. In printing this letter E. H. Coleridge altered the last sentence above and added a conclusion and signature.

have never ceased to remember you & with emotions of gratitude—
but immediately on my arrival at Sheffield I received a letter from
Mrs Coleridge with so alarming an account of her health that after
a short sojourn at Manchester I hastened homewards—& from that
moment to the present hour have been incessantly struggling with
such a series of domestic Sorrows & external disappointments, as
have depressed me beneath the *writing-point* in the thermometer
of mind.—I have now dropped the Watchman—and could not
drop it without expressing the warmest feelings of Gratitude to
you, Sir! & my other friends at Nottingham for the unexpected &
friendly hospitality with which you received the *itinerant Patriot*,
or the Zeal with which you must have promoted my interests since
that time—had the Miscellany succeeded in other towns in any
thing like the same proportion, I should have made my fortune—
I did not sell more even in Bristol.—

Looking down at my Legs accidentally, I cast my eye on a
memorandum that I have to thank you for a very handsome
present which I received at Sheffield—Mrs Fellowes is well, I trust
—& your little ones—you will present my grateful remembrances
to her

& believe me, | dear Sir, | Your obliged & grateful &c
S. T. Coleridge

127. *To John Thelwall*

Address: John Thelwall | Beaufort Buildings | Strand | London
MS. Pierpont Morgan Lib. Pub. with omis. Letters, *i. 159.*
Postmark: 14 May 1796.   *Stamped*: Bristol.

May 13th 1796

My dear Thelwall! you have given me 'the affection of a Brother':
and I repay you *in kind*. Your letters demand my friendship &
deserve my esteem: the Zeal, with which you have attacked my
supposed *Delusions*, proves that you are deeply interested for *me*,
and interested even to agitation for what you believe to be TRUTH.

You deem, that I have treated 'systems & opinions with the
furious prejudices of the conventicle, & the illiberal dogmatism of
the Cynic—'—that I have layed 'about me on this side & on that
with the sledge-hammer of abuse.' I have, you think, imitated the
'old sect in politics & morals' in their 'outrageous violence,' and
have 'sunk into the clownish fier[c]eness of intolerant prejudice.'—
I have 'branded' the presumptuous children of Scepticism 'with
vile epithets & hunted them down with abuse.'—'*These be hard
words, Citizen! & I will be bold to say, they are not to be justified*'

by the unfortunate page which has occasioned them. The only passage in it which appears *offensive* (I am not now enquiring concerning the *truth* or *falsehood* of this or the remaining passages) is the following. 'You have studied Mr G.'s Essay on politic. Just.—; but to think fil. aff. folly, grat. a crime, marr. injust. and the promis. interc. of the sexes right & wise, may class you among the despisers of vulgar prejudices, but cannot increase the probability that you are a *patriot*. But you act up to your principles—So much the worse. Your principles are villainous ones. I would not entrust my Wife or Sister to you—think you, I would entrust my Country ?'—[1]

My dear Thelwall! how are these opinions connected with the *Conventicle* more than with the Stoa, the Lyceum, or the grove of Academus? I do not perceive that to attack *adultery* is more characteristic of *Christian* Prejudices, than of the prejudices of the disciples of Aristotle, Zeno, or Socrates.—In truth, the offensive sentence 'your principles are villainous ones[']—was suggested by the *Peripatetic* Sage—who divides bad men into two Classes—the first he calls 'wet or intemperate Sinners'—men who are hurried into vice by their appetites but *acknowlege* their actions to be vicious—these are reclaimable. The second class he names—*dry* villains—Men who are not only vicious, but who (the steams from the polluted heart rising up & gathering round the head) have brought themselves & others to believe that *Vice* is *Virtue*.—We mean these men when we say—Men of bad *principles*.——*Guilt* is out of the Question—I am a Necessarian, and of course deny the possibility of it.——However a letter is not the place for reasoning —in some form or other, & by some channel or other, I shall publish my Critique on the New Philosophy—and I trust, shall demean myself not *ungently*, and disappoint your auguries.——One question only——Why should you not have intercourse with *the Wife* of your friend?—From the principles in your *heart*——Verily, Thelwall! I believe you—on your *heart* I should rest for my safety! But why not, I repeat, seduce my Wife from me?——Because it would be *criminal?* What more do we mean by *Marriage* than that state in which it would be criminal to tempt to, or permit, an act of inconstancy? But if criminal *at one moment*, criminal always: in other words, *Marriage is indissoluble*. For surely, if it would be wrong in *you* to solicit my *Wife*, it must be wrong in my *Wife* to solicit *you*—and if neither make advances, Marriage will be preserved indissoluble —You do not suppose, I attribute any magic to ceremonies—or think that the *Priest* married me ——Great indeed are the moral uses of Marriage—It is *Variety* that *cantharidizes us*. Marriage, that confines the appetites to one object,

[1] Cf. *Watchman*, III, 'Modern Patriotism'.

gradually causes them to be swallowed up in *affection*. Observe the face of an whoremonger or intriguer, and that of a married man—it would furnish physiognomic demonstration.——The real source of inconstancy, depravity, & prostitution, is *Property*, which mixes with & poisons every thing good—& is beyond doubt the Origin of all Evil.——'But you cannot be a Patriot unless you are a Christian.'—Yes! Thelwall! the disciples of Lord Shaftesbury & Ro[u]sseau, as well as of Jesus——but the man who suffers not his hopes to wander beyond the objects of sense will, in general, be *sensual*—& I again assert, that a Sensualist is not likely to be a Patriot.—Have I tried these opinions by the double test of argument & example—? *I think* so—the first would be too large a field—the second some following sentences of your letter force me to—— GERALD,[1] you insinuate is an *Atheist*—was he so, when he offered those solemn Prayers to God Almighty at the Scotch Convention?— And was this *Sincerity?*—. But Dr Darwin & (I suppose from his actions) Gerald think sincerity a folly & therefore vicious——Your Atheistic Brethren square their moral systems exactly according to their inclinations—Gerald & Dr Darwin are polite & good natured men & willing to arrive at good by attainable roads—they deem Insincerity a necessary virtue in the present imperfect state of our Nature. Godwin, whose very heart is cankered by the love of singularity & who feels no disinclination to wound by abrupt harshness, pleads for absolute Sincerity, because such a system gives him a frequent opportunity of indulging his misanthropy.— Poor Williams, the Welch Bard[2]—(a very meek man) brought the tear into my Eye by a simple narration of the manner in which Godwin insulted him, under the pretence of Reproof—& Thomas Walker[3] of Manchester told me, that his Indignation & Contempt were never more powerfully excited than by an unfeeling and insolent Speech of the said Godwin to the poor Welch Bard—*Scott* told me some shocking stories of Godwin—of his gross adulation to King, the money-lender—of his endeavors to seduce Mrs Reevely [Reveley]—&c—His base, & anonymous attack on you is enough for me—At that time I had prepared a letter to him, which I was about to have sent to the Morning Chronicle—& I convinced Dr Beddoes by passages from the Tribune of the calumnious nature

---

[1] Joseph Gerrald (1763–96) was found guilty of sedition in Mar. 1794 and sentenced to fourteen years' transportation. He was shipped to Botany Bay in May 1795 and died there of consumption in Mar. 1796. Coleridge had written sympathetically of him in *Conciones ad Populum*. See *Essays on His Own Times*, i. 18.

[2] Edward Williams (1746–1826), known as Iolo Morgannwg.

[3] Thomas Walker (1749–1817), founder of the Manchester Constitutional Society, was prosecuted for treasonable conspiracy in 1792, but was acquitted.

of the attack —I was once and only once in Company with God-
win——He appeared to me to possess neither the strength of
intellect that discovers truth, or the powers of imagination that
decorate falsehood—he talked futile sophisms in jejune language—
I like Holcroft a thousand times better, & think him a man of much
greater ability. Fierce, hot, petulant, the very High priest of
Atheism, he *hates* God 'with all his heart, with all his mind, with
all his soul, & with all his strength'. [']Every Man not an atheist
is only not a fool'——Dr Priestly ?—'there is a Petitesse in his
mind.—Hartley—Psha!—*Godwin*, Sir! is a thousand times a better
Metaphysician[']——But all this intolerance is founded in Benevo-
lence——: (I had almost forgotten that horrible story about his
Son.)¹—To return [to] GERALD——I have been informed by a
West-Indian (a Republican) that *to his knowlege* Gerald left a *Wife*
there to starve——and I well know that he was prone to intoxica-
tion, & an *Whore*monger. I saw myself a letter from Gerald to one
of his FRIENDS, couched in terms of the most abhorred Obscenity,
& advising a marriage with an old woman on account of her
money—Alas! alas! Thelwall—I almost wept—& poor Lovell
(who read it with me) was so much agitated that he left the
room——That story of his writing in favor of the slave-trade was
never *fully* cleared up——I mention these circumstances because
I conceive it possible to an exertion of ingenuity to deduce *their*
criminality even from Godwin's System of Morals.——

On the subject of using Sugar &c, I will write you a long &
serious letter—this grieves me more than your a[theism.] I hope,
I shall be able by severe & unadorned reasoning to convince you,
you are wrong.——Your remarks on my Poems are, I think, just
in general—there is a rage, & affectation of double Epithets—
'Unshuddered, unaghasted' is indeed truely ridiculous—But why
so violent against *metaphysics* in poetry? Is not Akenside's a
metaphysical poem? Perhaps, you do not like Akenside—well—
but I do—& so do a great many others—Why pass an act of
Uniformity against Poets?—I received a letter from a very sensible
friend abusing Love-verses—another blaming the introduction of
Politics, 'as wider from true poetry than the Equator from the
Poles.'—*Some for each*—is my Motto.—That Poetry pleases which
interests—*my* religious poetry interests the *religious*, who read it
with rapture—why? because it awakes in them all the associations
connected with a love of future existence &c—. A very dear friend
of mine, who is in my opinion the best poet of the age² (I will send

---

¹ Holcroft's sixteen-year-old son committed suicide after robbing his father
of £40.

² This refers to Wordsworth, whom Coleridge had met in the autumn of

you his Poem when published)[1] thinks that the lines from 364 to 375 & from 403 to 428 the best in the Volume—indeed worth all the rest—And this man is a Republican & at least a *Semi*-atheist.— Why do you object to *shadowy of truth?*[2] it is, I acknowlege, a Grecism—but, I think, an elegant one.—

Your remarks on the Della-crusca place of Emphasis are just in part—where we wish to point out the *thing*, & the *quality* is mentioned merely as a decoration, this mode of emphasis is indeed absurd—therefore I very patiently give up to critical vengeance *high* tree, *sore* wounds, & *rough* rock——but when you wish to dwell chiefly on the *quality* rather than the *thing*, then this mode is proper—& indeed is used in common conversation—who says— Good *Man*—? therefore *big* soul, *cold* earth, *dark* womb, & *flamy* child are [quite] right——and introduce a variety into the versification—[which is] an advantage, where you can attain it without any sacrifice of sense.——As to Harmony, it is all *association*— Milton *is harmonious* to me, & I absolutely nauseate Darwin's Poem.

Your's affectionately—S. T. Cole[ridge.]

Write me when you think you can come to Bristol—perhaps I may be able to fit up two Bed-rooms in my house—I will not give you your *board*—but you shall have it at *prime-cost*——Give my kind Love to Mrs Thelwall & kiss the dear Babies for me.

1795. On 24 Oct. 1795 Wordsworth told W. Mathews: 'Coleridge was at Bristol part of the time I was there. I saw but little of him. I wished indeed to have seen more—his talent appears to me very great.' *Letters of William and Dorothy Wordsworth: the Later Years*, ed. by E. de Selincourt, 3 vols., 1939, iii. 1333. The two men probably did not meet in 1796; but this letter shows they were in correspondence, either directly or through Cottle. Wordsworth by this time had not only read Coleridge's *Poems* but had communicated his impressions of *Religious Musings*.

[1] This poem was *Guilt and Sorrow; or Incidents upon Salisbury Plain*, the manuscript of which Wordsworth on 7 Jan. 1796 was planning to send to Cottle. By early March the poem was transmitted to Cottle, who gave it to Coleridge; and on 25 Mar. Azariah Pinney reported to Wordsworth that Coleridge has read the poem 'with considerable attention . . . [and] has interleaved it with white paper to mark down whatever may strike him as worthy your notice'. He has recommended publication and has formed a plan to distribute it through 'the People that sell the Watchman'. Coleridge must have kept the manuscript for some time, for it was not until late May that it was transmitted to Charles Lamb for delivery to Wordsworth. *Guilt and Sorrow* was not published until 1842, though a portion of it, *The Female Vagrant*, appeared in *Lyrical Ballads*, 1798. Cf. *Early Letters of William and Dorothy Wordsworth*, ed. E. de Selincourt, 1935, p. 149; B. Evans and Hester Pinney, 'Racedown and the Wordsworths', *Rev. of Eng. Studies*, Jan. 1932, pp. 12–13; and *Letters of Charles Lamb*, ed. E. V. Lucas, 3 vols., 1935, i. 8, 9.

[2] Cf. *Religious Musings*, line 396.

128. *To Joseph Cottle*

MS. Editor. Hitherto unpublished. **This fragment, the recto and verso of one sheet of Coleridge's letter, is all that remains of the holograph.**

[Nether Stowey.]   Tuesday Evening——[17 May 1796]

. . . & likewise Priestley's little Pamphlet on the Causes of Infidelity—all to his account.—He bids me tell you, that he settles with you half-yearly—that being the time when he attends the Bristol Fairs.—

By the Sherbourne Newsman (who leaves Brown's Shop about 9 on Monday Mornings) you will send a Copy of my Poems—directed to—Mr Richard Poole,[1] Sherbourne——*bound* as before, & put to Mr *Thomas Poole's* Account— . . .

I sincerely rejoice at Southey's safe arrival[2]—May the literary Republic rejoice!——The Sonnet on the next page was written by a friend of mine—

Please to send the inclosed letter immediately.

Your grateful & affectionate
S. T. Coleridge

129. *To Thomas Poole*

Address: Mr Thomas Poole
MS. British Museum. Pub. Letters, i. 164.

May 29th[3] [28] 1796

My dear Poole

This said Caravan does not leave Bridgewater till Nine——In the market-place stands the Hustings—I mounted it & pacing the boards mused on Bribery, False Swearing, and other *foibles* of Election Times.—I have wandered too by the River Parrot, which looks as filthy as if all the Parrots in the House of Commons had been washing their Consciences therein. Dear Gutter of Stowy! were I transported to Italian Plains, and lay by the side of a streamlet that murmured thro' an Orange-Grove, I would think of thee, dear Gutter of Stowy! and wish that I were poring on thee!——

So much by way of Rant.—I have eat three Eggs, swallowed

---

[1] Richard Poole had already read Coleridge's poems while visiting his brother Thomas at Nether Stowey. See Letter 124.

[2] Southey arrived in England on 14 May 1796 after a six months' residence in Portugal.

[3] Despite Coleridge's date, Letter 130 indicates that this letter was written on Saturday, 28 May.

sundries of Tea & Bread & Butter purely for the purpose of amusing myself—I have seen the Horses fed.—When at Cross, where I shall dine, I shall think of your happy dinner celebrated under the Auspices of Humble Independence supported by Brotherly Love!—

I am writing, you understand! for no wor[l]dly purpose but that of avoiding anxious Thoughts. Apropos of Honey Pie——Caligula or Elogabalus [*sic*] (I forget which) had a dish of Nightingales' tongues served up——What think you of the Stings of Bees?——

God bless you!——My filial love to your Mother & fraternity to your Sister—tell Ellen Cruikshanks that in my next parcel to you I will send my Haleswood Poem to her—Heaven protect her, & you, & Sara, & your Mother,

and (like a bad Shilling passed off between a handful of Guineas)
                    Your affectionate | Friend & Brother,
                                            S. T. Coleridge

P.S. Don't forget to send by Milton my old Clothes & Linen *that once was clean, & cetera*— | a pretty periphrasis that——

130. *To George Dyer*

Address: George Dyer | No. 10 | Clifford's Inn | Fleet Street | London
MS. Harvard College Lib. Pub. Chambers, Life, *335.*
Postmark: 3⟨1⟩ May 1796.   *Stamped*: Bristol.

                                    Sunday Evening—[29 May 1796]
My dear Sir

Last week I was on an affair of business at Stowy, about 50 miles from Bristol——I returned on Saturday Evening—& found that unfortunately Mrs Coleridge had sent the two letters with some other things in a parcel to me at Stowy, the morning before: which parcel arrived at Stowy about the time that I arrived at Bristol——I shall receive it on Thursday Morning—& as soon as I receive it, will write you.

How deeply I am affected by your kindness, you will conceive better than I can express.—You have already sent a sum amply sufficient to extricate me from my difficulties, & to provide for my expences till such time as my literary Industry will, I trust, find employment——

Deeply affected and almost agitated with that Gratitude, which if Philosophy discourage, Nature will more wisely compel, I remain

                            Your's sincerely & | affectionately
                                            S. T. Coleridge

131. *To John Fellows*

Address: John Fellows, Esq. | Nottingham
MS. Cornell University Lib. Hitherto unpublished.
Postmark: 1 June 1796.   *Stamped*: Bristol.

Tuesday May 31st 1796

My dear Sir

The Ladies, who have honored me by so delicate an act of liberality, will accept my sincerest acknowlegements. The Poems will be sent forthwith, directed to you & to be left at Mr Sutton's.[1]— The situation of a Tutor in a Gentleman's family I should embrace with avidity—but is it intended, that I should reside in the family? And if so, would not the circumstance of *my being married* present an impediment?——If this difficulty could be disposed of, I shall sing, 'Io Triumphe!'—

I expect your Election papers with some degree of Eagerness: and highly applaud your *truly moral* method of proceeding. I deeply regret, that Mr Hobhouse[2] had not pursued the same line of Conduct——but indeed the Bristolians rank very low in the orders of intellect; and form, I suspect, that subtle link, which (in the great chain of things) connects Man with the Brute Creation.— With the Poems I will send you all our Election Papers—. Mr Hobhouse spent about two thousand pound in Beer, & Cockades—that is—in making the Mob filthy & fine—& then found that *it would not do.*—Mr H. is a man of great abilities & uncommon Probity—— He is the author of some ingenious controversial Tracts in favor of the Unitarian Doctrines.—

The reports concerning the brutality of a certain Heir apparent towards his amiable wife *distress & agitate us as men;*[3] but open a fair prospect to the Friends of Liberty.—They who know how wonderfully the private Virtues of our present Sovereign have influenced the minds of people in general in favor of the most detestable measures, will conjecture what the effect may be of the contrary character of his Successor——.

Believe, my dear Sir! that I feel deeply your kind exertions in

---

[1] Included with this letter is a list of persons who subscribed to Coleridge's *Poems* at a guinea each, to compensate the author 'for his disappointment in The Watchman'.

[2] Benjamin Hobhouse (1757–1831) stood for Bristol in the general election of 1796 but was defeated.

[3] On 30 Apr. 1796 George, Prince of Wales, wrote to Princess Caroline, renouncing further cohabitation. See Coleridge's *On a Late Connubial Rupture in High Life, Poems*, i. 152, and Letter 134.

my behalf—Give my respectful remembrances to Mrs F— and to
Dr Smith, Mr Williams, Mr Hancock, &c—& believe me

> Your obliged & grateful
> S. T. Coleridge

132. *To the Committee of the Literary Fund*

MS. The Royal Literary Fund. Hitherto unpublished. On 13 May 1796 James
Martin wrote to the Committee of the Literary Fund as follows: 'Having been
informed, that Mr. Coleridge, a man of genius and learning, is in extreme
difficulties, proceeding from a sick family, his wife being ready to lie in, and
his mother in law, whom he has supported, being, as is supposed, on her
death-bed, I undertake to lay his case before you. Mr. Coleridge is of that
description of persons, who fall within the notice of your benevolent Institu-
tion. He is a man of undoubted talents, though his works have been unpro-
ductive, and, though he will in future be able to support himself by his own
industry, he is at present quite unprovided for, being of no profession. The
assistance, therefore, of the Literary Fund will be very acceptable to him. . . .
Mr. Coleridge is author of a volume of poems, lately published, and of some
prose writings.' On 19 May 1796 it was resolved by the Committee that 10
guineas be presented to Coleridge.

June 1796   [Endorsed 10 June 1796.]

Gentlemen,

I have received through the medium of a Friend ten guineas
delivered to the care of Mr Scot for my use. You will, I trust,
believe that I feel what I ought to feel for this relief so liberally and
delicately afforded me, and that in happier circumstances I shall
be proud to remember the obligation. With every ardent wish for
the prosperity of your benevolent and truly original Institution

> I subscribe myself | Your obliged and grateful
> Samuel Taylor Coleridge.

133. *To John Thelwall*

Address: John Thelwall | Beaufort Buildings | Strand | London.
MS. Pierpont Morgan Lib. Pub. Letters, *i. 166.*
Postmark: ⟨2⟩3 June 1796.   *Stamped*: Bristol.

Wednesday   June 22nd 1796

Dear Thelwall

That I have not written you, has been an act of self-denial, not
indolence. I heard that you were electioneering—and would not
be the occasion that any of your thoughts should diverge from
that focus.

I wish very much to see you. Have you given up the idea of
spending a few weeks or months at Bristol—you might be *making*

way in your review of Burke's Life & writings—& give us once or twice a week a lecture which I doubt not would be crowded. We have a large & every way excellent Library, to which I could make you a *temporary* Subscriber—that is—I would get a subscription-ticket transferred to you—.

You are certainly well-calculated for the Review, you meditate. Your answer to Burke[1] is, I will not say, the best—for that would be no praise—it is certainly the only good one; & it is a very good one. In style, and *in reflectiveness* it is, I think, your chef d'œuvre—. —. Yet the 'peripatetic'[2]—for which accept my thanks—pleased me more because it let me into *your heart*—the poetry is frequently *sweet* & possesses the *fire* of feeling, but not enough (I think) of the *light* of Fancy—

I am sorry, that you should entertain so degrading an opinion of me as to imagine that I *industriously* collected anecdotes unfavorable to the characters of great men—. No! Thelwall—but I cannot shut my ears—& I have never given a moment's belief to any one of those stories unless when they were related to me at different times by professed Democrats—. — My vice is of the opposite class—a precipitance in praise—witness my Panegyric on Gerald & that *black* gentleman, Margarot—in the Conciones[3]— & my foolish verses to Godwin in the Morning Chronicle.[4]—At the same time, Thelwall! do not suppose that I admit your *palliations*. Doubtless, *I* could fill a book with slanderous stories of *professed Christians*; but those very men would allow, they were acting contrary to Christianity—but, I am afraid, an atheistic bad Man manufactures his system of principles with an eye to his peculiar propensities:—and makes his actions the criterion of what is virtuous, not virtue the criterion of his actions. Where the *disposition* is not amiable, an acute understanding I deem no blessing—— To the last sentence in your letter I subscribe fully & with all my inmost affections—'He who thinks & *feels* will be virtuous: & he who is absorbed in self will be vicious—whatever may be his speculative opinions.'——Believe me, Thelwall! it is not his Atheism that has prejudiced me against Godwin; but Godwin who has perhaps *prejudiced* me against Atheism.——Let me see you— I already know a Deist, & Calvinists, & Moravians whom I love &

---

[1] John Thelwall, *The Rights of Nature against the Usurpation of Establishments: a Series of Letters on the recent Effusions of the Right Hon. Edmund Burke*, 1796.

[2] John Thelwall, *The Peripatetic, or, Sketches of the Heart, of Nature, and of Society*, 1793.

[3] Cf. *Essays on His Own Times*, i. 18–20. Margarot, a West Indian, was arrested, along with Gerrald, for sedition in 1793.

[4] Cf. *Morning Chronicle*, 10 Jan. 1795. *Poems*, i. 86.

reverence—& I shall leap forwards to realize my *principles* by
feeling love & honor for an Atheist.——By the by, *are* you an
Atheist?—For I was told, that Hutton was an atheist—& pro-
cured his three massy Quartos on the principles of Knowlege[1] in
the hopes of finding some arguments in favor of atheism—but lo!
I discovered him to be a profoundly pious Deist—'independent of
fortune, satisfied with himself, pleased with his species, confident
in his Creator.'—God bless you, my dear Thelwall!

   believe me with high esteem and *anticipated* tenderness
                              Your's sincerely—S. T. Coleridge

P.S. We have an hundred lovely scenes about Bristol, which would
make you exclaim—O admirable *Nature*! & me, O Gracious *God*!—

134. *To John Prior Estlin*

Address: Reverend J. P. Estlin | Mrs Smith's | Bridge end | Glamorganshire
MS. Bristol Central Lib. Pub. E. L. G. i. 51.
Stamped: Bristol.

                              Monday Morning   July 4th [1796]
My dear and highly-honored Friend

   I am alarmed lest I should be obliged to leave Bristol before you
come back, which, I assure you, would be chill and comfortless to
my feelings beyond expression.—On Friday last I received a
message from Perry, the Editor of the Morning Chronicle, thro'
Dr Beddoes, stating, that if I would come to town & write for him,
he would make me a regular compensation adequate to the main-
tenance of myself & Mrs Coleridge.—Grey, the co-editor with
Perry, died at the Hotwells, on Wednesday or Thursday.—
Dr Beddoes thought it a fine opening for me—& added that Perry
expected an immediate answer.—My feet began mechanically to
move towards your house—I was most uncomfortably situated.
You & Mrs Estlin out of Bristol—& Charles Danvers out of Bristol
—& even Mr Wade was absent. So I had nobody to speak to on
the subject except Mr Cottle—which I did, & he advised me to
write to Perry immediately, and accept his proposal. I did so, and
expect to morrow a letter from him with particulars / which I will
immediately acquaint you with.——My heart is very heavy: for
I love Bristol & I do not love London. Besides, local and temporary
Politics are my aversion—they narrow the understanding, they
narrow the heart, they fret the temper. But there are two Giants
leagued together whose most imperious commands I must obey
however reluctant—their names are, BREAD & CHEESE.——

[1] James Hutton, *Investigation of the Principles of Knowledge*, 3 vols., 1794.

I received from your Sister your kind note with Mr Hobhouse's
& Dr Disney's kindness.—You will believe, & will acquaint
Dr Disney, that I feel as I ought to do—I have myself written a
few lines to Mr Hobhouse.—

You have had delightful Weather—& you have that calm sun-
shine of the soul, that gives you senses to feel and enjoy it. I am
with you in Spirit:——and almost feel 'the sea-breeze lift my
youthful locks.'[1]—I would write Odes & Sonnets Morning &
Evening—& metaphysicize at Noon—and of rainy days I would
overwhelm you with an Avalanche of Puns & Conundrums
loosened by sudden thaw from the Alps of my Imagination.—My
most respectful & tenderest Love to dear Mrs Estlin—and ask
her—'If a Woman had murdered her Cousin, and there were no
other proof of her guilt except that she had an *half-barrel Cask* in
her possession—how would that convict her?[']—Answer. It
would be evident, that she had kild-er-kin.——As I know that now
she cannot mortify me by pretending not to enjoy the joke, she
will laugh most intemperately, do not ask her the next till a
quarter of an hour's intermission—why Satan sitting on a house-top
would be like a decayed Merchant?—Answer—Because he would
be imp-over-à-shed. Mr Wade was talking of Davies in Clare
Street—& asked me what I thought of a *religious Attorney*. Why
(quoth I) I should not doubt of his attachment to the *Law & the
Profits* (i.e. Prophets)—but should think his *Gospel*-faith rather
more questionable.——

My Love to Mr and Mrs Hort—& ask Hort (who *hates* a Conun-
drum)—Why a Murderer is like an unborn Jack-ass?—Answer.
He is an Ass-ass-in. i.e. Ass in an ass.—

You rejoice that the Prince & Princess are reconciled—altho' I
fear 'that never can true Reconcilement grow Where wounds of
deadly Wrong have pierced so deep.[']² I composed a few lines
lately on the Princess in which I simply expressed sympathy for
her without endeavoring to heap odium on her husband. Indeed
as the lines are *addressed to her* it would have been brutal to have
abused her husband to her Face.—

To an unfortunate Princess.[3]

I sigh, fair injur'd Stranger! for thy fate—
But what shall Sighs avail thee? Thy poor Heart
Mid all the pomp & circumstance of State
Shivers in nakedness! Unbidden start

---

[1] *Religious Musings*, line 251. [2] *Paradise Lost*, iv. 98–99.
[3] *Poems*, i. 152.

Sad Recollections of Hope's garish dream
That shap'd a seraph form, and nam'd it Love—
It's hues gay-varying, as the Orient Beam
Varies the neck of Cytherea's Dove.

To one soft accent of domestic Joy
Poor are the Shouts that shake the high-arch'd Dome:
The Plaudits, that thy *public* path annoy;
Alas! they tell thee—Thou'rt a Wretch *at home*!

Then o! retire and weep! Their very Woes
Solace the guiltless. Drop the pearly Flood
On thy sweet Infant, as the FULL-BLOWN Rose
Surcharg'd with dew bends o'er it's neighb'ring BUD!

And ah! that Truth some holy spell could lend
To lure thy Wanderer from the Syren's power:
Then bid your Souls inseparably blend,
Like two bright Dew-drops bosom'd in a flower!

S. T. C.

The Reviews have been wonderful—The Monthly has *cataracted* panegyric on my poems; the Critical has *cascaded* it; and the Analytical has *dribbled* it with very tolerable civility.[1] The Monthly has at least done justice to my Religious Musings—They place it 'on the very top of the scale of Sublimity.[']—!—!—!

I shall finish with some Verses which I addressed to Horne Tooke & the Company who met on June 28th to celebrate his Poll.—I begin by alluding to the comparatively small number which he polled in his first contest for Westminster—You must read the lines, two abreast.[2]

Britons! when last ye met, with distant streak
So faintly promised the pale Dawn to break;
So dim it stain'd the precincts of the Sky
E'en *Expectation* gaz'd with doubtful Eye.
But now such fair Varieties of Light
O'ertake the heavy-sailing Clouds of Night;
Th' Horizon kindles with so rich a red,
That, though the *Sun still hides* his glorious head,
Th' impatient Matin-bird *assur'd of Day*
Leaves his low nest to meet it's earliest ray;
Loud the sweet song of Gratulation sings,

---

[1] Cf. *Monthly Review*, June 1796, p. 194; *Critical Review*, June 1796, p. 209; *Analytical Review*, June 1796, p. 610.

[2] *Poems*, i. 150. John Horne Tooke (1736–1812), politician and philologist, published the first volume of his ῎Επεα Πτερόεντα, or the Diversions of Purley in 1786.

And high in air claps his rejoicing wings!
Patriot & Sage! whose breeze-like Spirit* first
The lazy mists of Pedantry dispers'd,
(Mists, in which Superstition's *pigmy* band
Seem'd Giant Forms, the Genii of the Land!)
Thy struggles soon shall wak'ning Britain bless,
And Truth & Freedom hail thy wish'd success.
Yes, *Tooke*! tho' foul Corruption's wolfish throng
Outmalice Calumny's imposthum'd Tongue,
Thy Country's noblest & *determin'd* Choice,
Soon shalt thou thrill the Senate with thy voice;
With gradual Dawn bid Error's phantoms flit,
Or wither with the lightning flash of Wit;
Or with sublimer mien & tones more deep
Charm sworded Justice from mysterious Sleep,
'By violated Freedom's loud Lament,
'Her Lamps extinguish'd & her Temple rent;
'By the forc'd tears, her captive Martyrs shed;
'By each pale Orphan's feeble cry for bread;
'By ravag'd Belgium's corse-impeded Flood,
'And Vendee steaming still with brothers' blood![']
And if amid the strong impassion'd Tale
Thy Tongue should falter & thy Lips turn pale;
If transient Darkness film thy aweful Eye,
And thy tir'd Bosom struggle with a sigh;
Science & Freedom shall demand to hear
Who practis'd on a Life so doubly dear;
Infus'd the unwholesome anguish drop by drop
Pois'ning the sacred stream, they could not stop!
Shall bid thee with recover'd strength relate
How dark & deadly is a Coward's Hate:
What seeds of Death by wan Confinement sown
When prison-echoes mock'd Disease's groan!
Shall bid th' indignant Father flash dismay
And drag th' unnatural Villain into Day,
Who to the sports of his flesh'd† Ruffians left
Two lovely Mourners of their Sire bereft!
'Twas wrong, like this, which Rome's *first Consul* bore—
So by th' insulted Female's name *he* swore
Ruin (& rais'd her reeking dagger high)
Not to the *Tyrants* but the *Tyranny*!!

* Ἔπεα πτερόεντα [S.T.C.].
† Dundas left thief-takers in Horne Tooke's House for three days—with his
two Daughters *alone*; for Horne Tooke keeps no servant.—[Note by S.T.C.]

God, who hath blessed you, bless you!——Mrs Coleridge begs her kindest Love to you all.——

Once more, may God bless you all—

& Your obliged & grateful & truly affectionate | Friend

S. T. Coleridge

135. *To Thomas Poole*

Address: Mr Thomas Poole | Stowy | near Bridgewater | Somerset—
MS. British Museum. Pub. Biog. Lit., *ed. H. N. Coleridge, 1847, ii. 368.*
Stamped: Bristol.

Monday Night. [4 July 1796]

My very dear Poole

Do not attribute it to Indolence that I have not written you. Suspense has been the real cause of my silence. Day after day I have confidently expected some decisive letter; and as often have been disappointed. 'Certainly I shall have one tomorrow noon, and then I will write.' Thus I contemplated the time of my silence in it's small component parts, forgetful into what a sum total they were swelling.—As I have heard nothing from Nottingham[1] notwithstanding I have written a pressing Letter, I have by the advice of Cottle & Dr Beddoes accepted a proposal of Perry's, the Editor of the Morning Chronicle—accepted it with a heavy & reluctant Heart.—On Thursday Perry was at Bristol for a few hours just time enough to attend the dying moments of his associate in the Editorship, Mr Grey—whom Dr Beddoes attended. Perry desired Dr Beddoes to inform me, that if I would come up to London and *write for him*, he would make me a regular compensation adequate to the maintenance of myself & Mrs Coleridge: and requested an immediate answer by the post—. Mr Estlin, & Charles Danvers, & Mr Wade are or were all out of town—I had no human creature to advise with except Dr Beddoes & Cottle. Dr Beddoes thinks it a good opening on account of Grey's Death; but I rather think, that Perry means to employ me as a mere Hireling without any *proportionate* Share of the Profits.—However as I am doing nothing & in the prospect of doing nothing settled, I was afraid to give way to the *omenings* of my heart, & accordingly, I accepted his proposal in *general terms*, requesting a line from him expressing the particulars *both of my occupation & proposed stipend*. This I shall receive tomorrow, I suppose—and if I do, I think of hiring a horse for a couple of days, & galloping down to you to have all your advice, which indeed if it should be for *rejecting* the proposals, I might receive by post—but if for finally accepting them—we

[1] See Letter 131, to John Fellows.

could not interchange Letters in a time sufficiently short for Perry's
needs, & so he would procure another person possibly—& at all
events I should not like to leave this part of England (perhaps for
ever!) without seeing you once more.—I am very sad about it—for
I love Bristol & I do not love London—& besides, local & temporary
politics have become my aversion. They narrow the Understanding,
and at least *acidulate* the Heart:—but those two Giants, yclept
BREAD & CHEESE, bend me into compliance.—I must do some-
thing. If I go, farewell Philosophy! Farewell, the Muse! Farewell,
my literary Fame!—

My poems have been reviewed. The *Monthly* has *cataracted*
panegyric on me—the *Critical cascaded* it—& the *Analytical
dribbled* it with civility: as to the British Critic,[1] they *durst not*
condemn and they would not praise—so contented themselves with
'commending me, as a *Poet*[']—and allowed me 'tenderness of
sentiment & elegance of diction.'—

I am so anxious & uneasy, that I really cannot write any further.
My kind & fraternal Love to Your Sister—& my filial respects to
your dear Mother—

and believe me to be | in my head, heart, & soul | Your's
most sincerely
S. T. Coleridge

136. *To John Fellows*

Address: John Fellowes Esq. | Nottingham
MS. Harvard College Lib. Pub. Letters Hitherto Uncollected, *ed. W. F.
Prideaux, 1913, p. 1.*
Postmark: 29 July 1796. *Stamped*: Tewkesbury.

Tewkesbury   Thursday Morning   July 28th 1796
Dear Sir

I received your parcel & a letter from Mrs Evans[2] on the same
day—as it was not possible for me to remain any longer in suspense
(having just then received a very handsome offer from Perry, the
Editor of the Morning Chronicle) I *immediately* set off with my wife
for Darley—from which place I am now returning.—Every thing
I saw of Mrs Evans made me consider the proposed situation an
object of my highest wishes—; but every *circumstance* seemed to
deny, that such wishes should be realized. Mr William Strutt was
cold, & his arguments (when he used *any* to Mrs Evans) dissuasive

[1] Cf. *British Critic*, May 1796, p. 549.
[2] Mrs. Elizabeth Evans was the daughter of Jedediah Strutt and the widow
of William Evans of Darley, Derbyshire.

—& the Grandfather Evans & Mr Walter Evans decisive in opposition—'twas, I assure you, a very trying week for the Widow. At length (on Tuesday morning) she determined, that the sacrifice of her children, which Mammon, gloomy as Moloch, required, should *not* be given—and the plan of education, which I proposed, is to be followed.—My salary is to be 150£ a year.—You will accept my gratitude for the interest which you have taken in my affairs. These, my dear Sir! are common words; but believe me, mine are not common feelings. The Poems Mrs Coleridge has sent directed for you to be left at Mr Sutton's——You will excuse the delay, imputing it to my anxieties & my daily expectation of being able to communicate something settled to you.—

Your Brother informed me that you are about to pitch your summer tents at Brighthelmstone—I need not say, how sincerely I wish you Health, Pleasure, & Happiness——

I return to Darley in the course of ten days—& have left Mrs Coleridge behind, as my hostage.—

You will present my kindest respects to Mrs Fellowes when you see her—

& believe me | Your obliged & grateful
S. T. Coleridge

137. *To Thomas Poole*

MS. British Museum. Pub. E. L. G. i. 56.

[Bristol.]   August [6], 1796   Saturday

My dear Poole

Read the inclosed.[1] I acknowlege one pang; but in no after emotion of vain regret have I apostatized from the divine philosophy, which I profess. The black clouds, which hide the Sun from my view, are they not big with fertility? and will they not drop it on me?——

I will write you from Derby.

Farewell, my beloved Friend!—Our dear Wade bids me tell you, that he loves and esteems you—You know that from *your own* heart.——

S. T. Coleridge

Send back Mrs Evans's Letter in the parcel——

---

[1] On his return to Bristol after a brief stay at Ottery, Coleridge found a letter, dated 3 Aug. 1796, from Mrs. Evans of Darley: 'The new and accumulated objections which have arisen to our plan since your departure, . . . [are so] overwhelming that I think the future happiness of the children as well as my own will be ruined by resistance.'

138. *To Josiah Wade*

Pub. Early Rec. *i. 173.*

Mosely, near Birmingham, [22 August] 1796.

My very dear Wade,

Will it be any excuse to you for my silence, to say, that I have written to no one else, and that these are the very first lines I have written ?

I stayed a day or two at Derby, and then went on in Mrs. [Evans's] carriage to see the beauties of Matlock. Here I stayed from Tuesday to Saturday, which time was completely filled up with seeing the country, eating, concerts, &c. I was the first fiddle, not in the concerts, but every where else, and the company would not spare me twenty minutes together. Sunday I dedicated to the drawing up my sketch of education, which I meant to publish, to try to get a school.

Monday I accompanied Mrs. E. to Oakover, with Miss W[illet], to the thrice lovely valley of Ham [Ilam]; a vale hung by beautiful woods all round, except just at its entrance, where, as you stand at the other end of the valley, you see a bare bleak mountain, standing as it were to guard the entrance. It is without exception the most beautiful place I ever visited, and from thence we pro-ceeded to Dove-Dale, without question, tremendously sublime. Here we dined in a cavern, by the side of a divine little spring. We returned to Derby quite exhausted with the rapid succession of delightful emotions.

I was to have left Derby on Wednesday; but on the Wednesday, Dr. Crompton, who had been at Liverpool, came home. He called on me, and made the following offer. That if I would take a house in Derby, and open a day-school, confining my number to twelve, he would send his three children. That, till I had completed my number, he would allow me One hundred a year; and when I had completed it, twenty guineas a year for each son. He thinks there is no doubt but that I might have more than twelve in a very short time, if I liked it. If so, twelve times twenty guineas is two hundred and forty guineas per annum; and my mornings and evenings would be my own: the children coming to me from nine to twelve, and from two to five: the two last hours employed with the writing and drawing masters, in my presence: so that only four hours would be thoroughly occupied by them. The plan to commence in November. I agreed with the Doctor, he telling me, that if, in the mean time, any thing more advantageous offered itself, I was to consider myself at perfect liberty to accept it.

On Thursday I left Derby for Burton. From Burton I took chaise, slept at Lichfield, and in the morning arrived at my worthy friend's, Mr. Thomas Hawkes, at Mosely, three miles from Birmingham, in whose shrubbery I am now writing. I shall stay at Birmingham a week longer.

I have seen a letter from Mr. William Roscoe (Author of the life of Lorenzo the magnificent; a work in two quarto Volumes, of which the whole First Edition sold in a month); it was addressed to Mr. Edwards, the minister here, and entirely related to me. Of me, and my composition[s], he writes in terms of high admiration, and concludes by desiring Mr. Edwards to let him know my situation and prospects, and saying, if I would come and settle at Liverpool, he thought a comfortable situation might be procured for me. This day Edwards will write to him.

God love you, and your grateful and affectionate friend,

S. T. Coleridge.

N.B. I preached yesterday.

139. *To Thomas Poole*

Address: Mr Thomas Poole | Stowey | near | Bridgewater | Somerset   *Single*
MS. British Museum. Pub. E. L. G. i. 56.
Stamped: Birmingham.

Monday Morning. [22 August 1796]

My beloved Friend

I was at Matlock, the place monodized by Bowles, when your letter arrived at Darley—& I did not receive it till near a week after.—Indeed, my very dear Poole! I wrote to you the whole truth—after the first moment I was perfectly composed, and from that moment to this have continued calm and light-hearted. I had just quitted you, and I felt myself rich in your love & esteem—you do not know, how rich I feel myself—.—O ever found the same, And trusted, & beloved!——[1]

The last sentences of your letter affected me more than I can well describe. Words & phrases, which might perhaps have adequately expressed my feelings, the cold-blooded Children of this World have anticipated & exhausted in their unmeaning gabber of flattery. I use common expressions—but they do not convey common feelings.—*My heart has thanked you*.——In preaching on Faith yesterday—I said that Faith was infinitely better than Good Works—as the Cause is greater than the effect—as a fruitful Tree is better than it's Fruits & as a friendly Heart is of far higher value than the Kindnesses which it naturally and *necessarily*

[1] Akenside, *Pleasures of the Imagination* (Second Version), i, ll. 88–89.

prompts.——It is for that *friendly Heart* that I now have thanked you: and which I so eagerly accept of—for with regard to settlement, I am likely to be better off now than before—as I shall proceed to tell you.——

I arrived at Darley on the Sunday: Mrs Evans was much agitated when she met me—: I hastened to relieve her embarrassment.—I told her to feel nothing on my account: 'I cannot be said to have lost that which I never had, and I have gained what I should not otherwise have possessed, your Acquaintance & Esteem.' 'Say rather (she exclaimed) my Love and Veneration.'—Monday I spent at Darley—on the Tuesday, I & Mrs Coleridge, and a Miss Willet went with Mrs Evans's carriage to Matlock, where we stayed till Saturday. Miss Willet generally resides with Mrs Evans—& is an amiable young Old maid—young old maid—for she is only about 2 & 40. Mrs Evans did not herself accompany us—her husband having lingered & died at Matlock the last summer.—Sunday we spent at Darley—and on Monday Sara, and Mrs Evans, and myself visited Oakover, a seat famous for a few first-rates of Raphael & Titian—& from thence to Ilam, a quiet vale hung round with woods—beautiful beyond expression—& from thence to Dove-dale, a place beyond expression tremendously sublime. Here in a cavern at the head of a divine little fountain we dined on cold meat—and returned to Darley, quite worn out with the succession of sweet Sensations.—On Tuesday we were employed in packing up—& on Wednesday we were to have set off.—Mrs Evans behaved with great liberality—she put in my hand a number of bank notes, which amounted to 95£, and she gave Mrs Coleridge all her baby clothes, which, I suppose, from the largeness of their quantity & the richness of their lace &c are very valuable. But on the Wednesday Dr Crompton who had just returned from Liverpool called on me, and made me the following— That if I would take a House in Derby & open a Day-school confining my Number to 12 Scholars he would send three of his Children on these terms: till my number was completed, he would allow me 100£ a year for them—when my number was completed, he should give me 20 guineas a year for each of them: the children to be with me from 9 to 12, and from 2 to 5—the two last hours (i.e. from 3 to 5) to be employed with their writing or drawing Masters who are to be payed by the Parent.—He has not the least shadow of doubt but that I shall complete my number almost instantly.—Now 12 20 guineas = 240 guineas = 252£—and my evenings & mornings at my own disposal—good things.—So I accepted the Offer, it being understood, that if any thing better offered, I should accept it.——There was not a House to be got in

Derby—but I engaged with a Man for a House now building & which is to be completed by the 8th of October—for 12 pound a year—and the Landlord pays all the Taxes except the Poor Rates.—The Landlord is rather an intelligent fellow—and has promised me to Rumfordize the Chimneys.——The plan is to commence in November—the intermediate time I spend at Bristol—at which place I shall arrive by the blessing of God on Monday night next—this week I spend with Mr Hawkes at Mosely, near Birmingham—in whose Shrubbery I now write.—I arrived here on Friday—having left Derby on Thursday—I preached here yesterday.—

If Sara will let me, I shall see you for a few days in the course of a month.

Direct your next letter S. T. Coleridge, Oxford Street Bristol.

My love to your dear mother & Sister—& believe me affectionately | Your ever faithful Friend

S. T. Coleridge

I shall write to my mother & Brothe[rs to]morrow—

140. *To John Prior Estlin*

Address: *Revd* Mr Estlin | St Michael's Hill | Bristol
MS. Bristol Central Lib. Pub. Letters to Estlin, *ed. H. A. Bright, 11.*
Stamped: Birmingham.

Mosely, Birmingham
Monday Morning. [22 August 1796]

My dear and honoured friend

On my return from Ottery, (where I was received by my mother with transport, and by my Brother George with joy & tenderness, and by my other Brothers with affectionate civility) I found at Mr Wade's a letter for me from Mrs Evans—a most impassioned Letter, in which she informed me that after she had acquainted her Brothers &c that she had determined to hazard all consequences rather than lose me, they [the]n came forwards & divulged what before this they [h]ad kept secret from her,—that even her children's own fortunes were in great measure dependent on the will of the Grandfather—and that every thing the worst was to be expected from his implacable resentment.—She was therefore forced to give up the scheme:—and requested me to fly back to her immediately. I accordingly stept almost immediately into the Mail Coach—this was Saturday night—and arrived at Darley by dinner time on Sunday.—I hastened to relieve Mrs Evans's embarrassment.—'I cannot be said to have lost that which I never had—and I have gained what I should not otherwise have possessed

—your esteem & acquaintance.' 'Say rather['] (she exclaimed) 'my veneration & love.'——After this we spent a lovely week at Matlock—and then visited Ilam, the most beautiful of valleys, and Dove-dale, the most tremendous of Sublimities.—Mrs Evans behaved with great liberality—a little before I was about to quit her, she insisted on my acceptance of 95£, and she had given Mrs Coleridge all her baby clothes, which are, I suppose, very valuable.—Well, on the Wednesday, I was to have left Darley, when in the Morning Dr Crompton came home. From the time that I first left Darley after having settled with Mrs Evans, he had been absent at Liverpool.——He came to make me the following Offer— Viz—that if I would take a House in Derby, & open a day-school, confining my number to 12, he would send his three children on the following terms—: till I had completed my number, he would allow me 100£ a year for them—when I had procured my full number, 12, he should give 20 guineas for each, exclusive of writing masters, Drawing, &c.—The children to come at 9, and leave me at 12——to come again at 2 & leave me at 5—from 3 to 5 in each afternoon to be occupied with their writing masters &c.—— He had not a shadow of doubt on his mind that I should complete my number almost instantly.—If so 12 times 20 guineas = 240 guineas—and my mornings & evenings at my own disposal——is a good thing—So I accepted his proposal, it being understood, that if any thing better should offer, I am at liberty to accept it.—The plan is to commence in November—the intermediate time I spend at Bristol, where Mrs Coleridge will, of course, lie in.——

On Thursday, I left Derby & am now at Mr Hawkes's, at Mosely, near Birmingham—where I shall stay till Monday morning next— & shall be at Bristol, Monday night. I preached yesterday morning from Hebrews C. IV. v. 1 & 2nd. 'Let us therefore fear——heard it.' 'Twas my chef d'œuvre. I think of writing it down, & publishing it with two other sermons—one on the character of Christ, and another on his universal reign, from Isaiah XLV. 22 & 23.

I should like you to hear me preach them & lament that my political notoriety prevents my [reli]eving you occasionally at Bristol.—

Mrs Evans requested me to make you & Mrs Estlin know & love her—she says, that She already knows & loves you both—: for indeed, my dear, very dear friend!—I do love to talk about you.

Kiss the dear little ones for me—& give my love to Mrs Estlin— Mrs Estlin, who is *my Sister!*——Indeed, I feel myself *rich, very rich* in possessing your Love & Esteem.——

S. T. Coleridge

P.S. If you can afford time, give me a line or two.——

141. *To John Colson*

Address: Jn Colson | No. 23 | Bush Lane | Cannon Street | London
MS. Wellesley College Lib. Hitherto unpublished.
Postmark: 6 September 1796.   *Stamped*: Bristol.

Bristol, Oxford Street   Sunday, Septembr 4th. 1796

My dear Colson!—Have *Faith* in me—I say to you, have Faith in me!——You deserve not that whole heart of friendship which I have devoted to you, if you have suspected from my silence that my affection has been estranged or gratitude grown cool. But my dearest fellow! Hope, that ignis fatuus, has not ceased to dance her watry fire before me—cold unwarming meteor! and always left me up to the neck in some slough of disappointment——Add to these my sympathy for others' sorrows—Poor Allen! my heart bleeds for him! His Wife is dying—& expence upon expence is sucking him dry—dry—dry—the very marrow is drawn away from the bone!—Can you wonder then, that I have neglected *some* necessary business—and that when I have finished my 'letters of compulsion,' that I have dreamt away the leisure hours——dreamt of *you*, my Colson! not unfrequently—altho' I have not written you.——

Well—in all human probability I shall settle at Derby in November—& open a day-school there. I have some children promised me on handsome terms—& still hope, that I shall do well. Whether or no, I will trust in God!——Since I last wrote to you, many events have been heaped on each other.—I had settled to have been the Tutor of the children of a Lady of Fortune—it was settled—but the Grandfather & Guardians opposed it fiercely —& it seems, the *Law* has sharpened their claws to make vain all resistance on the part of the mother, who is a woman of great mind & very great heart!—She treated me with esteem, & affection, and unbounded generosity——gave me 95£ and to Mrs Coleridge—all her baby-clothes—& she wept when she parted with me, & called me her brother——I was about to depart when a Dr Crompton advised me to open a Day-school in Derby—which I shall do.—He will send three of his children & allow me 100£ a year for them.——

I have been into Devonshire & reconciled my[self] to my family & my family to me.—

Tom Poole is at Bristol at the Fair—leaves it to morrow—— Excellent man! My veneration for him increases with my knowlege.——

My Colson! this is a hard World because of Error & Vice—and you, I imagine, are placed in a situation to see much misery, & alas! a heart to sympathize—perhaps *too keenly*. Good young man, dear ingenuous Child of Sensibility! waste not yourself in *vain* efforts—for the sake of the miserable, whom your heart throbs to relieve, be prudent with regard to *yourself*—but above all things, I intreat you, my dear Colson! to preserve your faith in Christ! It is my wealth [in] poverty, my Joy in sorrow, my peace amid tumult; for all the evil, I have committed, my gracious Pardon, and for every virtue my exceeding great reward! I have *found* it to be so—& can smile with pity at the Infidel, whose vanity makes him dream that I should barter such a blessing for a few subtleties from the school of the cold-blooded Sophist!——

Mrs Coleridge, who is remarkably well, desires her love to you— God love you, & | Your affectionate
S. T. Coleridge

142. *To Thomas Poole*

Address: Mr Thomas Poole | Stowey | near | Bridgewater | Somerset.
MS. British Museum. Pub. with omis. Letters, *i. 168*.
Stamped: Bristol.

Saturday, September 24th, 1796

My dear, very dear Poole

The Heart, thoroughly penetrated with the flame of virtuous Friendship, is in a state of glory; but 'lest it should be exalted above measure, there is given it a Thorn in the flesh:'[1]—I mean, that where the friendship of any person forms an essential part of a man's happiness, he will at times be pestered by the little jealousies & solicitudes of imbecil Humanity.—Since we last parted I have been gloomily dreaming, that you did not leave me so affectionately as you were wont to do.—Pardon this littleness of Heart—& do not think the worse of me for it. Indeed my Soul seems so mantled & wrapped round by your Love & Esteem, that even a dream of losing but the smallest fragment of it makes me shiver—as tho' some tender part of my Nature were left uncovered & in nakedness.——

Last week I received a Letter from Lloyd[2] informing me that his Parents had given their *joyful* concurrence to his residence with me; but that if it were possible, that I could be absent three or four days; his Father wished particularly to see me.—I consulted Mrs Coleridge who advised me to go—saying, that she should not be ill for three weeks. Accordingly on Saturday night I went

[1] 2 Corinthians xii. 7.
[2] Charles Lloyd (1775–1839), the poet, had met Coleridge at Moseley, near Birmingham, a short time before. In an unpublished note Mrs. Coleridge says that Coleridge was introduced to Lloyd by Thomas Hawkes. Cf. Letter 139.

by the Mail to Birmingham—was introduced to the Father, who is a mild man, very liberal in his ideas, and in religion an *allegorizing Quaker*—I mean, that all the apparently irrational part of his Sect he allegorizes into significations, which for the most part you or I might assent to.—We became well acquainted—& he expressed himself 'thankful to Heaven,' that his Son was about to be with me. He said, he would write to me concerning money-matters, after his Son had been some time under my Roof.[1]——
On Tuesday Morning I was surprized by a Letter from Mr Maurice, our medical attendant, informing me that Mrs Coleridge was delivered on Monday, September 19th, 1796, half past two in the Morning, of a Son—& that both she & the Child were uncommonly well. I was quite annihilated with the suddenness of the information—and retired to my room to address myself to my Maker—but I could only offer up to him the silence of stupified Feelings.—I hastened home & Charles Lloyd returned with me.——When I first saw the Child, I did not feel that thrill & overflowing of affection which I expected——I looked on it with a melancholy gaze—my mind was intensely contemplative & my heart only sad.—But when two hours after, I saw it at the bosom of it's Mother; on her arm; and her eye tearful & watching it's little features, then I was thrilled & melted, & gave it the Kiss of a Father.[2]—

Mrs Coleridge was taken ill suddenly—& before the Nurse or the Surgeon arrived, delivered herself—the Nurse just came in time to take away the after-birth—& when the whole was over, Mr Maurice came.—My Sara had indeed (God be praised) a wonderfully favorable time——& within a few hours after her delivery, was, excepting weakness, perfectly well.—The Baby seems strong, & the old Nurse has over-persuaded my Wife to discover a Likeness of me in it's face——no great compliment to me—for in truth I have seen handsomer Babies in my Life time.—It's name is David Hartley Coleridge.—I hope, that ere he be a man, if God destine him for continuance in this life, his head will be convinced of, & his heart saturated with, the truths so ably supported by that great master of *Christian* Philosophy.—

Charles Lloyd wins upon me hourly—his heart is uncommonly pure, his affections delicate, & his benevolence enlivened, but not sicklied, by sensibility.—He is assuredly a man of great Genius;

[1] 'The original arrangement was that Charles [Lloyd] was to pay 80£. a year in return for board, lodging, instruction, and the companionship of his friend and mentor.' E. V. Lucas, *Charles Lamb and the Lloyds*, 1898, p. 20.
[2] Cf. the Sonnet, *To a Friend who asked, how I felt when the Nurse first presented my Infant to me*, *Poems*, i. 154, and Letter 146.

but it must be in tete a tete with one whom he loves & esteems, that his colloquial powers open—& this arises not from reserve or want of Simplicity; but from having been placed in situations, where for years together he met with no congenial minds, and where the contrariety of his thoughts & notions to the thoughts & notions of those around him induced the necessity of habitually suppressing his Feelings.——His Joy, & gratitude to Heaven for the circumstance of his domestication with me, I can scarcely describe to you—& I believe, that his fixed plans are of being always with me.—His Father told me, that if he saw that his Son had formed Habits of severe Economy, he should not insist upon his adopting any Profession—as then his fair Share of his (the Father's) Wealth would be sufficient for him.

My dearest Poole! can you conveniently receive us in the course of a week—? we can both sleep in one bed, which we do now.—— And I have much, very much, to say to you—& consult with you about—for my heart is heavy respecting Derby——and my feelings are so dim & huddled, that tho' I can, I am sure, communicate them to you by my looks & broken sentences, I scarcely know how to convey them in a letter. And Charles Lloyd wishes much to know you personally.——I shall write on the other side of the Paper two of Charles Lloyd's Sonnets which he wrote in one evening at Birmingham——The latter of them alludes to the conviction of the truth of Christianity, which he had received from me, for he had been, if not a Deist, yet quite a Sceptic—

Sonnet[1]

1

Ye overflowings of a restless Heart,
Why thus torment me? Wishes undefin'd,
Why thro' my breast so vehemently dart
Waking convuls'd commotions of the Mind?

O Stubborn Feelings! why do ye refuse
The blameless sympathies of social bliss?
Why pamp'ring lonesome anguish idly muse
Or mutter workings of obscure Distress?

Almighty Parent! what a Thing am I!
Shudd'ring with extacy yet dumb the while!
Thou, only Thou with chaos-piercing eye

[1] This and the following sonnet were included in *Poems, by S. T. Coleridge, second edition. To which are now added Poems by Charles Lamb, and Charles Lloyd,* 1797, pp. 177–8.

Can'st see me as I am!—My Father! rise
Sublime in love, and with thy calming smile
Hush thou my Spirit's stormy phantasies!

Sonnet

2

If the lone Breathings of the poor in heart,
If the still Gratitude of Wretchedness
Reliev'd when least expecting, have access
To thee, th' Almighty Parent! thou wilt dart
Thy loving-kindness on the offering meek
My Spirit brings, opprest with thankfulness
At this lone hour: for thou dost ever bless
The stricken mind, that sighs & cannot speak.

Omniscient Father! I have been perplex'd
With Scoffers link'd! yea, called them my Friends
That snare the Soul—but Doubt & black Despair
Are past! My heart, no longer sorely vex'd,
May now unshroud itself—it's aim extends
To Heaven!—For thou, my best Friend! dwellest there!

Let me hear from you by post immediately——& give my kind
Love to your Sister & dear Mother—& likewise my Love to that
young Man with the soul-beaming Face,[1] which I recollect much
better than I do his name——God bless you, my dear Friend!
　　　　　　　　　　believe [me] with deep affection your
　　　　　　　　　　　　　　　S. T. Coleridge

143. *To Charles Lamb*

Pub. Letters, *i. 171.* This letter was written in response to a request made by
Charles Lamb after the tragic death of his mother. 'Write', said Lamb, 'as
religious a letter as possible.' *Lamb Letters*, i. 39. Unfortunately, of the many
letters Coleridge wrote to Lamb during this period this is the lone survivor;
but Lamb's own letters show that Coleridge did much to rescue his friend from
despair.

[28 September 1796]

Your letter, my friend, struck me with a mighty horror. It rushed
upon me and stupefied my feelings. You bid me write you a religious
letter. I am not a man who would attempt to insult the greatness
of your anguish by any other consolation. Heaven knows that in
the easiest fortunes there is much dissatisfaction and weariness of

---

[1] Thomas Ward was Poole's apprentice and afterwards partner. He tran-
scribed many of Coleridge's letters, particularly those written from Germany.

spirit; much that calls for the exercise of patience and resignation; but in storms like these, that shake the dwelling and make the heart tremble, there is no middle way between despair and the yielding up of the whole spirit unto the guidance of faith. And surely it is a matter of joy that your faith in Jesus has been preserved; the Comforter that should relieve you is not far from you. But as you are a Christian, in the name of that Saviour, who was filled with bitterness and made drunken with wormwood, I conjure you to have recourse in frequent prayer to 'his God and your God;'[1] the God of mercies, and father of all comfort. Your poor father is, I hope, almost senseless of the calamity; the unconscious instrument of Divine Providence knows it not, and your mother is in heaven. It is sweet to be roused from a frightful dream by the song of birds and the gladsome rays of the morning. Ah, how infinitely more sweet to be awakened from the blackness and amazement of a sudden horror by the glories of God manifest and the hallelujahs of angels.

As to what regards yourself, I approve altogether of your abandoning what you justly call vanities. I look upon you as a man called by sorrow and anguish and a strange desolation of hopes into quietness, and a soul set apart and made peculiar to God! We cannot arrive at any portion of heavenly bliss without in some measure imitating Christ; and they arrive at the largest inheritance who imitate the most difficult parts of his character, and, bowed down and crushed underfoot, cry in fulness of faith, 'Father, thy will be done.'

I wish above measure to have you for a little while here; no visitants shall blow on the nakedness of your feelings; you shall be quiet, and your spirit may be healed. I see no possible objection, unless your father's helplessness prevent you, and unless you are necessary to him. If this be not the case, I charge you write me that you will come.

I charge you, my dearest friend, not to dare to encourage gloom or despair. You are a temporary sharer in human miseries that you may be an eternal partaker of the Divine nature. I charge you, if by any means it be possible, come to me.

I remain your affectionate
S. T. Coleridge

---

[1] John xx. 17.

144. *To Charles Lloyd, Senior*

Pub. Charles Lamb and the Lloyds, *20.*

[Kingsdown, Bristol.]   Saturday, 15th Oct., 1796

Dear Sir,—As the father of Charles Lloyd you are of course in some measure interested in any alteration of my schemes of life; and I feel it a kind of Duty to give you my reasons for any such alteration. I have declined my Derby connection, and determined to retire once for all and utterly from cities and towns: and am about to take a cottage and half a dozen acres of land in an enchanting Situation about eight miles from Bridgewater.[1] My reasons are—that I have cause to believe my Health would be materially impaired by residing in a town, and by the close confinement and anxieties incident to the education of children; that as my days would be dedicated to Dr. Crompton's children, and my evenings to a course of study with my admirable young friend, I should have scarcely a snatch of time for literary occupation; and, above all, because I am anxious that my children should be bred up from earliest infancy in the simplicity of peasants, their food, dress, and habits completely rustic. I never shall, and I never will, have any fortune to leave them: I will leave them therefore hearts that desire little, heads that know how little is to be desired, and hands and arms accustomed to earn that little. I am peculiarly delighted with the 21st verse of the 4th chapter of Tobit, 'And fear not, my son! that we are made poor: for thou hast much wealth, if thou fear God, and depart from all sin and do that which is pleasing in His sight.' Indeed, if I live in cities, my children (if it please the All-good to preserve the one I have, and to give me more), my children, I say, will necessarily become acquainted with politicians and politics—a set of men and a kind of study which I deem highly unfavourable to all Christian graces. I have myself erred greatly in this respect; but, I trust, I have now seen my error. I have accordingly snapped my squeaking baby-trumpet of sedition, and have hung up its fragments in the chamber of Penitences.[2]

Your son and I are happy in our connection—our opinions and feelings are as nearly alike as we can expect: and I rely upon the goodness of the All-good that we shall proceed to make each other better and wiser. Charles Lloyd is greatly averse from the common

[1] John Cruikshank had been commissioned to obtain a house for Coleridge at Adscombe, near Nether Stowey. The plan did not materialize. Cf. *Thomas Poole*, i. 174.

[2] Coleridge uses almost this same figure in a letter to his brother George in early 1798. See Letter 238.

run of society—and so am I—but in a city I could scarcely avoid it. And this, too, has aided my decision in favour of my rustic scheme. We shall reside near a very dear friend of mine, a man versed from childhood in the toils of the Garden and the Field, and from whom I shall receive every addition to my comfort which an earthly friend and adviser can give.

My Wife requests to be remembered to you, if the word 'remember' can be properly used. You will mention my respects to your Wife and your children, and believe that I am with no mean esteem and regard

Your Friend,
S. T. Coleridge.

145. *To Joseph Cottle*

Pub. Rem. *115.*

Stowey, Oct. 18th, 1796

My dear Cottle,

I have no mercenary feelings, I verily believe; but I hate bartering at any time, and with any person; with you it is absolutely intolerable. I clearly perceive that by giving me twenty guineas, on the sale of the second edition, you will get little or nothing by the additional poems, unless they should be sufficiently popular to reach a third edition, which soars above our wildest expectations. The only advantage you can derive therefore from the purchase of them on such terms, is, simply, that my poetry is more likely to sell when the whole may be had in one volume, price 5s., than when it is scattered in two volumes; the one 4s., the other possibly 3s. In short, you will get nothing directly, but only indirectly, from the probable circumstance, that these additional poems added to the former, will give a more rapid sale to the second edition than could otherwise be expected, and cause it possibly to be reviewed at large. Add to this, that by omitting every thing political, I widen the sphere of my readers. So much for you. Now for myself. You must see, Cottle, that whatever money I should receive from you, would result from the circumstances that would give me the same, or more—if I published them on my own account. I mean the sale of the poems. I can therefore have no motive to make such conditions with you, except the wish to omit poems unworthy of me, and the circumstance that our separate properties would aid each other by the union; and whatever advantage this might be to me, it would, of course, be equally so to you. The only difference between my publishing the poems on my own account, and yielding them up to you; the only difference I say, independent of the above stated differences, is, that, in one case, I retain the property for ever, in the other case, I lose it after two editions.

However, I am not solicitous to have any thing omitted, except the sonnet to Lord Stanhope and the ludicrous poem;[1] I should like to publish the best pieces together, and those of secondary splendour, at the end of the volume, and think this is the best quietus of the whole affair.

Yours affectionately,
S. T. Coleridge.

146. *To Thomas Poole*

Address: Mr Thomas Poole | Stowey | near | Bridgewater | Somerset   *Single*
MS. British Museum. Pub. with omis. Biog. Lit., *ed. H. N. Coleridge, 1847, ii. 377.*
Stamped: Bristol.

November 1st 1796

My beloved Poole

Many *causes* have concurred to prevent my writing to you, but all together they do not amount to a *reason*. I have seen a narrow-necked Bottle so full of water, that when turned upside down not a drop has fallen out—. Something like this has been the case with me. My heart has been full, yea, crammed with anxieties about my residence near you. I so ardently desire it, that any disappointment would chill all my faculties, like the fingers of death. And entertaining [a] wish so irrationally strong, I necessarily have *day*-mair dreams that something will prevent it—so that since I quitted you, I have been gloomy as the month which even now has begun to lower and rave on us.—I verily believe, or rather, I have no doubt that I should have written you within the period of my promise, if I had not pledged myself for a certain gift of my Muse to poor Tommy: & alas! she has been too 'sunk on the ground in dimmest heaviness' to permit me to trifle.—Yet intending it hourly I deferred my letter a la mode the procrastinator!—Ah! me—I wonder not that the Hours fly so sweetly by me—for they pass unfreighted with the duties which they came to demand!——

I am frightened at not hearing from Cruikshanks——Has Lord Thing a my bob—I forget the animal's name—refused *him*—or has Cruikshanks forgotten *me*?[2]—I wrote a long Letter to Dr Crompton & received from him a very kind Letter which I will send you in the parcel I am about to convey by Milton.—

---

[1] *Written after a Walk before Supper, Poems,* i. 37. Neither this poem, which is quoted in Letter 19, nor the sonnet to Earl Stanhope was printed in Coleridge's *Poems* of 1797.

[2] The cottage at Adscombe belonged to Lord Egmont.

My poems are come to a second Edition, that is the first Edition is sold.—I shall alter the lines of the Joan of Arc & make a *one* poem entitled the progress of European Liberty, a vision—the first line—Auspicious Reverence! hush all meaner song, Till we the deep &c—& begin the Volume with it.[1] Then the Chatterton—Pixies Parlour—Effusion 27th—Effusion 28th—To a young Ass—Tell me on what holy ground—The Sigh—Epitaph on the Infant—The Man of Ross—Spring in a Village—Edmund—Lines with a poem on the Fr. Revolution—Seven Sonnets; namely those at pages 45, 59, 60, 61, 64, 65, 66. Shurton Bars—My pensive Sara!—Low was our pretty Cot—Religious Musings—. These in the order I have placed them——then another title page, with Juvenilia on it & an advertisement signifying that the poems were retained from the desire of some friends; but that they are to be considered as being in the Author's own opinion of very inferior merit. In this sheet will be 1 Absence—2 Fayette—3 Genevieve—4 Kosciusko—5 Autumnal Moon—6 to the Nightingale—7 Imitation of Spencer—8 Poem written in Early Youth,—all the others will be finally & totally omitted.[2]—It is strange that in the Sonnet to Schiller I wish to die—*die* that nothing may stamp me *mortal*—this *Bull* never struck me till Charles Lloyd mentioned it—the Sense is evident enough—but the word is ridiculously ambiguous.——.——

Charles Lloyd is a very good fellow & most certainly a young man of great Genius—he desires his kindest Love to you. I will write again by Milton: for I really can write no more now—I am so depressed. But I will fill up the letter with poetry of mine, or Charles Lloyd's, or Southey's.

Is your Sister married?——May the Almighty bless her! May he enable her to make all her new friends as pure, and mild, and amiable as herself! I pray in the fervency of my Soul!——Is your dear Mother well?——My filial respects to her. Remember me to Ward.——David Hartley Coleridge is stout, healthy, & handsome. He is the very miniature of me /

Your grateful & affectionate Friend & Brother,

S. T. Coleridge

Sonnet

My Bible! scarcely dare I open thee!
Rememb'ring how each eve I wont to give

---

[1] This poem was not published until 1817, when it appeared under the title, *The Destiny of Nations. A Vision.* See Letters 163, 164, 172, 177, 178, 194, and 233 for references to this poem by various titles and for two explanations of its non-appearance in Coleridge's 1797 volume.

[2] This tentative plan was modified when the volume was published in 1797.

The due text holily, while she did live
The pious Woman! & to Misery
Tho' thou dost bring glad tidings, still thy page
So plainly speaks of her, I lov'd—how well!
And kindling Virtue doth so amply tell
Of her most virtuous, that 'twere hard to assuage
The pang, that thou wilt wake! Yet, hallow'd Book!
Tho' for a time my bosom thou wilt wring,
Thy high & gracious promises will bring
Best consolation! Come then, I will look
In thy long-clasped Volume, there to find
Haply, tho' lost her form, my best friend's mind!

C. Lloyd.

This is a very rough-cast Sonnet; but the beauty & goodness of the sentiments redeem it from it's faults & make it dear to the good.—

Both the Sonnets are on his Grandmother—[1]

November 1st

As o'er the dying embers oft I cower
When my tir'd Spirits rest, & my Heart swells
Lull'd by domestic Quiet, Memory dwells
On that blest tide, when thou the evening hour
Didst gladden. As upon th' accustom'd chair
I look, it seems as if thou still wert there!
Kirtled in snowy Apron thy dear Knees
Propt on the fender'd Hearth my Fancy sees,
O'er which exchanging souls we wont to bend;
And as I lift my head, thy features send
A cheering smile to me! but in it's flight
O'er my rain-pelted Sash a Blast of Night
Sweeps surlily! Starting, my Fancy creeps
To the bleak Dwelling, where thy cold corse sleeps!

C. Lloyd

Inscription for the Cenotaph at Ermenonville.[2]— Cenotaph, a tomb erected to the *memory* of a person—from κενός empty & ταφή sepulchre.

---

[1] These two sonnets of Lloyd's were printed in Coleridge's *Poems*, 1797, pp. 203 and 206.

[2] Southey's *Poet. Works*, iii. 108.

Stranger! the MAN OF NATURE sleeps not here:
Enshrin'd far distant by his * rival's side
His relics rest, there by the giddy throng
With blind Idolatry alike rever'd!
Wiselier directed have thy pilgrim feet
Explor'd the scenes of Ermenonville. ROSSEAU
Lov'd these calm haunts of Solitude & Peace;
Here he has heard the murmurs of the stream,
And the soft rustling of the poplar grove
When o'er their bending Boughs the passing Wind
Swept a grey shade. Here if thy breast be full,
If in thine eye the tear devout should gush,
His Spirit shall behold thee, to thine home
From hence returning, purified of heart.

R. Southey.

* Voltaire,—in the pantheon at Paris [S.T.C.]

This is beautiful—but instead of Ermenonville & Rosseau put Vauclusa & Petrarch.

Explor'd Vauclusa's scenery. Petrarch lov'd
These quiet haunts &c——Would not the lines be applicable equally:—it is not sufficiently *peculiar* to Rosseau—I am astonished how an *admirer* of Rosseau could put so little *thought* in an inscription to his Memory.

I do not particularly admire Rosseau—Bishop Taylor, Old Baxter, David Hartley & the Bishop of Cloyne are *my men*.[1]

Sonnet

written on receiving letters informing me of the birth of a Son, I being at Birmingham.[2]

When they did greet me Father, sudden Awe
Weigh'd down my spirit! I retir'd and knelt
Seeking the throne of grace, but inly felt[3]
No heavenly visitation upwards draw
My feeble mind, nor cheering ray impart.
Ah me! before the eternal Sire I brought
Th' unquiet Silence of confused Thought
And shapeless feelings: my o'erwhelmed Heart
Trembled: & vacant tears stream'd down my face.

[1] Jeremy Taylor (1613–67), Bishop of Down and Connor, Richard Baxter (1615–91), David Hartley (1705–57), and George Berkeley (1685–1753), Bishop of Cloyne, form indeed a heterogeneous group.

[2] *Poems*, i. 152.

[3] Seeking the throne of Mercy; but I felt [Cancelled version of line above.]

And now once more, O Lord! to thee I bend,
Lover of Souls! and groan for future grace,
That, ere my Babe youth's perilous maze have trod,
Thy overshadowing Spirit may descend
And he be born again, a child of God!

S. T. Coleridge

This Sonnet puts in no claim to poetry—(indeed as a composition
I think so little of them that I neglect[ed] to repeat them to you)
but it is a most faithful picture of my feelings on a very interesting
event——When I was with you, they were indeed, excepting this
first, in a rude & undrest state.

Sonnet

Composed on my journey home from Birmingham.[1]

Oft of *some unknown Past* such Fancies roll
Swift o'er my brain, as make the Present seem,
For a brief moment, like a most strange dream
When, not unconscious that she dreamt, the Soul
Questions herself in sleep! and Some have said
We liv'd ere yet this *fleshly* robe we wore.
O my sweet Baby! when I reach my door,
If heavy Looks should tell me, thou wert dead,
(As sometimes, thro' excess of Hope, I fear)
I think, that I should struggle to believe,
Thou wert a Spirit to this nether sphere
Sentenc'd, for some more venial crime to grieve—
Didst scream, then spring to meet Heaven's quick Reprieve,
While we wept idly o'er thy little Bier!

S. T. Coleridge

Almost all the followers of Fenelon believe that *men* are degraded
Intelligences, who had once all existed, at one time & together,
in a paradisiacal or perhaps heavenly state.—The first four lines
express a feeling which I have often had. The present has appeared
like a vivid dream or exact similitude of some *past* circumstances.

Sonnet

to a friend who wished to know *how I felt* when the Nurse first
present[ed] my Infant to me.[2]

Charles! my slow Heart was only *sad*, when first
I scann'd that face of feeble Infancy:

---

[1] *Poems*, i. 153. See Letters 156 and 164.   [2] *Poems*, i. 154.

For dimly on my thoughtful spirit burst
All I had been, and all my Babe might be!
But when I watch'd it on it's Mother's arm
And hanging at her bosom (she the while
Bent o'er it's features with a tearful smile)
Then I was thrill'd & melted, and most warm
Imprest *a Father's kiss*! And all beguil'd
Of dark Remembrance and presageful Fear
I seem'd to see an Angel's form appear—
'Twas even thine, beloved Woman mild!
So for the Mother's sake the Child was dear,
And dearer was the Mother for the Child!
S. T. Coleridge

God bless thee! my dearest, and most esteemed friend——
Friend of my Soul! and Brother of my Choice!

147. *To Benjamin Flower*

Address: Mr Benjamin Flower | Printer | Cambridge
MS. Mr. Paul Coleridge. Pub. Memories *by Stephen Coleridge, London, 1913,*
p. 211.
Postmark: 3 November 1796. *Stamped*: Bristol.

November 2nd 1796

My dear Sir

The above admirable poem was written by Southey, the Author of Joan of Arc—& I am happy that I have the opportunity of introducing it to your paper. My poems are entering on a second Edition—I shall leave out with some other things all the political allusions except those which occur in the Religious Musings (by the bye, I have to thank you for your very respectful mention of that poem in your pamphlet.)—

Will you be so kind as to procure Lunn's & Deigh[ton's] permission to have their names in the title-page. Your's I presume I may reckon on.—

My Wife was safely delivered of a boy—a fine fellow & stout—on Sept. 19th. I have named him David Hartley Coleridge, in honor of the great Master of Christian Philosophy.

I shall shortly be delivered of an Examination of Godwin's political Justice.[1] I have raised myself many enemies among the atheists by my prelusive skirmishes.

I hope, that Robert Hall is well—Why is he idle—? I mean,

[1] This 'Examination' was never written.

towards the Public. We want such men to rescue this *enlightened age* from general Irreligion. The stream of Knowlege has diffused itself into shallows.

> Believe me | your obliged & sincerely grateful Friend
> S. T. Coleridge

148. *To Joseph Cottle*

Pub. Early Rec. *i. 54.*

[3 November 1796][1]

Dear Cottle,

A devil, a very devil, has got possession of my left temple, eye, cheek, jaw, throat, and shoulder. I cannot see you this evening. I write in agony.

> Your affectionate Friend and Brother,
> S. T. C.

149. *To Robert Southey*

Address: Robert Southey
MS. Harvard College Lib. Hitherto unpublished.

[3 November 1796][2]

I hear that Albion's Longini (the British Critics, I mean) have manifested their unshaken Zeal for political & religious orthodoxy without any weak scrupulosity about the *means.* Have you got the Review, & can you lend it me for a few minutes?——Lend me the Monthly Magazine for half an hour—& if you can do it conveniently, your last proof-sheet—From the right temple to the tip of my right shoulder including eye, cheek, Jaws, teeth, & throat I am suffering more than Jupiter parturient of Pallas.——

> S. T. Coleridge

150. *To Joseph Cottle*

MS. New York Public Lib. Pub. E. L. G. i. 59.

[5 November 1796]

My dear Cottle

I feel pain in being disappointed—& still greater pain in the idea of disappointing—but I am seriously ill. The complaint, my

---

[1] Since Coleridge was taken ill Wednesday night, 2 Nov. 1796, this letter was probably written the next day. See Letter 151.

[2] Since this letter describes Coleridge's illness in almost exactly the same terms as in a letter to Poole of 5 Nov., it was probably written on Thursday, 3 Nov.

medical attendant says, is nervous—and originating in *mental* causes. I have a Blister under my right-ear—& I take Laudanum every four hours, 25 drops each dose.[1]

—God be praised for all things! A faith in goodness *makes* all Nature good!

Your's affectionately
S. T. Coleridge

151. *To Thomas Poole*

Address: Mr Thomas Poole | Stowey | near | Bridgewater | Somerset
MS. British Museum. Pub. Letters, *i. 172.*

Saturday night. November 5th—[1796]

Thanks, my heart's warm thanks to you, my beloved Friend! for your tender letter—indeed I did not deserve so kind a one—but by this time you have received my last.—

To live in a beautiful country & to inure myself as much as possible to the labors of the field, have been for this year past my dream of the day, my Sigh at midnight—but to enjoy these blessings *near you*, to see you daily, to tell you all my thoughts in their first birth, and to hear your's, to be mingling identities with you, as it were;—the vision-weaving *Fancy* has indeed often pictured such things, but *Hope* never dared whisper a promise!—Disappointment! Disappointment! dash not from my trembling hand this bowl, which almost touches my lips! Envy me not this immortal Draught, and I will forgive thee all thy persecutions—forgive thee! impious!—I will *bless thee*, black-vested Minister of Optimism! Stern Pioneer of Happiness!—Thou hast been '*the Cloud*' before me from the day that I left the flesh-pots of Egypt & was led thro' the way of a wilderness—the *cloud*, that hast been guiding me to a land flowing with milk & honey—the milk of Innocence, the honey of Friendship! I wanted such a letter as your's—: for I am very unwell. On Wednesday night I was seized with an intolerable pain from my right temple to the tip of my right shoulder, including my right eye, cheek, jaw, & that side of the throat——I was nearly frantic—and ran about the House naked, endeavouring by every means to excite sensations in different parts of my body, & so to weaken the enemy by creating a division. It continued from one in the morning till half past 5, & left me pale & fainty.—It came on fitfully but not so violently, several times on Thursday—and began

---

[1] Oh that S.T.C. had never taken more than 25 drops each dose! J.C. [Note in manuscript by Cottle.]

severer threats towards night, but I took between 60 & 70 drops
of Laudanum, and *sopped* the Cerberus just as his mouth began
to open. On Friday it only *niggled*; as if the Chief had departed as
from a conquered place, and merely left a small garrison behind,
or as if he evacuated the Corsica,[1] & a few straggling pains only
remained; but *this morning* he returned in full force, & his Name is
Legion!—Giant-fiend of an hundred hands! with a shower of
arrowy Death-pangs he transpierced me, & then he became a Wolf
& lay gnawing my bones.——I am not mad, most noble Festus!—
but in sober sadness I have suffered this day more bodily pain than
I had before a conception of—. My right cheek has certainly been
placed with admirable exactness under the focus of some invisible
Burning-Glass, which concentrated all the Rays of a Tartarean
Sun.—My medical attendant decides it to be altogether nervous,
and that it originates either in severe application, or excessive
anxiety.—My beloved Poole! in excessive anxiety, I believe, it
might originate!——I have a blister under my right-ear, and I take
25 drops of Laudanum every five hours: the ease & *spirits* gained
by which have enabled me to write you this flighty, but not
exaggerating, account——. With a gloomy wantonness of Imagina-
tion I had been coquetting with the hideous *Possibles* of Dis-
appointment—I drank fears, like wormwood; yea, made myself
drunken with bitterness! for my ever-shaping & distrustful mind
still mingled gall-drops, till out of the cup of Hope *I almost poisoned
myself with Despair!*

Your letter is dated November 2nd—I wrote to you November
1st—Your Sister was married on that day[2]—& on that day several
times I felt my heart overflowed with such tendernesses for her, as
made me repeatedly ejaculate prayers in her behalf!—Such things
are strange—it may be superstition to think about such corre-
spondences; but it is a superstition which softens the heart & leads
to no evil.—We will call on your dear Sister as soon as I am quite
well—& in the mean time I will write a few Lines to her. I am
anxious beyond measure to be in the country as soon as possible—
I would it were possible to get a temporary residence till Adscombe
is ready for us.—I would, that it could be, that we could have three
Rooms in Bill Poole's large House for the winter—— Will you try
to look out for a fit servant for us—simple of heart, *physiognomically*

[1] 'The news of the evacuation of Corsica by the British troops, which took
place on October 21, 1796, must have reached Coleridge a few days before the
date of this letter. Corsica was ceded to the British, June 18, 1794. A declara-
tion of war on the part of Spain (August 19, 1796) and a threatened invasion
of Ireland compelled the home government to withdraw their troops from
Corsica.' *Letters*, i. 174 n.

[2] Sarah Poole married Mr. King of Acton near Bristol.

handsome, & scientific in vaccimulgence? That last word is a new one; but soft in sound, and full of expression. Vaccimulgence!— I am pleased with the word.—Write to me all things about your-self—where I can not advise, I can console—and communication, which doubles joy, halves Sorrow.——

Tell me whether you think it at all possible to make any terms with William Poole—you know, I would not wish to touch with the edge of the Nail of my great toe the line which should be but half a barley corn out of the circle of the most trembling Delicacy! —I will write Cruikshanks tomorrow, if God permit me!—God bless & protect you, Friend! Brother! Beloved!

S. T. Coleridge

Sara's best love & Lloyd's——David Hartley is well, saving that he is sometimes inspired by the God Eolus, & like Isaiah, his 'bowells, sound like an Harp'! (My filial Love to your dear Mother / —love to Ward— / Little Tommy! I often think of thee!)

152. *To Thomas Poole*

Address: Mr Thomas Poole | Stowey | near | Bridgewater | Somerset
MS. British Museum. Pub. with omis. Letters, *i. 176.*
Stamped: Bristol.

November 7th [1796.]   Monday Night—

My dearest Poole

I wrote you on Saturday night under the immediate inspiration of Laudanum—& wrote you a *flighty* letter, but yet one most accurately descriptive both of facts & feelings. Since then my pains have been lessening—and the greater part of this day I have enjoyed perfect ease: only I am totally inappetent of food, and languid even to an inward Perishing.

I wrote John Cruikshanks this morning—& this moment I have received a letter from him. My letter written *before* the receipt of his contains every thing, I could write in *answer* to it—and I do not like to write him superfluously, lest I should break in on his domestic terrors & solitary broodings, with respect to Anna Cruikshanks!——May the Father & Lover of the Meek preserve that meek Woman, and give her a Joyful and safe deliverance!!

I wrote this morning a short note of congratulatory kindliness to your Sister: & shall be eager to call on her, when LEGION shall have been thoroughly exorcised from my Temple & Cheek.—— Tell Cruikshanks that I have received his Letter, & thank him for it.

A few lines in your last letter betokened, I thought, a wounded spirit. Let me know the particulars, my beloved Friend!——I shall forget & lose my own anxieties, while I am healing your's with cheerings of Sympathy.

I met with the following Sonnet in some very dull poems, among which it shone like a solitary Star, when the night is dark, and *one* little space only of Blue uninvaded by the floating Blackness—or if a *terrestrial* Simile be required, like a red Carbuncle on a Negro's Nose. From the languor & exhaustion, to which Pain & my frequent Doses of Laudanum have reduced me, it suited the feeble temper of my Mind—& I have transcribed it on the other page.

I amused myself the other day (having some *paper* at the Printer's which I could employ no other way) in selecting 28 Sonnets, to bind up with Bowles's—I charge sixpence for them, and have sent you five to dispose of.——I have only printed two hundred, as my paper held out to no more; and dispose of them privately, just enough to pay the printing.—The Essay, which I have written at the beginning, I like.[1]

Menu's Ordinances[2] exhibit a mournful picture of an hideous Union of Priest-craft & Despotism. The man who told George Dyer, that it would furnish unanswerable arguments against the divine Legation of Moses, spoke what he did not himself believe— or rather perhaps believed it because he wished it. The first Chapter contains sublimity—& next to the first the last is the best.—I have likewise sent you Burke's pamphlet which was given to me—it has all his excellencies without any of his faults.—This parcel I send tomorrow morning, inclosed in a parcel to Bill Poole of Shurton.——

God love you, my affectionate Brother—

& your affectionate
S. T. Coleridge

[1] Two copies of the *Sonnets from Various Authors* have survived. The copy in the Victoria and Albert Museum (described by Wise, *Bibliography*, pp. 31–35) is bound up at the end of a copy of the fourth edition of W. L. Bowles's *Sonnets, and Other Poems*, 1796; that in the Huntington Library, bearing Charles Lloyd's signature on the title-page of Bowles's *Poems* and again on the *Sonnets*, is bound up with a copy of the third edition of Bowles's *Sonnets, with Other Poems*, 1794. Of the sonnets, 4 are by Coleridge, 4 by Lamb, 4 by Southey, 4 by Lloyd, 3 by Bowles, 2 by Charlotte Smith, and 1 each by John Bamfield [Bampfylde], Thomas Warton, Henry Brooks, William Sotheby, Thomas Dermody, Thomas Russell, and Anna Seward. Coleridge reprinted in somewhat altered form his introductory essay on the sonnet in *Poems*, 1797, pp. 71–74.

[2] *Institutes of Hindu Law; or the Ordinances of Menu*, translated by Sir William Jones, 1794.

Sonnet

With pensive Joy the moment I survey
When welcome Death shall set my Spirit free.
My Soul! the Prospect brings no fear to thee;
But soothing Fancy rises to pourtray
The dear and parting words, my Friends will say:
With secret Pride their heaving Breast I see,
And court the Sorrows that will flow for me.
And now I hear my lingering Knell decay,
And mark the Hearse! Methinks, with moisten'd eye
CLARA beholds the sad Procession move
That bears me to the Resting-place of Care,
And sighs 'Poor Youth! thy Bosom well could love,
'And well thy Numbers picture Love's despair![']
Vain Dreams! yet such as make it sweet to die.

I shall expect a letter from you——I have the wind & the hiccups as if the Demon of Hurricanes were laying waste my trullibub-plantation.——

153. *To John Thelwall*

Address: J. Thelwall | Beaufort Buildings | The Strand | London
MS. Pierpont Morgan Lib. Pub. E. L. G. i. 59.
Postmark: November 14, 1796.

Sunday November 13th 1796

My dear Thelwall

I ought indeed to have written to you and have felt no little pain from having omitted it. But the Post will not wait while I am writing apologies & excus[es] and I wish to speak of & concerning your affairs. This only let me say—if I could have written any thing pleasant, I would not have omitted or delayed.

The Sketch of your plan I like well. The origin of Property & the *mode of removing it's* evils—form the last Chapter of my Answer to Godwin, which will appear now in a few weeks—We run on the same ground, but we drive different Horses. I am daily more and more a religionist—you, of course, more & more otherwise. I am sorry for the difference, simply because it impoverishes our sympathies: for indeed it does not lessen my esteem & friendship.—I will bestir myself *assiduously* & *immediately* by personal exhortation & by letter & in the course of a few days, I hope & trust, I shall be able to give you tidings of the resuscitation of virtue among us. But *immediately* write me the size of your intended work, price &c &c—in short, send me your printed proposals.

Dr Beddoes mentioned your letter to me, & meant to have written you—but he has been immersed in business & he could write nothing cheering. He respects you. I think, that temporary pamphlets must be bad speculations. They are 'grass that in the morning' &c—But what is the *price* of your answer, & size—write immediately that I may know particulars: the price of that which you *have* published. I think I shall be able to get off about 30 for you, almost immediately.

Dr Fox[1] is a very good man—& when you send me the proposals &c, I will call upon him. I would mention names to you; but I know of none who would not rather be influenced by letters from me, than from you; because those, whom I know in different places, are all *personally* attached to me——& the world is not yet virtuous enough, to suppose that the nakedness of a good cause is sufficient—but, depend on it, I will write immediately & every where: that is to say, immediately I hear from you.

Have you, my dear Thelwall!—no plan for your future Life? What is the state of your body? Are you sickly, or strong? Is your body so weakened by exertion & anxiety, as to make *stimulants* (such as wine & constant *animal* food) necessary to your Health? How many dear Little ones have you?—I should like to know all things *about* you—for *you*, I am confident, I know already.—— *My* plan is formed—but of myself hereafter.—You mention'd to me that you are not a man of Greek & Roman Literature—have you read *variously* in your own language? I mean, have you been in the university phrase *a Fag?* Or rather have you read little, but reflected much?—I ask these perhaps impertinent Questions because I wish to see you engaged in some *great* works—& for these various & profound study is assuredly a thing needful.—

My Wife & little one (his name David Hartley) are marvellously well—Give my love to your's—

Write *immediately*, and believe me with great sincerity | Your
affectionate
S. T. Coleridge

I was glad to hear from Colson that you abhor the morality of my Sonnet to Mercy[2]—it is indeed detestable & the poetry is not above mediocrity. What a foul song Horne Tooke has committed!— It has done harm—the aristocrats glory in it, the worthy among *us* shudder, the ignorant *whet* their *knives.*

---

[1] Dr. Edward Long Fox kept a private asylum in Bristol. Cottle says that Dr. Fox, 'in admiration of Mr. C's talents, presented him with FIFTY POUNDS' in 1796. (*Early Rec.* ii. 163.) Coleridge printed *An Answer to 'A Letter to Edward Long Fox, M.D.'* in Dec. 1795. Cf. Wise, *Bibliography*, 16–18.

[2] Later entitled *Pity.* Cf. *Poems*, i. 93.

154. *To Charles Lloyd, Senior*

Pub. Charles Lamb and the Lloyds, *26.*

Monday, November 14th [1796]

Dear Sir,—I received your letter, and thank you for that interest
which you take in my welfare. The reasons which you urge against
my present plan are mostly well-founded; but they would apply
equally against any other scheme of life which *my* Conscience
would permit me to adopt. I might have a situation as a Unitarian
minister, I might have lucrative offices as an active Politician; but
on both of these the Voice within puts a firm and unwavering
negative. Nothing remains for me but schoolmastership in a large
town or my present plan. To the success of both, and indeed even
to my *subsisting* in either, health and the possession of my faculties
are necessary Requisites. While I possess these Requisites, *I know,*
I can maintain myself and family in the COUNTRY; the task of
educating children suits not the activity of my mind, and the
anxieties and confinement incident to it, added to the living in a
town or city, would to a moral certainty ruin that Health and those
faculties which, as I said before, are necessary to my gaining my
livelihood in *any* way. Undoubtedly, without fortune, or trade, or
profession it is *impossible* that I should be in any situation in which
I must not be dependent on my own health and exertions for the
bread of my family. I do not regret it—it will make me *feel* my
dependence on the Almighty, and it will prevent my affections
from being made earthly altogether. I praise God in all things, and
feel that to His grace alone it is owing that I am *enabled* to praise
Him in all things. You think my scheme *monastic rather than
Christian.* Can he be deemed monastic who is married, and em-
ployed in rearing his children?—who *personally* preaches the truth
to his friends and neighbours, and who endeavours to instruct tho'
Absent by the Press? In what line of Life could I be more *actively*
employed? and what titles, that are dear and venerable, are there
which I shall not possess, God permit[ting] my present resolutions
to be realised? Shall I not be an Agriculturist, an Husband, a
Father, and a *Priest* after the order of *Peace*? an *hireless* Priest?
'Christianity teaches us to let our lights shine before men.' It does
so—but it likewise bids us say, Our Father, lead us not [into]
temptation! which how can he say with a safe conscience who
voluntarily places himself in those circumstances in which, if he
believe Christ, he must acknowledge that it would be easier for a
Camel to go thro' the eye of a needle than for HIM to enter into the
Kingdom of Heaven? Does not that man *mock* God who daily

prays against temptations, yet daily places himself in the midst of the most formidable? I meant to have written a few lines only respecting myself, because I have much and weighty matter to write concerning my friend, Charles Lloyd; but I have been seduced into many words from the importance of the general truths on which I build my conduct.

While your Son remains with me, he will, of course, be acquiring that knowledge and those powers of Intellect which are necessary as the *foundation* of excellence in all professions, rather than the immediate science of *any. Languages* will engross one or two hours in every day: the *elements* of Chemistry, Geometry, Mechanics, and Optics the remaining hours of study. After tolerable proficiency in these, we shall proceed to the study of *Man* and of *Men*—I mean, Metaphysics and History—and finally, to a thorough examination of the Jewish and Christian Dispensations, their doctrines and evidences: an examination necessary for all men, but peculiarly so to your son, if he be destined for a medical man. A Physician who should be even a Theist, still more a *Christian*, would be a rarity indeed. I do not know *one*—and I know a *great many* Physicians. They are *shallow* Animals: having always employed their minds about Body and Gut, they imagine that in the whole system of things there is nothing but Gut and Body. . . .

['Here followed an account of Charles Lloyd's health, which was just then so "unsatisfactory" as to shut out anything but amusement. In his anxiety, Coleridge called in Dr. Beddoes.']¹

I chose Dr. Beddoes, because he is a *philosopher*, and the knowledge of *mind* is essentially requisite in order to the well-treating of your Son's distemper. . . . Such is Dr. Beddoes's *written* opinion. But he *told* me, that your Son's cure must be effected by Sympathy and Calmness—by being in company with some one before whom he *thought aloud* on all subjects, and by being in situations perfectly according with the tenderness of his Disposition. . . .

I hope your Health is confirmed, and that your Wife and children are well. Present my well-wishes. You are blessed with children who are *pure in Heart*—add to this Health, Competence, Social Affections, and Employment, and you have a complete idea of Human Happiness.

Believe me, | With esteem and friendly-heartedness, |
Your obliged
S. T. Coleridge.

¹ Comment by E. V. Lucas, op. cit. 30.

155. *To Thomas Poole*

Address: Mr Thomas Poole | Stowey | near | Bridgewater | Somerset
MS. British Museum. Pub. E. L. G. i. 61.
Stamped: Bristol.

Tuesday November 15th 1796 half past five

My dearest Poole

Since the receipt of your last letter I have written you *twice*: and for this week past I have been punctually at the door of the Post office, every Evening at five o'clock, anxiously expecting to hear from you. My anxieties eat me up. I entreat you, write me; if it be only to say, that you have nothing to write. Have you thought concerning my suggestions in the letter, I wrote during my illness?—Yes!—I am sure, you have. Let me know the Result of your Reflections.—

Charles Lloyd has been very ill, and his distemper (which may with equal propriety be named either Somnambulism, or frightful Reverie, or *Epilepsy from accumulated feelings*) is alarming. He falls all at once into a kind of Night-mair: and all the Realities round him mingle with, and form a part of, the strange Dream. All his voluntary powers are suspended; but he perceives every thing & hears every thing, and whatever he perceives & hears he perverts into the substance of his delirious Vision. He has had two principal fits, and the last has left a feebleness behind & occasional flightiness. Dr Beddoes has been called in.—

I want consolation, my friend! my Brother! Write & console me. My Wife & Child are very well.

Remember me to Cruikshanks—I hope, his domestic Anxieties have been happily terminated.

Your affectionately grateful
S. T. Coleridge

P.S. Estlin informs me, that he has received 15 guineas on my account; but declined mentioning the names. I suppose, it is from those of whom you spoke to me while we were riding that Sunday to Mr Newton's.——

If I should be likely to find out any temporary residence near you, I would immediately walk down to Stowey, to look about for it.——

But write!——

156. *To John Thelwall*

Address: John Thelwall | Beaufort Buildings | Strand | London
MS. Pierpont Morgan Lib. Pub. with omis. Letters, *i. 178.*
Postmark: 21 November 1796.   *Stamped*: Bristol.

Saturday Nov. 19th [1796]
Oxford Street, Bristol

My dear Thelwall

Ah me! literary *Adventure* is but bread and cheese *by chance!*
I keenly sympathize with you—sympathy, the only poor consola-
tion I can offer you. Can no plan be suggested? I mention one not
as myself approving it; but because it was mentioned to me—
Briefly thus—If the Lovers of Freedom in the principal towns
would join together by eights or tens, to send for what *books* they
want directly to you, & if you could place yourself in such a line
that you might have books from the different Publishers at Book-
sellers' price.—Suppose now, that 12 or 14 people should agree
together that a little order book should be kept in the *Shop* of one
of them—& when any one of these wanted a book, to write it down.
And as soon as enough were ordered, to make it worth the carriage,
to write up to you for them?——I repeat, that I mention the plan
merely because it was mentioned to me. Shame fall on the friends
of Freedom if they will do nothing better! If they will do nothing
better, they will not do even this!—And the plan would disgust
the Country Booksellers, who ought not to be alienated.

Have you any connection with the Corresponding Society
Magazine—I have not seen it yet—Robert Southey is one of it's
benefactors—Of course, you have read the Joan of Arc. Homer is
the Poet for the Warrior—Milton for the Religionist—Tasso for
Women—Robert Southey for the Patriot. The first & fourth books
of the Joan of Arc are to me more interesting than the same number
of Lines in any poem whatsoever.—But you, & I, my dear Thelwall!
hold different *creeds* in poetry as well as religion. N'importe.—By
the bye, of your works I have now all, except your essay on animal
vitality which I never had, & your *poems* which I bought on their
first publication, & lost them. From those poems I should have
supposed our poetical *tastes* more nearly alike, than I find, they
are.—The poem on Sols [*sic*] flashes Genius thro' Strophe 1.
Antistrophe I. & Epode I.—the rest I do not perhaps understand
——only I *love* these two lines—

Yet sure the Verse that shews the friendly mind
To Friendship's ear not harshly flows.—

Your larger *Narrative* affected me greatly. It is admirably written—& displays strong Sense animated by Feeling, & illumined by Imagination—& neither in the thoughts or rhythm does it encroach on poetry.——

There have been two poems of mine in the New Monthly magazine[1]—with my name—indeed, I make it a scruple of conscience never to publish any thing, however trifling, without it. Did you like them? The first was written at the desire of a beautiful little Aristocrat—Consider it therefore, as a Lady's Poem. Bowles (the bard of my idolatry) has written a poem lately without plan or meaning—but the component parts are divine. It is entitled—Hope, an allegorical Sketch. I will copy two of the Stanzas, which must be peculiarly interesting to you, virtuous High-Treasonist, & your friends, the other Acquitted Felons!—

> But see as one awaked from deadly Trance
> With hollow and dim eyes and stony stare
> CAPTIVITY with faltering step advance!
> Dripping & knotted was her coal-black Hair,
> For she had long been hid, as in the Grave:
> No sounds the silence of her prison broke,
> Nor one Companion had she in her Cave
> Save TERROR's dismal Shape, that no word broke,*
> But to a stony Coffin on the Floor
> With lean and hideous finger pointed evermore.
>
> The lark's shrill song, the early Village Chime,
> The upland echo of the winding Horn,
> The far-heard Clock that spoke the passing time,
> Had never pierc'd her Solitude forlorn:
> At length releas'd from the deep Dungeon's gloom
> She feels the fragrance of the vernal Gale,
> She sees more sweet the living Landscape bloom
> And whilst she listens to Hope's tender tale,
> She thinks, her long-lost Friends shall bless her sight,
> And almost faints with Joy amidst the broad Day-light!

> * for broke read spoke, as in Bowles.

The last line is indeed exquisite.——

Your portrait of yourself interested me—As to me, my face, unless when animated by immediate eloquence, expresses great Sloth, & great, indeed almost ideotic, good nature. 'Tis a mere carcase of a face: fat, flabby, & expressive chiefly of inexpression.——

---

[1] These were, *On a Late Connubial Rupture in High Life, Monthly Magazine,* Sept. 1796, p. 647, and *Reflections on entering into Active Life,* ibid., Oct. 1796, p. 712.

Yet, I am told, that my eyes, eyebrows, & forehead are physio-
gnomically good—; but of this the Deponent knoweth not. As to
my shape, 'tis a good shape enough, if measured—but my gait is
awkward, & the walk, & the *Whole man* indicates *indolence capable
of energies.*—I am, & ever have been, a great reader—& have read
almost every thing—a library-cormorant—I am *deep* in all out of
the way books, whether of the monkish times, or of the puritanical
aera—I have read & digested most of the Historical Writers—;
but I do not *like* History. Metaphysics, & Poetry, & 'Facts of
mind'—(i.e. Accounts of all the strange phantasms that ever
possessed your philosophy-dreamers from Tauth [Thoth], the
Egyptian to Taylor, the English Pagan,) are my darling Studies.—
In short, I seldom read except to amuse myself—& I am almost
always reading.——Of useful knowlege, I am a so-so chemist, & I
love chemistry——all else is *blank,*—but I *will* be (please God) an
Horticulturist & a Farmer. I compose very little—& I absolutely
hate composition. Such is my dislike, that even a sense of Duty is
sometimes too weak to overpower it.

I cannot breathe thro' my nose—so my mouth, with sensual
thick lips, is almost always open. In conversation I am impassioned,
and oppose what I deem [error] with an eagerness, which is often
mistaken for personal asperity——but I am ever so swallowed up
in the *thing*, that I perfectly forget my *opponent.* Such am I. I am
just about to read Dupuis' 12 octavos,[1] which I have got from
London. I shall read only one Octavo a week—for I cannot *speak*
French at all, & I read it slowly.——

My Wife is well & desires to be remembered to you & your Stella,
& little ones. N.B. Stella (among the Romans) was a Man's name.
All the *Classics* are against you; but our Swift, I suppose, is
authority for this unsexing.—

My little David Hartley Coleridge is marvellously well, & grows
fast.—I was at Birmingham when he was born—I returned
immediately on receiving the unexpected news (for my Sara had
strangely miscalculated) & in the Coach wrote the following
Sonnet.[2] It alludes in it's first lines to a *Feeling* which if you never
have had yourself, I cannot explain to you.

> Oft of some *Unknown Past* such fancies roll
> Swift o'er my brain, as make the Present seem,
> For a brief moment, like a most strange Dream
> When, not unconscious that [s]he dreamt, the Soul

---

[1] C. F. Dupuis, *Origine de tous les Cultes, ou Religion universelle.* 7 vols. in
12, 1795.

[2] *Poems*, i. 153. For a further discussion of this sonnet see Letter 164.

Questions herself in sleep: and Some have said
We liv'd ere yet this *fleshly* robe we wore.*
O my sweet Baby! when I reach my Door
If heavy Looks should tell me, thou wert dead,
(As sometimes, thro' excess of Hope, I fear)
I think, that I should *struggle* to believe
Thou wert a Spirit to this nether Sphere
Sentenc'd for some more venial crime to grieve;
Didst scream, then spring to meet heaven's quick reprieve
While we wept idly o'er thy little Bier!

  * Alluding to Plato's doc[trine] of Pre-existence [S.T.C.]

My feeling is more perspicuously, tho' less poetically, expressed
thus—take which you like.

Oft o'er my brain mysterious Fancies roll
That make the Present seem (the while they last)
A dreamy Semblance of some Unknown Past
Mix'd with such feelings, as distress the [Soul]
Half-reas'ning in her sleep: &c
Which do you like the best?—

Sonnet II[1]

To a Friend who asked me *how* I felt when the Nurse first presented
the Child to me.

Charles! my slow Heart was only *sad*, when first
I scann'd that face of feeble Infancy:
For dimly on my thoughtful spirit burst
All I had been, and all my babe might be!
But when I watch'd it on it's Mother's arm
And hanging at her bosom (She the while
Bent o'er it's features with a tearful smile)
Then I was *thrill'd*, & *melted*, and most warm
Imprest a Father's Kiss—and all beguil'd
Of dark Remembrance and presageful Fear
I seem'd to see an Angel's form appear——
'Twas even thine, beloved Woman mild!
So for the Mother's sake the Child was dear,
And dearer was [the] Mother for the Child!——

Write on the receipt of this—& believe me, as ever, with affec-
tionate esteem | Your sincere Friend
      S. T. Coleridge

  [1] *Poems*, i. 154.

P.S. I have inclosed a five guinea note——The five Shillings over please to [la]y out for me thus—In White's (of Fleet Street or the Strand, I forget which—O! the Strand, [I] believe—but I don't know which) well, in White's Catalogue are the following Books

> 4674. Iamblichus, Proclus, Porphyrius &c, One shilling & six-
> pence, One little volume—
> 4686 Juliani Opera, three shillings——

Which two books you will be so kind as to purchase for me & send down with the 25 pamp[h]lets. But if they should unfortunately be sold, in the same Catalogue are

		s	d
2109	Juliani Imp. Opera—	12	6
676	Iamblichus de Mysteriis	10	6
2681	Sidonius Apollinaris	6	0

& in the Catalogue of Robson, the Bookseller in New Bond Street,

	s	d	
Plotini Opera, a Ficino,—£1	1	0	——making all together

	s	d	
£2	10	0	——

If you can get the two former little books, costing only four & sixpence, I will [r]est content with them—if they are gone, be so kind as to purchase for me [t]he others, I mentioned to you, amounting to two pound, ten shillings—and, as in the course of next week I shall send a small parcel of books & manuscripts to my very dear Charles Lamb of the India House, I shall be [en]abled to convey the money to you in a letter, which he will leave at your house.——I make no apology for this commission—because I feel (to use a vulgar phrase) that I would do as much for you.

P.S. Can you buy them time enough to send down with your pamphlets? If not, make a parcel per se.

I hope, your hurts from the fall are not serious—You have given a *proof* now that you are no *'Ippokrite*——but I forgot, that you are not a Greekist, & perchance, you hate puns—but in Greek krités signifies a judge, & hippos an Horse—Hippocrite, therefore, may mean a *Judge of Horses*—My dear fellow! I laugh more, & talk more nonsense in a week, than [mo]st other people do in a year—& I *let* puns [in]offensively [in the presenc]e of grave men, who smile, like verjuice putred.

Farewell!

(I have inclosed the five pound—write when you have received it.)

157. *To Thomas Poole*

Address: Mr Thomas Poole | Stowey | near | Bridgewater | Somerset
MS. British Museum. Pub. E. L. G. i. 63.
Stamped: Bristol.

Monday Morning [28 November 1796]

My beloved friend! pardon the childish impatience which I have betrayed. The Sailor, who has borne cheerily a circumnavigation, may be allowed to feel a little like a coward, when within sight of his expected & wished for port.

We shall be more than content to live a year in the house you mention. It is not a beauty, to be sure; but it's vicinity to you shall overbalance it's Defects.—Pray, take it for us, for a year—I would it were possible, that we could get into it in three weeks—for we must quit our house on Christmas day, & it will be awkward to take Lodgings for a week—and expensive.

I will *instruct* the maid in *cooking*—Charles Lloyd continues well & desires his kind remembrance to you—So does Sara—& little Hartley has just left off sucking for half a second, & sends a half-formed smile to you—

Love to your mother—Your's affection[ately]

S. T. Coleridge

P.S. We shall rejoice to be bruised by the right-fist of your Love, in these ten days.

158. *To Charles Lloyd, Senior*

Pub. Charles Lamb and the Lloyds, *31.*

Sunday, December 4, 1796

Dear Sir,—I think it my duty to acquaint you with the nature of my connection with your Son. If he be to stay with me, I can neither be his tutor or fellow-student, nor in any way impart a regular system of knowledge. My *days* I shall devote to the acquirement of *practical* husbandry and horticulture, that as 'to beg I am ashamed,' I may at least be able 'to dig': and my evenings will be fully employed in fulfilling my engagements with the 'Critical Review' and 'New Monthly Magazine.' If, therefore, your Son occupy a room in my cottage, he will be there merely as a Lodger and Friend; and the only money I shall *receive* from him will be the sum which his *board* and *lodging* will cost *me*, and which, by an accurate calculation, I find will amount to half a guinea a week, exclusive of his washing, porter, cyder, spirits, in short any potation beyond table-beer—these he must provide himself with. I shall keep no servant.

I must add that Charles Lloyd must *furnish* his own bedroom. It is not in my power to do it myself without running into debt; from which may Heaven amid its most angry dispensations preserve me!

When I mentioned the circumstances which rendered my literary engagement impracticable, when, I say, I first mentioned them to Charles Lloyd, and described the severe process of simplification which I had determined to adopt, I never dreamt that he would have desired to continue with me: and when at length he did manifest such a desire, I dissuaded him from it. But his feelings became vehement, and in the present state of his health it would have been as little prudent as humane in me to have given an absolute refusal.

Will you permit me, Sir! to write of Charles Lloyd with freedom? I do not think he ever will endure, whatever might be the consequences, to practise as a physician, or to undertake any commercial employment. What weight your authority might have, I know not: I doubt not he would struggle to submit to it—but would he *succeed* in any attempt to which his temper, feelings, and principles are inimical? . . . What then remains? I know of nothing but agriculture. If his attachment to it *should* prove permanent, and he really acquired the steady dispositions of a practical farmer, I think you could wish nothing better for him than to see him married, and settled *near you* as a farmer. I love him, and do not think he will be well or happy till he *is* married and settled.

I have written plainly and decisively, my dear Sir! I wish to avoid not only evil, but the *appearances* of evil. This is a world of calumnies! Yea! there is an imposthume in the large tongue of this world ever ready to break, and it is well to prevent the contents from being sputtered into one's face. My Wife thanks you for your kind inquiries respecting her. She and our Infant are well—only the latter has met with a little accident—a burn, which is doing well.

To Mrs. Lloyd and all your children present my remembrances, and believe me in all esteem and friendliness,

Yours sincerely
S. T. Coleridge.

159. *To John Colson*

MS. Harvard College Lib. Hitherto unpublished.

Thursday December 8th 1796

My dear Colson

Your long silence did indeed make me uneasy. I attributed it to your anxieties, which (Judging of your mind by my own) I supposed to have exerted a *narcotic* influence on you.—I shall leave Bristol within ten days: I hope, I shall see you before that time. Believe me, there is no human face, the sight of which will kindle up more Joy in mine & my Sara's. Sara never speaks of you, but as 'DEAR Colson![']

I will write you a long letter by to morrow's post respecting myself, & cottage.—I am glad, Cruikshanks has not payed—'twas a foolish flight of kindness. Desire Parsons to strike it off his accompt Book.

The two guineas was payed to a Mr White, for a dozen of his 'Falstaff's original Letters'[1] which I disposed of for him here. 'Tis a truly laughable book.——Poor Allen! my heart bleeds over his distresses. The money, which I remitted him, demanded his esteem, not gratitude. I write, '*esteem*'—for in this rascally world, a man deserves *esteem* merely for being *honest*: and indeed it was only *honesty* in me. For I received from him more than I have been able to return, when I was in the army. He was perpetually sending me from Oxford money, & Tea, & Sugar, & a variety of other things, & twice came down, and wept over 'the thought-be-wilder'd Man'[2] with tears of brotherly affection.—When I forget to love him, the best & kindest thing that God's Mercy can do for my soul, will be to forget *me*.

My dearest Colson! the moment you receive this letter, if possible, walk to Robson's, the bookseller, in Bond Street—(New Bond Street, I believe) and buy for me a pamphlet entitled 'an Essay on the Prosodies of the Greek & Latin Languages'—dedicated to Lord Thurlow.[3] 'Tis a three shilling touch, I believe. I had to review & have lost it—& it is of the *utmost* consequence to me to have it *directly*. So pack it up & send it by *tomorrow's* Mail. You see, my dear Colson! *why* I have desired you to take so long a walk in such a peremptory mode of Begging.

If you see Tom Poole, give my kind Love to him. His absence from Stowey is an unfortunate thing for me. I dined with Captn King last Saturday. He is a good tempered Man, with sufficient sense, & very handsome——

God love you & your's.
S. T. Coleridge

---

[1] James White, *Original Letters of Sir John Falstaff and His Friends*, 1796.
[2] Cf. *To the Rev. W. L. Bowles*, line 7, *Poems*, i. 84.
[3] Coleridge reviewed this essay of Samuel Horsley's in the *Critical Review* for Feb. 1797. See *Rev. of Eng. Studies*, July 1951, pp. 238–47.

160. *To Thomas Poole*

Address: Mr Thomas Poole | Stowey | near | Bridgewater | Somerset—
MS. British Museum. Pub. Letters, *i. 183.*
Stamped: Bristol.

Sunday Morning [11 December 1796]

My beloved Poole

The sight of your villainous hand-scrawl was a great comfort to me. How have you been diverted in London? What of the Theatres? And how found you your old friends?—I dined with Mr King yesterday week. He is, quantum suff., a pleasant man—and (my wife says) very handsome.—Hymen lies in the arms of Hygeia, if one may judge by your Sister. She looks remarkably well.—But has not she *caught* some complaint in the *head*?—Some *scurfy* Disorder?—For her *Hair* was filled with an odious white *Dandruff*.

About myself, I have so much to say, that I really can say nothing. I mean to work *very hard*—as Cook, Butler, Scullion, Shoe-cleaner, occasional Nurse, Gardener, Hind, Pig-protector, Chaplain, Secretary, Poet, Reviewer, and omnium-botherum shilling-scavenger—in other words, I shall keep no Servant, and will cultivate my Land-acre, and my wise-acres, as well as I can. The motives, which led to this determination, are numerous & weighty; I have thought much & calmly; and calculated time & money with unexceptionable accuracy; and at length determined not to take the charge of Charles Lloyd's mind on me. Poor fellow! he still hopes to live with me——is now at Birmingham.——I wish, that little Cottage by the road side were gettable—? That with about two or three rooms——. It would quite do for us—as we shall occupy only *two rooms*—. I will write more fully on the receipt of your's —— God love you

&

S. T. Coleridge

161. *To Benjamin Flower*

Address: Mr Benjamin Flower | Printer | Cambridge
MS. Huntington Lib. Pub. E. L. G. i. 63.
Postmark: 13 December 1796.   *Stamped*: Bristol.

Sunday Night. [11 December 1796]

My much esteemed Friend

I truly sympathize with you in your severe Loss, and pray to God that he may give you a sanctified use of your Affliction. The death of a young person of high hopes and opening faculties impresses me less gloomily, than the Departure of the Old. To my more natural Reason, the former *appears* like a *transition*; there seems an *incompleteness* in the life of such a person, contrary to the general order of nature; and it makes the heart say, 'this is not all.' But when an old man sinks into the grave, we have seen the bud, the blossom, and the fruit; and the unassisted mind droops in melancholy, as if *the Whole* had come and gone.—But God hath been merciful to us, and strengthened our eyes thro' faith, and Hope may cast her anchor in a certain bottom, and the young and old may rejoice before God and the Lamb, weeping as tho' they wept not, and crying in the Spirit of faith, Art thou not from everlasting, O Lord God my Holy One? We shall not die!——I have known affliction, yea, my friend! I have been myself sorely afflicted, and have rolled my dreary eye from earth to Heaven, and found no comfort, till it pleased the Unimaginable High & Lofty One to make my Heart more tender in regard of religious feelings. My philosophical refinements, & metaphysical Theories lay by me in the hour of anguish, as toys by the bedside of a Child deadly-sick. May God continue his visitations to my soul, bowing it down, till the pride & Laodicean self-confidence of human Reason be utterly done away; and I cry with deeper & yet deeper feelings, O my Soul! thou art wretched, and miserable, & poor, and blind, and naked!——The young Lady, who in a fit of frenzy killed her own mother, was the Sister of my dearest Friend, and herself dear to me as an only Sister. She is recovered, and is acquainted with what she has done, and is very calm. She was a truly pious young woman; and her Brother, whose soul is almost wrapped up in her, hath had his heart purified by this horror of desolation, and prostrates his Spirit at the throne of God in believing Silence. The Terrors of the Almighty are the whirlwind, the earthquake, and the Fire that precede the still small voice of his Love. The pestilence of our lusts must be scattered, the strong-layed Foundations of our Pride blown up, & the stubble & chaff of our Vanities burnt, ere we can give ear to the inspeaking Voice of Mercy, 'Why *will* ye die?'——

My answer to Godwin will be a six shilling Octavo; and is designed to shew not only the absurdities and wickedness of *his* System, but to detect what appear to me the defects of all the systems of morality before & since Christ, & to shew that wherein they have been right, they have exactly coincided with the Gospel, and that each has erred exactly where & in proportion as, he has deviated from that perfect canon. My last Chapter will attack the credulity, superstition, calumnies, and hypocrisy of the present race of Infidels. Many things have fallen out to retard the work; but I hope, that it will appear shortly after Christmas, at the farthest. I have endeavoured to make it a cheap book; and it will contain as much matter as is usually sold for eight shillings. I perceive, that in the New Monthly Magazine the Infidels have it all hollow. How our ancestors would have lifted up their hands at th[at] modest proposal for making experiments in favor of Idolatry!

Before the 24th of this month I will send you my *poetic endeavor*[1]—it shall be as good as I can make it. The following Lines are at your service, if you approve of them.

LINES to a Young Man of Fortune who abandoned himself to an indolent and causeless Melancholy.[2]

> Hence that fantastic Wantonness of Woe,
> O Youth to partial Fortune vainly dea[r!]
> To plunder'd WANT's half-shelter'd Hovel go,
> Go, and some hunger-bitten Infant hear
> Moan haply in a dying Mother's Ear;
> Or when the cold and dismal fog-damps brood
> O'er the rank Church-yard with sear elm-leaves strew'd
> Pace round some WIDOW's grave, whose dearer Part
> Was slaughter'd where o'er his uncoffin'd limbs
> The flocking Flesh-birds scream'd! Then, while thy Heart
> Groans, and thine eyes a fiercer Sorrow dims,
> Know (and the Truth shall kindle thy young Mind)
> What Nature makes thee mourn, she bids thee heal:
> O Abject! if to sickly Dreams resign'd
> All effortless thou leave Earth's common weal
> A prey to the thron'd Murderers of Mankind!
> *Bristol, Dec. 11th,* ~~1796~~

S. T. COLERIDGE.

Do you keep a Shop in Cambridge?——I seldom see *any* paper. Indeed, I am out of heart with the French. In one of the numbers of my Watchman I wrote 'a remonstrance to the French Legislators':[3] it contain'd *my* politics, & the splendid Victories of the French since that time have produced no alterations in them. I am tired of reading butcheries and altho' I should be unworthy the name of Man, if I did not feel my Head & Heart awfully interested

[1] Coleridge's *Ode to the Departing Year*, was first printed in the *Cambridge Intelligencer*, 31 Dec. 1796, under the title, *Ode for the last day of the Year 1796.* Cf. *Poems*, i. 160.

[2] First published in the *Cambridge Intelligencer*, 17 Dec. 1796. Cf. *Poems*, i. 157.

[3] Cf. *Watchman*, No. VIII, 27 Apr. 1796.

in the final Event, yet, I confess, my Curiosity is worn out with regard to the particulars of the Process.—The paper, which contained an account of the departure of your friend, had in it a Sonnet written during a Thunder-storm.[1] In thought & diction it was sublime & fearfully impressive. I do not remember to have ever read so fine a *Sonnet*—Surely, I thought, this burst from no common feelings agitated by no common sorrow!—Was it your's?—

A young man of fortune, (his name, Gurney) wrote & published a book of horrible Blasphemies, asserting that our blessed Lord deserved his fate more than any malefactor ever did Tyburn (I pray heaven, I may incur no Guilt by transcribing it!)—& after a fulsome panegyric adds that the name of *Godwin* will soon supersede that of Christ.—Godwin wrote a letter to this Man, thanking him for his *admirable* work, & soliciting the honor of his personal friendship!!!—

With affectionate Esteem | Your's sincerely
S. T. Coleridge

At the close of this week I go with my Wife & Baby to Stowey, near Bridgewater, Somersetshire: where you will for the future direct to me. Whenever there is any thing particular, I shall be thankful for your Paper.

S. T. C.

162. *To Thomas Poole*

Address: Mr Thomas Poole | Stowey | near Bridgewater | Somerset
MS. British Museum. Pub. with omis. Letters, *i. 184.*
Stamped: Bristol.

[Endorsed 12 December 1796]

You tell me, my dear Poole! that my residence near you would give you great pleasure; and I am sure, that if you had any objections on your own account to my settling near Stowey, you would have mentioned them to me.[2] Relying on this, I assure you that a Disappointment would try my philosophy. Your Letter did indeed give me unexpected and most acute pain. I will *make* the Cottage do. We want but three rooms.—If Cruikshanks have promised more than his circumstances enable him to perform, I am sure, that I can get the other purchased by my friends in Bristol—I mean, the place at Adscombe. I wrote him pressingly

[1] For this sonnet see *Monthly Repository*, vol. viii, 1834, p. 656.

[2] 'A possible habitation, no more than a poor cottage, had been found at Stowey. But a new trouble had arisen. Poole himself had begun to feel qualms as to Coleridge's adaptability to a purely country life, and these, rather indiscreetly at this late stage, he expressed.' Chambers, *Life*, 63.

on this head some ten days ago; but he has returned me no answer. Lloyd has obtained his Father's permission & will return to me. He is willing to be his own Servant. As to Acton, 'tis out of the Question.—In Bristol I have Cottle & Estlin (for Mr Wade is going away) willing & eager to serve me—but how they can serve me more effectually at Acton, than at Stowey, I cannot divine. If I live at Stowey, you indeed *can* serve me effectually, by assisting me in the acquirement of agricultural practice.—If you can instruct me to manage an acre and a half of Land, and to raise on it with my own hands all kinds of vegetables, and grain, enough for myself & my Wife, and sufficient to feed a pig or two with the refuse, I hope, that you will have served me *most* effectually, by placing me out of the necessity of being served. I receive about forty guineas yearly from the Critical Review & New Monthly magazine. It is hard if by my greater works I do not get twenty more. I know how little the human mind requires when it is tranquil—and in proportion, as I should find it difficult to simplify my wants, it becomes my duty to simplify them. For there must be a vice in my nature, which woe be to me if I do not cure. The less meat I eat, the more healthy I am; and strong Liquors of any kind always & perceptibly injure me.—Sixteen shillings would cover all the weekly expences of my Wife, infant, and myself—this I say from my Wife's own calculation.

But whence this sudden revolution in your opinions, my dear Poole? You saw the Cottage, that was to be our temporary residence, and thought, we might be *happy* in it—and now you hurry to tell me, that we shall not even be *comfortable* in it.—You tell me, I shall be too far from my *friends*—i.e. Cottle & Estlin—for I have no other in Bristol—in the name of Heaven, *what can* Cottle or Estlin do for me? Or indeed what can any body [do] for me?—They do nothing who do not teach me how to be independent of any except the Almighty Dispenser of Sickness & Health!—And too far from the Press——With the printing of the Review & Magazine I have no concern—and if I publish any work on my own account, I will send a fair & faultless Copy, and Cottle promises to correct the Press for me.—Mr King's Family may be very worthy sort of people, for aught I know; but assuredly I can employ my time wiselier, than to gabble with my tongue to Beings, with whom neither my Head or Heart can commune.—My habits & feelings have suffered a total alteration. I *hate* company except of my dearest friends; and systematically avoid it, and when in it keep silence as far as social Humanity will permit me. Lloyd's Father in a letter to me yesterday enquired, how I should live without any companions?——I answered him, not an hour before

I received your letter—— 'I shall have six companions—My Sara, my Babe, my own shaping and disquisitive mind, my Books, my beloved Friend, Thomas Poole, & lastly, Nature, looking at me with a thousand looks of Beauty, and speaking to me in a thousand melodies of Love. If I were capable of being tired with all these, I should then detect a Vice in my Nature, and would fly to habitual Solitude to eradicate it.'—Yes! my friend! while I opened your letter, my heart was glowing with enthusiasm towards you—how little did I expect that I should find you earnestly & vehemently persuading me to prefer Acton to Stowey, and in return for the loss of *your* Society recommending *Mr King's* Family as 'very pleasant Neighbors'! Neighbors!—Can mere Juxta-position form a neigh-bourhood? As well should the Louse in my Head call himself my friend, and the Flea in my Bosom style herself my Love!——

On Wednesday Week we must leave our House: so that if you continue to dissuade me from settling near Stowey, I scarcely know what I shall do.—Surely, my beloved Friend! there must be some reason, which you have not yet told me, which urged You to send this hasty and heart-chilling Letter! I suspect that something has passed between your Sister & dear Mother—(in whose illness I sincerely sympathize with you.)——

I have never considered my settlement at Stowey in any other Relation than it's advantages to myself, and they would be great indeed. My objects (assuredly, wise ones) were to learn agriculture (& where should I get instruction except at Stowey) and to be where [I] can communicate in a literary way?——

I must conclude—I pray you let me hear from [you] immediately—

God bless you &

S. T. Coleridge.

163. *To Thomas Poole*

Address: Mr Thomas Poole | Stowey | near | Bridgewater | Somerset
MS. British Museum. Pub. with omis. Letters, i. *187.* This letter was begun on Monday night, 12 December 1796, a few hours after Letter 162, and was completed the following morning.
Stamped: Bristol.

Tuesday December 13th 1796

Monday Night.

I wrote the former Letter immediately on the receipt of your's, in the first Flutter of Agitation. The tumult of my Spirits has now subsided; but the Damp struck into my very Heart; and there I feel it. O my God! my God! when am I to find rest! Disappoint-ment follows Disappointment; and Hope seems given to me merely

to prevent my becoming callous to Misery!—Now I know not
where to turn myself. I was on my way to the city Library when
I found your letter at the Post-office—I opened it at the Library
& wrote an answer to it there. Since I have returned, I have been
poring into a book as a shew for not looking at my Wife & the
Baby! By God, I dare not look at them. Acton! the very name
makes me grind my Teeth!—What am I to do there? 'You will
have a good Garden, you may, I doubt not, have ground.' But am
I not ignorant, as a child, of every thing that concerns the Garden,
& the Ground? And shall I have one human Being there, who will
instruct me? The House too—what should I do with it? We want
but two rooms, or three at the furthest— & the country around is
intolerably flat. I would as soon live on the Banks of a Dutch
Canal!—And no one human being near me, for whom I should,
or could, care a rush! No one walk, where the beauties of Nature
might endear solitude to me! There is one Ghost, that I *am* afraid
of; with that I should be perpetually haunted in this same cursed
Acton, the hideous Ghost of departed Hope.—O Poole! how could
you make such a proposal to me?——I have compelled myself to
reperuse your Letter, if by any means I may be able to penetrate
into your motives. I find three reasons assigned for my not settling
at Stowey. The first, the distance from my friends, & the Press.
This I answered in the former letter—As to my friends, what can
they do for me—& as to the Press, even if Cottle had not promised,
to correct it for me, yet I might as well be 50 miles from it, as 12,
for any purpose of correcting the Printer's copy.—Secondly, the
Expence of moving. Well, but I must move to Acton: and what
will the difference be?—Perhaps, three guineas.—Ought a Friend
to have advised another Friend to live at a distance from him, and
as a reason to urge that the latter would save three guineas by
it?——I would give three guineas, that you had not assigned this
Reason.—Thirdly, the wretchedness of that Cottage, which alone
we can get.—But surely, in the house, which I saw, *two* rooms may
be found, which by a little green List, and a carpet, and a slight
alteration in the fireplace, may be made to exclude the cold: and
this is all, we want. Besides, it will be but for a while. If Cruik-
shanks cannot buy & repair Adscombe, I have no doubt, that my
friends here & at Birmingham would, some of them, purchase it.
So much for the Reasons—; but these cannot be the real reasons.
I was with you for a week, and then we talked over the whole
scheme, & you approved of it, & I gave up Derby—More than
9 weeks have elapsed since then—and you saw & examined the
Cottage, which we expected to live in for a while, & you knew every
other of these reasons, if reasons they can be called. Surely, surely,

my friend! something has occurred which you have not mentioned to me. Your Mother has manifested a strong dislike to our living near you—or some thing or other—for the reasons, you have assigned tell me nothing except that there are reasons, which you have not assigned. Pardon me if I write vehemently—I meant to have written calmly; but Bitterness of Soul came upon me. Mrs Coleridge has observed the workings of my face, while I have been writing; and is intreating to know what is the matter—I dread to shew her your Letter—I dread it. My God! my God! what if she should dare to think, that my most beloved Friend is grown cold towards me!—

Tuesday Morning, Eleven o'clock. After an unquiet & almost sleepless Night, I resume my pen.—As the sentiments over Leaf came from my Heart, I will not suppress them.—I would keep a Letter by me, which I wrote to a mere acquaintance, lest any thing unwise should be found in it—but my friend ought to know not only what my Sentiments are, but what all my feelings were.—I am indeed perplexed & cast down.——My first plan, you know, was this——My family was to have consisted of Charles Lloyd, my Wife, & Wife's Mother, my Infant, the Servant, & myself—My means of maintaining them—Eighty pound a year from Charles Lloyd, & forty from the Review & Magazine / : my time was to have been divided into four parts—1. Three hours after breakfast to studies with C. Ll.— 2. the remaining hours till Dinner to our Garden— 3. From after dinner till Tea to Letter-writing, and domestic Quietness. 4. From Tea till Prayer time to the Reviews, Magazines, & other literary Labors.——In this plan I calculated nothing on my Garden, but amusement. In the mean time I heard from Birmingham that Lloyd's Father had declared, that He should insist on his Son's returning to him at the close of one twelvemonth. What am I to do then?—I shall be again afloat on the wide sea unpiloted & unprovisioned. I determined to devote *my whole day* to the acquirement of practical horticulture, to part with Lloyd immediately, & live without a servant.—Charles Lloyd intreated me to give up the Review & Magazine, & devote the evenings to him. But this would be to have given up a permanent for a temporary Situation, and after subtracting 40£ from C. Ll's 80£ in return for the Review Business, & then calculating the expence of a servant, a less severe mode of general Living, & Lloyd's own Board & Lodging, the remaining 40£ would make but a poor figure—& what was I to do at the end of the Twelve-month?——In the meantime Mrs Fricker's Son could not be got out, as an apprentice—he was too young, and premiumless, & no one would take him: & the old Lady herself manifested a great

aversion to leaving Bristol. I recurred therefore to my first promise
of allowing her 20£ a year——but all her furniture must of course
be returned, and enough only remains to furnish one bedroom—& a
kitchen-parlour. If Charles Lloyd & the Servant went with me I
must have bought new furniture to the amount of 40 or 50£, which
if not Impossibility in person, was Impossibility's first Cousin.—
We determined to live by ourselves. We arranged our time, money,
& employments—we found it not only practicable *but easy*—&
Mrs Coleridge entered with enthusiasm into the Scheme. To
Mrs Coleridge the Nursing & Sewing only would have belonged—
the rest I took upon myself—& since our resolution have been
learning the practice.—With only two rooms, & two people—their
wants severely simple—& no great labor can there be in their
waiting upon themselves. Our Washing we should put out.——I
should have devoted my whole Head, Heart, & Body to my Acre
& a Half of Garden Land—& my evenings to Literature.—Mr &
Mrs Estlin approved, admired, & applauded the scheme—&
thought it not only highly virtuous, but highly prudent.—In the
course of a year & a half I doubt not, that I should feel myself
independent, for my bodily strength would have increased & I
should have been weaned from animal food, so as never to touch
it but once a week—& there can be no shadow of Doubt, that an
acre & a half of Land divided properly & managed properly would
maintain a small family in *every thing*, but cloathes & rent.—What
had I to ask of my friends? Not money—for a temporary relief of
my Wants is nothing—removes no gnawing of anxiety, & debases
the dignity of the Man. Not their Interest—What could their
Interest (supposing they had any) do for me? I can accept no place
in State, Church, or Dissenting Meeting. Nothing remains possible,
but a School, or Writer to a Newspaper, or my present Plan.—I
could not love the man, who advised me to keep a School or write
for a Newspaper. He must have a hard Heart! What then could I
ask of my friends! What of Mr Wade?—Nothing. What of Mr
Cottle? Nothing. What of Mr Estlin? Nothing. What of Thomas
Poole? O! a great deal.—Instruction, daily advice, Society—every
thing necessary to my feelings & the realization of my innocent
Independance.——You know, it would be impossible for me to
learn *every* thing myself—to pass across my Garden once or twice
a day, for five minutes, & set me right, & cheer me with the sight
[of] a friend's face, would be more to me than hundreds.——Your
Letter was *not* a kind one—One week only, & I must leave my
House—& yet in one week you advise me to alter the plan which
I had been three months forming & in which you must have known
by the Letter, I wrote you, during my illness, that I was interested

even to an excess & violence of Hope—& to abandon this plan for darkness & a renewal of anxieties, which might be fatal to me! Not one word have you mentioned how I am to live, or even exist—supposing I were to go to Acton. Surely, surely, you do not advise me to lean with the whole weight of my Necessities on the Press?—— Ghosts indeed! I should be haunted with Ghosts enough—the Ghosts of Otway & Chatterton, & the phantasms of a Wife broken-hearted, & a hunger-bitten Baby! O Thomas Poole! Thomas Poole! if you did but know what a Father & Husband must feel, who toils with his brain for uncertain bread! I dare not think of it—The evil Face of Frenzy looks at me!——The Husbandman puts his seed in the Ground & the Goodness, Power, & Wisdom of God have pledged themselves, that he shall have Bread, and Health, & Quietness in return for Industry, & Simplicity of Wants, & Innocence. The AUTHOR scatters his seed—with aching head, and wasted Health, & all the heart-leapings of Anxiety—& the Folly, the Vices, & the Fickleness of Man promise him Printers' Bills & the Debtors' Side of Newgate, as full & sufficient Payment.—

Charles Lloyd is at Birmingham—I hear from him daily—In his Yesterday's Letter he says—'My dearest Friend! every thing seems clearing around me. My Friends enter fully into my views. They seem altogether to have abandoned any ambitious views on my account. My Health has been very good ever since I left you; & I own, I look forward with more pleasure than ever to a permanent connection with you. Hitherto, I could only look forward to the pleasures of a Year—all beyond was dark & uncertain. My Father now completely acquiesces in my abandoning the prospect of any Profession, or Trade. If God grant me Health, there now remains no Obstacle to a completion of my most sanguine Wishes.'——Charles Lloyd will furnish his own Room, & feels it his Duty to be in all things his own Servant.—He will put up a Press Bed—so that one Room will be his Bed Chamber & Parlour—& I shall settle with him the hours & seasons of our being together, and the hours & seasons of our being apart. But I shall rely on him for nothing except his own maintenance.

As to the Poems, they are Cottle's Property, not mine.—There is no obstacle from me—no new Poems *intended* to be put into the Volume, except 'the Visions of the Maid of Orleans,' which is ready for them. But Cottle puts them to Press, when the Printing of Southey's Poems is finished—i.e. in about a week.—But Literature, tho' I shall never abandon it, will always be a secondary Object with me—My poetic Vanity & my political Furore have been exhaled; and I would rather be an expert, self-maintaining Gardener than a Milton, if I could not unite both.

My *Friend!* wherein I have written impetuously, pardon me! & consider what I have suffered, & still am suffering, in consequence of your Letter. There were two sentences in it which wounded me more deeply than the rest—'Mr King's Family you will find very pleasant Neighbours'—and 'We shall be excellent Friends'—I can scarcely persuade myself, that they were your Sentences.— *Finally, my Friend! if your opinion of me, & your attachment to me remain unaltered, and if you have assigned the true Reasons, which urged you to dissuade me from a settlement at Stowey, and if indeed provided such settlement were consistent with my good & happiness, it would give you unmixed Pleasure, I adhere to Stowey & consider the time from last Evening as a distempered Dream. But if any circumstances have occurred that have lessened your Love, or Esteem, or Confidence, or if there be objections to my settling at Stowey on your own account, or any other objections than what you have urged, I doubt not, you will declare them openly & unreservedly to me,* in your answer to this, which I shall expect with a total incapability of doing or thinking of, any thing, till I have received it.—Indeed, indeed, I am very miserable——

God bless you & your affectionate

                                   S. T. Coleridge

164. *To John Thelwall*

MS. *New York Public Lib. Pub. with omis.* Letters, *i. 193.*

                    December 17th. Saturday Night. [1796]

My dear Thelwall

I should have written you long ere this, had not the settlement of my affairs previous to my leaving Bristol, and the organization of my *new plan* occupied me with bulky anxieties that almost excluded every thing but Self from my thoughts. And, besides, my Health has been very bad, and remains so—A nervous Affection from my right temple to the extremity of my right shoulder almost distracted me, & made the frequent use of Laudanum absolutely necessary. And since I have subdued this, a Rheumatic Complaint in the back of my Head & Shoulders, accompanied with sore throat, and depression of the animal Spirits, has convinced me that a man may change bad Lodgers without bettering himself. I write these things not so much to apologize for my silence, or for the pleasure of complaining, as that you may know the reason why I have not given you 'a strict account' how I have disposed of your Books. This I will shortly do, with all the Veracity, which, that solemn Incantation *'upon your honor'* must necessarily have conjur'd up.—

Your second & third part promise great things—I have counted the subjects, and by a nice calculation find that eighteen Scotch Doctors would write fifty four Quarto Volumes; each chusing his Thesis out of your Syllabus. May you do good by them; and moreover enable yourself to do more good—I *should* say—to continue to do good. *My farm* will be a garden of one acre & an half; in which I mean to raise vegetables & corn enough for myself & Wife, and feed a couple of snouted & grunting Cousins from the refuse. My evenings I shall devote to Literature; and by Reviews, the Magazine, and other shilling-scavenger Employments shall probably gain 40£ a year—which Economy & Self-Denial, Goldbeaters, shall hammer till it cover my annual Expences. Now in favor of this scheme I shall say nothing: for the more vehement my ratiocinations were previous to the experiment, the more ridiculous my failure would appear; and if the Scheme deserve the said ratiocination, I shall *live down* all your objections. I doubt not, that the time will come when all our Utilities will be directed in one simple path. That Time however is not come; and imperious circumstances point out to each one his particular Road. Much good may be done in all. I am not *fit* for *public* Life; yet the Light shall stream to a far distance from the taper in my cottage window. Meantime, do *you* uplift the *torch* dreadlessly, and shew to mankind the face of that Idol, which they have worshipped in Darkness!

And now, my dear fellow! for a little sparring about Poetry. My first *Sonnet is obscure*;[1] but you ought to distinguish between obscurity residing in the uncommonness of the thought, and that which proceeds from thoughts unconnected & language not adapted to the expression of them. When you *do* find out the meaning of my poetry, can you (in general, I mean) alter the language so as to make it more perspicuous—the thought remaining the same?— By 'dreamy semblance' I *did* mean semblance of some unknown Past, like to a dream—and not 'a semblance *presented* in a dream.'— I meant to express, that oftimes, for a second or two, it flashed upon my mind, that the then company, conversation, & every thing, had occurred before, with all the precise circumstances; so as to make Reality appear a Semblance, and the Present like a dream in Sleep. Now this thought is obscure; because few people have experienced the same feeling. Yet several have—& they were proportionably delighted with the lines as expressing some strange sensations, which they themselves had never ventured to com-

[1] *Sonnet, Composed on a journey homeward; the author having received intelligence of the birth of a Son. Sept. 20, 1796. Poems, i. 153. See also Letter 156.*

municate, much less had ever seen developed in poetry. (—The lines I have since altered to—

> Oft o'er my Brain does that strange Rapture roll
> Which makes the Present (while it's brief fits last)
> Seem a mere Semblance of some Unknown Past,
> Mix'd with such feelings, as distress the Soul
> When dreaming that she dreams.)

Next as to 'mystical'—Now that the thinking part of Man, i.e. the Soul, existed previously to it's appearance in it's present body, may be very wild philosophy; but it is very intelligible poetry, inasmuch as Soul is an orthodox word in all our poets; they meaning by 'Soul' a being inhabiting our body, & playing upon it, like a Musician inclosed in an Organ whose keys were placed inwards.— Now this opinion I do not hold—not that I am a Materialist; but because I am a Berkleian——Yet as you who are not a Christian wished you were, that we might meet in Heaven, so I, who do not believe in this descending, & incarcerated Soul, yet said, if my Baby had died before I had seen him, I should have *struggled* to believe it.——Bless me! a commentary of 35 lines in defence of a Sonnet!— And I do not like the Sonnet much myself——. In some (indeed in many of my poems,) there is a garishness & swell of diction, which I hope, that my poems in future, if I write any, will be clear of—; but seldom, I think, any *conceits*.—In the second Edition now printing I have swept the book with the expurgation Besom to a fine tune—having omitted nearly one third.—As to Bowles, I affirm, that the manner of his accentuation in the words 'broad dāy-līght[']¹ (thrēē lōng Sȳllables) is a beauty, as it admirably expresses the Captive's *dwelling* on the sight of Noon—with rapture & a kind of Wonder.

> The common Sun, the Air, the Skies,
> To Him are opening Paradise.
>   Gray.²

But supposing my defence not tenable, yet how a blunder in metre stamps a man, Italian or Della Cruscan, I cannot perceive.—— As to my own poetry I do confess that it frequently both in thought & language deviates from 'nature & simplicity.' But that Bowles, the most tender, and, with the exception of Burns, the only *always-natural* poet in our Language, that *he* should not escape the charge of Della Cruscanism / this cuts the skin & *surface* of my Heart.—— 'Poetry to have it's highest relish must be *impassioned*!' true! but

¹ Cf. Letter 156, the last line of the passage quoted from Bowles.
² *Ode on the Pleasure arising from Vicissitude*, lines 51–52.

first, Poetry ought not always to have it's *highest* relish, & secondly, judging of the cause from it's effect, Poetry, though treating on lofty & abstract truths, ought to be deemed *impassioned* by him, who reads it with impassioned feelings.—Now Collins' Ode on the poetical character—that part of it, I should say, beginning with—'The Band (as faery Legends say) Was wove on that creating Day,' has inspired & whirled *me* along with greater agitations of enthusiasm than any the most *impassioned* Scene in Schiller or Shakspere——using 'impassioned' in it's confined sense for writings in which the human passions of Pity, Fear, Anger, Revenge, Jealousy, or Love are brought into view with their workings.—— Yet I consider the latter poetry as more valuable, because it gives *more general* pleasure—& I judge of all things by their Utility.—— I feel strongly, and I think strongly; but I seldom feel without thinking, or think without feeling. Hence tho' my poetry has in general a *hue* of tenderness, or Passion over it, yet it seldom exhibits unmixed & simple tenderness or Passion. My philosophical opinions are blended with, or deduced from, my feelings: & this, I think, peculiarizes my style of Writing. And like every thing else, it is sometimes a beauty, and sometimes a fault. But do not let us introduce an act of Uniformity against Poets—I have room enough in *my* brain to admire, aye & almost equally, the *head* and fancy of Akenside, and the *heart* and fancy of Bowles, the solemn Lordliness of Milton, & the divine Chit chat of Cowper: and whatever a man's excellence is, that will be likewise his fault.

There were some verses of your's in the last monthly Magazine,— with which I was much pleased. Calm good sense combined with *feeling*, & conveyed in harmonious verse, & a chaste & pleasing Imagery.—I wish much, very much to see your other poem. As to your Poems which you informed me in the accompanying letter that you had sent in the same parcel with the pamphlets,— whether or no your Verses had more than their *proper number of Feet*, I cannot say; but certain it is, that somehow or other they *marched off*. No 'Poems by John Thelwall' could I find.—

When I charged you with anti-religious Bigotry, I did not allude to your Pamphlet; but to passages in your Letters to me, & to a circumstance which Southey, I *think*, once mentioned—that you had asserted, that the *name* of God ought never to be introduced in poetry:[1] which, to be sure, was carrying hatred to your Creator very far indeed!

My dear Thelwall! 'It is the principal felicity of Life, & the chief

[1] Southey misrepresented me—my maxim was & is that the name of God should not be introduced into Love Sonnets—[Note written on manuscript by John Thelwall.]

Glory of Manhood to speak out fully on all subjects.' I will avail
myself of it—I will express *all* my feelings; but will previously take
care to make my feelings benevolent. Contempt is Hatred without
fear—Anger Hatred accompanied with apprehension. But because
Hatred is always evil, Contempt must be always evil—& a good
man ought to speak *contemptuously* of nothing. I am sure a wise
man will not of opinions which have been held by men, in *other*
respects at least, confessedly of more powerful Intellect than him-
self. 'Tis an assumption of *infallibility*; for if a man were wakefully
mindful that what he now thinks foolish, he may himself hereafter
think wise, it is not in nature, that he should *despise* those who now
believe what it is possible he may himself hereafter believe——&
if he deny this possibility, he must *on that point* deem himself
infallible & immutable.—Now in your Letter of Yesterday you
speak with *contempt* of two things, Old Age & the Christian
Religion:—this Religion was believed by Newton, Locke, &
Hartley, after intense investigation, which in each had been pre-
ceded by unbelief.—This does not *prove* it's truth; but it should
save it's followers from *contempt*—even though thro' the infir-
mities of mortality they should *have lost their teeth*. I call that man
a Bigot, Thelwall, whose intemperate Zeal for or against any
opinions leads him to contradict himself in the space of half-a-
dozen lines. Now this you appear to me to have done.—I will write
fully to you now; because I shall never renew the Subject. I shall
not be idle in defence of the Religion, I profess; & my books will
be the place, not my letters.—You say the Christian is a *mean*
Religion: now the Religion, which Christ taught, is simply 1 that
there is an Omnipresent Father of infinite power, wisdom, & Good-
ness, in whom we all of us move, & have our being & 2. That when
we appear to men to die, we do not utterly perish; but after this
Life shall continue to enjoy or suffer the consequences & [natur]al
effects of the Habits, we have formed here, whether good or evil.—
This is the Christian *Religion* & all of the Christian *Religion*. That
there is *no fancy* in it, I readily grant; but that it is mean, &
deficient in *mind*, and *energy*, it were impossible for me to admit,
unless I admitted that there *could be* no dignity, intellect, or force
in any thing but *atheism*.—But tho' it appeal not, itself, to the
fancy, the truths which it teaches, admit the highest exercise of it.
Are the 'innumerable multitude of angels & archangels' less
splendid beings than the countless Gods & Goddesses of Rome &
Greece?—And can you seriously think that Mercury from Jove
equals in poetic sublimity 'the mighty Angel that came down from
Heaven, whose face was as it were the Sun, and his feet as pillars
of fire: Who set his right foot on the sea, and his left upon the

earth. And he sent forth a loud voice; and when he had sent it forth, seven Thunders uttered their Voices: and when the seven Thund[ers] had uttered their Voices, the mighty Angel lifted up his hand to Heaven, & sware by Him that liveth for ever & ever, that TIME was no more?[']¹ Is not Milton a *sublimer* poet than Homer or Virgil? Are not his Personages more sublimely cloathed? And do you not know, that there is not perhaps *one* page in Milton's Paradise Lost, in which he has not borrowed his imagery from the *Scriptures*?—I allow, and rejoice that *Christ* appealed only to the understanding & the affections; but I affirm that, after reading Isaiah, or St Paul's Epistle to the Hebrews, Homer & Virgil are disgustingly *tame* to me, & Milton himself barely tolerable. You and I are very differently organized, if you think that the following (putting serious belief out of the Question) is a mean flight of impassioned Eloquence; in which the Apostle marks the difference between the Mosaic & Christian Dispensations—'For ye are not come unto the Mount that might be touched' (i.e. a *material* and earthly place) 'and that burned with fire; nor unto Blackness, and Tempest, and the sound of a Trumpet, and the Voice of Words, which voice they who heard it intreated that it should not be spoken to them any more; but ye are come unto Mount Sion, and unto the city of the living God, to an innumerable multitude of Angels, to God the Judge of all, and to the Spirits of just Men made perfect!'²——*You* may prefer to all this the Quarrels of Jupiter & Juno, the whimpering of wounded Venus, & the Jokes of the celestials on the lameness of Vulcan—be it so (The difference in our tastes it would not be difficult to account for from the different feelings which we have associated with these ideas)——I shall continue with Milton to say, that

Sion Hill

Delights *me* more, and Siloa's Brook that flow'd
Fast by the oracle of God!

'Visions fit for Slobberers.' If infidelity do not lead to Sensuality, which in every case except your's I have observed it to do, it always takes away all respect for those who become unpleasant from the infirmities of Disease or decaying Nature. Exempli gratiâ—The *Aged* are '*Slobberers*'—The *only* Vision, which Christianity holds forth, is indeed peculiarly adapted to these *Slobberers*—Yes! to these lonely & despised, and perishing SLOB- BERERS it proclaims, that their 'Corruptible shall put on *Incorruption,* & their Mortal put on *Immortality*.'³

¹ Cf. Revelation x. 1–6.   ² Hebrews xii. 18–19, 22–23.
³ 1 Corinthians xv. 53.

In reading over this after an interval of 23 Years I was wondering what I

'Morals for the Magdalen & Botany Bay.' Now, Thelwall! I presume that to preach morals to the virtuous is not quite so requisite, as to preach them to the vicious. 'The Sick need a Physician.' Are morals, which would make a Prostitute a Wife, & a Sister; which would restore her to inward peace & purity; are morals, which would make Drunkards sober, the ferocious benevolent, & Thieves honest, *mean morals*? Is it a despicable trait in our Religion, that it's professed object is 'to heal the broken-hearted, and give Wisdom to the Poor Man?'—It preaches *Repentance*—what repentance? Tears, & Sorrow, & a repetition of the same crimes?—No. A 'Repentance unto good works'—a repentance that completely does away all superstitious terrors by teaching, that the *Past* is nothing in itself; that if the Mind *is* good, that it *was* bad, imports nothing. 'It is a religion for Democrats.' It certainly teaches in the most explicit terms the rights of Man, his right to Wisdom, his right to an equal share in all the blessings of Nature; it commands it's disciples to go every where, & every where to preach these rights; it commands them never to use the arm of flesh, to be perfectly non-resistant; yet to hold the promulgation of *Truth* to be a Law above Law, and in the performance of this office to defy 'Wickedness in high places,' and cheerfully to endure ignominy, & wretchedness, & torments, & death, rather than *intermit* the performance of it; yet while enduring ignominy, & wretchedness, & torments & death to feel nothing but sorrow, and pity, and love for those who inflicted them; wishing their Oppressors to be altogether such as they, 'excepting these bonds.'— Here is *truth* in theory; and in practice a union of energetic *action*, and more energetic *Suffering*. For activity amuses; but he, who can *endure* calmly, must possess the seeds of true Greatness. For all his animal spirits will of necessity fail him; and he has only his *Mind* to trust to.——These doubtless are morals for all the Lovers of Mankind, who wish to *act* as well as *speculate*; and that you should allow this, and yet not three lines before call the same *Morals mean*, appears to me a gross self-contradiction, symptomatic of Bigotry.—I write freely, Thelwall! for tho' *personally* unknown, I really love you, and can count but few human beings, whose hand I would welcome with a more hearty Grasp of Friendship. I suspect, Thelwall! that you never read your Testament since your Understanding was matured, without carelessness, & previous contempt, & a somewhat like Hatred—Christianity

could have said that looked like contempt of age. May not slobberers have referred not to age, but to the drivelling of decayed intellect—which is surely an ill guide in matters of understanding and consequently of faith [?] J. T. 1819. [Note written on manuscript by John Thelwall.]

regards morality as a process—it finds a man vicious and un-
susceptible of noble motives; & gradually leads him, at least,
desires to lead him, to the height of disinterested Virtue—till in
relation & proportion to his faculties & powers, he is perfect 'even
as our Father in Heaven is perfect.' There is no resting-place for
Morality. Now I will make one other appeal, and have done for
ever with the subject.—There is a passage in Scripture which
comprizes the whole process, & each component part, of Christian
Morals. Previously, let me explain the word Faith—by Faith I
understand, first, a deduction from experiments in favor of the
existence of something not experienced, and secondly, the motives
which attend such a deduction. Now motives being selfish are only
the beginning & the *foundation*, necessary and of first-rate impor-
tance, yet made of vile materials, and hidden beneath the splendid
Superstructure.——

'Now giving all diligence, add to your Faith *Fortitude*, and to
Fortitude Knowlege, and to Knowlege Purity, and to Purity
*Patience, and to Patience ‡Godliness, and to Godliness Brotherly-
kindness, and to Brotherly-kindness Universal Love.'[1]

---

* Patience. Permit me, as a definition of this word to quote one sentence
from my first Address.—Page 20: [*Conciones ad Populum.*] 'Accustomed to
regard all the affairs of Man, as a Process, they never hurry & they never
pause.' In his not possessing *this* virtue, all the horrible excesses of Robespierre
did, I believe, originate. [Note by S.T.C.]

‡ Godliness: the belief, the habitual, & efficient belief, that we are always
in the presence of our universal Parent.—I will translate literally a passage
from a German Hexameter Poem [Voss's *Luise*]——It is the Speech of a
Country clergyman on the birth-day of his Daughter—The *latter part* fully
expresses the Spirit of Godliness, & it's connection with Brotherly-Kindness.
(Pardon the harshness of the Language—for it is translated totidem verbis.[)]
'Yes! my beloved Daughter! I am cheerful, cheerful as the Birds singing in
the Wood here, or the Squirrel that hops among the aëry branches around it's
young in their Nest. To day it is eighteen years since God gave me my Beloved,
now my only child, so intelligent, so pious, and so dutiful. How the Time flies
away! Eighteen years to come—how far the Space extends itself before us!
and how does it vanish when we look back upon it! It was but yesterday, it
seems to me, that as I was plucking flowers here, & offering praise, on a sudden
the joyful Message came, "A Daughter is born to us". Much since that time
has the Almighty imparted to us of Good and of Evil. But the Evil itself was
Good; for his Loving-kindness is infinite. Do you recollect (*to his Wife*) as it
once had rained after a long Drought, and I (Louisa in my arms) was walking
with thee in the freshness of the Garden, how the Child snatched at the rain-
bow, and kissed me, and said—Papa! there it rains flowers from Heaven! Does
the blessed God strew these, that we children may gather them up? Yes! I
answered—full-blowing and heavenly Blessings does the Father strew, who
stretched out the Bow of his Favor: flowers & fruits that we may gather them
with thankfulness & joy. *Whenever I think of that great Father then my Heart*

---

[1] 2 Peter i. 5–7.

I hope, whatever you may think of Godliness, you will like the *note* on it.—I need not tell you, that Godliness is God*like*-ness, and is paraphrased by Peter—'that ye may be partakers of the divine nature.'—i.e. act from a love of order, & happiness, & not from any self-respecting motive—from the *excellency*, into which you have exalted your *nature*, not from the *keenness* of *mere prudence.*

——'add to your faith fortitude, and to fortitude knowlege, and to knowlege purity, and to purity patience, and to patience Godliness, and to Godliness brotherly kindness, and to brotherly kindness universal Love.' Now, Thelwall! [Can you after reading this consciously repeat that these words are fit only for Prostitutes & hardened Rogues?—][1] Putting *Faith* out of the Question, (which by the by is not mentioned as a virtue but as the leader to them) can you mention a virtue which is not here enjoined—& supposing the precepts embod[ied] in the practice of any one human being, would not Perfection be personified?—I write these things not with any expectation of making you a Christian—I shou[ld smile] at my own folly, if I conceived it even in a friendly day-dream. But [I do wish to see a progression in your *moral* character, & I *hope* to see it —for while you so frequently appeal to the passions of Terror, & Ill nature & Disgust, in your popular writings, I must be blind not to perceive that you present in your daily & hourly practice the *feelings* of *universal Love.*][2] 'The ardor of undisciplined Benevolence seduces us into malignity.'—And while you accustom yourself to speak so *contemptuously* of Doctrines you do not accede to, and Persons with whom you do not accord, I must doubt whether even your *brotherly-kindness* might not be made more perfect. That is surely *fit* for a man which his mind after sincere examination approves, which animates his conduct, soothes his sorrows, & heightens his Pleasures. Every good & earnest Christian declares that all this is true of the *visions* (as you please to style them, God knows why) of Christianity——Every earnest Christian therefore

*lifts itself up, and swells with active impulse towards all his Children, our Brothers who inhabit the Earth around us; differing indeed from one another in powers and understanding, yet all dear Children of the same Parent, nourished by the same Spirit of Animation, and ere long to fall asleep; to fall asleep, and again to wake in the common Morning of the Resurrection; all who have loved their fellow-creatures, all shall rejoice with Peter, and Moses, and Confucius, and Homer, and Zoroaster, with Socrates who died for truth, and also with the noble *Mendlesohn, who teaches that the divine one was never crucified.'* * A German, Jew by parentage, and *Deist* by election. He has written some of the most acute books possible in favor of natural Immortal[ity] and Germany deems him her profoundest Metaphysician, with the exception of the most unintelligible Emanuel Kant.—[Note by S.T.C.]

[1, 2] The words in brackets have been inked out in the manuscript.

is on a level with *slobberers*. Do not charge me with dwelling on *one* expression—these expressions are always indicative of the habit of feeling.—You possess fortitude, and purity, & a large portion of brotherly-kindness & universal Love—drink with unquenchable thirst of the two latter virtues, an[d] *acquire* patience; and then, Thelwall! should *your* System be true, all that can be said, is that (if both our Systems should be found to increase our own & our fellow-crea[tures'] happiness)—Here lie or did lie *the all* of John Thelwall & S. T. Coleridge—they were both humane, & happy, but the former was the more knowing: & if my System should prove true, we, I doubt not, shall both meet in the kingdom of Heav[en,] and I with transport in my eye shall say—'I·*told* you so, my *dear* fellow.' But seriously, the faulty habit of feeling, which I have endeavoured to point out in you, I have detected in at least as great degree in my own practice & am struggling to subdue it.—

I rejoice, that the Bankrupt Honesty of the Public has paid even the small Dividend—you mention. As to your second part, I will write you about it, in a day or two, when I give you an account how I have disposed of your first.—My dear little Baby is well; and my Wife thinks, that he already begins to flutter the callow wings of his Intellect. O the wise heart & foolish head of a Mother! Kiss your little Girl for me, & tell her, if I knew her, I would love her; and then I hope in your next letter you will convey *her* Love to me and my Sara.—Your dear Boy, I trust, will return with rosy cheeks. Don't you suspect, Thelwall! that the little Atheis[t,] Madam Stella, has an abominable *Christian* kind of a *Heart?*—My Sara is much interested about her; and I should not wonder if they were to be sworn sister-seraphs in the heavenly Jerusalem. Give my Love to her.

I have sent you some loose sheets which Charles Lloyd & I printed together, intending to make a Volume, but I gave it up, & cancelled them.[1]—Item—a Joan of Arc, with only the passage of my writing cut out for the Printers—as I am printing it in my second Edition, with very great alterations & an addition of four hundred lines, so as to make it a complete & independent Poem— entitled The Progress of Liberty—or the Visions of the maid of Orleans.—Item—a sheet of Sonnets collected by me for the use of a few friends, who payed the printing——There you will see my opinion of Sonnets.[2]—Item, Poems by C. Lloyd on the death of one of your 'Slobberers'—a very venerable old Lady, & a Quaker.[3] The Book is drest like a rich Quaker, in costly raiment but un-

---

[1] For Lamb's criticism of this work, which has completely vanished, see *Lamb Letters*, i. 67–71.

[2] Cf. Letter 152.   [3] *Poems on the Death of Priscilla Farmer*, 1796.

ornamented. The loss of her almost killed my poor young friend: for he doted on her from his Infancy.—Item, a Poem of mine on Burns, which was printed to be dispersed among friends. It was addressed to Charles Lamb.[1]—Item—(Shall I give it thee, Blasphemer? No. I won't—but) to thy Stella I do present the poems of my [Bowles] for a keep-sake.[2]——Of this parcel I do intreat thy acceptance. I have another Joan of Arc—so you have a *right* to the one inclosed.—Postscript—Item, a humourous Droll on S. Ireland,[3] of which I have likewi[se a]nother. Item—A strange Poem written by an Astrologer here, who *was* a man of fine Genius, which, at intervals, he still discovers.—But, ah me! Madness smote with her hand, and stamped with her feet and swore that he should be her's—& her's he is.—He is a man of fluent Eloquence & general knowlege, gentle in his manners, warm in his affections; but unfortunately he has received a few rays of supernatural Light thro' a crack in his upper story. I *express* myself unfeelingly; but indeed my heart always achs when I think of him. Item, some Verses of Robert Southey's to a College Cat.—And finally the following Lines by thy affectionate Friend

S. T. Coleridge

Sonnet[4]

to a young man who abandoned himself to a causeless & indolent Melancholy.

Hence that fantastic Wantonness of Woe,
　　O Youth to partial Fortune vainly dear!
To plunder'd Want's half-shelter'd Hovel go,
　　Go, and some hunger-bitten Infant hear
　　Moan haply in a dying Mother's Ear;
Or seek some WIDOW's grave, whose dearer Part
　　Was slaughter'd, where o'er his uncoffin'd Limbs
The flocking Flesh-birds scream'd! Then, while thy Heart
　　Groans, and thine eyes a fiercer Sorrow dims,
Know, and the Truth shall kindle thy young mind,
　　What Nature makes thee mourn, she bids thee heal:
O Abject! if to sickly Dreams resign'd
　　All effortless thou leave Earth's common weal
A Prey to the thron'd Murderers of Mankind!

---

[1] Cf. *To a Friend, who had declared his intention of writing no more poetry.*
'First published in a Bristol newspaper in aid of a subscription for the family of Robert Burns.' *Poems*, i. 158.
[2] See Letter 165 to Mrs. Thelwall.
[3] James White's *Original Letters of Falstaff* were prefaced by a dedication to 'Master Samuel Irelaunde'. The dedication was probably written by Lamb.
[4] Cf. *Poems*, i. 157.

After the five first lines these two followed,

Or when the cold & dismal fog-damps brood
O'er the rank Church-yard with sear Elm-leaves strew'd,
Pace round some WIDOW'S grave &c—— Were they rightly
omitted ?

I love Sonnets; but *upon my honor* I do not love *my* Sonnets.

N.B. Direct your Letters

S. T. Coleridge | Mr Cottle's | High Street | Bristol.

165. *To Mrs. John Thelwall*

MS. Victoria and Albert Museum. Pub. Wise, Bibliography, *32.* This letter is
written on the fly-leaf of W. L. Bowles's *Sonnets, and Other Poems*, 4th edition,
1796. Bound up with the Bowles volume is one of two surviving copies of the
pamphlet, *Sonnets from Various Authors*, which Coleridge printed for private
circulation. See Letter 152.

Sunday Morning December the eighteenth 1796

Dear Mrs Thelwall

I entreat your acceptance of this Volume, which has given me
more pleasure, and done my heart more good, than all the other
books, I ever read, excepting my Bible. Whether you approve or
condemn my poetical taste, the Book will at least serve to remind
you of your unseen, yet not the less sincere,

Friend

Samuel Taylor Coleridge

166. *To Thomas Poole*

Address: Mr Thomas Poole | Stowey | near | Bridgewater | Somerset
MS. British Museum. Pub. Letters, *i. 208.*
Stamped: Bristol.

Sunday Morning. [18 December 1796][1]

My dear Poole

I wrote to you with improper impetuosity; but I had been
dwelling so long on the circumstance of living near you, that my
mind was thrown by your letter into the feelings of those distressful
Dreams, where we imagine ourselves falling from precipices. I
seemed falling from the summit of my fondest Desires; whirled
from the height, just as I had reached it.

We shall want none of the Woman's Furniture—we have enough

[1] The similarity between the health details here and in Letter 164 settles
the date.

for ourselves. What with boxes of Books, and Chests of Drawers,
& Kitchen-Furniture, & Chairs, and our Bed and Bed-linen, &c &c,
we shall have enough to fill a small Waggon—& to day I shall make
enquiry among my trading acquaintance, whether or no it would
not be cheaper to hire a Waggon to take them straight down to
Stowey, than to put them in the Bridgewater Waggon—taking in
the double trouble & expence of putting them in the Drays to
carry them to the Public Waggon, & then seeing them packed again
—& again to be unpacked & packed at Bridgewater: I much
question, whether our goods would be good for anything.

I am very poorly; not to say ill. My face monstrously swoln; my
recondite Eye sits quaintly behind the flesh-hill; and looks as little,
as a Tomtit's. And I have a sore throat that prevents me from
eating aught but spoon-meat without great pain—& I have a
rheumatic complaint in the back part of my head & Shoulders.—
Now all this demands a small portion of Christian Patience, taking
in our present circumstances——My Apothecary says it will be
madness for me to walk to Stowey on Tuesday, as in the furious
Zeal of a new convert to Economy, I had resolved to do. My Wife
will stay a week, or fortnight after me; I think it not improbable,
that the Weather may break up by that time.——However, if I
do not get worse, I will be with you by Wednesday or Thursday[1]
at the furthest—so as to be there before the Waggon.——Is there
any *grate* in the House?—I should think, one might Rumfordize
one of the chimneys—I shall bring down with me a dozen yards of
Green List.—I can endure cold, but not a cold room! If we can but
contrive to make two rooms *warm*, & *wholesome*, we will laugh in
the faces of Gloom & Ill-lookingness.

I shall lose the Post, if I say a word more.—You thoroughly &
in every nook & corner of your Heart forgive me for my letters?—
Indeed, indeed, Poole! I know no one whom I esteem more, no
one friend whom I love so much—but bear with my Infirmities!

God bless you & | Your grateful & affectionate

S. T. Coleridge

167. *To Thomas Poole*

Pub. Poems, *ii. 1113.* When Coleridge published the *Ode on the Departing Year*
as a pamphlet, he prefaced to it this dedicatory letter addressed 'To Thomas
Poole, of Stowey'.

Bristol,   December 26, 1796

My dear Friend—

Soon after the commencement of this month, the Editor of the
Cambridge Intelligencer (a newspaper conducted with so much

---

[1] Actually Coleridge did not leave for Nether Stowey until 31 Dec. 1796.

ability, and such unmixed and fearless zeal for the interests of Piety and Freedom, that I cannot but think my poetry honoured by being permitted to appear in it), requested me, by Letter, to furnish him with some Lines for the last day of this Year. I promised him that I would make the attempt; but, almost immediately after, a rheumatic complaint seized my head, and continued to prevent the possibility of poetic composition till within the last three days. So in the course of the last three days the following Ode was produced. In general, when an Author informs the Public that his production was struck off in a great hurry, he offers an insult, not an excuse. But I trust that the present case is an exception, and that the peculiar circumstances, which obliged me to write with such unusual rapidity, give a propriety to my professions of it: nec nunc eam apud te jacto, sed et ceteris indico; ne quis asperiore limâ carmen examinet, et a confuso scriptum et quod frigidum erat ni statim traderem.[1] (I avail myself of the words of Statius, and hope that I shall likewise be able to say of any weightier publication, what *he* has declared of his Thebaid, that it had been tortured[2] with a laborious Polish.)

For me to discuss the *literary* merits of this hasty composition were idle and presumptuous. If it be found to possess that Impetuosity of Transition, and that Precipitation of Fancy and Feeling, which are the *essential* excellencies of the sublimer Ode, its deficiency in less important respects will be easily pardoned by those, from whom alone praise could give me pleasure: and whose minuter criticisms will be disarmed by the reflection, that these Lines were conceived 'not in the soft obscurities of Retirement, or under the Shelter of Academic Groves, but amidst inconvenience and distraction, in sickness and in sorrow.'[3] I am more anxious, lest the *moral* spirit of the Ode should be mistaken. You, I am sure, will not fail to recollect, that among the Ancients, the Bard and the Prophet were one and the same character; and you *know*, that although I prophesy curses, I pray fervently for blessings.

Farewell, Brother of my Soul!

> ——O ever found the same,
> And trusted and belov'd![4]

Never without an emotion of honest pride do I subscribe myself
> Your grateful and affectionate Friend,
> S. T. COLERIDGE.

[1] Adapted 'from an apology addressed "Meliori suo", prefixed to the Second Book of the *Silvae*', by Statius. Cf. *Poems*, ii. 1113 n.

[2] *Multâ cruciata limâ.* [Note by S.T.C.] *Silv.*, lib. iv. 7. 26.

[3] Dr. Johnson, Preface to the *Dictionary of the English Language*.

[4] Akenside's *Pleasures of the Imagination* (Second Version), i, ll. 88–89.

168. *To Robert Southey*

Address: Robert Southey | No. 8 | West-gate Buildings | Bath
MS. Lord Latymer. Pub. E.L.G. i. 67.

Tuesday Morning [27 December 1796]

I thank you, Robert Southey! for your poems; and by way of
return present you with a collection of (what appear to me) the
faults.—'The Race of Banquo' and 'To the Genius of Africa'
ought to have rescued the ode from your very harsh censure.[1] The
latter is perfect, saving the last line, which is one of James Jennings's
new thoughts; and besides, who after having been whirled along by
such a tide of enthusiasm can endure to be impaled at last on the
needle-point of an Antithesis?[2] Of the Inscriptions I like the first
and last the least:[3] all the rest almost equally, and each very much.
In the spirited & most original Lines to your own Miniature
'wrong'—*rhymes* with—'solitary song.'[4]—You, I doubt not, have
associated feelings dear to you with the ideas—'this little picture
was for ornament design'd' &c——and therefore do right in retain-
ing them. To me &, I suppose, to most strangers the four last lines
appear to drag excrementitiously——the Poem would conclude
more satisfactorily at 'Spirit of Spenser! was the Wanderer
wrong?' The fault of the four Lines *seems* to be that having
digressed you do not *lead* yourself to your subject, but without
ceremony take a huge *leap* back again. Now tho' it is always well
to *leave* the subject on the mind, yet rather than use such means
I would forego it.——'The poem on the Death of an old Spaniel'
will, I doubt not, be set to music by angelic & archangelic Dogs
in their state of exaltation. It is a poem which will do good—and
that is saying a great deal.—In the ode to Contemplation 'the
smoke long shadowing play' is scarcely accurate—[']the smoke's
long shadow' would surely be more natural & perspicuous?—
[']The Musings on a Landscape' is a delicious poem.——The
words To HIM begin the Line awkwardly, to *my* ear.——The final
pause at the end of the first two Syllables of a line is seldom
tolerable, except when the first two Syllables form a trochee—the

[1] In his prefatory remarks (*Poems,* 1797) Southey wrote: 'I now think the
Ode the most worthless species of composition as well as the most difficult.'
[2] The last stanza of *To the Genius of Africa,* including the offending line—
'And make Oppression groan opprest'—was later dropped.
[3] The first inscription, *For a Tablet at Godstow Nunnery,* Southey did not
include in his *Poetical Works,* 1838; the last, *For the Cenotaph at Ermenonville,*
was retained.
[4] Coleridge objected to the rhyme in the blank verse poem, *To my own
Miniature Picture.* Southey later dropped the offending lines.

reason, I apprehend, is, that to the ear they with the line foregoing make an Alexandrine.

—I have animadverted on those poems only which are my particular favorites—and now for the Penates, which if I were to abandon my judgment to the impulse of present Feelings, I should pronounce the most interesting poem of it's length in our Language.—I have detected two faults only, that a Man amid the miseries of a struggling Life should look back on the quiet happiness of childhood bears no resemblance to a Persian Monarch leaving the Luxuries of a Palace to revisit the cot where he had been a shepherd—.——But the *five first Lines* of the Poem—they are very, very *beautiful*; but (pardon my obtuseness) have they any *meaning?*[1] 'The Temple of Paean' does not, I presume, mean any real temple—but is only an allegorical building—expressing Poesy —either ancient or modern. If modern, how is it's wall ruined? If ancient, how do *you* hang up your silent harp on it? Does it allude to ancient Poetry, as expressing the subject of the Present Poem? yet you say, that you shall strike that 'high and solemn strain' *ere* you hang it up. (—Besides, is *Paean* the God of *Poetry?*—I think, that the ancients religiously confined the name to Apollo in his capacity of *Healer & Python-killer*: but of this I am not certain.) However, whether ancient or modern poesy be indicated, or whatever may [be] the import of each distinct image, your general meaning is clear—namely, that after this Song you will intermit the writing of Poetry / yet in the next lines you say, there may [its] strings make melancholy music——i.e. This one song, and then I will *discontinue* verse-writing—during which discontinuance I will write verses!—Is all this only my obtuseness & frigidity? or have you not faultily mixed spiritual with corporeal, allegorical meanings with meanings predicable only of catgut & rosin, bricks & mortar?—A Tempest may shake an aged pile—but what has a tempest to do with ancient poetry?—If there were any respectable God with a respectable name who presided over the Law, or the affairs of active Life in general, you would have acted wiselier (I speak not dogmatically, but merely say, I think, you would have acted wiselier) if you had hung up your harp on the

---

[1] The lines to which Coleridge objected are:

> Yet one Song more! one high and solemn strain
> Ere PAEAN! on thy temple's ruined wall
> I hang the silent harp: there may its strings,
> When the rude tempest shakes the aged pile,
> Make melancholy music. One Song more!

In reprinting the poem, *Hymn to the Penates*, in 1838, Southey changed *Paean* to *Phoebus*.

walls of his Temple—& added—yet shall it's strings, (if any ruder storm is abroad) make melancholy music. i.e. Tho' I intermit my poetry in consequence of the calls of Business, yet if any particular occasion arise, I will *unhang* my harp.—What if you *left* the harp in the fane of Vacuna? If these observations strike you as just, I shall be sorry, they did not strike me when you *read* the poem! But indeed the lines sound so sweet, and *seem* so much like sense, that it is no great matter. 'Tis a handsome & finely-sculptur'd Tomb——& few will break it open with the sacrilegious spade & pick-ax of Criticism to discover, whether or no it be not a *Cenotaph.*

—I have been in bed for these two days—the effect of a dire cold & feverish complaint—but I am better now—& leave Bristol on Thursday——

S. T. Coleridge.

169. *To John Prior Estlin*

Address: Revd J. P. Estlin | at Mr Bishop's | No. 21 Essex Street | Strand | London
MS. Victoria University Lib. Pub. Letters to Estlin, *25.*
Postmark: 31 December 1796.   *Stamped*: Bristol.

December 30th 1796

My dear Friend

I am not yet gone; but I go *with* Mrs Coleridge tomorrow morning.—I thought it advisable to get some review-books off my hands first.——I hope, that you and dear Mrs Estlin arrived safe! God bless you both!—My Heart must be cold in the grave, when it ceases to thrill & warm at the mention of your names.—You met me

> sever'd from those amities
> Which grow upon the Heart, and roughly push'd
> Naked & lonely to Life's stormy verge——

And you cloath'd that heart with new affections, and drew me back to serenity.—Enough!

> The farewell tear, which even now I pay,
> Best thanks you; and whene'er of pleasures flown
> My Heart some sweeter Image would renew,
> Lov'd honor'd FRIENDS! I will remember *you!*

—I have printed *that* Ode—I like it myself—A parcel of them will have arrived at Parsons's, in Pater-noster Row, at the same time you receive this Letter. It occupies two sheets Quarto—& is priced One Shilling.—If you think, after perusal, that the composition does credit to the Author of the Religious Musings (pardon my vanity) you will recommend it to your friends. I have taken my motto, you will see, from Æschylus—ἐφημίοις φροιμίοις— are—bloody Presages, I believe——but I have sent away my Scapula.[1]—You know, I am a *mottophilist,* and almost a motto-*manist*——I love an apt motto to my Heart.—Παρακοπά (page 9) is a good word—it is commonly, but loosely, rendered, *madness*—— it means properly an *excision* of mind—so that we see but *one* side, and are blind to noon day evidence on the other.—

Have you preached your anti-atheistical Sermon?—Do you print it in London?[2]—Let me hear (directing to me, Stowey near Bridgewater, Somerset.)

Present our respects to Mr & Mrs Bishop—I hope to hear shortly, that *he* is safely delivered—for I am sure, his *heart* is in a state of parturience that demands sympathy equally with the '*to come*' of your lovely Sister-in-law.

Present my respects to Dr Disney—& my affectionate Regards to Mr Frend, if you see him.

My David Hartley laughs, cries, & sucks with all imaginable vivacity.

Heaven love you

& your grateful | & affectionate
S. T. Coleridge

P.S. I have adopted your objection to 'urg'd his flight'—it certainly *meant* nothing.

170. *To John Thelwall*

Address: John Thelwall | Mr Hardy's | Tavistock Street | Covent Garden | London
MS. Pierpont Morgan Lib. Pub. with omis. Letters, i. 210.
Postmark: 2 January 1797. *Stamped:* Bristol.

Decemb. 31st. 1796

Enough, my dear Thelwall, of Theology. In my book on Godwin I compare the two Systems—his & Jesus's—& that book I am sure you will read with attention.—I entirely accord with your opinion of Southey's Joan—the 9th book is execrable—and the poem tho' it frequently reach the *sentimental,* does not display, the *poetical, Sublime.* In language at once natural, perspicuous, & dignified, in manly pathos, in soothing & sonnet-like description, and above all, in character, & *dramatic* dialogue, Southey is unrivalled; but as certainly he does not possess opulence of Imagination, lofty-paced

---

[1] Joannes Scapula, *Lexicon Graeco-Latinum Novum,* 1580.
[2] *The Nature and Causes of Atheism,* 1797.

Harmony, or that *toil* of thinking, which is necessary in order to plan *a Whole*. Dismissing mock humility, & hanging your mind as a looking-glass over my Idea-pot, so as to image on the said mind all the bubbles that boil in the said Idea-pot, (there's a damn'd long-winded Metaphor for you) I think, that an admirable Poet might be made by *amalgamating him & me*. I *think* too much for a *Poet*; he too little for a *great* Poet. But he abjures *thinking*—& lays the whole stress of excellence—on *feeling*.—Now (as you say) they must go together.—Between ourselves, the *Enthusiasm* of Friendship is not with S. & me. We quarreled—& the quarrel lasted for a twelvemonth—We are now reconciled;[1] but the cause of the Difference was solemn—& 'the blasted oak puts not forth it's buds anew'—we are *acquaintances*—& feel *kindliness* towards each other; but I do not *esteem*, or LOVE Southey, as I must esteem & love the man whom I dared call by the holy name of FRIEND! —and vice versâ Southey of me— I say no more—it is a painful subject—& do you say nothing—I mention this, for obvious reasons—but let it go no farther.——It is a painful subject. Southey's direction at present is—R. Southey, No. 8, West-gate Buildings, Bath, but he leaves Bath for London in the course of a week.

You imagine that I know Bowles personally—I never *saw* him but once; & when I was a boy, & in Salisbury *market-place*.

The passage in your letter respecting your Mother affected me greatly.—Well, true or false, Heaven is a less gloomy idea than Annihilation!—Dr Beddoes, & Dr Darwin think that *Life* is utterly inexplicable, writing as Materialists—You, I understand, have adopted the idea that it is the result of organized matter acted on by external Stimuli.—As likely as any other system; but you *assume* the thing to be proved—the '*capability* of being stimulated into sensation' *as* a *property* of organized matter—now 'the Capab.' &c is *my* definition of *animal Life*——Monro believes in a plastic immaterial Nature—all-pervading—

> And what if all of animated Nature
> Be but organic harps diversely fram'd
> That tremble into *thought* as o'er them sweeps
> Plastic & vast &c[2]—

---

[1] 'In the end of September, Southey took the first step, and sent over a slip of paper with a word or two of conciliation. The paper contained a sentence in English from Schiller's Conspiracy of Fiesco at Genoa. *Fiesko! Fiesko! du räumst einen Platz in meiner Brust, den das Menschengeschlecht, dreifach genommen, nicht mehr besetzen wird.* Fiesco! Fiesco! thou leavest a void in my bosom, which the human race, thrice told, will never fill up. Act V. Sc. 16.' *Biog. Lit.*, ed. H. N. Coleridge, 1847, ii. 376.

[2] See *The Eolian Harp*, lines 44–47, *Poems*, i. 102.

(by the bye—that is my favorite of *my* poems—do *you* like it?)
Hunter that the *Blood* is the Life—which is saying nothing at all—
for if the blood were *Life*, it could never be otherwise than Life—
and to say, it is *alive*, is saying nothing—& Ferriar believes in a
Soul, like an orthodox Churchman—So much for Physicians &
Surgeons—Now as to the Metaphysicians, Plato says, it is *Har-
mony*—he might as well have said, a fiddle stick's end—but I love
Plato—his dear *gorgeous* Nonsense! And *I, tho' last not least, I* do
not know what to think about it—on the whole, I have rather made
up my mind that I am a mere *apparition*—a naked Spirit!—And
that Life is I myself I! which is a mighty clear account of it. Now
I have written all this not to expose my ignorance (that is an acci-
dental effect, not the final cause) but to shew you, that I want to
see your Essay on Animal Vitality—of which Bowles, the Surgeon,
spoke in high Terms—Yet *he* believes in a *body* & a *soul*. Any book
may be left at Robinson's for *me*, 'to be put into the next parcel
sent to Joseph Cottle, Bookseller, Bristol.'——Have you received
an Ode of mine from Parsons's? In your next letter tell me what
you think of the *scattered* poems, I sent you—send me any poems,
and I will be minute in Criticism——for, O Thelwall! even a long-
winded Abuse is more consolatory to an *Author's* feelings than a
short-breathed, asthma-lunged Panegyric.——Joking apart, I
would to God we could sit by a fireside & joke vivâ voce, face to
face—Stella & Sara, Jack Thelwall, & I!——As I once wrote to
my dear *friend*, T. Poole, 'repeating'

> Such Verse as Bowles, heart-honour'd Poet, sang,
> That wakes the Tear yet steals away the Pang,
> Then or with Berkley or with Hobbes romance it
> Dissecting Truth with metaphysic lancet.
> Or drawn from up those dark unfathom'd Wells
> In wiser folly clink the Cap & Bells.
> How many tales we told! What jokes we made!
> Conundrum, Crambo, Rebus, or Charade;
> Ænigmas, that had driven the * Theban mad,
> And Puns then best when exquisitely bad;
> And I, if aught of archer vein I hit,
> With my own Laughter stifled my own Wit.[1]

* Œdipus. [Note by S.T.C.]

[1] *Poems*, ii. 976.

171. *To Thomas Poole*

MS. British Museum. Pub. Poems, *ii. 978.* This invitation is scribbled on the back of a Prospectus of Coleridge's course of six lectures on the English Rebellion and the French Revolution, to begin on 23 June 1795.

[Endorsed Jany ⟨17⟩97.]

To T. Poole

Plucking flowers from the Galáxy
On the pinions of Abstraction
I did quite forget to ax 'e
Whether you have an objaction
With us to swill 'e and to swell 'e
And make a pig stie of your belly.
A lovely limb most dainty
Of a ci-de vant Mud-raker,
I makes bold to acquaint 'e
We've trusted to the Baker:[1]
And underneath it Satis
Of that subtérrene Apple
By the Erudite 'clep'd, *taties,*
With which if you'd wish to grapple;
As sure as I am a sloven
The clock will not strike twice one,
When the said Dish will be out of the Oven,
And the Dinner will be a nice one.

    P.S. Besides, we've got some cabbage—
        You Jew-dog, if you linger
        May the Itch in pomp of Scabbage
        Pop out between each finger.

172. *To Joseph Cottle*

Address: Mr. Cottle   Bookseller | High-Street | Bristol   *Single*
MS. Harvard College Lib. Pub. with omis. and as three separate letters, Early Rec. *i. 188, 219, and 229.* The postscript which Cottle added (ibid. i. 189) does not appear either in this or any other manuscript.
Stamped: Bridgewater.

[Friday] Morning [6 January 1797][2]

My dear Cottle

We arrived safe—our house is set to rights—we are all, Maid, Wife, Bratling, & self, remarkably well——Mrs Coleridge likes

---

[1] 'The "miserable cottage" did not possess an oven.' *Thomas Poole,* i. 211 n.
[2] This letter was written a few days after Coleridge's arrival at Nether

Stowey, & loves Thomas Poole, & his Mother, who love her——a
communication has been made from our Orchard into T. Poole's
Garden, & from thence to Cruikshanks's, a friend of mine & a young
married Man, whose Wife is very amiable; & she & Sara are already
on the most cordial terms—from all this you will conclude, *that
we are happy.*—I have not been unmindful of you, and my engage-
ments—& but that Milton, the carrier, passed by on Wednesday
Morning two hours earlier than his usual time, you would have
received a parcel—Now I wish you to adopt for my sake as a poet
& for Biggs's sake as a printer, the following plan—which was
suggested by Thomas Poole——not to *page* the volume; but
merely in the last page instead of Finis to put the number of pages

256 pages. | thus.

but instead thereof to put over the pages in the centre No. 1.
No. 2. etc—as for instance the Visions of the Maid of Arc, notes &
introduction, will comprise exactly four sheets, reckoning that
there are *actually* in each page eighteen lines, which I find is the
case in Southey's—(bye the bye what a *divine* poem his Musings
on a Landscape after Gaspar Poussin is!—I love it almost better
than the Hymn to the Penates.)—Now [ov]er every page of these
64 pages (No. 1.)—then Chatterton (No. 2)—etc[1]——This will
answer three ends—it will be new—it will be *uniform* / whereas
sticking the Titles over the pages, some very long titles, others
short, others without any, is hateful to the eye—& lastly,[2] it will
give me that opportunity which I so much wish, of sending my
Visions of the Maid of Arc & my correcting of the Joan of Arc, to
Wordsworth, who lives not above 20 [40] miles from me & to
Lamb, whose *taste & judgment* I see reason to think more correct &
philosophical than my own, which yet I place pretty high.[3]—Of
my last Ode I have received criticisms from these Quarters,[4] which

Stowey. Since Coleridge speaks of having missed Milton the carrier on Wednes-
day and tells Cottle the *Ode on the Departing Year* as published in pamphlet
form on 31 Dec. 1796 would have been better if he had had the advantage
of Lamb's criticism, sent from London on 2 Jan. 1797, Friday, 6 Jan. 1797,
seems a safe conjecture.

[1] The 1797 edition of Coleridge's *Poems* did not quite follow these sug-
gestions. The pages and not the poems are numbered. See also Letter 180.

[2] Cottle omits the preceding part of this sentence, substituting the intro-
ductory clause, 'If you delay the press'. *Early Rec.* i. 229.

[3] Ultimately Lamb's unfavourable opinion of *The Destiny of Nations* was
in part responsible for Coleridge's abandonment of the poem for the 1797
volume. See Letter 178.

[4] This is further evidence that Wordsworth and Coleridge were in corre-
spondence. See Letter 127.

if I had seen before it's publication would have brought my Ode much nearer to perfection.—This therefore is my wish & intention —but at all events you may depend on receiving from Milton on Thursday next the Prefaces[1] & six hundred lines of the first poem— it will consist of eight hundred twenty more or less—but the Notes will be numerous.——This then must be the order of the Volume.

Title page,
Dedicatory Sonnet,[2]   { first half-sheet
   Table of Contents
   Prefaces (for I   { second half-sheet.
   make two)

Then

No. 1. The Progress of Liberty, or the Visions of the Maid of Orleans.[3] (Four sheets.—

No. 2. Monody on Chatterton.

No. 3 Songs of the Pixies

No. 4. The Rose.   (page 80.

No. 5. The Kiss   (page 82.

No. 6 To a young Ass

No. 7 Domestic Peace   (p. 77.

No. 8 The Sigh

No. 9 Epitaph on an Infant.   (No. 9. over the page; but let number 10. *begin* in the *same* page——

No. 10. The Man of Ross.

No. 11 The Spring in a Village—

No. 12. Edmund

No. 13 Lines with a Poem on the French Revolution.

No. 14. Lines with an unfinished Poem.

No. 15. The Sonnets— / which   (there will be 10
     I will send you   (6 already printed—
                          (4 new.——

No. 16. Shurton Bars.

No. 17. My pensive Sara! thy soft cheek reclin'd

No. 18. Low was our pretty Cot.

No. 19 The flower in February. Sweet Flower! that peeping &c—

[1] In the 1797 volume Coleridge reprinted with alterations the Preface of 1796 and also added a second Preface.

[2] In 1797 a blank verse *Dedication to the Reverend George Coleridge* replaced the proposed 'Dedicatory Sonnet'.

[3] This poem was omitted in 1797, the *Ode on the Departing Year* being the first poem after the dedication.

No. 20 The Hour, when we shall meet again.
No. 21 The Poem to Charles Lloyd
No. 22 Ode on the Departing Year.
No. 23. Religious Musings.

Then—No. 24. No. 25. No. 26.

Charles Lamb's Poems   Divided into three numbers—
Sonnets—Fragments—Ode—
Then—my Juvenile pieces—unnumbered, to shew how little I
value them—with a short Advertisement.

The notes will be printed at the bottom of the page—& I write
exactly the same number of words in a line as are printed in the
lines of Southey's notes—so that I *know*, I am accurate in giving
five sheets to Title, Preface, & Visions of the Maid of Orleans.—
You may therefore On Monday Morning send my Chatterton &
Songs of the Pixies to the Press——In the Chatterton make the
following alterations[1]—Page 1st inclose the two last lines in a
parenthesis/. Page. 2nd. omit bosom-startling. Yet oft ('tis Nature's
call). Page 3rd. Line the 3rd—let line be Line—i.e. 1 into L.
Page 4th. line the 3rd omit, aye, as——Light-hearted Youth! he
hastes along, And meditates the future Song, How dauntless Ælla
fray'd the Dacyan Foes: See! as floating &c. And instead of He—
line 4th. & See instead of And—line 6th——then omit the eight
last lines of this Page. / —Page 5th instead of Clad in Nature's &c
put Yes! in Nature's rich array—

His eyes dance rapture, & his bosom glows!
Yes! in Nature's rich array &c

Page 5th line 4th Most fair instead of How fair—& in the last line
of the Page—light-flushing instead of that lighten'd—

And Joy's wild gleams light-flushing o'er thy face.

Page 6. line 7th omit *death-cold*. Page 7th line 2nd omit *thrilling*——
& at the end of the Monody put—October, 1794. Songs of the
Pixies.[2] Page 16. / After the words 'on which occasion,' [a]dd 'and
at which time,' / page 18. Streaks the East [w]ith purple Light—

---

[1] All of the suggested alterations in the *Monody on the Death of Chatterton*
were followed in 1797, with the exception of lines 41 and 54. Coleridge directed
that line 41 read, 'Yes! in Nature's rich array', but it was printed, 'Yes! Clad in
Nature's rich array'. In line 54 *light-flashing* appeared instead of *light-flushing*.

[2] All of the suggested changes in the *Songs of the Pixies* were followed
in 1797, except: *froths* not altered to *froth* (line 72); *The purpling* not altered
to *Th' impurpling* (line 107); and *August, 1793* was not added at the end of the
poem.

instead of Purples the East with streaky Light. [I]n the 12th line
scented instead of lily-scented. Page 20. Solemn Thought instead
of solemn thought—i.e. capitals in the Initial letters. Page 21.
Wild instead of wildly-bow'rd. Page 22. Omit the comma after
[w]aves & alter froths into froth. Page 24. Obeisance instead of
obedience. Page 25th line 4th Th' impurpling instead of The
purpling—[A]t the end—put—August, 1793.—The Rose (p. 80.)
omit the word 'the' before dew—.—Inebriate with dew.—The
Kiss (p. 82) needs [n]o alteration. In the Ass. p. 92. line 9th. 'thy
Master' instead of 'her Master' [a]nd line eleventh alter to For
much I fear me, that *He* lives, like thee. Line 13th alter to 'How
askingly it's footsteps hither bend[']——P. 93. last line alter [to]
The aching of pale FASHION's vacant breast!—& then put December,
1794.[1] Domestic Peace & the Sigh need no alteration—& these will
last Biggs till Thursday Morning—when if you will send down
your young man to the Bear Inn, Red Cliff Street, to ask for
Milton, the Stowey Carrier, you will find a parcel containing the
book of my poems interleaved with the alterations—& likewise
the Prefaces & Poem which I shall send to you *for your criticisms.*—
Let me hear from you, my friend!—& tell me about my Ode—it is
very strange that Parsons has not advertised it.—Is Southey gone
to London yet? I think that the Poems from p. 7 to 28. 49 to 52.
67 to 74. 83 to 98. 121 to 128. 135 to 144. 163 to 182——would have
appeared to more advantage in the volume of Lovell & Southey—
that they do not rise much above mediocrity[2]—that the Poems
from 29 to 48. from 55 to 64. from 77 to 82. 99 to 116—129 to 134.
145 to 153—187 to 198—are worthy the author of Joan of Arc[3]—&
that from 154 to 158—203 to 220 deserve to have been [pu]blished
after the Joan of Arc, as proofs of *progressive* genius.[4]—

God bless you & S. T. C.

[1] The changes requested for *The Rose,* &c., were all made in the *Poems* of
1797.

[2] Coleridge refers to the following poems in Southey's 1797 volume: *The
Triumph of Woman; Ode written on the 1st. of January;* two poems entitled,
*Birth-Day Ode; Humphrey and William; John, Samuel, and Richard; Sappho;
Ode written on the 1st. Decr.; To Contemplation; To Horror; Mary;* and *Donica.*

[3] Coleridge refers to the following poems: *Poems on the Slave Trade,* six
sonnets; *To the Genius of Africa; To my own Miniature Picture; The Pauper's
Funeral; Inscriptions* (1–8); *Elinor; Frederic;* ten sonnets; *Written on a
Sunday Morning; Ode on the Death of a Favorite Spaniel; The Soldier's
Wife; The Widow; The Chapel Bell; The Race of Banquo;* and *Rudiger.*

[4] Coleridge refers to *Musings on a Landscape of Gaspar Poussin* and *Hymn
to the Penates.*

173. *To John Prior Estlin*

MS. Bristol Central Lib. Pub. with omis. Letters, *i. 213.*

[January 1797]

My dear Friend

I was indeed greatly rejoiced at the first sight of a letter from you; but it's contents were painful. Dear, dear Mrs Estlin!—Sara burst into an agony of tears, that she HAD been so ill.—Indeed, indeed, we hover about her—& think, & talk of her, with many an interjection of prayer.—I do not wonder that you have acquired a distaste to London—your associations must be painful indeed.— But God be praised! you shall look back on those sufferings, as the vexations of a dream! Our friend, T. Poole, particularly requests me to mention how deeply he condoles with you in Mrs Estlin's illness, how fervently he thanks God for her recovery.—I assure you he was extremely affected.——We are all remarkably well— & the child grows fat & strong. Our House is better than we ex- pected—there is a comfortable bedroom & sitting room for C. Lloyd,[1] & another for us—a room for Nanny, a kitchen, and outhouse. Before our door a clear brook runs of very soft water; and in the back yard is a nice *Well* of fine spring water. We have a very pretty garden, and large enough to find us vegetables & employment. And I am already an expert Gardener—& both my Hands can exhibit a callum, as testimonials of their Industry. We have likewise a sweet Orchard; & at the end of it T. Poole has made a gate, which leads into his garden—& from thence either thro' the tan yard into his house, or else thro' his orchard over a fine meadow into the garden of a Mr Cruikshanks, an old acquaintance, who married on the same day as I, & has got a little girl a little younger than David Hartley. Mrs Cruikshanks is a sweet little woman, of the same size as my Sara—& they are extremely cordial. T. Poole's Mother behaves to *us*, as a kind & tender Mother—She is very fond indeed of my Wife.—So that, you see, I ought to be happy—& thank God, I am so.——

I may expect your sermon I suppose, in the course of a fort- night—Will you send me introductory Letter[s] to Mr Howell[2] of Bridgewater & Toulmin[3] of Taunton? I have fifty things to

---

[1] Late in 1796 Charles Lloyd returned to Birmingham on a visit to his family, but by 16 Jan. 1797 he was with Lamb in London. (*Lamb Letters,* i. 90.) Early in February he came to Stowey, stayed a fortnight with Poole, and settled in the Coleridge cottage on the 22nd. (*Charles Lamb and the Lloyds,* 37–38.)

[2] Mr. Howell, the Unitarian minister at Bridgwater.

[3] Joshua Toulmin (1740–1815), a staunch Socinian and liberal, was a Uni- tarian minister at Taunton for thirty-eight years.

write—but the carrier is at the door——To poor John give our
love——and our kind love to Miss Estlin—& to all friends—To
Mrs Estlin my heart is so full, that I know not what to write——
Believe me with gratitude, with filial respect, & fraternal affection

Your sincere *friend*

S. T. Coleridge.

174. *To Thomas Poole*

Address: Mr T. Poole
MS. Victoria University Lib. Pub. Letters, *i. 4*. This is the first of five auto-
biographical letters written at Poole's request. (Cf. Letters 179, 208, 210, 234.)
With these letters may be read the autobiographical notes in Chapter I of
James Gillman's *Life of Coleridge*, 1838.

Feb. 6, 1797 Monday.[1]

My dear Poole

I could inform the dullest author how he might write an interest-
ing book—let him relate the events of his own Life with honesty,
not disguising the feelings that accompanied them.—I never yet
read even a Methodist's 'Experience' in the Gospel Magazine
without receiving instruction & amusement: & I should almost
despair of that Man, who could peruse the Life of John Woolman[2]
without an amelioration of Heart.—As to my Life, it has all the
charms of variety: high Life, & low Life, Vices & Virtues, great
Folly & some Wisdom. However what I am depends on what I
have been; and you, MY BEST FRIEND! have a right to the narra-
tion.—To me the task will be a useful one; it will renew and deepen
my reflections on the past; and it will perhaps make you behold
with no unforgiving or impatient eye those weaknesses and defects
in my character, which so many untoward circumstances have
concurred to plant there.——

My family on my Mother's side can be traced up, I know not,
how far—The Bowdens inherited a house-stye & a pig-stye in the
Exmore Country, in the reign of Elizabeth, as I have been told—&
to my own knowlege, they have inherited nothing better since
that time.—On my father's side I can rise no higher than my
Grandfather, who was dropped, when a child, in the Hundred of
Coleridge in the County of Devon; christened, educated, &
apprenticed by the parish.—He afterwards became a respectable

---

[1] 'When Coleridge resided at Stowey he agreed to write his life in a series
of letters to be addressed to me—I was to receive a letter every Monday
morning—' [MS. note by Tom Poole.]

[2] The Journal of John Woolman (1720–72), the Quaker abolitionist, was
published in Philadelphia in 1774 and in London in 1775.

Woolen-draper in the town of South Molton.[1] / I have mentioned
these particulars, as the time may come in which it will be useful
to be able to prove myself a genuine Sans culotte, my veins un-
contaminated with one drop of Gentility. My father received a
better education than the others of his Family in consequence of
his own exertions, not of his superior advantages. When he was
not quite 16 years old, my Grandfather became bankrupt; and by
a series of misfortunes was reduced to extreme poverty. My father
received the half of his last crown & his blessing; and walked off
to seek his fortune. After he had proceeded a few miles, he sate
him down on the side of the road, so overwhelmed with painful
thoughts that he wept audibly. A Gentleman passed by, who knew
him: & enquiring into his distresses took my father with him, &
settled him in a neighb'ring town as a schoolmaster. His school
increased; and he got money & knowlege: for he commenced a
severe & ardent student. Here too he married his first wife, by
whom he had three daughters; all now alive. While his first wife
lived, having scraped up money enough, at the age of 20 he walked
to Cambridge, entered at Sidney College, distinguished himself for
Hebrew & Mathematics, & might have had a fellowship: if he had
not been married.—He returned—his wife died—Judge Buller's
Father gave him the living of Ottery St Mary, & put the present
Judge to school with him—he married my Mother, by whom he
had ten children of whom I am the youngest, born October 20th
[21], 1772.

These sketches I received from my mother & Aunt; but I am
utterly unable to fill them up by any particularity of times, or
places, or names. Here I shall conclude my first Letter, because I
cannot pledge myself for the accuracy of the accounts, & I will not
therefore mingle them with those, for the accuracy of which in the
minutest parts I shall hold myself amenable to the Tribunal of
Truth.—You must regard this Letter, as the first chapter of an
history; which is devoted to dim traditions of times too remote
to be pierced by the eye of investigation.——

Your's affectionately
S. T. Coleridge

[1] 'Probably a mistake for Crediton.' *Letters,* i. 5 n.

175. *To Richard Brinsley Sheridan*[1]

Address: Richard Brinsley Sheridan Esq. | M. P. | London
MS. Harvard College Lib. Hitherto unpublished.
Stamped: Bridgewater.

Stowey, near Bridgewater.   Feb. 6th, 1797

Dear Sir

I received a letter last Saturday from a friend[2] of the Revd W. L.
Bowles, importing that *You* wished me 'to write a tragedy on
some popular subject.'[3] I need not say, that I was gratified and
somewhat elated by the proposal; and whatever hours I can win
from the avocations, by which I earn my immediate subsistence,
shall be sacred to the *attempt*. The *attempt* I shall make more
readily, as I have reason to believe, that I can hope without
expecting, and of course meet rejection without suffering dis-
appointment. Indeed I have conceived so high an idea of what a
Tragedy ought to be, that I am certain I shall myself be dis-
satisfied with my production; and I can therefore safely promise,
that I will neither be surprized or wounded, if I should find *you*
of the same opinion. I should consider myself well paid for my
trouble by the improvement which my mind would have received
from it, as an Exercise; and by the honor conferred on me by *your*
having proposed it.

The phrase 'popular subject' has a little puzzled me. Mr Bowles
perhaps will be able to inform me, whether you meant by it to
recommend a fictitious and domestic subject, or one founded on
well-known History. The four most popular Tragedies of Shake-
spear (Lear, Othello, Hamlet, and Romeo and Juliet) are either
fictitious, or drawn from Histories and parts of History unknown
to the Many: and the impression from Schiller's 'Fiesco' is weak
compared to that produced by his 'Robbers.' There are however
great advantages in the other scale. The Spectators come with a
prepared Interest.——

I shall not cease to remember this your kind attention to me;
and am pleased, that I have to add the feeling of individual
obligation to the deeper and more lofty gratitude, which I owe you
in common with all Europe.——

S. T. Coleridge

[1] Richard Brinsley Sheridan (1751–1816), dramatist and parliamentary
orator.

[2] Probably William Linley. Cf. Letter 211.

[3] In compliance with Sheridan's request, Coleridge wrote *Osorio*. See Letters
209 and 212.

176. *To John Thelwall*

Address: Mr. Thelwall | . . . [address heavily inked out] [Readdressed in another hand] Mr. Hardy's | Tavistock Street | Covent Garden
MS. Pierpont Morgan Lib. Pub. with omis. Letters, *i*. 214.
Postmark: 9 February 1797. *Stamped*: Bridgewater.

Stowey, near Bridgewater, Somerset.   Feb. 6th 1797.

I thank you, my dear Thelwall, for the parcel, & your Letters.
Of the contents I shall speak in the order of their importance.
First then, of your scheme of a school. I approve it; and fervently
wish, that you may find it more easy of accomplishment, than my
fears suggest. But try, by all means, try. Have hopes without
expectations—hopes to stimulate exertion, not expectations to
hazard disappointment.—Most of our patriots are tavern & parlour
Patriots, that will not avow their principles by any decisive action;
& of the few, who would wish to do so, the larger part are unable,
from their children's expectancies on rich Relations &c &c.—May
there remain enough for your Stella to employ herself on! Try, by
all means, try! For your comfort, for your progressiveness in
literary excellence, in the name of every thing that is happy, and
in the name of every thing that is miserable I would have you do
any thing honest, rather than lean with the whole weight of your
necessities on the Press. Get bread, & cheese, cloathing & housing
independently of it; & you may then safely trust to it for beef and
strong beer. You will find a country Life a happy one; and you
might live comfortably with an hundred a year. Fifty £ you might,
I doubt not, gain by *reviewing*; & furnishing miscellanies for the
different magazines; you might safely speculate on twenty pound
a year more from your compositions published separately—
$50+20 = 70£$—& by severe economy, a little garden labor, & a
pig stie, this would do—and if the education scheme did not suc-
ceed, and I could get *engaged* by any one of the Reviews & the New
Monthly Magazine, I would *try* it: & begin to farm by little & slow
degrees.—You perceive that by the Press I mean merely *writing
without a certainty.* The other is as secure as any thing else could
be to *you*. With health & spirits it would stand; & without health
& spirits every other mode of maintenance, as well as reviewing,
would be impracticable.—You are going to Derby! I shall be with
you in Spirit.—Derby is no common place; but where you will find
citizens enough to fill your lecture room puzzles me.——Dr Darwin
will no doubt excite your respectful curiosity. On the whole, I
think, he is the first *literary* character in Europe, and the most
original-minded Man. Mrs Crompton is an Angel; & Dr Crompton
a truly honest & benevolent man, possessing good sense & a large

portion of *humour*. I never think of him without respect, & tenderness; never (for thank heaven! I abominate Godwinism) without gratitude. William Strutt is a man of stern aspect, but strong, very strong abilities: Joseph Strutt every way amiable. He deserves his *Wife*—which is saying a great deal—for she is a sweet-minded Woman, and one that you would be apt to recollect whenever you met or used the words lovely, handsome, beautiful &c—'While smiling Loves the shaft display, And lift the playful torch elate.'— Perhaps, you may be so fortunate as to meet with a Mrs Evans whose seat is at Darley, about a mile from Derby. Blessings descend on her! Emotions crowd on me at the sight of her name— We spent five weeks at her house—a sunny spot in our Life!— My Sara sits and thinks and thinks of her, & bursts into tears—& when I turn to her, says—I was thinking, my dear! of Mrs Evans & Bessy. (—(i.e.) her daughter). I mention this to you, because things are charactered by their effects. She is no common Being who could create so warm & lasting an interest in *our* hearts: for *we* are no common people. Indeed, indeed, Thelwall! she is without exception the greatest WOMAN, I have been fortunate enough to meet with in my brief pilgrimage thro' Life.——

At Nottingham you will surely be more likely to obtain audiences; & I doubt not, you will find a hospitable reception there. I was treated by many families with kindliness, by some with a zeal of affection. Write me if you go & when you go.——

Now for your pamphlet.—It is well-written; & the doctrines sound, altho' sometimes, I think, deduced falsely—for instance— p. (111) It is *true* that all a man's children, 'however begotten, whether in marriage or out,' are his heirs in nature, and ought to be so in true policy; but instead of tacitly allowing that I meant by it to encourage what Mr B. & the Priests would call licentiousness, (and which surely, Thelwall! in the *present state of society* you must allow to be *injustice*, inasmuch as it deprives the woman of her respectability in the opinions of her neighbors) I would have shewn that such a law would of all others operate most powerfully *in favor* of *marriage*; by which word I mean not the effect of spells uttered by conjurors, but *permanent* cohabitation useful to Society as the best conceivable means (in the present state of Soc. at least:) of ensuring nurture & systematic education to infants & children. We are but frail beings at present; & want such motives to the practice of our duties. Unchastity *may* be no vice—I think, it is—but it may be no vice, abstractly speaking—yet from a variety of causes unchaste women are almost without exception careless Mothers. *Wife* is a solemn name to me because of it's influence on the more solemn duties of *Mother*.—Such passages—

(page 30 is another of them) are offensive. They are mere *assertions*, and of course can convince no person who thinks differently: and they give pain & irritate.——I write so frequently to you on this subject, because I have reason to *know* that passages of this order did give very general offence in your first part; & have operated to retard the sale of the second.—If they had been arguments, or necessarily connected with your main argument, I am not the man, Thelwall! who would oppose the filth of prudentials merely to have it swept away by the indignant torrent of your honesty. But as I said before, they are mere *assertions*; & certainly their truth is not self-evident.——Without [*sic*] the exception of these passages the pamphlet is the best, I have read, since the commencement of the war; warm, not fiery; well-reasoned without being dry; the periods harmonious yet avoiding metrical harmony; and the ornaments so disposed as to set off the features of truth without turning the attention on themselves.—I account for it's slow sale partly from your having compared yourself to Christ in the first (which gave great offence to my knowlege, altho' very foolishly, I confess) & partly from the sore & fatigued state of men's minds which disqualifies them for works of principle that exert the intellect without agitating the passions.—But it has not been reviewed yet—has it?——I read your narrative—& was almost sorry, I had read it—: for I had become much interested, & the abrupt 'no more' jarred me.——I never heard before of your variance with Horne Tooke.—Of the poems the two Odes are the best[1]—Of the two Odes the last, I think——it is in the best style of Akenside's best Odes.—Several of the sonnets are pleasing—& whenever I was pleased, I paused, & imaged you in my mind in your captivity.——*My* Ode by this time you are conscious that you praised too highly—you wrote to me in the warmth of a first impression. With the exception of 'I unpartaking of the evil thing' which line I do not think *injudiciously* weak, I accede to all your remarks, & shall alte[r] accordingly——Your remark that the line on the Empress had more of Juvenal than Pindar *flashed itself* on my mind——I had admired the line before; but I became immediately of your opinion—& that criticism has convinced me that your nerves are exquisite *electrometers* of Taste.[2]—You forgot to point out to me, that the whole Childbirth of Nature is at once ludicrous & disgusting—an epigram smart yet bombastic.—The Review of Bryant's pamphlet[3] is good—the sauce is better than

---

[1] See *Poems written in Close Confinement*, 1795, pp. 13–22.
[2] For this figure see also Letters 195 and 464.
[3] Jacob Bryant (1715–1804) published a treatise against the doctrines of Thomas Paine.

the Fish.——Speaking of Lewis's death,[1] surely, you forget that
the Legislature of France were to act by *Laws* and not by general
morals—; & that they violated the Law which they themselves
had made. I will take in the Corresponding Society Magazine.——
That good man, James Losh, has just published an admirable
pamphlet translated from the French of Benjamin Constant
entitled 'Considerations on the Strength of the present Govern-
ment of France'.[2] 'Woe to that country where crimes are punished
by crimes, and where men murder in the name of Justice.'—I apply
this to the death of the mistaking but well-meaning Lewis.——I
never go to Bristol—from seven to half past eight I work in my
garden; from breakfast till 12 I read & compose; then work again—
feed the pigs, poultry &c, till two o'clock—after dinner work again
till Tea—from Tea till supper *review*. So jogs the day; & I am
happy. I have society—my *friend*, T. Poole and as many acquaint-
ances as I can dispense with——there are a number of very pretty
young women in Stowey, all musical—& I am an immense favorite:
for I pun, conundrumize, *listen*, & dance. The last is a recent
acquirement—. We are *very* happy—& my little David Hartley
grows a sweet boy—& has high health—he laughs at us till he
makes us weep for very fondness.—You would smile to see my
eye rolling up to the ceiling in a Lyric fury, and on my knee a
Diaper pinned, to warm.——I send & receive to & from Bristol
every week—& will transcribe that part of your last letter & send
it to Reed.

I raise potatoes & all manner of vegetables; have an Orchard; &
shall raise Corn with the spade enough for my family.—We have two
pigs, & Ducks & Geese. A Cow would not answer the keep: for we
have whatever milk we want from T. Poole.

—God bless you & your affectionate

S. T. Coleridge

Sara's love to you, amorous Jeffery Ruddell![3]—& my Love to
Stella.—

[1] Louis XVI was guillotined at Paris, 21 Jan. 1793.
[2] Henri Benjamin Constant's pamphlet, *De la force du gouvernement actuel et de la nécessité de s'y rallier*, was published in 1796. James Losh's translation is not listed in the British Museum Catalogue.
[3] Geoffrey de Rudel, the troubadour, fell in love with the Countess of Tripoli without having seen her.

177. *To Joseph Cottle*

Pub. Early Rec. *i. 137.*

Stowey, [Early February 1797]
My dear Cottle,

I feel it much, and very uncomfortable, that, loving you as a brother, and feeling pleasure in pouring out my heart to you, I should so seldom be able to write a letter to you, unconnected with business, and uncontaminated with excuses and apologies. I give every moment I can spare from my garden and the Reviews (i.e.) from my potatoes and meat, to the poem, [*The Destiny of Nations*][1] but I go on slowly, for I torture the poem, and myself, with corrections; and what I write in an hour, I sometimes take two or three days in correcting. You may depend on it, the poem and prefaces will take up exactly the number of pages I mentioned, and I am extremely anxious to have the work as perfect as possible, and which I cannot do, if it be finished immediately. The Religious Musings, I have altered monstrously, since I read them to you, and received your criticisms. I shall send them to you in my next. The Sonnets I will send you with the Musings. God love you!

From your affectionate friend,
S. T. Coleridge.

178. *To Joseph Cottle*

Pub. Rem. *130, where the text is more complete than in* Early Rec. *i. 230.*

[*Circa* 10 February 1797][2]
My dear Cottle,

The lines which I added to my lines in the 'Joan of Arc,' have been so little approved by Charles Lamb, to whom I sent them, that although I differ from him in opinion, I have not heart to finish the poem.

. . . So much for an 'Ode,' [*Departing Year*] which some people think superior to the 'Bard' of Gray, and which others think a rant of turgid obscurity; and the latter are the more numerous class. It is not obscure. My 'Religious Musings' I know are, but not this 'Ode.'

[1] Cottle's text supplies *Religious Musings* in brackets, but Coleridge obviously refers to *The Destiny of Nations*.

[2] On 5 Feb. 1797 Lamb sent Coleridge some severe criticisms on *The Destiny of Nations*; on 13 Feb., realizing that he had disheartened Coleridge, he acknowledged the justice of some of Coleridge's objections and urged him to go on with the poem. *Lamb Letters,* i. 92–100. This letter, therefore, must have been written about 10 Feb. 1797.

179. *To Thomas Poole*

Address: Mr Thomas Poole
MS. Victoria University Lib. Pub. with omis. Letters, *i. 6.* This is the second of the autobiographical letters.

Sunday   March 1797

My dear Poole

My Father, (Vicar of, and Schoolmaster at, Ottery St. Mary, Devon) was a profound Mathematician, and well-versed in the Latin, Greek, & Oriental Languages. He published, or rather attempted to publish, several works: 1st, Miscellaneous Dissertations arising from the 17th and 18th Chapters of the Book of Judges; II. Sententiae excerptae, for the use of his own School; 3rd (& his best work) a Critical Latin Grammar; in the preface to which he proposes a bold Innovation in the names of the Cases. My father's new nomenclature was not likely to become popular, altho' it must be allowed to be both sonorous and expressive— exempli gratiâ—he calls the ablative the Quippe-quare-quale-quia-quidditive Case!—My Father made the world his confidant with respect to his Learning & ingenuity: & the world seems to have kept the secret very faithfully.—His various works, uncut, un-thumbed, have been preserved free from all pollution, except that of his Family's Tails.—This piece of good-luck promises to be hereditary: for all *my* compositions have the same amiable *home-staying* propensity.—The truth is, My Father was not a first-rate Genius—he was however a first-rate Christian. I need not detain you with his Character—in learning, good-heartedness, absentness of mind, & excessive ignorance of the world, he was a perfect *Parson Adams.*—My Mother was an admirable Economist, and managed exclusively.—My eldest Brother's name was John: he went over to the East Indies in the Company's Service; he was a successful Officer, & a brave one, I have heard: he died of a consumption there about 8 years ago. My second Brother was called William—he went to Pembroke College, Oxford; and afterwards was assistant to Mr Newcome's School, at Hackney. He died of a putrid fever the year before my Father's death, & just as he was on the eve of marriage with Miss Jane Hart, the eldest Daughter of a very wealthy Druggist in Exeter.—My third Brother, James, has been in the army since the age of sixteen—has married a woman of fortune—and now lives at Ottery St Mary, a respectable Man. My Brother Edward, the wit of the Family, went to Pembroke College; & afterwards, to Salisbury, as assistant to Dr Skinner: he married a woman 20 years older than his Mother. She is dead:

& he now lives at Ottery St Mary, an idle Parson. My fifth Brother, George, was educated at Pembroke College, Oxford; and from thence went to Mr Newcome's, Hackney, on the death of William. He stayed there fourteen [ten] years: when the living of Ottery St Mary[1] was given him—there he now has a fine school, and has lately married Miss Jane Hart; who with beauty, & wealth, had remained a faithful Widow to the memory of William for 16 years.—My Brother George is a man of reflective mind & elegant Genius. He possesses Learning in a greater degree than any of the Family, excepting myself. His manners are grave, & hued over with a tender sadness. In his moral character he approaches every way nearer to Perfection than any man I ever yet knew—indeed, he is worth the whole family in a Lump. My sixth Brother, Luke (indeed the seventh, for one Brother, the second, died in his Infancy, & I had forgot to mention him) was bred as a medical Man—he married Miss Sara Hart: and died at the age of 22 [25], leaving one child, a lovely Boy, still alive. My Brother Luke was a man of uncommon Genius,—a severe student, & a good man.——— The 8th Child was a Sister, Anne—she died a little after my Brother Luke—aged 21.

> Rest, gentle Shade! & wait thy Maker's will;
> Then rise *unchang'd*, and be an Angel still!

The 9th Child was called Francis: he went out as a Midshipman, under Admiral Graves—his Ship lay on the Bengal Coast—& he accidentally met his Brother John—who took him to Land, & procured him a Commission in the Army.—He shot himself (having been left carelessly by his attendant) in a delirious fever brought on by his excessive exertions at the siege of Seringapatam: at which his conduct had been so gallant, that Lord Cornwallis payed him a high compliment in the presence of the army, & presented him with a valuable gold Watch, which my Mother now has.—All my Brothers are remarkably handsome; but they were as inferior to Francis as I am to them. He went by the name of 'the handsome Coleridge.' The tenth & last Child was S. T. Coleridge, the subject of these Epistles: born (as I told you in my last) October 20th, 1772.

From October 20th, 1772 to October 20th, 1773.———Christened Samuel Taylor Coleridge—my Godfather's name being Samuel Taylor Esq. I had another Godfather, his name was Evans: & two Godmothers; both called 'Monday' [Mundy].—

From October 20th, 1773 to October 20th 1774.———In this year

---

[1] 'George Coleridge was Chaplain Priest, and Master of the King's School, but never Vicar of Ottery St. Mary.' *Letters*, i. 8 n.

I was carelessly left by my Nurse—ran to the Fire, and pulled out a live coal—burnt myself dreadfully—while my hand was being Drest by a Mr Young, I spoke for the first time (so my Mother informs me) & said—'Nasty Doctor Young'!—The snatching at fire, & the circumstance of my first words expressing hatred to professional men, are they at all *ominous*? This Year, I went to School—My Schoolmistress, the very image of Shenstone's, was named, Old Dame Key—she was nearly related to Sir Joshua Renyolds [*sic*].—

From October 20th 1774 to October 1775. I was inoculated; which I mention, because I distinctly remember it: & that my eyes were bound—at which I manifested so much obstinate indignation, that at last they removed the bandage—and unaffrighted I looked at the lancet & suffered the scratch.—At the close of this Year I could read a Chapter in the Bible.

Here I shall end; because the remaining years of my Life *all* assisted to form *my particular mind*—the three first years had nothing in them that seems to relate to it.

[Signature cut off]

180. *To Joseph Cottle*

Address: Mr Cottle | Bookseller | High-street | Bristol   *Single*
MS. *Harvard College Lib. Pub. with omis. and as two separate letters*, Early Rec. *i. 213 and 232*. In the manuscript the Preface to the 1797 edition of Coleridge's *Poems* and two poems precede this letter.
Stamped: Bridgewater.

Friday Morning [10 March 1797]

If, my dear Cottle! you have not sent the prefaces to the press you will substitute the one now sent[1] for that sent by T. Poole.— If you do not like these Verses;[2] or if you do not think them worthy of an Edition in which I profess to give nothing but my choicest fish, pick'd, gutted, and clean'd; get somebody to write them out, & send them with my compliments to the Editor of the New Monthly Magazine.[3]—But if you think as well of them as I do, (most probably from parental dotage for my last-born) . . .[4] you must

[1] The 'Preface to the second Edition' which Coleridge included in this letter is dated 6 Mar. 1797. Since the manuscript version is the same as that printed in the 1797 *Poems*, I have omitted it. Cf. *Poems*, ii. 1145.

[2] See end of letter for 'these Verses'.

[3] The first of these two poems, *To an unfortunate Woman*, which was omitted from the 1797 volume, was first printed in the *Morning Post*, 7 Dec. 1797; the second, *Allegorical Lines on the same subject*, was published in the 1797 *Poems*, 105, under the title, *To an Unfortunate Woman*.

[4] Four lines inked out on manuscript, apparently by Cottle. They read in part: be so kind as to shew them to Mr & to Mrs Estlin—if either of them,

print them immediately following the Kiss, according to the order
which I sent you by Letter—only *paging*, instead of *Numbering*.

I suppose, I shall hear from you tomorrow.——Public affairs
are in strange confusion—I am afraid that I shall prove at least as
good a prophet as bard—O doom'd to fall, enslav'd & vile:[1]—but
may God make me a foreboder of evils never to come!—I have
heard from Sheridan, desiring me to write a Tragedy——I have no
genius that way—Robert Southey has—and highly as I think of
his Joan of Arc, I cannot help prophesying, that he will be known
to posterity as Shakespear's great Grandson, and only as Milton's
great great grand nephew-in-law.—I think, that he will write a
Tragedy; and Tragedies.——

Charles Lloyd has given me his Poems, which I give to you on
condition that you print them *in this volume*—after Charles Lamb's
poems——the Title-page, which by the bye must not be printed
till all the rest is, thus—Poems by S. T. Coleridge, second Edition,
to which are added Poems by Charles Lamb, and C. Lloyd.—
Charles Lamb's poems will occupy about 40 pages: C. Lloyd's at
least a hundred—altho' only his choice fish——A poem on Christ-
mas which he has written lately is exquisite—Now supposing that
the poems, which I myself have added, are only sufficient to make
up for the different type & number of lines in each page, in the two
Editions—my poems will occupy only 132 pages, that being two
thirds of the present——to this add 140—and you have 272
pages——72 more than the former Edition.——So much for the
priceableness of the Volume—Now for the saleability, Charles
Lloyd's connections will take off a great many more than a
hundred, I doubt not.——So that in no way can you miss my
omitted Lines——in the table of *my* contents put the added poems
in Italics, with a note saying so—God bless you—& S. T. Coleridge.

To an unfortunate Woman, whom I knew in the days of her
Innocence. Composed at the Theatre.[2]

> Maiden! that with sullen brow
> Sit'st behind those Virgins gay,
> Like a scorch'd and mildew'd bough
> Leafless mid the blooms of May;
>
> Inly-gnawing, thy Distresses
> Mock those starts of wanton glee,
> And thy inmost soul confesses
> Chaste Affection's Majesty.

upon whose taste I have almost an implicit reliance, . . . to their being un-
worthy of my Edition— . . .

[1] Line 121 of the early versions of the *Ode on the Departing Year*.
[2] *Poems*, i. 171.

Loathing thy polluted Lot,
Hie thee, Maiden! hie thee hence:
Seek thy weeping Mother's cot
With a wiser Innocence![1]

Mute the *Lavrac and forlorn,
While she moults those firstling plumes,
That had skimm'd the tender corn
Or the Beanfield's od'rous blooms:

Soon with renovated Wing
Shall she dare a loftier flight,
Upwards to the Day-star sing
And embathe in heavenly Light!

* the Lark [S.T.C.]

    Allegorical Lines on the same subject.[2]

Myrtle-Leaf, that ill-besped
Pinest in the gladsome ray,
Soil'd beneath the common tread
Far from thy protecting Spray;

When the Scythesman[3] o'er his sheaf
Caroll'd in the yellow Vale,
Sad I saw thee, heedless Leaf!
Love the dalliance of the Gale.

Lightly didst thou, poor fond[4] Thing!
Heave and flutter to his sighs;
While the Flatt'rer, on his wing
Woo'd and whisper'd thee to rise.

Gaily from thy mother stalk
Wert thou danc'd and wafted high;
Soon on this unshelter'd walk
Flung to fade, and rot, and die![5]

---

[1] With the wreck of Innocence! [MS. emendation in Cottle's handwriting; not adopted by Coleridge.]

[2] *Poems*, i. 172.

[3] Rustic [MS. emendation in Cottle's handwriting; authorized by Coleridge.] Cf. Letter 181.

[4] foolish [MS. emendation in Cottle's handwriting; authorized by Coleridge.] Cf. Letter 181.

[5] Flung to wither and to die! [MS. emendation in Cottle's handwriting; authorized by Coleridge, but not carried out in the 1797 *Poems*.] Cf. Letter 181.

181. *To Joseph Cottle*

MS. Harvard College Lib. Pub. with omis. and as two separate letters, Early Rec. *i. 197 and 224.* The sentence, 'I like your lines on Savage', appears in *Early Rec.* i. 233, as a postscript to one of the two letters Cottle made of Letter 180 of this edition.

Wednesday Morning [15 March 1797]   Ten o'clock.

My dearest Cottle

I write under great anguish of mind, Charles Lloyd being very ill. He has been seized with his fits three times in the space of seven days; and just as I was in bed, last night, I was called up again—and from 12 o clock at night to *five* this morning he remained in one *continued* state of *agoniz'd Delirium*. What with the bodily toil exerted in repressing his frantic struggles, and what with the feelings of anguish for his agonies, you may suppose that I have forced myself from bed with aching temples & a feeble frame. I was not in bed till after five.—However, I will hastily tell you what is to be done with the poems.—

The Ode must be reprinted—T. Poole says, that rather than the first poem in the book should appear with so many horrid blunders, you shall put a guinea to his account towards the expence—& *I* will scrape up another.—

O'er Nature struggling in portentous birth is printed after Weep & Rejoice—instead of before it, as the Sense, the Poetry, & (what might have directed you) the correspondent Metre of the second antistrophe demanded—and you have in page 15 retained one of those two lines, for which two I had substituted this one, By livid fount &—in consequence, the passage is nonsense, imprimis, & (secondly) there is a line without a rhyme.—Besides this, there are a multitude of small typographical blunders—& one or two very foolish alterations.——Mr Lloyd's poems are to be printed after mine in the order put in page 16 of the copy of my Ode——

The first poem on the Unfortunate Woman will do well for the monthly Magazine—the second therefore only shall be printed in my poems—with this title—

Allegorical Lines to an unfortunate Woman,
whom I had known in the days of her Innocence.

Your remarks are perfectly just on it[1]—except that, in this country, T. P. informs me, Corn is *as often* cut with a Scythe, as with a hook. However for Scythesman read Rustic—for 'poor fond

---

[1] In *Early Rec.* i. 219–24 Cottle prints what purports to be his letter of criticism to Coleridge.

thing[']—read—foolish Thing,——& for Flung to fade & rot & die—read Flung to wither & to die!—Ill-besped is indeed a sad blotch—but after having tried at least a hundred ways before I sent the poem to you, and as many more since,—I find it incurable.—This first poem is but a so so composition—I wonder, I could be so blinded by the ardor of recent composition, as to see any thing in it.——I will send it myself to the Editor.—

I like your lines on Savage—. . .[1] We offer petitions, not as supposing that we influence the immutable—but because to petition the Supreme Being is the way, most suited to our nature, to stir up the benevolent affection in our own heart—Christ positively commands it—& in St Paul, &c you will find unnumbered instances of prayers for individual Blessings for Kings, rulers, countries, &c &c——We indeed should always join to our petition—But thy will be done, Omniscient, All-loving, Immutable God!——Milton waits impatiently—

S. T. Coleridge

182. *To Josiah Wade*

Address: Mr. Wade | at Mrs. Wade's Pershore, Worcestershire [*Readdressed*] at Mrs. Cooper's Queen Square No. 48—Bristol
Transcript Coleridge family. Pub. E.L.G. i. 72.

Stowey near Bridgewater   March 16th 1797.

My dear Friend

If any set of circumstances can excuse me for suffering so kind, so very kind, a letter as your last, to remain so long unanswered, these circumstances are ready to plead for me—In the first place, my review business had been suffered to accumulate so as to excite great discontent in my employers; for this last three weeks I have been compelled to devote great part of my time to it—Secondly Cottle has been clamorous about my new Edition, and transcribings, alterations, &c, &c, have been forced on me by necessity—Thirdly Sheridan has sent to me to write a Tragedy, which he promises me to introduce on Drury Lane Theatre with every possible advantage, and wishes me to sketch out one immediately and send him the *sketch*, when he will give me his opinion of it. But fourthly poor Charles Lloyd has been ill indeed—within these ten days he has had five fits, all of them followed by a continued and agonizing Delirium of five or six hours.—So that what with bodily struggles and mental anguish and loss of sleep from sitting up with him, my temples ache, and my frame is feeble.—My dear

---

[1] One sentence inked out in MS.

dear Wade! never believe so very ill of me as to suspect that my epistolary silence originates in want of affection.—I detest profession, but it eases my heart to tell you, how often I think and talk of you and of the unwearied kindness you have shewn me: indeed it is a common theme after supper. I speak of you with both my eyes and heart full—brimfull—We are well—the baby and Mrs. Coleridge remarkably so—in my next, which I will write before I receive an answer to this, I will give you a minute account of our Cottage and mode of life.

You are a good Prophet—my God! into what a state have the Scoundrels brought this devoted kingdom—If the House of Commons would but melt down their faces, it would greatly assist the copper Currency—We should have *brass* enough.[1]

Our love to Mrs. Wade—I rejoice to hear that you are likely to settle in Bristol—as then I shall hear from you and be more in the way of seeing you——

T. Poole desires his love—be particular in your next about Ann Wade—Our David Hartley is a very Seraph in Clouts—and laughs, till he makes us cry for very overflowing joy and tenderness.

God Almighty love you and | Your ever grateful Friend
S. T. Coleridge

You see in what a hurry I write.

183. *To William Lisle Bowles*

Address: Revd W. L. Bowles | Donhead | near Shaftsbury | Wilts.
MS. Professor C. B. Tinker. Pub. A Wiltshire Parson and His Friends, *by Garland Greever, 1926, p. 29.*

Thursday Morning. [16 March 1797][2]

Dear Sir

But that I am not likely to have another opportunity of transmitting the accompanying trifles to you, I would not intrude on you at a moment, when your heart is necessarily occupied with it's own feelings.—You have the nightly prayers of my little family for the restoration of your dear Mother's health. To me the death of the aged has a more mournful effect than that of the young. Accustomed to observe a completeness in all the works of Nature, the departure of the Latter seems more of a *transition*—the heart is dissatisfied, & says, *this cannot be all.* But of the aged we have seen the bud, the blossom, & the fruit—& the whole circle of existence appears completed.—But praise & thanksgiving to

---

[1] Cottle added this paragraph as a postscript to Letter 185 of this edition. Cf. *Early Rec.* i. 240.

[2] This letter was written before the death of Bowles's mother on 25 Mar. 1797, and the reference to Lloyd's seizures suggests mid-March.

him who sent light & immortality into the world, bidding the corruptible put on incorruption, & the mortal immortality: for the young & old alike rejoice before God & the Lamb.—

The poems of Mr Lloyd will, I think, please you—the Woman, whom they lament, approached as near perfection, as human nature admits.—His affection for her was almost too great—for her death has had the most melancholy effects on his health—he fell into a nervous complaint, which has terminated in a species of epileptic seizures.—He is at present domesticated in my cottage.

My Ode you will read with a kindly forbearance as to it's *political* sentiments.—The base of our politics is, I doubt not, the same. We both feel strongly for whomever our imaginations present to us in the attitude of suffering.—I confess, that mine is too often a '*stormy* pity.'

The plan I had sketched for my tragedy is too chaotic to be transmitted at present—but immediately I understand it myself, I will submit it to you: & feel greatly obliged to you for your permission to do it.—It is 'romantic & wild & somewhat terrible'— & I shall have Siddons & Kemble in my mind—but indeed I am almost weary of the Terrible, having been an hireling in the Critical Review for these last six or eight months—I have been lately reviewing the Monk, the Italian, Hubert de Sevrac[1] & &c & &c— in all of which dungeons, and old castles, & solitary Houses by the Sea Side, & Caverns, & Woods, & extraordinary characters, & all the tribe of Horror & Mystery, have crowded on me—even to surfeiting.—

I rejoice to hear of your new Edition—Why did you ever omit that sublime Sonnet, Thou, whose stern Spirit loves the awful storm—?[2] I should have pleaded hard too for the first, Bereave me not[3]—& still more vehemently for the Sonnet to Harmony[4]—

---

[1] Professor Garland Greever, on the basis of this letter, identifies four reviews as Coleridge's: those of Ann Radcliffe's *The Mysteries of Udolpho* and *The Italian*, of Mary Robinson's *Hubert de Sevrac*, and of M. G. Lewis's *The Monk*; but Mr. C. I. Patterson convincingly shows that only the review of *The Monk* is indubitably Coleridge's. In a letter dated 1828 Coleridge confirms Mr. Patterson's contention. The reviews of *The Monk* and of Bishop Horsley's tract, *On the Prosodies of the Greek and Latin Languages*, Coleridge says, 'were perfected into Print'. (Both of these reviews appeared in the February issue of the *Critical Review* for 1797.) Coleridge adds that he 'likewise had written some half a score or more of what, I thought, clever & epigrammatic & devilishly severe Reviews', but that 'a Remark made by Miss Wordsworth', to whom he had read one of them, 'occasioned my committing the whole Batch to the Fire'. See Garland Greever, *A Wiltshire Parson*, 165–200; C. I. Patterson, 'The Authenticity of Coleridge's Reviews of Gothic Romances', *Journal of Eng. and Ger. Philology*, Oct. 1951, pp. 517–21; and E.L.G. ii. 407.

[2] *At Dover, 1786.*   [3] *At Oxford, 1786.*   [4] *Music.*

the only description of the effect of Music that suited my ex-
perience—or rose above commonplace—[In Sonn]et xvi (as they
now stand) the parenthesis always [interr]upts the tide of my
feelings[1]—We describe [for o]*thers*—not when we speak *to* the object
described—perhaps I may be wrong—but I am sure, you will
excuse my freedom—I do not like your alteration of Evening—it
seems now to possess less *oneness* than it did before—in the 18th[2]
you use 'hope' in two ways—once as an abstract—he with new
hope—once as an impersonation—Sweet Hope!—is this an imper-
fection?—I could write a great deal about your late alterations—
but I will not detain you any more—

believe me | very sincerely | Your's
S. T. Coleridge

I shall be anxious to your [hear?] of your dear Parent's
Health.—

184. *To Joseph Cottle*

From a catalogue of Browne and Browne, Booksellers, Newcastle-upon-Tyne.
Pub. E.L.G. i. 70.

[Early April 1797]

My dearest Cottle

I love and respect you as a brother, and my memory deceives
me woefully, if I have not evidenced by the animated tone of my
conversation, when we have been *tête-à-tête*, how much your com-
pany interested me. But when last in Bristol the day I meant to
have devoted to you was such a day of sadness, that I could *do
nothing.*—On the Saturday, the Sunday, and the ten days after
my arrival at Stowey[3] I felt a depression too dreadful to be
described

So much I felt my genial spirits droop!
My hopes all flat, nature within me seem'd
In all her functions weary of herself.[4]

Wordsworth's conversation,[5] &c roused me somewhat; but even

---

[1] *Distant View of England from the Sea.*

[2] *Hope.*

[3] Coleridge was in Bristol on 23 Mar. See Letter 185, headnote.

[4] *Samson Agonistes,* 594–6.

[5] On 19 Mar. 1797 Wordsworth had left Racedown for Bristol, from whence
he expected to return in about a fortnight. Cf. *Early Letters,* 165. He may
have seen Coleridge in Bristol; but it is certain from Coleridge's letter that
Wordsworth visited Stowey, probably early in April, on his way back to Race-
down. See Letter 190, which shows that Poole also met Wordsworth at this
time.

now I am not the man I have been—and I think never shall. A
sort of calm hopelessness diffuses itself over my heart.—Indeed
every mode of life which has promised me bread and cheese, has
been, one after another torn away from me—but God remains.
I have no immediate pressing distress, having received ten pounds
from Lloyd's father at Birmingham.[1]—I employ myself now on a
book of Morals in answer to Godwin, and on my Tragedy. David
Hartley is well, and grows.—Sara is well and desires a sister's
love to you.

Tom Poole desires to be kindly remembered to you. I see they
have reviewed Southey's Poems and my Ode in the Monthly
Review.[2] Notwithstanding the Reviews, I, who in the sincerity of
my heart am *jealous* for Robert Southey's fame, regret the publica-
tion of that volume. Wordsworth complains, with justice, that
Southey writes *too much at his ease*[3]—that he seldom 'feels his
burthened breast

Heaving beneath th' incumbent Deity.'

He certainly will make literature more *profitable to him* from the
fluency with which he writes, and the facility with which he pleases
himself. But I fear, that to posterity his wreath will look un-
seemly—here an ever living amaranth, and close by its side some
weed of an hour, sere, yellow, and shapeless—his exquisite beauties
will lose half their effect from the bad company they keep. Besides
I am fearful that he will begin to rely too much on *story* and *event*
in his poems, to the neglect of those *lofty imaginings*, that are
peculiar to, and definitive of, the poet. The *story* of Milton might
be told in two pages—it is this which distinguishes an *Epic Poem*
from a *Romance in metre*. Observe the march of Milton—his severe
application, his laborious polish, his deep metaphysical researches,
his prayers to God before he began his great poem, all that could
lift and swell his intellect, became his daily food. I should not
think of devoting less than 20 years to an Epic Poem. Ten to collect
materials and warm my mind with universal science. I would be
a tolerable Mathematician, I would thoroughly know Mechanics,
Hydrostatics,   Optics,   and   Astronomy,   Botany,   Metallurgy,
Fossilism, Chemistry, Geology, Anatomy, Medicine—then the
mind of man—then the *minds of men*—in all Travels, Voyages and

---

[1] Charles Lloyd left Nether Stowey, presumably before 23 Mar., since
Coleridge was in Bristol on that date. Shortly afterwards Lloyd was placed
under the care of Dr. Erasmus Darwin, in a sanatorium at Lichfield. *Lamb
Letters*, i. 107.

[2] See *Monthly Review*, Mar. 1797.

[3] Cottle (*Early Rec.* i. 191) omits the names of both Wordsworth and Southey
and prints: 'There are some Poets who write too much at their ease.'

Histories. So I would spend ten years—the next five to the com-
position of the poem—and the five last to the correction of it.

So I would write haply not unhearing of that divine and rightly-
whispering Voice, which speaks to mighty minds of predestinated
Garlands, starry and unwithering. God love you,

S. T. Coleridge.

185. *To Josiah Wade*

Pub. Early Rec. *i. 240*. In introducing this fragment Cottle remarks: 'A little
before this time [i.e. 10 May 1797; see Letter 188], a curious, or, rather,
ludicrous occurrence happened to Mr. C. during a pedestrian excursion of his
into Somersetshire.' *Early Rec.* i. 239. The fragment probably belongs to a
letter of 1797. On 23 March 1797 Coleridge signed for the first two volumes
of J. J. Brucker's *Historia Critica Philosophiae*, 6 vols., 1766–7, at the Bristol
Library, but he did not take the books with him until 6 April (see Letter
187). It would seem, therefore, that he was in Bristol on 23 March and again
on 6 April. Since he returned in dejected spirits to Stowey after the March visit
(see Letter 184), he was in no mood to write in so jesting a manner as in this
fragment, which may have been written after the second visit to Bristol.

[*Circa* 8 April 1797]

My dear friend,

I am here [Stowey] after a most tiresome journey; in the course
of which, a woman asked me if I knew one Coleridge, of Bristol.
I answered, I had heard of him. 'Do you know, (quoth she) that
that vile jacobin villain drew away a young man of our parish, one
Burnet,' &c. and in this strain did the woman continue for near
an hour; heaping on me every name of abuse that the parish of
Billingsgate could supply. I listened very particularly; appeared
to approve all she said, exclaiming, 'dear me!' two or three times,
and, in fine, so completely won the woman's heart by my civilities,
that I had not courage enough to undeceive her. . . .

S. T. Coleridge.[1]

186. *To Joseph Cottle*

Pub. Rem. *140, where the text is more complete than in* Early Rec. *i. 246*. This
letter, as printed by Cottle, is obviously a composite of parts of several letters.
The first paragraph refers to Burnett's illness at his home in Huntspill,
which probably explains Coleridge's presence there. The second paragraph
sends a message to Mrs. Coleridge, even though the letter is headed
'Stowey'; this paragraph, therefore, probably belongs to a letter written

---

[1] The postscript Cottle printed here is a paragraph taken from Letter 182.

before Coleridge settled in Nether Stowey. The third paragraph presumably belongs to the Stowey period, though mice may have plagued the Coleridges at Clevedon or elsewhere. The postscript may be from a letter written in Stowey. Did Cottle group together Coleridge's comments on kittens, mice, and dogs for reasons known only to himself?

Stowey.   [Early April 1797?]

My dear friend,

I found George Burnet ill enough, heaven knows, Yellow Jaundice,——the introductory symptoms very violent. I return to Bristol on Thursday, and shall not leave till *all be done.*

Remind Mrs. Coleridge of the kittens, and tell her that George's brandy is just what smuggled spirits might be expected to be, execrable! The smack of it remains in my mouth, and I believe will keep me most horribly temperate for half a century. He (Burnet) was bit, but I caught the Brandiphobia.[1] [obliterations] . . . (—scratched out, well knowing that you never allow such things to pass, uncensured. A good joke, and it slipped out most impromptu-ishly.)

The mice play the very devil with us. It irks me to set a trap. By all the whiskers of all the pussies that have mewed plaintively, or amorously, since the days of Whittington, it is not fair. 'Tis telling a lie. 'Tis as if you said, 'Here is a bit of toasted cheese; come little mice! I invite you!' when, oh, foul breach of the rites of hospitality! I mean to assassinate my too credulous guests! No, I cannot set a trap, but I should vastly like to make a Pitt—fall. (Smoke the Pun!) But concerning the mice, advise thou, lest there be famine in the land. Such a year of scarcity! Inconsiderate mice! Well, well, so the world wags.

Farewell, S. T. C.

P.S. A mad dog ran through our village, and bit several dogs. I have desired the farmers to be attentive, and to-morrow shall give them, in writing, the first symptoms of madness in a dog.

I wish my pockets were as yellow as George's phiz!

[1] 'It appears that Mr. Burnet had been prevailed upon by smugglers to buy some prime cheap brandy, but which Mr. Coleridge affirmed to be a compound of Hellebore, kitchen grease, and Assafoetida! or something as bad.' *Rem.* 140.

187. *To G. Catcott*

Address: Mr G.. Catcott Sub-Libran.
MS. Bristol Central Lib. Pub. Early Rec. *i. 211.* In printing this letter Cottle changed '*one shilling & three pence*' to 'five shillings', in the first sentence; and at the close of the letter he inserted the word 'expensive' before 'notes & letters'.

[*Circa* 6 May 1797][1]

Mr Catcott

I beg your acceptance of the enclosed letters. You must not think lightly of the present; as they cost me, who am a very poor man, *one shilling & three pence.*—For the future, all letters to me from the Library must be thus directed—

S. T. Coleridge | Mr Cottle's | Bookseller, | High Street | Bristol.

With respect to the Bruckers; altho' by accident they were register'd on the 23rd of March, yet they were not removed from the Library for a fortnight after—: and when I received your first letter on this subject,[2] I had had the two Volumes *just three weeks.* Our learned & ingenious Committee may read thro' two quartos— i.e. *two thousand and four hundred pages of close printed Greek & Latin* in three weeks, for aught I know to the contrary: I pretend to no such intenseness of application or rapidity of Genius.——I must beg you to inform me by Mr Cottle, [wha]t length of time is allowed by the rules & *customs* of our institution for each book— whether the contents, as well as the size, are consulted in apportioning the times—or whether, customarily, any time at all is *apportioned*, except where the Committee, in *individual* cases, chuse to deem it proper.—I subscribe to your Library, Mr Catcott! not to read novels, or books of quick reading & easy digestion— but to get books, which I can not get else where—books of massy knowlege——& as I have few books of my own, I read with a common place book—so that if I be not allowed a longer period of time for the perusal of such books, I must contrive to get rid of my

---

[1] In the Register of the Bristol Library Society it is noted that Coleridge was charged with the Brucker volumes from 23 Mar. to 11 May 1797. The entries also show that letters from the Library were sent to Coleridge on 26 Apr. and 5 May. See George Whalley, 'The Bristol Library Borrowings of Southey and Coleridge, 1793–8', *The Library, Trans. Biblio. Soc.*, Sept. 1949, pp. 114–32. Coleridge's letter was probably written immediately on receipt of the library's second communication.

[2] The 'first letter' from the Bristol Library on 26 Apr. 1797 reads: 'Sir, I am directed by the COMMITTEE to remind you that Brucker, Hist. Crit. Phil. Vol. 1st & 2nd was registered in your Name, on the 23 Day of March ulto. G. Catcott Sub-Librarian.' [MS. Harvard.]

subscription, which would be a thing perfectly useless, except as far as it gives me an opportunity of reading your little notes & letters—.

Your's in christian fellowship
S. T. Coleridge

188. *To Joseph Cottle*

Addrrss: Mr Cottle | Bookseller.
MS. Edinburgh University Lib. Pub. E.L.G. i. 75. Cottle makes two letters of this manuscript. Cf. *Early Rec.* i. 211 and 239.

[10 May 1797]

My dear dear Cottle

Have patience—& *every thing* shall be done. I think entirely of your Brother;[1] in two days, I will think entirely *for you*—and by Wednesday next you shall have Lloyd's other poem, & all Lamb's —*besides &c*—I have written *1500* lines of *my Tragedy*—T. Poole is in extacies with it—he says, it has passion, well-conducted plot, stage-effect, & the spirit of poetic language without the *technicalities.*—

S. T. Coleridge

I have not received the Poet's Fate.[2]
Take the enclosed to the Library[3]—I have sent a Curious Letter to G. Catcott.—A dog, he has all together made me pay 5s for postage—

189. *To Joseph Cottle*

Pub. Early Rec. *i. 147.* Cottle introduces this fragment thus: 'I then pressed him to dedicate his Poems to one of his relatives, his brother George, of whom he occasionally spoke with peculiar kindness.' Since the *Dedication. To the Reverend George Coleridge, of Ottery St. Mary, Devon,* was dated 26 May 1797, this note must have been written not long before. In one copy of the 1797 *Poems* Coleridge wrote: 'N.B. If this volume should ever be delivered according to its direction, *i.e.* to Posterity, let it be known that the Reverend George Coleridge was displeased and thought his character endangered by the Dedication.—S. T. Coleridge.' *Poems*, i. 173 n.

[*Circa* 15 May 1797]

You, I am sure, will be glad to learn, that I shall follow your advice.

[1] 'My brother, [Amos Cottle] when at Cambridge, had written a Latin poem for the prize: the subject, "Italia, Vastata", and sent it to Mr. Coleridge . . . in MS. requesting the favor of his remarks.' *Rem.* 136 n.
[2] Cf. George Dyer, *The Poet's Fate. A Poetical Dialogue*, 1797. Pantisocracy and Coleridge are mentioned in the footnotes, pp. 26–27.
[3] Referring, apparently, to the Brucker volumes, which were returned on 11 May.

190. *To Joseph Cottle*

Address: Mr Cottle | Bookseller | High Street | Bristol
MS. Harvard College Lib. Pub. Letters, *i. 220.*
Stamped: Crewkhern.

Thursday. [8 June 1797]

My dear Cottle

I am sojourning for a few days at Racedown, the mansion of our friend Wordsworth: who has received Fox's Achmed[1]——he returns you his acknowlegements & presents his kindliest respects to you. —I shall be home by Friday—not tomorrow—but the next Friday. If the Ode on the departing Year be not reprinted, please to *omit* the lines from 'When shall scepter'd Slaughter cease'—to—For still does Madness roam on Guilt's bleak dizzy height—inclusive. The first Epode is to end at the words 'Murderer's fate.'[2]—Wordsworth admires my Tragedy—which gives me great hopes. Wordsworth has written a Tragedy himself.[3] I speak with heart-felt sincerity & (I think) unblinded judgement, when I tell you, that I feel myself a *little man by his* side; & yet do not think myself the less man, than I formerly thought myself.—His Drama is absolutely wonderful. You know, I do not commonly speak in such abrupt & unmingled phrases—& therefore will the more readily believe me. —There are in the piece those *profound* touches of the human heart, which I find three or four times in 'The Robbers' of Schiller, & often in Shakespere—but in Wordsworth there are no *inequalities*. T. Poole's opinion of Wordsworth is—that he is the greatest Man, he ever knew—I coincide.[4]——

It is not impossible, that in the course of two or three months I may see you——

God bless you &
S. T. Coleridge

Of course, with the lines you omit the notes that relate to them.

---

[1] In 1797 Cottle published *Poems, containing the Plaints, Consolations, and Delights of Achmed Ardebeili, a Persian Exile,* by Charles Fox, 1749–1809.

[2] These lines, which had appeared earlier in the *Cambridge Intelligencer,* were not included in the 1797 edition. Cf. *Poems,* i. 163 n.

[3] Referring, of course, to *The Borderers.*

[4] This statement proves conclusively that Poole, like Coleridge, had formed an estimate of Wordsworth prior to June 1797. Letter 184 shows that Wordsworth had stopped at Nether Stowey on his return to Racedown from Bristol, probably in early April. Coleridge's 'sojourn' at Racedown reported at the beginning of this letter was, therefore, a return visit.

191. *To John Prior Estlin*

Address: Revd J. P. Estlin | St Michael's Hill | Bristol
MS. Bristol Central Lib. Pub. Letters to Estlin, *38.* The upper half of pages 1
and 2 of the manuscript has been cut off.
Stamped: Crewkhern.

[9 June 1797]

... of this month—I wished to have written you when it was decided.
—These causes dissolved in that universal menstruum of apologies,
my indolence—made me delay my letter, till, I fear, I write at a
time, when even a letter from a friend will intrude on your fears &
anxieties. Believe me, I share them—no hour passes, in which
I do not think of, with an eagerness of mind,—dear Mrs Estlin. I
feel, at times, sad & depressed on her account—on mine own, I
might have said. For, God knows! these are not the times, when
we can fear for a dear friend with a moderate fear!——

I am at present sojourning for a few days with Wordsworth, at
Racedown Lodge, near Crewkherne: & finishing my Tragedy.
Wordsworth, who is a strict & almost severe critic, thinks *very*
highly of it—which gives me great hopes. . . .

... I have been led to believe.—Where there are two ministers,
they ought to be either as Brothers—one soul in two heads—or as
Father & Son.——

I breakfasted with Dr Toulmin last Monday—the more I see of
that man, the more I love him. I preached for Mr Howel the
Sunday before—My sermon was admired—but *admired* sermons,
I have reason to think, are not those that do most good.—I
endeavored to awaken a Zeal for Christianity by shewing the
contemptibleness & evil of lukewarmness.

—T. Poole gives me notice that you have, a midsummer's 20
guineas for me, which those have contributed who believe that
they are enabling me to benefit my fellow-creatures in proportion
to my powers.—Will you be so kind as to call on Mrs Fricker, and
give her five guineas in *my name*—and to transmit five guineas to
Mrs Coleridge.—I hope, & trust, that this will be the last year,
that I can conscientiously accept of those contributions, which in
my present lot & conscious of my present occupations, I feel no
pain in doing.—

If this Mr Reynell settles with me,[1] it will at least provide my
immediate household expences—&, if my Tragedy succeed, Io
triumphe!—

[1] Richard Reynell, who paid a visit to Stowey in Aug. 1797, did not settle
with the Coleridges. See *Ill. London News*, 22 Apr. 1893, for his letter describing
Wordsworth, Burnett, the Coleridges, and the cottage.

Give my heart-felt love to dear, dear Mrs Estlin—and kiss dear Anna, and Alfred & Caroline for me. My kindest remembrances to Mr & Mrs Hort—& believe me

your obliged, & truly affectionate Friend
S. T. Coleridge

192. *To John Prior Estlin*

Address: Revd J. P. Estlin | St Michael's Hill | Bristol
MS. Bristol Central Lib. Pub. E.L.G. i. 75.
Stamped: Crewkhern.

Saturday Morning. [10 June 1797]

My dear Friend

I wrote to you yesterday—& to day I must write again.—I shall have quite finished my Tragedy in a day or two; & then I mean to walk to Bowles, the poet, to read it to him, & have his criticisms——& then, accordingly as he advises, I shall either transmit the play to Sheridan, or go to London & have a personal interview with him.—At present, I [am] almost shillingless—I should be glad therefore, if you could transmit me immediately a *five pound note* of the bank of England, directed—

S. T. Coleridge, | Race-down Lodge | near | Crewkherne.—

I calculate that by this time your anxieties are past—mine will continue till I hear from you.

This is a lovely country—& Wordsworth is a great man.—He admires your sermon against Payne[1] much more than your last— I suppose because he is more inclined to Christianity than to Theism, simply considered.— The lines over leaf, which I have procured Miss Wordsworth to transcribe, will, I think, please you.—

When I arrive at Bowles's, I will write again—giving you a minute account of the bard——

God bless *you*, and *your's*—& all of us!—

Most affectionately | Your obliged friend
S. T. Coleridge

her eye
Was busy in the distance, shaping things
That made her heart beat quick. Seest thou that path?
(The green-sward now has broken its grey line;)
There, to and fro she paced; through many a day

---

[1] *Evidences of revealed religion, and particularly Christianity, stated, with reference to a pamphlet called: The Age of Reason, in a discourse delivered December 25, 1795.*

Of the warm summer: from a belt of flax
That girt her waist, spinning the long-drawn thread
With backward steps. Yet, ever as there passed
A man, whose garments shewed the Soldier's red,
Or crippled mendicant in Sailor's garb,
The little child, who sat to turn the wheel,
Ceased from his toil, and she, with faultering voice,
Expecting still to learn her husband's fate,
Made many a fond inquiry; and when they,
Whose presence gave no comfort, were gone by,
Her heart was still more sad—And by yon gate
That bars the traveller's road, she often sat,
And if a stranger-horseman came, the latch
Would lift; & in his face look wistfully,
Most happy, if from aught discovered there
Of tender feeling, she might dare repeat
The same sad question——Meanwhile, her poor hut
Sank to decay: for he was gone, whose hand,
At the first nippings of October frost,
Closed up each chink, and with fresh bands of straw
Checquered the green-grown thatch; and so she sat
Through the long winter, reckless and alone,
Till this reft house by frost, and thaw, and rain
Was sapped; and, when she slept, the nightly damps
Did chill her breast, and in the stormy day
Her tattered clothes were ruffled by the wind,
Even by the side of her own fire. Yet still
She loved this wretched spot, nor would for worlds
Have parted hence: and still, that length of road,
And this rude bench one torturing hope endeared,
Fast rooted at her heart; and, Stranger, here
In sickness she remained, and here she died,
Last human tenant of these ruined walls—[1]

193. *To Joseph Cottle*

Address: Mr Cottle.
MS. Edinburgh University Lib. Pub. E.L.G. i. 77.

June 29—1797

My very dear friend

I unfortunately gave away the loose sheets, you sent me—what shall I do?—There are many errata—C. Lamb will probably be

---

[1] *Excursion*, i. 880–916.

here in about a week—Could you not contrive to put yourself in a Bridgewater Coach—& T. Poole would fetch you in a one horse Chair to Stowey——What delight would it not give us.—By all means omit that one line—& if you like, the objectionable part in the first advertisement——I do not admit your reasoning against the latter part of the dedication—the possible *error* or intemperance to which I alluded—was—All nations curse thee! &c &c——in the Ode[1]—

I returned from Wordsworth's last night—God love you & eke

your affectionate *friend*

S. T. Coleridge.

If Lamb *is* to come, I will write you when—

194. *To Joseph Cottle*

Pub. Early Rec. *i. 230.*

Stowey, [Late June] 1797[2]

My dear Cottle,

I deeply regret, that my anxieties and my slothfulness, acting in a combined ratio, prevented me from finishing my 'Progress of Liberty, or Visions of the Maid of Orleans,' with that Poem at the head of the volume, with the Ode in the middle, and the 'Religious Musings' at the end. . . .

In the 'Lines on the Man of Ross', immediately after these lines,

'He heard the widow's heaven-breathed prayer of praise,
He mark'd the shelter'd orphan's tearful gaze,'

Please to add these two lines;

'And o'er the portioned maiden's snowy cheek,
Bade bridal love suffuse its blushes meek.'

And, for the line,

'Beneath this roof, if thy cheer'd moments pass,'

I should be glad to substitute this,

'If near ['neath] this roof thy wine-cheer'd moments pass.'

[1] Cf. line 139 of the *Departing Year.*

[2] Since the changes which Coleridge requests for the *Lines on the Man of Ross* 'came too late for admission' in the 1797 *Poems (Early Rec.* i. 231), this letter must have been written in June. See Letter 195.

195. *To Joseph Cottle*

Address: Mr Cottle | Bookseller | High Street | Bristol
MS. Harvard College Lib. Pub. with omis. Chambers, Life, 77. Cottle mangled
this letter 'even beyond his wont', making a separate letter of two parts,
printing another section as a postscript to Letter 301 of this edition, and trans-
ferring the names of C. Lamb, Wordsworth, and Dr. Parr to Letter 118 of this
edition. See *Early Rec.* i. 161, 252, and 256.
Stamped: Bridgewater.

[*Circa* 3 July 1797][1]

My dear friend

These are the errors,[2] or the alterations—Now, I conceive, that
as the volumes are bound, you might employ a boy for sixpence
or a shilling to go thro' them & with a fine pen, and dainty ink,
make the alterations in each volume—I am confident, it would
not cost more than printing the errata,—and then the Errata may
remain, as it is *now already* printed.[3]—*I wish, it could be so*: for
really, nobody scarcely does look at the table of Errata——the
Volume is a most beautiful one——you have determined that the
three Bards shall walk up Parnassus, or the Hill of Fame, in their
best Bib & Tucker. Give my Love to your Brother Amos—I condole
with him—but it is the fortune of War—the finest poem, I ever
wrote, lost the prize[4]—& that which gained it, was contemptible
—but an ode may *sometimes* be too bad for the prize; but VERY
OFTEN *too good*.

Wordsworth & his exquisite Sister are with me—She is a woman
indeed!—in mind, I mean, & heart—for her person is such, that
if you expected to see a pretty woman, you would think her ordin-
ary—if you expected to find an ordinary woman, you would think
her pretty!—But her manners are simple, ardent, impressive—.

> In every motion her most innocent soul
> Outbeams so brightly, that who saw would say,
> Guilt was a thing impossible in her.[5]—

Her information various—her eye watchful in minutest observation

---

[1] Arriving from Racedown on 28 June, Coleridge almost immediately
returned there, bringing the Wordsworths back to Stowey on 2 July. Since
he does not mention the accidental scalding of his foot, which occurred on
4 July, or Charles Lamb, who arrived on 7 July, this letter was probably
written on 3 July. See Chambers, *Life*, 77, and Letter 197.

[2] See end of letter for the Errata.

[3] 'According to an Advertisment in *The Morning Post* the book was pub-
lished on October 28th, 1797.' Wise, *Bibliography*, 39.

[4] Coleridge apparently refers to his *Greek Ode on Astronomy*, which failed
to win a Browne Medal in 1793. See Letter 28.

[5] For these lines, descriptive of Joan of Arc, see *Destiny of Nations*, 173–5.

of nature—and her taste a perfect electrometer—it bends, protrudes, and draws in, at subtlest beauties & most recondite faults.
——She with her Brother desire their kindest respects to you—If you can pick up a Hamlet, an Othello, & a Romeo & Juliet, separately, in *numbers*, or an odd volume—Wordsworth would thank you to get it for him——

T. Poole will be collecting the names of the persons, who want my poems here—when I have got them, I will send the Number & you will put it to Poole's account—For myself I want one, for C. Lamb *one*, for Wordsworth in *your* name *one*, for my Brother *one*, and one I shall send with a sonnet to Dr *Parr*—

God love you | & your ever affectionate
S. T. Coleridge

Errata[1]

P. 22. For 'light-flashing' read 'light-flushing'

P. 52. The Man of Ross is altogether misprinted; and cannot be made intelligible in these Errata.

P. 78. Line 3. for 'blissful' read 'happy' & for 'anguish'd' read 'mournful'. Line 9 for 'thy margin's willowy maze' read 'thy marge with willows grey'. Line 11. place a full stop after 'transparence'— and instead of 'to the gaze' read 'on my way' and Line 7. for 'blaze' read 'ray'

P. 87. Line 11. Omit the full stop.

P. 92. Line 10. For the colon put a comma.

P. 97. Scratch out these three lines

'Where melodies round honey-dropping flowers
'Footless & wild like birds of Paradise
'Nor pause nor perch hovering on untamed wing[']

and put a full stop instead of a Comma at 'Fairy-land.'—

P. 105. Line 7. omit the comma at 'sad' & Line 8. for 'gale' read 'Gale'.

P. 109. Scratch out the 9th & 10th lines.

Religious Musings Line 71. alter to
'Fear, a wild-visaged Man with starting eye'.

Alter Lines 77 and 78 to these

'While Faith's whole armour girds his limbs! And thus
'Transfigur'd, with a deep and dreadless awe,
'A solemn hush of spirit, he beholds[']

---

[1] In the manuscript these errata, which are in Dorothy Wordsworth's handwriting, precede the letter. See Wise, *Bibliography*, 39, for a description of the errata slip inserted in some copies of the 1797 *Poems*.

P. 145—There is a line omitted; after 376 it ought to have been
'Up the fine fibres thro' the sentient brain
'Roll subtly-surging. Pressing on his steps
Lo! PRIESTLEY there &c—and a colon instead of a comma at the word 'Sage'.

P. 180. For 'When I this performed' read 'When I had this perform'd'

P. 186. Line 9. after 'boundeth' insert the word 'on'

196. *To Thomas Poole*

Address: Mr T. Poole
MS. British Museum. Pub. Ill. London News, *22 April 1893, p. 500.* On 14 July 1797 the lease for Alfoxton (usually spelled Alfoxden), a house some three miles from Nether Stowey, was signed by Wordsworth, and he and Dorothy settled there the same day. (Cf. *Early Letters,* 170.) Coleridge was visiting there on the 17th. *Thomas Poole,* i. 232–3.

[*Circa* 17 July 1797]

My dear Poole

We have taken a fore quarter of Lamb from your Mother—which you will be so kind, according to your word, or (as the wit said to a minister of state) *notwithstanding your promise,* to send over to the Foxes [Alfoxden] to morrow morning by a boy—

I pray you, come over if possible by eleven o'clock that we may have Wordsworth's Tragedy read under the Trees—

S. T. Coleridge

197. *To Robert Southey*

Address: Robert Southey | at Mrs Barnes's | Burton, near Ringwood | Hampshire   Single
MS. Lord Latymer. Pub. with omis. Letters, *i. 221.*
Stamped: Bridgewater

[*Circa* 17 July 1797]

Dear Southey

You are acting kindly in your exertions for Chatterton's sister:[1] but I doubt the success. Chatterton's or Rowley's poems were never popular—the very circumstance which made them so much talked of—their *ancientness*—prevented them from being generally read——in the degree, I mean, that Goldsmith's poem or even

[1] *The Works of Thomas Chatterton,* to which Cottle contributed 'most of the editorial part', and Southey 'advice and a preface', did not appear until 1803. Jack Simmons, *Southey,* 68.

Rogers's thing upon memory has been.—The sale was *never* very great.—Secondly, the London Edition & the Cambridge Edition, which are now both of them the property of London Booksellers, are still on hand—& these Booksellers will 'hardly exert their interest for a rival.' *Thirdly, these are bad times.* Fourthly, all who are sincerely zealous for Chatterton, or who from knowlege of her are interested in poor Mrs Newton, will come forwards first——& if others should drop in but slowly, Mrs Newton will either receive no benefit at all from those, her friends, or one so long procrastinated from the necessity of waiting for the complement of subscribers, that it may at last come too late.—For these reasons I am almost inclined to think, *a subscription* simply would be better.——It is unpleasant to cast a damp on any thing; but that benevolence alone is likely to be beneficent, which *calculates.*—If however you continue to entertain higher hopes, than I—believe me, I will shake off my sloth, & use my best muscles in gaining subscribers. I will certainly write a preliminary Essay, and I will *attempt* to write a poem on the life & death of Chatterton, but the Monody *must not be reprinted.*—Neither this or the Pixies' Parlour would have been in the second Edition, but for dear Cottle's solicitous importunity. Excepting the last 18 lines of the Monody, which tho' deficient in chasteness & severity of diction, breathe a pleasing spirit of romantic feeling, there are not 5 lines in either poem, which might not have been written by a man who had lived & died in the self-same St Giles's Cellar, in which he had been first suckled by a drab with milk & Gin.—The Pixies is the least disgusting; because the subject leads you to expect nothing—but on a life & death so full of heart-giving *realities*, as poor Chatterton's to find such shadowy nobodies, as cherub-winged DEATH, Trees of HOPE, bare-bosom'd AFFECTION, & simpering PEACE—makes one's blood circulate like ipecacuanha [*sic*].—But so it is. A young man by strong feelings is impelled to write on a particular subject—and this is all, his feelings do for him. They set him upon the business & then they leave him.—He has such a high idea, of what Poetry ought to be, that he cannot conceive that such things as his natural emotions may be allowed to find a place in it—his learning therefore, his fancy, or rather conceit, and all his powers of buckram are put on the stretch—. It appears to me, that strong feeling is not *so* requisite to an Author's being profoundly pathetic, as taste & good sense.—

Poor old Wag!——*his mother* died of a dish of a clotted Cream, which my mother sent her as a present.

I rejoice that your poems are all sold.[1]—In the ballad of Mary,

[1] *Poems by Robert Southey*, 1797.

the Maid of the Inn, you have properly enough made the diction colloquial—but *'engages* the eye', applied to a *gibbet* strikes me as *slipsloppish*—from the unfortunate meaning of the word *'engaging'*.[1] —Your praise of my Dedication gave me great pleasure—From the 9th to the 14th the five lines are flat & prosish—& the versification ever & anon has too much of the rhyme or couplet cadence— & the metaphor on the diverse sorts of friendship is *hunted down*[2]— but the poem is dear to me, and in point of *taste* I place it next to 'Low was our pretty cot [']' which I think the best of my poems.—

I am as much a Pangloss as ever—only less *contemptuous*, than I used to be, when I argue how unwise it is to feel contempt for any thing——

I had been on a visit to Wordsworth's at Racedown near Crewkherne—and I brought him & his Sister back with me & here I have *settled them*—. By a combination of curious circumstances a gentleman's seat, with a park & woods, elegantly & completely *furnished*—with 9 *lodging rooms*, three parlours & a Hall—in a most beautiful & romantic situation by the sea side—4 miles from Stowey—this we have got for Wordsworth at the rent of 23£ *a year, taxes included*!!—The park and woods are *his* for all purposes *he* wants them—i.e. he may walk, ride, & keep a horse in them— & the large gardens are altogether & entirely his.——Wordsworth is a very great man—the only man, to whom *at all times* & in *all modes of excellence* I feel myself inferior—the only one, I mean, whom I *have yet met with*—for the London Literati appear to me to be very much like little Potatoes—i.e. *no great Things*!—a compost of Nullity & Dullity.—

Charles Lamb has been with me for a week—he left me Friday morning.— / The second day after Wordsworth came to me, dear Sara accidently emptied a skillet of boiling milk on my foot, which confined me during the whole time of C. Lamb's stay & still prevents me from all *walks* longer than a furlong.—While Wordsworth, his Sister, & C. Lamb were out one evening; / sitting in the arbour of T. Poole's garden, which communicates with mine, I wrote these lines,[3] with which I am pleased——

> Well—they are gone: and here must I remain,
> Lam'd by the scathe of fire, lonely & faint,
> This lime-tree bower my prison. They, meantime,

---

[1] Southey later altered the line to 'His irons you still from the road may espy'. See *Poet. Works*, 1838, vi. 9.

[2] See lines 20–30, *Poems*, i. 174.

[3] *Poems*, i. 178. Another copy of these lines was sent in a letter to Charles Lloyd, which has not come to light. See Campbell, *Poetical Works*, 591, for the version sent to Lloyd.

My friends, whom I may never meet again,
On springy* heath, along the hill-top edge,
Wander delighted, and look down, perchance,
On that same rifted Dell, where many an Ash[1]
Twists it's wild limbs beside the ferny rock,
Whose plumy ferns** for ever nod and drip
Spray'd by the waterfall. But chiefly Thou,
My gentle-hearted CHARLES! thou, who hast pin'd
And hunger'd after Nature many a year
In the great City pent, winning thy way,
With sad yet bowed soul, thro' evil & pain
And strange calamity.—Ah slowly sink
Behind the western ridge; thou glorious Sun!
Shine in the slant beams of the sinking orb,
Ye purple Heath-flowers! Richlier burn, ye Clouds!
Live in the yellow Light, ye distant Groves!
And kindle, thou blue Ocean! So my friend
Struck with joy's deepest calm, and gazing round
On the wide view,† may gaze till all doth seem
Less gross than bodily, a living Thing
That acts upon the mind, and with such hues
As cloathe the Almighty Spirit, when he makes
Spirits perceive His presence!
                              A Delight
Comes sudden on my heart, and I am glad
As I myself were there! Nor in this bower
Want I sweet sounds or pleasing shapes. I watch'd
The sunshine of each broad transparent Leaf
Broke by the shadows of the Leaf or Stem,
Which hung above it: and that Wall-nut Tree
Was richly ting'd: and a deep radiance lay
Full on the ancient ivy which usurps
Those fronting elms, and now with blackest mass

---

* *elastic*, I mean.—[S.T.C.]
** The ferns, that grow in moist places, grow five or six together & form a complete 'Prince of Wales's Feather'—i.e. plumy.—[S.T.C.]
† You remember, I am a *Berkleian*.—[S.T.C.]

[1] Wand'ring well-pleas'd, look down on grange or dell
    Or deep fantastic [*originally* that deep gloomy] Rift, where many an Ash
[Cancelled version of lines 6 and 7.]
    Cf. *Kubla Khan*, line 12, 'But oh! that deep romantic chasm'. Should the 'wild, romantic dell' near Alfoxden described in *This Lime-Tree* join the combe at Culbone as a possible influence on *Kubla Khan*? See *Thomas Poole*, i. 233; *Early Letters*, 170–1; W. Sypher, 'Coleridge's Somerset: a Byway to Xanadu', *Philological Quarterly*, Oct. 1939, p. 353; and Letter 209.

Makes their dark foliage gleam a lighter hue
Thro' the last twilight.—And tho' the rapid bat
Wheels silent by and not a swallow twitters,
Yet still the solitary humble-bee
Sings in the bean flower. Henceforth I shall know
That nature ne'er deserts the wise & pure,
No scene so narrow, but may well employ
Each faculty of sense, and keep the heart
Awake to Love & Beauty: and sometimes
'Tis well to be bereav'd of promis'd good
That we may lift the soul, & contemplate
With lively joy the joys, we cannot share.
My Sister & my Friends! when the last Rook
Beat it's straight path along the dusky air
Homewards, I bless'd it; deeming, it's black wing
Cross'd, like a speck, the blaze of setting day,[1]
While ye stood gazing; or when all was still,
Flew creaking o'er your heads, & had a charm
For you, my Sister & my Friends! to whom
No sound is dissonant, which tells of Life!

I would make a shift by some means or other to visit you, if I thought, that you & Edith Southey would return with me.—I think, indeed I almost am certain that I could get a one horse chair free of all expence—I have driven about the country a great deal lately—& brought back Miss Wordsworth over forty miles of execrable road: & have been always a very cautious & am now no inexpert, whip.—And Wordsworth at whose house I now am for change of air has commissioned me to offer you a suit of rooms at this place, which is called 'All-foxen'—& so divine and wild is the country that I am sure it would increase your stock of images—& three weeks' absence from Christ-Church will endear it to you—& Edith Southey & Sara may not have another opportunity of seeing each other—& Wordsworth is very solicitous to know you—& Miss Wordsworth is a most exquisite young woman in her mind, & heart.— I pray you, write me immediately, directing Stowey near Bridgewater, as before.—God bless you & your

affectionate S. T. Coleridge

I heard from C. Lamb of Favell & Legrice. Poor Allen![2] I know

---

[1] Had cross'd the flood [*originally* orb] & blaze of setting day, [Cancelled version of line above.]

[2] Robert Allen had been appointed Assistant Surgeon to the Second Royals, then stationed in Portugal.

nothing of it—As to Rough, he is a *wonderful fellow.*—And when I returned from the army, *cut* me for a month, till he saw that other people were as much attached [to] me as before.

198. *To John Prior Estlin*

Address: Revd J. P. Estlin | St Michael's Hill | Bristol
MS. Bristol Central Lib. Pub. E.L.G. i. 78.
Stamped: Bridgewater.

Stowey—Sunday. [23 July 1797]

My dear Friend

I would accept your kind invitation immediately, but that I have a bad foot—A scald imperfectly healed—& I walked with it—after one day's walking I was obliged to return—with a wound in my foot.—But if possible, I will ride to Bristol at the end of the week.——Heaven forbid that there should not be worse vices of the mind than Prejudice—for *all* of us, more or less, must necessarily be prejudiced.—The worst vice of the Intellect, I believe, is *malignant* Prejudice— & next to this, or perhaps co-equal with it, is *Indifference.*—I have sometimes feared, from the dislike, the encreasing dislike, which I find in myself, to all *chirurgical operations,* that my mind is verging to this state—it is certainly much nearer to it, than to any disquietude & restlessness of Temper concerning errors, which do not appear directly connected with vice & misery.—I judge so much by the *fruits,* that I feel a constant yearning towards the belief that such tenets are *not* errors.—Now all this applies to the present case. I cannot as yet reconcile my intellect to the sacramental Rites; but as I do not see any ill-effect which they produce among the Dissenters, and as you declare from your own experience that they have *good* effects, it is painful to me even simply *to state my dissent*—and more than this I have not done, and, unless Christianity were attacked on this head by an Infidel of real learning & talents, more than this I do not consider myself as bound to do.—I never even state my dissent unless to Ministers who urge me to undertake the ministry.—My conduct is this—I omit the rites,—and wish to say nothing about it—every thing that relates to Christianity is of importance; but yet all things are not of equal importance; and when the Incendiaries have surrounded the building, it is idle to dispute among ourselves whether an old Stair-case was placed in it by the original Architect, or added afterwards by a meaner Hand.——But notwithstanding this, it's little comparative importance, I cannot, I must not, play the hypocrite—If I performed or received the Lord's supper, in my present state of mind, I should indeed be eating & drinking condemnation. But this I need not say to you.——As to Norwich, it is an *ugly* place, and an extravagantly *dear* place—& it is very, very far different from all I love, animate & inanimate—& parties run high —and I am wearied with politics, even to soreness.—I never knew a passion for politics exist for a long time without swallowing up, or absolutely excluding, a passion for Religion—. Perhaps I am wrong: but so I think.—However, I trust to see you by the end of the week.—To Mrs Estlin remember me affectionately— and kiss for me the dear little ones.—May Heaven love you and him who ever feels for you the mingled affections of Son, Brother, & Friend—

S. T. Coleridge

199. *To Thomas Poole*

Address: Mr T. Poole
MS. British Museum. Pub. E.L.G. i. 80.

Wednesd. July. [26?] 1797

My dear Poole

If you are at leisure, will you send by Nanny the Coat &c, which you mentioned to me—as I wish to have it made fit for me by next Sunday—Sara bids me likewise remind you of some Stockings, half silk & half-cotton, which *you* could not wear /—

——You shall be my Elijah—& I will most reverentially catch the Mantle, which you have cast off.——

Why should not a Bard go tight & have a few neat things on his back? *Ey?—Eh!—Eh!*

God bless you | &
S. T. Coleridge

200. *To Josiah Wade*

Address: Mr Wade | No 6 Berkley Place Bristol
Transcript Coleridge family. Pub. E.L.G. i. 80.

Aug—1. [17]97

My very dear Friend

I meant to have surprized you by a visit at Berkley Place—and therefore did not immediately answer your letter—Were I going on a Journey to Paradise I would defer it, to have the pleasure of seeing you a week at Stowey. I pray you come—do, do, my dear Wade! In very sincerity I know nothing in the ordinary events of life that would give me so great pleasure—Your letter cheered

me. I was gloomy at your silence—You misunderstood my letter.
I meant only to say, that I should write so quick, that you *could
not* answer my first before you would receive my second letter.
From this I was prevented by reviews and a strange Visitor—
and then I knew not where to direct to you, my dear fellow! do not
let there be such pauses in our correspondence. I will pledge myself
to write you once every *fortnight*—if you will repay my letters.

What can I say to you of your dear Baby? I heard of it, only
from your Letter. A Tear came into my eye—and I have sighed
many times since, when I have been walking alone:—and the
pretty Lamb has passed across my Memory.—And all the comfort
we can offer on such occasions, is sympathy.

Sara has had a miscarriage—but in so very early a stage, that
it occasioned but little pain, one day's indisposition and no con-
finement.—Indeed, the circumstance is quite unknown, except to
me. My little Hartley grows a beautiful child.—T. Poole would be
most joyful to behold your face.

John Thelwall is a very warm hearted honest man—and dis-
agreeing, as we do, on almost every point of religion, of morals, of
politics, and of philosophy; we like each other uncommonly well—
He is a great favorite with Sara. *Energetic Activity*, of *mind* and of
heart, is his Master-feature. He is prompt to *conceive*, and still
prompter to *execute*—. But I think, that he is deficient in that
patience of mind, which can look *intensely* and *frequently* at the
same subject. He believes and disbelieves with impassioned con-
fidence——I wish to see him *doubting* and *doubting*. However, he
is the man for *action*—he is intrepid, eloquent, and—honest.—
Perhaps the only *acting* Democrat, that *is* honest[1] for the *Patriots*
are ragged cattle—a most execrable herd—arrogant because they
are ignorant, and boastful of the strength of reason, because they
have never tried it enough to know its *weakness*.—O my poor

[1] Thelwall arrived at Stowey on 17 July, visiting the Coleridges and at
Alfoxden for ten days. (*Thomas Poole*, i. 232.) He was in Bristol by early
August, for Wade, writing to Coleridge on 10 Aug., said: 'Thank you for the
character of Thelwall. So far as I was able to judge it is very just. He dined
with me on his return—we went down to Pill by water & walk'd back. Some
People would accuse him of too much levity; but you know my opinion is that
there is, "a time for all things"—we went out to be merry & laugh—'.
In his poem, *Lines written at Bridgewater, in Somersetshire, on the 27th of
July, 1797,* Thelwall contemplates the possibility of living near the households
at Nether Stowey and Alfoxden:

> [Then] by our sides
> Thy Sara, and my Susan, and, perchance,
> Allfoxden's musing tenant, and the maid
> Of ardent eye, who, with fraternal love,
> Sweetens his solitude.

Country! The Clouds cover thee—there is not one spot of clear blue in the whole heaven.

My love to all whom you love—and believe [me] with brotherly affection, with esteem and gratitude, and every warm emotion of the heart,

Your faithful
S. T. Coleridge

201. *To Joseph Cottle*

Pub. Early Rec. *i. 253.* This letter is particularly baffling. The reference to Cottle's ill health, also mentioned by Wordsworth on 16 Aug. 1797 (*Early Letters*, 172), and the paragraph concerning Thelwall's trunk suggest that the letter was written in August 1797. Herbert Croft, however, was imprisoned for debt in 1795 and in 1797 was living abroad. Cottle, therefore, has again combined passages from different letters.

Stowey, [Early August 1797]

My very dear Cottle,

Your illness afflicts me, and unless I receive a full account of you by Milton, I shall be very uneasy, so do not fail to write.

Herbert Croft is in Exeter goal! This is unlucky. Poor devil! He must now be unpeppered. We are all well. W[ordsworth][1] is well. Hartley sends a grin to you! He has another tooth!

In the waggon, there was brought, from Bath, a trunk, in order to be forwarded to Stowey, directed, 'S. T. Coleridge, Stowey, near Bridgewater.' This, we suppose, arrived in Bristol on Tuesday or Wednesday, last week. It belonged to Thelwall. If it be not forwarded to Stowey, let it be stopped, and not sent.

Give my kind love to your brother Robert, and *ax* him to put on his hat, and run without delay to the inn, or place, by whatever bird, beast, fish, or man distinguished, where Parsons's Bath waggon sets up.

From your truly affectionate friend,
S. T. Coleridge

202. *To John Thelwall*

Address: Mr Thelwall | to be left at the Post Office | Swansea | Glamorganshire
MS. Pierpont Morgan Lib. Pub. Letters, *i. 231.*
Stamped: Bridgewater.

Saturday Evening [19 August 1797].[2]   Bridgewater

My dear Thelwall

Yesterday morning I miss'd the Coach; and was ill, and could

---

[1] Printed as 'Wordsworth' in *Rem.* 145.

[2] Coleridge's reference to the assizes, which were held on 19 Aug. 1797, establishes the date of this letter, which in turn dates Letters 203 and 204.

not walk. This Morning the Coach was completely full: but I was
not ill, and so did walk—and here I am, foot-sore, very; and
weary, somewhat.—With *regard to the business*, I mentioned it at
Howell's; but I perceive, he is absolutely powerless—*Chubb* I
would have called on—but these are the assizes—and I find, he is
surrounded in his own house by a mob of visitors, whom it is
scarcely possible for him to leave—long enough at least for the
conversation, I want with him.—I will write him tomorrow morning
—& shall have an answer the same day—which I will transmit to
you on Monday, but you *cannot* receive it till Tuesday night—if
therefore you leave Swansea before that time, or in case of accident,
before Wednesday Night—leave directions with the Post Master
to have your letter forwarded——I go for Stowey immediately[1]—
which will make my walk 41 miles. The Howells desire to be remem-
bered to you kindly—

I am sad at heart about you on many accounts; but chiefly
anxious for this present business.—The Aristocrats seem determined
to persecute, *even Wordsworth*.[2]—But we will at least not yield
without a struggle—and if I cannot get you near me, it shall not
be for want of a tryal on my part.—But perhaps, I am passing the
worn-out spirits of a *fag*-walk, for [the r]eal aspect of the business.—
God love you & believe me | Affectionately Your *friend*

S. T. Coleridge

203. *To John Chubb*

Address: Mr John Chubb | Bridgewater
MS. Mr. John B. Chubb. Pub. E.L.G. i. 82.
Stamped: Bridgewater.

[20 August 1797]

Dear Sir

I write to you on the subject of Thelwall. He has found by
experience, that neither his own health or that of his Wife &
children can be preserved in London; and were it otherwise, yet
his income is inadequate to maintain him there. He is therefore

---

[1] On his arrival at Stowey, Coleridge found Richard Reynell there on a visit.
Reynell's letter to his sister also describes Coleridge's journey from Bristol:
'On my arrival at Stowey and at Mr. Coleridge's house I found he was from
home, having set out for Bristol to see Mrs. Barbauld a few days before. . . .
He returned on Saturday evening after a walk of about 40 miles in one day
apparently not much fatigued.'
[2] See A. J. Eagleston, 'Wordsworth, Coleridge, and the Spy', *Coleridge*, ed.
by Edmund Blunden and E. L. Griggs, 1934, pp. 73–87; George W. Meyer,
'Wordsworth and the Spy Hunt', *American Scholar*, Winter 1950–1, pp. 50–56;
Thomas Poole, i. 235–43; and *Biog. Lit.*, ch. x.

under the necessity of fixing his residence in the Country. But by his particular exertions in the propagation of those principles, which *we* hold sacred & of the highest importance, he has become, as you well know, particularly unpopular, thro' every part of the kingdom—in every part of the kingdom therefore some odium, & inconvenience must be incurred by those, who should be instrumental in procuring him a cottage there—but are Truth & Liberty of so little importance that we owe no sacrifices to them? And because with talents very great, & disinterest[ed]ness undoubted, he has evinced himself, in activity & courage, superior to any other patriot, must his country *for this* be made a wilderness of waters to him?——There are many reasons for his preferring this to any other part of the kingdom / he will here find the society of men equal to himself in talents, & probably superior in acquired knowlege—of men, who differ from each other very widely in many very important opinions, yet unite in the one great duty of unbounded *tolerance.*—If the day of darkness & tempest should come, it is most probable, that the influence of T. would be very great on the lower classes—it may therefore prove of no mean utility to the cause of Truth & Humanity, that he had spent some years in a society, where his natural impetuosity had been disciplined into patience, and salutary scepticism, and the slow energies of a *calculating* spirit.——

But who shall get him a cottage here? I have *no power*—& T. Poole is precluded from it by the dreadful state of his poor Mother's health, & by his connection with the Benefit Club[1]—the utilities of which he estimates very high, & these, he thinks, would be materially affected by any activity in favor of T.—Besides, has he not already taken his share of odium—? has he not already almost alienated, certainly very much cooled, the affections of some of his relations, by his exertions on *my* account?—And why should *one* man do *all*?——But it must be left to every man's private mind to determine, whether or no his *particular* circumstances do or do not justify him in keeping aloof from all interference in such subjects.——J. T. is now at Swansea, and expects an answer from me respecting the possibility of his settling here—he requested me to write to you—I have done it—& you will be so kind (if in your power, *to day*) to give me one or two lines, briefly informing me whether or no *your* particular circumstances enable you to exert

---

[1] This club is referred to by a government agent reporting to the Home Office on 16 Aug. He speaks of 'the inhabitants of Alfoxton House' as 'a Sett of violent Democrats', alludes to the activities of both Coleridge and Thelwall, and finds Poole 'the more dangerous from his having established. . . what He stiles *The Poor Man's Club*'. A. J. Eagleston, op. cit. 82–83.

yourself in taking a cottage for him—*any where* 5 or 6 miles round
Stowey.—He means to live in perfect retirement—neither taking
pupils or any thing else—— /

It is painful to ask that of a person which he may find it equally
distressing to grant or deny— / But I do not ask any thing; but
simply lay before you the calculations on *one* side of the subject—/
Your own mind will immediately suggest those on the other side—/
& I doubt not, you will decide according [to] the preponderance——

Believe me with respect &c

S. T. Coleridge

204. *To John Thelwall*

Address: Mr Thelwall | to be left at the Post office | Swansea | Glamorganshire
Cross Post
MS. Pierpont Morgan Lib. Pub. Letters, *i. 232.*
Stamped: Bridgewater.

[21 August 1797]

Dear Thelwall

This is the first hour, that I could write to you any thing decisive.
—I have received an answer from Chubb, intimating that he
would undertake the office of procuring you a cottage, provided it
was thought *right*, that you should settle *here*; but *this*—(i.e.—the
whole difficulty—) he left for T. Poole & me to settle.—And he
acquainted Poole with this determination—. Consequently, the
whole returns to it's former situation—& the hope, which I had
entertained, that you could have settled here without any, the
remotest interference of Poole, *has vanished.* To such interference
on his part there are insuperable difficulties—the whole Malignity
of the Aristocrats will converge to him, as to the *one* point—his
tranquillity will be perpetually interrupted——his business, &
his credit, hampered & distressed by vexatious calumnies—the
ties of relationship weakened—perhaps broken—& lastly, his poor
Mother made miserable—the pain of the Stone aggravated by
domestic calamity & quarrels betwixt her son & those neighbours
with whom & herself there have been peace & love for these fifty
years.—Very great odium T. Poole incurred by bringing *me* here—
my peaceable manners & known attachment to Christianity had
almost worn it away—when Wordsworth came & he likewise by
T. Poole's agency settled here— / You cannot conceive the tumult,
calumnies, & apparatus of threatened persecutions which this
event has occasioned round about us. If *you* too should come, I am
afraid, that even riots & dangerous riots might be the consequence
— / *either* of us separately would perhaps be tolerated—but *all*

three together—what can it be less than plot & damned conspiracy —a school for the propagation of demagogy & atheism?—And it deserves examination whether or no as moralists we should be justified in hazarding the certain evil of calling forth malignant passions for the contingent good, that might result from our living in the same neighbourhood?—Add to which, that in point of the *public interest* we must put into the balance the Stowey Benefit Club— / of the *present* utility of this T. Poole thinks highly—of it's *possible* utility *very, very* highly indeed— / —but the interests, nay, perhaps almost the existence of this club is interwoven with his character—as a peaceable & *undesigning* Man—certainly, any future & greater excellence, which he hopes to realize, in & through this society, will vanish like a dream of the morning.—If therefore you can get the land & cottage near Bath, of which you spoke to me, I would advise it—on many accounts—but if you still see the arguments on the other side in a stronger light than those which I have stated,——come! but not yet!—come in two or three months —take lodgings at Bridgewater—familiarize the people to your name & appearance—and when the *monstrosity* of the thing is gone off, & the people shall have begun to consider you, as a man whose mouth won't eat them—& whose pocket is better adapted for a bundle of sonnets than the transportation or ambush-place of a French army—then you may take a *house*—but indeed—I say it with a very sad, but a very clear conviction—at *present* I see that much evil & little good would result from your settling here.——/

I am unwell—this business has indeed preyed much on my spirits—and I have suffered for you more than I hope & trust you will suffer yourself——

> God love you &
> Your's—
> S. T. Coleridge

205. *To Joseph Cottle*

Pub. Early Rec. *i.* 234.

[August 1797]

I shall now stick close to my Tragedy (called Osorio,) and when I have finished it, shall walk to Shaftesbury to spend a few days with Bowles.[1] From thence I go to Salisbury, and thence to Christchurch, to see Southey.

[1] Coleridge set off to see Bowles on 6 Sept. *Early Letters*, 172.

206. *To Thomas Poole*

Address: Mr Poole
MS. British Museum. Hitherto unpublished.

[Endorsed August 30th, ⟨17⟩97]

My dearest Poole

I had quite forgotten the Bristol fair[1]—and this very evening, I was anticipating the delight of coming upon you tomorrow, with

Fifth Act.

— — — —

Finis

I have but a very few lines to do.—

Tobin[2] is engaged to dine tomorrow at Bridgewater—the which he deeply regrets; but he cannot disentangle himself. God love you, my best and dearest Friend!

Your's—
S. T. Coleridge

207. *To Robert Southey*

[Addressed by Charles Lloyd] Mr. Robert Southey | No 8 West-Gate buildings | Bath
MS. Lord Latymer. Hitherto unpublished. A letter from Charles Lloyd to Southey occupies pages 1 and 2 of the manuscript, Coleridge's letter pages 3 and 4. It was at this time that Coleridge must have met Tom Wedgwood, who was to play so great a part in his life.
Stamped: Bridgewater.

[15 September 1797][3]

Dear Southey

That little poem[4] is to me the most affecting of all your little pieces—I beseech you, do not alter the latter part—the line & a half

that disrobes
The Earth of all it's bright, day-borrow'd hues—

---

[1] The Bristol fair was held for eight days, beginning 1 Sept.

[2] James Webbe Tobin, a Bristol friend of both Coleridge and Wordsworth. He later settled in London. He is not to be confused with his brother, John Tobin, the dramatist, who left Bristol in 1787, and whom Coleridge first mentions in 1803. See Letter 499–A.

[3] There is nothing in Coleridge's letter to suggest when it was written but Lloyd's letter affords a clue:

N. Stowey Friday morning

Dear Southey

I went yesterday over to Wordsworth's with the hope of hearing the remaining acts of his tragedy, but was disappointed in finding him ill &

[*See p. 346 for note 4.*]

says nothing more than 'that discolouring shade' and is an anti-climax to two, the most pleasing lines, I recollect any where— 'day-borrow'd['] —I do not like independent of this objection—it is [a wo]rd not *'in keeping'* with the other part. [H]ome*ward*ly & heaven *ward*—come rather too close together, for a fastidious ear. —The lines 'nor could her heart'—down to—[']insolent pity.'— are so common-place & say so little that has not been said in the same language before, that I cannot but think that the poem would be better without them. What follows is altogether exqui-site—very, very pathetic—/ but the idea of the infant's ingratitude would be more forcible, if the infant's *age* were definitely introduced, any where in the poem—& the phrase 'became indifferent to her'— is *ambiguous*—and may mean—that she cared not for the child— as well as that the child cared not for her.—

God love you | &
S. T. Coleridge

208. *To Thomas Poole*

Address: Mr Thomas Poole
MS. Victoria University Lib. Pub. Letters, *i. 10.* This is the third of the auto-biographical letters.

October 9th, 1797

My dearest Poole

From March to October—a long silence! but [as] it is possible, that I may have been preparing materials for future letters, the time cannot be considered as altogether subtracted from you.

From October 1775 to October 1778.

These three years I continued at the reading-school—because I

incapable of reading it—He & his Sister very much press'd me to stay over to morrow as the Wedgwoods are coming to spend two days with them— This, as you may suppose was no great inducement, but as Wordsworth has promis'd to read me his tragedy, not having any important reason to alledge, for not accepting his invitation I intend staying till Monday— Coleridge is unwell with a sore throat— Still I have not heard from Birmingham!— My love to Edith—

God bless you!
C. Lloyd Jr.

Since Tom and John Wedgwood arrived at Alfoxden on 15 or 16 Sept., Lloyd's letter and therefore Coleridge's must have been written on Friday, 15 Sept. 1797. See R. B. Litchfield, *Tom Wedgwood*, 1903, p. 51. Consider also an un-published letter from Tom Wedgwood to Poole, dated from Alfoxden, 18 Sept. 1797: 'It gave us real concern to miss seeeing you last night.' Southey was at Bath on 16 Sept. See E. K. Chambers, *A Sheaf of Studies*, 1942, p. 63.

[4] Coleridge refers to Southey's English Eclogue, *Hannah*, written at Burton and published in 1799. Southey made some of the suggested alterations.

was too little to be trusted among my Father's School-boys—. After breakfast I had a halfpenny given me, with which I bought three cakes at the Baker's close by the school of my old mistress— & these were my dinner on every day except Saturday & Sunday —when I used to dine at home, and wallowed in a beef & pudding dinner.—I am remarkably fond of Beans & Bacon—and this fond- ness I attribute to my father's having given me a penny for having eat a large quantity of beans, one Saturday—for the other boys did not like them, and as it was an economic food, my father thought, that my attachment & penchant for it ought to be encouraged. ——My Father was very fond of me, and I was my mother's darling—in consequence, I was very miserable. For Molly, who had nursed my Brother Francis, and was immoderately fond of him, hated me because my mother took more notice of me than of Frank—and Frank hated me, because my mother gave me now & then a bit of cake, when he had none—quite forgetting that for one bit of cake which I had & he had not, he had twenty sops in the pan & pieces of bread & butter with sugar on them from Molly, from whom I received only thumps & ill names.—So I became fretful, & timorous, & a tell-tale—& the School-boys drove me from play, & were always tormenting me—& hence I took no pleasure in boyish sports—but read incessantly. My Father's Sister kept an *every-thing* Shop at Crediton—and there I read thro' all the gilt- cover little books that could be had at that time, & likewise all the uncovered tales of Tom Hickathrift, Jack the Giant-killer, &c & &c &c &c —/—and I used to lie by the wall, and *mope*—and my spirits used to come upon me suddenly, & in a flood—& then I was accustomed to run up and down the church-yard, and act over all I had been reading on the docks, the nettles, and the rank-grass. —At six years old I remember to have read Belisarius, Robinson Crusoe, & Philip Quarle [Quarll]—and then I found the Arabian Nights' entertainments—one tale of which (the tale of a man who was compelled to seek for a pure virgin) made so deep an impression on me (I had read it in the evening while my mother was mending stockings) that I was haunted by spectres, whenever I was in the dark—and I distinctly remember the anxious & fearful eagerness, with which I used to watch the window, in which the books lay— & whenever the Sun lay upon them, I would seize it, carry it by the wall, & bask, & read—. My Father found out the effect, which these books had produced—and burnt them.—So I became a *dreamer*—and acquired an indisposition to all bodily activity—and I was fretful, and inordinately passionate, and as I could not play at any thing, and was slothful, I was despised & hated by the boys; and because I could read & spell, & had, I may truly say, a memory

& understanding forced into almost an unnatural ripeness, I was flattered & wondered at by all the old women—& so I became very vain, and despised most of the boys, that were at all near my own age—and before I was eight years old, I was a *character*—sensibility, imagination, vanity, sloth, & feelings of deep & bitter contempt for almost all who traversed the orbit of my understanding, were even then prominent & manifest.

From October 1778 to 1779.—That which I began to be from 3 to 6, I continued from 6 to 9.—In this year I was admitted into the grammer school, and soon outstripped all of my age.—I had a dangerous putrid fever this year—My Brother George lay ill of the same fever in the next room.——My poor Brother Francis, I remember, stole up in spite of orders to the contrary, & sate by my bedside, & read Pope's Homer to me—Frank had a violent love of beating me—but whenever that was superseded by any humour or circumstance, he was always very fond of me—& used to regard me with a strange mixture of admiration & contempt—strange it was not—: for he hated books, and loved climbing, fighting, playing, & robbing orchards, to distraction.—

My mother relates a story of me, which I repeat here—because it must be regarded as my first piece of wit.—During my fever I asked why Lady Northcote (our neighbour) did not come & see me. —My mother said, She was afraid of catching the fever—I was piqued & answered—Ah—Mamma! the four Angels round my bed an't afraid of catching it.—I suppose, you know the old prayer—

Matthew! Mark! Luke! & John!
God bless the bed which I lie on.
Four Angels round me spread,
Two at my foot & two at my bed [head]—

This prayer I said nightly—& most firmly believed the truth of it. —Frequently have I, half-awake & half-asleep, my body diseased & fevered by my imagination, seen armies of ugly Things bursting in upon me, & these four angels keeping them off.—In my next I shall carry on my life to my Father's Death.—

God bless you, my dear Poole! | & your affectionate
S. T. Coleridge.

209. *To John Thelwall*

Address: Mr John Thelwall | Derby
MS. Pierpont Morgan Lib. Pub. with omis. Letters, *i. 228.* This letter tends to establish the date of *Kubla Khan*.

Although the note Coleridge prefixed to *Kubla Khan* when it was published

in 1816 asserts that the poem was written during a retirement 'to a lonely farm-house' in the summer of 1797, another note, which he added to an autograph copy of the poem now in the possession of Lady Crewe, points to the autumn of 1797: 'This fragment with a good deal more, not recoverable, composed, in a sort of Reverie brought on by two grains of Opium, taken to check a dysentery, at a Farm House between Porlock & Linton, a quarter of a mile from Culbone Church, in the fall of the year, 1797.' This letter to Thelwall tends to confirm the second note. The brief absence mentioned in the opening sentence probably refers to the solitary retirement near Porlock, where *Kubla Khan* was composed. The passage in the first paragraph con-cerning his yearning for 'something *great*—something *one & indivisible*',—a passage echoed in the next letter—shows that he was preoccupied with sublimity at this time, and he demonstrates his argument by citing a few lines from *This Lime-Tree Bower my Prison*. The line recalling 'rocks or water-falls, mountains or caverns' is reminiscent of *Kubla Khan*, and the wish he expresses, 'to float about along an infinite ocean cradled in the flower of the Lotos', suggests the effect of opium. Furthermore, the phrase quoted from *Osorio*, 'the *fall of the* year', parallels the use of that expression in the Crewe manuscript cited above; and the opening lines of the long quotation from *Osorio* portray an autumnal scene, possibly near Porlock—indeed, Professor Wylie Sypher, who identifies the farmhouse where *Kubla Khan* was written as Ash Farm, says 'it overlooks the very panorama that Coleridge seems to have described in [these lines from] *Osorio*' ('Coleridge's Somerset: a Byway to Xanadu', *Philological Quarterly*, Oct. 1939, pp. 353–66). Thus it seems safe to assume that *Kubla Khan* was composed in Oct. 1797, a few days before this letter was written, and not, as E. H. Coleridge and J. D. Campbell suggest, in May 1798. See *Poems*, i. 295, and *Poetical Works*, xlii.
Postmark: 16 October 1797. *Stamped*: Bridgewater.

Saturday Morning. [14 October 1797]

My dear Thelwall

I have just received your letter—having been absent a day or two—& have already, before I write you, written to Dr Beddoes—I would to heaven, it were in my power to serve you—but alas! I have neither money or influence—& I suppose, that at last I must become a Unitarian minister as a less evil than starvation—for I get nothing by literature—& Sara is in the way of repairing the ravages of war, as much as in her lies.——You have my wishes, & what is very liberal in me for such an atheist reprobate, my prayers.——I can *at times* feel strongly the beauties, you describe, in them-selves, & for themselves—but more frequently *all things* appear little—all the knowlege, that can be acquired, child's play——the universe itself—what but an immense heap of *little* things?—I can contemplate nothing but parts, & parts are all *little*—!—My mind feels as if it ached to behold & know something *great*—some-thing *one & indivisible*—and it is only in the faith of this that rocks or waterfalls, mountains or caverns give me the sense of sublimity or majesty!—But in this faith *all things* counterfeit infinity!—'Struck with the deepest calm of Joy' I stand

Silent, with swimming sense; and gazing round
On the wide Landscape gaze till all doth seem
Less gross than bodily, a living Thing
Which acts upon the mind, & with such Hues
As cloath th' Almighty Spirit, when he makes
Spirits perceive his presence![1]——

It is but seldom that I raise & spiritualize my intellect to this
height—& at other times I adopt the Brahman Creed, & say—It is
better to sit than to stand, it is better to lie than to sit, it is better
to sleep than to wake—but Death is the best of all!—I should much
wish, like the Indian Vishna, [Vishnu] to float about along an
infinite ocean cradled in the flower of the Lotos, & wake once in a
million years for a few minutes—just to know that I was going to
sleep a million years more. I have put this feeling in the mouth of
Alhadra my Moorish Woman——She is going by moonlight to the
house of Velez—when the Band turn off to wreck their vengeance
on Francesco—

But
                                        'She mov'd steadily on
Unswerving from the path of her resolve.'[2]——

A moorish Priest (who has been with her & then left her to seek the
men) had just mentioned the owl—
    'It's note comes dreariest in the *fall of the* year'—/this dwells on
her mind—& she bursts into this soliloquy[3]—

The hanging Woods, that touch'd by Autumn seem'd
As they were blossoming hues of fire & gold,
The hanging Woods, most lovely in decay,
The many clouds, the Sea, the Rock, the Sands,
Lay in the silent moonshine—and the Owl,
(Strange, very strange!) the Scritch-owl only wak'd,
Sole Voice, sole Eye of all that world of Beauty!—
Why, such a thing am I?——Where are these men?
I need the sympathy of human faces
To beat away this deep contempt for all things
Which quenches my revenge!—O would to Alla,

---

[1] Cf. *This Lime-Tree Bower my Prison*, lines 38–43, *Poems*, i. 180.

[2] *Osorio*, Act v, Scene i, lines 8–9, *Poems*, ii. 583.

[3] This passage from Act v of *Osorio* (lines 37–56), with its emphasis on
'the *fall of the* year', was probably composed in Oct. 1797, and may have an
association with Coleridge's 'retirement' near Porlock. Although Coleridge
had earlier noted that *Osorio* was almost finished, Letter 211 shows that he
was still working over it after his September visit to Bowles. See Letters 205
and 206.

The Raven & the Seamew were appointed
To bring me food—or rather that my Soul
Could drink in life from the universal air!
It were a lot divine in some small skiff
Along some Ocean's boundless solitude
To float for ever with a careless course,
And think myself the only Being alive!

I do not wonder that your poem procured you kisses & hospi-
tality—It is indeed a very sweet one—and I have not only admired
your genius more, but I have loved YOU better, since I have read
it.—Your sonnet—(as you call it—& being a free-born Briton who
shall prevent you from calling 25 blank verse lines a Sonnet, if you
have taken a bloody resolution so to do)—your Sonnet I am much
pleased with— / but the epithet 'downy' is probably more appli-
cable to Susan's upper lip than to her Bosom—& a mother is so
holy & divine a being, that I cannot endure any *corporealizing*
epithets to be applied to her or any part of her—besides, damn
epithets!—. The last line & a half I suppose miswritten—what can
be the meaning of 'or scarce one Leaf To cheer etc. &c—'?—
'Cornelian Virtues'——pedantry!—[']The melancholy fiend'—
villainous in itself—& inaccurate—it ought to be the fiend that
makes melancholy—I should have written it either thus (or perhaps
something better)

but with matron cares
Drives away heaviness, & in your smiles—& &c——

A little *compression* would make it a beautiful poem. *Study com-
pression!*—

I presume you mean Decorum by *Harum Dick*. An affected fellow
at Bridgewater called Truces, Trusses—I told him I admired his
pronunciation—for that lately they had been found 'to suspend
ruptures without curing them'—.— There appeared in the Courier
the day before yesterday a very sensible vindication of the conduct
of the Directory.[1] [Di]d you see it?——

Your news respecting Mrs E. did not *surprize* me—I *saw* it even
from the first week I was at Darley——As to the other event, our
non-settlement at Darley, I suspect, had little or rather *nothing* to
do with it——but the *cause* of our non-settlement there, might
perhaps— / —O God! O God!——I wish—(but what is the use of
wishing?) I wish that Walter Evans may have talent enough to

---

[1] No such article appeared in the *Courier* on Thursday, 'the day before
yesterday'; but Coleridge must refer to an article, 'Justification of the late
conduct of the Directory', which was published in the *Courier* on Tuesday,
10 Oct. 1797.

appreciate Mrs Evans![1]—but I suspect, his intellect is not tall enough even to measure her's!——Hartley is well—& *will not* walk or run, having discovered the art of crawling with wonderful ease & rapidity!——Wordsworth & his Sister are well—

I want to see your Wife—God bless her!——

Oh! my Tragedy—it is finished, transcribed, & to be sent off to day[2]—but I have no hopes of it's success—or even of it's being acted.—

God bless [you] &
S. T. Coleridge

210. *To Thomas Poole*

Address: Mr T. Poole
MS. Victoria University Lib. Pub. with omis. Letters, i. *13*. This is the fourth of the autobiographical letters.

[Endorsed Octr 16th, ⟨17⟩97]

Dear Poole

From October 1779 to Oct. 1781.——I had asked my mother one evening to cut my cheese *entire*, so that I might toast it: this was no easy matter, it being a *crumbly* cheese—My mother however did it— / I went into the garden for some thing or other, and in the mean time my Brother Frank *minced* my cheese, 'to disappoint the

---

[1] Walter Evans had married Mrs. Evans of Darley. Cf. Letter 136.

[2] Two copies of *Osorio* were sent off, the first to William Linley, Sheridan's brother-in-law, on 14 Oct., the second via Bowles to Sheridan two days later (see Letter 211). On 2 Dec. Coleridge wrote that he had received a letter from Linley 'the long & the short of which is that Sheridan rejects the Tragedy' (cf. Letter 213). Coleridge had met Linley when he visited Bowles in Sept. 1797 and addressed the following sonnet to him:

To Mr William Linley

While my young cheek preserves it's healthful hues
And I have many friends, who hold me dear—
LINLEY! methinks, I would not *often* hear
Such melodies as thine, lest I should lose
All memory of the wrongs and sore distress
For which my miserable brethren weep:
But should uncomforted misfortunes steep
My daily bread in tears and bitterness,
And if in Death's dread moment I should lie
With no beloved face by my bed side
To catch the last glance of my closing eye—
O God! such songs breath'd by my angel guide
Would make me pass the cup of anguish by,
Mix with the blest, nor know that I had died!

S. T. Coleridge

Donhead | September 12th, | 1797 [MS. Buffalo Public Lib.]

favorite'. I returned, saw the exploit, and in an agony of passion flew at Frank—he pretended to have been seriously hurt by my blow, flung himself on the ground, and there lay with outstretched limbs——I hung over him moaning & in a great fright—he leaped up, & with a horse-laugh gave me a severe blow in the face—I seized a knife, and was running at him, when my Mother came in & took me by the arm— / I expected a flogging—& struggling from her I ran away, to a hill at the bottom of which the Otter flows—about one mile from Ottery.— There I stayed; my rage died away; but my obstinacy vanquished my fears—& taking out a little shilling book which had, at the end, morning & evening prayers, I very devoutly repeated them—thinking *at the same time* with inward & gloomy satisfaction, how miserable my Mother must be! —I distinctly remember my feelings when I saw a Mr Vaughan pass over the Bridge, at about a furlong's distance—and how I watched the Calves in the fields beyond the river. It grew dark— & I fell asleep—it was towards the latter end of October—& it proved a dreadful stormy night— / I felt the cold in my sleep, and dreamt that I was pulling the blanket over me, & actually pulled over me a dry thorn bush, which lay on the hill—in my sleep I had rolled from the top of the hill to within three yards of the River, which flowed by the unfenced edge of the bottom.—I awoke several times, and finding myself wet & stiff, and cold, closed my eyes again that I might forget it.——In the mean time my Mother waited about half an hour, expecting my return, when the *Sulks* had evaporated—I not returning, she sent into the Church-yard, & round the town—not found!—Several men & all the boys were sent to ramble about & seek me—in vain! My Mother was almost distracted—and at ten o'clock at night I was *cry'd* by the crier in Ottery, and in two villages near it—with a reward offered for me. —No one went to bed—indeed, I believe, half the town were up all one night! To return to myself—About five in the morning or a little after, I was broad awake; and attempted to get up & walk —but I could not move—I saw the Shepherds & Workmen at a distance—& cryed but so faintly, that it was impossible to hear me 30 yards off——and there I might have lain & died—for I was now almost given over, the ponds & even the river near which I was lying, having been dragged.—But by good luck Sir Stafford North-cote, who had been out all night, resolved to make one other trial, and came so near that he heard my crying—He carried me in his arms, for near a quarter of a mile; when we met my father & Sir Stafford's Servants.—I remember, & never shall forget, my father's face as he looked upon me while I lay in the servant's arms—so calm, and the tears stealing down his face: for I was the child of his old age.——My Mother, as you may suppose, was out-rageous with joy—in rushed a *young Lady*, crying out—'I hope, you'll whip him, Mrs Coleridge!'—This woman still lives at Ottery—& neither Philosophy or Religion have been able to conquer the antipathy which I *feel* towards her, whenever I see her.—I was put to bed—& recovered in a day or so—but I was certainly injured—For I was weakly, & subject to the ague for many years after—.—

My Father (who had so little of parental ambition in him, that he had destined his children to be Blacksmiths &c, & had accom-plished his intention but for my Mother's pride & spirit of aggran-dizing her family) my father had however resolved, that I should be a Parson. I read every book that came in my way without distinction—and my father was fond of me, & used to take me on his knee, and hold long conversations with me. I remember, that at eight years old I walked with him one winter evening from a farmer's house, a mile from Ottery——& he told me the names of the stars—and how Jupiter was a thousand times larger than our world—and that the other twinkling stars were Suns that had worlds rolling round them—& when I came home, he shewed me how they rolled round— / . I heard him with a profound delight & admiration; but without the least mixture of wonder or incredulity. For from my early reading of Faery Tales, & Genii &c &c—my mind had been habituated *to the Vast*——& I never regarded *my senses* in any way as the criteria of my belief. I regulated all my creeds by my conceptions not by my *sight*—even at that age. Should children be permitted to read Romances, & Relations of Giants & Magicians, & Genii?——I know all that has been said against it; but I have formed my faith in the affirmative.—I know no other way of giving the mind a love of 'the Great', & 'the Whole'. —Those who have been led to the same truths step by step thro' the constant testimony of their senses, seem to me to want a sense which I possess—They contemplate nothing but *parts*—and all *parts* are necessarily little—and the Universe to them is but a mass of *little things*.[1]—It is true, that the mind *may* become credulous & prone to superstition by the former method—but are not the Experimentalists credulous even to madness in believing any absur-dity, rather than believe the grandest truths, if they have not the testimony of their own senses in their favor?—I have known some who have been *rationally* educated, as it is styled. They were marked by a microscopic acuteness; but when they looked at great things, all became a blank & they saw nothing—and denied

---

[1] The similarity between the foregoing passage and Letter 209 has been obscured, since E. H. Coleridge printed the autobiographical letters at the beginning of his edition, thus placing them out of their chronological order.

(very illogically) that any thing could be seen; and uniformly put the negation of a power for the possession of a power—& called the want of imagination Judgment, & the never being moved to Rapture Philosophy!——

Towards the latter end of September 1781 my Father went to Plymouth with my Brother Francis, who was to go as Midshipman under Admiral Graves; the Admiral was a friend of my Father's.— My Father settled my Brother; & returned Oct. 4th, 1781—. He arrived at Exeter about six o'clock—& was pressed to take a bed there by the Harts—but he refused—and to avoid their intreaties he told them—that he had never been superstitious—but that the night before he had had a dream which had made a deep impression. He dreamt that Death had appeared to him, as he is commonly painted, & touched him with his Dart. Well he returned home—& all his family, I excepted, were up. He told my mother his dream —; but he was in high health & good spirits—& there was a bowl of Punch made—& my Father gave a long & particular account of his Travel, and that he had placed Frank under a religious Captain &c—/ At length, he went to bed, very well, & in high Spirits.—A short time after he had lain down he complained of a pain in his bowells, which he was subject to, from the wind—my mother got him some peppermint water—and after a pause, he said—'I am much better now, my dear!'—and lay down again. In a minute my mother heard a noise in his throat—and spoke to him—but he did not answer—and she spoke repeatedly in vain. Her *shriek* awaked me —& I said, 'Papa is dead.'—I did not know [of] my Father's return, but I knew that he was expected. How I came to think of his Death, I cannot tell; but so it was.—Dead he was—some said it was the Gout in the Heart—probably, it was a fit of Apoplexy / —He was an Israelite without guile; simple, generous, and, taking some scripture texts in their literal sense, he was conscientiously indifferent to the good & the evil of this world.—

God love you & S. T. Coleridge

211. *To William Lisle Bowles*

Address: The Revd W. L. Bowles | Donhead
MS. Yale University Lib. Pub. A Wiltshire Parson, *by Garland Greever, 1926, 32.*

Stowey near Bridgewater.   Monday, Oct. 16th, 1797
My dear Sir

At last I send you the Tragedy complete & neatly transcribed— I have sent another to Mr Linley.—I endeavoured to strike out the character of Warville, the Englishman; and to substitute some more interesting one—but in vain!—So I have altered his name, made him a German, and a nothing at all. Perhaps, I had better have given Albert a *confidential Servant*—*he* might have cleaned Albert's shoes, &c—whereas what Maurice does or *can* do, is not quite so clear.—In truth, I have fagged so long at the work, & see so many imperfections in the original & main plot, that I feel an indescribable disgust, a sickness of the very heart, at the mention of the Tragedy. If there be any thing with which I am at all satisfied, it is—the style. I have endeavoured to have few sentences which *might not* be spoken in conversation, avoiding those that are *commonly* used in conversation.——You, I know, will forward it to Mr Sheridan with all speed; and will be so kind as to write to him on the subject.——Excepting for the money which would be gained if it succeeded, I am not conscious of a wish relating to the piece. It is done: and I would rather mend hedges & follow the plough, than write another. I could not avoid attaching a pecuniary importance to the business; and consequently, became anxious: and such anxieties humble & degrade the mind.—

I hope you are well—give my respects to Mrs Bowles, & believe me with great sincerity

Your obliged
S. T. Coleridge

P.S. I should very much wish to see your Progress of Discovery before it is printed—you might be sure, that I would shew it to no human being, except my Wife.——

You will be so kind as with the Tragedy to transmit this little volume to Mr Sheridan.[1]

212. *To Joseph Cottle*

Address: Mr Cottle | Bookseller| High Street | Bristol
MS. Harvard College Lib. Pub. with omis. E. K. Chambers, A Sheaf of Studies, *1942, p. 43.* Cottle took his usual liberties with this manuscript, printing it as three communications. See *Early Rec.* i. 139, 251, and 288. The top half of pages 1 and 2 of the holograph has been torn off.
Stamped: Bridgewater.

[*Circa* 20 November 1797][2]

. . .Southey's poem[3] is very [plea]sing—no. . .a little digressive.—

[1] Presumably, *Poems by S. T. Coleridge*, 1797.
[2] The reference to the introduction of Wordsworth's play to Harris, the manager of Covent Garden (see postscript), suggests that this letter was written about 20 Nov. 1797, before which date *The Borderers* was dispatched to London. Cf. *Early Letters*, 174.
[3] *To A. S. Cottle*, published only in A. S. Cottle, *Icelandic Poetry*, 1797, pp. xxxi–xlii.

From the beginning to the Words—Of Earth & Heaven—!—It is exquisite— / Regner's tale has been hackneyed by Southey in other poems, and by 20 before Southey.—From 'Were I, my Friend! a solitary man'—to Fill'd with the firs' faint odour—! is in Southey's best manner—rich—almost delicious!—Let me except the two lines 'That loathes the commerce[']——to 'hollow Gaieties! —['] It may be very well; but we have had too much of it.—What follows to 'the deeds of men[']—is well conceived, but expressed in an every-day Manner—it wants the vividness of an original mind.—From thence to 'wretched wife'—a sublime & deep Eloquence!——The conclusion of the Paragraph is very well; but Southey himself has hackneyed it. He may reply as Martial did to the Man who laughed at his worn-out Toga—Vetus, at meum.—*Old,* but my own.—To the. . .& awful Invective against Things as they are?—He himself is the best Judge.——I am translating the Oberon of Wieland—it is a difficult Language, and I can translate at least as fast as I can construe.—I pray you, as soon as possible, procure for me a German-English Grammar—I believe, there is but one—*Widderburne's,* I think—but I am not certain.—I have written a ballad of about 300 lines[1]—& the Sketch of a Plan of General Study:—and I have made a very considerable Proficiency in the French Language, and study it daily—and daily study the German—so that I am not, & have not been, idle.——I have heard nothing about my Tragedy, except some silly remarks of Kemble's, to whom Linley shewed it—it does not appear to me that there is a shadow of probability that it will be accepted.—It gave me no pain—& great pleasure in finding that it gave me no pain. I had rather hoped than believed, that I was possessed of so much philosophical capability.—Sheridan, most certainly, has not used me with common Justice. The proposal came from himself—and altho' this circumstance did not bind him to accept the Tragedy, it certainly bound him to pay every & that the earliest, attention to it.—I suppose, it lies snugly in his green Bag—if it have not emigrated to the Kitchen or the Cloāca.

I sent three mock Sonnets in ridicule of my own, & Charles Lloyd's, & Lamb's,[2] &c &c—in ridicule of that affectation of un-affectedness, of jumping & misplaced accent on common-place epithets, flat lines forced into poetry by Italics (signifying how well & *mouthis[h]ly* the Author would read them) puny pathos &c &c—

---

[1] Apparently *The Ancient Mariner,* see Letters 218 and 233, and E. K. Chambers, 'Some Dates in Coleridge's *Annus Mirabilis*', *A Sheaf of Studies,* 1942, pp. 42–59.

[2] *Sonnets attempted in the Manner of Contemporary Writers,* first published *Monthly Magazine,* Nov. 1797. Cf. *Poems,* i. 209.

the instances are almost all taken from mine & Lloyd's poems ——I signed them Nehemiah Higginbottom. I think they may do good to our young Bards.—

God love you &
S. T. Coleridge.

P.S. I have procured for Wordsworth's Tragedy an Introduction to Harris, the Manager of Convent-garden—who has promised to read it attentively and give his answer immediately—and if he accept it, to put it in preparation without an hour's delay.—

213. *To Thomas Poole*

Address: Mr T. Poole | Stowey | near | Bridgewater
MS. British Museum. Pub. E.L.G. i. 83.
Stamped: Bristol.

Saturday Evening [Endorsed Decem. 2d 1797]

My dear Poole

I write from Cottle's shop to request you if there have arriv'd any letters for me to send them addressed to Cottle's High Street —I have been several times at King's—he & your Sister are remarkably well—Sara & I go there on Wednesday, stay for a day or two, and homeward for Stowey—I received a letter from Linley, the long & the short of which is that Sheridan rejects the Tragedy —his *sole* objection is—the obscurity of the three last acts.——

The Estlins, & Cottle, and Wade all desire to be kindly remembered to you—My love to your dear Mother & to Ward—& believe me, as ever, your's, my best & dearest Friend! most affectionately,

S. T. Coleridge

214. *To Robert Southey*

Address: Mr Southey | No. 23 | East Street | Red Lion Square | London
MS. Lord Latymer, Pub. with omis. Letters, i. 251 n.
Postmark: 8 December 1797. *Stamped*: Bristol.

Thursday Morning [7 December 1797]

I am sorry, Southey! very sorry that I wrote or published those Sonnets[1]—but 'sorry' would be a tame word to express my feelings,

---

[1] Coleridge refers to his Nehemiah Higginbottom sonnets, the second of which, *To Simplicity*, Southey assumed to be in ridicule of himself. This sonnet brought Southey's animosity into the open, and Lamb, to whom Coleridge also wrote that it 'was not composed with reference to Southey', vehemently rejected the denial: 'It was a lie too gross for the grossest ignorance to believe.'

if I had written them with the motives which you have attributed to me.—I have not been in the habit of treating our separation with levity—nor ever since the first moment thought of it without deep emotion—and how you could apply to yourself a Sonnet written to ridicule infantine simplicity, vulgar colloquialisms, and lady-like Friendships—I have no conception. Neither I believe could a passage in your writings have suggested to me or any man the notion of *your* 'plaining plaintively'.[1] I am sorry that I wrote them; because I am sorry to perceive a disposition in you to believe evil of me, and a disposition to teach others to believe Evil—of which your remark to Charles Lloyd was a painful instance.[2]—I say this to you; because I shall say it to no other being.——I feel myself wounded: and write ac[cordingly]—

I believe in my letter to Lloyd I forgot to mention that the Editor of [the] Morning Post is called Stuart[3]—and that he is the Brother in law of Mackintosh[4]——

Your's sincerely
S. T. Coleridge

[1] *To Simplicity*, line 11, 'Now of my false friend plaining plaintively.'

[2] Although Lloyd had left the Coleridges in the spring of 1797 with no ill feelings and seems to have been on friendly terms when he visited Stowey in Sept. 1797 (see Letter 207), by 11 Nov. he had written a novel, *Edmund Oliver*, the hero of which resembles Coleridge in personal appearance and undergoes experiences in love, in the army, and in the use of opium not unlike Coleridge's. Southey, whose quarrel with Coleridge of 1795 was only superficially healed, probably provided material for Lloyd's novel—a justifiable inference, since Lloyd was living with Southey during its composition and since Southey had himself planned a novel by the same name in 1796. Coleridge apparently did not learn of *Edmund Oliver* until its appearance in Apr. 1798 (see Letter 243).

[3] Daniel Stuart (1766–1846) had purchased the *Morning Post* in 1795. An astute journalist, he raised that paper into prominence. Later he was equally successful with the *Courier*. Stuart was soon to be on the most intimate terms with Coleridge, whose contributions to the *Morning Post* began on 7 Dec. 1797.

[4] James Mackintosh (1765–1832), philosopher, politician, and historian, in 1789 married Daniel Stuart's sister, who died eight years later. In Apr. 1798 Mackintosh married Catherine Allen, a sister of Mrs. John and Mrs. Josiah Wedgwood. Coleridge seems never to have been drawn to Mackintosh and came to speak of him with an asperity which may have arisen from Mackintosh's unfavourable estimate of Wordsworth as a poet. See Letter 402. Among the papers of Lord Latymer, however, there is a letter from Mackintosh to Coleridge, in which it is proposed that Coleridge contribute to the *Morning Post*. Mackintosh may have influenced the Wedgwoods in their determination to offer financial assistance to Coleridge.

No 19 Sale Street, Lincoln's Inn, London, Novr 17th, 1797.

Sir

In common with every man of taste & feeling I have long been an admirer of your genius, but it was not till my late visit to Mr Wedgewood's that I felt an interest in your Character almost equal to my admiration of your

215. *To Josiah Wedgwood*

MS. Wedgwood Museum. Pub. E.L.G. i. 84. On 23 December 1797, Thomas and Josiah Wedgwood, sons of the potter, sent a draft for £100 to Coleridge (see Letter 231). On 27 December 1797 Coleridge wrote the following letter of acceptance; reconsidering the matter, he later returned the draft in a long letter dated 5 January 1798 (see Letter 217). On 10 January 1798, the Wedgwoods offered Coleridge an annuity of £150, 'independent of every thing but the wreck of our fortune, an event which we hope is not very likely to happen' (see headnote to Letter 222 for the Wedgwoods' letter). On 17 January 1798 (Letter 222) Coleridge wrote to Josiah Wedgwood accepting the annuity.

Stowey near Bridgewater.
Decemb. 27th,[1] 1797

Dear Sir

I received your letter, with the enclosed order, yesterday. You have relieved me from a state of hesitation & perplexity; and have

extraordinary powers. From the reports of Dr Beddoes & of my amiable Friend Miss Allen I found that you were no less interesting as a man than as a poet & I heard with the most sincere regret that like many other good men & great poets you had not been so kindly treated by fortune as by nature. Had I been possessed of opulence I should certainly have thought your permission to assist you one of the greatest honours of my life & the power of aiding such a Man to be the chief enjoyment & blessing of wealth. But I am poor & the great & wealthy of our days seem to have a different taste in the employment of their riches from that which I flatter myself would actuate me if I were in their place.—On my return to town I found an easy opportunity of procuring a very small Stipend for you which I thought might with very little exertion from you contribute to make you somewhat more easy. When I went to Cote House again Dr Beddoes at my desire wrote to you & by your answer I saw that you were not averse from the proposal. The Newspaper is the Morning Post. The political tone is such as cannot be disagreeable to your feelings or repugnant to your Principles. The Proprietor who is no stranger to your Character & talents is ashamed of offering you so small a pittance but he pleads in excuse that the large establishment of parliamentary reporters makes this season of the year peculiarly expensive & that if the Connexion proves agreeable to both parties after a fair trial he will very gladly increase the salary. He has already ordered the Paper to be sent to you & he informs me that verses or political Essays as you may chance to be inclined will be equally agreeable to him. You will observe the address proper for your letters at the bottom of the Paper. Will you do me the favour of communicating to me the name of your tragedy that I may urge the irresolute good nature of Sheridan to bring it forward as soon as possible. Suffer me to add that if by any means within my narrow power either now or hereafter I can shew you in any degree my esteem for your virtue & my admiration for your genius you will do me [the grea]test plea[s]ure & honour [by po]inting it out to me.

[Conclusion and signature cut off manuscript.]

[1] If Coleridge received Josiah Wedgwood's letter and the draft for £100 on Christmas Day, this letter must have been written on 26 Dec. Cf. Letters 216 and 231. In both letters, however, he speaks of a delay in answering.

given me the tranquillity & leisure of independence for the next two years.—I am not deficient in the ordinary feelings of gratitude to you and Mr T. Wedgewood; but I shall not find them oppressive or painful, if in the course of that time I shall have been acquiring knowlege for myself, or communicating it to others; if either in act or preparation I shall have been contributing my quota to the cause of Truth & Honesty.——

I am | with great respect & affection— | Your obliged &c
S. T. Coleridge

216. *To John Prior Estlin*

Address: Revd J. P. Estlin | St Michael's Hill | Bristol
MS. Bristol Central Lib. Pub. Letters to Estlin, *46.*
Stamped: Bridgewater.

Saturday Morning [30 December 1797]
My dear Friend

On the morning of Christmas day I received Mr Row's[1] letter to you: on Thursday night, eleven o'clock, I received from Mr I. Wood of Shrewsbury an invitation in the name of Mr Row's Congregation, accompanied with a very kind note from Mr Row. On this subject I now entreat your friendly advice: and in order to enable you to give it, I must retrace my life for the last three months.—At the commencement of this period I began to feel the necessity of gaining a regular income by a regular occupation. My heart yearned toward the ministry; but I considered my scruples, as almost insurmountable Obstacles to my conscientious performance of it's duties.—Another plan presented itself; that of joining with Mr Montague[2] in a project of Tuition. Our scheme was singular & extensive: extensive, for we proposed in three years to go systematically, yet with constant reference to the nature of *man*, thro' the mathematical Branches, chemistry, Anatomy, the laws of Life, the laws of Intellect, & lastly, thro' universal History, arranging separately all the facts that elucidate the separate states of Society, savage, civilized & luxurious: singular, for we proposed ourselves, not as Teachers, but only as Managing Students. If by this plan I

---

[1] John Rowe, the Unitarian minister at Shrewsbury, was resigning his post to join Estlin in Bristol.

[2] Basil Montagu (1770–1851), the friend of Wordsworth, was called to the bar in May 1798. It was Montagu who precipitated the Wordsworth–Coleridge quarrel in 1810.

could at once subsist my family for three years, and enable myself
to acquire such a mass of knowlege, it would doubtless be prefer-
able to all other modes of action for me, who have just knowlege
enough of most things to feel my ignorance of all things. The
probability however of it's success was very small—before I left
Stowey, it dwindled yet more—& when at Bristol, in all the de-
spondency of the new taxes, the plan appeared absolutely romantic.
In the mean time my conversations with you had certainly weak-
ened my convictions on certain subjects, or at least deadened their
efficacy—I made up my mind to be a Dissenting Minister—&
offered to supply Mr Row's place for a few Sundays at Shrewsbury,
to see whether I liked the place and whether the congregation liked
me, and would endure my opinions, which softened & modified as
they had been, did still retain a degree of *peculiarity*.—I returned
to Stowey, & wrote to Montague, that if indeed he should procure,
& *immediately* procure, the eight pupils at 100£ a year, they board-
ing & lodging at their own expence (for this was his plan) I would
join him gladly.—But as I did not perceive the *slightest chance* of
this, unless it were done *immediately*, I should accept some situa-
tion, as Dissenting Minister—and that I had no time for delay or
wavering.—/Well!—on Christmas day Morning I received two let-
ters—one from you, i.e.—Mr Row's letter to you—one in an un-
known hand, but which I supposed to be upon some newspaper
business—& did not open it till some time after I had read &
pondered the former.—In this I saw the features of *contingency* very
strongly marked, & (as I always do on such occasions) to prevent
disappointment I checked my hopes. Mr *Kentish* was to be applied
to—I had heard that he was not very comfortably situated at
Exeter—& as to Norwich, the same motive which inclined me not
only to prefer Shrewsbury, but Shrewsbury out of the question, to
reject Norwich, I naturally supposed would have it's influence on
him—the salary being so much more, the country more delightful,
& provisions of all kinds so much cheaper.—Supposing that he
declined it, still it was uncertain whether the congregation would
elect *me*: & that part of Mr Row's letter (Without some indepen-
dence Mr C. is almost the only man I would wish to settle here &c)
increased my doubts.—I did not refuse to think, that by gentleness,
& intellectual efforts I should compel their respect when they
became acquainted with me—: but I thought it probable, that such
a congregation, in a town so violently aristocratic, would be deter-
red from electing me by the notoriety of my *political* conduct, & by
the remaining peculiarities of my religious creed.—My mind was
lost & swallowed up in musing on all this; when I carelessly opened
the second letter. It proved to be from Mr Josiah Wedgewood—

The following is a Copy—Dear Sir, My Brother Thomas & myself had separately determined that it would be right to enable you to defer entering into an engagement, we understand you are about to form, from the most urgent of motives. We therefore request, you will accept the inclosed Draft with the same simplicity with which it is offered to you.—Dear Sir, sincerely Your's

Josiah Wedgewood

P.S. As the draft is payable to the Bearer of it, I shall be obliged to you to acknowlege the receipt of it to me at Penzance.—
The inclosed Draft was for an hundred pound.—Well! what was I to do ? This hundred pound joined with the guinea per week which I gain from the Morning Post & which only takes me up two days in the week would give me the leisure & tranquillity of independence for the two next years—at the end of which time by systematic study I should be better fitted for any profession than I am at present.——Without this, unless I am elected at Shrewsbury which I thought more than uncertain, I shall remain necessitous & dependent, and be compelled to fag on in all the nakedness of Talent without the materials of Knowlege or systematic Information.—But if I accept it, I certainly bind myself to hold myself free for some time at least for the co-execution of the Plan of general Study with Montague: and in the realization of which I understand that the Wedgewoods are actively interesting themselves: as conceiving it likely to be of general Benefit.——And this letter was to be answered *immediately.* My friend T. Poole strenuously advised me to accept it—considering how contingent the Shrewsbury plan appeared—I however lingered, I may truly say, almost a sleepless man, Monday night, and Tuesday night & Wednesday night, regularly sitting up till the post came in, which is not till past eleven —anxiously hoping to receive some letter more decisive respecting Shrewsbury.—On the Thursday *Morning* I was obliged to acknowlege the receipt of the Draft—having already delayed it beyond all limits of propriety.—Well—after a storm of fluctuations, Poole still retaining his opinions, & urging them more decisively, I accepted the Draft in a letter expressive of manly gratitude—and on the Thursday Night I received the letter from Mr Wood!—The distress of my mind since then has been inexpressible.—The plan which with the eagerness of Friendship you had been exerting yourself to secure for me—how can I bear to think that it should perish in your hand, the very moment you had caught it ?—Yet on the other hand if I send back the Draft I shall lose the esteem of the Wedgewoods & their friends, to whom I shall appear deficient not only in consistency, but even in common probity. It will appear to them,

that I had accepted the Draft in words which implied that it had relieved me from a state of great uncertainty—whereas in truth, I had accepted it to console myself for a disappointment.—Write immediately——

S. T. Coleridge

217. *To Josiah Wedgwood*

Address: Josiah Wedgewood Esq. | Penzance | Cornwall
MS. Wedgwood Museum. Pub. E.L.G. i. 85.
Stamped: Bridgewater.

Stowey [near Br]idgewater.
J[an.] 5th, 1798

Dear Sir

By the inclosed you will understand the occasion of this Letter. Your Brother and yourself will be pleased with my conduct, if I shall make it appear probable to you, that the purposes, for which you sent and I accepted so large a Bill, will be better answered by my returning than by my retaining it. You wished to remove those urgent motives which might make it necessary for me to act in opposition to my principles: you wished to give me leisure for the improvement of my Talents at the same time that my mind should be preserved free from any professional Bias which might pervert, or at least hamper, the exertion of them. I will state to you with great Simplicity all that has passed thro' my mind on these subjects. The affectionate esteem, with which I regard your character, makes this openness pleasant to me: and your Kindness seems to have authorized the freedom, which I am about to take in being so diffuse concerning my own affairs.

If a man considered himself as acting in opposition to his principles *then only* when he gave his example or support to actions and institutions, the existence of which produces *unmingled* evil, he might perhaps with a safe conscience perpetrate any crime and become a member of any Order. If on the other hand a man should make it *his principle* to abstain from all modes of conduct, the general practice of which was not permanently useful, or at least absolutely harmless, he must live, an isolated Being: his furniture, his servants, his very cloathes are intimately connected with Vice and Misery. To preserve therefore our moral feelings without withdrawing ourselves from active life we should, I imagine, endeavor to discover those evils in society which are the most pressing, and those of which the immediate Removal appears the most practicable: to the removal of these we should concenter our energies, for the removal of them be prepared to make any sacrifices. In other things we *must* compound with a large quantity of evil—taking care to select from the modes of conduct, which may be within our choice, those in which we can do the most good with the least evil. Now I shall apply this to myself. As far as I am able to decide, the most pressing evils & those of which the speedy removal is the most practicable, are these—the union of Religion with the Government, and those other political Institutions & abuses which I need not name; but which not only produce much evil directly & per se, but likewise perpetuate the causes of most other evils. Do not think me boastful when I assert that rather than in any way support any of these, I would undergo Poverty, Dependence, & even Death. There remain within my choice two Sources of Subsistence: the Press, and the Ministry. Now as to the Press, I gain at present a guinea a week by writing for the Morning Post—and as my expences, living as I now do, will not exceed 100£ a year—or but little more, even including the annual 20£, for which my wife's mother has a necessity—I could by means of your kindness subsist for the two next years, & enjoy leisure & external comfort. But anxiety for the future would remain & increase, as it is probable my children will come fast on me: and the Press, considered as a Trade, is perhaps only not the worst occupation for a man who would wish to preserve any delicacy of moral feeling. The few weeks that I have written for the Morning Post, I have felt this ——Something must be written & written immediately—if any important Truth, any striking beauty, occur to my mind, I feel a repugnance at sending it garbled to a newspaper: and if any idea of ludicrous personality, or apt antiministerial joke, crosses me, I feel a repugnance at rejecting it, because *something must be written,* and nothing else suitable occurs. The longer I continue a hired paragraph-scribbler, the more powerful these Temptations will become: and indeed nothing scarcely that has not a *tang* of personality or *vindictive* feeling, is pleasing or interesting, I apprehend, to my Employers. Of all things I most dislike party politics—yet this sort of gypsie jargon I am compelled to fire away.—To the *ministry* I adduced the following objections at the time that I decided against entering into it.—It makes one's livelihood hang upon the profession of *particular opinions:* and tends therefore to warp the intellectual faculty ; to fasten convictions on the mind by the agency of it's wishes; and if Reason should at length dissever them, it presents strong Motives to Falsehood or Simulation.—Secondly, as the subscriptions of the Congregation form the revenue, the minister is under an inducement to adapt his moral exhortations to their wishes rather than to their needs. (Poor Pilkington of Derby was, I believe, obliged to resign on account of his sermons respecting Riches & Rich Men.) Thirdly, the routine of Duty brings on a certain sectarian mannerism, which generally narrows the Intellect itself, and always narrows the sphere of it's operation. In answer to these objections it may be observed: first, that I see the contingency of these evils very distinctly, and in proportion to my clear perception of them it is probable that I shall be able to guard against them. Secondly, the Press, considered as a *Trade*, presents still greater temptations—& this is not a controversy concerning absolute, but concerning *comparative* good. Thirdly, the income of that place, which is now offered to me, does not depend on the congregation, but is an estate. This weakens certainly, tho' as certainly it does not remove, the second objection. Fourthly—The principal of these objections are weak or strong in proportion to the care & impartiality with which the particular opinions had been formed previously to the assumption of the ministerial office; inasmuch as the probability of a change in these opinions is thereby proportionally lessened. Now, not only without any design of becoming an hired Teacher in any sect but with decisive intentions to the contrary I have studied the subject of natural & revealed Religion—I have read the works of the celebrated Infidels—I have conversed long, & seriously, & dispassionately with Infidels of great Talents & information—& most assuredly, my faith in Christianity has been confirmed rather than staggered. In teaching it therefore, at present, whether I act *beneficently* or no, I shall certainly act bene*volent*ly. Fifthly—The *necessary* creed in our sect is but short—it will be necessary for me, in order to my continuance as an Unitarian Minister, to believe that Jesus Christ was the Messiah—in all other points I may play off my intellect *ad libitum*. Sixthly—that altho' we ought not to brave temptations in order to shew our strength, yet it would be slothful and cowardly to retire from an employment, because tho' there *are* no temptations at present, there *may be* some hereafter. —In favor of my assuming the ministerial office it may be truly said, that it will give me a regular income sufficient to free me from all anxiety respecting my absolute wants, yet not large enough to exempt me from motives, even of a pecuniary nature, for literary exertion. I can afford to dedicate three or twice three years to *some one work*, which *may be* of benefit to society, and will certainly be uninjurious to my own moral character: for I shall be positive at least that there is no falsehood or immorality in it proceeding from haste or necessity.—If I do enter on this office, it will be at Shrewsbury—I shall be surrounded by a fine country, no mean ingredient in the composition of a poet's happiness—I shall have at least five days in every week of perfect leisure—120£ a year—a

good house, valued at 30£ a year—and if I should die & without
any culpable negligence or extravagance have left my family in
want, Congregations are in the habit of becoming the guardians.
Add to this, that by Law I shall be exempted from military service
—to which, Heaven only knows how soon we may be dragged. For I
think it not improbable, that in case of an invasion our government
would serve all, whom they chose to suspect of disaffection, in the
same way that good King David served Uriah—'Set ye Uriah in
the forefront of the hottest Battle, & retire ye from him, that he
may be smitten & die.' I do not wish to conceal from you that I
have suffered more from fluctuation of mind on this than any former
occasion: and even now I have scarcely courage to decide absolutely.
It is chilling to go among *strangers*—& I leave a lovely country,
and one friend so eminently near to my affections that his society
has almost been consolidated with my ideas of happiness. However
I shall go to Shrewsbury, remain a little while amongst the congre-
gation: if no new argument arise against the ministerial office, and
if the old ones assume no new strength, there I shall *certainly* pitch
my *tents*, & *probably* shall build up my permanent Dwelling.—What-
ever is conducive to a man's real comforts is in the same degree
conducive to his utility—a permanent income not inconsistent
with my religious or political creeds, I find necessary to my quiet-
ness—without it I should be a prey to anxiety, and Anxiety, with
me, always induces Sickliness, and too often Sloth: as an overdose
of Stimulus proves a narcotic. You will let me know of the arrival
of the Bill: and it would give me very great pleasure to hear, that
I had not forfeited your esteem by first accepting, & now returning
it. I acted, each time, from the purest motives possible on such an
occasion: for, my public usefulness being incompatible with personal
vexations, an enlightened Selfishness was in this case the only
species of Benevolence left to me—

Believe me, dear Sir! with no ordinary feelings of esteem and
affection for you & your family, sincerely your's

S. T. Coleridge

218. *To John Prior Estlin*

Address: Revd J. P. Estlin | St Michael's Hill | Bristol
MS. Bristol Central Lib. Pub. E.L.G. i. 91.
Stamped: Bridgewater.

Saturday Morning [6 January 1798]

My dear friend

After much & very painful hesitation I have at length returned
the Draft to Mr Wedgewood with a long letter explanatory of my

conduct——The first sunny morning that I walk out, at Shrewsbury, will make my heart die away within me—for I shall be in a *land of Strangers*! For I shall have left a Friend whose sympathies were perfect with my manners, feelings & opinions—and what is yet more painful, I shall have left him unconvinced of the *expediency* of my going, public or personal.—I could not *stay* with an easy conscience; but whether I shall be happy so far removed from any who love me, I know not. This I know—I will make myself contented by struggling to do my Duty.——

I have written to Mr Wood & to Mr Row—promising to be at Shrewsbury by the latter end of next week. To morrow I perform Mr Howel's duty—the good old man has gone to London with his daughter to seek surgical assistance for her.

I am now, utterly without money: and my account stands thus. —I owe Biggs 5£—Parsons, the Bookseller, owes me more than this considerably; but he is a rogue, & will not pay me.—I have not payed Mrs Fricker her quarterly allowance—in short—

	£	S	D
Biggs	5″	0″	0
Mrs Frick.	5″	5″	0
A quarter's Rent due Dec. 25th, 1797	2″	2″	0
Maid's Wages	1″	1″	0
Shoemaker	1″	13″	0
Coals	2″	6″	0
Chandler—	0″	12″	0
Sundries	0″	12″	0
	£18″	11″	0

This is all I owe in the world: now in order to pay it I must borrow ten pound of you, 5£ of Mr Wade,[1] and will sell my Ballad to Phillips who I doubt not will give me 5£ for it[2]—I suppose, that my Friends will not withdraw their annual subscription of 5£ *this year*—Afterwards of course I should not want it—So that, you see, I propose to anticipate your's, Mr Hobhouse's, & Mr Wade's Subscriptions.——

God love you! I will be with you—as soon as Riches, instead of

[1] The following endorsement appears on the address sheet of this manuscript: Jany—8—98 | Rec'd of Mr. Estlin Fifteen Guineas | on Coleridge's acct. | *J. Wade*

[2] Coleridge refers to *The Ancient Mariner*. It did not appear in the *Monthly Magazine*, of which Richard Phillips was the proprietor.

making *themselves* wings, shall make a pair for *my* shoulders—at present, I am absolutely unfledged.—

Your's with filial & fraternal affection

S. T. Coleridge

My affectionate remembrances to Mrs Estlin.—

219. *To Josiah Wade*

Address: Mr. Wade | No. 6 Barclay Parade, Bristol
Transcript Coleridge family. Pub. E.L.G. i. 90.

Saturday [6 January 1798]

My very dear Friend

This last fortnight has been eventful—I received an hundred pounds from Josiah Wedgewood, in order to prevent the necessity of my going into the Ministry—I have received an invitation from Shrewsbury to be the Minister there—and after the fluctuations of mind which have for nights together robbed me of Sleep, & I am afraid of Health, I have at length returned the order to Mr Wedgewood with a long letter explanatory of my conduct, & accepted the Shrewsbury Invitation—so I shall be with you by the middle of next week—But I am moneyless, & want 20£—for 10£ I have written to Mr Estlin, 5£ I will get, somehow or other from the Editor of the New Monthly Magazine, and 5£ I must borrow of you, if you can lend it me with perfect convenience, but, I beseech [you], do not put yourself out of your way in these hard times— for [if] it be not perfectly convenient to you, I doubt not, I shall be able to get it somewhere or other—

My dear friend, T. Poole, is not convinced of the *expediency*, either to the public or myself, of my returning the Draft & accepting the congregation—It would have been a heart sadning thing to have parted from him in any way, but to part from him, he not satisfied that there is any necessity or propriety in my parting from him, is *very* painful.—But more of this when we meet—let me hear from you immediately—God love you

S. T. Coleridge

220. *To John Prior Estlin*

Address: Revd J. P. Estlin | St Michael's Hill | Bristol   by favor of Mr Kell.
MS. Cornell University Lib. Pub. Letters to Estlin, *45*.

Sunday Night [14 January 1798]

My very dear Friend

After a fatiguing Journey I arrived here on Saturday night—I left Worcester 6 o'clock, Saturday Morning—and we did not reach

Shrewsbury till Saturday night, 8 o'clock. I preached, of course,
morning & afternoon—like Mr Row much—he is a sensible,
christian-hearted man—& I am very well.—What more can I
write?—If you were to pay the post, it would go against my
conscience to leave so much space unfilled, & give you so little
for your money—but as it will cost you nothing, why should I stand
wringing my dish clout of a brain in order to squeeze out a few
dirty drops not worth the having—Give my kind love to Mrs
Estlin &

> believe me with fraternal & filial esteem & affection
> Your S. T. Coleridge

221. *To John Prior Estlin*

Address: Revd J. P. Estlin | St Michael's Hill | Bristol   *Single*
MS. Bristol Central Lib. Pub. E.L.G. i. 92.
Stamped: Shrewsbury.

[16 January 1798]

My very dear Friend

I answer your letter to Mr Row—because it is probable that I
must say all that he would say—and that I shall have to say what
he could not say for me.—We have talked over the affair seriously
—and at the conclusion of our conversations our opinions have
nearly coincided.—First of all I must give you the *information*,
which I have received on this affair—& then I will proceed to make
some direct observations on your very kind letter. In a letter full
of elevated sentiments Mr Josiah Wedgewood offers me from him-
self & his brother Thomas Wedgewood 'an annuity of 150£ for life,
legally secured to me, *no condition whatever being annexed.*'—|——
You seemed by the phrase of 'a family in this neighbourhood' to
suppose that the offer proceeded from or included the Wedgewoods
at Cote House—this is not the case. Josiah Wedgewood lives in
Staffordshire.

Now nothing can be clearer than that I cannot accept the
Ministerial Salary at Shrewsbury & this at the same time. For as I
am morally certain that the Wedgewoods would not have thought
it their duty, or rather would have found it to be *not* their duty, to
have offered me 150£ yearly, if I had been previously possessed of
an 150£ regular income—it follows indisputably, that I cannot
accept the first 150£ with the determination to accept the latter
150£ immediately after.—But (independently of the *animus donan-
tis* which is conclusive in this case) were I to accept the salary at
Shrewsbury, I *would not* accept the annuity from the Wedgewoods.
—Many deserve it equally; and few would want it less.——It is

almost equally clear to me, that as two distinct & incompatible objects are proposed to me, I ought to chuse between them—with reference to the advantages of each—& not make the one a dernier resource if the other should fail.—No, anteriorly to the decision of the Congregation here, I will send the Wedgewoods a definitive answer, either accepting or declining the offer—If I accept it, I will accept it *for itself*—and not to console me for a disappointment in the other object, which I should have preferred if I could have ensured it.—Now then I can state clearly the Question on which I am to decide——

'Shall I refuse 150£ a year for life, as certain, as any fortune can be, for (I will call it) another 150£ a year, the attainment of which is not yet certain, and the duration of which is precarious?—'

You answer—'Yes!—the cause of Christianity & practical Religion demands your exertions. The powers of intellect, which God has given you, are given for this very purpose, that they may be employed in promoting the best interests of mankind.'—

Now this answer would be decisive to my understanding, & (I think you know enough of me to believe me when I say that were the annuity 1500£ a year instead of 150£,) it should be decisive on my conduct, if I could see any reason why my exertions for Christianity & practical Religion depend—I will not say, on my being at Shrewsbury, but—on my becoming a stipendiary & regular minister.—It makes me blush, I assure you, sitting *alone* as I now am, at the idea of mentioning two such names as I am about to do, with any supposeable reference to my own talents, present or to come / but *the kind* is *not altered* by *the degree*—Did Dr HARTLEY employ himself for the promotion of the best interests of mankind? Most certainly. If instead of being a physician he had been an hired Teacher, that he would not have taught Christianity *better*, I can certainly say—& I suspect, from the vulgar prejudices of mankind that his name might have been less efficacious.—That however is a Trifle. A man who thinks that Lardner defended Christianity because he received 50 or 60£ a year for preaching at Crouched Friars, [Crutched Friars][1] must be such a booby that it cannot be of much consequence what he thinks—but—*Lardner!*— do you really think, my dear Friend! that it would have been of much detriment to the Christian world if the author of the Credibility &c had never received nor accepted the invitation at Crouched Friars?—Surely not.—I should be very unwilling to think that my efforts as a Christian Minister depended on my preaching

[1] Nathaniel Lardner (1684–1768), nonconformist divine and biblical scholar, became assistant to Dr. Harris at the meeting-house in Poor Jewry Lane, Crutched Friars, in Sept. 1729.

regularly in one pulpit.—God forbid!—To the cause of Religion
I solemnly devote all my best faculties—and if I wish to acquire
knowlege as a philosopher and fame as a poet, I pray for grace
that I may continue to feel what I now feel, that my greatest
reason for wishing the one & the other, is that I may be enabled
by my knowlege to defend Religion ably, and by my reputation
to draw attention to the defence of it.—I regard every experiment
that Priestly made in Chemistry, as giving *wings* to his more sublime
theological works.—I most assuredly shall preach often—and it is
my present purpose alternately to assist Dr Toulmin & Mr Howel,
one part of every Sunday, while I stay at Stowey.—'I know (you
say) that it was from the purest motives that he thought of entering
into the ministry'——My motives were as pure as they could be,
or ought to be. Surely an *especial* attachment to a society, which
I had never seen, was not one of them—neither if I were to permit
myself to be elected the Minister here, should I consider the salary
as the payment of my services, i.e. my stated & particular services
to the People *here*, but as a means of enabling myself to employ
all my time both for their benefit & that of *all* my fellow-beings.—
Two modes of gaining [a] livelihood were in my power—The press
without reference to Religion—& Religion without reference to the
Press.—(By the *Press as a Trade* I wish you to understand, review-
ing, newspaper-writing, and all those things in which I proposed no
fame to myself or permanent good to society—but only to gain
that bread which might empower me to do both the one and the
other on my vacant days.—) I chose the latter—I preferred, as more
innocent in the first place, & more *useful* in the second place, the
ministry as a Trade to the Press as a Trade.—A circumstance arises
—& the necessity ceases for my taking up either—that is—as a
means of providing myself with the necessaries of Life.—Why should
I not adopt it?——But you continue—'and I cannot but rejoice
that he has it in his power to demonstrate this (i.e. the purity of
my motives) to the satisfaction of others.'—It is *possible* then that
some may say, 'while he wanted money, he was willing to preach
the gospel in order to get [it]—when that want ceased, his zeal
departed.'—Let them say it—I shall answer most truly—While I
could not devote my time to the service of Religion without
receiving money from a particular congregation, I subdued the
struggles of reluctance, & would have submitted to receive it—
Now I am enabled—as I have received freely, freely to give.—If
in the course of a few years I shall have appeared neglectful of the
cause of Religion, if by my writings & preachings I shall not have
been endeavouring to propagate it, then & not till then the charge
will affect me.—I have written you as the thoughts came upper-

most—I might say a great deal more. I might talk of Shrewsbury in particular & state particular reasons of attachment to Stowey— but I chose to confine myself to generals.—Anterior to any con- versation Mr Row thought on the whole that I ought to accept the annuity—He desires me to say, that he will leave this place on the Wednesday of next week, for Bristol—I will serve for him as long as he chuses.

Your's most affectionately S. T. Coleridge

P. S. To this add that the annuity is independent of my health, &c &c—the salary dependent not on health but on 20 caprices of 20 people.—

222. *To Josiah Wedgwood*

Address: Josiah Wedgewood, Esq. | Penzance | Cornwall
MS. Wedgwood Museum. Pub. E.L.G. i. 96. Coleridge's letter was written in answer to the following letter from the Wedgwoods, which arrived in Stowey after Coleridge's departure for Shrewsbury. Poole opened it and had a copy prepared and sent to Coleridge.
Stamped: Shrewsbury.

Penzance Jany 10th. 1798.

Dear Sir

In the absence of my Brother who has an engagement this morning, I take up the pen to reply to your letter received yesterday. I cannot help regretting very sincerely that at this critical moment we are separated by so great a length of the worst road in the kingdom. It is not that we have found much difficulty in deciding how to act in the present juncture of your affairs, but we are apprehensive that deprived of the benefit of conversation, we may fail somewhat in explaining our views & intentions with that clearness & persuasion which should induce you to accede to our proposal without scruple or hesitation,—nay, with that glow of pleasure which an accession of merited good fortune & the observation of virtuous conduct in others, ought powerfully to excite in the breast of healthful Sensibility.—Writing is painful to me. I must endeavor to be concise; yet to avoid abruptness. My Brother & myself are possessed of a considerable superfluity of fortune; squandering & hoarding are equally distant from our inclinations. But we are earnestly desirous to convert this superfluity into a fund of beneficence & we have now been accustomed, for some time, to regard ourselves rather as Trustees than Proprietors. We have canvassed your past life, your present situation & prospect; your character & abilities. As far as certainty is com- patible with the delicacy of the estimate, we have no hesitation in declaring that your claim upon the fund appears to come under more of the conditions we have prescribed to ourselves for it's disposal, & to be every way more unobjectionable than we could possibly have expected. This result is so congenial with our heart-felt wishes that it will be a real mortification to us if any misconception or distrust of our intentions, or any unworthy diffidence of yourself, should interfere to prevent it's full operation in your favor.

[Tom Wedgwood.]

(373)

After what my brother Thomas has written I have only to state the proposal we wish to make to you. It is that you shall accept an annuity for life of £150 to be regularly paid by us, no condition whatsoever being annexed to it. Thus your liberty will remain entire, you will be under the influence of no professional bias, & will be in possession of a 'permanent income not inconsistent with your religious & political creeds' so necessary to your health & activity.

I do not now enter into the particulars of the mode of securing the annuity &c. that will be done when we receive your consent to the proposal we are making, and we shall only say now that we mean the annuity to be independent of every thing but the wreck of our fortune, an event which we hope is not very likely to happen, though it must in these times be regarded as more than a bare possibility.

Give me leave now to thank you for the openness with which you have written to me, & the kindness you express for me, to neither of which can I be indifferent, and I shall be happy to derive the advantages from them that a friendly intercourse with you cannot fail to afford me.

> I am very sincerely yours
> Josiah Wedgwood

Shrewsbury   Jan. 17th, 1798

Dear Sir

Yesterday morning I received the letter which you addressed to me in your own and your brother's name. Your benevolence appeared so strange & it came upon my mind with such suddenness, that for a while I sat and mused on it with scarce a reference to myself, and gave you a moral approbation almost wholly unmingled with those personal feelings which have since filled my eyes with tears—which do so even now while I am writing to you. What can I say? I accept your proposal not unagitated but yet, I trust, in the same worthy spirit in which you made it.—. I return to Stowey in a few days. Disembarrassed from all pecuniary anxieties yet unshackled by any regular profession, with powerful motives & no less powerful propensities to honourable effort, it is my duty to indulge the hope that at some future period I shall have given a proof that as your intentions were eminently virtuous, so the action itself was not unbeneficent.

With great affection & esteem | I remain | Your's sincerely
> S. T. Coleridge

223. *To Thomas Poole*

Address: Mr T. Poole | Stowey | near | Bridgewater | Somerset
MS. British Museum. Hitherto unpublished.
Stamped: Shrewsbury.

[17 January 1798]

My best dear Friend

I have written to Josiah Wedgewood by this post, & accepted the offer.—Such benevolence is something so new, that I am not

certain that I am not dreaming: I sit & muse upon it in the abstract, & it seems so strange that I cannot apply it to myself—nor has my heart yet felt any of the swell & glow of personal feelings. —Well—I will receive them on my return by reflection from your's ——I shall or rather I must stay here two Sundays longer; because Mr Row is going to Bristol to seek a House.——Estlin is ardent for my *declining* Wedgewood's offer—he wrote *at* me in a letter to Mr Row, which accompanied your letters—Row read Estlin's letter, and advised me without a moment's hesitation to *accept* the offer. —The people here are dressy & fond of expence—& the women very handsome—the Parsons of the Church of England, many of them, Unitarians & democrats—and the People hot-headed Aristocrats ——this is curious, but it is true.—The Congregation is small, and my reputation had cowed them into vast respectfulness—but one shrewd fellow remarked that he would rather hear me *talk* than *preach.*——
My love to our dear Mother—& to Ward—

Your's most affectionately—
S. T. Coleridge

224. *To Isaac Wood*

Address: Mr. Isaac Wood, | High Street, | Shrewsbury.
Pub. Christian Reformer, *Nov.–Dec. 1834, p. 838.*

Shrewsbury, Jan. 19, 1798

Dear Sir,

'Freely have ye received, freely give,' is a precept in which the practice and spirit of every Christian Minister ought to be moulded. I do not hesitate to affirm it as my opinion, that both Christianity and the preaching of Christianity would exist in a much purer state, if, like St. Paul, we made tents for our bread, and preached the Gospel for conscience' sake. There is a congruity, not wholly fanciful, in purchasing things necessary for the body by the labour of the body, and things necessary for the mind by the labour of the mind. Food, raiment and lodging seem the appropriate remunerations for manual industry; respect, esteem, affection, and the consciousness of doing good for knowledge, or learning, or piety, or disinterested zeal. But, alas! this beautiful order of things, if not rendered impossible by the present state of society, is in most instances incompatible with our present modes of education. I will instance my own case. A scholastic education, continued to the age of twenty-three, made my bodily faculties obtuse and weak in proportion as it had given variety and acuteness to my intellectual powers, and, of course, presented insuperable objections, both of mind and body, to my obtaining sustenance for myself and a family by my labour either in the manufactory or the field. At this time I formed those religious and political opinions which exclude me, I thank God, from the Law and the Church. The profession of Physic remained; but I could not afford the previous expenses, and (to avail myself of a vulgar proverb) 'the horses would have starved while the grass was growing.' There lay before me, then, either *the Press as a trade*, or the *Ministerial Office*. (By *the Press as a trade*, I wish you to understand the writing for newspapers, reviews and magazines—all those literary exertions in which I proposed neither my own reputation nor the permanant good of society, but only as innocently as possible to gain such a salary as might enable me to do both the one and the other on my vacant days.) Perceiving, or appearing to myself to perceive, that some general evils, and some particular discomforts would result from my becoming a salaried minister, I adopted the former. But I soon discovered my mistake. I did not indeed alter my opinion essentially respecting the nature and consequences of hired *preaching*, but I saw more clearly the nature and consequences of hired *writing*. I found it the situation of all others in which a delicacy of moral feeling and moral perception would with the greatest difficulty be preserved. I found that the temptations to do evil were many, and the anxieties and uncertainties of the occupation so great, that they would soon have sapped the very faculties by which alone that occupation could be made profitable to myself, and on which alone can be founded my future utility to my fellow-creatures. I therefore subdued the struggles of reluctance, and with the purest motives possible on such an occasion, I determined to choose the ministry, not as in itself an absolute good, but as far more innocent, far more useful than the other mode of employment; and at that time my choice lay only between these two, and one or the other of them I was under the immediate impulse both of duty and necessity to choose. Still, however, I should have conformed so far to that precept with which I commenced my letter, that I should have regarded the salary I received, not as payment for my particular services to the congregation from whom I received it, but only as the means of enabling myself to pursue a *general* scheme of Christian warfare, of which those particular services would have formed only a part. Within these few days the state of my circumstances has been altered; and with the simple and cottage life to which I have accommodated my habits, I am enabled to defend that cause to which I have solemnly devoted my best efforts, when and how and where it appears best to me; and, as I have received the gospel

freely, freely to give it. Of course I retire from the candidateship
for the ministerial office at Shrewsbury; and have deemed it proper
to inform your society of it, before I placed myself within the
contingency of their election, and antecedently to my being accepted
or rejected. I have an humble trust, that many years will not pass
over my head before I shall have given proof in some way or other
that active zeal for Unitarian Christianity, not indolence or indiffer-
ence, has been the motive of my declining a local and stated settle-
ment as preacher of it. My friends Mr. Howell and Dr. Toulmin are
both in the descent of life, and both at a small distance from me; and
it is my purpose to relieve one or the other every Sunday.—You will
be kind enough to convey this information to the society in the way
you think best. I have developed my motives to you with all the
openness and simplicity of a confidential and private letter; but I
have not the least objection to your communicating it publicly.

As this, my dear Sir, may very probably be the close of our
short-lived correspondence, I cannot conclude it without expressing
my great and unfeigned esteem for you, as sincerely believing you
to be a man whose natural dispositions have made him a *well-
wisher* to his fellow-men, and whose zeal and clearness of intellect
have enabled him to be in no ordinary degree their *benefactor*.—
May God bless you, and

S. T. Coleridge

225. *To William Wordsworth*

Address: W. Wordsworth Esq. | Allfoxden | Stowey, near | Bridgewater |
Somerset.   *Single*
MS. Bristol Central Lib. Pub. Letters, i. 234.
Stamped: Shrewsbury.

Tuesday Morning. Jan. [23,] 1798

My dear Wordsworth

You know, of course, that I have accepted the magnificent
liberality of Josiah & Thomas Wedgewood. I accepted it on the
presumption that I had talents, honesty, & propensities to per-
severant effort. If I have hoped wisely concerning myself, I have
acted justly.[1] But dismissing severer thoughts, believe me, my dear
fellow! that of the pleasant ideas, which accompanied this unex-
pected event, it was not the least pleasant nor did it pass thro' my
mind the last in the procession, that I should at least be able to

---

[1] Wordsworth's comment on Coleridge's good fortune is somewhat unen-
thusiastic: 'No doubt you have heard of the munificence of the Wedgwoods
towards Coleridge. I hope the fruit will be good as the seed is noble.' *Early
Letters*, 188.

trace the spring & early summer of Alfoxden with you; & that
wherever your after residence may be, it is probable that you will
be within the reach of my Tether, lengthened as it now is.——The
country round Shrewsbury is rather tame—My imagination has
cloathed it with all it's summer attributes; but I still can see in
it no possibility beyond that of *Beauty*.—The Society here were
sufficiently eager to have me, as their Minister, and, I think,
would have behaved kindly & respectfully—but I perceive clearly,
that without great courage & perseverance in the use of the mono-
syllable, *No*! I should have been plunged in a very Maelstrom of
visiting—whirled round, and round, and round, never changing
yet always moving.—Visiting with all it's pomps & vanities is the
mania of the place; & many of the congregation are both rich &
expensive.—I met a young man, a Cambridge undergraduate—
talking of plays &c, he told that an acquaintance of his was printing
a translation of one of Kotzebu's Tragedies, entitled, Beniowski[1]
——The name startled me, and upon examination I found that the
story of my 'Siberian Exiles' has been already dramatized.—If
Kotzebu has exhibited no greater genius in it than in his Negro
slaves, I shall consider this as an unlucky circumstance—but the
young man speaks enthusiastically of it's merits. I have just read
the Castle Spectre[2]—& shall bring it home with me.—I will begin
with it's defects, in order that my 'But' may have a charitable
transition.—1. Language—2. Character. 3. Passion. 4. Sentiment.
5. Conduct——1. Of styles some are pleasing, durably and on
reflection—some only in transition—and some are not pleasing
at all—And to this latter class belongs the Castle Spectre. There
are no felicities in the humourous passages; and in the serious ones
it is Schiller Lewis-ized—i.e. a flat, flabby, unimaginative Bombast
oddly sprinkled with colloquialisms. 2.—No character at all. The
author in a postscript lays claim to *novelty* in *one* of his characters—
that of Hassan.—Now Hassan is a negro, who *had* a warm &
benevolent heart; but having been kidnapped from his country &
barbarously used by the Christians, becomes a Misanthrope.—
This is all!!——3. Passion—horror! agonizing pangs of Conscience!
Dreams full of hell, serpents, & skeletons! starts & attempted
murders &c &c &c; but, positively, not *one* line that marks even a
superficial knowlege of human feelings, could I discover. 4. Senti-
ments are moral & humourous. There is a book called the Frisky

[1] *Count Benyowsky; or the Conspiracy of Kamtschatka. A Tragi-comedy.*
Translated from the German by W. Render, 1798.

[2] M. G. Lewis's *Castle Spectre* was produced at Drury Lane in 1797. Cole-
ridge's copy of the play, according to E. H. Coleridge, is dated 20 Jan. 1798.
Cf. *Letters*, i. 236 n.

Songster, at the end of which are two chapters—the first containing *Frisky* Toasts & Sentiments—the second, *Moral* Toasts:—and from these chapters I suspect, that Mr Lewis has stolen all his sentimentality, moral & humourous. A very fat Friar, renowned for Gluttony & Lubricity, furnishes abundance of jokes (all of them abdominal vel si quid infra) Jokes that would have stunk, had they been fresh; and alas! they have the very saeva mephitis of *antiquity* on them.—BUT—5—the Conduct of the Piece is, I think, *good*—except that the first act is *wholly* taken up with explanation & narration.——This Play proves how accurately you conjectured concerning *theatric* merit. The merit of the Castle Spectre consists wholly in it's *situations*. These are all borrowed, and all absolutely *pantomimical*; but they are admirably managed for stage effect. There is not much bustle; but *situations* for ever. The whole plot, machinery, & incident are borrowed—the play is a mere patchwork of plagiarisms—but they are very well worked up, & for stage effect make an excellent *whole*.—There is a pretty little Ballad-song introduced—and Lewis, I think, has great & peculiar excellence in these compositions. The simplicity & naturalness is his own, & not imitated; for it is made to subsist in congruity with a language perfectly modern—the language of his own times, in the same way that the language of the writer of 'Sir Cauline'[1] was the language of *his* times. This, I think, a rare merit: at least, I find, *I* cannot attain this innocent nakedness, except by *assumption* —I resemble the Dutchess of Kingston, who masqueraded in the character of 'Eve before the Fall' in flesh-coloured Silk.——This play struck me with utter hopelessness—it would be [easy] to produce these situations, but not in a play so for[cibly] as to admit the permanent & closest beauties of style, passion & character. To admit pantomimic tricks the plot itself must be pantomimic— Harlequin cannot be had unaccompanied by the Fool.——

I hope to be with you by the middle of next week— I must stay over next Sunday, as Mr Row is obliged to go to Bristol to seek a House. He & his Family are honest, sensible, pleasant people. My kind Love to Dorothy—& believe me | with affectionate esteem |

Your's sincerely
S. T. Coleri[dge]

[1] It was from 'Sir Cauline' that S. T. C. borrowed not only the archaic words found in 'The Ancient Mariner' but also the name 'Christabel', which name, however, occurs only in the stanzas interpolated by Percy. (See *Reliques*.) MS. note by J. D. Campbell.

226. *To Joseph Cottle*

Address: Mr Cottle | Bookseller | High Street | Bristol   by favor of the Revd Mr Rowe
MS. Cornell University Lib. Pub. with omis. Early Rec. i. 307.

[24 January 1798][1]

My very dear Cottle

The moment I received Mr Wedgewood's letter, I accepted his *offer*—how a contrary report could arise, I cannot guess— / —I hope to see you at the close of next week—I have been respectfully & kindly treated at Shrewsbury, & am well, & now & ever

Your grateful & affectionate | Friend
S. T. Coleridge

—Send the inclosed as soon as possible to Mr Wade.—

227. *To Thomas Wedgwood*

MS. Wedgwood Museum. Pub. Tom Wedgwood, *58.*

Shrewsbury
Friday Night—twelve o'clock [26 January 1798]

My dear Sir—I have this moment received your letter—and have scarcely more than a moment to answer it by return of post. If kindly feelings can be repaid by kindly feelings, I am not your debtor— / —I would wish to express the something that is big at my heart, but I know not how to do it without indelicacy. As much abstracted from personal feelings, as is possible, I honor & esteem you for that which you have done—I must, of *necessity*, stay here till the close of Sunday next—On Monday Morning I shall leave it & on Tuesday will be with you at Cote House—

Very affectionately your's
S. T. Coleridge

228. *To Thomas Poole*

Address: Mr T. Poole | Stowey | near | Bridgewater, | Somerset
MS. British Museum. Pub. E.L.G. i. 97.
Stamped: Shrewsbury.

Saturday Morning [27 January 1798]

My dearest Poole

I thank you, heart-wise, for the Joy you have in my joy——. I received a very affectionate letter from Thomas Wedgewood last

[1] In Letter 221 Coleridge said that Mr. Rowe 'will leave this place on the Wednesday of next week, [24 Jan.] for Bristol'. The address shows that Rowe was to deliver this letter to Cottle.

night—& answered it immediately. He desires me to meet him at
Cote House—I shall therefore leave this place on Monday Morning
—& shall, God willing, breakfast with him on Tuesday Morning—on
which day I will write you——The people here absolutely *consume*
me—the Clergymen of the Church are eminently courteous, &
some of them come & hear me. If I had stayed, I have reason to
think that I should have doubled the congregation almost immedi-
ately.——With two sermons to meditate in each week, with many
letters to write, with invitations for dinner, tea, & supper in each
day, & people calling in, & I forced to return morning calls, every
morning, you will not be surprized, tho' you will be vexed to hear,
that I have written nothing for the Morning Post—but I shall
write immediately to the Editor.—

I long to be at home with you, & to settle & persevere in, some
mode of repaying the Wedgewoods thro' the medium of Mankind
——/ I wish to be at home with you indeed, indeed——my Joy is
only in the bud here—I am like that Tree, which fronts me——The
Sun shines bright & warm, as if it were summer—but it is not
summer & so it shines on leafless boughs. The beings who know
how to sympathize with me are my foliage.——

My filial love to your dear Mother | & believe me, my
best dear friend! | ever, ever most affectionately your's
S. T. Coleridge

P.S. My love to Ward, the Coryphaeus of Transcribers & Re-
scribers!! when the evil times come, I will use all my Interest to
save him from the Proscribers.—That joke is like the last drop of
greasy water wrung out of an afternoon dishclout—it came with
difficulty & might as well have stayed behind.——

229. *To the Editor of the 'Monthly Magazine'*

Pub. Monthly Magazine, *January 1798, p. 8.* In September and October 1796
and December 1797 three communications to the editor of the *Monthly Maga-
zine,* signed 'B.', 'Crito', and 'A.B.C.D.', discussed Coleridge's *Monody on the
Death of Chatterton.*

Shrewsbury   [January 1798]
Sir

I hope, that this letter may arrive time enough to answer its
purpose. I cannot help considering myself as having been placed
in a very ridiculous light, by the gentlemen who have remarked,
answered, and rejoined, concerning my monody on Chatterton. I
have not seen the compositions of my competitors,[1] (unless indeed

[1] Crito (*Monthly Magazine,* Oct. 1796) had said: 'There were at least, two

the exquisite poem of Warton's, entitled 'The Suicide' refer to this subject) but this I know, that my own is a very poor one. It was a school exercise, somewhat altered; and it would have been omitted in the last edition of my poems, but for the request of my friend, Mr. Cottle, whose property those poems are. If it be not in your intention to exhibit my name on any future month, you will accept my best thanks, and not publish this letter, but if Crito and the Alphabet-Men should continue to communicate on this subject, and you should think it proper, for reasons best known to yourself, to publish their communications, then I depend on your kindness for the insertion of my letter; by which, it is possible, those your correspondents may be induced to expend their remarks, whether panegyrical or vituperative, on nobler game than on a poem which was, in truth, the first effort of a young man, all whose poems a candid critic will only consider as first efforts.

Your's with due respect,
S. T. Coleridge

230. *To John Thelwall*

Address: Mr Thelwall | Llynswen, [Llyswen] | Brecknockshire | to be left at the three Cocks in the | road to Brecknock—By the Hay Bag.
MS. Pierpont Morgan Lib. Pub. E.L.G. i. 99.
Stamped: Bristol.

Tuesday, Jan. 30th, 1798

My dear Thelwall

Two days after I received your letter—that to which you allude in your last—I returned you an answer, directed J. Thelwall, Derby. In it I informed you of Dr Beddoes' answer to me—'how he had applied to those, whom he had entertained hopes from, without success; but was ready to contribute his own quota'——and that I wrote back to Dr B. ['] that I believed you would probably accomplish your plan by the assistance of your friends; but that if you had occasion for his *individual* assistance, I would inform him as soon as I heard from you.'—And I did not hear from you—and it appears, that you did not receive my letter; for which I am sorry—but I have lately had a letter from me to Mr Wedgewood intercepted, and I suspect the *country* post masters grievously.——

My Wife & Baby are well—and I shall probably kiss my *youngest* boy in April.—As to myself, I received an invitation from Shrews-

monodies written on CHATTERTON, superior to the poem in question.' A.B.C.D. replying to Crito (*Monthly Magazine*, Dec. 1797) supposed that the two poems were written by Warton and Amwell, but he affirmed 'that MR. COLERIDGE, in his monody, eminently excels his competitors'.

bury to be the Unitarian Minister, and at the same time an order for 100£ from Thomas & Josiah Wedgewood—I accepted the former, & returned the latter in a long letter explanatory of my motives—& went off to Shrewsbury, where they were on the point of electing me unanimously & with unusual marks of affection, when I received an offer from T. & J. Wedgewood—of an annuity of 150£ to be legally settled on me.—Astonished, agitated, & feeling as I could not help feeling, I accepted the offer—in the same worthy spirit, I hope, in which it was made—And this morning I have returned from Shrewsbury, & am now writing in Cottle's Shop— / I received your letter this morning, & have lost no time in answering it.—I shall be at Stowey in a few days; from whence I write to you of my plans &c—& likewise concerning you.— Unhusbandize your lips, & give the kiss of *fraternal* love to Stella, for me—

I am hurried off—& can only say that I think of you often—& never without affectionate Esteem—

S. T. Coleridge

231. *To George Coleridge*

Address: Revd G. Coleridge | Ottery St Mary
MS. Lady Cave. Hitherto unpublished.

Stowey near Bridgewater   Feb. 8th [9]¹ 1798

My dear Brother

The interval, since I received your letter, has been crowded with events of great importance to me. On Christmas Day I received a letter from Mr Josiah Wedgewood—of which the following is a copy—(Note. The late Mr Wedgewood had three sons, John, a Banker, who resides at Cote House, a magnificent Seat near Bristol—Josiah, who carries on the Pottery in Staffordshire—and Thomas, a single man, & in no line of business)

Launceston, Decembr. 23, 1797

Dear Sir

My Brother Thomas, & myself had separately determined that it would be right to enable you to defer entering into an engagement, we understand you are about to form from the most urgent of motives. We therefore request, that you will accept the inclosed draft with the same simplicity, with which it is offered to you—

I remain, dear Sir sincerely your's

Josiah Wedgewood.

¹ Coleridge apparently was confused over the date, for in the next letter he tells Estlin, 'I arrived at Stowey, on Friday last, by dinner time', i.e. 9 Feb.

The inclôsed draft was for an 100£——After some hesitation I returned an answer, accepting it—but on the day after I received an invitation from the Unitarian congregation at Shrewsbury to become their minister—and having taken a week maturely to deliberate on the subject, I at last returned the draft to Mr Wedgewood in a letter, of which No. 1. is a copy.[1]—I immediately set off for Shrewsbury—on the eleventh of January—arrived there the 13th—and on the 16th I received from Josiah & Thomas Wedgewood a letter, of which No. 2 is a copy.[2]—I returned an answer, expressing human & manly feelings of gratitude, & accepted the offer.—I of course addressed a letter to the society, declining the office, & explaining my motives—but did not leave Shrewsbury till Monday 29th of Jan.—I received a very complimentary & affectionate letter from the Society, expressing their regret for their own loss, but approving my motives—& they requested that I would publish the six sermons, which I had preached to them—/ which I declined, having preached them extempore, & consequently, not able to appreciate their real merits—

——I stayed a week at Cote House, & have just returned home. Disembarrassed from pecuniary anxieties yet unshackled by any regular profession, with powerful motives, and, I trust, no less powerful propensities to honorable effort, I indulge the hope, that at some future period I shall have given some proof, that as the *intentions* of the Wedgewoods were eminently pure, so the action itself was not unbeneficent.

We received pain from hearing of the sickness which you have had—We hope, it is past, and that you have no other toils than that of the school.—God be praised, both Mrs Coleridge & my child enjoy, & have enjoyed, compleat health.—

As to my Tragedy, the story is briefly this—Last year in the spring Sheridan wrote to me thro' Bowles (the poet) requesting me in very pressing & complimentary language to write a Tragedy —he promised me his assistance in adapting it for the stage, & that he would bring it on with every possible advantage.—I knew the man's character too well, to suffer myself to be inflated by hope— however I set myself in good earnest about it, finished the piece in a much better style than I had supposed myself capable of doing, & transmitted it to Sheridan, in October—From that time to this I have received no answer from him, altho' I have written to him —& the only intelligence, I have received, was from Linley, Sheridan's brother in law, who told me that Sheridan spoke to him in extravagant terms of it's merits.—In all probability, Mrs

[1] See Letter 217.
[2] See headnote to Letter 222 for the Wedgwoods' letter.

Sheridan has made thread-papers with it.—It has not given me
one pang: for some who know Sheridan intimately, had prepared
me to expect it.—

Give my love to Mrs G. Coleridge—& to my Brothers—& my
Duty to my Mother.—I intreat my Brother James's acceptance of
the accompanying prints—I am told, they are great likenesses,
and as he is a musical man, may perhaps be interesting to him.—
They were *payed* to me by a bankrupt bookseller, in commutation
for some money which he owed me——

Your affectionate & grateful Brother,

S. T. Coleridge

232. *To John Prior Estlin*

Address: Revd J. P. Estlin
MS. Bristol Central Lib. Pub. Letters to Estlin, *59.*

Tuesday night—[13 February 1798]

My dear Friend

If you have never been a slave to the superstition of impulses,
you will marvel to hear that I arrived at Stowey, on Friday last,
by dinner time.——I left Mr Wedgewood's on Thursday evening,
just time enough to keep an engagement, I had made, to sup with a
Mr Williams of Nottingham, at the White Lion.—There I slept—
awoke at 5 in the morning, and was *haunted* by a strange notion
that there was something of great importance that demanded my
immediate presence at Stowey. I dressed myself, and walked out
to dissipate the folly—but the Bridgewater Coach rattling by, &
the Coachman asking me if I would get in—I took it for an omen
—the superstitious feeling recurred—and in I went—came home,
& found—my wife & child in very good health!—However, as I
must necessarily be in Bristol, in a few weeks, I the less regret my
strange & abrupt departure.

T. Poole informs me that there is a letter for me at your house—
if so, be so kind as to send it to Mr Cottle's for me.——

T. Wedgewood did not speak a word to me about *the circum-
stance*—only that I should *hear* from him. So I know nothing
relating to myself so far, which you do not know.——

Have you given over the thoughts of editing Butler's analogy[1]
with notes?——If the Unitarian Society would publish it in their
tracts, I would willingly & *immediately* undertake it *with you*—
adding a disquisition on Hume's system of Causation—or rather
of non-causation. This is the pillar, & confessedly, the *sole* pillar,

---

[1] Joseph Butler's *Analogy* first appeared in 1736.

of modern Atheism—if we could clearly & manifestly detect the sophisms of *this* system, I think, that Butler's Analogy *aided* by well-placed notes would answer irresistably all the objections to Christianity founded on a priori reasonings—& these are the only reasonings that infidels use even with plausibility.—I have sent you Payne's Letter to Erskine[1]—it was sent to me privately by the Editor of the Morning Post—for they do not venture to *publish* it. —There are some ludicrous blunders—exemp. gratiâ—This erudite Philosopher mistakes Moses's Autograph for the publication of the Law—& asserts that the *Law* was not known till Hilkiah (Chronicles, Ch. *34.*) *pretended* to have found it—Mr Ireland[2] *pretended* to have found a *copy* of Lear in Shakspere's own hand— ergo—we have proof that the Tragedy was *not* composed by Shakespere, & never heard of till the 37th year of the reign of George the third!— / .—Erudite Logician!—— / There is annexed a Sermon in defence of Deity with one or two good remarks in it— but the *proof* is very idle, & the definition of Deity—i.e. a being whose power is equal to his will—in all probability applies equally to a Maggot. There is however one argument against the *Bible* quite *new*—'I (the said Thomas Payne) could write a better book myself'—& therefore it cannot be the word of God—. Now unless we suppose Mr Payne mistaken (which is hard to suppose on a subject where he must be so impartial a judge, i.e. his own genius) this argument is quite unanswerable!!

I mentioned the unitarian Society, because I propose to myself no pecuniary profit, but could not sustain, on the other hand any pecuniary loss.

My kind love to Mrs Estlin—& believe me | with gratitude, esteem, & fervent affection | ever, ever your's

S. T. Coleridge

233. *To Joseph Cottle*

Address: Mr Cottle
MS. Jesus College Lib., Cambridge. Pub. with omis. E.L.G. i. 100.

Feby 18—1798

My dear Cottle

[I pray you, when you send a parcel, do always write *one* line

---

[1] Paine published his *Letter to Erskine* in June 1797. Erskine was counsel for the prosecution in the case against Thomas Williams, publisher of Paine's *Age of Reason*. To Paine's *Letter* was appended a *Discourse to the Society of Theophilanthropists*, later published as *Atheism Refuted*.

[2] In Dec. 1795 Samuel Ireland published the forgeries of his son, W. H. Ireland, as *Miscellaneous Papers and Legal Instruments under the hand and seal of William Shakespeare, including the tragedy of King Lear, and a small fragment of Hamlet, from the original MSS. in the possession of Samuel Ireland.*

at least—I always must pay like damnation.][1] I have finished my ballad—it is 340 lines.[2] I am going on with the Visions[3]—all together (for I shall print two scenes of my Tragedy, as fragments)[4] I can add 1500 lines— / Now what do you advise?—Shall I add my Tragedy, & so make a second Volume—? or pursue my first intention of inserting the 1500 in the 3rd Edition?[5]—If you should advise a second volume, should you wish—i.e.—find it convenient —to be the purchaser / ? I ask this question, because I wish you to know the true state of my present circumstances— / I have received nothing yet from the Wedgewoods & my money is utterly expended. A friend of mine wanted 5 guineas for a little while, which I borrowed of Poole as for myself—& do not therefore like to apply to him. Mr Estlin has some little money, I believe, in his hands; but I received from him before I went to Shrewsbury 15£—& I believe that this was an *anticipation* of the 5 guinea presents, which my friends would have made me, in March. But (this affair of the Mr Wedgewoods turning out) the money in Mr Estlin's hand must go towards repaying him that sum which he suffered me to anticipate—Meantime I owe Biggs 5£ which lies heavy on my thoughts—And Mrs Fricker has not been payed her last quarter which lies still heavier. As to myself, I can contrive to go on here— but this 10£ I must pay some how, that is, 5£ to Biggs, and 5£ to Mrs Fricker.——This week I purpose to offer myself to the Bridgewater congregation as assistant minister—without any salary, directly or indirectly.—But say not a word of this to any one, unless you see Mr Estlin.——I pray you, if you have not 5£ conveniently to spare, call on Mr Estlin & get it in my name as *borrowed*, & transmit it to Mrs Fricker—for that must be payed.——

God love you | &
S. T. Coleridge

234. *To Thomas Poole*

Address: Mr T. Poole
MS. Victoria University Lib. Pub. with omis. Letters, *i. 18.* This is the fifth and last of the autobiographical letters.

[Endorsed Feby 19th 1798]
From October 1781 to October 1782.

After the death of my father we, of course, changed houses, & I

[1] Passage in brackets inked out in MS.
[2] Coleridge apparently refers again to *The Ancient Mariner*, though that poem when 'finished' in 1798 had 658 lines.
[3] i.e. *The Destiny of Nations.*
[4] Two scenes from *Osorio, The Foster-mother's Tale* and *The Dungeon*, appeared in *Lyrical Ballads*, 1798.
[5] No such '3rd Edition' appeared at this time.

remained with my mother till the spring of 1782, and was a day-scholar to Parson Warren, my Father's successor— / He was a booby, I believe; and I used to delight my poor mother by relating little instances of his deficiency in grammar knowlege—every detraction from his merits seemed an oblation to the memory of my Father, especially as Parson Warren did certainly *pulpitize* much better.—Somewhere, I think, about April 1792, [1782] Judge Buller, who had been educated by my Father, sent for me, having procured a Christ's Hospital Presentation.—I accordingly went to London, and was received by my mother's Brother, Mr Bowden, a Tobacconist & (at the same [time]) clerk to an Underwriter. My Uncle lived at the corner of the Stock exchange, & carried on his shop by means of a confidential Servant, who, I suppose, fleeced him most unmercifully.—He was a widower, & had one daughter who lived with a Miss Cabriere, an old Maid of great sensibilities & a taste for literature——Betsy Bowden had obtained an unlimited influence over her mind, which she still retains—Mrs Holt (for this is her name now) was, when I knew her, an ugly & an artful woman & not the kindest of Daughters—but indeed, my poor Uncle would have wearied the patience & affection of an Euphrasia. —He was generous as the air & a man of very considerable talents —but he was a Sot.—He received me with great affection, and I stayed ten weeks at his house, during which time I went occasionally to Judge Buller's. My Uncle was very proud of me, & used to carry me from Coffee-house to Coffee-house, and Tavern to Tavern, where I drank, & talked & disputed, as if I had been a man— /. Nothing was more common than for a large party to exclaim in my hearing, that I *was a prodigy*, &c &c &c—so that, while I remained at my Uncle's, I was most completely spoilt & pampered, both mind & body. At length the time came, & I donned the *Blue* coat & yellow stockings, & was sent down to Hertford, a town 20 miles from London, where there are about 300 of the younger Blue coat boys—At Hertford I was very happy, on the whole; for I had plenty to eat & drink, & pudding & vegetables almost every day. I stayed there six weeks; and then was drafted up to the great school at London, where I arrived in September, 1792 [1782]—and was placed in the second ward, then called Jefferies's ward; & in the under Grammar School. There are twelve Wards, or dormitories, of unequal sizes, beside the Sick Ward, in the great School—& they contained, all together, 700 boys; of whom I think nearly one third were the Sons of Clergymen. There are 5 Schools, a Mathematical, a Grammar, a drawing, a reading, & a writing School—all very large Buildings.—When a boy is admitted, if he read very badly, he is either sent to Hertford or to the Reading-

School—(N.B. Boys are admissible from 7 to 12 years old)—If he learn to read tolerably well before 9, he is drafted into the lower Grammar-school—if not, into the writing-school, as having given proof of unfitness for classical attainment.—If before he is eleven he climbs up to the first form of the lower Grammar-school, he is drafted into the head Grammar School—if not, at 11 years old he is sent into the writing School, where he continues till 14 or 15—and is then either apprenticed, & articled as clerk, or whatever else his turn of mind, or of fortune shall have provided for him. Two or three times a year the Mathematical Master beats up for recruits for the King's boys, as they are called—and all, who like the navy, are drafted into the Mathematical & Drawing Schools—where they continue till 16 or 17, & go out as Midshipmen & Schoolmasters in the Navy.—The Boys, who are drafted into the head Grammar School, remain there till 13—& then if not chosen for the university, go into the writing school. Each dormitory has a Nurse, or Matron—& there is a head Matron to superintend all these Nurses. —The boys were, when I was admitted, under excessive subordination to each other, according to rank in School—& every ward was governed by four Monitors, (appointed by the *Steward*, who was the supreme Governor out of School—our Temporal Lord) and by four *Markers*, who wore silver medals, & were appointed by the head Grammar Master, who was our supreme Spiritual Lord. The same boys were commonly both Monitors & Markers— We read in classes on Sundays to our *Markers*, & were catechized by them, & under their sole authority during prayers, &c—all other authority was in the monitors; but, as I said, the same boys were ordinarily both the one & the other.—Our diet was very scanty—Every morning a bit of dry bread & some bad small beer —every evening a larger piece of bread, & cheese or butter, whichever we liked—For dinner—on Sunday, boiled beef & broth— Monday, Bread & butter, & milk & water—on Tuesday, roast mutton, Wednesday, bread & butter & rice milk, Thurday, boiled beef & broth—Friday, boiled mutton & broth—Saturday, bread & butter, & pease porritch—Our food was portioned—& excepting on Wednesdays I never had a belly full. Our appetites were *damped* never satisfied—and we had no vegetables.—

S. T. Coleridge

235. *To Joseph Cottle*

Address: Mr Cottle | Bookseller | *Bristol*
MS. Mr. W. L. Lewis. Pub. with omis. Letters, *i. 238.*
Stamped: Bridgewater.

Stowey, Wednesday Morning. [7 March 1798]

My dear Cottle

I have been confined to my bed for some days thro' a fever occasioned by the stump of a tooth which baffled chirurgical efforts to eject it; & which by affecting my eye affected my stomach, & thro' that my whole frame. I am better—but still weak in consequence of such long sleeplessness & wearying pains—weak, very weak.—I thank you, my dear Friend! for your late kindness—and in a few weeks will either repay you in money or by verses, as you like.—With regard to Lloyd's verses, it is curious that *I* should be applied to—to be 'PERSUADED to RESIGN,['] and in ho[pe] that I might 'CONSENT to GIVE UP' a number of poem[s] which were published at the earnest request of the author[, who] assured me that the circumstance was 'of no trivial import to his happiness.'
——Times change, & people change; but let us keep our souls in quietness!——I have no objection to any disposal of C. Lloyd's poems except that of their being republished with mine.[1] The motto, which I had prefixed 'Duplex &c' from Groscollius[2] has placed me in a ridiculous situation[3]—but it was a foolish & presumptuous start of affectionateness, and I am not unwilling to incur punish-

---

[1] Southey certainly, and possibly Lamb took umbrage at the Nehemiah Higginbottom sonnets, and it is difficult to suppose that Lloyd was not deeply wounded by Coleridge's ill-timed burlesque. When he learned of the plan to issue a new edition of the poems of Coleridge, Lamb, and Lloyd, he asked that his own poems be omitted; he and Lamb, too, planned a collaborative venture, which appeared during 1798 as *Blank Verse, by Charles Lamb and Charles Lloyd*. This letter shows that Coleridge was hurt by Lloyd's action, probably more deeply than he cared to reveal to Cottle.

[2] In the manuscript Cottle twice underlined the word 'Groscollius' and wrote '(fictitious)' above it.

[3] The motto for the 1797 edition of the *Poems* of Coleridge, Lamb, and Lloyd was: 'Duplex nobis vinculum, et amicitiae et similium junctarumque Camoenarum; quod utinam neque mors solvat, neque temporis longinquitas! *Groscoll. Epist. ad Car. Utenhov. et Ptol. Lux. Tast.*' When Cottle asked concerning the meaning of the motto, Coleridge replied: 'It was all a hoax. Not meeting with a suitable motto, I invented one, and with references purposely obscure.' (*Rem.* 164.) Groscollius, Carolus Utenhovius, and Ptolomoeus Luxius Tastaeus were scholar friends of the Scottish poet and historian George Buchanan (1506–82). In the light of the separate publication in 1798 of Lamb's and Lloyd's poems Coleridge's motto indeed loses its significance: 'We have a double bond: that of friendship and of our linked and kindred Muses: may neither death nor length of time dissolve it.'

ments due to my folly.—By past experiences we build up our moral being.——How comes it that I have never heard from dear Mr Estlin, my fatherly & brotherly friend? This idea haunted me during my sleepless nights, till my sides were sore in turning from one to the other, as if I were hoping to turn away from the idea. —The Giant Wordsworth—God love him!—even when I speak in the terms of admiration due to his intellect, I fear lest tho[se] terms should keep out of sight the amiableness of his manners——he has written near 1200 lines of a blank verse, superior, I hesitate not to aver, to any thing in our language which any way resembles it.[1] Poole (whom I feel so consolidated with myself that I seem to have no occasion to speak of him out of myself) thinks of it as likely to benefit mankind much more than any thing, Wordsworth has yet written.——With regard to my poems I shall prefix the Maid of Orleans, 1000 lines—& three blank verse poems, making all three, about 200—/ and I shall utterly leave out perhaps a larger quantity of lines: & I should think, it would answer to you in a pecuniary way to print the third Edition *humbly* & cheaply. My alterations in the Religious Musings will be considerable, & will lengthen the poem.——Oh! Poole desires you *not* to mention his house to any one unless you hear from him again; as since I have been writing a thought has struck us of letting it to an inhabitant of the village— which we should prefer, as we should be certain that his manners would be severe, inasmuch as he would be a Stow-ic.

God bless you & S. T. C.

236. *To the Editor of the 'Morning Post'*

Pub. Morning Post, *10 March 1798.*

[Early March 1798]
Sir, I am not absolutely certain that the following Poem[2] was written by EDMUND SPENSER, and found by an angler buried in a fishing-box—

'Under the foot of Mole, that mountain hoar,
''Mid the green alders, by the Mulla's shore.'

But a learned Antiquarian of my acquaintance has given it as his opinion, that it resembles SPENSER's minor Poems as nearly as *Vortigern and Rowena*[3] the Tragedies of WILLIAM SHAKESPEARE.—

[1] Wordsworth's long projected but never completed *Recluse*. See *Early Letters*, 188, 190.
[2] *The Raven, Poems*, i. 169.
[3] W. H. Ireland's pseudo-Shakespearian play.

The Poem must be read in *recitative*, in the same manner as the Aegloga Secunda of the Shepherd's Calendar.

Cuddy.

237. *To John Wicksteed*

Address: John Wicksteed | Wem near | Shrewsbury
Transcript British Museum. Pub. E.L.G. i. 101.

March 9th 1798

I will relate to you Sir! with simplicity all of my conversation respecting Mr Arthur Aikin,[1] which I can recollect. You may, I think, rely on the *substance*; but I do not pledge myself for the identical words. Indeed, when I hear a man pretending to minute accuracy in the retailing of conversations, I am in the habit of suspecting that he is deceiving himself. I at least, who at Shrewsbury talked much on many subjects, should find it impossible; especially as the circumstance, on which you have written, made no very deep impression on my mind.——I was supping at Mr Hart's —: to the best of my present recollection, I did not then know that Mr Arthur Aikin had ever been a Minister in any place, still less of his particular connection with the Town of Shrewsbury—Some one (I forget who) asked me, what I thought of Mr Arthur Aikin? I answered, that I had never seen either him or any of his works; but that from what I had heard from a literary Man in London I concluded that he was a booby—a booby, I think, I said—if not that, it was some phrase equally indefensible. By the warmth, which I had excited, I perceived gradually the morass, into which I had been walking; and retraced my steps as well as I could. But 'As well as we can' is, you know, awkward enough on such occasions; and this awkwardness & confusion are too light a punishment for the folly & presumption which places us there. A few minutes after, a Lady present spoke of a friend of mine, Mr Estlin, with considerable asperity, upon almost as slight grounds as I had before spoken of Mr Arthur Aikin. I defended my friend; and then animadverting on my own rashness with sufficient severity concluded by moralizing on the silliness & cruelty of pronouncing harsh opinions of men with whom we are slightly or not at all acquainted. The next morning, or the morning after, I met the younger Miss Hart; & again apologized to her for my words, and my apology consisted wholly in self-condemnation—This is all I remember; but whatever I said, I must have said *professedly* from hearsay—and as to bad-

---

[1] Arthur Aikin (1773–1854), nephew of Mrs. Barbauld and a scientific writer, was trained for the Unitarian ministry, but apparently never took a pulpit.

ness of heart or moral character in any way, I never spoke or even thought of it—However, whatever else I said, 'si quid dixissem contra spiritum caritatis universae, id indictum volo.' I had received a letter from a friend in London in which he wrote—'George Dyer is going into Scotland with that booby, Arthur Aikin'—and another acquaintance once told me, that he had met young Aikin occasionally at Edingburgh; that he was ['] a sullen cold blooded fellow; but very acute.'—These were the only ideas that I could in any way have connected with his name; & I accuse myself of an obtuseness in my moral associations in not making his relationship to that great and excellent woman Mrs Barbauld counteract the unkindly feeling, which the foolish and contradictory tittle-tattle of my two acquaintances had produced in my mind to his disfavor. But regret is a waste of our faculties—from the past experiences we constitute the present moral existence.——

Pardon me, if I read without believing your account of the infra-human folly of 'numbers of the good people of Shrewsbury' in their feelings of admiration towards me—It must have been exaggerated to you by a glass that has magnified to monstruosity.—I am sure that I discovered enough good sense in them with whom I conversed, and who alone could retail my conversation, to justify me in pronouncing it impossible. But if the fact should ever approximate to your statement of it, I assure you it would be neither 'amusing' to me or 'ludicrous'—The errors of my fellow-creatures ordinarily incline me to reflectiveness; or if my meditations be imbued with any passion, it is with that of sorrow—it would be especially so with reference to persons, whom my good wishes and grateful thoughts will always follow, wherever I may be.—

You have written Sir! with warmth, and I am neither surprised nor offended by it; no, nor by the imperious tone, to which the supposed injury your friend had received from my rashness, seems to entitle you, and which you have accordingly assumed. But ordinarily it is a great waste of time, intellect & feeling to be hunting old conversations about characters any way known—we had better be discussing the opinions which have made such characters known. Among whom, but the very foolish, can a Man's character be injured by a vague assertion or an unproved story?—and to be injured among the foolish is, for aught I know, an advantage—it preserves you from their *praise*.—Besides the nature of the human memory is such that no man can at all times accurately keep distinct two sentences spoken near about the same time, even tho' they should have had different references, or distinguish himself between what he said and what at the same time he said it, he had *in his thoughts* to say likewise—or, but I should exhaust a much

larger space of paper than remains to me and your patience to boot,
if I went on to enumerate the various causes of that very evident
fact, that the persons of veracity, who endeavour to repeat a
conversation, will each repeat it a different way. People in general
are not sufficiently aware how often the imagination creeps in and
counterfeits the memory—perhaps to a certain degree it does
always blend with our supposed recollections—You will excuse these
desultory remarks or attribute them to my old vice of preaching—
although preaching is *not* my trade nor 'reverend' a prefix to my
name which I voluntarily admit—I have answered your letter by
the return of post—

farewell   S. T. Coleridge—

P.S. On looking for your address I perceive it is Wem. I have
therefore opened my letter to beg that you will tell young Mr
Haseloed [Hazlitt] that I remember him with respect due to his
talents and that the wish which I expressed of seeing him at
Stowey still lives within me—

238. To George Coleridge

Address: Revd G. Coleridge | Ottery St Mary | Devon
MS. Coleridge Cottage, Nether Stowey. Pub. with omis. Letters, *i. 239.*
Stamped: Bridgewater.

[Circa 10 March 1798][1]

My dear Brother

An illness, which confined me to my bed, prevented me from
returning an immediate answer to your kind & interesting Letter.
My indisposition originated in the stump of a tooth over which
some matter had formed: this affected my eye, my eye my stomach,
my stomach my head; and the consequence was a general fever—
and the sum of pain was considerably increased by the vain
attempts of our Surgeon to extract the offending stump. Laudanum
gave me repose, not sleep: but YOU, I believe, know how divine
that respose is—what a spot of inchantment, a green spot of
fountains, & flowers & trees, in the very heart of a waste of Sands![2]
—God be praised, the matter has been absorbed; and I am now

---

[1] This letter clearly follows Letter 235 (7 Mar.), since Coleridge is now
recovering from his illness, and closely parallels Letter 240, in which the same
recovery is mentioned. It seems to precede Letter 240, since there Mrs. Cole-
ridge's confinement is spoken of as 'within a month', while here as 'within
5 or 6 weeks'. It was probably written during the Alfoxden visit of 9–18 Mar.,
as was Letter 240. See *Journals of Dorothy Wordsworth*, ed. by E. de Selincourt,
2 vols., 1952, i. 11, 14. It is worth noting that Berkeley Coleridge was not born
until 14 May.   [2] Cf. *Kubla Khan.*

recovering a pace, and enjoy that *newness* of sensation from the fields, the air, & the Sun, which makes convalescence almost repay one for disease.——I collect from your letter, that our opinions and feelings on political subjects are more nearly alike, than you imagine them to be. Equally with you (& perhaps with a deeper conviction, for my belief is founded on actual experience) equally with you I deprecate the moral & intellectual habits of those men both in England & France, who have modestly assumed to themselves the exclusive title of Philosophers & Friends of Freedom. I think them at least *as* distant from greatness as from goodness. If I know my own opinions, they are utterly untainted with French Metaphysics, French Politics, French Ethics, & French Theology.—As to THE RULERS of France, I see in their views, speeches, & actions nothing that distinguishes them to their advantage from other animals of the same species. History has taught me, that RULERS are much the same in all ages & under all forms of government: they are as bad as they dare to be. The Vanity of Ruin & the curse of Blindness have clung to them, like an hereditary Leprosy. Of the French Revolution I can give my thoughts the most adequately in the words of Scripture—'A great & strong wind rent the mountains & brake in pieces the rocks *before* the Lord; but the Lord was not in the wind; and after the wind an earthquake; but the Lord was not in the earthquake: and after the earthquake a Fire—& the Lord was not in the fire:' and now (believing that no calamities are permitted but as the means of Good) I wrap my face in my mantle & wait with a subdued & patient thought, expecting to hear 'the still small Voice,'[1] which is of God.—In America (I have received my information from unquestionable authority) the morals & domestic habits of the people are daily deteriorating: & one good consequence which I expect from revolutions, is that Individuals will see the necessity of individual effort; that they will act as kind neighbours & good Christians, rather than as citizens & electors; and so by degrees will purge off that error, which to me appears as wild & more pernicious than the παγχρυσοῦν and panacaèa of the old Alchemists—the error of attributing to Governments a talismanic influence over our virtues & our happiness—as if Governments were not rather effects than causes. It is true, that all effects react & become causes—& so it must be in some degree with governments—but there are other agents which act more powerfully because by a nigher & more continuous agency, and it remains true that Governments are more the *effect* than the *cause* of that which we are.—Do not therefore, my Brother! consider me as an enemy to Governments & Rulers: or as one who say[s] that they

[1] 1 Kings xix. 11–13.

are evil. I do not say so—in my opinion it were a species of blasphemy. Shall a nation of Drunkards presume to babble against sickness & the head-ach?—I regard Governments as I regard the abscesses produced by certain fevers—they are necessary consequences of the disease, & by their pain they increase the disease; but yet they are in the wisdom & goodness of Nature; & not only are they physically necessary as effects, but also as causes they are *morally* necessary in order to prevent the utter dissolution of the patient. But what should we think of the man who expected an absolute *cure* from an ulcer that only prevented his dying?—— Of GUILT I say nothing; but I believe most stedfastly in original Sin; that from our mothers' wombs our understandings are darkened; and even where our understandings are in the Light, that our organization is depraved, & our volitions imperfect; and we sometimes see the good without *wishing* to attain it, and oftener *wish* it without the energy that wills & performs—And for this inherent depravity, I believe, that the *Spirit* of the Gospel is the sole cure—but permit me to add, that I look for the *spirit* of the Gospel 'neither in the mountain, nor at Jerusalem'——.

You think, my Brother! that there can be but two *parties* at present, for the Government & against the Government.—It may be so—I am of no party. It is true, I think the present ministry weak & perhaps unprincipled men; but I could not with a safe conscience vote for their removal; for I could point out no substitutes. I think very seldom on the subject; but as far as I have thought, I am inclined to consider the Aristocrats as the more respectable of our three factions, because they are more decorous. The Opposition & the Democrats are not only vicious—they wear the *filthy garments* of vice.

> He that takes
> Deep in his soft credulity the stamp
> Design'd by loud Declaimers on the part
> Of Liberty, themselves the slaves of Lust,
> Incurs derision for his easy faith
> And lack of Knowlege—& with cause enough.
> For when was public Virtue to be found
> Where private was not? Can he love the whole
> Who loves no part? He be a *nation's* friend
> Who is, in truth, the friend of no man there?
> Can he be strenuous in his country's cause
> Who slights the charities, for whose dear sake
> That country, if at all, must be belov'd?

Cowper.[1]—

[1] *The Task*, v. 496–508.

I am prepared to suffer without discontent the consequences of my follies & mistakes—: and unable to conceive how that which I am, of Good could have been without that which I have been of Evil, it is withheld from me to regret any thing: I therefore consent to be deemed a Democrat & a Seditionist. A man's character follows him long after he has ceased to deserve it—but I have snapped my squeaking baby-trumpet of Sedition & the fragments lie scattered in the lumber-room of Penitence. I wish to be a good man & a Christian—but I am no Whig, no Reformist, no Republican—and because of the multitude of these fiery & undisciplined spirits that lie in wait against the public Quiet under these titles, because of them I chiefly accuse the present ministers —to whose folly I attribute, in great measure, their increased & increasing numbers.—You think differently: and if I were called on by you to prove my assertions, altho' I imagine I could make them appear plausible, yet I should feel the insufficiency of my data. The Ministers may have had in their possession facts which may alter the whole state of the argument, and make my syllogisms fall as flat as a baby's card-house—And feeling this, my Brother! I have for some time past withdrawn myself almost totally from the consideration of *immediate* causes, which are infinitely complex & uncertain, to muse on fundamental & general causes—the 'causae causarum.'—I devote myself to such works as encroach not on the antisocial passions—in poetry, to elevate the imagination & set the affections in right tune by the beauty of the inanimate impregnated, as with a living soul, by the presence of Life—in prose, to the seeking with patience & a slow, very slow mind 'Quid sumus, et quidnam victuri gignimur[']—What our faculties are & what they are capable of becoming.—I love fields & woods & mounta[ins] with almost a visionary fondness—and because I have found benevolence & quietness growing within me as that fondness [has] increased, therefore I should wish to be the means of implanting it in others—& to destroy the bad passions not by combating them, but by keeping them in inaction.

> Not useless do I deem
> These shadowy Sympathies with things that hold
> An inarticulate Language: for the Man
> Once taught to love such objects, as excite
> No morbid passions, no disquietude,
> No vengeance & no hatred, needs must feel
> The Joy of that pure principle of Love
> So deeply, that, unsatisfied with aught
> Less pure & exquisite, he cannot chuse
> But seek for objects of a kindred Love

In fellow-natures, & a kindred Joy.
Accordingly, he by degrees perceives
His feelings of aversion softened down,
A holy tenderness pervade his frame!
His sanity of reason not impair'd,
Say rather that his thoughts now flowing clear
From a clear fountain flowing, he looks round—
He seeks for Good & finds the Good he seeks.

                                    Wordsworth.[1]—

I have layed down for myself two maxims—and what is more I am in the habit of regulating myself by them—With regard to others, I never controvert opinions except after some intimacy & when alone with the person, and at the happy time when we both seem awake to our own fallibility—and then I rather state *my* reasons than argue against his.—In general conversation & general company I endeavor to find out the opinions common to us—or at least the subjects on which difference of opinion creates no uneasiness—such as novels, poetry, natural scenery, local anecdotes & (in a serious mood and with serious men) the general evidences of our Religion.——With regard to myself, it is my habit, on whatever subject I think, to endeavour to discover all the good that has resulted from it, that does result, or that can result—to this I bind down my mind and after long meditation in this tract, slowly & gradually make up my opinions on the quantity & the nature of the Evil.—I consider this as a most important rule for the regulation of the intellect & the affections—as the only means of preventing the passions from turning the Reason into an hired Advocate.——I thank you for your kindness—& purpose in a short time to walk down to you[2]—but my Wife must forego the thought, as she is within 5 or 6 weeks of lying-in.—She & my child (whose name is David Hartley) are remarkably well.——You will give my duty to my Mother—& my love to my Brothers, to Mrs J. & G. Coleridge—. Excuse my desultory style & illegible scrawl: for I have written you a long letter, you see—& am, in truth, too weary to write a fair copy, or re-arrange my ideas—and I am anxious that you should know me as I am——

                    God bless you | & your affectionate Brother
                                                S. T. Coleridge

---

[1] These lines originally formed part of the conclusion to *The Ruined Cottage*. See *Poetical Works of William Wordsworth*, ed. by E. de Selincourt and Helen Darbishire, 5 vols., 1940–9, v. 400–1.

[2] Coleridge paid a brief visit to Ottery St. Mary in April, and by the 18th had returned to Stowey. See *Journals of Dorothy Wordsworth*, i. 15, and G. M. Harper, *William Wordsworth*, 2 vols., 1923, i. 342.

239. *To Joseph Cottle*

[Addressed by Dorothy Wordsworth] Mr Cottle | Bookseller | High Street | Bristol
MS. Mr. A. G. B. Randle. Pub. with omis. Early Rec. *i. 297.*
Stamped: Bridgewater.

[*Circa* 13 March 1798][1]

My dear Cottle

I regret that aught should have happened to have disturbed our tranquillity respecting Lloyd—I am willing to believe myself *in part* mistaken—& so let all things be as before.—I have no wish respecting those poems, either for or against their republication with mine.—As to the third Edition, if there be occasion for it *immediately*, it must be published with some alterations but no additions or omissions.—The Pixies, Chatterton, and some dozen others shall be printed at the end of the volume under the title of Juvenile Poems——& in this case I will send you the volume immediately.—But if there be no occasion for the volume to go to the press for ten weeks, at the expiration of that time I would make it a volume worthy of me, and omit utterly near one half of the present volume—a sacrifice to pitch-black Oblivion.—Whichever be the case, I will repay you the money you have payed for me *in money*—& in a few weeks—as if you should prefer the latter proposal (i.e. the not sending me to the press for 10 weeks) I should *insist* on considering the additions however large as mere *payment* to you for the omissions—which indeed would be but strict justice.——

I am requested by Wordsworth to put the following questions— What *could* you conveniently & *prudently*, and what *would* you, give for

[1] On the manuscript of Coleridge's letter Dorothy Wordsworth wrote the following undated note:
Dear Cottle,
    We have sent you the Malvern hill[s] by the Bristol coach from Bridgewater —The great Coat and the waistcoat we shall send by Milton next Week. Mr and Mrs Coleridge have been here a few days—I wish you were of the party. Wm. begs his best love—God bless you Dear Cottle
                                        Yours most truly
                                            Dorothy Wordsworth
We have received the books for which we are much obliged to you. They have already completely answered the purpose for which William wrote for them. He will either send them at the time appointed, or, as they are Pinney's, write to him & explain—Remember me kindly to your Mother & sisters.
Since the Coleridges were at Alfoxden from 9 Mar. to 18 Mar., and since Dorothy Wordsworth says they 'have been here a few days', this letter must have been written during their visit.

1   Our two Tragedies—with small prefaces containing an analysis of our principal characters. Exclusive of the prefaces, the Tragedies are together 5000 lines—which *in the printing* from the dialogue form & directions respecting actors & scenery is at least equal to 6000.—To be delivered to you within a week of the date of your answer to this letter—& the money, which you offer, to be payed to us at the end of four months from the same date—none to be payed before—all to be payed then.—

2   Wordsworth's Salisbury Plain & Tale of a Woman which two poems with a few others which he will add & the notes will make a volume [of . . . pages.—][1] This to be delivered to you within 3 weeks of the date of your answer—& the money to be payed, as before, at the end of four months from the same date.—

Do not, my dearest Cottle! harrass yourself about the imagined great merit of the compositions—or be reluctant to offer what you can *prudently* offer, from an idea that the poems are worth more— / But calculate what you *can* do with reference, simply to yourself—& answer as speedily as you can—and believe me your sincere, grateful, & affectionate Friend & Brother

S. T. Coleridge

N.B. The Tragedies to be published in one volume.—

240. *To Joseph Cottle*

Address: Mr Cottle | Bookseller | High Street | Bristol
MS. Mr. A. G. B. Randle. Pub. with omis. Early Rec. i. 300.
Stamped: Bridgewater.

[*Circa* 17 March 1798][2]

My dear Cottle

I never involved *you* in the bickering—and never suspected you, in any one action of your life [(except that of '*our poems*')][3] of practising any guile against any human being except yourself—Your letter supplied only one in a Link of circumstances that informed me of some things & perhaps deceived me in others[4]——I shall write to day to Lloyd.——

---

[1] Words in brackets inked out in manuscript.

[2] This letter was written towards the end of the Alfoxden visit of 9–18 Mar. The allusion to 'the Tragedies' places it shortly after Letter 239; the reference to the lectures in Bristol and the remarks concerning Mrs. Coleridge's physician parallel comments in Letter 241.

[3] Passage in brackets inked out in manuscript.

[4] From this and the preceding letter it would seem that Cottle was also involved in Coleridge's misunderstanding with Lloyd and Lamb, an inference perhaps borne out by Lamb in dedicating his Works to Coleridge in 1818: 'My friend Lloyd and myself came into our first battle (authorship is a sort of

You will be so kind as not to communicate the contents of my last letter, concerning the Tragedies &c, to any one.——There is no occasion.——I do not think, I shall come to Bristol for these lectures[1]——I ardently wish for the knowlege—but Mrs Coleridge is within a month of her time—and I cannot, I ought not to leave her—especially, as her Surgeon is not a John Hunter, nor our house likely to perish from a plethora of comforts. Besides, there are other things that might disturb that evenness of benevolent feeling which I wish to cultivate. I am much better—& at present, at Allfoxden—and my new & tender health is all over me like a voluptuous feeling.—

God bless you—I do not much like to make you pay the postage for this scrawl; but you requested it—

S. T. Coleridge

241. *To Josiah Wade*

Pub. Early Rec. *i. 296.*

March 21st, 1798

My very dear friend,

I have even now returned from a little excursion[2] that I have taken for the confirmation of my health, which had suffered a rude assault from the anguish of a stump of a tooth which had baffled the attempts of our surgeon here, and which confined me to my bed. I suffered much from the disease, and more from the doctor; rather than again put my mouth into his hands, I would put my hands in a lion's mouth. I am happy to hear of, and should be most happy to see, the plumpness and progression of your dear boy; but—yes, my dear Wade, it must be a but, much as I hate the word but. Well,—but I cannot attend the chemical lectures. I have many reasons, but the greatest, or at least the most ostensible reason, is, that I cannot leave Mrs. C. at that time; our house is an uncomfortable one; our surgeon may be, for aught I know, a lineal descendant of Esculapius himself, but if so, in the repeated trans-

---

warfare) under cover of the greater Ajax. How this association . . . came to be broken,—who snapped the threefold cord,—whether yourself (but I know that was not the case) grew ashamed of your former companions,—or whether (which is by much the more probable) some ungracious bookseller was author of the separation,—I cannot tell.'

[1] Dr. Thomas Beddoes 'opened his course [of Chemical Lectures] early in the spring of 1798'. J. E. Stock, *Memoirs of the Life of Thomas Beddoes*, 1811, p. 145.

[2] The 'little excursion' must have been, as Chambers suggests, the visit to Alfoxden of 9–18 Mar. (*Life*, 101).

fusion of life from father to son, through so many generations, the wit and knowledge, being subtle spirits, have evaporated. . . .
Ever your grateful and affectionate friend,
S. T. Coleridge

242. *To Joseph Cottle*

Pub. Early Rec. *i. 311.*

[Early April 1798][1]

My dear Cottle,

Neither Wordsworth nor myself could have been otherwise than uncomfortable, if any but yourself had received from us the first offer of our Tragedies, and of the volume of Wordsworth's Poems. At the same time, we did not expect that you could with prudence and propriety, advance such a sum, as we should want at the time we specified. In short, we both regard the publication of our Tragedies as an evil. It is not impossible but that in happier times, they may be brought on the stage: and to throw away this chance for a mere trifle, would be to make the present moment act fraudulently and usuriously towards the future time.

My Tragedy employed and strained all my thoughts and faculties for six or seven months: Wordsworth consumed far more time, and far more thought, and far more genius. We consider the publication of them an evil on any terms; but our thoughts were bent on a plan for the accomplishment of which, a certain sum of money was necessary, (the whole) at that particular time, and in order to this we resolved, although reluctantly, to part with our Tragedies: that is, if we could obtain thirty guineas for each, and at less than thirty guineas Wordsworth will not part with the copy-right of his volume of Poems. We shall offer the Tragedies to no one, for we have determined to procure the money some other way. If you choose the volume of Poems, at the price mentioned, to be paid at the time specified, i.e. thirty guineas, to be paid sometime in the last fortnight of July, you may have them; but remember, my dear fellow! I write to you now merely as a bookseller, and intreat you, in your answer, to consider yourself only; as to us, although money is necessary to our plan, [that of visiting Germany][2] yet the plan

[1] This letter follows Letters 239 and 240, since Wordsworth and Coleridge have now abandoned their plan to publish their Tragedies. On 12 Apr. Wordsworth wrote to Cottle inviting him to visit Alfoxden, and Coleridge's letter seems to have been written early in the same month. The clause, 'if thou comest in May', suggests that this letter belongs to April.

[2] This seems to be Cottle's interpolation. Wordsworth wrote to James Losh on 11 Mar. of the proposed visit to Germany (*Early Letters*, 189), but there is no evidence that either he or Coleridge had mentioned it to Cottle.

is not necessary to our happiness; and if it were, W. would sell his Poems for that sum to some one else, or we could procure the money without selling the poems. So I entreat you, again and again, in your answer, which must be immediate, consider yourself only.

Wordsworth has been caballed against *so long and so loudly*, that he has found it impossible to prevail on the tenant of the Allfoxden estate, to let him the house, after their first agreement is expired, so he must quit it at Midsummer; whether we shall be able to procure him a house and furniture near Stowey, we know not, and yet we must: for the hills, and the woods, and the streams, and the sea, and the shores would break forth into reproaches against us, if we did not strain every nerve, to keep their Poet among them. Without joking, and in serious sadness, Poole and I cannot endure to think of losing him.

At all events, come down, Cottle, as soon as you can, but before Midsummer, and we will procure a horse easy as thy own soul, and we will go on a roam to Linton and Linmouth, which, if thou comest in May, will be in all their pride of woods and waterfalls, not to speak of its august cliffs, and the green ocean, and the vast valley of stones, all which live disdainful of the seasons, or accept new honours only from the winter's snow. At all events come down, and cease not to believe me much and affectionately your friend,

S. T. Coleridge

243. *To Charles Lamb*

Transcript Dorothy Wordsworth, in Lord Latymer's possession. Pub. with omis. Letters, i. 249. The transcript contains four slight additions in Coleridge's handwriting. Because there had been so much misunderstanding through Lloyd's tattling and Southey's animosity, Coleridge took the precaution of preserving a copy of his letter.

[Early May 1798][1]

Dear Lamb

Lloyd has informed me through Miss Wordsworth[2] that you

[1] This letter belongs to early May 1798, since Coleridge refers to *Edmund Oliver*, published in April, and since Wordsworth, in a letter dated 9 May, tells Cottle he has received 'Charles Lloyd's works', but has not read the novel, though Dorothy has done so (*Later Years*, iii. 1339–40). A letter from Lloyd to Southey, misdated 4 Apr. 1797, the year certainly being 1798 and the month and day possibly being in error as well, may refer to this letter of Coleridge's: 'Coleridge has written a very odd letter to Lamb. I don't know what may be his sentiments with regard to our conduct, but I can perceive that he is bent on dissociating himself from us—particularly Lamb I think he has used unkindly' (*Lamb Letters*, i. 104 n.).

[2] Reverting to the events of this spring in a notebook entry dated 3 Nov. 1810, Coleridge showed how Lloyd's gossip had involved Dorothy Wordsworth:

intend no longer to correspond with me. This has given me little
pain; not that I do not love and esteem you, but on the contrary
because I am confident that your intentions are pure. You are
performing what you deem a duty, & humanly speaking have that
merit which can be derived from the performance of a painful
duty.—Painful, for you could not without some struggles abandon
me in behalf of a man who wholly ignorant of all but your name
became attached to you in consequence of my attachment, caught
his from *my* enthusiasm, & learnt to love you at my fire-side, when
often while I have been sitting & talking of your sorrows & affec-
tions [afflictions], I have stopped my conversations & lifted up wet
eyes & prayed for you. No! I am confident, that although you do
not think as a wise man, you feel as a good man.

From you I have received little pain, because for you I suffer
little alarm—I cannot say this for your friend—it appears to me
evident that his feelings are vitiated, & that his ideas are *in their
combinations*, merely the creatures of those feelings. I have received
letters from him & the best & kindest wish which as a christian I
can offer in return is that he may feel remorse.

Some brief resentments rose in my mind, but they did not
remain there; for I began to think almost immediately; & my
resentments vanished. There has resulted only a sort of fantastic
scepticism concerning my own consciousness of my own rectitude.
As dreams have impressed on him the sense of reality, my sense
of reality may be but a dream. From his letters it is plain, that he
has mistaken the heat & bustle & swell of self-justification for the
approbation of his conscience. I am certain that *this* is not the case
with me, but the human heart is so wily & so inventive, that pos-
sibly it may be cheating me, who am an older warrior, with some
newer stratagem.—When I wrote to you that my sonnet to simpli-
city was not composed with reference to Southey you answered me
(I believe these were the words) 'It was a lie too gross for the
grossest ignorance to believe,' & I was not angry with you, because
the assertion, which the grossest Ignorance would believe a lie the
Omniscient knew to be truth—This however makes me cautious
not too hastily to affirm the falsehood of an assertion of Lloyd's,
that in Edmund Oliver's love-fit, debaucheries, leaving college &
going into the army he had no sort of allusion to, or recollection of,
my love-fit, debaucheries, leaving college, & going into the army

'[Lloyd] even wrote a letter to D. W., in which he not only called me a villain,
but appealed to a conversation which passed between him & *her*, as the grounds
of it—and as proving that this was her opinion no less than his—She brought
over the *letter* to me from Alfoxden with tears—I laughed at it—' Chambers,
A Sheaf of Studies, 68.

& that he never thought of my person in the description of Edmund Oliver's person in the first letter of the second volume.[1] This cannot appear stranger to me than my assertion did to you; & therefore I will suspend my absolute faith——I write to you not that I wish to hear from you, but that I wish you to write to Lloyd & press upon him the propriety, nay, the necessity of his giving me a meeting either tête à tête or in the presence of all whose esteem I value.[2] This I owe to my own character—I owe it to him if by any means he may even yet be extricated. He assigned as reasons for his rupture, my vices, and he is either right or wrong; if right it is fit that others should know it & follow his example—if wrong he has acted very wrong. At present, I may expect every thing from his heated mind, rather than continence of language; & his assertions will be the more readily believed on account of his former enthusiastic attachment, though with wise men this would cast a hue of suspicion over the whole affair, but the number of wise men in the kingdom would not puzzle a savage's arithmetic—you may tell them in every count on your fingers. I have been unfortunate in my connections. Both you & Lloyd became acquainted with me at a season when your minds were far from being in a composed or natural state & you clothed my image with a suit of notions & feelings which could belong to nothing human. *You* are restored to comparative saneness, & are merely wondering what is become of the Coleridge with whom you were so passionately in love. *Charles Lloyd's* mind has only changed its disease, & he is now arraying his ci-devant angel in a flaming Sanbenito—the whole ground of the garment a dark brimstone & plenty of little Devils flourished out in black. O me! Lamb, 'even in laughter the heart is sad'—My kindness, my affectionateness *he* deems wheedling, but if after reading all my letters to yourself & to him you can suppose him wise in his treatment & correct in his accusations of me, you think worse of human nature than poor human nature, bad as it is, deserves to be thought of.

God bless you & S. T. Coleridge[3]

[1] *Edmund Oliver*, published by Cottle and dedicated to Lamb, deeply lacerated Coleridge's feelings. Unlike Dorothy—'She thinks it contains a great deal, a *very* great deal of excellent matter but bears the marks of a too hasty composition', Wordsworth reported to Cottle—Coleridge saw through its thin disguise. He recognized, apparently for the first time, the extent of the animosity against himself and the part Southey must have played in the genesis of *Edmund Oliver*. See especially Letter 248, in which Coleridge says that Lloyd's 'infirmities have been made the instruments of another man's darker passions'.

[2] No such meeting took place, though Wordsworth soon tried 'to bring back poor Lloyd' to Stowey. (See Letter 248.)

[3] No answer to this letter has been preserved, but it shows that there was

244. *To William Wordsworth*

Address: Mr Wordsworth | Allfoxden
MS. Dove Cottage. Pub. E. L. Griggs, 'Wordsworth through Coleridge's Eyes',
Wordsworth, *ed. by G. T. Dunklin, 1951, p. 48.*

May 10th, 1798

In stale blank verse a subject stale
I send *per post* my *Nightingale*;[1]
And like an honest bard, dear Wordsworth,
You'll tell me what you think, my Bird's worth.
My opinion's briefly this—
His *bill* he opens not amiss;
And when he has sung a stave or so,
His breast, & some small space below,
So throbs & swells, that you might swear
No vulgar music's working there.
So far, so good; but then, 'od rot him!
There's something falls off at his bottom.
Yet, sure, no wonder it should breed,
That my Bird's Tail's a tail indeed
And makes it's own inglorious harmony
AEolio crepitû, non carmine.

S. T. Coleridge

considerable correspondence, now lost, among Coleridge, Lamb, and Lloyd.
Some time after receiving it Lamb, on hearing that Coleridge was going to
Germany, sent him a sarcastic letter containing eight burlesque scholastic
theses, and on 28 July he included these theses in a note to Southey (*Lamb
Letters*, i. 123–7). Lucas suggests that Lamb and Lloyd may have concocted
this letter while they were together in Birmingham from 23 May to 6 June,
a suggestion borne out by Coleridge's remark to Cottle on showing it to him:
'These young visionaries will do each other no good' (ibid. i. 125 n. and *Early
Rec.* i. 301). Coleridge wisely refrained from replying to Lamb, but the friendship
was not renewed until early 1800.

To Lloyd, of course, must go much of the blame for Coleridge's quarrel
with Lamb. Lloyd was an inveterate and often malicious talebearer, and he
carried gossip first to Southey, then to Lamb, and finally to Cottle and Dorothy
Wordsworth. His conduct, Coleridge later wrote in his notebook, 'was not that
of a fiend, only because it was that of a madman' (Chambers, *A Sheaf of
Studies*, 68). And Lamb, too, was later to blame Lloyd in a letter to Coleridge:
'He is a sad Tattler; ... he almost alienated you ... from me, or me from you,
I don't know which' (*Lamb Letters*, ii. 267–8).

[1] *The Nightingale; a Conversation Poem, April, 1798, Poems,* i. 264.

245. *To John Prior Estlin*

Address: Revd J. P. Estlin | St Michael's Hill | Bristol
MS. Bristol Central Lib. Pub. Letters, i. 246.
Stamped: Bridgewater.

Monday, May 14th, 1798

My dear Friend

I ought to have written to you before; and have done very wrong in not writing. But I have had many sorrows; and some that bite deep, calumny & ingratitude from men who have been fostered in the bosom of my confidence![1]—I pray God, that I may sanctify these events; by forgiveness, & a peaceful spirit full of love.—This morning, half past one, my Wife was safely delivered of a fine boy;[2] she had a remarkably good time, better if possible than her last; & both she & the Child are as well as can be.—By the by, it is only 3 in the morning now.—I walked in to Taunton & back again; & performed the divine services for Dr Toulmin. I suppose you must have heard that his daughter in a melancholy derangement suffered herself to be swallowed up by the tide on the sea-coast between Sidmouth & Bere.—These events cut cruelly into the hearts of old men; but the good Dr Toulmin bears it like the true practical Christian—there is indeed a tear in his eye, but *that* eye is lifted up to the heavenly father!——I have been too neglectful of practical religion—I mean, actual & stated prayer, & a regular perusal of scripture as a morning & evening duty! May God grant me grace to amend this error; for it is a grievous one!—Conscious of frailty I almost wish (I say it confidentially to you) that I had become a stated Minister: for indeed I find true Joy after a sincere prayer; but for want of habit my mind wanders, and I cannot *pray* as often [as] I ought. Thanksgiving is pleasant in the performance; but prayer & distinct confession I find most serviceable to my spiritual health when I can do it. But tho' all my doubts are done away, tho' Christianity is my *Passion*, it is too much my *intellectual* Passion: and therefore will do me but little good in the hour of temptation & calamity.——

My love to Mrs E. & the dear little ones: & ever, O ever believe me

with true affection & gratitude | Your filial Friend

S. T. Coleridge

---

[1] In a notebook entry for 3 Nov. 1810 Coleridge says that his suffering over the quarrel with Lamb and Lloyd prevented his finishing *Christabel*. Chambers, *A Sheaf of Studies*, 68.

[2] Berkeley Coleridge.

246. *To Thomas Poole*

Address: Mr Thomas Poole | Mr R. Poole's | Sherborn
MS. British Museum. Pub. Letters, *i. 248.*
Stamped: Bridgewater.

Monday, May 14th, 1798   Morning, 10 o clock——
My dearest Friend

I have been sitting many minutes with my pen in my hand, full of prayers & wishes for you & the house of affliction in which you have so trying a part to sustain—but I know not what to *write.* May God support you! may he restore your Brother—but above all I pray that he will make us able to cry out with a fervent sincerity, Thy Will be done!—I have had lately some sorrows that have cut more deeply into my heart than they ought to have done—& I have found Religion & *commonplace Religion* too, my restorer & my comfort—giving me gentleness & calmness & dignity! Again, and again may God be with you, my best dear Friend!—O believe me, believe me, my Poole! dearer, to my understanding & affections unitedly, than all else in this world!——It is almost painful & a thing of fear to tell you that I have another boy—it will bring upon your mind the too affecting circumstance of poor Mrs Richard Poole![1]—The prayers which I have offered for her have been a relief to my own mind—I would that they could have been a consolation to her.—Scripture seems to teach us that our fervent prayers are not without efficacy even for others—and tho' my Reason is perplexed, yet my internal feelings impel me to a humble Faith, that it is possible & consistent with the divine attributes.——

Poor Dr Toulmin! he bears his calamity like one in whom a faith thro' Jesus is the *Habit* of the whole man, of his affections still more than of his convictions. The loss of a dear child in so frightful a way cuts cruelly with an old man—but tho' there is a tear & an anguish in his eye, that eye is raised to heaven.

Sara was safely delivered at half past one this morning—the boy is already almost as large as Hartley. She had an astonishingly good time, better if possible than her last; and excepting her weakness, is as well as ever. The child is strong, & shapely—& has the paternal beauty in his upper lip.—God be praised for all things!——
						Your affectionate & entire Friend
						S. T. Coleridge

---

[1] Poole's brother Richard was on his death-bed, and Mrs. Richard Poole had just given birth to a baby.

247. *To George Coleridge*

Address: Revd G. Coleridge | Ottery St Mary | Devon
MS. Lady Cave. Pub. E.L.G. i. 104.
Stamped: Bridgewater.

May 14th, Monday. 1798

My dear Brother

By an odd jumble of accidents I did not receive the parcel till within a few days— / My wife was this morning delivered of a very fine boy—she had a remarkably good time & both she and the child are as well as can be. May God be praised!——

Believe me, I am truly anxious to hear concerning your little one; my little Hartley has had an ugly cough & feverish complaint which made me fear the whooping cough; but it was only the effect of teething, at least, so we hope.——Yesterday I walked in to Taunton to perform the divine services for poor Dr Toulmin whose daughter in a melancholy derangement suffered herself to be swallowed up by the tide on the coast between Sidmouth & Bere. Good old Man! he bears it like one in whom Christianity is an habit of feeling in a still greater degree than a conviction of the understanding. He sanctifies his calamity; but it is plain, that it has cut deep into his heart.—And then from a Mrs Stone I heard all at once the death of Mr William Lewis: remembering the man, & remembering the conversation we had concerning him in the churchyard walk, and considering as it were in a glance of the imagination his bulk & stature, & then the horrid manner of his death—it so overpowered me that I felt as if I had been choked, and then burst into an agony of tears. I scarcely remember ever to have been so deeply affected.—

I will write again in a few days, and send you the Tragedy, &c &c—Sheridan has again promised to fit it for the stage & bring it on, which promise he will as certainly break as

I am

your affectionate & grateful | Brother
S. T. Coleridge

Present my duty to my Mother & my Wife's Duty—My kindest love to Mrs G. Coleridge & a dear kiss for the little one. Mrs S. Coleridge's thanks & love to her & Mrs J. Coleridge.—My kind love to Edward & the Major—& the Major's Quintetto,[1] God bless their beautiful faces!—I have written a *poem* lately which I think even the Major (who is no admirer of the art) would like.[2]——

[1] The 'Major's Quintetto' were James, John Taylor, Bernard Frederick, Francis George, and Frances.
[2] Probably *Fears in Solitude, written in April 1798, during the alarm of an invasion, Poems*, i. 256.

Pray let me hear from you; what was I to send beside the Tragedy & the Historical Grammar? There was something else: & I have forgotten it.—

248. *To John Prior Estlin*

Address: Revd J. P. Estlin | St Michael's Hill | Bristol
MS. Bristol Central Lib. Pub. Letters, *i. 245.*

May, [18, 1798.][1] Friday Morning
My dear Friend

I write from Cross—to which place I accompanied Mr Wordsworth, who will give you this letter. We visited Cheddar—but his main business was to bring back poor Lloyd, whose infirmities have been made the instruments of another man's darker passions.— But Lloyd, (as we found by a letter that met us on the road) is off for Birmingham / Wordsworth proceeds lest possibly Lloyd may not be gone[2]—& likewise to see his own Bristol Friends, as he is so near them.——I have now known him a year & some months, and my admiration, I might say, my awe of his intellectual powers has increased even to this hour—& (what is of more importance) he is a tried good man.—On one subject we are habitually silent—we found our data dissimiliar, & never renewed the subject / It is his practice & almost his nature to convey all the truth he knows without any attack on what he supposes falsehood, if that falsehood be interwoven with virtues or happiness—he loves & venerates Christ & Christianity—I wish, he did more—but it were wrong indeed, if an incoincidence with one of our wishes altered our respect & affection to a man, whom we are as it were instructed by our great master to say that not being against us he is for us.——His genius is most *apparent* in poetry—and rarely, except to me in tete a tete, breaks forth in conversational eloquence.——

My best & most affectionate wishes attend Mrs Estlin & your little ones—&

believe me with filial & fraternal | Friendship | Your grateful
S. T. Coleridge

[1] According to Dorothy Wordsworth's journal, she, Wordsworth, and Coleridge left for Cheddar on Wednesday, 16 May, and slept at Bridgwater. The next entry, again mentioning the visit to Cheddar and Cross, is obviously misdated Thursday, 22 May, for 17 May. (*Journals*, i. 16.) This letter, written from Cross on 18 May, was to be delivered by Wordsworth on his arrival in Bristol.

[2] In June, as a result of Cottle's efforts to effect a reconciliation, Lloyd wrote to Cottle: 'I love Coleridge, and can forget all that has happened' (*Early Rec.* i. 304). It was, however, a long time before Coleridge could view with equanimity the baseness of Charles Lloyd.

249. *To Thomas Poole*

Address: Mr T. Poole
MS. British Museum. Pub. Letters, *i. 249.*

Sunday Morning [20 May 1798]

My dearest Poole

I was all day yesterday in a distressing perplexity whether or no it would be wise or consolatory for me to call at your house—or whether I should write to your mother, as a christian Friend—or whether it would not be better to wait for the exhaustion of that grief, which must have it's way.—

So many unpleasant & shocking circumstances have happened to me or to my immediate knowlege within the last fortnight, that I am in a nervous state & the most trifling thing makes me weep— / Poor Richard! May Providence heal the wounds which it hath seen good to inflict!——

Do you wish me to see you to day? Shall I call on you? shall I stay with you?—or had I better leave you uninterrupted?——In all your Sorrows as in your joys, I am, indeed, my dearest Poole, a true & faithful Sharer!—

May God bless & comfort you all!—

S. T. Coleridge

250. *To Joseph Cottle*

Address: Mr Cottle | Bookseller | No 5 | Wine Street | Bristol
MS. Harvard College Lib. Pub. with omis. Early Rec. *i. 315.*

Monday Morning [28 May 1798][1]

My dear Cottle

You know what I think of a letter—how impossible it is to *argue* in it. You must therefore take simple statements, & in a week or two I shall see you & endeavor to *reason* with you.

Wordsworth & I have *maturely weigh'd* your proposal, & this is our answer—W. would not object to the publishing of Peter Bell *or* the Salisbury Plain, singly; but to the publishing of *his poems*

---

[1] On 18 May, as Letter 248 shows, Wordsworth went to Bristol. While he was away Hazlitt arrived for a three-week visit to Stowey, lasting from *circa* 20 May to 11 June; and a day or two after Hazlitt's arrival Wordsworth himself returned from Bristol. Possibly Cottle came with him; at all events, Cottle's visit, during which plans for the publication of *Lyrical Ballads* were formulated, probably took place in late May. Furthermore, on 31 May Dorothy wrote to her brother that 'William has now some poems in the Bristol press' (*Early Letters*, 192). Coleridge's letter, therefore, must have been written on 28 May, immediately following Cottle's visit, or at latest on Monday, 4 June.

in two volumes he is decisively repugnant & oppugnant—He deems
that they would want variety &c &c—if this apply in his case, it
applies with tenfold force to mine.—We deem that the volumes
offered to you are to a certain degree *one work*, in *kind tho' not in
degree*, as an Ode is one work—& that our different poems are as
stanzas, good relatively rather than absolutely:—Mark you, I say
in kind tho' not in degree.—The extract from my Tragedy will have
no sort of reference to my Tragedy, but is a Tale in itself, as the
ancient Mariner.—The Tragedy will not be mentioned— / As to the
Tragedy, when I consider it [in] reference to Shakespear's & to *one*
other Tragedy, it seems a poor thing; & I care little what becomes
of it—when I consider [it] in comparison with modern Dramatists,
it *rises*: & I think it too bad to be published, too good to be
squandered.—I think of breaking it up; the planks are sound, &
I will build a new ship of old materials.—The dedication to the
Wedgewoods[1] would be indelicate & *unmeaning.*—If after 4 or 5
years I shall have finished some work of some importance, which
could not have been written but in an unanxious seclusion—to
them I will dedicate it, for the Public will have owed the work to
them who gave me the power of that unanxious Seclusion.——As
to anonymous Publications, depend on it, you are deceived.—
Wordsworth's name is nothing—to a large number of persons mine
stinks——The Essay on Man, Darwin's[2] Botanic Garden, the
Pleasures of memory, & many other most popular works were
published anonymously.——However, I waive all *reasoning*; &
simply state it as an unaltered opinion, that you should proceed as
before, with the ancient Mariner.—

The picture shall be sent.[3] For your love-gifts & book-loans
accept our hearty love—The Joan of Arc is a divine book.[4]—It
opens lovelily——I hope that you will *take off* some half dozen of
our poems in great paper, even as the Joan of Arc.——Cottle, my
dear Cottle, I meant to have written you an Essay on the Meta-
physics of Typography; but I have not time.—Take a few hints
without the abstruse reasons for them with which I mean to favor
you—18 lines in a page, the lines closely printed, certainly, *more
closely* than those of the Joan—(Oh by all means closer! W. Words-
worth)[5] *equal ink*; & *large margins*. That is *beauty*—it may even
under your immediate care mingle the sublime!——

---

[1] In printing this letter Cottle inserted here the phrase, 'which you recom-
mend'. *Early Rec.* i. 316.
[2] Cottle deleted 'Darwin's' and substituted 'the' in the manuscript.
[3] The earliest known portrait of Wordsworth by W. Shuter.
[4] The second edition of Southey's *Joan of Arc* appeared in 1798.
[5] The sentence in parentheses is in Wordsworth's handwriting.

And now, my dear Cottle! may God love you & me who am ever with most unauthorish feelings your true friend

S. T. Coleridge

I walked to Linton the day after you left us, & returned on Saturday.—I walked in one day & returned in one— /

251. *To Thomas Poole*

Address: Mr T. Poole | Stowey | near | Bridgewater | Somerset
MS. British Museum. Pub. with omis. Thomas Poole, *i. 271.*
Stamped: Cobham.

Saturday. June 16th, 1798

My dear Poole

I arrived in Bristol on Monday Evening,[1] spent the next day at Estlin's, who opposed my German Expedition furore perreligioso, amicissimo furore.—At Brentford I arrived Wednesday Evening— and was driven by Mr Purkiss[2] great part of the way to Stoke, on Thursday Evening—: and here I am, well, &c &c. Mr Josiah Wedgewood & Wife left us this morning, being obliged to go to Bristol; for Dr Beddoes has alarmed him concerning the state of his wife's health; so I stay with Tom & the Miss Wedgewoods. / — Purkiss is a *gentleman* with the free & cordial & interesting manners of the man of literature. His colloquial diction is uncommonly pleasing, his *information* various, his *own* mind elegant & acute /: all these are but *general* expressions; but this I can say, that if he liked me as well as I liked him, I have left very agreeable thoughts & feelings in the mind of an excellent man. And I like Mrs Purkiss.

The Wedgewoods received me with joy & affection. I have been metaphysicizing so long & so closely with T. Wedgewood, that I am a caput mortuum, mere lees & residuum; but if I do not write now, you will not receive the letter, heaven knows when / for the post here is quite uncertain.——Godwin has expressed to the Wedgewoods a vehement desire of being re-introduced to me—so I shall see him next week.—I shall step into London on Monday / there are some letters from Wedgewood to me; be so kind as to open them, & to give me an account whether any thing be contained in them except his various determinations concerning his

---

[1] Hazlitt, his visit to Stowey over, accompanied Coleridge to Bristol. Writing to his father he says: 'I have just time to let you know that I shall set out on my way home this evening. Mr. Coleridge is gone to Taunton to preach for Dr. Toulmin. He is to meet me at Bridgwater, and we shall proceed from thence to Bristol tomorrow morning.' P. P. Howe, *The Life of William Hazlitt*, 1947, pp. 43–44.

[2] Samuel Purkis, Poole's friend, was living in Brentford, near London.

going to Bristol / —direct—Mr Coleridge, Josiah Wedgewood's Esq. Stoke, near Cobham, Surry.—This place is a noble large house, in a rich pleasant country / but the little Toe of Quantock is better than the head & shoulders of Surry & Middlesex. These dull places however have the effect of liveliness from their being a variety to me.—May you say the same by this letter—for it is scarcely worth the postage.—God bless you, my Friend,

       & believe me with gratitude & constancy   your's ever,

                                  S. T. Coleridge

252. *To Thomas Poole*

Address: Mr T. Poole | Stowey near | Bridgewater
MS. British Museum. Pub. E.L.G. i. 106.
Stamped: Bristol.

                                   August 3rd 1798

My dearest Poole

I arrived safely, &c.—With regard to Germany, these are my intentions, if not contravened by superior arguments.—I still think the realization of the scheme of high importance to my intellectual utility; and of course to my moral happiness. But if I go with Mrs C. & little ones, I must *borrow*—an imprudent, perhaps an immoral thing— : and the uncertainties attendant on all human schemes; the uncertainty of our happiness, comfort, cheap living &c when in Germany; and the unsettled state of Germany itself; force on me the truth that I ought not to hazard any considerable sum.—I propose therefore, if, as I guess, Mrs Coleridge's wishes tend the same way, to go myself (comparatively a trifling expence) stay 3 or 4 months, in which time I shall at least have learnt the language / then, if all is well, all comfortable, and I can rationally propose to myself a scheme of weighty advantages—to fetch over my family ——if not to return, with my German for my pains; & the wisdom that 3 or 4 months sojourn among a new people must give to a watchful & thinking man.—Make up your mind on my scheme—I shall return in a week.—All, whom I have seen, are well. Wordsworth & his Sister, Wade & Cottle, desire their best love to you— / I shall dart into Wales, and return per viam Swansea usque ad Bridgwater sive Cummage—absent a week from date hereof.[1]—

        God bless you & your ever affectionate & grateful,

                                  S. T. Coleridge

---

[1] Coleridge did, in fact, 'dart into Wales' in the company of the Wordsworths, Dorothy later noting that 'Mr Coleridge proposed it to us one evening and we departed the next morning at six o'clock' (*Early Letters*, 201). While in Wales they paid a visit to Thelwall at Llyswen (*Later Years*, ii. 959).

Wordsworth has not forgotten his promise about his Tragedy. I have been very anxious about poor Cruckshanks—doubtful, very doubtful about the bottom of his affairs!—May his better Genius protect him!—

253. *To Thomas Poole*

Address: Mr Thomas Poole | Nether Stowey | Bridgewa[ter] | Somerse[t]
MS. British Museum. Pub. Letters, *i. 258.*
Postmark: 17 September 1798.

[15 September 1798]

My very dear Poole

We have arrived at Yarmouth[1] just time to be hurried into the packet—and 4 or 5 letters of recommendation have been taken away from me, owing to their being wafered.—Wedgewood's luckily were not.—

I am on the point of leaving my native country for the first time —a country, which, God Almighty knows, is dear to me above all things for the love I bear to you.—Of many friends, whom I love and esteem, my head & heart have ever chosen you as the Friend— as the one being, in whom is involved the full & whole meaning of that sacred Title—God love you, my dear Poole! and your faithful &

most affectionate

S. T. Coleridge

P.S.—We may be only 2 days, we may be a fortnight going—the same of the pacquet that returns—so do not let my poor Sara be alarmed, if she do not hear from me.—I will write alternately to you & to her, twice every week, during my absence.——May God preserve us & make us continue to be joy & comfort & wisdom & virtue to each other, my dear, dear Poole!——

254. *To Mrs. S. T. Coleridge*

Address: Mrs Coleridge | Nether Stowey, Bridgewater, | Somersetshire, | England.
MS. New York Public Lib. Pub. with omis. Letters, *i. 259.*
Postmark: Foreign Office, 1 October 1798.

I.

Tuesday Night, 9' o clock. Sept. 18th, 1798

Over what place does the Moon hang to your eye, my dearest Sara? To me it hangs over the left bank of the Elbe; and a long

---

[1] On 14 Sept. 1798 Coleridge, John Chester of Stowey, and the Wordsworths left London. They arrived in Yarmouth the next day and sailed for Germany on 16 Sept. *Dorothy Wordsworth Journals*, i. 19.

trembling road of moonlight reaches from thence up to the stern of
our Vessel, & there it ends. We have dropped anchor in the middle
of the Stream, 30 miles from Cuxhaven, where we arrived this
morning at eleven o'clock, after an unusually fine passage of only
48 hours—.—The Captain agreed to take all the passengers up to
Hamburgh for ten guineas— / my share amounted only to half a
guinea. We shall be there if no fogs intervene tomorrow morning.—
Chester was ill the whole voyage, Wordsworth shockingly ill, his
Sister worst of all—vomiting, & groaning, unspeakably! And I
neither sick or giddy, but gay as a lark. The sea rolled rather high;
but the motion was pleasant to me. The stink of a sea cabbin in a
packet, what from the bilge water, & what from the crowd of *sick*
passengers, is horrible. I remained chiefly on deck.——We left
Yarmouth, Sunday Morning, Sept. 16th, at eleven o'clock— /
Chester & [the] Wordsworths ill immediately—Our passengers were
‡ Wordsworths, ✝ Chester, S. T. Coleridge, A Dane, Second Dane,
Third Dane, A Prussian, an Hanoverian & ‡ his Servant, a German
Taylor & his ‡ Wife, a French ‡ Emigrant, & ‡ french Servant,
‡ two English Gentlemen, and ‡ a Jew.—All those with the prefix
✝ were sick; those marked ‡ horribly sick.—The view of Yarmouth
from the sea is interesting—besides, it was English Ground that
was flying away from me.—When we lost sight of land, the moment
that we quite lost sight of it, & the heavens all round me rested
upon the waters, my dear Babies came upon me like a flash of
lightning—I saw their faces so distinctly!—This day enriched me
with characters—and I passed it merrily. Each of these characters,
I will delineate to you in my Journal, which you & Poole, alternately,
will receive regularly as soon as I arrive at any settled place—
which will be in a week. Till then I can do little more than give you
notice of my safety, & my faithful affection to you / but the Journal
will commence from the day of my arrival at London, & give every
day's occurrence, &c—I have it written, but I have neither paper,
or time, to transcribe it. I trust nothing to memory.—The Ocean
is a noble Thing by night; a beautiful white cloud of foam at
momently intervals roars & rushes by the side of the Vessel, and
Stars of Flame dance & sparkle & go out in it—& every now and
then light Detachments of Foam dart away from the Vessel's side
with their galaxies of stars, & scour out of sight, like a Tartar Troop
over a Wilderness!——What these Stars are, I cannot say—the
sailors say, that they are the Fish Spawn which is phosphorescent.—
/ The noisy Passengers swear in all their languages with drunken
Hiccups that I shall write no more—& I must join them.—Indeed,
they present a rich feast for a Dramatist.——My kind love to dear
Mrs Poole / with what wings of swiftness would I fly home if I

could but find something in Germany to do her good!——Remember me affectionately to Ward—& my love to the Chesters, Bessy, Susan & Julia / & to Cruckshanks, & to Ellen & Mary when you see them—& to Lavinia Poole, & Harriet & Sophy. And be sure you give my kind love to Nanny—I associate so much of Hartley's Infancy with her, so many of his figures, looks, words & antics with her form, that I can never cease to think of her, poor Girl! without interest.—Tell my best good Friend, my dear Poole! that all his manuscripts with Wordsworth's Tragedy are safe in Josiah Wedgewood's hands—& they will be returned to him together.—Good night, my dear, dear Sara!—'every night when I go to bed & every morning when I rise' I will think of you with a yearning love, & of my blessed Babies!——Once more, my dear Sara! good night.——

Did you receive my letter, *directed* in a different hand, with the 30£ Bank Note?—The Morning Post & Magazine will come to you as before. If not regularly, Stewart desires that you will write to him.

Wednesday afternoon, 4 o'clock

We are safe in Hamburgh—an ugly City that stinks in every corner, house, & room worse than Cabbin, Sea sickness, or bilge Water!— The Hotels are all crowded—with great difficulty we have procured a very filthy room at a large expence; but we shall move tomorrow. —We get very excellent Claret for a Trifle—a guinea sells at present for more than 23 shillings here.—But for all particulars, I must refer your patience to my Journal—& I must get some proper paper. / I shall have to pay a shilling or eighteen pence with every letter.—N.B.—Johnson, the Bookseller, without any poems sold to him; but purely out of affection conceived for me, & as part of any thing I *might* do for him, gave me an order on Remnant at Hamburgh for 30 pound.[1]——The Epea Pteroenta, an Essay on Population,[2] and a History of Paraguay, will come down for me directed to Poole / & for Poole's Reading— / Likewise, I have desired Johnson to print in Quarto a little Poem [of mine,[3] one of

---

[1] Soon after his arrival in Hamburg Coleridge took advantage of Johnson's kindness.

Hamburgh, Septr 21st 1798. For 25£ sterling Two months after Date pay this my first of Exchange (Second not paid) to the order of Mr William Remnant Twenty five pounds Sterling, value received, and place the same to Account as advised by

S. T. Coleridge

To Mr Joseph Johnson, | Bookseller, St Paul's Church Yard | London. [MS. private possession.]

[2] J. Horne Tooke, *ΕΠΕΑ ΠΤΕΡΟΕΝΤΑ* or the Diversions of Purley, Parts I and II, 1798, and T. R. Malthus, *Essay on Population*, 1798.
[3] *Fears in Solitude, Written in 1798, during the Alarm of an Invasion. To*

which Quartos must] be sent to my Brother, [Revd G C Ottery St
Mary, carriage paid——]¹ I pray you, my Love! read Edgeworth's
Essay on Education²—read it heart & soul—& if you approve of
the mode, teach Hartley his Letters—I am very desirous, that you
should begin to teach him to read—& they point out some easy
modes.——J. Wedgewood informed me that the Edgeworths were
most miserable when Children, & yet the Father, *in his book*, is ever
vapouring about their *Happiness!*—!—However there are very
good things in the work—& some nonsense!——

Kiss my Hartley, & Bercoo Baby Brodder / Kiss them for their
dear Father, whose heart will never be absent from them many
hours together!—My dear Sara—I think of you with affection &
a desire to be home / & in the full & holiest sense of the word, &
after the antique principles of *Religion* unsophisticated by philo-
sophy will be, I trust, your Husband faithful unto Death.

[S T Coleridge]

[Wednesday night 11 o'clock—The sky & colours of the clouds
are quite English just as if I were coming out of T Poole's home-
ward with you in] my arm.

255. *To Thomas Poole*

Transcript Thomas Ward copy-book, New York Public Lib. Hitherto unpublished.

Hamburg Friday Septr 28th 1798

My dear dear Poole

The Ocean is between us & I feel how much I love you! God bless
you my dear Friend—Since I last wrote to Sara, I have been
wandering about & about to find Lodgings—I have given up all
thought of going to Eisenach or Weimar, and shall settle with
Chester for three months or possibly four at Ratzeburg, 7 German
(i.e. 35 English Miles) from Hamburg—We go tomorrow & my
address is—Mr Coleridge | at the | Pastor Unruke, | Ratzeburg, |
Germany,—

Get a German Map and find me out—Ratzeburg is a most beautiful
place and North-east of Hamburg—On Sunday Morning I begin

which are added, France, an Ode; and Frost at Midnight, 1798. This little work
was printed by Johnson, which may explain why he gave Coleridge the order
on Remnant.

¹ A few lines cut from the manuscript, presumably for Coleridge's autograph
on the opposite page. The words enclosed in brackets have been supplied from
a transcript made by Thomas Ward.

² *Practical Education*, a joint work of Maria Edgeworth and her father,
Richard Edgeworth, appeared in two volumes in 1798.

my Journal, and you will receive, or Sara, the first Sheet by the next Mail—Did you receive my letter from Yarmouth? Did Sara receive the Bank note of £30 from London?—The price of Lodging and Boarding is very high—we shall pay 36 marks a week for two rooms, for bread, butter, milk, dinner, & supper—& find ourselves washing, tea & wine—this is at the rate of 60 pounds a year each, English Money—We are not imposed on in this—but the Cheapness of Germany is a Hum!—at least of the Northern Parts.—Wordsworth & his Sister have determined to travel on into Saxony, to seek cheaper places[1]—God knows whether he will succeed—to him who means to stay two or three years, it may answer—To me who mean to return in 3 months, the having no travelling expences will nearly pay for my Lodging and Boarding—For Chester & I shall reach Ratzeburg (Luggage & all) for 16 shillings—Our Journey to Eisenach and back again could not have cost less than £30—A Mark is 16 pence but then an English Guinea is always 17 marks & now it is 17 marks and ninepence—and Bills of Exchange for pounds sterling are reckoned in the same proportion——I have not been idle—you will soon see in the Morning Post the Signature of *Cordomi*[2]—Let me hear from you and tell me of every thing—&

[1] After a short stay together in Hamburg, Wordsworth and Coleridge separated, Coleridge and Chester setting off for Ratzeburg on 30 Sept. Three days later the Wordsworths moved on to Goslar (*Dorothy Wordsworth Journals*, i. 28, 31, and 34). The decision to settle in separate places in Germany was, as this letter shows, a perfectly justifiable one, and relations continued as amicable as before. Between the two poets, too, a voluminous correspondence, now lost, was carried on: 'I hear as often from Wordsworth as letters can go backward & forward,' Coleridge wrote to Mrs. Coleridge on 14 Jan. 1799.

At home in England, however, the separation of the two poets was greeted with enthusiasm. 'The Wordsworths', Poole wrote to Coleridge on 8 Oct. 1798, 'have left you—so there is an end of our tease about amalgamation etc, etc. I think you both did perfectly right—it was right for them to find a cheaper situation, and it was right for you to avoid the expence of travelling, provided you are where *pure German* is spoken. You will of course frequently hear from Wordsworth—when you write remember me to him and to his sister.' Josiah Wedgwood, too, expresses satisfaction in an unpublished letter to Poole, dated 1 Feb. 1799: 'I have received one long & interesting letter from Coleridge. . . . I think his expedition seems to have answered to him and I hope that Wordsworth & he will continue separated. I am persuaded that Coleridge will derive great benefit from being thrown into mixed society.' And Lamb, not without maliciousness, wrote to Southey when he heard the news: 'I hear that the Two Noble Englishmen have parted no sooner than they set foot on German earth, but I have not heard the reason—possibly, to give novelists an handle to exclaim, "Ah me! what things are perfect?"' (*Lamb Letters*, i. 141).

[2] No contributions to the *Morning Post* for this period have been identified. Two poems, *Something Childish, but very Natural* and *Home-sick. Written in Germany*, were first published with the signature 'Cordomi' in the *Annual Anthology*, 1800. (Cf. *Poems*, i. 313–14.) Coleridge quoted the first poem in Letter 276, the second in Letter 277.

give me your Opinion &c—I expect that Stuart will pay me very
handsomely for what I mean to do—I have spent some time with
Klopstock; but I shall anticipate nothing. I associate none but
kindly feelings with Stowey—& therefore tell all whom you meet
that I desire my love to them—but to your dear Mother and Ward
particularly, for they are with you and of you—Tell my dear Sara
that I am well, very well—and so is Chester—Go to my house and
kiss my dear babies for me—my Friend, my best Friend, my
Brother, my Beloved—the tears run down my face——God love
you &

S T Coleridge

Chester's love and duty to his Mother &c &c &c——The People
here for this last week have been frantic with Joy for Nelson's
Victories[1] &c—

256. *To Mrs. S. T. Coleridge*

Transcript Thomas Ward copy-book, New York Public Lib. The journal part
of this letter was revised and published as *Satyrane's Letters*, i. See *The Friend*,
No. 14, 23 November 1809, and *Biog. Lit.*, 1817, ii. 183–204.

Ratzeburg Octbr 3d 1798   Wednesday

My dearest love /

At length out of the filth, the noise and the tallow-faced Roguery
of Hamburg, I sit down, in quietness to fulfil my promise——No
little fish thrown back again into the water—no Fly unimprisoned
from a boy's hand, could more buoyantly enjoy it's element, than
I this clear & peaceful house, situated in this wholesome Air! with
this lovely view of the Town, woods and lake of Ratzeburg from
the window, at which I write.—In London I visited Mrs Barbauld;
but before that I had introduced myself to Johnson, the Bookseller,
who received me civilly the first time, cordially the second, affec-
tionately the third—& finally took leave of me with tears in his
eyes.—He is a worthy Man.—At Yarmouth I had some long con-
versations with George Burnet——
    Sunday Septr 16th 1798—Eleven o'clock—The Packet set sail,
& for the first time in my life I beheld my native land retiring from
me——my native Land to which I am convinced I shall return
with an intenser affection—with a proud Nationality made rational
by my own experience of its Superiority.—My dear dear Babies—
I told you how, when the land quite disappeared, they came upon
my eye as distinctly as if they had that moment died and were
crossing me in their road to Heaven!——Chester began to look

[1] Coleridge refers, of course, to the battle of the Nile, 1 Aug. 1798.

(420)

Frog-coloured and doleful—Miss Wordsworth retired in confusion
to the Cabin—Wordsworth soon followed—I was giddy, but not
sick, and in about half an hour the giddiness went away, & left only
a feverish Inappetence of Food, arising I believe, from the accursed
stink of the Bilge water, & certainly not decreased by the Sight of
the Basons from the Cabin containing green and yellow specimens
of the inner Man & brought up by the Cabin-boy every three
minutes—I talked and laughed with the Passengers—then went to
sleep on the deck—was awaked about three o'clock in the After-
noon by the Danes, who insisted in very fluent but not very correct
English, that I should sit down and drink with them——Accord-
ingly I did—My name among them was Docteur Teology—(i.e.
Theology)—& dressed as I was all in black with large shoes and
black worsted stockings, they very naturally supposed me to be a
Priest.—I rectified their mistake—what then? said they—Simply
I replied, *un Philosophe.*—Well, I drank some excellent wine &
devoured Grapes & part of a pine-apple—

> Good things I said, good things I eat,
> I gave them wisdom for their meat.——

And in a short time became their Idol—Every now and then I
entered into the feelings of my poor Friends below, who in all the
agonies of sea-sickness heard us most distinctly, spouting, singing,
laughing, fencing, dancing country dances—in a word being Bac-
chanals——The Dane (so by way of eminence I shall call a short
thin limbed Man with white hair and farthing face slightly marked
with the small pox). The Dane nearly tipsy got me to himself
towards the Evening, & began to talk away in most magnific style,
& as a sort of pioneering to his own Vanity flattered *me* with such
Grossness!—the *most highest superlativities* an Englishman can con-
ceive would be mere debasements in comparison——The following
conversation I noted down immediately & is as accurate as the
detail of a conversation can possibly be—(Dane) 'Vat imagina-
tion! vat language! vat fast science! vat eyes!—vat a milk vite
forehead!—O my Heafen! You are a God!—Oh me! if you should
tink I flatters you—no, no, no—I hafe ten tousand a year—yes—
ten tousand a year—ten tousand pound a year!—vell, vat's that?
a mere trifle!—I 'ouldn't give my sincere heart for ten times the
money.—Yes! you are a God!——I a mere Man!—But my dear
Friend! tink of me as a Man. Is I not speak English very fine? Is
I not very eloquent?' (STC) 'Admirably, Sir! most admirably!——
Believe me, Sir! I never heard even a Native talk so fluently.'
(Dane squeezing my hand most vehemently) 'My *dear* Friend! vat
an affection & *fidelity* we hafe for each other!—But tell me, do tell

me—Is I not now & den speak some fault? Is I not in some wrong?—' (STC) 'Why, Sir! perhaps it might be observed by nice Critics in the English Language that you occasionally use the word "is" instead of "am"——In our best Companies We generally say "am I" not "Is I"—Excuse me Sir!—It is so mere a Trifle'—(Dane) 'O! o! o!—Is—is—is—Am—am—am—ah—hah—yes—yes —I know—I knows'—(STC) 'Am, art, is; are, are, are' (Dane) 'O yes! I know, I know——Am, am, "am" is the presens, and "is" the Perfectum—Yes! yes. yes! and "are" is the Plusquam perfectum' (STC. bridling in my face with a curb rein) 'And "art" Sir! is?' (Dane) 'My dear Friend! it is dhe plusquam perfectum' ——(then swinging my hand about & cocking his little bright hazle eyes at me, that danced with vanity and wine) 'You see, my dear Friend! *I* hafe some learning'—(STC) Learning Sir!—Who dares suspect it! Who can hear you talk for a minute, who can even look at you without perceiving it? (Dane) 'My dear Friend!' (then with a somewhat humbler look & in a reasoning tone of voice) I could not talk so of Presens & Imperfectum & Futurum and Plusquam plueperfectum and all dat my *dear* Friend! widout some learning! ——(STC) To be sure, you could not——! Lord! Lord! Sir!—A Man like you cannot talk on any subject without shewing the Depth of his information—! (Dane) [']Now I will tell you, my dear Friend! There did happen about me what de whole History of Denmark record no instance about no body else—I is—I AM dhe only instance. ! Dhe Bishop did ask me all dhe questions about all dhe Religion, in dhe Latin Grammar'—(STC) 'Grammar, Sir?—the language, I presume—?' (Dane a little offended) 'Yes! Grammar is language, and language is Grammar[']—(STC) 'Ten thousand pardons—it is a blunder of my own.'— (Dane) 'Vell, and I was only fourteen of my years'—(STC) 'only fourteen years old?['] (Dane) 'Yes, only fourteen years old—& he asked me all questions, Religion & Philosophy and all in dhe Latin Tongue.—& I answered him all, every one, my dear Friend!—all in dhe Latin Tongue!'—— (STC) 'A Prodigy!' (Dane) 'No! no! no! he was a Bisehoff—a Bisehoff![']— (STC, not knowing what he meant) 'Yes! a Bishop.' —(Dane) 'Yes! a Bishop, not a Prédigé—' (STC) 'What is a Prédigé, my dear Friend?'—(Dane) 'A Prediger—a Priest that must preach efery sontay—It was a Bishop' / STC (N.B. I have since discovered that Prediger is the German word for an inferiour Priest—however I now replied) 'My dear Sir! We have misunderstood each other. I said that your answering in Latin was a Prodigy, that is, a thing that is wonderful! that does not often happen!' (Dane) 'often! dhere is not von instance recorded in dhe whole History of Denmark.' (STC) 'And since then, Sir'—(Dane) [']I was

sent ofer to dhe West Indies—to an Island, & dhen I had no more
to do wid books—no, no!—I put my genius anodher way—& my
dear Friend! I hafe made ten tousand a year——is not dhat genius,
my dear Friend! But vat is money?—I tink dhe poorest Man alive
my equal—Yes! my dear Friend! my little fortune is pleasant to
my generous heart because I can do good—no Man with so little a
fortune ever did so much generosity!—no person—no man person,
no woman person ever denies it.—But we are Gotte's Children'——
/ Here the Hanoverian interrupted us, and the Danes and the Prus-
sian joined us—The Prussian was a hale Man, tall, strong, & stout—
and 60 years old—a travelling Merchant—full of stories and gesti-
culations, & buffoonery—but manifestly with the soul as well as
the look of a Mountebank, who while he is making you laugh picks
your pocket.—Amid all his droll looks and droll gestures, there
remained *one* look, in his face, that never laughed—and that one
look was the Man—the other looks were but his Garments—The
Hanoverian was a pale, fat, bloated, young Man, whose Father lives
in Soho Square in London—his name Eckand—and he has made a
large fortune as an army Contractor—The Son emulated the Eng-
lish in Extravagance &c—was a good-natured fellow not without
information & literature; but a most egregious Coxcomb.—He had
attended constantly the house of Commons & Kemble & Mrs Sid-
dons, at Drury Lane, had spoken, as he informed me, with con-
siderable applause in several debating Societies—was perfect in
Walker's pronouncing Dictionary; and with an accent, which
strongly reminded me of the Scotchman in Roderic Random, who
professed to teach the true English Pronunciation. He was con-
stantly deferring to my superiour Judgment whether or no I had
spoken this or that word with propriety, or 'the true delicacy'——
His great ambition seemed to be towards Oratory & he introduced
most liberally in all his conversation those cant phrases which dis-
figure the orations of our legislators—as 'while I am on my legs'
&c &c &c—Of the two Danes not yet described, (N.B. one a Swede,
not a Dane) one of them, the Brother of the Dane, a Man with a
fair, white and unhealthy face, and white hair, looked silly, said
little, and seemed to be absolutely dependent on his Brother—the
second was a fiery featured, scurvy faced Man, his Complexion the
colour of a red hot poker that is beginning to cool—a blackish red
—he was however by far the best informed & most rational of the
whole Party, & quite the Gentleman; but appeared miserably
dependent on the Dane. This Man, the Swede, for reasons that
will soon appear I distinguish by the name of 'Nobility.'——The
Englishman was a genteel Youth who spoke German perfectly and
acted often as Interpreter of the Prussian's jokes for me—The Jew

was in the Hold, & the French Man was so ill that I could observe
nothing of him or concerning him except the affectionate attentions
of his Servant to him—The poor Fellow was very sick himself, &
every now and then ran to the side of the vessel, discharged his
stomach and returned in the twinkling of an eye to his sick Master
—now holding his head—now wiping his forehead, and in the most
soothing terms telling him he would soon be better; and his eye
was always affectionate towards his Master.——Sunday Afternoon
7 o'clock—The Sea rolled higher, & the Dane by means of the
greater agitation *turned out of doors* enough of what he had been
drinking to make room for a great deal more. His favourite drink
was Sugar and Brandy—i.e. a very little water with a great deal of
Brandy, sugar and nutmeg—His Servant boy, a black eyed Mulatto,
had a goodnatured round face, exactly the colour of the peel of the
fruit of the walnut——The Dane again got me to himself; we sate
together in the ship's boat that lay on the Deck, and here began a
conversation most truly ludicrous—he told me that he had made a
large fortune in the Island of Santa Cruz, & was returning to Den-
mark to enjoy it—talked away in the most magnific style, till the
Brandy aiding his Vanity, & garrulity aiding the Brandy, he talked
like a Madman; entreated me to come and see him in Denmark—
there I should find in what a style he would live, his influence with
the Government of Denmark, and he would introduce me to the
young King &c &c &c—so he went on dreaming aloud; and then
turning the conversation to Politicks, declaimed like a Member of
the Corresponding Society about the Rights of Man; & how not-
withstanding his fortune he thought the poorest Man alive his
Equal—! 'All are equal, my dear Friend! all are equal—we are all
Gotte's Children—The Poorest Man hafe the same rights with me
—Jack! Jack! some more sugar and Brandy!——dhere is dat fellow
now—he is a Mulatto; but he is a Man—he is my equal—dhat's
right, Jack! here you Sir! shake hands with dhis Gentleman—shake
hands with me you dog!—Dhere, dhere, we are all equal, my dear
Friend!—Do I not speak like Socrates?—Socrates & Plato & Aris-
totle—they were all Philosophers, all very great Men—and so was
Homer & Virgil, but they were Poets—Yes! I know all about it—
but what can any body say more dhan dhis—we are all equal—we
are all Gotte's Children—Dho I have ten tousand a year, I am no
more dhan the meanest Man alive—I have no pride, and yet my
dear Friend! I can say do! and it is done! Ha! Ha! Ha! my dear
Friend!—Now dhere, is dhat Gentleman—(pointing to 'Nobility')
he is a Swedish Baron—you shall see—Ho! Ho! Ho! (calling to him)
get me, will you, a bottle of wine from the cabin.['] (Swede) Here,
Jack! go and get your Master a bottle of wine from the Cabin—

(Dane) No! no! no!—do *you* go now—you go yourself—you go now
—(Swede) Pshaw!—(Dane) Now go, go I pray you.——*And the
Swede went!*——After this the Dane talked about Religion, and
supposing me to be in *the continental sense* of the expression what
I had called myself—'Un Philosophe',—he talked of Deity in a
declamatory style very much resembling some Parts of Payne's
devotional Rants in the Age of Reason—& then said, 'what damn'd
Hypocrism all Jesus Christ's Business was,['] and ran on in the
commonplace style about Christianity—and appeared withered
when I professed myself a Christian. I sunk 50 fathoms immediately
in his Graces—however I turned the conversation from a subject
on which I never think myself allowed not to be in earnest—I found
that he was a Deist disbelieving a future state—The Dane retired
to the Cabin, and I wrapped myself up in my great Coat, lay in the
Boat, and looked at the water, the foam of which, that beat against
the Ship & coursed along by it's sides, & darted off over the Sea,
was full of stars of flame——I was cold, and the Cabin stunk, and I
found reason to rejoice in my great Coat, which I bought in London,
and gave 28 shillings for—a weighty, long, high caped, respectable
rug—The Collar will serve for a night Cap, turning over my head
—I amused myself with two or three bright stars that oscillated
with the motion of the sails—fell asleep—woke at one o'clock Mon-
day Morning, and, it raining, I found myself obliged to go down to
the cabin—accordingly 'I descended into Hell and rose again' the
next morning after a most sound sleep—my nose, the most placable
of all our Senses, reconciled & insensible of the stink——

Monday Septr 17th.—Eat a hearty breakfast—talked much with
the Swede, who spoke with contempt of the Dane, as a Fool, purse-
mad—but he confirmed the Dane's boasts concerning the largeness
of his Fortune, which he had acquired partly as a Planter, and
partly as an Advocate—that is—a Barrister—From the Dane and
from himself I gathered that he was indeed a Swedish Nobleman,
who had squandered his Fortune in high living and Gaming, & had
sold his estates to the Dane, on whom he was absolutely dependent
—He seemed to suffer little pain, if any, from the Dane's Insolence
—was very humane & attentive to Miss Wordsworth, performing
all the most disagreeable offices for her with the utmost delicacy
and gentleness. Indeed, his manners and conversation were in a
very high degree pleasing, and I struggled to believe his Insensi-
bility respecting the Dane, Philosophical fortitude——The Dane
quite sober; but still his Character oozed out at every pore—We
dined &c—& I partook of the Hanoverian's & Dane's wines, &
Pine apples—told them some hundred Jokes, and passed as many
of my own /. Danced all together a sort of wild dance on the Deck

—Wordsworth and Sister bad as ever—The Dane, insolent with wine, every quarter of an hour or perhaps oftener would hollo to the Swede in these words—'Ho! Nobility, go and do such a thing— Mr Nobility, do that,' &c—and so the Swede went by the name of Nobility.——About 4 o'clock I saw a wild duck swimming on the waves—a single solitary wild duck—You cannot conceive how interesting a thing it looked in that round objectless desart of waters—In the evening till dark talked with the Hanoverian— Sails lowered, for fear we should run foul on the land in the night— (the land is so flat that it can only be seen at a very small distance) ——went to bed—awaked at 4 o'clock in the morning on Tuesday Septr 18th by the cry of Land! Land!——It was an ugly Island Rock at a distance on our left, called Helgoland.——About nine o'clock we saw the Main-land, which seemed as scarce able to hold it's head above water——low, flat, and dreary—so low that it *edged* the water— low, flat, and dreary, with light houses & land marks that seemed to give a language & character to the dreariness —We entered the mouth of the Elbe, having first passed closely the Island Newerck [Neuwerk]—can see but one bank, namely, the right——saw a Church—thanked God for my safe voyage, and thought most affectionately and with many tears of my wife and babies, and of my Friend—and of my Friends at Bristol—dear good Mr and Mrs Estlin, and Wade, whose heart has been ever so firm towards me.—Eleven o'clock—arrive at Cuxhaven, which if you cannot find in the map, you will at least find the name of Ritzebuttel, which is almost the same place—Here the ship dropped Anchor, and the boat was hoisted out, which carried the Hanoverian and a few others over to Cuxhaven—The Captain agreed to take us all up to Hamburg for ten guineas—hauled anchor and passed gently up the river—At Cuxhaven in clear weather both sides of the river may be seen—we could see only the right bank—Passed a Multitude of English Merchant Ships that had been for nine days waiting for a wind—Saw both banks; and both neat and flat; very neat and quite artificial—On the left bank saw a Church or two in the distance—on the right bank it was Steeple, and Windmill, and Cottage, and Windmill & house, and Steeple, and Windmill, & Windmill, and neat house, and Steeple. These are the objects; and this was the succession of them—About 40 miles from Cuxhaven we passed a most lovely Island, about a mile and a half in length, wedge shaped—very green and woody, and with a nice farm-house on it.—From Cuxhaven to this place the shore was very green, and not inelegantly planted with Trees—where there were no Trees, it bore a striking resemblance to the Shore from Huntspill to Cummage.—But five miles before we arrived at this Island, the night came on, and (for the navigation of the Elbe is a most perilous one) we dropped anchor 35 miles from Cuxhaven.—I began a letter to my dearest Sara—the moon over the left bank of the Elbe—a deep black cloud above it—and a thin, very thin black cloud, like a strip of black crape stretched across it——The line of Moonlight on the water, which had been so bright, glimmered very dim—We saw lights in the houses on the right bank, two or three; I felt the striking contrast between the silence of this majestic Stream whose banks are populous with Men & Women & Children, & flocks and herds—the Silence by night of the peopled river, contrasted with the ceaseless noise, the uproar, and the loud agitations of the desolate solitude of the ocean——The Passengers below have retired to bed, and left me to all my best Feelings—The Prussian this night had displayed all his talents to captivate the Dane, who had adopted him into his Train of Dependents—The *English* Youth interpreted the Prussian's stories to me—they were all obscene and abominable; but some sufficiently witty, and a few valuable as philosophical facts of the manners of the Countries, concerning the natives of which he related them—His person, countenance, manners & conversation all coincided—cold, tho' libidinous; cunning and calculative amid the roar of his boisterous Buffoonery.—The German Taylor and his little Wife were both Characters; but these and some other things of less consequence I have reserved that I may have something to talk of when once more I sit in the great Arm Chair at Poole's over his strong beer—God bless him——

Wednesday Septr 19th. Hauled the Anchor at 5 o'clock in the morning—at six a thick fog came on & we were obliged to drop it again—and we were fearful that it would continue all Day; but about nine it cleared and we passed that beautiful Island—We had but very little wind & did not go more than 4 miles an hour—— The Shores became more beautiful; green and the Trees close to the water, with neat houses and sharp Steeples peering over them, some of the Steeples white, some black, & some red. There is the greatest profusion of Churches on the right bank.—The Trees and Houses are very low; sometimes the low trees overtopping the yet lower houses; sometimes the low houses overtopping the lower Trees—Both the right & left Banks are green to the very brink, & level with the water, like a park Canal.

Forty six miles from Cuxhaven and 16 from Hamburg (English miles) the Village of Veder [Wedel?] with a black Steeple—it stands on the left bank which belongs all the way to Denmark—Close by the Village of Veder and without any Church the village of Schulau, wild & pastoral—and then the left bank rises at once 40 feet at least above the water, and stood a perpendicular sandy Facing

with thin patches of green like some parts of the shore near Shurton
Bars. I look[ed] up the River along the same bank, and saw at some
distance high lands, brown and barren with scars of naked sand—
We now saw boats with Fishermen in them, and the Sea-gulls
flying round and round about them—We reach those high lands,
and come to Blankenese, a very wild Village scattered amidst
scattered Trees in three divisions over three Hills—the Village in
three divisions; yet seemingly continuous——Each of the three
hills stands towards the River, a facing of bare sand; and a great
number of Boats with bare Poles stood in Files along the Banks,
in a sort of fantastic Harmony with the steep facings of bare Sand.
Between each Facing is a Dell green & woody, and one a deep Dell.
It is a large Village made up of *Individual* houses, each house sur-
rounded with Trees and with a separate path to it—A village with
a Labyrinth of Paths—A Neighbourhood of houses is the best name
I can find to give it—Fishermen dwell here, and it is celebrated for
making boats called Blankenese Boats. Here first we saw the Spires
of Hamburg—From Blankenese up to Altona the left bank of the
Elbe very pretty—high and green, prettily planted with Trees—
houses near the water . . .[1] of Trees—and Summer houses and
Chinese things all up the high Banks—all neat and comfortable,
like a rural Place cut into Shapes & *townified* for the citizens who
come here from Altona and Hamburg to smoke their pipes on
Saturdays and Sundays—The Boards of the houses (i.e. the Farm
houses) are left unplaistered, painted green and black, like some
old houses in England—

—— Wednesday 4 o'clock—got ourselves out of the Vessel into
a Boat at Altona, half a mile from Hamburg—passed with trouble
the huge masses of Shipping that choke the wide Elbe from Altona
up to Hamburg—and are now safe at the boom [baum]-house
Hamburg——

Chester and I are well—and comfortable. But I wish hourly for
my dear Sara, & my Babes. God bless her & her faithful & affec-
tionate Husband

S T Coleridge

257. *To Mrs. S. T. Coleridge*

Transcript Thomas Ward copy-book, New York Public Lib. Pub. Letters, *i. 262.*
The first part of this letter is missing from the transcript.

Octbr 20th 1798

. . . But I must check these feelings & write more collectedly.—I
am well, my dear Love!—very well—and my situation is in all

[1] Word missing in transcript.

respects comfortable—My Room is large, & healthy—The house commands an enchanting prospect—The Pastor is worthy and a learned Man—a Widower with 8 Children, 5 of whom are at home —The German Language is spoken here in the utmost purity—The Children often stand round my Sopha and chatter away—& the little one of all corrects my pronunciation with a pretty pert lisp & self sufficient tone, while the others laugh with no little joyance.— The Gentry and Nobility here pay me almost an adulatory attention——There is a very beautiful little Woman, less I think than you—a Countess Kilmansig [Kielmansegge]—her Father is our Lord Howe's Cousin. She is the wife of a very handsome Man, and has two fine little Children—I have quite won her heart by a German Poem which I wrote. It is that sonnet 'Charles! my slow heart was only sad when first '[1]—& considerably dilated with new images & much superior in the German to it's former dress—It has excited no small wonder here for it's purity and harmony—I mention this as a proof of my progress in the language—indeed it has surprised myself—but I want to be home—and I work hard—very hard, to shorten the time of absence—The little Countess said to me—'O! Englishmen be always sehr gut Fathers and Husbands.—I hope dat you will come and lofe my little babies, and I will sing to you and play on the guitar & the Piano Forte—and my dear Huspan he spracts sehr gut English and he lofes England better than all the world'—(sehr gut is very good; spract speaks or talks)—She is a sweet little Woman, and what is very rare in Germany, she has perfectly white regular, french Teeth——I could give you many instances of the ridiculous partiality or rather madness for the English—One of the first things, which strikes an Englishman, is the German cards—They are very different from ours—the Court Cards have two heads, a very convenient thing, as it prevents the necessity of turning the cards and betraying your hand—& are smaller & cost only a penny—yet the Envelope, in which they are sold, has Wahrliche Englisch Karten—i.e. Genuine *English* Cards. ——I bought some sticking plaister yesterday; it cost two pence— a very large piece; but it was three halfpence farthing too dear— for indeed it looked like a nasty rag of black Silk which Cat or Mouse dung had stained & spotted——but this was Königl. Pat: Engl: Im: Plaister—i.e. Royal Patent *English Ornament* Plaister—They affect to write English over their doors—One house has English Lodgement and Caffee Hous!—But the most amusing of all is an advertisement of a quack Medicine of the same Class with Dr Solomon's & Brody's——For the spirits and all weakness of mind and body—What think you? 'A wonderful and secret Essence

[1] *Poems*, i. 154. The German version has not come to light.

extracted with patience & God's blessing from the English Oaks, and from that part thereof, which the heroic Sailors of that Great Nation call the Heart of Oak. This invaluable & infallible Medicine has been godlily extracted therefrom by the slow processes of the Sun & magnetical Influences of the Planets & Fixed Stars.'—This is a literal Translation—At the Concert, when I entered, the Band played 'Britannia! rule the waves'—and at the dinner which was given in honor of Nelson's Victory, 21 guns were fired by order of the military Governour, and between each Firing the Military Band played an English Tune—I never saw such enthusiasm, or heard such tumultuous shouting, as when the Governour gave as a toast, 'The Great Nation.'—By this Name they always designate England, in opposition to the same title self-assumed by France. The Military Governour is a pleasant Man, & both he & the Amtmann (i.e. the Civil Regent) are particularly attentive to me—I am quite domesticated in the house of the latter—his first wife was an English Woman, and his partiality for England is without bounds.—— God bless you, my love! write me a very, very long letter—write me all that can cheer me—all that will make my eyes swim & my heart melt with tenderness!

Your faithful & affectionate Husband
S. T. Coleridge

P.S.—A Dinner lasts not uncommonly three Hours!—

258. *To Thomas Poole*

Address: Mr T. Poole | Nether Stowey | Somersetshire | England   Payed to Cuxhaven fr Ritzbuttel
MS. New York Public Lib. Part of the journal in this letter was revised and published in *Satyrane's Letters*, ii. See *The Friend*, No. 16, 7 December 1809, and *Biog. Lit.* 1817, ii. 205–17. The manuscript is torn and the words in brackets have been supplied from a transcript made by Thomas Ward. *Postmark*: 10 November 1798.

October 26th—1798

3rd of the Journal—8th including all.[1]

My best and dearest Friend

My spirit is more feminine than your's—I cannot write to you without tears / and I know that when you read my letters, and when you talk of me, *you* must often 'compound with misty eyes'—. May God preserve me for your friendship, and make me worthy of it! I received your letter yesterday—since I last wrote, I have been

[1] Actually the second part of the journal. Only six letters to Poole and Mrs. Coleridge from 15 Sept. to 26 Oct. have come to light.

on a tour to Travemunde on the Baltic Sea, & the places adjoining to which circumstance you must attribute my silence.—My last landed me on the Elbe-stairs at the Baum-house, Hamburgh.— While I was standing on the stairs, I was amused by the passage boat which goes once or twice a day from Hamburg to Haarburg, across the River—it was crammed with all people of all nations in all sorts of dresses, the Men with pipes of all shapes and fancies, strait and wreathed, simple and complex, long and short, cane, clay, porcelain, wood, tin, silver, and ivory—*one*, a mere hot-spice-gingerbreadcake-man's Stump Whiffer, and *many* with silver chains & with silver *bole*-covers.—Well, but to adopt the Journal Form Sep. 19th Afternoon.——Wordsworth had introduced himself to a kind of confidential acquaintance with the French Emigrant who appeared a man of sense & was in his manners a most complete gentleman. He seemed about 50. It was agreed that if possible we should house together—Wordsworth & the Emigrant went in search of an Hotel—the Emigrant's Servant, Chester, & Miss Wordsworth stayed with the luggage—and I dashed into the town to deliver my letters of recommendation. I had two from Wedgewood, 1. to Mr Von Axen, and one to a Mr Chatterley.—I dashed on; and very naturally began to *wonder* at *all* things—some for being so like, and some for being so unlike, the things in England. Dutch Women with large umbrella Hats shooting out half a yard before them, and with a prodigal *plumpness* of petticoat *behind*—the Hamburghers with caps, plated on the cawl with silver or gold, or both, fringed with lace, & standing *round before* their eyes, like a canopy-veil—the Hanoverian Women with the fore part of the Head bare, then a stiff lace standing upright like a Wall, perpendicular on the Cap; and the Cap behind *tailed* with a monstrous quantity of Ribbon which lies or tosses on the Back. 'Their Visnomies seem'd like a goodly Banner Spread in defiance of all Enemies!'[1]—The Young Men dashing *English* Bucks—the Ladies, all in English Dresses & in the newest Fashions—and all rouged.—I looked in at the windows as I passed—gentlemen & ladies drinking Coffee or playing Cards, and *all* the Gentlemen *Smoking* at the same Time. The Streets narrow and stinking, without any appropriate path for the foot-passengers—the Gable Ends of the Houses, all towards

the street; some in the ordinary Triangular form, ⋀—but most

of them ⌐⌐ notched and *shapified* with more than Chinese

---

[1] Spenser, *Amoretti*, v.

Grotesqueness.—Above all, both here and at Altona, I was struck with the *profusion* of windows—so large & so many that the Houses look all Glass. Mr Pitt's Tax would greatly improve the Architecture of Hamburgh; but the Elbe & the Country round will be still more benefited by the last Conflagration. For it is a foul City!——

I moved on & crossed a multitude of ugly Bridges, the water intersecting the City every where & furnishing to an Architect the *capabilities* of all that is beautiful & magnificent in human Edifices —such it might have been; it might have been more than the Rival of Venice; & it is——Huddle and Ugliness, Stink and Stagnation! Close by many of the Bridges I observed great Water wheels—huge deformities, but yet they produced motion in the air & the water, & therefore appeared pleasing to me.—I met with many who talked broken English—& at last, after some vagaries, I arrived at the Jungfr' Stieg (Maidens' Walk) where the Von Axens reside.—It is a walk or promenade, planted with treble rows of Elm Trees, which are slim & dwarf, on account of their being pruned & cropped every year—and this Walk occupies one side of a Square piece of water, with many Swans on it, quite tame / & there were Gentlemen, in pretty pleasure-boats, rowing the Ladies.—It pleased me much—; but I observed that it was not *lamped* round. If it were, it would make a beautiful appearance by night!——I delivered my letter to Mr Von Axen who embarrassed me by his sad and solemn Politeness, & his broken English—I left him rather abruptly & called on Remnant, an English Bookseller for whom I had a letter from Johnson—he was not at home / thro' Streets & Streets, or rather thro' Lanes & Lanes, I trudged to Chatterley's / amused as I went on by the *wicker*-waggons (with moveable forms in them, one behind the other, across the waggon)! These Waggons are the Hackney Coaches of Hamburgh—(tho' there were Hackney Coaches likewise; but the Waggons appeared far more numerous). They were quite uncovered, & in shape something like the old Grecian Cars, only much larger / that is, long, & *narrow* compared with the length—I saw several parties of Eight in them besides the Coach Man.—Amused too by the signboards on the Shops—all the articles sold within are painted in a grotesque confusion on these Boards, & in general were painted very exactly.—Well, I arrived at Chatterley's—an odd beast! He read Mr Wedgewood's letter, & asked me drily if I would take a cup of Tea.—'Yes!'— / An old Woman, his domestic, poured into her hand out of the Tea Cannister what *I thought* a very small portion—'Oh! Oh! Oh! Oh!' exclaimed Chatterley—& she returned part of it into the Tea Cannister!——Well, I drank a couple of dishes, & agreed that I would call again on the morrow morning—& now the Emigrant's Servant came & guided

me to Der Wilder Man i.e. The Savage—an hotel not of the
genteelest Class.—But Wordsworth & the Emigrant had trudged
over & over the City—& every House was *full*! However they were
drinking some excellent Claret, & I joined them with no small
glee—.—The Emigrant had one large Room in which himself &
Servant were to sleep, & in which it was agreed that we should all
breakfast & drink Tea—there was a Bed room for Chester & me,
with two beds in it—and one for Miss Wordsworth.—Wordsworth
had procured one for himself at Sea Man's Hotel where Baldwin
lodged, the Brother of Losh's Wife, & a college Acquaintance of
Wordsworth's. My bed room looked into and commanded the
Market Place of Hamburgh; and close by, as close as close can be,
is the great huge church of St Nicholas, with shops & houses built
up against it; out of which *Wens and Warts*, or rather, out of which
unseemly *Corns*, it's high huge Steeple rises, *necklaced* near the Top
with a Round of large Gilt Balls.—The Hotel is certainly well fitted
for a stranger—this Steeple must be quite a Pole-Star.—— / —The
Emigrant was of the Noblesse, & was an intimate Friend of the
Abbe De Lisle, the famous Poet—he had been a man of large For-
tune, out of which he had rescued a considerable part. He talked
with rapture of Paris under the Monarchy—& seemed not a little
enamoured of London, where he had lived in style, & where his
favorite Niece resided, a married woman. But some Emigrants,
whom he had offended, I believe, by some refusals in the money-
way, conspired against him, accused him of being connected with
the governing Party, & tho' they could prove nothing; yet they
had interest enough to have him sent away by the Duke of Port-
land. So he was obliged to sell out of the Stocks at a great loss—&
leave the Country. He seemed very deeply *cut* at heart—a man
without hopes or wishes—yet a melancholy Frenchman is almost a
merry Englishman, & we found no lack of vivacity in him, & his
manner was exceedingly delightful. He carried with him a sort of
travelling furniture & toilet—all of silver or gold—indeed every
part of his moveables evinced the Man of Fortune.—He meant to
take a House near Hamburgh.—The Swedish Nobleman called on
me, from the Dane / & in his name pressed me to come to the 'King
of England'—the great superb Hotel of Hamburgh— / & here I
might have had a room in the Dane's suit[e] of apartments, & have
been one of his Table.—But I remembered Godwin's excuse for
feeding on that scoundrelly money-lender, Ki[ng—] (the Proprietor
of that ex[ecrable ve]hicle of Jacobinism, the Telegraph)—and tho'
I should have liked to [have studied] *the man* a little more, yet I did
not think it right or reputa[ble— so] I refused the offered Kindness.
——Went to be[d—We both] instead of Bed Cloaths had two feather

beds one above & one below—/both ou[r Sheets] stunk prodigiously
of the Soap, with which they had been washed.—I awo[ke at] two
o'clock, & was struck by the awful *Echo* of the Clock in the huge
Ch[urch,] which I heard distinctly. The Echo was loud, & long, and
trembling.——[Slept again,] and, (Thursday, Sept. 20th—)

Sept. 20th, I was awaked by the distressful Cries of Poultry
crowing [& clucking] & screaming in the market place. I looked out,
and saw a large crowd of Market-people / and saw among other
articles large Heaps of Hares & Game Fowl, for Sale.—I reviewed
my Expences from Yarmouth to Hamburgh—

L.	S.	D	
0″	3″	6	Fee to the Searcher.
0″	12″	6	Pass port.
0″	6″	0	Bill at the Inn.
0″	1″	0	Porterage to the Pier
0″	3″	0[1]	Boat to the Pacquet. N.B. Every Passenger pays half a crown [for himself and 1 shilling for every box] or [parcel he may have—]
3″	3″	0	Passage Money.
1″	1″	0	Provision-money. N.B. Wordsworths & Chester provisioned themselves; but I would advise every one to provision with the Captain—it is but a guinea, & you may be at Sea a fortnight.——
0″	10″	6	Fees to the Mate, Steward, & Sailors. N.B. This is the least Sum possible.——
0″	10″	6	Passage from Cuxhaven to Altona. Had I gone in any other way, than in the Pacquet, this would have cost at least a guinea—probably more / and it is *very rare indeed* that the pacquets go up to Hamburgh. So I was in luck.——
0″	1″	0	Boat for self & portmanteau from Altona to Hamburgh.——
0″	2″	0	Porterage from the Boat to the Inn. N.B. Of course, I payed *the share*—tho' my own baggage was not the 20th part.—I mention this, merely to account for the largeness of the Sum.——

Sum-Total. £.6″ 14″ 6.—P.S. For Babies they charge nothing on
board the Pacquet—Children above 5 years old pay half price.——

My next Sheet will recommence with Thursday, Sept. 20th—/—.
We are very well, & very comfortable. My progress in the language

---

[1] In Coleridge's notebook this item reads 3/6, thus making the 'Sum-Total'
correct.

is rapid & surprizes the people here not a little. Every one pays me the most assiduous attentions—I have attended some Conversations at the Houses of the Nobility—stupid things enough.—It was quite a new thing to me to have Counts & Land-dr[osten] bowing & scraping to me—& Countesses, old & young, complimenting & amusing me.—But to be an Englishman is in Germany to be an Angel—they almost worship you. I wrote to Mrs Coleridge some ludicrous instances of the Rage for England.—It is absolutely false that the literary Men are Democrats in Germany—Many *were*; but like me, have *published* Abjurations of the French—among which number are Klopstock, Goethe, (the author of the Sorrows of Werter) Wieland, Schiller & Kotzebu.—The German is a noble Language—a very noble Language. If you had time, I should recommend you strenuously to look over the German Grammar, & devote half an hour in every day to construing five or six lines of German. There are Grammar & Dictionary & Meisner's Dialogues among my Books.—I cannot endure to have an enjoyment in which you cannot partake / and it will furnish an immense store of Enjoyment for your Retirement, and Old Age.——I have written to a learned Physician in Hamburgh about the Palliate for the Stone— Sir John Sinclair is such an old [wo]man that I have no hopes. Most certainly, Beddoes would have heard of it.—However, God grant, it may be true!——My dear Love to your Mother—indeed, indeed, I love her as a Mother.—Love to Ward—& My dear Poole! my Heart is quite full of you.

> [God bless you
> & S. T. Coleridge—]

N.B. The present King of Prussia is quite adored in Germany; & deserves to be so. He is a *good Man.* May he continue to be so.

259. *To Mrs. S. T. Coleridge*

Address: Mrs Coleridge | Nether Stowey | Somersetshire | England   Pay'd to Cuxhaven.
MS. New York Public Lib. Part of the journal in this letter was revised and published in *Satyrane's Letters*, ii. See *The Friend*, No. 16, 7 December 1809, and *Biog. Lit.* 1817, ii. 217–21. Coleridge prints in *Satyrane's Letters*, ii, a long passage on drama, of which he says, 'I might have written this last sheet without having gone to Germany'; and since the passage does not appear in the German letters, I suspect he wrote it after he returned to England. *Postmark*: Foreign Office, 21 November 1798.

Nov. 8th, 1798

My dearest Love

After an eight weeks' Run of fine weather we are at last visited by the chilly, misty Rains of November—and the Lake looks turbid, and the purple of the woods has degenerated into a shabby Dirt-colour. My best dear Sara! what an impassable Hog-stye, what a Slough of Despond must Lime-Street be—vocal with the Poor-house Nightingales!——But however let me recommence my Journal—

Thursday Morn. Sept. 20th—10 o clock. I called on Mr Chatterley. He introduced me to his Partner, Mr Klopstock; or as we ludicrously named him, YOUNG Klopstock.—He is indeed younger than his Brother / altho' an old man.——Well—he could not speak a word of English; but was kind and courteous. I went and fetched Words-worth; and he and Klopstock talked in French—which K. spoke fluently, altho' with a most glorious havock of Genders & Syntax. ——K. took us to Professor Ebeling—Now what a *Professor* is, I know not; but I will enquire & inform you when I give an account of the German Universities & the condition of their Literary Men. ——The Professor was a lively intelligent Man—lively altho' deaf —he spoke English very decently / but it was [an] effort to talk with him—as we were obliged to drop all our Pearls into a huge Ear-trumpet.—He informed us that Pacha Oglou[1] was not a Rebel, but a Turkish Constitutionalist, at the head of the Party who oppose all the Innovations & Gallicisms of the Seraglio. He is a sturdy Mahometan, supported by the Nobles & Men of Law—and ready to submit, if the Grand Seignior will reduce his Government to the practices of his Ancestors.—This information he had received from a Mr Hawkins who had just returned from Constantinople, who likewise affirms that the Modern Greeks are an estimable and interesting People; very many among them remember the glory of their ancestors; they are impatient of the Turkish Yoke, but detest French Men & French Manners.——He told us a good Italian Pun. —When Buonaparte was in Italy, he was on some occasion exceed-ingly irritated by the Perfidy of the Italians, & said in a large Com-pany—Ay!—'their own Proverb is most true.'—The Italians are 'tutto Ladrones' [tutti ladroni] (that is—all Bandittimen, or Thieves.—) An Italian Lady present answered—Non tutto [tutti]; mais [ma] Buona Parte. Not all; but a good Part.——The following anecdote is more valuable; & is true: whereas to my mind the Pun sounds very much like a *Might be* good Thing.——Hoche[2] had received much information concerning the Face of the Country from a very accurate Map, the Maker of which, he had been in-formed, lived at Dusseldorf.—At the storming of Dusseldorf by the French Army Hoche ordered the House & Property of this man to be preserved; & finding that he had fled, said—'He had no reason

---

[1] Pasvan Oglu, Turkish governor of Vidin.
[2] Lazare Hoche (1768–97), the French general.

to flee / the French Nation make war *for* such men, not *against*
them!'——You remember Milton's Sonnet—'The great Emathian
Conqueror bade spare The House of Pindarus'— / Altho' a Snail-
trailing Mapmaker may not be put alongside of the Theban Eagle,
yet this does not prevent Hoche from being as great a man as
Alexander—

From the Professor's Klopstock took us to Wagon-house—i.e.—
a place where second Hand Travelling-Machines were on Sale.—
All very dear—none under 30 pound.——

Young Klopstock is a sort of Merchant in the agency Line; (as
indeed are most of the Hamburghers) and he is the Proprietor of
one of the Hamburgh Newspapers.—We saw at his house a fine
Bust of his Brother—there was a solemn and heavy Greatness in
the Countenance which corresponded with my preconceptions of
his style & genius.—I saw likewise there a very, very fine picture
of Lessing. His eyes were uncommonly like mine—if any thing,
rather larger & more prominent—But the lower part of his face &
his nose—O what an exquisite expression of elegance and sensibility!
—There appeared no depth, weight, or comprehensiveness in the
Forehead.—The whole Face seemed to say, that Lessing was a man
—of quick & voluptuous Feelings; of an active but light Fancy;
acute; yet acute not in the observation of actual Life, but in the
arrangements & management of the Ideal World—(i.e.) in taste,
and in metaphysics.——

Thursday. 3 o / clock. Dined at the Saxe Hotel; because, it being
French, we expected it would be cheap. But we had a miserable
Dinner; and were detestably cheated.— 6 o-clock. We went to the
French Comedy.—Most truly stupid & ridiculous. The following is
a sketch.—First Act informs us that a Court Martial is to be held
on a Count Vatron who had drawn his Sword on the Colonel whose
Sister he had married. The Officers plead in behalf of Count Vatron
—in vain!—His wife—the Colonel's Sister—pleads—with most
tempestuous agonies—in vain! She falls into Hysterics & faints
away.——Second Act—Sentence of Death passed—the Wife frantic
& Hysterical as before.—Third Act— / Wife frantic—Soldiers just
going to fire—the Handkerchief dropped—when 'Reprieve![']
'Reprieve'—is cried out—& in comes the Prince Somebody—
and pardons the Count—& the Wife is frantic with Joy.—That's
all!——The afterpiece was flat; but with some pretty Music.

Thursday Night.—Saw in the Streets not one Prostitute / I found
afterwards that they all live in one Street near Altona; and never
appear out of their Houses, as Prostitutes.—(N.B. Altona is a large
town; bearing the same relation to Hamburgh, as Islington to
London. / But it belongs to the King of Denmark—& the Ham-

burghers (they say) named it for that Reason, Altona—which in low German signifies, Too near.)——Amused by the Watchmen who chant a sort of Night-Song, ringing not unmusically, a small Bell at Intervals.—(N.B.) At Ratzeburgh the Watchman blows a Tune on a Horn, every half-hour thro' the Night. / —The Doors of all the Houses have Bells, both at Hamburgh & Ratzeburgh, & wherever else I have been.—A little Iron Rod, the length of my hand, is fastened to the Top of the Door, thus —The Bell hangs on one side of the Door—& bends in the shape of a Canopy over the Iron Rod. Of course whenever you open or shut the Door, the Iron Rod strikes the Bell—and there is from Morning to Night an incessant kling, kling, klang / quite wearisome till you cease to observe it.—Bürger alludes to this in the Lenore where the Knight first comes to the Chamber—

And horch! und horch! den Pfortenving—And hark! and hark the
                                                    Gate-Bell
Ganz lose, leise, klingklingkling!¹   All softly, lowly, kling-
                                                 klingkling.—

N.B.—Bürger of all the German Poets pleases me the most, as yet —the Lenore is greatly superior to any of the Translations. Bürger's wife was unchaste, & he died of a broken Heart—She is now a Demirep & an Actress at Hamburgh!—A *Bitch*!!——

Friday, Septem. 21st. We consumed the morning in carriage-hunting:—and dined at our Hotel at the Ordinary—a mark a head. —This was the Dinner, & all the Dinners I have since seen, resemble it as nearly as English Dinners resemble one another in different Houses.——First—Soup.—(N.B. It was good *Broth*; but every Thing here is called *Soup*.—)—A long Interval.——Some hung Beef, with unsalted boiled Beef, cut out in slices & handed round in a plate—each man takes what he likes with his fork.—Then two large Dishes of Vegetables were handed round—The first, Carrots drest in butter—not unpleasantly: & at the same time, great French Beans with their seeds in them, stewed in some condiment, I knew not what.—The vegetables are never brought to Table *simple* as with us.—Another long Interval—'And Patience, at a German Ordinary, Smiling at Time!'——Then were handed round in a plate as before Slices of roast-beef, roasted dry & ragged—A good Sallad—then Slices of Roast Pork with stewed Prunes, & other sweet Fruit stewed—.——Then cheese, and Butter, with plates of Orleans Plumbs by way of Desert: *and*—Apples.—It appears from Shake-

---

¹ G. A. Bürger, *Lenore*, lines 101–2.

spear's Plays that in his time the Eng[lish][1] drest their dishes as the
Germans do now—as for instance, the Merry Wives [of] Windsor—
'Slender. I bruised my shin with playing with sword & dagger for
a dish [of stewed] prunes; & by my Troth I cannot abide the smell
of Hot Meat since.'——So in the [same Piece—] 'Evans.—I will
make an end of my dinner: there's pippins & cheese yet to come[.']

I have now dined at all the Gentlemen's & Noblemen's Houses
w[ithin] two or three miles of Ra[tzebur]gh—& the dinners have
been always [begun by] Soup—sometimes made of Flesh, some-
times of Fruit—in short, it [is always the first] Thing.—I believe,
I have tasted 20 kinds of Soup.—The flesh Soup is good Broth &
the Meat is introduced afterwards—not the better for it's avant-
courier.—Besides this, the most common Soups are / — 1 Wine
Soup—made of the common Wine, (resembling pleasant Cyder but
with the vinous flavor) of Water, sugar, Eggs & Carraway Seeds.—
2 Water Soup—the same as Water gruel.—3. Plum Soup—made
of bruised Plums, Sugar, Eggs & Water. 4 Raisin Soup.—Made of
Water-gruel with Currants & Raisins in it, and a little wine. 5. Rice
Soup:—it is Rice-milk. 6. Kreutzer [Grütze ?] Soup. Milk with a sort
of Millet, called Kreutzers—(there are large Fields of the Plant which
flowers in June—& then for half a mile together you may see one
sheet of white blossoms that send forth an odour sweeter, they say,
than the Bean blossom.—) 7. Beer Soup.—Made of Beer, Eggs, Sugar,
& crumbled Bread. /——Well—first Soup.—Then the Table is *covered*
with small dishes, & *exactly resembles* a Saturday's Scrap Dinner in
a large Family——a long Interval—then Fish is handed round—
another Interval——then Pies & Tarts—another Interval—then
a large Joint of Roast Meat——another Interval—then Cheese,
Butter, Fruits, & Sweetmeats.——There is placed for every two
Persons a bottle of common wine, either white or red—the white
I have described before; & the Red is a distant Relation of Claret
—/ But during the Dinner the Servants hand round Glasses of
richer wines—at the Lord of Culpin's they came in this order.—
1. Claret. 2. Madeira. 3. Port. 4. Frontiniac. 5. A Spanish Wine—I
have forgot the name. 6 Old Hock. 7. Mountain. 8. Champaign.
9. Old Hock again. 10th & last.—Punch.—Each *Man* drank a glass
of each / but this is the custom only on high days & great Feasts.—
They change the Plates often; but seldom or never the Knives and
Forks—not even after Fish.—I however always send away my
knife and fork with the Plate / and the Servants consider me as an
Englishman.—All the men have a hideous custom of picking their
Teeth with their forks—Some hold up their napkins before their

---

[1] Manuscript torn; the words in brackets in this and the following paragraph
are supplied from a transcript made by Thomas Ward.

mouths while they do it—which is shocking—and adds a moral
Filth to the action by evincing that the Person is conscious of the
Filth of the Action.—And the Top of their Teeth, the breadth of
the Top, is commonly black & yellow with a Life's *Smoking*—the
Women too have commonly bad Teeth. In *every* House every
Person, Children & all, have always a folded Napkin put on the
Plate / but it is not always very clean.——Carpets are very un-
common. As far as my experience goes hitherto, I like the Stoves
very well.—Chester & I could not conceive at first what they were.
We saw in every Room a great high Thing of a strange Shape,
made of Dutch Tiles—or black Tiles—or ebony—from seven to
ten feet high—Till I went to Ratzeburgh, I imagined them to be
ornamental Furniture.—I wish very much I could draw—how
many awkward round about Sentences which after all convey no
true ideas, would three lines with a pencil save me:—and I too am
especially a very awkward Describer of Shapes & Dresses.——

We are well, My dear Love!——My next letter will recommence
with Friday, Sept. 21st—N.B. Yet Goose is always stuffed with
Plums & Prunes in great quantities—it is indeed a Plum & Prune
Pie, of which the Goose is the *Crust*.——

We have not heard from the Wordsworths—to my great Anxiety
& inexpressible Astonishment. Where they are, or why they are
silent, I cannot even guess.——O my love! I wish you were with
me— / —I have received no information that can be relied upon
concerning the medicine, Sir John Sinclair mentions— / but I will
not give up the Search / tho' I believe it to be all idle.—How a man
ought to weigh such Sentences before he publishes them!—it is no
good thing to trifle with the Hopes of them who are in Agony!——

I have not yet heard from you, my Love! But I hope that
tomorrow or next day will bring me a letter— / God love you &
your most aff. & faithful Husband, S. T. Coleridge.—

My love to dear Mrs Poole,—to Bessy, Susan, & Julia Chester—
to Lavinia, &c at the Farm—to Mr & Mrs Roskilly—&c—

260. *To William Wordsworth*

Pub. Memoirs of William Wordsworth, *by Christopher Wordsworth, 2 vols., 1851, i. 132.*

[*Circa* 17 November 1798][1]

You have two things against you: your not loving smoke; and
your sister. If the manners at Goslar resemble those at Ratzeburg,

[1] Since on 8 Nov. Coleridge told his wife that he had not heard from Words-
worth (Letter 259), and since he wrote to Poole on 20 Nov. (Letter 261) that
Wordsworth had written from Goslar, 'where he arrived six weeks ago'
(6 Oct.), this letter belongs to *circa* 17 Nov.

it is almost necessary to be able to bear smoke. Can Dorothy endure smoke? Here, when my friends come to see me, the candle nearly goes out, the air is so thick.

261. *To Thomas Poole*

Address: Mr Thomas Poole | Nether Stowey | Somersetshire | England *single* payed to Cuxhaven
MS. New York Public Lib. Part of the journal in this letter was revised and published in *Satyrane's Letters*, iii. See *The Friend*, No. 18, 21 December 1809, and *Biog. Lit.* 1817, ii. 237–53.
Postmark: Foreign Office, 10 December 1798.

Ratzeburgh. Novemb. 20th, 1798

My beloved Poole—How comes it that I hear from none of you? —Since your's of the 8th of October, there has been a dreary Silence. Am I not a Friend, a Husband, a Father?—And do there not belong to each of these it's own longings and inquietudes?— The Post comes in here four times a week; and for these last three Weeks four times every week have I hoped and hoped for a letter, till my heart is almost weary of hoping—and no hour passes in which my anxiety about you does not for a few minutes turn me away from my studies.—I fear that you have not written; and I fear that you have written—: if the latter be the Case, *you* may be blaming *me*—& Sara imagining that I do not feel my own & her absence as I ought to feel it.—

Friday, Sept. 21st. Wordsworth & I accompanied Klopstock to his Brother's who lives ten minutes walk from the Gates, in a row of little Summer-houses—so they appear—with ugly rows of cropped & meagre Elms before them.—Whatever beauty may be before the Poet's Eyes at present, it must certainly be purely of his own creation—thought I, as I entered the House.—We waited a few minutes in a neat little parlour, ornamented with Prints, the subjects of which were from Klopstock's Odes.—The Poet entered. —I was much disappointed in his countenance. I saw no Likeness to the Bust.—. There was no *comprehension* in the Forehead—no *weight* over the eyebrows—no expression of peculiarity, either moral or intellectual, in the eyes;—there was no *massiveness* in the general Countenance.—He is not quite so tall as I am—his upper jaw is toothless, his under jaw all black Teeth; and he wore very large half-boots, which his legs completely filled. They were enormously swelled.—He was lively, kind and courteous. He talked in French with Wordsworth—&, with difficulty, spoke a few sentences to me in English.—We were with him somewhat more than an hour. He began the conversation by expressing his rapture, in a

very voluble utterance, at the surrender of the French in Ireland[1]
—and his sanguine belief in Nelson's Victory.—He talked as a
most vehement Anti-gallican.—The Subject changed to Poetry—
& I enquired, in Latin, concerning the history of German Poetry,
& of the elder German Poets.—To my great astonishment he
confessed, he knew very little on the subject—he had indeed read
occasionally one or two of their elder writers—but not as to be able
to speak of their merits.—He told me that Professor Ebeling would
probably give me every information of this kind—the subject had not
particularly excited his curiosity.—(N.B. He answered in French,
& Wordsworth interpreted it to me)—He shewed us a superb
Edition of his works in Quarto—two Volumes containing his Odes
are all that are yet printed—. The price is £2, the volume / nearly
twice as dear as the same sort of Books in England. From whence I
conclude that they import the Paper from England, & that
Printers capable of the Beautiful in Printing are few & of course
have their own Prices. He talked of Milton & Glover;[2] & thought,
Glover's blank Verse superior to Milton's!—Wordsworth & myself
expressed our surprize—& Wordsworth explained his definition &
ideas of harmonious Verse, that it consisted in the arrangement of
pauses & cadences, & not in the even flow of single Lines—Klop-
stock assented, & said that he meant only in single Lines that
Glover was the Superior. He said, he had read Milton, in a prose
Translation, when he was 14.—*I understood this myself, & Words-
worth interpreted Klopstock's French, as I had already construed it.*
He appeared to know very little of Milton—or indeed of our Poets
in general. He spoke with great Indignation of the English Prose
Translation of his Messiah—All the Translations had been bad, very
bad—but the English was no Translation—there were pages on
pages, not in the Original—: & half the Original was not to be
found in the Translation. Wordsworth told him that *I* intended to
translate a few of his Odes as specimens of German Lyrics—he then
said to me in English, 'I wish, you would render into English some
select Passages of the Messiah, & *revenge* me of your Countryman.'
—It was the liveliest Thing, which he produced in the whole
Conversation. He told us that his first Ode was fifty years older
than his last. I looked at him with much emotion—I considered
him as the venerable Father of German Poetry; as a good man;
as a Christian; with legs enormously swelled; seventy four years
old; yet active and lively in his motions, as a boy; active, lively,
chearful and kind and communicative—and the Tears swelled

[1] On 8 Sept. 1798 General Humbert, who had conducted a French expedi-
tion to Ireland, surrendered to Cornwallis.
[2] Richard Glover (1712–85), author of *Leonidas*, a blank verse epic.

into my eyes; and could I have made myself invisible and inaudible, I should have wept outright.—In the picture of Lessing there was a Toupee Periwig which enormously injured the effect of his Physiognomy—Klopstock wore the same, powered, &c— / it had an ugly look; & Powder ever makes an old man's face look dirty.— It is an honor to Poets & Great Men that you think of them as parts of Nature; and any thing of Trick & Fashion wounds you in them as much as when you see Yews clipped into miserable peacocks.—The Author of the Messiah should have worn his own Grey Hair.—Powder and the Periwig were to the Eye what *Mr* Milton would be to the Ear—. —Klopstock talked what appeared to me great nonsense about the superior power which the German Language possessed, of *concentering meaning.* He said, he had often translated parts of Homer & Virgil line by line; and a German Line was always sufficient for a Greek One.—He observed that in English we could not do this.—I answered that in English we could commonly render 1 Greek line in a line & a half English; & that I conjectured, that a Line and a half English contained no more words than *one* German Hexameter.—He did not understand me well— & I was glad of it.—It *appeared* to me great nonsense—& since I have read so many of the German Poets, I find that it really *was* nonsense. I have translated some German Hexameters into English —& three lines English will express four lines German. The reason is evident—our language abounds in monosyllables.——We took our leave. We did not see Klopstock's Wife.—He never had any children—& this is his second Wife.—Klopstock possesses a pension from the Court of Denmark, or rather I believe from the Bernstorff Family—It was procured for him by his Friend, Count Stolberg the Poet—whose Sister was Bernstorff's Wife. I need not tell you, that this Bernstorff was the great & good Prime Minister of Denmark—whose name smells like a sweet Odor thro' the whole North of Europe / & his Son succeeds him in his office, & tho' not in Talents, yet in Virtue.—

At the beginning of the French Revolution Klopstock wrote some fiery Odes in praise of France—he received high & honorary Presents from the French Republic, &, like our Priestley, was invited to the French Legislature, which he declined.—But when French Liberty metamorphosed herself into a Fury, he sent back the Presents with an Ode, expressing his Recantation—& his abhorrence of the French Proceedings.—And since then, he has [been] more than enough an Antigallican.——

I will anticipate a little.—On Sunday 23rd I went to Ratzeburgh —& stayed there till Thursday— / In this Interval Wordsworth dined at the Country house of Klopstock's Brother—& the Poet

& his Wife dined with him.—The Wife had been a great Beauty,
& retained the proofs of it—but according to [him & Miss] W.—
She was vain & haughty—& gratified her pride by manifestly
exercising her authority over the Poet, as if conscious alwa[ys]
who it was over whom she was ruling.— So much for her.—
Wordsworth had a long [&] various Conversation on literature
with Klopstock—but it [was] (& Wordsworth agrees with me) all
very *commonplace*! He [s]poke in high terms of Wieland, as the
greatest Master of the German Language; but when prest on the
subject of his immorality, he confessed that *he* would not have
written the Oberon.—He spoke with the keenest *contempt* of
Schiller's Productions; & said, they could not retain their fame
many years.—Of Kant he said, that he was a Mountebank & the
Disgrace of Germany—an unintelligible Jargonist.—And that his
New Lights were going out very fast in Germany. (N.B. / *I* meet
every where tho', with some SNUFFS that have a live spark in them
—& fume under your nose in every company.—All are Kantians
whom I have met with.)—Of our poets he knew very little. He
spoke of Shakespeare's absurdities in a manner which proved he
had felt but little from his beauties.—Of Gray he knew nothing
but his Elegy—An Englishman some years back had given him
Collins's Poems, with which he was pleased.—He spoke of his own
Odes as excelling chiefly in lyric Construction; & therein thought
himself a successful Imitator of the Ancient Lyric.—Wordsworth
confessed, he had never discovered either sense or beauty in the
construction of Horace's Odes; but of this Klopstock would not
even hear!—Now here comes a melancholy Story:—as it implies a
littleness & vanity in the Old Poet that is painful to contemplate.
—He said, he had first planned the Messiah when he was Seventeen
—that he meditated on the Plan three years before he wrote a
Line— / & that he had never seen Milton till he had finished his
Plan.—This was a flat self-contradiction; but he appeared, according
to Wordsworth, very fearful lest he should be considered as an
Imitator of *Milton*!——— /—I was vexed to the Heart to hear this
Story—& the Wordsworths & I strive to believe that it was a
mistake on our part; but we cannot. However, we shall never
mention it except to our most intimate Friends who do not live in
or about London.——

Well—so much for that.——Well, he meditated three years on
the Plan—& then began to write; at first, in measured Prose, like
the Telemachus, in which he succeeded tolerably well—At last the
Thought struck him that the Ancient Hexameter would suit the
German Language. There had been already some specimens of
German Hexameter; but most miserable ones.—He set himself to

work, & in the course of a day or two had constructed 20 German Hexameters; & was so pleased with them that from henceforward he wrote only in Hexameters.—He published, thro' the urgency of Friends, the six first Books in his 23rd year:—& they were received with rapture.—Such is the History of the Messiah from the Poet's own Mouth.—Perhaps, you will ask, Have you read any of Klopstock's Poetry?—But a little, & that little was *sad Stuff*!—They call him the German Milton—a very *German* Milton indeed!—A sensible young man here assures me that Kl.'s poetical Fame is going down Hill.——

I have heard from Wordsworth—He is at Goslar—where he arrived six weeks ago / & his violent hatred of letter-writing had caused his ominous silence—for which he accuses himself in severe terms.—Goslar is an old decaying city at the Foot of the Hartz Mountain[s]—provisions very cheap, & lodgings very cheap; but no Society—and therefore as he did not come into Germany to learn the Language by a Dictionary, he must remove: which he means to do at the end of the Month. His address is—la grande Rue de Goslar en Basse Saxe.—Dorothy says—'William works hard, but not very much at the German.'—This is strange—I work at nothing else, from morning to night— / —It is very difficult to combine & arrange the German Sentences—and I make miserable Havoc with the Genders—but yet my progress is more rapid than I could myself have believed.—We are well—very well. —There is a fine lovely Frost.——

God love you, & my Sara & Babes—Love to your dear Mother.

S. T. Coleridge

262. *To Mrs. S. T. Coleridge*

Transcript Thomas Ward copy-book, New York Public Lib. Pub. with omis. Letters, *i. 265.* Part of the journal in this letter was revised and published in *Satyrane's Letters*, iii. See *The Friend*, No. 18, 21 December 1809, and *Biog. Lit.* 1817, ii. 232–4.

Ratzeburg, Novr 26th. 1798

Another, and another, and yet another Post day; and still Chester greets me with, 'No letters from England'! A Knell, that strikes out regularly four times a week—How is this my Love?— Why do you not write to me? — Do you think to shorten my absence by making it insupportable to me?—Or perhaps you anticipate that if I received a letter, I should idly turn away from my German to *dream* of you—of you & my beloved babies!—Oh yes!—I should indeed dream of you for hours and hours; of you, and of beloved Poole, and of the Infant that sucks at your breast, and of my dear dear Hartley—You would be *present*, you would be with me in the Air that I breathe; and I should cease to see you only when the tears rolled out of my eyes, and this naked un-domestic Room became again visible—But oh with what leaping and exhilarated faculties should I return to the objects & realities of my mission.— But now—nay, I cannot describe to you the gloominess of Thought, the burthen and Sickness of heart, which I experience every post day—Through the whole remaining day I am incapable of every thing but anxious imaginations, of sore and fretful feelings—The Hamburg Newspapers arrive here four times a week; and almost every Newspaper commences with, '*Schreiben aus London*—They write from London'—This day's, with schreiben aus London, vom *Nov 13*—But I am certain that you have written more than once; and I stumble about in dark and idle conjectures, how and by what means it can have happened that I have not received your Letters—I recommence my Journal, but with feelings that approach to disgust—for in very truth I have nothing in-teresting to relate——

Saturday Septr 22d—Wordsworth and we were in a state of doubt and oscillation whether we should proceed to Weimar or fix ourselves in some village near Hamburg—We were frightened at the expences of travelling to Weimar, extra post, as these expences were represented by English Travellers. Baldwin told us that it probably *would* cost 60 and *must* cost *forty* guineas—Remnant & the Germans affirmed this to be a prodigious hyperbole, & Remnant assured us that it was impossible that the Journey, (extra post, that is, the same as post chaises in opposition to stage Coaches) should cost us all four, provisions and all, & including all con-ceivable impositions, more than 15£—What a difference!—But Wordsworth says he can believe no Man—The laxity and inaccuracy of Men's minds are so astonishing—Young Klopstock recom-mended Ratzeburg to us, & offered a letter of introduction—and we accepted it, and I was appointed the Missioner.———

Septr 23d. Sunday —Shops, half of them, open as on other days. A French Comedy at Night—; but this is the third time only that the Theatres have been open on Sundays. The Hamburghers had been struggling for it for years, but it had been refused by the Aldermen as indecent.—One gate too is to be openable at Night—hitherto the gates have been all shut at 9 in Summer, & 5 in Winter, & no person from highest to lowest permitted to go out or in——I observed a Woman ironing, & others at *work*—I felt myself inclined to a strict Sabbatism; for I observe that where the Rich *may* play, the poor *must* work.—I entered the Church of St Nicholas—

observed a huge picture, I suppose 16 feet high, of St Christopher
with our Saviour on his shoulders—I should not have understood
it, but for the note relative to the saint in Southey's Travels in
Spain & Portugal—There was the largest Organ that I ever beheld
—& the whole Church was profuse in all ornaments except Wor-
shippers—It was an inconceivably thin Congregation—In other
parts of Germany none pretend not to be Infidels, except the
Pastors & the Peasantry—but in Hamburgh they are not *Irreli-
gionists*, only they *have no Religion*——

Septr 23d.—Sunday 5 o'clock—afternoon—I set off in the stage
for Ratzeburg—The vehicle bore a sort of rude resemblance to an
English stage coach—but it was larger—It held the same pro-
portion and likeness as an Elephant's ear to the human. On the
Top were naked boards of different colours, some painted, some
not—as if they had been parts of different Wainscoats—Instead
of Windows there were leathern curtains with a little eye of glass
in them—The Coach Doors and the Back-seats were thus windowed;
and as these Curtain Windows would not come close, it was terribly
cold.—And yet this thing of a Coach had it's finery—for it was
lined with *cut velvet*!—The four horses were harnessed simply with
ropes, which, when they stopped, lay upon the Ground—I payed
4 marks for my fare—As we entered the Vicinity of Hamburgh, I
was much struck with the neat and festal lightness of the Country
houses—Some were houses of entertainment, some private houses;
but all were neat & crowded with neat holliday-dressed People—I
observed some Boys playing in a farm-yard—One sat on a high
post and swung round and round $\overset{.*}{\underset{}{\not\!\!/\!\!/}}$ a black Skin—the others
shouting and running with *forward* hands, round and round the
post—but the particulars of the play I could not learn—There was
a German in the Coach, who talked a little Latin, & was very kind
and civil to me—Whenever the Coach stopped, I went up to the
Cottages, or rather Bauer-houses, & the alehouses—they were alike,
except in size—one great Room like a Barn with a hay loft over it
—the straw & hay dangling in tufts through the Boards, which
formed the Ceiling of the great Room & the floor of the Loft—
From this huge Room, which is paved like a street, sometimes one,
sometimes two rooms are *inclosed*—and these are commonly floored
—In the large Room the Cattle, the Pigs & Poultry, Men, Women
& Children live very amicably— but yet it seemed clean and
comfortable.—One house I measured—it was an hundred feet in

length and 48 in breadth: *Door* $\boxed{\begin{smallmatrix}2\\3 & 4\end{smallmatrix}}$ Door—1—

Apartments won from the Room—2.2—Stalls for the Cattle &c—3

—the breadth where the stalls were not—48 feet—4—the breadth where the stalls were, 32 feet—Of course the stalls were on each side 8 feet in breadth—the faces of the Cows &c were towards the room, indeed in it _//////_ ;——(What a Genius for painting I possess! I cannot help admiring the exquisite Elegance of my own drawing—it wants nothing but colours to make it surpass the original.) The Woodwork of these buildings on the outside, un-plaistered as in the old houses among us, & being painted red & green, they cut & tesselate the house very prettily—From within three miles of Hamburgh almost to Molln, which is 30 miles, it was a dead flat, only varied by woods in the Distance—near Molln it became more beautiful—There was a small Lake planted round with Groves—exactly like a Nobleman's seat among us.—There was a palace in view, belonging to the King of England and tenanted by the Inspector of the Forests.—We were nearly the same time travelling from Hamburgh to Ratzeburg 35 miles, as from London to Yarmouth 126—However we arrived there Monday Septr 24th. 9 o'clock—It appeared at a little distance like a cluster of neat red houses, on the opposite side of the lake, & near the head of it—but as we approached, it appeared more and more near the middle of it—& this too was a delusion. For Ratzeburg is an Island in the lake, and there are seven miles of water above it, and only 1/2 beneath it—the lake runs nearly from south to north—But I will describe Ratzeburg more fully hereafter—Suffice it at present to say that I was enchanted with the appearance—Here a ludicrous circumstance occurred—I had never asked Klopstock the Name of the Gentleman, but only took the letter—Accordingly when I arrived at Ratzeburgh, I consulted the direction—but lo! it was in German Characters—which, (the written) I cannot even now read. However there was one word which I made out, & which from it's situation I took for the name—this was Wohlgebohrne.—So I began to enquire where Mr Wohlgebohrne lived—No body knew such a Person—I was a little frightened and shewed my letter—A Grin!— The address was to the Amtman Braunes—An Amtman is a sort of perpetual Mayor—at once the Mayor & the Justice of Peace;— and Wohlgebohrne or 'Well born' is one of the common titles of Civility, & means no more than our Esqr—Well I delivered my letter to the Amtman, who spoke English very well & received me very kindly——Here I must conclude—or I shall be too late for the post—let your letters be thus directed,

Mr Coleridge | Ratzeburg | (7 Ger: miles from Hamburgh) |
Germany

Chester is well, & we are comfortable except from anxiety—My

best love to Mrs Poole and to all Friends—God bless you my dear love—& your affectionate and faithful Husband
      S T Coleridge—N.B. My love to Nanny.——

We have a deep snow and a hard frost, and I am learning to skate—There are Balls and Concerts every week—& I am pressed by all the Ladies to dance.—But if I could, I am in no dancing Mood.——

263. *To Mrs. S. T. Coleridge*

Transcript Thomas Ward copy-book, New York Public Lib. Pub. Letters, *i. 266.*

Sunday Evening/ Decr 2d. 1798

God, the Infinite, be praised that my Babes are alive. His mercy will forgive me that late and all too slowly I raised up my heart in thanksgiving.[1]—At first and for a time, I wept as passionately as if they had been dead—and for the whole day the weight was heavy upon me, relieved only by fits of weeping.—I had long expected, I had passionately expected, a letter; I received it, and my frame trembled—I saw your hand, and all feelings of mind and body crowded together—had the news been chearful & only, 'We are as you left us'—I must have wept, to have delivered myself of the stress and tumult of my animal sensiblity—But when I read the danger and the agony—My dear Sara!—my love! my Wife!——God bless you & preserve us—I am well; but a stye, or something of that kind, has come upon & enormously swelled my eye-lids, so that it is painful and improper for me to read or write!—In a few days it will now disappear—& I will write at length—(now it forces me to cease)—tomorrow I will write a line or two on the other side of the page to Mr Roskilly[2]——

I received your letter Friday, November 31st.[30th.]—I cannot well account for the slowness—O my babies!—Absence makes it painful to be a Father!—

My Wife, believe and know that I pant to be home & with you.
      S. T. Coleridge

Decr. 3d.—My eyes are painful—but there is no doubt, but they will be well in two or three days—I have taken physic, eat very little flesh—& drink only water—but it grieves me that I cannot read—I need not have troubled my poor eyes with a superfluous love to my dear Poole—

---

[1] In a letter of 1 Nov. 1798 Mrs. Coleridge wrote of Berkeley Coleridge's illness, disfigurement, and recovery from an inoculation with small-pox.

[2] The Rev. Mr. Roskilly, curate at Nether Stowey, had been promoted to be rector of Kempsford in Gloucestershire.

264. *To Mr. Roskilly*

Transcript Thomas Ward copy-book, New York Public Lib. Pub. Letters, *i. 267.*

Ratzeburg   Germany   Decr 3d 1798
My dear Sir

There is an honest heart out of Great Britain that enters into your good fortune with a sincere and lively Joy—May you enjoy life and health—all else you have—a good Wife—a good conscience, a good temper, sweet children and Competence!—The first glass of wine I drink shall be a bumper—not to you! no!—but to the Bishop of Gloucester! God bless him!

Sincerely your Friend
S. T. Coleridge

265. *To William Wordsworth*

Pub. Memoirs of Wordsworth, *i. 138.* This fragment and the one which follows are undated. They seem to have been written about the same time. Since the letter to Coleridge from William and Dorothy Wordsworth (*Early Letters*, 203) in answer to Letter 266 mentions Coleridge's eyes, and since on 3 December Coleridge said, 'My eyes are painful—' (Letter 263), these two fragments probably belong to early December 1798.

[Early December 1798]

With regard to measures, I am convinced that *our* language is, in some instances, better adapted to these metres than the *German:* e.g. '*a*' and '*the*' are better short syllables than '*ein*' and '*der;*' '*not*' than '*nicht.*' . . . Is the German, in truth, adapted to these metres? I grievously suspect that it is all pure pedantry. Some advantages there, doubtless, are, for we cannot fall foul of any thing without advantages.

266. *To William Wordsworth*

Pub. Memoirs of Wordsworth, *i. 138.*

[Early December 1798]

As to the German Hexameters, they have in their very essence grievous defects. It is possible and probable that we receive organically very little pleasure from the Greek and Latin hexameters; for, most certainly, *we* read all the spondees as iambics or trochees. But then the words have a fixed quantity. We know it; and there is an effect produced in the brain similar to harmony without passing through the ear-hole. The same words, with different meanings, rhyming in Italian, is a close analogy. I suspect

that great part of the pleasure derived from Virgil consists in this
satisfaction of the judgment. 'Majestate manûs' begins an hexa-
meter; and a very good beginning it is. 'Majestate magnâ' is read
exactly in the same manner, yet that were a false quantity; and a
schoolmaster would conceit that it offended his *ear*. Secondly, the
words having fixed quantities in Latin, the lines are always of equal
length in *time;* but in German, what is now a spondee is in the next
line only two-thirds of a dactyl. Thirdly, women all dislike the
hexameters with whom I have talked. They say, and in my opinion
they say truly, that only the two last feet have any discernible
melody; and when the liberty of two spondees, 'Jovis incrementum,'
is used, it is absolute prose.[1]

When I was ill and wakeful, I composed some English hexa-
meters:[2]

William, my teacher, my friend! dear William and dear Dorothea!
Smooth out the folds of my letter, and place it on desk or on table;
Place it on table or desk; and your right hands loosely half-closing,[3]
Gently sustain them in air, and extending the digit didactic,
Rest it a moment on each of the forks of the five-forkéd left hand,
Twice on the breadth of the thumb, and once on the tip of each
    finger;
Read with a nod of the head in a humouring recitativo;
And, as I live, you will see my hexameters hopping before you.
This is a galloping measure; a hop, and a trot, and a gallop!

All my hexameters fly, like stags pursued by the stag-hounds,
Breathless and panting, and ready to drop, yet flying still onwards.[4]
I would full fain pull in my hard-mouthed runaway hunter;
But our English Spondeans are clumsy yet impotent curb-reins;
And so to make him go slowly, no way have I left but to lame him.

William, my head and my heart! dear Poet that feelest and thinkest!
Dorothy, eager of soul, my most affectionate sister!
Many a mile, O! many a wearisome mile are ye distant,
Long, long, comfortless roads, with no one eye that doth know us.
O! it is all too far to send to you mockeries idle:
Yea, and I feel it not right! But O! my friends, my beloved!
Feverish and wakeful I lie,—I am weary of feeling and thinking.
Every thought is worn *down*,—I am weary, yet cannot be vacant.
Five long hours have I tossed, rheumatic heats, dry and flushing,

---

[1] For Wordsworth's reply, see *Early Letters*, 203.
[2] *Poems*, i. 304.
[3] False metre. [Note by S. T. C.]
[4] '*Still* flying onwards', were perhaps better. [Note by S. T. C.]

Gnawing behind in my head, and wandering and throbbing about me,
Busy and tiresome, my friends, as the beat of the boding night-spider.[1]

I forget the beginning of the line:

> . . . my eyes are a burthen,
Now unwillingly closed, now open and aching with darkness.
O! what a life is the eye! what a fine and inscrutable essence!
Him that is utterly blind, nor glimpses the fire that warms him;
Him that never beheld the swelling breast of his mother;
Him that ne'er smiled at the bosom as babe that smiles in its slumber;
Even to him it exists, it stirs and moves in its prison;
Lives with a separate life, and 'Is it the spirit?' he murmurs:
Sure, it has thoughts of its own, and to see is only its language.

There was a great deal more, which I have forgotten, as I never wrote it down. No doubt, much better might be written; but these will still give you some idea of them. The last line which I wrote I remember, and write it for the truth of the sentiment, scarely less true in company than in pain and solitude:

William, my head and my heart! dear William and dear Dorothea! You have all in each other; but I am lonely, and want you!

267. *To William Wordsworth*

Address: M. Wordsworth, | Chez Madame la Veuve Dippermaer, [Deppermann] | Dans la Grande Rue, | Goslar, Basse Saxe.
Pub. Memoirs of Wordsworth, *i. 137.*

Ratzeburg, Dec. 10. 1798

. . . The blank lines gave me as much direct pleasure as was possible in the general bustle of pleasure with which I received and read your letter. I observed, I remember, that the 'fingers woven,'[2] &c., only puzzled me; and though I liked the twelve or fourteen first lines very well, yet I like the remainder much better. Well, now I have read them again, they are very beautiful, and leave an affecting impression. That

> Uncertain heaven received
> Into the bosom of the steady lake,[3]

---

[1] False metre. [Note by S. T. C.]
[2] *There was a Boy*, line 7, Wordsworth, *Poet. Works*, ii. 206.
[3] Ibid., lines 24–25.

I should have recognised any where; and had I met these lines running wild in the deserts of Arabia, I should have instantly screamed out 'Wordsworth!'. . . .

268. *To William Wordsworth*

Pub. Memoirs of Wordsworth, *i. 138.*

[December 1798][1]

. . . I am sure I need not say how you are incorporated into the better part of my being; how, whenever I spring forward into the future with noble affections, I always alight by your side. . . .

269. *To Thomas Poole*

Address: Mr T. Poole | Nether Stowey | Somersetshire | England   Pay'd to Cuxhaven
MS. New York Public Lib. Pub. with omis. Letters, *i. 267.* A small part of the journal was revised and published in *Satyrane's Letters,* iii. See *The Friend,* No. 18, 21 December 1809, and *Biog. Lit.* 1817, ii. 236–7. The manuscript is torn and the passages in brackets have been supplied from a transcript made by Thomas Ward.
Postmark: Foreign Office, 19 January 1799.

January 4th, 1799—Morning, 11 o'clock

My Friend, my dear Friend!

Two Hours have past, since I received your Letter—it was so frightfully long since I received one!!—My body is weak and faint with the Beating of my Heart.—But every thing affects one, more than it ought to do, in a foreign Country. I cried myself blind about Berkley, when I ought to have been on my knees in the joy of thanksgiving.—The waywardness of the Pacquets is wonderful —On the 7th of Decemb. Chester received a letter from his Sister, dated Nov. 27th—: your's is dated Nov. 22nd, & I received it only this morning. I am quite well; calm, & industrious. I now read German as English—that is, without any *mental* translation, as I read—I likewise understand all that is said to me, & a good deal of what they say to each other. On very trivial, and on metaphysical Subjects I can talk *tolerably*—so so!—but in that conversation, which is between both, I bungle most ridiculously.—I owe it to my industry that I can read old German, & even the old low-

[1] Christopher Wordsworth in introducing this fragment notes that the letter of which it is an excerpt deals with some plan for the future settlement of Wordsworth and Coleridge 'in neighbourhood to each other'; and since Coleridge's letter to Poole of 4 Jan. 1799 shows that a plan for settling in the same vicinity in England had already been under discussion, this fragment must belong to Dec. 1798.

german, better than most of even the educated Natives—it has greatly enlarged my knowlege of the English Language.—It is a great bar to the amelioration of Germany that thro' at least half of it, and that half composed almost wholly of Protestant States, from whence alone amelioration can proceed, the Agriculturists & a great part of the Artisans talk a language as different from the language of the higher classes (in which all books are written,) as the Latin is from the Greek. The differences are greater than the affinities, & the affinities are darkened by the difference of pronunciation & spelling.—I have written twice to Mr Jos. Wedgewood[1]—& in a few days will follow a most voluminous letter, or rather series of letters, which will comprise a history of the Bauers, or Peasants—collected not so much from books, as from oral communications from the Amtman here—(An Amtman is a sort of perpetual Land-mayor— / —uniting in himself *Judge* & Justice of Peace over the Bauers of a given District.)——. I have enjoyed great advantages in this place; but I have payed dear for them. Including *all expences* I have not lived at less than two pound a week—Wordsworth (from whom I receive long & affectionate letters) has enjoyed scarcely one advantage, but his expences have been considerably less than they were in England.—Here I shall stay till the last week in January, when I shall proceed to GOTTINGEN, where, all expences included, I can live for 15 shillings a week —for these last two months I have drank nothing but water & I eat but little animal food—at Gottingen I shall hire lodging for two months, buy my own cold beef at an eating-house, & dine in my chamber which I can have at a dollar a week.—And here at Gottingen I must endeavor to unite the advantages of advancing in German, & doing something to repay myself.—My dear Poole! I am afraid, that, supposing I return in the first week of May, my whole expences from Stowey to Stowey, including books & cloathes, will not have been less than 90 POUND!—And if I buy ten pounds worth more of books it will have been an hundred. / I despair not by that intense application & regular use of my time, to which I have now almost accustomed myself, that by three months' residence at Gottingen I shall have *on paper* at least *all* the materials, if not the whole of the structure, of a work that will repay me.— The work I have planned—& I have imperiously excluded all waverings about other works—! That is the disease of my mind— it is comprehensive in it's conceptions & wastes itself in the con-

---

[1] Writing to Coleridge on 20 Jan. 1799, Josiah Wedgwood said: ' I have just received your letter of the 29th Novr and I find by it that a former from Hamburgh has not come to me, and I do not now expect to receive it.' Neither of Coleridge's letters has come to light.

templations of the many things which it might do!—I am aware
of the disease, & for the next three months, if I cannot cure it I
will at least suspend it's operation. This Work is a Life of Lessing
—& interweaved with it a true state of German Literature, in it's
rise & present state.——I have already written a little life, from
three different biographies, divided it into years—& at Gottingen
I will read his works regularly, according to the years in which
they were written, & the controversies, religious & literary, which
they occasioned.[1]—But of this say nothing to any one.——The
Journey to Germany has certainly *done me good*—my habits are less
irregular; & my *mind* more in my *own power*! But I have much
still to do!——

I did indeed receive great joy from Roskilly's good fortune—&
in a little note to my dear Sara I joined a note of congratulation to
Roskilly.—Cruckshank!—O Poole! you are a noble heart as ever
God made!——Poor Cruckshank—he is passing thro' a fiery discip-
line, and I would fain believe, that it will end in his peace and
utility.—/—Wordsworth is divided in his mind, unquietly divided,
between the neighbourhood of Stowey & the N. of England. He
cannot think of settling at a distance from *me*, & I have told him
that I *cannot* leave the vicinity of Stowey. His chief objection to
Stowey is the want of Books—the Bristol Library is a *hum* & will
do us little service, & he thinks that he can procure a house near
Sir Gilford [Gilfrid] Lawson's by the Lakes, & have free access to
his immense Library.—I think it better once in a year to walk to
Cambridge, in the summer vacation—perhaps, I may be able to get
rooms for nothing—& there for a couple of months read like a
Turk on a given plan, & return home with a mass of materials
which with dear *independent* Poetry will fully employ the remaining
year.—But this is idle prattling about the Future. But indeed it is
time to be looking out for a house for me——it is not possible, I
can be either comfortable or useful in so small a house as that in
Lime street—. If Woodland can be gotten at a reasonable Price, I
would have it:—I will now finish my long neglected Journal——

On Thursday, Sept. 27th, 1798, I returned by extra-post as far
as Empfelde a little village half way between Ratzeburgh & Ham-
burgh—from Empfelde I walked to Hamburgh—thro' deep sandy
roads & a dreary Flat—the soil every where white & hungry &
excessively pulverized. But the approach to Hamburgh, that is, a
mile or two before you reach it, is exceedingly sweet. The light cool
Country Houses, *which you can look thro'* ; & the gardens behind,
with Trees in piazzas; every house with neat rails before it, & green

---

[1] Coleridge's projected study of Lessing, to which so many references occur
in succeeding letters, was never carried out.

seats within the rails—every thing, nature & all, neat & *artificial*— & it pleased me far more than if the Houses & Gardens & Pleasure-fields had been in a better Taste. For this better Taste would have been mere *apery*— / the narrow-minded, ignorant, money-loving Merchant of Hamburgh could only have *adopted*, he could not have *enjoyed*, the wild simplicity of Nature / and the mind begins to love nature first of all by imitating human conveniences *in* nature—but this is a *step* in intellect tho' a low one; & were it not, all around me spoke of innocent enjoyment in *sensitive* Comfortableness; and I enter'd with joy & sympathy into the enjoyments even of the narrow-minded & money-loving Merchants of Hamburgh. With these thoughts I reached the vast Ramparts of the city—they are huge, green Cushions, one rising above the other, and Trees growing in the interspaces, eloquent of a long Peace.—I found Wordsworth at the inn—out of spirits & disgusted with Hamburgh & Hamburghers, & resolved to seek cheaper residence more to the South.——Sept. 28th——After dinner, I walked with Wordsworth to Altona—we found the Prostitutes all in one Street—we had seen none even in the streets, & no beggars. We walked on the ramparts —O what a divine Sunset! There were woods in the Distance—A rich sandy Light (nay, much deeper than sandy) was over the woods that blackened in this blaze: a *brassy* Mist seemed to *float* on that part of the woods which lay immediately under the intenser part of the Blaze. The Trees on the Ramparts & the moving People between the Trees were cut &—I want a word—patched (shall I say) by the brassy Splendor— all else was obscure—in the same manner as the Trees were divided into portions of obscurity & brassy Light, so were the Bodies of the men & women that moved up & down thro' them.—It was a fairy Scene—& what added to the effect, among the People there was a very beautiful Child riding on a saddled goat with a splendid Bridle.—Chester & self resolved to stay over the Saturday because this Saturday was the Feast of St Michael, the Patron Saint of Hamburgh; and we were informed that there would be splendid Processions &c. Satur. 29th. Feast of St Michael, but no processions!—Only two or three sermons preached to nobody in two or three churches, all silent & solemn, as a Sunday at Bristol; & St Michael & his Patronage cursed by the higher Classes, because the French Comedy is prohibited on this day—Sunday, Sept. 30th Left Hamburgh in an extra-post at seven o'clock. These Extra-posts answer to Post-chaises in England; they are uncovered wicker-carts,—a dust-cart, an English Dustcart— on my word, I do not exaggerate—is a piece of finery compared with him [them]—& the Horses! Were one of your Plough-mares to see one of these, she would believe that it was the Skeleton-Ghost of her Grandfather!—Where ever we stopped, the Postillion fed his horses with the brown rye-bread which he eat himself—he and his Horses breakfasted together on the same diet in a most amusing manner—only the Horses had no gin to their water, & the Postillion no water to his Gin!—Changed post at Emfelde, & of course, more Germanorum, stopped two Hours.—The Inns are always Farms—and both on Inns, Stables, & Farms there are ALWAYS nailed up at both Gables two pieces of wood cross each other thus *a*

the Gable. bb. the Cross.— the crosses often shaped

into [horns &] horses heads . This, they believe univer-

sally, keeps of[f] the Evil Spirit who in a ball of fire would come into their chimnies.—Here *all* the higher classes, except the Clergy *perhaps*, are Infidels—& all the *People* grossly superstitious.—From Emfelde to Ratzeburgh our journey is comprized in two lines—We rode in wicker waggon with our Goods / O'er damn'd bad roads thro' damn'd delightful Woods. These woods were sometimes like walls to the road—sometimes they opened on one side & left us, formed curves & prospects in the distance—Sometimes both sides grad-[ually] went off & we found ourselves in a large circle formed by distant woods—[The] area once a green & lovely Pasturage Farm —but more often dry & drear[y Fields of] Rye stubble. We observed a cruel Custom—[The] Cattle in the roads were [chai]ned horn to hoof, & so had their heads ever on the g[round—] I have observed similar Cruelties in the Isle of Anglesea in Wales—& where ever fences & general agriculture are bad, there they will always exist.—In the great Stables here where the Cattle are wintered the Cattle have the head ever chained, low down in a state of most unnatural Constraint.—On Sunday Evening we arrived at Ratzeburg, & we took possession of our Lodgings.——Here ends my Journal—After this time one day was like another—in my next letter I will describe Ratzeburg, & give you my Journey to Lubec & the Baltic Sea.—Then shall follow the customs of the better classes wherein they differ from the English—& then the Customs, Superstitions, modes of Marriage &c of the Bowers.—Chester begs that you take up 25£ from his Brother, & [remit it for him to Mr Wedgwood, & I shall draw for it in a Draught on Mr Wedgwood through the Von Axens—Chester is well & comfortable & begins to make progress—not in speaking—but in reading—He begs his kind remembrances to you——

I am pestered every ball night to dance, which very *modestly* I refuse—They dance a most infamous dance called the Waltzen—There are perhaps 20 couple—the Man & his Partner embrace each other, arms round waists, & knees almost touching, & then whirl round & round, the whole 20 couple, 40 times round at least, to lascivious music. This they dance at least three times every ball night—There is no Country on the Earth where the married Women are chaste like the English—here the married Men intrigue or whore—and the Wives have their Cicisbeos. I entreat you, suspect *me* not of any Cicisbeo affair——I am no Puritan; but yet it is not customs or manners that can extinguish in me the Sacredness of a married Woman, or quench the disgust I feel towards an Adultress—It is here as in France—the single Women are chaste, but Marriage seems to legitimate Intrigue—This is the chief moral objection I have to Infidels—In Individuals it may not operate—but when it is general, it always taints the domestic Happiness of a People——].

Sara, I suppose, is at Bristol—On Monday I shall write to her. ——The Frost here has been uncommonly severe / for two days it was twenty degrees under the Freezing Point.—Wordsworth has left Goslar, & is on his road into higher Saxony to cruise for a pleasanter place. He has made but little progress in the Language —.—I am interrupted—& if I do not conclude, shall lose the Post. —.Give my kind love to your dear Mother—O that I could but find her comfortable on my return—to Ward remember me affectionately—likewise remember [me] to James Cole, & my grateful remembrances to Mrs Cole for her kindness during my Wife's domestic Troubles.—To Harriet, Sophia, & Lavinia Poole—to the Chesters—to Mary & Ellen Cruikshank——in short, to all to whom it will give pleasure remember me affectionately and my dear, dear Poole—

God bless us!—

S. T. Coleridge

[P.S. The Amtman who is almost an Englishman & an Idolizer of our nation, desires to be kindly remembered to you—He told me yesterday that he had dreamt of you the night before.]

270. *To Mrs. S. T. Coleridge*

Address: Mrs Coleridge | Nether Stowey | Somersetshire | England　　pay'd to Cuxhaven　　[Readdressed in another hand] No 17 Newfoundland Street | Bristol

MS. New York Public Lib. Pub. with omis. Letters, i. 271. Small parts of this letter were revised and published in *Satyrane's Letters*, ii and iii. See *The*

Friend, Nos. 16 and 18, 7 and 21 December 1809, and *Biog. Lit.*, 1817, ii. 213–14 and 234–6.
Postmark: Foreign Office, 6 March 1799.

Monday, Jan. 14th, 1799. Ratzeburg

My dearest Love—

Since the wind changed & it became possible for me to have Letters, I lost all my tranquillity. Last evening I was absent in company, & when I returned to Solitude, [was] restless in every fibre. A novel, which I attempted to read, seemed to interest me so extravagantly, that I threw it down—& when it was out of my hands, I knew nothing of what I had been reading. This morning I awoke long before Light, feverish & unquiet—I was certain in my mind, that I should have a Letter from you; but before it arrived my restlessness & the irregular pulsation of my Heart had quite wearied me down—& I held the letter in my hand like as if I was stupid, without attempting to open it.—'Why don't you read the letter?' said Chester—& I read it.—Ah little Berkley—I have mis-givings—but my duty is rather to comfort you, my dear dear Sara! —I am so exhausted that I could sleep.—I am well; but my spirits have left me—I am completely home-sick. I must walk half an hour—for my mind is too scattered to continue writing.——I entreat & entreat you, Sara! take care of yourself—if you are well, I think I could frame my thoughts so that I should not sink under other losses—. You do right in writing me the Truth—Poole is kind—but you do right, my dear! In a sense of *reality* there is always comfort—the workings of one's imagination ever go beyond the worst that nature afflicts us with—they have the terror of a superstitious circumstance.—I express myself unintelligibly—/ Enough, that you write me always the whole Truth. Direct your next letter thus—An den Herrn Coleridge, a la Post restante, Gottingen, Germany.—If God permit, I shall be there before this day three weeks—and I hope, on May day, to be once more at Stowey. My motives for going to Gottingen, I have written to Poole—. I hear as often from Wordsworth as letters can go back-ward & forward in a country where 50 miles in a day & night is *expeditious* Travelling!—He seems to have employed more time in writing English [tha]n in studying German—No wonder!—for he might as well have been in England as at Goslar, in the situation which he chose, & with his *unseeking* manners——He has now left it, and is on Journey to Nordhousen. His taking his Sister with him was a wrong Step—it is next to impossible for any but married women or in the suit of married women to be introduced to any company in Germany. Sister [here] is considered as only a name for Mistress.—Still however *male* acquainta[nce] he might have had—& had I been at Goslar, I *would* [have] had them—but [W., God] love him! seems to have lost his spirits & [almost his] inclination [for] it. In the mean time his expences have been almost less than [if he had] been in England. / Mine have been . . . [1] very great; but I do not despair of returning to England, with somewhat to pay the whole.—O God! I do languish to be at home!—

I will endeavor to give you some idea of Ratzeburgh; but I am a wretched Describer.—First, you must conceive a Lake, running from South to North, about 9 miles in Length, and of very various breadths—the broadest part may be perhaps two or three miles, the narrowest scarce more than half a mile.—About a mile from the southernmost point of the lake, i.e. from the beginning of the Lake —is the Island-town of Ratzeburgh.

● is Ratzeburgh 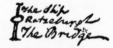 is our House / on the Hill—from the bottom of the Hill there lies on the lake a slip of Land, scarcely two stone throws wide, at the end of which is a little Bridge with a superb military Gate—and this Bridge joins Ratzeburgh to the slip of Land—You pass thro' Ratzeburgh up a little Hill & down the little Hill, and this brings you to another Bridge, narrow but of an immense length, which communicates with the other shore.

The water to the South of Ratzeburgh is called the little Lake, & the other the large Lake, tho' they are but one piece of water.— This little Lake is very beautiful—the Shores just often enough green & bare to give the proper effect to the magnificent Groves, which mostly fringe them. The views vary almost every ten steps, such & so beautiful are the turnings & windings of the Shore—they unite beauty & magnitude, & can be best expressed by feminine Grandeur!—At the north of the great Lake, and peering over, you see the seven church-towers of Lubec, which is twelve or 14 miles from Ratzeburgh—yet you see them as distinctly as if they were not 3 miles from you. The worse thing is that Ratzeburgh is built entirely of bricks & tiles—& is therefore all red—a clump of brick dust red—it gives you a strong idea of perfect neatness; but it is not beautiful.—In the beginning or middle of October, I forget which, we went to Lubec in a boat—For about two miles the shores

---

[1] MS. blurred; two or three words obliterated.

of the Lake are exquisitely beautiful, the woods now running into the water, now retiring in all angles.[1] After this the left shore retreats,[1] the lake acquires it's utmost breadth & ceases to be beautiful—at the end of the lake is the River, about as large as the River at Bristol—but winding in infinite Serpentines thro' a dead flat, with willows & reeds, till you reach Lubec—an old fantastic Town. We visited the churches at Lubec—they were crowded with gawdy gilded Figures, & a profusion of Pictures, among which were always portraits of the popular Pastors who had served the Church. The Pastors here wear white ruffs, exactly like the pictures of Queen Elizabeth. There were in the Lubec Churches a very large attendance; but almost *all women*. The genteeler people dress'd precisely as the English; but behind every Lady sat her maid, the caps with gold & silver cawls. All together a Lubec Church is an amusing sight. In the evening I wished myself a painter, just to draw a German Party at Cards—One man's long Pipe rested on the Table, smoking half [a y]ard from his mouth by the fish-dish; another who w[as] shuffling, and of course had both hands employed, held his pipe in his Teeth, and it hung down between his Thighs even to his ancles—& the distortion which the attitude & effort occasioned made him a most ludicrous Phiz.— . . .[2] [I would, had] it been possible, have loitered a week in those churches; & found incessant amusement. Every picture, every legend cut out in gilded wood-work, was a history of the manners & feelings of the ages, in which such works were admired & executed.—The Sun both rises & sets over the little Lake by us / & both rising & setting presents most lovely spectacles—In October Ratzeburg used at Sunset to appear completely beautiful—A deep red light spread over all, in complete harmony with the red town, the brown red woods, & the yellow red Reeds on the skirts of the Lake & on the Slip of Land. A few boats paddled by single persons used generally to be floating up & down in the rich Light. But when first the Ice fell on the Lake, & the whole Lake was frozen, one huge piece of thick transparent Glass, O my God! what sublime scenery I have beheld.—[3] Of a morning I have seen the little [lake] covered with Mist; when the Sun peeped over the Hill, the Mist broke in the middle; and at last stood as the waters of the red Sea are said to have done when the Israelites passed—& between these two walls of Mist the Sunlight *burnt* upon the Ice in a strait *road* of golden Fire, all across the lake—intolerably bright, & the walls of Mist

---

[1] Two small sketches at these points have not been reproduced.
[2] 8½ lines inked out in manuscript.
[3] See *The Friend*, No. 19, 28 Dec. 1809, for a revised version of this passage, entitled *Christmas out of Doors*.

partaking of the light in a multitude of colours.—About a month
ago the vehemence of the wind had shattered the Ice[1]—part of it,
quite smattered, was driven to shore & had frozen anew; this was
of a deep blue & represented an agitated sea—the water, that ran
up between the great islands of Ice, shone of a yellow green (it was
at sunset) and all the scattered islands of *smooth* ice were *blood*;
intensely bright *Blood*: on some of the largest Islands the Fisher-
men were pulling out their immense nets thro' the Holes made in
the Ice for this purpose, & the Fishermen, the net-poles, & the
huge nets made a part of the Glory! O my God! how I wished you
to be with me!—In skating there are three pleasing circumstances
—the infinitely subtle particles of Ice, which the Skate cuts up, &
which creep & run before the Skater like a low mist, & in sun
rise or sun set become coloured; 2nd the Shadow of the Skater in
the water seen thro' the Transparent Ice, & 3rd the melancholy
undulating sound from the Skate not without variety; & when
very many are skating together, the sounds and the noises give an
imp[ulse to] the icy Trees, & the woods all round the lake *tinkle*!—
It is a plea[sant] Amusement to sit in an ice-stool (as they are
called) and be driven along [the ice] by two Skaters—I have [done]
so, faster than most horses can gallop.——As to the customs here,
[they are] nearly the same as in England—except that [the men]
never sit after dinner, [but dri]nk at dinner, which often lasts
three or four hours; & in noble families is divided into three Gäng[e]
—that is—walks. When you have sat about an hour, you rise up,
each Lady takes a Gentleman's arm, and you walk about for a
quarter of an Hour—in the mean time another course is put upon
the table; & this in great dinners is repeated 3 times. A man here
seldom sees his wife till dinner—they take their coffee in separate
rooms, & never eat at breakfast; only as soon as they are up, they
take their coffee—& about 11 o clock eat a bit of bread & butter;
& with the coffee, the men at least take a pipe. (Indee[d, a] pipe at
Breakfast is a great addition to the comforts of Life: I shall [smoke]
at no other time in England. *Here* I smoke four times a day—1 at
breakfast, 1 half an hour before dinner, 1 in the afternoon at Tea,
and one just before bed time—but I shall give it all up, unless, as
before observed, you should happen to like the smoke of a pipe at
Breakfast.) Once when I first came here, I smoked a pipe imme-

[1] In *The Friend* Coleridge inserted the following beautiful passage: 'During
the whole night, such were the thunders and howlings of the breaking ice, that
they have left a conviction on my mind, that there are Sounds more sublime
than any Sight *can* be, more absolutely suspending the power of comparison,
and more utterly absorbing the mind's self-consciousness in it's total attention
to the object working upon it.'

diately after dinner; the Pastor expressed his surprize: I expressed mine that he could smoke before breakfast—'O—Herr Gott! (i.e. Lord God) quoth he—it is delightful—it invigorates the frame, & *it cleans out the moutt so!*' A common amusement at the German Universities is for a number of young men to smoke out a Candle— i.e. to fill a room with Tobacco-smoke till the Candle goes out.— Pipes are quite the rage—a pipe of a particular kind, that has been smoked for a year or so, will sell here for twenty Guineas—the same pipe, when new, costs about four or five. They are called Meerschaums.

Price of Provisions &c at Hamburgh, & the same holds good, with very little variation of Ratzeburgh, & Lubec. Beef per pound—   from 3d to 5d—that is, in summer the best beef is about 3d, about Christmas 5d

Mutton	ditto
Veal	from 5d to 7d
Pork—	4d to 6d
A fat goose	4 Shillings
A Turkey	7 to 9 Shillings
Fowls	14 pence a couple

Bread nearly the same as in England.

Cheese /	4d a pound
English Cheese /	16d.
Eggs—	6d a dozen.

Vegetables & Fruit, dearer than in London.

Soap	6d a pound
Candles	8d a pound

N.B. Most Housekeepers make their own Soap & Candles.

Coffee	22 pence a pound.

Sugar, two Shillings a pound

Tea execrable and adulterated—8 Shillings, *pnd*

Ordinary wine,	7d or 8d a bottle, when bought in the cask.
Good Claret,	16d
Best Claret	2 Shillings
Old Hock from	2 to 9 Shillings
Best Brandy	20d the bottle
Rum	16d
Gin	10d
Common Spirit	6d or 7d.

Fish *cheap in Spring.*—

Game, sold in the markets; but I could not hear the price.

Salt, excessively cheap—cheap as dirt.

English Cloth more than one third as dear as in England; but the making up is cheaper.—German Cloth comes cheap, as cheap again.

Firing, extravagantly dear—.

The Amtman here in his house has six stoves, & the Kitchen fire, and besides two large loads of Turf he uses more than an hundred pounds' worth (sterling) of wood. Wood is 14 dollars the fathom: a dollar is 3 marks, & a mark is sixteen pence. House Rent in Lubec is much of a muchness with the House rent at Bristol; *but there are no taxes*—at Ratzeburg the same as at Stowey; but at Hamburgh, O my God! the meanest House in any part of the town lets for 100£ a year, & some (nothing very handsome either) for 300£.—Servants' wages here are very small—if there are two Servants, the upper has about 50 Shillings a year, the under-maid not thirty—& they eat but little flesh, & never taste Tea or Coffee or Beer. A man can keep a Coach, Coachman, & two Horses, for 40£ a year, including all expences.—In short, with 1 or 200 a year you cannot live better, in Germany than in England; but if you [have] 1000£ a year you can live twice as well: on account of no Taxes, & servants.

God bless you, my dear Love!—I will soon write again—My dear Love to Poole & his Mother—

S. T. Coleridge

Perhaps, you are in Bristol / however, I had better direct it to Stowey.—My love to Martha & your Mother, & your other Sisters. —Once more, my dearest Love, God love & preserve us thro' this long absence!—O my dear Babies!—my Babies!—

271. *To Josiah Wedgwood*

Address: Josiah Wedgewood Esq. | Stoke House | near | Cobham | Surry | England   pay'd to Cuxhaven

MS. New York Public Lib. Pub. E. L. G. i. 116.

As early as 4 January 1799 Coleridge planned to send Josiah Wedgwood 'in a few days' a series of letters on the history of the Bauers (Letter 269); again on 21 May he wrote to Wedgwood that he had lying by his side 'six huge *Letters*', all but one having been written three months previously. He had planned to send them by a Cambridge man, Hamilton, whom he had met at Göttingen on 16 February, but Hamilton's departure being delayed, Coleridge decided to carry them to England himself (Letters 272 and 283). The next we hear of these letters is on 1 November 1800, when Coleridge told Wedgwood that they would soon be published in a volume of his German tour. To save the labour of transcription he had sent them off to the printers as they were written, 'your name of course erased' (Letter 362). No such publication appeared, and the following letter, numbered I on the manuscript, is all that survives of Coleridge's history of the Bauers.

[February 1799]

I.

It is difficult to give a definite idea of the word Bauer without

running thro' the origin & history of this Class. Under the Roman
Empire there existed nothing analogous to it. The free Citizens
were either independent Proprietors of Land, or lived in towns &
Cities—the agricultural labor was performed by Slaves, as in the
West India Islands. Gibbon calculates the number of the Subjects
of the first Emperors at 120 millions, of which he computes one
Half to have been Slaves. These seem to have been treated more
humanely under the Emperors, than during the Republic.—Of this
I have been able to conceive two causes—: first, the Roman Empire
had grown so large that it became the Policy of the Emperors to
make no further conquests—& the *Peace* of the whole civilized
World, the consequence of this Policy, operated in the same man-
ner on the Roman Slavery, as an actual abolition of the African
Trade would operate on the West India Slavery.—It stopped up
the source: & made the masters from the advanced Price of the
Slaves, &c more attentive to their well-being—& in a generation or
two they became to a certain degree naturalized in the countries
where they laboured & the idea *Enemy* ceased to associate itself
with that of Slave.—Secondly, the Roman Empire was too large,
& too incongruous in it's parts, for that *national* Religion, which
built on national Events & working on the imagination thro'
definite forms and on the feelings thro' incessant association of the
mythology with the Laws & Scenes, which were *exclusively* theirs,
had effected wonders on the Greeks & early Romans! for this it was
grown too large. It gradually therefore suffered the National Reli-
gion to sink into contempt, & took up a World-Religion—such as
had always existed in Asia, from the *largeness* of the Asiatic Em-
pires. To this cause I am inclined to attribute the easy Propagation
of Christianity—which was in truth the World-Religion common
to the great Empires in Asia, divested of Asiatic forms & ceremo-
nies.—The consequence of Christianity or a World-Religion as
opposed to a *National* Religion appears to me universally this—
Personal and domestic Duties are far better attended to, but
Patriotism & all Enthusiasm for the aggrandisement of a country
as a country, are weakened or extinguished.—In Greece & Rome
on the contrary, under the influence of a *national* Religion, we find
sorry Fathers, bad Husbands, & cruel Masters; but glowing &
generous Patriots.—In Christian Countries an excellent Private
Character totally devoid of all public Spirit is the most common of
characters.—But on this subject a man might write a volume &
bring out some curious observations on the March of Things in
France; & how far a Passion for Statues &c will be able to smuggle
a sort of Idolatry into the Feelings altho' it *may be* too late in the
World to introduce it into the understanding.—The more I think,

the more I am convinced that the greatest of differences is produced when in the one case the feelings are worked upon thro' the Imagination & the Imagination thro' definite Forms (i.e. the Religion of Greece & Rome); & in the other case where the Feelings are worked upon by Hopes & Fears purely individual, & the Imagination is kept barren in definite Forms & only in cooperation with the Understanding labours after an obscure & indefinite Vastness— / this is Christianity.—My dear Friend! I have made something like a digression—but it is the first, & shall be the last—The influence of the World-Religion operated slowly on the Roman Character; but it did operate & produced finally laws & regulations in favor of the Slaves; still Slavery continued. But soon after the Northern Nations had shattered the Roman Empire, Slavery began to transmute itself into Vassalage—a state of Dependence more suited to a wild people who had not yet learnt to be luxurious, and on whom the doctrines of the Christian Priests worked with greater effect while according to the Testimony of Tacitus the Slaves in the German Nations were properly speaking, Vassals, *i.e.* the Master gave the Servant House & Land, & received in return a given share of the Produce, retaining however an arbitrary power of dispossession &c.—N.B. I mean this whenever I use the word Vassals. At first the Northern Nations adopted absolute Slavery, which they had learnt from the Romans, but soon they formed part of their Slaves into Vassals, & in the year 1200 *Slavery* was wholly abolished throughout Germany & Italy, and in 1300, or somewhat earlier throughout France & Spain.—In England Vassalage instead of Slavery appears to have been general, still earlier, than in Italy or Germany.— / —.

It appears however that the *German* Conquerors did by no means either make Slaves or Vassals of the Nations which they conquered — / the *Sclavonian* Nations, who conquered Poland & Russia, *did*. —And it is probable that the huge Body of Polish Nobles (the only free men in the country) are the descendants of the conquering Army / & the Wretches who form the Polish Peasantry, the conquered People.—It remains therefore difficult to account for the amazing Proportion of Vassals in France, & Spain, countries conquered by the *German* Tribes; & still more for the still greater Number of Vassals in Germany, which had never been conquered. It is evident from this that altho' Vassalage originated in Slavery, yet in the middle ages the Vassals were not the descendants of Slaves.—I find in the History of Hungaria by Palma[1] a distinct

---

[1] Carolus Franciscus Palma, *Notitia Rerum Hungaricum*, 3 vols., 3rd ed., 1785. Professor Francis Christensen has brought to my attention the fact that the names of nine of the twelve characters of Coleridge's *Zapolya* and the only

account of the introduction of Vassalage in that country—& I believe that Hungary is the only Country in which it was ever distinctly & suddenly introduced.—Hungary had been conquered in 884 by an Asiatic Tribe, amounting to 20,000 men. The smallness of their number made these conquerors adopt, in part, the mildness of the German Tribes—to the conquered nation they left un-touched their personal Freedom, and permitted them the posses-sion of their Estates, on the condition of receiving $\frac{1}{9}$ of the yearly Profits. This the 20,000 divided among themselves / & the descen-dants of these 20,000 are the present Hungarian Nobility; at least, with such mixtures as 900 years necessarily bring along with them.

In this state things continued till 1514, when Pope Leo X com-missioned the Cardinal Thomas Baxato [Bakócz] to preach up a crusade against the Turks. 80,000 Hungarians assembled them-selves under the holy banner, & being in distress for provisions, they plundered the cities, Ofen & Pesth—& irritated by the execu-tion of some of the Ringleaders, they elected a George Dofa [Dozsa] for King—& declared war against the Nobles; but they were completely routed, & the King Bladislaus [Wladislaus] & the Senate of Nobles hereupon declared all the Country People of Hungary for Vassals—leaving them no power of alienating their property & laying them under heavy Services & Taxes—in short, they declared the whole of their Possessions to be the *Estates* of the Nobles, & the original Proprietors as parts of the Estate & transferable with the same.—This accounts for the state of Vassa-lage in Hungary; but in France, Spain, Germany, & Italy we find no such events on record; & it is a certain fact, that the original German Conquerors did not introduce Vassalage. In Spain & in many parts of Italy they admitted the conquered people to fully equal Rights with themselves—& in France altho' they reserved to themselves political superiority, yet the laws of property they left unaltered.—They took from the natives nearly one third of the Lands; but these they possessed in the same manner as the natives possessed the remaining two thirds.—Yet in Spain, Italy, France, & the unconquered Germany throughout the middle ages we find the most oppressive Vassalage universal.—We must attri-bute this phaenomenon therefore to (I) the constant civil wars, in

place-name other than Illyria are from Hungarian history. Sarolta, for example, is the name of the mother of the first king of Hungary and Zapolya the name of the last national king. The rebellion under Dozsa which Coleridge mentions in this letter was put down by John Zapolya and Stephen Bathory (the Old Bathory and Bethlen Bathory of Coleridge's play) at Temesvar (Coleridge's Temeswar). Generally Coleridge's spelling of the proper names is close to Palma's. (Professor Christensen studied Coleridge's dramatic works in his doctoral dissertation, 'Three Romantic Poets and the Drama', Harvard, 1934.

which Vassalage was uniformly the lot of all Prisoners, to whom
was immediately allotted house & Land & they were obliged to
cultivate the same for the advantage of the conquerors.—2ndly to
the introduction of feudal Tenures.—At first the Chief allotted or
lent out his *peculiar* Domains on easy conditions.—The Possessors
of these feudal Tenures were constantly favoured at the expence
of their fellow-subjects—hence many voluntarily subjected them-
selves & properties—these again by means of the civil wars & the
horrid abuses of the courts of Justice obtained secondary Vassals—
& in this state of things we find the origin of the Aristocracy of the
Nobles.—The great & favoured Vassals formed the Nobles—and
accordingly as they made themselves independant of the Crown,
as in England & great part of Germany, or were retained or
brought back again, under the power of the same, as in France, so
arose either mixed or absolute Monarchy.—The secondary Vassals
are the Bauers.—3rdly to the absence of Commerce & Manufac-
tures.—In purely agricultural states, in which from any cause
Vassalage had taken root, the number of Vassals must constantly
increase.—For unproperty persons could in such states find no
other means of subsistence than by voluntarily subjecting them-
selves—for accustomed to vassals the great Proprietors would
form no idea of Farmers, or Hired Servants.—But the number of
unproperty Persons must necessarily increase in every a[gri]cul-
tural State, where in order to keep estates in the family the rights
of Pri[mogenitur]e will be always established.—In Germany, the
Laws compelled ev[ery un]property man to arrange himself as
Vassal under so[me] Proprietor—who became answerable for him
&c.—4thly to Superstition [&] the influence of the Clergy.—It was
generally believed that the Vassals of the Church had a better
chance of heaven—& it is pretty certain, that upon earth at least,
they were better used & less liable to the devastations of War.—It
is said, that at the moment of the French Revolution there existed
in France a million & a half Vassals on the lands belonging to the
Clergy.——

It appears then, that soon after the Irruption of the Northern
Nations Slavery changed into Vassalage; but the number of Vas-
sals became far greater than that of Slaves had been.——At first,
at least in the case of those who had been made vassals thro' Con-
quest or Civil war, the Lord gave house & land indeed, & was
payed by a share of the Produce (a far less horrid state than that
of Slaves on Roman or West India Plantations)—but he retained
a power of possession over the person of the Vassal, & could dispose
of him to other estates.—(This is still the case in many of the
Russian Dominions.) This however had been always regarded as

tyranny, and from the year 983 the Clergy, following the example
of the Bishop of Constanz, struggled to introduce the glebae ad-
scriptio—by which the Vassal or Bondman was rendered insepar-
able from his Family & from the estate.—This is the first allevia-
tion of the Vassalage of the Peasants.—About the same time, the
Princes & Nobles who prided themselves in keeping open tables
for a large retinue, found the old method of receiving from their
Vassals shares of the natural Produce inconvenient & precarious—
they gave therefore to these Vassals certain pieces of Land which
should be wholly their's—& instead of rent exacted SERVICES—
that is every Vassal with his Cattle & Family worked a given
number of days on the Estate of his Lord.——This by fixing the
idea of a distinct [right] may be considered as the second alleviation.
—The third is the jus ad glebam, which where combined with the
glebae adscriptio, is still vassalage; but vassalage beginning to
border on Freedom. To this some districts of Germany arrived
very early in the *middle* ages; & I believe, there are still parts in
Mecklenburg where the Vassals have not even yet arrived to it.—
(The Duke of Mecklenburg, our Queen's Brother, is, by the by, a
fine mixture of Fool & Tyrant / & Vassalage is in his dominions
more cruel than in any part of Europe, except Russia & Russian
Poland.)

Of a formal Emancipation of the Vassals thro' Government
History gives not one Example from the year 1247 (when Matilda,
wife of Otto, Duke of Brunswick, stated by law a sum of money
which being offered, no Vassal in the country of Luneburg could
be refused his Freedom) till the reign of Frederic I of Prussia, who
formally abolished Vassalage in his Westphalian Dominions.—Yet
in this interspace it had been insensibly abolishing throughout
Germany—so that before the Edict of Fred. I. the number of
Vassals was trifling compared to that of free Peasants.—This
alteration must be ascribed 1st to the Crusades, when multitudes
were freed on condition of becoming Soldiers—or, more accurately,
to make them become voluntary & of course, braver Soldiers—&
many bought their Freedom for a trifling Sum of their Lords who
took all means of raising money for that expedition.—2—The
Introduction of the Roman Law produced many happy effects on
the state of property, & smoothed the way to the Emancipation.
3rdly Still however the state of Vassalage continued frequent &
cruel to the beginning of the 16th Century when the obstinate &
bloody Peasants-war contributed still more powerfully to their
general Emancipation—4thly To these must be added, & perhaps,
as the most powerful cause, the rise of Towns, & Cities, of com-
merce & Manufactures, which made it in the first place possible &

even easy for the Vassals to procure money to buy their Freedom—
& secondly, by affording safe places of Refuge to Fugitives, dis-
posed the Lords to sell that Freedom, which if not sold would
probably be taken.——/ —Traces of Vassalage still exist in Hol-
stein, Lausitz, and Silesia—the latter is curious, as Frederic the
Great gave all the Silesian Peasants *jus ad glebam*, & security of
Inheritance; & limited the Ransom-money (which, being offered,
perfect Freedom must be given) at a Ducat; i.e. 7 Shillings Ster-
ling.——In Mecklenburg it is still universal—& in Pommerania /
if the present great & good King of Prussia, who is deservedly
idolized in Germany, has not abolished it.—If he has not, it may
be considered as certain, that he shortly will do it.——In the next,
I will give the distinct History of the Hanoverian Bauers to the
present day—& in a third the account of them, as they are, in
agriculture, size of property, education, &c &c &c &c— / — / ——
Your grateful & affectionate Friend
S. T. Coleridge

272. *To Mrs. S. T. Coleridge*

Address: Mrs Coleridge | Nether Stowey | Somersetshire | England   Payed
to Cuxhaven   [Readdressed in another hand] Mrs Coleridge | No 17 New-
foundland Street | Bristol
MS. New York Public Lib. Pub. with omis. Letters, *i. 277*. The manuscript is
torn and the words in brackets have been supplied from a transcript made by
Thomas Ward.
Postmark: Foreign Office, 21 March 1799.

(bey dem Rademacher Göring, in der Burg Strasse, Göttingen)
March 12th [10], 1799, Sunday Night.
My dearest Love

It has been a frightfully long Time, since we have heard from
each other. I have not written, simply because my letters could
have gone no further than Cuxhaven; & would have stayed there,
to the [no] small hazard of their being lost.—Even yet the Mouth of
the Elbe is so much choked with Ice, that the Pacquets for England
cannot set off. Why need I say, how anxious this long Interval of
Silence has made me? I have thought & thought of you, and pic-
tured you & the little ones so often & so often, that my Imagination
is tired, down, flat and powerless; and I languish after Home for
hours together, in vacancy; my *feelings* almost wholly unqualified
by *Thoughts*. I have, at times, experienced such an extinction of
Light in my mind, I have been so forsaken by all the *forms* and
colourings of Existence, as if the *organs* of Life had been dried up;
as if only simple BEING remained, blind and stagnant!—After I

From a pastel portrait made in Germany in 1799 and now in the possession of Mrs. C. S. Gardner

have recovered from this strange state, & reflected upon it, I have thought of a man who should lose his companion in a desart of sand where his weary Halloos drop down in the air without an Echo.—I am deeply convinced that if I were to remain a few years among objects for whom I had no affection, I should wholly lose the powers of Intellect—Love is the vital air of my Genius, & I have not seen one human Being in Germany, whom I can conceive it *possible* for me to *love*—no, not one. To my mind, they are an unlovely Race, these Germans!—We left Ratzeburg Feb. 6th, on a Wednesday Evening, 7 o'clock—we have no analogy in England for a German Stage Coach, so perfectly wretched is it—such a Temple of all the Winds of Heaven!! This was not the coldest night in the Century, because the night following was two Degrees colder—the oldest man living remembers not such a night as Thursday, Feb. 7th. This whole winter I have heard incessant complaints of the unusual Cold; but I have felt very little of it. But *that Night*—My God! [Now] I know what the *Pain* of Cold is, & what the Danger!—The pious Care of the German Governments that none of their loving Subjects should be suffocated, is admirable!—On Friday Morning when the Light dawned, the Coach looked like a shapeless Idol of Suspicion with an hundred Eyes— for there were at least so many holes in it!—And as to *rapidity*, we left Ratzeburg at 7, Wed. Evening, & arrived at Lunenburg—i.e. 35 English miles—at 3 o'clock on Thursday Afternoon—This is a fair Specimen. In England I used to laugh at the 'Flying Wa[g-gons;]' but compared with a German Post Coach the metaphor is perfectly justifiable, & f[or the f]uture I shall never meet a flying Waggon without thinking respectfully of [it's] speed.—The whole Country from Ratzeburg almost to Einbeck, i.e. 155 English miles, is a flat objectless hungry heath, bearing no marks of cultivation, except close by the Towns—& the only remarks, which suggested themselves to me, were—that it was cold—very cold—shocking Cold—'never felt it so cold in my life[']—Meine Seele! es ist kalt! —abscheulich kalt! widernatürlich kalt! ganz erstaunend kalt, &c & & &c. Hanover is 115 miles from Ratzeburg—we arrived there Saturday Evening, having slept Friday Night at Celle (a large tolerably handsome Town.)—The Herr von Döring, a Noble-man who resides at Ratzeburg, & distinguished me by constant attentions & civilities, gave me letters to his Brother in law at Hanover—& by the manner in which his Brother-in-law received me I found that they were not *ordinary* letters of recommendation. He pressed me exceedingly to stay a week in Hanover, but I refused —& left it on Monday Noon—in the mean time however he had introduced me to all the great People, & presented me, 'as an

English Gentleman of first-rate Character & Talents,' to Baron
Steinberg, the Minister of State, & to Von Brandes, the Secretary
of State & Governor of the Gottingen University.—The first was
amazingly *perpendicular*; but civil & polite, & gave me letters to
Heyne, the Head-Librarian at Gottingen, &, in truth, the real
Governor of Gottingen.—Brandes gave me letters likewise to Heyne
& Blumenbach,[1] who are his Brothers in law.—I had likewise other
letters given me. Baron Steinberg offered to present me to the
Prince (*Adolphus*) who is now in Hanover; but I deferred the honor
till my return.—I shall make Poole laugh, when I return, with the
visiting Card which the Baron left at my Inn.—I reasoned against
the doctrine of Rights in the Presence of Brandes, who is an
Author & a vehement aristocrat, & so delighted him that he has
written me a complimentary letter——Description is not my Fort;
but descriptions of Towns & Cities—I abhor even to *read* them!—
Besides, I saw nothing particular in Hanover—it is a neat town,
well-lighted, neither handsome or ugly, about the size of Taunton,
(perhaps a little larger) & contains about 16,000 Inhabitants. *It
being the seat of the Government*, the Inhabitants, at least the
Gentry, dance and game & commit adultery——there is a Tobacco
Manufacture & a *Library with some curious books*.—(N.b.—I hold
the *last line* for a master-piece of *informative* & *discriminative*
Description.)—The two things worth seeing are—I. A Conduit
representing Mount Parnassus, with statues of Apollo, the Muses,
& a great many others, flying Horses, Rhinoceroses, & Elephants
—& 2. A Bust of Leibnitz.—The first for it's excessive absurdity,
ugliness, & indecency—absolutely, I could write the most humo-
rous Octavo Volume containing the Description of it with a Com-
mentary!—The second—i.e. the Bust of Leibnitz—impressed on
my whole soul a sensation which has ennobled and enriched it!—
It is the face of a God!—& Leibnitz *was* almost more than a man
in the wonderful capaciousness of his Judgment & Imagination!
——Well—we left Hanover on Monday Noon—after having payed
a most extravagant Bill. We lived with Spartan Frugality & payed
with Persian Pomp—. But I was an Englishman & visited by half
a dozen Noblemen, & the Minister of State!—the Landlord could
not dream of affronting me by anything like a reasonable charge!
—On the road we stopped with the Postillion always, & our ex-
pences were nothing—Chester & I made a very hearty dinner of
cold Beef &c—& both together payed only fourpence—Coffee &
Biscuits only three pence a piece—in short—a man may travel
cheap in Germany—but he must avoid great towns, [& not be

---

[1] Johann Friedrich Blumenbach (1752–1840), physiologist and founder of
anthropology.

visi]ted by Ministers of State!—The country, as I said, was dreary;
but the Inhabitants were, one & all, warmly clothed—I must say,
that I have seen very few objects of misery in the whole Hanoverian
Dominions.—In the little Pot houses & Cottages where we stopped
was a wonderful uniformity——their Diet consisted generally of
Potatoes (always very small, but extremely good) soup, and a sort
of sausage made of Grits (Grits or Gerts, I don't [know] how to
spell the word) pigs' fat, and pigs' blood.—These were universal &
form a very nutritious & very economic food.—The most frequent
soups which we observed in the cottages were 1—a soup of Water,
Barley or Buckwheat, Onions & Potatoes. 2—of water, and
vetc[hes, w]ith clumps of the above described sausage.—The
Bread is every where [a blac]k *sour* Bread, of which I am grown
very fond, & prefer it to [any other].—White Bread is so uncom-
mon, that at a *fair* in a little Vi[llage,] instead of Sweetmeats &
Gingerbread, as in England, there were in Trays, covered with nice
white napkins, Rolls & *Twists* of *White* Bread.—There was in the
whole fair neither Gingerbread or Sweetmeat.—Vetches are eaten
all over Germany, by Rich as well as Poor—I like them very much.
In good truth, my Taste & Stomach are very *catholic*, & adapt
themselves with great ease to all sorts of [Diets—In a] village,
some four miles from Einbeck we stopped about 4 o clock in the
morning—it was pitch dark, & the Postillion *led* us into a room
where there was not a ray of Light—we could not see our hands—!
but it felt extremely warm.—At length & suddenly, the Lamp came
—& we saw ourselves in a Room, 13 Strides in length, strewed with
straw—& lying by the side of each other on the straw twelve *Jews*
—I assure you, it was curious.—Their dogs lay at their Feet—
there was one very beautiful Boy among them, fast asleep, with the
softest conceivable opening of the Mouth, with the white Beard of
his Grandfather upon his right cheek, a fair rosy cheek!——I asked
the Landlord how much they payed for their night's Lodging—he
told me, a Metier a piece—that is—an halfpenny. The Jews are
horribly, unnaturally oppressed & persecuted all throughout Ger-
many.——The Cottagers every where in Germany use little Lamps
instead of Candles—if it be cheaper here, where all make their own
Candles, surely it must be vastly cheaper in England.——We were
frequently obliged to stop in the night—the road & track being
completely *lost* in the Snow. In these cases the Postillions *smoked on*
with undisturbed Phlegm, & simply said—Schwer Noth!—that is
—the Epilepsy!—This oath is universal in Germany—'a curious
fact, Tom'! Bye the bye, Swearing is almost unknown among gen-
teel People here.—It is a general Prejudice *here*, that the English
are monstrous Eaters—in England, that the Germans are Devils

for Drinking!—The fact is, that a German eats more than *any two* Englishmen, but is exceedingly sober—and I have reason to believe that no Country in God's Earth labours under the tremendous curse of Drunkenness equally with England.—About Einbeck the country becomes Hilly & amphitheatrical—& the Hills are cleft, woody, & run into each other / but there is neither stately River nor Lake.—The country soon ceases to be beautiful—however it continues tolerable, till we arrived at Gottingen, a most emphatically ugly Town in a plain surrounded by naked Hills, that are neither high or interesting—175 miles from Ratzeburg.—We arrived in the evening of Tuesday, Feb. 12th.—That my Descriptions of the Country are so uninteresting, is owing, partly to the *intense Cold* which obliged us to fasten up the Coach as much as possible—& partly, to the Depth of the Snow, which not only concealed the shapes of Things, but by the Glitter & by the Sameness checked & discouraged me from watching them.——I forgot to say, that Schwer Noth is pronounced exactly Swear not!—& at first this equivocation has an odd effect to an English Man who is ignorant of the Language.—— / —While we were drinking Tea, we heard a loud, very very loud Smacking of Whips—ran to the Window, & lo! 30 Sledges full gallop, one after the other, each with one or two Ladies—I must draw the Sledge.

a the Student who sits [or] rather stands astride behind the Sledge, & (the reins running each side the [sledge) &] so manages the first Horse—.—b.—the Ladies in the Sledge. c c c—the Reins—(N.B. No[t in] the Sledge, as in the *Picture*.) d d. the first Horse.— c. c. c. c. c. the Reins—aga[in—] d d d. the second Horse, at least 10 yards from the first. e e the Postillion [who] rides on the second Horse.—All, Ladies, Student, Sledge, Horses, & Postillion, a[re] drest in all imaginable Pomp—the Horses have Bells, & the Noise of the Whips is [inconceivable—] This is a darling [amuse]ment of the Students; but a very expensive one. I found afterw[ards] that young Parry, [Hobhous]e's Nephew, was at the head of this Party —& he to[ld me] that his share [alone cost] him 35 dollars—somewhat more than 5 gui[neas—] N.b. They gave refre[shments &c su]ch as Wine, Cakes &c.——

Wednesday Morning we sought out Lodgings & took four very neat Rooms, [at the] rate of 25 Shillings a month, the Landlord to find us Plates, Knives, & [Forks] & our Tea Things—We likewise agreed with the House opposite to us [for] a Dinner Portion, for 19 Shillings a month. This is amply sufficient for us Bo[th,] both for dinner & Supper. Consequently for lodging & boarding *for both* we only pay two guineas & 2 Shillings, a month—to these expences you must add bread, butter, wood, tea, & washing, & a trifle for the maid. Coffee is half a crown a pound, but it [is] not good. The Tea is *very good*; but you give 13 Shillings a pound for [it—Sugar is] half a crown a pound—Butter a Shilling, or 11d—Washing somewhat cheaper than in England—fire wood very expensive; but in the course of a week or so we shall be able to do without it— our rooms are so warm.—In the lodgings we were a little cheated— we might have had four magnificently furnished Rooms in the best House in Gottingen at the Rate of fourteen *Louis* a year—A Louis is about 16*s* & 3*d*.—In short, you may live very cheap at Gottingen; but one must be always on the watch against being cheated. Every human Being from the highest to the lowest is in a conspiracy against you—commercial Integrity is quite unknown in Germany, & cheating in business is a national, & therefore not an individual crime / for a German is educated to consider it as *right*. This day I called with my Letters on the Professor Heyne, a little, hopping, over-civil, sort of a Thing who talks very fast & with fragments of coughing between every ten words—however, he behaved very courteously to me.—The next day I took out my Matricula & commenced Student of the University of Gottingen —for which I payed 15 Shillings—without this I could not have used the Library &c—. Heyne has honoured me so far, that he has given me the Right, which properly only the Professors have, of sending to the Library for an indefinite number of Books, in *my own* name.[1]—He told me that he wished the English had never been at Göttingen—they had introduced expensive habits &c—— Friday Afternoon 3 Englishmen called on me, who gave me a melancholy picture of Gottingen—of it's dullness—of the impossibility of being introduced into mixed societies, &c &c—I went with them & visited the Library, which without doubt is the very first in the World both in itself, & in the management of it.—It consists of two *immense* large Rooms, ornamented with busts & Statues—some Antiques, some Copies of Antiques—there are very fine Copies of all the best ancient Statues—but of the Library more hereafter.—On Saturday Evening I went to the Concert where a Student declaimed a Monodrama to Music—at first, it struck me as if a Parson was preaching during the chimes—; but after a little while I liked it. It was declaiming—i.e. impassioned Reading—not like *Recitativo*—but *Reading*—the Music sometimes

---

[1] For Coleridge's borrowings between 21 Feb. and 16 June 1799 see Alice D. Snyder, 'Books borrowed by Coleridge from the Library of the University of Göttingen, 1799', *Modern Philology*, Feb. 1928, pp. 377–80.

accompanying, but more often filling up the pauses of the Voice.—
Here the other Englishmen introduced themselves—three had
known my Friends at Cambridge & were eager to make my acquain-
tance—: for they were Cambridge men—two others were the
Parries,[1] the Nephews of Mr Hobhouse, & acquaintances of Mr
Estlin—.—After the Concert Hamilton,[2] a Cambridge man, took
me, as his Guest, to the Saturday Club—where *what is called* the
first Class of Students meet & sup once a week—Here were all the
nobility, & three Englishmen, Hamilton, Brown, & Kennet.—Such an
Evening I never passed before—roaring, kissing, embracing, fighting,
smashing bottles & glasses against the wall, singing—in short, such
a scene of uproar I never witnessed before, no, not even at Cam-
bridge.—I drank nothing—but all, except two of the Englishmen,
were drunk—& the party broke up a little after one o/clock in the
morning. I thought of what I had been at Cambridge, & of what I
was—of the wild & bacchanalian Sympathy with which I had
formerly joined similar Parties, & of my total inability now to do
aught *but meditate*—& the feeling of the deep alteration in my
moral Being gave the scene a melancholy interest to me!—There
were two Customs which I had never seen before—the one they
call *Smollets* [Schmollis], & consists in two men drinking a glass of
wine under each other's arm, & then kissing & embracing each other
—after which they always say *Thou* to each other. The other cus-
tom was this—when all were drunk & all the Bottles smashed, they
brought a huge Sword, sung a Song round it, then each fixed his Hat
on the sword, Hat over Hat, still singing—& then all kissed & em-
braced each other, still singing.—This Kissing is a most loathsome
Business—& the English are known to have such an aversion to
it, that it is never expected of them.—

We are quite well. Chester will write soon to his Family—in the
meantime he sends Duty, Love, & Remembrances to all to whom
they are due.—I have drank no wine or fermented liquor now for
more than 3 months—in consequence of which I am apt to be
costive & wakeful; but then I never feel any oppression after
dinner & my Spirits are much more equable—blessings which I
deem inestimable!—My dear Hartley!—My Berkley—how in-
tensely I long for you!—My Sara—O my dear Love! To Poole—
God bless him!—To dear Mrs Poole, & Ward kindest Love—& to
all Love & Remembrance.

                                                        S. T. Coleridge

(Mr Coleridge, in der Burg Strasse, Göttingen, Germany.)

[1] Charles and Frederick Parry, brothers of Sir William Parry, the arctic
explorer.
[2] Anthony Hamilton of St. John's College, Cambridge.

273. *To Mrs. S. T. Coleridge*

[Addressed in another hand][1] Mr Coleridge | Greata Hall | Keswick   To be delivered to Mr Jackson

MS. British Museum. Hitherto unpublished. This fragment, which is headed 'Gottingen', is all that remains of what was probably a letter to Mrs. Coleridge. Coleridge here defines the term Professor, as he had promised in Letter 259.

[March 1799]
Gottingen

Gottingen had been a considerable town long before George the second made it a university—so early as 1475 there was calculated to be 800 *Master* Manufacturers of Cloth & Stuffs. Before the year 1400 it had been admitted into the Hanseatic League, & remained in it till the year 1572. But both town & manufactory received injuries in the famous thirty years war, from which it has never recovered.—A Sovereign Prince in order to establish a University in his Dominions must receive the imperial Privilege: this privilege George the IId received from the Emperor Charles VIth; Jan. 13th. 1733—the University commenced in October 1734 & having been presented with complete rights of Jurisdiction, distinct from the civil power & dependent only on the *Government*, it was solemnly consecrated 17th Sept. 1737. From the name of it's founder it is called the Georgia Augusta University; & the King of England is always the Rector Magnificentissimus. The Prorector is elected annually from out of the ordinary Professors—or rather they take it by turns. During his office he is an Imperial Count Palatine, and as such has the right (I quote from the charter) 'to nominate Notaries & laureate Poets, to legitimate Bastards, restore their honour to the Infamous' &c &c.——— / —*A Professor* is one who has received from the Government & University that especial Degree which authorizes him to teach publickly in the particular department or faculty, of which he is Professor.—The Ordinary Professors (Professores ordinarii) are not only authorized to read lectures—but are salaried by the Government so to do.—Since the foundation of this University it has [ha]d a succession of the most eminent men in Germany as it's ordinary Professors—among which the names of Mosheim, Gesner, Haller, Michaelis, Pütter, Kästner, Heyne, Letz or Less,[2] Blumenbach, Lichtenburg, Plank, Eichhorn, Meiners, and Jacobi are as well known to the Literati throughout Europe, as to their own Countrymen.—The Professors are divided into

---

[1] The address indicates that this manuscript was forwarded to Coleridge at Keswick in 1800, when he was planning to publish his German tour. See Letters 340 and 362.

[2] i.e. Gottfried Less (1736–97), biblical scholar.

four Faculties—I the theological, consisting of 3 & sometimes 4 members, 2 the Jurists, of 4 members, the Medicinists, of 3 & (4) the Philosophers of 8—Sum total 18 or 19.—These are the Professores ordinarii—the number of those who can teach but are not appointed to do so, is in each faculty indefinite.— The Professores ordinarii of the first faculty in all processions &c wear a black *robe*, of the second a light Scarlet, of the third a deep Red—& the [Philo]sophers march in Purple—with drum, fife, & trumpet, too! too! too! [Each of the fa]culties takes it in his turn yearly to be the President of. . .

274. *To Thomas Poole*

Address: Mr T. Poole | Nether Stowey | Somersetshire | England   Pay'd to Cuxhaven

MS. British Museum. Pub. with omis. Letters, *i. 282.*

Postmark: Foreign Office, 3 May 1799.

April 6th, 1799

My dearest Poole

Your two letters, dated, Jan. 24th and March 15th, followed close on each other. I was still enjoying 'the livelier impulse and the dance of thought'[1] which the first had given me, when I received the second.—At the time, in which I read Sara's lively account of the miseries which herself and the infant had undergone, all was over & well—there was nothing to *think* of—only a mass of Pain was brought suddenly and closely within the sphere of my perception, and I was made to suffer it over again. For this bodily frame is an imitative Thing, and touched by the imagination gives the hour that is past, as faithfully as a repeating watch.—But Death— the death of an Infant—of one's own Infant![2]—I read your letter in calmness, and walked out into the open fields, oppressed, not by my feelings, but by the riddles, which the Thought so easily proposes, and solves—never! A Parent—in the strict and exclusive sense a *Parent*—! to me it is a *fable* wholly without meaning except in the *moral* which it suggests—a fable, of which the Moral is God. Be it so—my dear dear Friend! O let it be so! La nature (says Pascal) 'La Nature confond les Pyrrhoniens, et la raison confond les Dogmatistes. Nous avons une impuissance à prouver,

---

[1] *Fears in Solitude*, line 220.

[2] Berkeley Coleridge died of consumption on 10 Feb. 1799. Poole at first thought it desirable to spare Coleridge's feelings by concealing the news; but later he thought better of his decision, perhaps fearing that Coleridge would hear of the baby's death from other sources, and on 15 Mar. wrote a tender letter containing the ill tidings.

invincible à tout le Dogmatisme: nous avons une idée de la vérité, invincible à tout le Pyrrhonisme.' I find it wise and human to believe, even on slight evidence, opinions, the contrary of which cannot be proved, & which promote our happiness without hampering our Intellect.—My Baby has not lived in vain—this life has been to him what it is to all of us, education & developement! Fling yourself forward into your immortality only a few thousand years, & how small will not the difference between one year old & sixty years appear!—Consciousness—! it is no otherwise necessary to our conceptions of future Continuance than as connecting the *present link* of our Being with the one *immediately* preceding it; & *that* degree of Consciousness, *that* small portion of *memory*, it would not only be arrogant, but in the highest degree absurd, to deny even to a much younger Infant.—'Tis a strange assertion, that the Essence of Identity lies in *recollective* Consciousness—'twere scarcely less ridiculous to affirm, that the 8 miles from Stowey to Bridge-water consist in the 8 mile stones. Death in a doting old age falls upon my feelings ever as a more hopeless Phaenomenon than Death in Infancy / ; but *nothing* is hopeless.—What if the vital force which I sent from my arm into the stone, as I flung it in the air & skimm'd it upon the water—what if even that did not perish! —It was *life*—! it was a particle of *Being*—! it was *Power!*—& *how could* it perish—? *Life, Power, Being!*—organization may & probably *is*, their *effect*; their *cause* it *cannot* be!—I have indulged very curious fancies concerning that force, that *swarm* of motive Powers which I sent out of my body into that Stone; & which, one by one, left the untractable or already possessed Mass, and——but the German Ocean lies between us.—It is all too far to send you such fancies as these!——'Grief' indeed,

> Doth love to dally with fantastic thoughts,
> And smiling, like a sickly Moralist,
> Finds some resemblance to her own Concerns
> In the Straws of Chance, & Things Inanimate![1]

But I cannot truly say that I grieve—I am perplexed—I am sad—and a little thing, a very trifle would make me weep; but for the death of the Baby I have *not* wept!—Oh! this strange, strange, strange Scene-shifter, Death! that giddies one with insecurity, & so unsubstantiates the living Things that one has grasped and handled!—/ Some months ago Wordsworth transmitted to me a most sublime Epitaph / whether it had any reality, I cannot say.—Most probably, in some gloomier moment he had fancied the moment in which his Sister might die.

[1] *Osorio*, v. i. 11–14.

To Thomas Poole

Epitaph[1]

A Slumber did my spirit seal,
  I had no human fears:
She seem'd a Thing, that could not feel
  The touch of earthly years.

No motion has she now, no force;
  She neither hears nor sees,
Mov'd round in Earth's diurnal course
  With rocks, & stones, and trees!

April 8th, 1799.

I feel disappointed beyond doubt at the circumstance of which you have half informed me, deeply disappointed; but still we can *hope*. If you live at Stowey, & my moral & intellectual Being grows & purifies, as I would fain believe, that it will—there will be always a motive, a strong one to their coming.[2] In your next letter, I pray you, be more minute.—As to your servants & the people of Stowey in general—Poole, my Beloved! you have been often unwisely fretful with me when I have pressed upon you their depravity.—Without religious joys, and religious terrors nothing can be expected from the *inferior* Classes in society—whether or no any *class* is strong enough to stand firm without them, is to me doubtful.—There are favoured *Individuals*, but not *Classes*. Pray, where is Cruikshanks? & how go his affairs?—and what good Luck has Sam. Chester had?— / —In this hurly burly of unlucky Things, I cannot describe to you how pure & deep Joy I have experienced from thinking of your dear Mother!—O may God Almighty give her after all her agonies now at last a long, rich, yellow Sunset, in this, her evening of Life!—So good, and so virtuous, and with such an untameable Sensibility *to enjoy* the blessings of the Almighty— surely God in heaven never made a Being more capable of enjoying with a deeper Thankfulness of Earth Life & it's Relations!—

With regard to myself I am very busy, very busy indeed!—I attend several Professors, & am getting many kinds of knowlege; but I stick to my Lessing—The Subject more & more interests me, & I doubt not in the least, that I shall wholly clear my expences by the end of October.—I am sorry to tell you, that I find that work as hard as I may I cannot collect all the vast quantity of Materials which I must collect, in less than six weeks—if I would do myself

---

[1] *Poet. Works*, ii. 216.
[2] Poole had informed Coleridge of an unrealized plan of the Wedgwoods to buy an estate near Stowey. See Letter 283.

justice; & perhaps, it may be 8 weeks. — / The materials which I have & shall have would of themselves make a quarto volume; but I must not work quite so hard as I have done / it so totally dries up all my colour.—With regard to the house at Stowey, I must not disguise from you that to live *in* Stowey, & in that house which you mention, is to me an exceedingly unpleasant Thought. Rather than go any where else assuredly I would do it—& be glad / but the thought is unpleasant to me.—I do not like to live *in* a Town—still less in Stowey where excepting yourself & Mother there is no human being attached to us & few who do not dislike us.—Besides, it [is] a sad Tyranny that all who live in towns are subject to—that of inoculating all at once &c &c. And then the impossibility of keeping one's children free from vice & profaneness—& &c.—

If I do not send off this letter now, I must wait another week— What must I do?—How you will look, when you see the blank Page!—My next shall make up for it—

Heaven bless you
& S. T. Coleridge

275. *To Mrs. S. T. Coleridge*

Transcript Thomas Ward copy-book, New York Public Lib. Pub. Letters, *i. 284.*

Gottingen in der Wende Strasse   April 8th. 1799—

It is one of the discomforts of my absence, my dearest Love! that we feel the same calamities at different times—I would fain write words of consolation to you; yet I know that I shall only fan into new activity the pang which was growing dead and dull in your heart—Dear little Being!—he had existed to me for so many months only in dreams and reveries, but in them existed and still exists so livelily, so like a real Thing, that although I know of his Death, yet when I am alone and have been long silent, it seems to me as if I did not understand it.—Methinks, there is something awful in the thought, what an unknown Being one's own Infant is to one!—a fit of sound—a flash of light—a summer gust, that is as it were *created* in the bosom of the calm Air, that rises up we know not how, and goes we know not whither!—But we say well; it goes! it is gone!—and only in states of Society in which the revealing voice of our most inward and abiding nature is no longer listened to, (when we sport and juggle with abstract phrases, instead of representing our feelings and ideas) only then we say it *ceases*! I will not believe that it ceases—in this moving stirring and harmonious Universe I *cannot* believe it!—Can cold and darkness

come from the Sun? where the Sun is not—there is cold and dark-
ness!—But the living God is every where, & works every where—
and where is there room for Death?—To look back on the life of
my Baby, how short it seems!—but consider it referently to non-
existence, and what a manifold and majestic Thing does it not
become?—What a multitude of admirable actions, what a multi-
tude of *habits* of actions it learnt even before it saw the light? and
who shall count or conceive the infinity of its thoughts and feelings,
it's hopes and fears, & joys, and pains, & desires, & presentiments,
from the moment of it's birth to the moment when the Glass,
through which we saw him darkly, was broken—and he became
suddenly invisible to us?—Out of the Mount that might not be
touched, and that burnt with fire, out of Darkness, and blackness
and tempest, and with his own Voice, which they who heard
entreated that they might not hear it again, the most high God
forbad us to use his *name vainly*—And shall we who are Christians,
shall we believe that he himself uses his own power vainly?—That
like a child he builds palaces of mud and clay in the common road,
and then he destroys them, as weary of his *pastime*, or leaves them
to be trod under by the Hoof of Accident?—That God works by
general laws are to me words without meaning or worse than
meaningless—Ignorance and Imbecillity, and Limitation must
wish in generals—What and who are these horrible shadows neces-
sity and general law, to which God himself must offer *sacrifices*—
hecatombs of Sacrifices?—I feel a deep conviction that these
shadows exist not—they are only the dreams of reasoning Pride,
that would fain find solutions for all difficulties without Faith!—
that would make the discoveries which lie thick sown in the path
of the eternal Future unnecessary; and so conceiting that there is
sufficiency and completeness in the narrow present, weakens the
presentiment of our wide and ever widening Immortality!—God
works in each for all—most true—but more comprehensively true
is it, that he works in all for each.—I confess that the more I think,
the more I am discontented with the doctrines of Priestly. He
builds the whole and sole hope of future existence on the words and
miracles of Jesus—yet doubts or denies the future existence of
Infants—only because according to his own System of Materialism
he has not discovered how they can be made *conscious*—But Jesus
has declared that *all* who are in the grave shall arise—and that
those who should arise to perceptible progression must be ever as
the Infant which he held in his Arms and blessed!—And although
the *Man* Jesus had never appeared in the world, yet I am Quaker
enough to believe, that in the heart of every Man the Christ would
have revealed himself, the Power of the Word, that was even in

the Wilderness—To me who am absent this Faith is a real con-
solation—& the few, the slow, the quiet tears which I shed, are the
Accompaniments of high and solemn Thought, not the workings
of Pain or Sorrow—When I return indeed, and see the vacancy
that has been made—when no where any thing corresponds to the
form which will perhaps for ever dwell on my mind, then it is
possible that a keener pang will come upon me—Yet I trust, my
Love!—I trust, my dear Sara! that this event which has forced us
to think of the Death of what is most dear to us, as at all times
probable, will in many and various ways be good for us—To have
shared—nay, I should say—to have divided with any human
Being any one deep Sensation of Joy or of Sorrow, sinks deep the
foundations of a lasting love—When in Moments of fretfulness
and Imbecillity I am disposed to anger or reproach, it will, I trust,
be always a restoring thought—'We have wept over the same little
one—& with whom am I angry?—with her who so patiently and
unweariedly sustained my poor and sickly Infant through his long
Pains—with her—who, if I too should be called away, would stay
in the deep anguish over my death-pillow! who would never forget
me!'—Ah, my poor Berkley!—A few weeks ago an Englishman
desired me to write an Epitaph on an Infant who had died before
it's Christening—While I wrote it, my heart with a deep misgiving
turned my thoughts homewards—

> On an Infant, who died before it's Christening—[1]
>
> Be rather than be *call'd* a Child of God!
> Death whisper'd. With assenting Nod
> It's head upon the Mother's breast
> The baby bow'd, and went without demur,
> Of the Kingdom of the blest
> Possessor, not Inheritor!——

It refers to the second Question in the Church Catechism—

We are well, my dear Sara—I hope to be home at the end of 10
or 11 weeks—If you should be in Bristol, you will probably be
shewn by Mr Estlin three letters which I have written to him all
together—& one to Mr Wade—Mr Estlin will permit you to take
the letters to Stowey that Poole may see them, & Poole will return
them—

I have no doubt but I shall repay myself by the work which I am
writing, to such an amount, that I shall have spent out of my income
only 50 pounds at the end of August—My love to your Sisters—&
love & duty to your Mother—God bless you my love! and shield

[1] *Poems*, i. 312.

us from deeper Afflictions, or make us resigned unto them (and perhaps the latter Blessedness is greater than the former).

Your affectionate & faithful | Husband
S T Coleridge

276. *To Mrs. S. T. Coleridge*

Address: Mrs Coleridge | Nether Stowey | Somersetshire | England   Payed
to Cuxhaven
MS. New York Public Lib. Pub. with omis. Letters, *i. 288.*
Postmark: Foreign Office, 6 May 1799.

Göttingen, bey Hüne in der Wende Strasse.
April 23rd 1799

My dear Sara

Surely it is unnecessary for me to say, how infinitely I languish to be in my native Country & with how many struggles I have remained even so long in Germany!—I received your affecting letter, dated Easter Sunday; and had I followed my impulses, I should have packed up & gone with Wordsworth & his Sister, who passed thro', & only passed thro', this place, two or three days ago.—If they burn with such impatience to return to their native Country, they who are all to each other, what must *I* feel, with every thing pleasant & every thing valuable, & every thing dear to me at a distance—here, where I may truly say, my only amusement is—to labour!—. But it is in the strictest sense of the word impossible that I can collect what I have to collect, in less than six weeks from this day; yet I read & transcribe from 8 to 10 hours every day. Nothing could support me but the knowlege that if I return now, we shall be embarrassed & in debt; & the moral certainty that having done what I am doing, we shall be more than *cleared*: / not to add that so large a work with so great a variety of information from sources so scattered, & so little known even in Germany, will, of course, establish my character—for industry & erudition, certainly; & I would fain hope, for reflection & genius.— This day in June I hope, & trust, that I shall be in England—! O that the Vessel could but land at Shurton Bars!—Not that I should wish to see you & Poole immediately on my Landing— No!—the sight, the touch of my native Country were sufficient for one *whole Feeling*—one most deep unmingled Emotion! But then & after a lonely walk of the three miles—*then*, first of *all* whom I knew, to see you, & my *Friend*!—It lessens the delight of the thought of my Return, that I must get at you thro' a tribe of *acquaintances*, *damping* the freshness of one's Joy!—My poor little Baby!—at this moment I see the corner of the Room where his cradle stood—

& his cradle too—and I cannot help seeing *him in* the cradle. Little lamb! & the snow would not melt on his limbs!—I have some faint recollection that he had that difficulty of breathing once before I left England—or was it Hartley?—/— 'A child! a child! is born, and the fond heart Dances: and yet the childless are more happy!'—/— In Christmas[1] I saw a custom which pleased & interested me here—the children make little Presents to their Parents, & to one another; & the Parents to the Children. For three or four months before Christmas the Girls are all busy, & the boys save up their pocket-money, to make or purchase these presents— What the present is to be, is cautiously kept secret, & the Girls have a world of contrivances to conceal it—such as, working when they are out on visits & the others are not with them, & getting up in the morning long before light, &c.—Then on the Evening before Christmas Day one of the parlours is lighted up by the Children, into which the Parents must not go; a great yew-bough is fastened on the Table at a little distance from the wall, a multitude of little Tapers are fastened in the bough, but not so as to burn it till they are nearly burnt out—& coloured paper &c hangs & flutters from the twigs.——Under this bough the Children lay out in great neatness the presents they mean for their parents; still concealing in their pockets what they intend for each other. Then the Parents are introduced—& each presents his little gift—& then they bring out the others & present them to each other, with kisses, & embraces.—Where I saw the Scene, there were 8 or 9 children of different ages; and the eldest Daughter & the Mother wept aloud for joy & tenderness; & the tears ran down the face of the Father, & he clasped all his children so tight to his breast, as if he did it to stifle the Sob that was rising within him.—I was very much affected. And the Shadow of the Bough on the wall, on the wall & arching over on the Ceiling, made a pretty picture—& then the raptures of the very little ones, when at least [last] the Twigs & thread leaves began to catch fire, & *snap*—O that was a delight for them!— / On the next day, in the great parlour, the Parents lay out on the Tables the presents for the children / a scene of more sober joy succeeds / as on this day, after an old custom, the Mother says privately to each of her Daughters, & the Father to each of his Sons, that which he has observed most praiseworthy & that which he has observed most faulty in their conduct—. Formerly, & still in all the little Towns & villages through the whole of North Germany, these Presents were sent by all the parents of the village to some one Fellow who in high Buskins, a white Robe, a Mask, &

[1] The following passage was published almost verbatim in *The Friend*, No. 19, 28 Dec. 1809, under the title *Christmas within Doors*.

an enormous Flax Wig personates Knecht Rupert—i.e. the Servant
Rupert. On Christmas night he goes round [to] every house, & says
that Jesus Christ, his Master, sent him there—the Parents & older
children receive him with great pomp of reverence, while the little
ones are most terribly frightened / he then enquires for the children,
& according to the character which he hears from the Parent, he
gives them the intended Presents, as if they came out of Heaven
from Jesus Christ—or if they should have been bad children, he
gives the Parents a rod, & in the Name of his Master Jesus recom-
mends them to use it frequently.—About 7 or 8 years old, the
children are let into the secret; & it is curious, how faithfully they
all keep it!—There are a multitude of strange wild superstitions
among the Bauers—these still survive in spite of the efforts of the
Clergy who in the north of Germany, i.e. in the Hanoverian,
Saxon, & Prussian Dominions are almost all Deists. But they make
little or no impressions on the Bauers, who are wonderfully
religious & fantastically superstitious; but not in the least priest-
rid.—But in the Catholic Countries of Germany the difference is
vast indeed!—I met lately an intelligent & calm-minded man who
had spent a considerable time at Marburg, in the Bishoprich of
Paderborn, in Westphalia. He told me, that Bead-prayers to the
Holy Virgin are universal & universally too are magical Powers
attributed to one particular formula of words which are absolutely
jargon / at least, the words are to be found in no known Language.
The Peasants believe it however to be a prayer to the Virgin, &
happy is the man among them who is made confident by a Priest
that he can repeat it perfectly; for heaven knows, what terrible
calamity might not happen, if any one should venture to repeat it,
& blunder.—Vows, & Pilgrimages to particular Images, are still
common among the Bauers / if any one die before the performance
of his vow, they believe that he hovers between Heaven & Earth,
and at times *hobgoblins* his relations till they perform it for him.
Particular Saints are believed to be eminently favorable to parti-
cular Prayers—& he assured me solemnly that a little before he
left Marburg, a *Lady* of Marburg had prayed, & given money to
have *the public Prayers*, at St Erasmus's Chapel to St Erasmus—
for what, think you?—That the Baby, with which she was then
pregnant, might be a Boy with white Hair & rosy Cheeks.—When
their Cows, Pigs, or Horses are sick they take them to the Domi-
nican Monks who prescribe *texts out of holy books*, & perform
exorcisms.—When men or women are sick, they give largely to
the Convent, who, on good conditions, dress them in Church-robes,
& lay a particular & highly-venerated Crucifix on their Breasts / &
perform a multitude of antic Ceremonies.—In general, my In-

former confessed, that they *cured* the persons—which he seemed to think extraordinary, but which I think very natural. Yearly on St Blasius' Day unusual multitudes go to receive the Lord's Supper; & while they are receiving it, the Monks hold a Blasius Taper (as it [is] called) before the Forehead of the kneeling Person, & then pray to St Blasius to drive away all head-achs for the ensuing year.—Their wishes are often expressed in this form—'Mary, Mother of God, make her Son *do so and so.*'——Yet with all this, from every information which I can collect (& I have had very many opportunities of collating various accounts) the Peasants in the Catholic Countries of Germany, but especially in Austria, are far better off, & a far happier & livelier race than those in the Protestant Lands.—/—I fill up the sheet with scattered information, / put down in the order in which I happened to see them.— The Peasant children where ever I have been, are dressed warm & tight; but very ugly the dress looks; a frock-coat, some of coarse blue cloath, some of Plaid, buttoned behind—the Row of Buttons running down the Back, & the seamless buttonless fore-part—'t has an odd look!——When the Peasants marry, if the Girl is of a good character, the Clergyman gives her a virgin Crown—(a tawdry ugly thing made of gold & silver Tinsel, like the Royal Crowns in Shape)—this they wear, with cropped, powdered, & pomatumed Hair— / in short, the Bride looks Ugliness personified.—While I was at Ratzeburg, a girl came to beg the Pastor to let her be married in this crown—& she had had two Bastards!— The Pastor refused, of course.—I wondered that a reputable Farmer should marry her; but the Pastor told me that where a female Bauer is the heiress, her having had a bastard does not much stand in her way / and yet tho' little or no infamy attaches to it, the number of Bastards is but small / 2 in 70 has been the average at Ratzeburg among the Peasants.—By the bye, the Bells in Germany are not rung as our's with ropes—but two men stand, one on each side of the Bell—& each pushes the Bell away from him with his foot.—In the Churches, what is a Baptismal Font in our churches, is a great Angel with a Bason in his hand;—he draws up & down with a chain, like a Lamp—. In a particular part of the Ceremony down comes the great Stone Angel with the Bason, presents it to the Pastor who having taken *quant. suff.*, up flies my Angel to his old place in the Ceiling. You cannot conceive, how droll it looked.——The Graves, in the little village Church yards, are square; and in square or parallelogrammic wooden cases—they look like Boxes without lids—& Thorns & Briars are woven over them, as is done in some parts of England. Perhaps, you recollect that beautiful passage in Jeremy Taylor's Holy Dying / '& the

Summer brings briars to bud on our graves'—.—The Shepherds,
with iron-soled boots, walk before their Sheep (as in the East)—
you know, our Saviour says—My Sheep follow me.—So it is here—
the Dog and [the S]hepherd walk first, the Shepherd with his
romantic fur-C[ap] & general[ly k]nitting a pair of white worsted
Gloves—he walks on, & his dog by him, & then follow the Sheep,
winding along the roads in a beautiful *Stream*! In the fields I
observed a multitude of poles with bands & trusses of Straw tied
round the higher part, & the top—on enquiry we found that they
were put there for the Owls to perch on— / And the Owls?—O—
they catch the Field mice, who do amazing damage in the light
soil all throughout the north of Germany.—/—The Gallows near
Gottingen like that near Ratzeburg is three great Stone Pillars,
square like huge Tall chimneys, & connected with each other at the
top by three iron bars with hooks to them—& near them is a
wooden pillar with a wheel on the top of it, on which the head is
exposed, if the Person instead of being hung is beheaded.—I was
frightened at first to see such a multitude of bones & Skeletons of
Sheep, Oxen, & Horses, & bones, as I imagined, of Men for many,
many yards all round the Gallows—/—I found that in Germany
the Hangman is by the laws of the Empire *infamous*—these Hang-
men form a cast—& their Families always marry with each other
&c—and that all dead Cattle—who have died belong [to] them—
& are carried by the Owners to the Gallows & left [by] them there—
When their cattle are bewitched or otherwise desperately sick, the
Peasants take them, & tie them to the Gallows—Drowned Dogs,
& Kittens, &c are thrown there; in short, the Grass grows rank,
& yet the Bones overtop it.—The fancy of human bones must, I
suppose, have arisen in my ignorance of comparative Anatomy.——
    God bless you, my Love!—I will write again speedily.—When
I was at Ratzeburgh, I wrote one wintry night in bed but never
sent you three stanzas which, I dare say, you will think very silly;
& so they are: & yet they were not written without a yearning,
yearning, yearning *Inside*—for my yearning affects more than my
heart—I feel it all within me.[1]

1

        If I had but two little wings
        And were a little feath'ry Bird,
          To *you* I'd fly, my Dear!
        But Thoughts, like these, are idle Things—
          And I stay here.

[1] *Poems*, i. 313. The lines are an imitation of the German folk song, *Wenn
ich ein Vöglein wär.*

2

But in my sleep to *you* I fly,
I'm always with you in my sleep—
   The World is all one's own.
But then one wakes—and where am I ?
   All, all alone!

3

Sleep stays not tho' a Monarch bids,
So I love to wake ere break of Day ;
   For tho' my Sleep be gone,
Yet while 'tis dark, one shuts one's lids,
   And still dreams *on*!

If Mrs Southey be with you, remember me with all kindness / &
thankfulness for their attention to you & Hartley.[1]——To dear
Mrs Poole give my filial love—My love to Ward.—Why should I
write the name of Tom Poole except for the pleasure of writing
it ?—It grieves me to the heart that Nanny is not without [*sic*]
you. I cannot bear changes——Death makes enough!—God bless
you, my dear dear Wife, &
      believe me with eagerness to clasp you to my heart, your
                            faithful Husband
                            S. T. Coleridge

Here is a letter from Chester for his mother / she must pay you
half the Postage. *We* save a shilling by sending a double letter—for
double, or treble, in Germany there is no difference in the P[ostag]e.
I have received four letters—three in one / & p[aid no] more than
for a s[ingle one.]

---

[1] Southey had undertaken the interment of Berkeley Coleridge and had
extended every kindness to Mrs. Coleridge. 'Edith and Southey', Mrs. Cole-
ridge wrote to Coleridge on 24 Mar., 'have behaved towards me with particular
kindness ; in my trouble after the loss of my child Southey brought a Coach
and carried me and Hartley over to Westbury where they both strove to
amuse me and the child, who is excessively fond of them both as they are of
him.' Perhaps, however, Southey's unfavourable opinion of *Lyrical Ballads*,
as shown by his review of the volume in the *Critical Review* for Oct. 1798, was
reflected in Mrs. Coleridge's tactless comment in her letter: 'The Lyrical
Ballads are not esteemed well here, but the Nightingale and the River Y
[Wye].' Even more pointedly Mrs. Coleridge wrote to Poole: 'The Lyrical
Ballads are laughed at and disliked by all with very few excepted.' Her letter
to Coleridge also reports on the literary activities of Lamb, Lloyd, and
Southey, information which in the light of their recent mistreatment of him,
Coleridge can hardly have relished.

277. *To Thomas Poole*

Address: [M]r T. Poole | Nether Stowey | Somersetshire | England   pay'd
to Cuxhaven
MS. British Museum. Pub. with omis. Letters, *i. 295.* The manuscript is torn
and the words in brackets have been supplied from a transcript made by
Thomas Ward.
Postmark: Foreign Office, 17 May 1799.

May 6th 1799, Monday Morning

My dear Poole, my dear Poole! I am homesick.—Society is a
burthen to me; and I find relief only in labour. So I read & tran-
scribe from morning to night / & never in my life have I worked so
hard as this last month: for indeed I must sail over an ocean of
matter with almost spiritual Speed, to do what I have to do in the
time, in which I *will* do it, or leave it undone!— / O my God! how
I long to be at home—My *whole Being* so yearns after you, that
when I think of the moment of our meeting, I catch the fashion of
German Joy, rush into your arms, and embrace you—methinks,
my *Hand* would swell, if the whole force of my feeling were crowded
there.—Now the Spring comes, the vital sap of my affections rises,
as in a tree!—And what a gloomy Spring! But a few days ago all
the new buds were covered with snow; & every thing yet looks so
brown & wintry, that yesterday the Roses (which the Ladies
carried on the Ramparts, their Promenade) beautiful as they were,
so little harmonized with the general face of Nature that they
looked to me like silk & paper Roses.—But these leafless spring
Woods / O how I long to hear your *whistle* to the Rippers!——
There are a multitude of Nightingales here / poor things! they
sang in the Snow / —I thought of my own verses on the Nightingale,
only because I thought of Hartley, my *only* child!—Dear Lamb!
I hope, *he* won't be dead, before I get home.—There are moments
in which I have such a power of Life within me, such a conceit of
it, I mean—that I lay the Blame of my Child's Death to my
absence—*not intellectually*; but I have a strange sort of sensation,
as if while I was present, none could die whom I intensely loved—
and doubtless *it* was no absurd idea of your's that there may be
unions & connections out of the visible world.——Wordsworth &
his Sister passed thro' here, as I have informed you— / I walked
on with them 5 english miles, & spent a day with them. They were
melancholy & hypp'd—W. was affected to tears at the thought of
not being near me, wished me, of course, to live in the North of
England near the Sir Frederic Vane's great Library / —I told him,
that independent of the expence of removing, & the impropriety
of taking Mrs Coleridge to a place where she would have no

acquaintance, two insurmountable objections, the Library was
no inducement—for I wanted old books chiefly, such as could be
procured any where better than in a Gentleman's new fashionable
Collection / —Finally, I told him plainly, that *you* had been the
man in whom *first* and in whom alone, I had felt an *anchor*! With
all my other Connections I felt a dim sense of insecurity & un-
certainty, terribly uncomfortable / —W. was affected to tears, very
much affected; but he deemed the vicinity of a Library absolutely
necessary to his health, nay to his existence. It is painful to me too
to think of not living near him; for he is a *good* and *kind* man, &
the only one whom in *all* things I feel my Superior—& you will
believe me, when I say, that I have few feelings more pleasurable
than to find myself in intellectual Faculties an Inferior / . But my
Resolve is fixed, *not to leave you till you leave me!* I still think that
Wordsworth will be disappointed in his expectations of relief from
reading, without Society—& I think it highly probable, that where
I live, there he will live, unless he should find in the North any
person or persons, who can feel & understand him, can reciprocate
& react on him.—My many weaknesses are of some advantage to
me; they unite me more with the great mass of my fellow-beings—
but dear Wordsworth appears to me to have hurtfully segregated
& isolated his Being / Doubtless, his delights are more deep and
sublime; / but he has likewise more hours, that prey on his flesh &
blood.—/—With regard to Hancock's House, if I can get no place
within a mile or two of Stowey, I must try to get that—but I
confess, I like it not!—not to say, that it is not altogether pleasant
to live directly opposite to a person who had behaved so rudely to
Mrs Coleridge, & whose Relation to your family necessarily makes
me feel that rudeness, and remember it. But these are in the eye of
reason all Trifles—& if no other House can be got, in my eye too
they shall be Trifles.——
There have happened a multitude of Suicides in Germany
within thes[e] last months; I have heard of eleven / and many of
them curious enough. I relate the following, because I am sure of
it's accuracy, & because it is quite *German*—i.e. it has quite a
Schiller-ish, *Charles de Moorish Gloss* about it.—On the 3rd of
Feb. Herlt, a Subaltern Officer in the Catholic Cours at Dresden,
made a pleasure party in a Sledge with a woman with whom he
lived in criminal connection, called Wilhelmine Pfeifer. The[y]
went to the Heller, a little place in the midst of Woods two english
miles from Dresden, to a Pleasure house there— / here they feasted
most gloriously, & enjoyed themselves / & in conclusion, Herlt
shot the Girl dead, & then himself.—He was a native of Bohemia,
and had married a Tradesman's Daughter of Leibsic—but had

lived unhappily with her, & became addicted to gambling & Drinking &c—he had long declared his intention of destroying himself, to which the impossibility of being divorced, it was supposed, had impelled him. This however is contradicted by himself in a letter directed to his wife, which was found after his death on the table in the place where he shot himself, acquainting her with his Intention. The following is an extract from this letter— 'Forgive me—for ever!—In yonder World perhaps we see each other again. My Death was unavoidable—I and Thou are not the Causes; but Wicked Men; and the wickedest of all is Lieutenant Slawianowsky.' (N.B. On the news of Herlt's Suicide this man went off privately, & has not been heard of since.) 'Death must have it's Causes; mine has *it's*, has many causes which I will hold in silence. It may be easily supposed, that the Prospect into Futurity is a terrible one to me. But complain not. This Destiny was appointed me by the same being who appointed the Heavens & the Earth, and at the same time. I die as one who dies on a sick bed of a six months' Sickness. Since Michaelmas I too have been sick, & now I return again [to] the all-vivifying Being. From my Childhood Happiness has fled from me, [and] Misfortune persecuted me, especially in my Marriage. I utter no complaint against thee; for I knew that thou wert a weak Woman! Now & hereby receiv'st [thou] intelligence of my Death. The woman, with whom I am, I found by accident, loved her from day to day more impetuously, and we are, as thou seest, inseparable. Our Love cannot be legalized by Priests according to human ordinances—in it's fitness to our being / it has legalized itself. This is not the reason why I leave this world. Thou knowest, how Mankind have treated me, how they have stripped me of my little Property. I am in debt; thou knowest how my Creditors surround me. Would to God that by living for years on bread & water I could satisfy their wishes. Entreat the Lieutenant Colonel in the name of all the Saints and of all the Departed that have ever lived upon Earth, that he procure us to be *buried*, let the spot of earth be where it will. (N.B. This has been done.) Provide for thine & my Child as a mother. He has lost a Father; a Father whom his fellow-men made miserable. The portrait of my Wilhelmine must S. carry to her Mother, & tell her, that we are insepara[ble] thro' the great all vivifying Being.— The Death hour strikes—& we go! My Wilhelmine, last Being to me, for us both there is but one Grave.—'— At the bottom of this letter Wilhelmine wrote the following, which in the original is in a wild irregular Verse—'To die with Herlt is my Will, I hope with exultation with thee, my Herlt! to die! And there in yonder Glory with thee to take possession of our Inheritance! I loved thee in life impetuously, in death I love thee far more. Thou, whom I have found faithful, come with me—let us go in triumph and ask Happiness of the Being that made us. Beautiful was the hour, in which thy fidelity was rewarded. (I presume, she means the hour of her first seduction by Herlt.) Thy resolve leads thee to the Cavern of Death; but a voice will echo there and call thee to a nobler Existence, the voice of him who in love destined thee to this Hour. I too am near to the Dwelling of the Grave. Thou hast led me to the Heller / there my Soul takes it's departure, goes full of Joy with thee and in thee in an inconceivable Inseparability to the spiritual World.—Come, my Herlt![']——

In Tragedy we pronounce many things unnatural, only because we have drawn our notions of Nature from persons in a calm, or only moderately agitated state / but in all violent states of *Passion* the mind *acts & plays a part*, itself the actor & the spectator at once! —My God! to think that this Girl should find a delight in the moment of Death in putting these thoughts into Rhyme; or rather from the wild nature of the verse the Rhymes perhaps half-led her to the Thoughts!—/—I have a number of affecting Stories of this kind to tell you, of winter Evenings.——O Poole! I am homesick. —Yesterday, or rather, yesternight, I dittied the following hobbling Ditty; but my poor Muse is quite gone—perhaps, she may return & meet me at Stowey.[1]

> 'Tis sweet to him, who all the week
> Thro' city crowds must push his way,
> To stroll alone thro' fields and woods
> And hallow thus the Sabbath day.
>
> And sweet it is, in summer bower
> Sincere, affectionate, and gay,
> One's own dear Children feasting round,
> To celebrate one's marriage day.
>
> But what is all to *his* delight,
> Who having long been doom'd to roam
> Throws off the Bundle from his Back
> Before the Door, of his own Home?
>
> H[ome sickness] is no baby pang,
> [This feel] I hourly more and more:
> The[re's healing] only in thy wings,
> Thou Breeze, that play'st on Albion's shore!

[1] *Poems*, i. 314.

The Professors here are exceedingly kind to all the Englishmen;
but to me they pay [the most] *flattering* attention—Especially,
Blumenbach and Eichhorn.—Nothing can be conce[ived more]
delightful than Blumenbach's lectures / & in conversation he is
indeed a most i[nteresting] man. / The learned Orientalist, Tychson,
has given me instruction in the Gothic, [and] Theotiscan Lan-
guages,[1] which I can now read pretty well; & hope in the cou[rse
of a] year to be thoroughly acquainted with all the Languages of
the north, both [GERMAN] & Celtic. For I find being learned is a
mighty easy thing, compared with [any study] else. My God! a
miserable Poet must he be, & a despicable Metaphysician [whose]
acquirements have not cost more trouble & reflection than all the
lea[rning of] Tooke, Porson, & Parr united. With the advantage
of a great Lib[rary] Learning is nothing, methinks—merely a sort
of excuse for being [idle—Yet a] man gets reputation by it; and
reputation gets money—& for reputa[tion I don't care] a damn,
but money—yes—Money I must get, in all honest [ways—there-
fore] at the end of two or three years if God grant me life expect to
see me come out with some horribly learned book, full of manu-
script quotations from Laplandish and Patagonian Authors—
possibly, on the striking resemblance between the Sweogothic &
Sanscrit Languages, & so on!——N.B. Whether a sort of Parch-
ment might not be made out of old Shoes; & whether Apples should
not be engrafted on Oak Saplings; as then the Fruit would be the
same as now, but the wood far more valuable?—*Two ideas of mine.*
To extract Aqua fortis from Cucumbers is a discovery not yet made;
but Sugar from Bete, O! all Germany is mad about it. I have seen
the Sugar, sent to Blumenbach from Achard, the great Chemist;
& it is good enough. They say that an hundred pound weight of
Bete will make 12 pound of Sugar; & that there is no expence in
the preparation. It is the Beta altissima, belongs to the Beta
vulgaris, and in Germany is called Runkel-rübe. Its leaves re-
semble those of the common red Bete.—It is in shape like a clumsy
nine pin, & about the size of a middling Turnip—the flesh is white,
but has rings of a reddish Cast. I will bring over a quantity of the
Seed.—/ Likewise hath the Apothecary Cavette Sobies at Lille in
Flanders discovered a means to heat rooms without Fire, in a
pleasant & healthy manner. Take a tin vessel, the top of which
must have screws in order to be screwed down / lay in a few pieces
of Quick lime, which has been the moment before moistened with
cold water, shut the vessel, screw down the top; & in two minutes
the vessel will be burning hot, & it will keep a room in a comfortable

---

[1] See *Biog. Lit.*, ch. x, for Coleridge's comments on Thomas Christian
Tyschen (1758–1834), and on the Theotisc language.

& equable warmth for 2 Hours.——The Price of meat for Hanover
as appointed by the Government for the month of May 1799—

> A pound of Beef   L   S   D
> of the 1st sort —0 ... 0 ...   4
> of the 2nd sort—0 ... 0 .... $3\frac{1}{2}$
> of the 3rd sort— 0 ... 0 ..... $2\frac{1}{2}$
> A pound of Veal
> of the 1st ——————$3\frac{1}{2}$
> of the ordinary sort ———$2\frac{3}{4}$
> a pound of Mutton
> of the 1st sort —————$4\frac{1}{2}$
> —— 2nd sort —————$3\frac{3}{4}$
> —— 3rd sort ——————$3\frac{1}{4}$
> A Pound of Pork
> may not cost more [of
> whatever sort it is than]   3 pence.

For Gottingen.

		D	
Wheat, 4 Shillings the Bushel	Beef,	$3\frac{1}{4}$	the pound
Rye, three & eightpence.	Veal, best	$3\frac{1}{4}$	
Barley half a crown.	Veal, ordinary	$2\frac{1}{4}$	
Oats two shillings & 2d	Veal of 3rd sort	2	
Peas—the same.	Pork	$3\frac{1}{4}$	
Beans the same	Mutton	$3\frac{1}{4}$	
	Venison	$3\frac{1}{4}$	

So you see, meat here is three pence farthing a pound in general;
—but People here complain bitterly of the dearness.

[A Stupid l]etter—I believe, my late proficiency in Learning has
somewhat stupified me but live in hopes of one better worth the
postage. In the last week of June, I trust, you will see me.—
Chester is well, & desires love & duty to his family.—I have a
frightful Cold, which gives my Nose such a fecundity as beggars
me in handkerchiefs—I dry them, & use them three Lavas deep.
Else I am well.—To your dear Mother & to Ward give my kind
Love——& to all who ask after me.—

My dear Poole! don't let little Hartley die before I come home.—
That's silly—true—& I burst into tears as I wrote it.

Your's   S. T. Coleridge.

278. *To Mrs. S. T. Coleridge*

MS. British Museum. Pub. Thomas Poole, *i. 300.* This note was written on the address sheet of the preceding letter to Poole.

[6 May 1799]

My dear Sara

On Saturday next I go to the famous Harz Mountains—about 20 english miles from Gottingen—to see the mines & other curiosities. On my return I will write you all that is writable.—God bless you, my dear dear dear Love! & your affectionate & ever faithful

Husband   S. T. Coleridge.

With regard to money, my Love! Poole can write to Mr Wedgewood if it is not convenient for him to let you have it.

279. *To Charles Parry*

MS. McGill University. Hitherto unpublished.

[Early May 1799][1]

My dear Parry

Don't be afraid that I intend to keep it—let not your Conscience alarm you—I will bring it tomorrow with me—/. I pray you, lend me for this Evening the map of the Harz / and tomorrow morning you shall see what you shall see /

S. T. Coleridge

280. *To Mrs. S. T. Coleridge*

Address: Mrs Coleridge | Nether Stowey | Somersetshire | England   Payed to Cuxhaven
MS. New York Public Lib. Pub. with omis. New Monthly Magazine, *October 1835.* Parts of this and the following letter were printed in the *Amulet* in 1829, as 'Over the Brocken'. The manuscript is badly torn, especially at the edges of the pages, and the words in brackets have been supplied from a transcript made by Thomas Ward.
Postmark: Foreign Office, 3 June 1799.

Clausethal, Friday Morning, May 17th, 1799

[My de]arest Love, I wished to give you some idea of the manner in which the Women in this part [of the] country carry their infants; and of the baskets in which they put their Burthens, & the manner of [bearing] the basket, which is kept to the back by a

---

[1] This letter was probably written not long before the Harz tour, which began on 11 May 1799.

A sketch drawn by Charles Parry at the beginning of a letter to Mrs. S. T. Coleridge, dated May 17th, 1799

broad stripe of cloth going under the arm[pits and over] the shoulders.—It is astonishing what burthens the Women here carry! These Baskets are universal both [in Götti]ngen, and all the Harz Country.—The Women wear long *strip'd* cotton cloaks, almost but not quite [so long] as your white Cloak / —The manner in which they fold them when they carry their infants [pre]sents commonly a most picturesque Drapery, & reminds you of the Statues of the ancients.—[This] little Sketch here Mr Parry was so kind as to draw for me / both objects were taken [imme]diately from Nature. / —I write to you from Clausethal, Friday Morning, May 17th, 1799.—[On] Saturday, May 11th, 10 o clock, we left Gottingen, 7 in Part[y]—Charles & Frederic Parry, Greenough,[1] Carlyon,[2] Chester, myself, and one German, the Son of Professor Blumenbach; an intelligent & well informed young man, especially in Natural History——. We ascended a hill, N.E. of Göttingen, & passed thro' areas surrounded by woods, the areas now closing in upon us, now opening & retiring from us, till we came to Hessen Dreisch, which belongs to the Prince of Hesse Cassel / Here I observed a great wooden Post with the french words, Pais Neutre (Neutral Country) on it—a precaution in case the French should march near. This miserable Post forcibly contrasted in my mind with the 'And Ocean 'mid his uproar [w]ild Speaks safety to his *Island* Child!['][3]—I bless God that my Country is an Island.— Here [we] dined on potatoes & pancakes—the pancakes throughout this part of the Country are [exce]llent, but tho' pancakes in shape, in taste they more resemble good *Yorkshire*, [or *batter* pu]dding. These & eggs you may almost always procure, when you can [procure] nothing else. They were brewing at the Inn—I enquired & found that they put [3] Bushels of Malt & five large Handfuls of Hops to the Hogshead.——The Beer [as] you may suppose, but indifferent stuff. Immediately from the Inn we passed into [a nar]row road thro' a very lofty Fir Grove / these tall Firs are branchless almost to the [top—c]onsequently no wood is so gloomy, yet none has so many spots & patches of [Su]nshine / the Soil consisted of great stones & rocks covered wholly & deeply with a bright-green Moss, speckled with the sunshine, & only orna-mented by the tender Umbrella three-*leaves* & virgin white *flower* of the Wood-sorrel—a most delightful acid to a thirsty foot-

---

[1] Charles Bellas Greenough (1778–1855), geographer and geologist. See Edith J. Morley, 'Coleridge in Germany', *Wordsworth and Coleridge*, ed. by E. L. Griggs, 1939, pp. 220–36, for Greenough's supplementary record of the Harz tour.

[2] Clement Carlyon (1777–1864), physician. His *Early Years and Late Reflections* (4 vols., 1836–58) gives a further description of this excursion.

[3] *Ode to the Departing Year*, 129–30.

To Mrs. S. T. Coleridge

traveller. / And now we emerged from the fir-grove, & saw a beautiful Prospect before us, with the little Village '*Wage*' [Waake] before us on the slope of a low Hill. We pass *thro'* this village & journey on for a mile or two thro' Coombes very much [li]ke those about Stowey & Holford, but still more like those at Porlock, on account of [the] great rocky fragments which jut out from the Hills both here & at Porlock & which [alas! w]e have not at dear Stowey!——And now a green Hill, smooth & green [with] young Corn, faces us; & we pass at it's foot, and the Coomb curves away into [a] new & broader Coomb green with Corn, both the bottom & the Hills—in no way interesting, except for the variety.—In the former Coombe there were two or three neat Cottages with a bit of cultivated Ground around them, & Walnut Trees close by the House, exactly like a Cottage or rather Farm-house in one of the Holford Coombes.—We passed thro' Rudolpshausen, a village near which is the Amtman's House & Farm-buildings.—The Government give the Amtmen but moderate salaries; but then they let them great Farms at a very very low Rent—so the Amtmen throughout the Han[over]ian Country are the great agriculturists, and form the only class that correspond[s to our G]entlemen-farmers. From them & in them originate all the innovations in the systems of agricultu[re here—] I have never seen in England farm-buildings so large, compact, & commodious for all the purp[oses of] storing, & stall-feeding as those of these Amtmen generally are.—They have commonly from a thou[sand to] 1500 English acres.——From Rudolph's Hausen (i.e. Houses) we came to Womar's Hausen, a Catho[lic] Village belonging to the Elector of Mayence, & the first Catholic Village I had seen—a crucifix, [i.e. a] wooden Image of Christ on the Christ [Cross], at the end of the Town & two others in the road [at a lit]tle distance from the Town. The greater part of the Children here were naked all but the Shirt, or rather the *relique* of a ci devant Shirt: but they were fat, healthy, & pl[ayful—] The Woman at the end wore a piece of Silver round her neck, having the figure of St Andrew on it—She gravely informed us, that St Andrew had been a Man of the Forest & born near this village, & that he was remarkably good to People with sore eyes.—Here we met some Students from the University of Halle, most adventurous Figures, with leather Jackets, long sabres, & great three cornered Hats, with small iron chains dangling from them—& huge Pipes in the mouth, the Boles of which absolutely mounted above the Forehead.—Poole would have called them Knights of the Times. I asked young Blumen-bach, if it was a Uniform. He said No!—but that it was a Student's *Instinct* to play a character, in some way or other / & that therefore in the universities of Germany whim & caprice were exhausted in planning [&] executing blackguardisms of Dress.—I have seen much of this at Gottingen; but beyond doubt Gottingen is a gentlemanly & rational place compared with the other Universities. Thro' roads no way rememb'rable we came to Gieboldshausen, over a bridge, on whic[h was] a mitred Statue with a great Crucifix in it's arms—/ the village long and ugly, [but the Church,] like most Catholic Churches, interesting—& this being Whitsun Eve, all were crowding to [it with] their Mass-books & Rosaries— the little babies commonly with coral Crosses hanging [on the] Breast.—Here we took a Guide / left the Village, ascended a Hill— & now the Woods rose u[p before] us in a verdure which surprized us like a Sorcery!—The Spring has burst forth with the [suddenness] of a Russian Summer / As we left Gottingen there were buds & here & there a Tree half-green; but here were Woods in full foliage, distinguished from summer only by the exquisite Freshness of their tender Green. We entered the Wood thro' a beautiful mossy Path, the Moon above us blending with the evening Lights; & every now & then a Nightingale would invite the others to sing / & some *one* other commonly answered, & said, as we supposed—It is yet somewhat too early!——For the Song was not continued.— We came to a square piece of Greenery compleatly *walled* on all four sides by the Beeches—again entered the Wood & having travelled about a mile emerged from it into a gran[d] Plain, Mountains in the distance, but ever by our road the Skirts of the Green-woo[d—] A very rapid River ran by our side. And now the Nightingales were all singing [and the] tender verdure grew paler in the moonlight—only the smooth parts of the R[iver] were still deeply purpled with the reflections from the fiery red Lights in the West.—So surrounded & so impressed, we arrived at Poele [Pöhlde], a dear little Cluster of Houses in the middle of a semi-

circle of woody Hills the area of the semicircle scarcely broader than the breadth of the Village—the Trees still for the most part Beech.—We left it, & now the Country ceased to be interesting, and we came to the town of Schlachtfeld [Scharzfeld] belonging to Hanover / Here we had Coffee & Supper, & with many a patriotic Song (for all of my Companions sing very sweetly, & are thorough Englishmen) we closed the Evening & went to Sleep in our Cloaths on the Straw laid for us in the Room / This is the only Bed which is procurable at the village Inns in Germany / . At half past seven, Whitsunday Morning, we left Schlachtfeld, passed thro' a broad Coomb, turned up a smooth Hill on the Right, & entered a Beech Wood / & after a few hundred yards we came to

the Brink of an enormous Cavern—which we descended—It went
under Ground 800 feet, consisted of various apartments, dripping,
stalactitious, & with mock chimnies; but I saw nothing unusual,
except in the first apartment, or, as it were, antichamber. You
descend from the Wood by steps cut into the Rock, pass under a
most majestic natural Arch of Rock, & then you come into the
Light—for this antichamber is open at the Top for a space of
20 yards in length, & 8 in breadth—the open space of an oval
Form / and on the edges the Beeches grow & stretch their arms
over the Cavern, but do not wholly form a ceiling. Their verdure
contrasted most strikingly with the huge Heap of Snow which lay
piled in this antichamber of the Cavern into a white Hill, im-
perfectly covered with withered Leaves.—The sides of this anti-
chamber were wet stones in various angles, all green with dripping
Moss.—Reascended—journeyed thro' the wood with various
ascents & descents; & now descending we came to a *Slope* of
Greenery, almost perfectly round with walls [of woods, and]
exactly 170 Strides in diameter. As we entered this sweet Spot, a
[hoary Ruin peeped over] the opposite Woods in upon us—. We
reentered the Woods, & still desce[nding came to a little] Brook
where the Wood left us / & we ascended a smooth green Hill, on
the Top of which [stood the] Ruined Castle. When we had nearly
reached the Top, I layed down by a black & blaste[d Trun]k, the
remains of a huge hollow Tree, surrounded by wild Gooseberry
Bushes, & looked back [on the] Country, we had passed. Here again
I could see my beautiful *Rotundo* of Greenery—the rest [of the
v]iew was woody Hills swelling over woody Hills in various out-
lines.—The Ruin had nothing [obs]ervable in it / but here let me
remark, that in all the Ruins I have seen in Germany, [and] this
is no small number, I have never discovered the least vestige of
Ivy.—The Guide [inf]ormed us that the Castle had been besieged
in the year 1760 by a French army of [110]00 men under General
Beaubecour, who had pitched camp on the opposite Hills—[and
was] defended for eleven days by 80 Invalids under Prince Ysen-
burg, & at last taken by Treachery, & then dismantled &c ——.
From the top of the Hill a large Plain opened before us, with
villages—a little village Neuhof lay at the foot of the Hill; we
reached it, & then turned up thro' a valley on the left hand. The
Hills on both sides the valley were prettily wooded, & a rapid
lively river ran thro' it— / So we went for about 2 miles, and
almost at the end of the valley, or rather of it's first Turning, we
found the Village of Lauterberg—. Just at the entrance of the
Village two streams come out from two deep & woody Coombes
close by each other, meet & run into a third deep woody *Coomb*

opposite / *before you* a wild Hill which seems the end & the Barrier
of the valley; on *the right hand* low Hills now green with Corn, &
now wooded—; and on the left a [m]ost majestic Hill indeed! the
effect of whose simple outline *Painting* could not give / & how poor
a Thing are *Words*? We pass thro' this neat little Town, the majestic
Hill on the [left hand] soaring over the Houses, & at every inter-
space you see the *whole* of it, it's [Beeches, it's Firs, it's] Rocks,
it's scattered Cottages, & the one neat little Pastor's House at the
Foot [emb]osomed in Fruit-trees, all in Blossom/ the noisy Coomb-
brook dashing close by it.—We [leave] the Valley or rather the
first Turning on the left, following a stream—& so the vale winds
[on, the] river still at the foot of woody Hills, with every now [and]
then other smaller valleys on [right] & left crossing our Vale, &
ever before you the woody Hills running, like *Groo*[*ves* one] into
the other / Sometimes I thought myself in the *Coombes* about
Stowey, sometimes a[bout] Porlock, sometimes between Porlock
& Linton / only the Stream was somewhat larger / —sometimes
the Scenery resembled parts in the River Wye almost to Identity
except that the River was not quite so large.—We turn'd, &
turned & entering the fourth Curve of the Vale we perceived all
at once that we had been ascending—the Verdure vanished! All
the Beech Trees were leafless / & so were the silver Birches, whose
boughs always, winter & summer, hang so elegantly!—But low
down in the Valley, & in little companies on each [ban]k of the
River a multitude of black green Conical Fir Trees—with herds of
[Catt]le wandering about, almost every one with a cylindrical Bell
around it's neck [of no] inconsiderable size— / And as they moved
scattered over the narrow vale & [up] among the Trees on the Hill,
the noise was like that of a large City in the stillness [o]f the
Sabbath Morning, when all the Steeples all at once are ringing for
Church.—The whole was a melancholy & romantic Scene that was
quite new to me——Again we turned, passed three smelting
Houses which we visited—A scene of terrible Beauty is a furnace
of boiling Metal, darting out every moment blue, green, & scarlet
Lightning, like serpents' Tongues! And now we ascended a steep
Hill on the Top of which was St Andreas Burg, a Town built
wholly of Wood—We arrived here, Whitsunday Afternoon, May
12th, ½ past 4. Here we supped & slept / here we supped, & I not
being quite well procured a Bed—the others slept on Straw.——
We left St Andreas Burg, May 13th, 8 o clock, ascended still, the
Hill unwooded except here & there with a few stubby Fir Trees.—
We descended again to ascend far higher; & now we came to a most
beautiful Road that winded on the breast of the Hill, from whence
we looked down into a deep deep Valley or huge Bason full of Pines

& Firs, the opposite Hills full of Pines & Firs, & the Hill above us
on whose breast we were winding, likewise full of Pines & Firs.—
The Valley or Bason on our Right Hand into which we looked
down is called the Vale of Rauschenbach, that is, the Valley of the
Roaring Brook—& *roar* it did, indeed, most solemnly!——The
Road on which we walked was weedy with infant fir-trees, an inch
or two High— / And now on our left hand came before us a most
tremendous Precipice of [y]ellow & black Rock, called the Rehburg,
that is, the Mountain of the Roe.—A Deer-stealer [once] was, as is
customary in these cases throughout all Germany, fastened to a
Roe-buck, his feet [to] the Horns, & his head towards the Tail—&
then the Roe let loose.—The frighted Animal came [a]t length to
the brink of this Precipice, leaped down it, & dashed both himself
& the man to [a]toms.——Now again is nothing but Pines & Firs,
above, below, around us!—How awful is [the] deep Unison of their
undividable Murmur—What a *one* thing it is [—it is a sound] that
[im]presses the dim notion of the Omnipresent! In various Parts of
the deep [vale below us we be]held little dancing Waterfalls
gleaming thro' the branches; & now on our left ha[nd from the
very s]ummit of the Hill above us a powerful Stream flung itself
down, leaping & foaming, & no[w c]oncealed, & now not concealed,
& now half-concealed by the Fir Trees, till towards the Roa[d i]t
became a visible Sheet of Water, within whose immediate Neigh-
bourhood no Pine [cou]ld have permanent abiding-place!—The
Snow lay every where on the sides of [the Ro]ads, & glimmered in
company with the waterfall-foam—snow-patches & water breaks
[gli]mmering thro' the Branches in the Hill above, the deep Bason
below & the Hill opposite. Over the high opposite Hills so dark in
their Pine forests a far higher round barren stony Mountain looked
in upon the Prospect from a distant Country.——Thro' this
scenery we passed on, till our Road was crossed by a second
Waterfall or rather aggregation of lit[tle] dancing Waterfalls, one
by the side of the other, for a considerable breadth—& all cam[e at]
once out of the dark wood above, & rolled over the mossy rock-
fragments, little Firs growing in Islets scattered among them.—
The same scenery continued till we came to the Oder Teich, a lake
half made by man & half by nature— / it is two miles in length, &
but a few hundred yards in breadth, & winds between banks or
rather, thro' *high Walls* of Pine Trees / it has the appearance of
a most cal[m] & majestic River / it crosses the road, goes into a
wood, & there at once plunges [itself] down into a most magnificent
Cascade, & runs into the vale, to which *it* gives [the] Name of 'the
Vale of the Roaring Brook.'—We clomb down into the vale, &
stood at the bottom of the Cascade, & climbed up again by it's

side / —The rocks over which it plunged were unusually wild in their shape, giving fantastic resemblances of men & animals—& the fir-boughs by the side were kept almost in a *swing*, which unruly motion contrasted well with the stern Quietness of the huge Forest-sea every where else. / Here & else where we found large rocks of violet Stone which when rubbed or when the Sun shines strong on them, emit a scent which I could not [have] distinguished from violet. It is yellow–red in colou[r.]

My dear d[ear Love! & m]y Hartley! My blessed Hartley [!—by hill and wood] & Stream, I close my ey[es and] dream of you!——

If possib[le], I will this evening continue my little Tour in a second letter—

Your faithful Husband
S. T. Coleridge

281. *To Mrs. S. T. Coleridge*

Address: Mrs Coleridge | Nether Stowey | Somersetshire | England   Pay'd to Cuxhaven
MS. New York Public Lib. Pub. New Monthly Magazine, *October 1835.* The manuscript is badly torn, especially at the edges of the pages, and the words in brackets have been supplied from a transcript made by Thomas Ward.
Postmark: Foreign Office, 3 June 1799.

May 17th—Friday Night. [1799]

My dearest Love

These Letters, & the Descriptions in them, may possibly recall to *me* real forms, i[f I should] ever take it into my head to read them again; but I fear that to you they must be [insupportably] unmeaning—accumulated repetitions of the same words in almost the same Combinati[ons—but how] can it be otherwise? In Nature all things are individual; but a Word is but an arb[itrary Character] for a whole Class of Things; so that the same description may in almost all cas[es be applied] to twenty different appearances—& in addition to the difficulty of the Thing itse[lf I neither] am or ever was a good Hand at description.—I see what I write / but alas[! I cannot] write what I see. / —My last Letter concluded with the Oder Teich / from thence we enter[ed a second] Wood, & now the Snow met us in large masses, and we walked for two miles kn[ee deep in] it, with an inexpressible Fatigue, till we came to the Mount called Little Brock[en—here even] the Firs deserted us, or only now & then, a patch of them, wind-shorn; no [higher than] one's knee, matted & cowering to the Ground like the Thorn bushes on our highest Sea-hills.—The Soil was plashy & boggy / we

descended & came to the foot of the Great Brocken / without a
rival the highest Mountain in all the north of Germany, & the seat
of innumerable Superstitions. On the first day of May all the
Witches dance here at midnight / & those who go may see their
own Ghosts walking up & down with a little Billet on the Back,
giving the Names of those who had wished them there: for 'I wish
you on the Top of the Brock[en'] is a common Curse throughout
the whole Empire.—Well—we ascended, the soil boggy, & [at] last
reached the Height, which is 573 Toises above the level of the Sea.
We visited the Blocksberg, a sort of Bowling Green inclosed by
huge Stones, something like those at Stonehenge; & this is the
Witches' Ball-room / thence proceeded to the house on the [hill]
where we dined / & now we descended. My Toe was shockingly
swoln, m[y feet] bladdered, and my whole frame seemed going to
pieces with fatigu[e—however] I went on, my key-note Pain,
except when, as not unseldom happe[ned, I struck] my Toe against
a Stone or Stub—& this of course produced a *bravura* [of Torture—]
In the evening about 7 we arrived at Elbinrode [Elbingerode]—I
was really unwell. The [transition] from my late Habit of sitting &
writing for so many hours in the day to such in[tense] bodily
exercise had been too rapid & violent / I went to bed with chatter-
ing Teeth / beca[me] feverish-hot, & remained tossing about &
unable to sleep till two in the morning, [when] a perspiration burst
out on me, I fell asleep, & got up in the morning qui[te well—] At
the Inn they brought us an Album, or Stamm Buch, requesting
that we w[ould write] our names, & something or other as a re-
membrance that we had been there. I wrote the follow[ing] Lines,
which I send to you, not that they possess a grain of merit as
Poetry: but because they contain a true account of my journey
from the Brocken to Elbinrode.[1]

> I stood on Brocken's sovran height & saw
> Woods crowding upon woods, hills over hills,
> A *surging* Scene and only limited
> By the blue Distance. Wearily my way
> Downward I dragg'd thro' Fir-groves evermore,
> Where bright-green Moss heav'd in sepulchral forms,
> Speckled with sunshine; and, but seldom heard,
> The sweet Bird's Song became an hollow Sound;
> And the Gale murmuring indivisibly
> Preserv'd it's solemn murmur most distinct
> From many a Note of many a Waterbreak,
> And the Brook's *Chatter*; on whose islet stones

[1] *Poems*, i. 315.

The dingy Kidling with it's tinkling Bell
Leapt frolicsome, or old romantic Goat
Sat, his white Beard slow-waving! I mov'd on
With low & languid thought: for I had found
That grandest Scenes have but imperfect Charms,
Where the sight[1] vainly wanders nor beholds
One spot, with which the Heart associates
Holy Remembrances of Child or Friend,
Or gentle Maid, our first & early Love,
Or Father, or the venerable Name
Of our adored Country. O thou Queen,
Thou delegated Deity of Earth,
O 'dear dear' England, how my longing Eye
Turn'd Westward, shaping in the steady Clouds
Thy sands & high white Cliffs! Sweet Native Isle,
This Heart was proud, yea, mine Eyes swam with Tears
To think of Thee; & all the goodly view
From sov'ran Brocken, woods and woody Hills,
Floated away, like a departing Dream,
Feeble and dim.—Stranger! these Impulses
Blame thou not lightly; nor will *I* profane
With hasty Judgment or injurious Doubt
That man's sublimer Spirit, who can feel
That God is every where! the God who fram['d]
Mankind to be one mighty Brotherhood,
Himself our Father & the World our Ho[me!]

We left Elbinrode, May the 14th (N.[B. Rode] signifies a Place
from whence Roots [have] been grubbed up in order for building
or Plantation.—) We travelled for half a mile thro' a wild Country
of bleak stony Hills by our side with several Caverns, or rather
mouths of Caverns, visible in their Breasts, & now we came to
Rubell[and—] O it was a lovely Scene. Our road was at the foot
of low Hills & here were a few neat Cottages—behind us were high
hil[ls] with a few scattered Firs, & flocks [of] Goats visible on the
topmo[st crags—] On our right Hand—[a] fine shallow river of
about thirty yards broad / & beyond the Ri[ver a crescent] Hill[2]
clothed with firs that rise one above the other, like Spectators in an
[Amphitheatre—] We advanced a little farther; the Crags behind
us ceased to be visible; and now [the whole was on]e & complete;
all that could be seen was the cottages at the foot of the low green

---

[1] eye. [Cancelled word in line above.]
[2] A small, indistinct drawing appearing here in the manuscript has not
been reproduced.

Hill (cottages embosomed [in fruit trees] in blossom), the Stream,
& the little crescent of Firs.——I lingered here, & [unwillingly
lost sig]ht of it for a little while—the Firs were so beautiful, & the
masses [of Rocks, walls], & obelisks of Rocks, started up among
them, in the very places where if they [had not been, a] painter
with the Poet's Feeling, would have imagined them!—We crossed
the [River (it's] name Bode) entered the sweet wood, & came to the
mouth of the Cavern with the man [who shews i]t—it was a huge
place, 800 feet in length & more in depth; of many [different
apar]tments / the only thing that distinguished it from other
caverns was that the Guide [who was really a] character, had the
Talent of finding out & seeing uncommon Likenesses [in the
different] forms of the Stalactite: Here was a nun—this was
Solomon's Temple—[th]at was a Roman Catholic chapel—here
was a Lion's claw—nothing but flesh & blood wanting to make it
completely a claw / !—This was an organ & had all the notes of the
organ / &c & &c—but alas! with all possible straining my eyes,
ears, & my imagination I could see nothing but common Stalac-
tite;—& hear nothing but the dull *ding* of common Cavern Stones.
One thing was really striking—a huge Cone of Stalactite hung
from the roof [of] the largest apartment, & on being struck gave
perfectly the sound of a Death bell. [I was] behind, & heard it
repeatedly at some distance / & the effect was very much [in the]
Fairy Kind. /——Gnomes & Things unseen, That toll mock death
bells for mock funerals!—[After] this a little clear well, & a black
stream pleased me the most; & multiplied by [fifty and] coloured
ad libitum, might be well enough to *read of* in a novel or poem.——
We [returned & now] before the Inn on the green Plat around the
May pole the villagers were [celebrating Whit] Tuesday.—This
May Pole is hung as usual with garlands on the [top; and in these]
garlands Spoons & other little valuables are placed—the high
smooth [round pole is th]en well greased—& now he [who] can
climb up to the Top may have what [he can get] /—a very laugh-
able scene, as you may suppose of awkwardness, & agility / [and
fail]ures on the very brink of success.—Now began a Dance / the
Women [danced] very well / & in general I have observed through-
out Germany that the Women [in the] lower ranks degenerate far
less from the Ideal of a Woman than [the Men] from that of man. /
The Dances were Reels & the Walzen; but chiefly [the] latter.
This dance is in the *highest* circles sufficiently voluptuous; but here,
the motions etc were far *more* faithful Interpreters of the Passion
or rather appetite, which doubtless the Dance was intended to
shadow out.—Yet even after that giddy Round & Round is
over, the walking to music, the woman laying [her] arm with

confident affection on the man's shoulders, or (among the Rustics)
round [his] Neck, has something inexpressibly charming in it.—
The first Couple at the [Wa]lzen (pronounced Waltsen / z is pro-
nounced always ts) was a very fine tall Girl [of] 2 or 3 & 20, in the
full bloom & growth of limb & feature, & a fellow with [h]uge
Whiskers, a long Tail, & a woolen night-cap on:—he was a soldier,
[and] from the more than usual glances of the Girl, I presumed,
was her Lover.—He [w]as beyond compare the Gallant & the
Dancer of the Party—Next came two Bauern, one of whom in the
whole contour of his face & person, & above [all in] the laughably
would-be-frolicsome fling-out of his Heel irresistably reminded
[me of] Shakespear's Slender, & the other of his Dogberry—O two
such faces, [and two] such postures! O that I were an Hogarth!—
What an enviable Talent it is to have [a G]enius in Painting!—
Their Partners were pretty Lasses not so tall as the former, &
[d]anced uncommonly light & airy. The fourth Couple was a sweet
Girl of about 17, delicately slender & very prettily dressed, with
a full blown Rose in the white Ribbon that went round her Head
& confined her reddish-brown Hair—& her Partner *waltsed*—with
a pipe in his mouth! smoking all the while! / & during the whole of
[th]is voluptuous Dance the whole of his Face was a fair Personi-
fication of [*true*] *German Phlegm.*—After these, but I suppose, not
actually belonging to [the Par]ty, a little ragged Girl & a ragged
boy with his stockings about his [heels *w*]*altsed* & danced / waltsing
& dancing in the rear / most entertainingly. [B]ut what most
pleased me was a little Girl of about 3 or 4 years old, certainly not
[mor]e than 4, [who] had been put to watch a little Babe of exactly
a year old (for one of our party had asked) & who was just begin-
ning to run away.—The Girl teaching h[im to walk] was so ani-
mated by the Music that she began to waltse with him, & the [two
babes] whirled round & round hugging & kissing each other, as if
the Music had ma[de them mad—] I am no judge of music—it
pleased me! & Mr Parry who plays himself, as[sured me it was]
uncommonly good. There were two Fiddles & a Bass Viol / the
Fiddlers, but abov[e all, the] Bass Violist, most Hogarthian
Phizzes!—God love them!—I felt far more a[ffection for] them
than towards any other set of human beings whom I have met with
in Germ[any, I suppose,] because they looked so happy!——We
left them—as we go out of the Village the c[rescent shaped] Hill
of Firs sinks, & forms an irregular Wood / but the opposite Hill
rises, & bec[omes in it's] Turn a perfect Crescent, but of a far other
character—higher & more abrupt [and ornamented] not clothed
with Firs, the larger part of the Hill being masses & variously
[jutting Precipices] of Rocks, grey, sulphur-yellow, or mossy.—

Shortly after we meet with huge marble Rocks—& about a mile
from Rubelland we arrived at a manufactury where the marble is
polished. The veins of the Blankenburg marble have an exquisite
Beauty / a foot square is valued at half a crown. Young Blumen-
bach informed us that marble was a marine substance—that the
veins, at least the Brown & the Red Veins were true *Corals*, & the
white was the accidental Cement.—Here a huge Angle of Rock
comes out & divides the road / O[ur] path went on the left one way,
& the River the other. We left the River [Bode] unwillingly—for
it went immediately into a deep deep Pine wood, where [we] saw
high Pillars of Rock that, I don't [know] why, seemed to *live*
among the black Fi[r trees], & I wished to be it's companion. But
one always quits a dashing River unwil[lingly—] Our path led us
over a green Plain that heaved up & down [in hillocks] & Embreast-
ments of Earth / till we came to a Village, Hütten rode—[We left
it and] still the Country continued not particularly interesting, till
we arriv[ed at the foot] of a Hill, up which our Road winded with
many a scattered Fir by [the side of] the Road. We reached the
Top—& behold! now again the Spring meets us! [I look back] & see
the snow on the Brocken, & all between the black *mineral* G[reen
of] Pine-Groves, wintry, endlessly wintry / & the Beech & the
Birch, & the [wild Ash] all leafless—but lo! before us—a sweet
Spring! not indeed in the ful[l] youthful verdure as on our first
day's Journey, but timidly soft, half-[wintry—] and with here &
there spots & patches of Iron brown.—Interesting in the hig[hest]
degree is it to have seen in the course of two or three days so many
diffe[rent] climates with all their different Phaenomena!—The
vast plain was before us, Rocks on the Right Hand, a huge Wall of
Rocks—! on the left & curving round into the front view, Hills of
Beeches, soft surges of woody Hills. At the feet of the Hill lay the
Castle & Town of Blankenburg, with all it's orchards of blossoming
Fruit Trees. Blankenberg is a considerable Town, containing 500
Houses & 3000 Inhabitants; & belongs to the Duke of Bruns-
wick.—Immediately opposite to our Inn is the House in which the
unfortunate Louis the 18th [lived] during 21 months—he left
Blankenberg last February, in consequence of a Lordship have
[having] been given him by the Emperor of Russia, in Livonia.—
Some enquiries which we had m[ade] concerning him at Rubeland
had occasioned a suspicion of our being Spies, [&] one fellow whom
we asked answered us—'I'll die for my King & Country / & wh[at]
sort of French Fellows are you?' Hence we were shy of the Sub-
ject; but our Landlord, a most communicative Fellow, soon re-
lieved us—& for at least two hours talked incessantly of the King,
with whose most minute daily occupations he had made himself as

well acquainted or better, than I am with Poole's.—These are a chapter of Contents for his Conversation—1. His majesty was very religious—had prayers in his house every day, & an open Service there on Tuesdays, Thursdays, & Saturdays. 2. He kept a regular mistress, a large fine tall Woman of a fair Complexion, a French Woman, whose Husband at the sa[me] time lived in the House, observing the most distant Civilities & Respect tow[ard] his Wife. 3. A Washerwoman's Daughter however of Blankenberg, by the name of Hase, had struck his Majesty's Eye—a young Girl of no unimpregnable [chastity—and on]ce or twice a Week his Majesty was graciously accustomed to send one of his [Nobles for her]— on the first interview he presented her with 12 Laub Dollars (about [50 Shillings) wh]ich she had shewn with much glee to our Land- lord.—Afterwards his [presents declined]/. 4. He had 83 persons in his Household, 8 of whom were Dukes—[& his daily ex]pences were an hundred Dollars (about 20£)—& he received his money [always from H]amburg, & our Landlord had been informed by his Relation the Post Master, [that he rec]eived regularly 40,000 Dollars (6000£) at a time. 5. He never on any [occasion r]ode out of his own Gardens, & had so much personal Fear of Regicides [that he had] a subterraneous secret Passage under his House. 6. The number of his [Coaches was 15—a]ll very handsome, & all ball-proof, & the Blinds likewise Ball-proof. [7. He] had 70 Horses; & at one time 7 Princesses in the same House with him. The quantity of meat used & wasted in the Household was prodi- gious—there were [eve]ry week two Oxen regularly consumed. 8. Twice a week his Majesty bathed in [G]ravy-soup, for which purpose 80 pounds of Beef were constantly used—which [so]up with the meat was after given to the Poor. 9. He ordered his Sur- geons & [Phy]sicians to attend the poor gratis. 10. And wept when he quitted the [pla]ce——/—/ We went & visited the Castle which was shewn us by a young Woman. [Suc]h an immense number of ugly Rooms with such an immense number [of pic]tures, not *one* of which possessed the least merit, or rather not *one* of which [whi]ch was not a despicable Daub!—And almost all obscene!— So false is it [th]at our ancestors were more innocent than we—/ The Passions are much the same in all ages—but Obscenity & Indelicacy are the fit & peculiar Company of Ignorance & Bar- barous Manners.—One thing amused me—the young Woman opened a Room, pointed to us to go in, & then herself turned up another pair of Stairs—/ On entering we perceived a parcel of execrable Daubs on execrable Subjects / but the half-modesty of the Girl was interesting. There was no Reason on earth for her shewing us the Room—& many which she herself [stood] looking at with great calmness were not a whit better. / We returned, [and spent] the Evening with a round of old English Songs, of which God Save [the] King & Rule Britannia were, as you may suppose repeated no small number [of] Times—for being abroad makes every man a Patriot & a Loyalist—almost a [Pitti]te!

God bless you, my Love & S. T. Coleridge
& good night!

282. *To Thomas Poole*

Address: Mr T. Poole | Nether Stowey | Somersetshire | England   Pay'd to
Cuxhaven
MS. British Museum. Pub. E.L.G. i. 107.
Postmark: Foreign Office, 3 June 1799.

Sunday Morning, 1/2 past 8/ May 19th, 1799
My dearest Poole
I arrived at Göttingen last night, 9 o'clock, after a walk of thirty miles—somewhat disappointed at finding no letters for *me*, but *surprized* that Chester had none. Surely, his family do not behave over-attentively towards him!—We have been absent 8 months and 10 days; & he has received *one* Letter from them!—Well—now to conclude my all too uninteresting Journal.—In my second letter to Sara I was still at Blankenburg—We left it on Wednesday Morning, May 15th taking first one survey more of the noble view which it commanded.—I stood on the Castle Hill, on my Right a Hill half-wood, half rock, of a most grand outline (the rude sketch of it's outline is given in that little Drawing at the top of my first letter to Sara)[1] then a plain of young Corn—then Rocks——walls and towers / And pinnacles of Rock, a proud domain / Disdainful of the Seasons! these formed the right hand. On the left and curving round till they formed the front view, Hills here green with leafy Trees, here still iron-brown, dappled as it were with coming Spring & lingering Winter; not (like the single Hill) of abrupt & grand outlines, but rising & sinking yet on the whole still rising, in a *frolic Surginess*.—In the Plain (or Area of the view) young Corn, herds of Cattle, troops of Goats, & shepherds at the head of *Streams* of Sheep.——We left the town, proceeded thro' the Plain, & having walked about half a mile, turned to contemplate the backward view, to which was now added the Towers & castle of Bermburg, that looked in upon us from the distance, on our right hand as we *then* stood.—We proceeded; and a mile from Blankenburg we came to a small Lake quite surrounded with Beech-trees, the margins of the Lake solid marble

[1] See Letter 281, where this drawing is indicated but not reproduced.

Rock—two or three Stone-thrushes were flitting about those rocky margins. Our road itself was, for a few strides, occupied by a pretty little one arched Bridge, under which the Lake emptied itself, and at the distance of ten yards from the bridge, on our right hand, plunged itself down, (it's stream only once broken by a jutting rock nearly in the midst of the fall) into a chasm of 30 feet in depth and somewhat more in length (a chasm of black or mossy Rocks) & then ran under ground.—We now entered the Woods, the morning thick & misty—we saw a number of wild deer, & at least fifty Salamanders.— / The salamander is a beautiful Lizard, perfectly harmless (I examined several in my naked hand.) Its length from six to seven Inches, with a *Nightingale's* Eye, and just 22 yellow streaks on it's glossy-black Skin. That it can live in the Fire, is a fable; but it is true, that if put on burning Coals, for the first, or even the *second* time, it emits a liquid so copiously as to extinguish the Coals.—So we went, up hill & down dale, but all thro' woods, for four miles, when we came to a sort of Heath stubby with low trunks of old fir-trees—& here were Women in various groups sowing the Fir-seed: a few ceasing from their work to look at us / Never did I behold aught so impressively picturesque, or rather *statue*-esque, as these Groups of Women in all their various attitudes—The thick mist, thro' which their figures came to my eye, gave such a soft *Unreality* to them! These lines, my dear Poole, I have written rather for my own pleasure than your's—for it is impossible that this misery of words can give to you, that which it may yet perhaps be able to recall to me.—What can be the cause that I am so miserable a Describer? Is it that I understand neither the practice nor the principles of Painting?—or is it not true, that others have really succeeded?—I could half suspect that what are deemed fine descriptions, produce their effects almost purely by a charm of words, with which & with whose combinations, we associate *feelings* indeed, but no distinct *Images*.—/ From these Women we discovered that we had gone out of our way precisely 4 miles / so we laughed, & trudged back again, & contrived to arrive at Werninger rode about 12 o'clock.—This belongs to the Princely Count Stolberg, a Cousin of the two Brothers, the Princely Counts Stolberg of Stolberg,[1] who both of them are Poets & Christians—good Poets, real Christians, & most kind-hearted Princes— / what a combination of rarities for Germany!——The Prince—Count Stolberg at Werninger rode gave on this day a feast to his People—& almost all the family of the Stolbergs were assembled—the nobles & people were shooting for a prize at a

[1] Counts Christian and Friedrich Leopold Stolberg. Coleridge translated the latter's *Hymne an die Erde. Poems*, i. 327.

Stuffed Bird placed on the Top of a high May-pole. A nobleman
of the Family, who had been lately at Göttingen, recognized Parry,
& was about to have introduced us; but neither our dress or time
permitting it, we declined the honour.—In this little town there
is a School with about 12 or 13 poor Scholars in it, who are main-
tained by the Tenants & citizens—they breakfast with one, dine
with another, & sup with a third / managing their visits so as to
divide the Burthen of their maintenance according to the capa-
bilities of the People, to whose tables they solicit admission.—
Thro' a country not sufficiently peculiarized to be worth describing
we came to Drubeck, a pretty village—far off on the right hand a
semicircular Vale of an immense extent: / close by on the left, it's
figure the Concave of a Crescent, a high woody Hill, the *heights*
cloathed with firs with an intermixture of Beeches yellow-green in
their opening Foliage; but below these & flowing adown the Hill
into the valley, a noble Stream of Beeches, of freshest verdure.
We enter[ed] the wood, passed woods & woods, every now & then
coming to little spots of Greenery of various sizes & shapes, but
always walled by Trees; & always as we entered, the first object
which met us was a Mount of wild outline, black with firs soaring
huge above the woods. / One of these Greeneries was in shape a
Parallelogram, walled on three sides by the silver-barked weeping
Birches, on the fourth by Conical Firs—a rock on the Fir-side rose
above the Trees just within the wood, & before us the huge Fir-
mount / it was a most impressive Scene!—Perhaps, not the less so
from the mistiness of the wet Air.——We travelled on & on, O what
a weary way! now up, now down, now with path, now without it /
having no other guides than a map, a compass, & the foot-paces
of the Pigs, which had been the day before driven from Hartzburg
to Dribbock [Drübeck] / where there had been a Pig-Fair.—This
intelligence was of more service to us than Map or Compass.—At
length we came to the foot of the huge Fir-mount roaring with
woods, & winds, & waters!—And now the Sky cleared up, and
masses of crimson Light, fell around us from the fiery west, & from
the Clouds over our heads that *reflected* the western fires.—We
wound along by the feet of the Mount, & left it behind us, close
before us a high hill, a high hill close on our right, & close on our
left a hill—we were in a circular Prison of Hills / and many a mass
of Light, moving & stationary, gave life & wildness to the Rocks
& Woods that rose out of them.—But now we emerged into a new
scene!—close by our left hand was a little Hamlet, each House
with it's orchard of Blossom-Trees, in a very small & very narrow
coomb / : the Houses were built on the lowest part of the Slope of
the steeply-shelving Hills, that formed the Coomb; but on our

right hand was a huge Valley with rocks in the distance & a steady Mass of Clouds that afforded no mean substitute for a Sea. / On each side, as ever, high woody Hills—but majestic River, or huge Lake—O that was wanting, here & every where !—And now we arrived at Hartsburg / —Hills ever by our sides, in all conceivable variety of forms & garniture—It were idle in me to attempt by words to give their projections & their retirings & how they were now in Cones, now in roundnesses, now in tonguelike Lengths, now pyramidal, now a huge Bow, and all at every step varying the forms of their outlines; / or how they now stood abreast, now ran aslant, now rose up behind each other / or now, as at Harzburg, presented almost a Sea of huge motionless waves / too multiform for Painting, too multiform even for the Imagination to remember them / yea, my very sight seemed *incapacitated* by the novelty & Complexity of the Scene. / Ye red lights from the Rain Clouds! Ye gave the whole the last magic Touch! / I had now walked five & thirty miles over roughest Roads & had been sinking with fatigue / but so strong was the stimulus of this scene, that my frame seemed to have drank in a new vitality; for I now walked on to Goslar almost as if I had risen from healthy sleep on a fine spring morning: so light & lively were my faculties.——On our road to Goslar we passed by several Smelting Houses & Wire Manufacturies, & one particularly noticeable where they separate the Sulphur from the Ores. The night was now upon us / & the white & blue flares from this Building formed a grand & beautiful Object—& so white was the flame, that in the manufactury itself All appeared quite like a natural Day light. (It is strange, that we do not adopt some means to render our artificial Lights more white.)—As the Clock struck ten we entered the silent City of Goslar / and thro' some few narrow Passages, called Streets by Courtesy, we arrived at our Inn— / my Companions scarcely able to speak—too tired even to be glad that the Journey was over / a journey of 40 miles, including the way which we lost. / On Thursday, May the 16th, we saw the Vitriol Manufactory, & the Dome Church at Goslar. The latter is a real Curiosity—it is one of the oldest, if not the oldest, in Germany. The first thing that strikes you on entering it is a picture of St Christopher wading thro' the River with Jesus Christ (a boy with a globe in his hand) on his Shoulders—this is universal in all the Churches that I have seen ; but noticeable here for the *enormous* size of the Picture ! & for the conceit of putting in the hand of the Giant Saint a fir Tree 'with which the Mast of some tall ammiral Hewn on Norwegian Hills, were but a wand '[1]—! & giving this huge fir Tree a crack in the middle, the face of the holy Giant with a

---

[1] *Paradise Lost*, i. 293–4.

horrid Grin of Toil & Effort corresponding with the said Crack in
proof of the huge weight of the disguised Deity.—The next was an
Altar of the God Croto[Krodo]—the only assured antiquity of German
Heathenism. On this altar human sacrifices were offered—it is of
metal, brass I believed, with diamond holes all around it, & sup-
ported by four grotesque animals.—Then two stone-baboons with
monk's Cowls on them, grinning at each other—said to have been
likewise the work of the said savage Pagans, when the Monks first
preached Christianity in Germany / —Then an altar-piece by the
celebrated Lucas Cranach / in which the faces of the Apostles are
marvellously ugly, but lively & natural.—It is an admirable
Painting.—Then tombs & thrones of Emperors & Queens &
Princesses (for Goslar was formerly the Seat of the Saxon Emperors
of Germany), the hole where the Devil entered, & how he set two
Bishops by the Ears & how they fought in this church & how one
killed the other—a huge Crown of Bell-metal 7 strides in Diameter
given by the victor Bishop for Penance— / Alto Relievo of the
Monk who had poisoned an Emperor in the Lord's Supper / & the
under petticoat of leather which the Devil took from the Woman
who rose from her bed at midnight, supposing it to be matin time,
entered the church, began praying &c, wondered rather to see the
Church so full / when all at once she heard the Clock strike 12,
cried aloud, 'God & Christ'—Rausch rausch rausch! [raus?]—All
nothing but Ghosts—off flew the woman, but as she ran over the
threshold, she tripped, fell down, & ere she could get up again, the
Devil had pulled off her petticoat.—I was much interested by this
ruinous old Church—half Lutheran, half Catholic—the occasion
of which I will explain when I come home. / —We left this ugly
silent old desert of a City, & strolled on thro' hill & dale of Pines,
up which the little mists crept like smoke from Cottage chimneys—
till we came to Clausthal, a large Town with a number of mines
around it, one of which all but myself descended / I had before read
a most minute Description of the said Mine; & from the same con-
cluded that I should see nothing new after what I had seen at
Stowey / & fr[om Che]ster's account my conclusion was perfectly
right. / So I stayed at home & wr[ote tw]o letters to Sara.—I saw
the whole process of Mint[ing] here (for all the [Han]overian
Money is here minted) & other little uncu[rious] Curiosities, which
I have ever found hideously stupid.—We were such a hospital of
bruised Toes, swelled ancles, bladdered soles, & excoriated Heels,
that we stayed in this town till Saturday Morning, May 18th.—We
passed up & down over little Hills thro' a pine-covered Country,
still looking down into deep & wild Coombes of Pine & Fir Trees
(I scarcely know the difference between Pine & Fir) till we came to

Lehrbech, a little village of wood with wooden tiles on the house tops, lying in the bottom of a narrow Coomb, three or four of the Houses scattered upon the Slopes of the Hills, that formed the Coomb.—The Coomb is rich with the green green Beeches; the Slope of the Hills have Beeches & Firs intermixed; but the heights are wholly the property of the Firs. From here we proceeded to Osterode, a hilly pleasant country, the soil heav'd up & down in hillocks with many a little dell & hollow, & the pine trees picturesquely scattered. Osterode is a large & very ugly town, the people looking dirtier & poorer than is common in Germany— Over the Town Hall is the Rib of a Giant / —these are common in the inland towns of Germany. They are generally Whales' Ribs— in the dark ages it was of course extremely unusual for any man to leave his plough, as the song says, to go ploughing the wild seas / when any did, they were of course ambitious to bring something curious home, as a present to their Countrymen / & this is no doubt the origin of these Whale ribs.—From Osterode we proceeded to Catlenburg / Mem. the view of the Amtshouse on a woody Hill, part of the wood cleared / & the space occupied by a fine Garden. From henceforwards the views became quite English, except that in England we have water ever in our views, either sea or lake or river—& we have elmy hedges—& single Cottages—& gentlemen's seats—& many a house, the dwelling of Knowlege & virtue, between the Cottage & the Gentleman's Seat— / Our fields & meadows too are so green, that it is comm[on h]ere for novellists & describers to say when they praise a prospect 'It had a British Greenness'—all this & more is wanting in Germany / but their woods are far finer, & their hills more diversified, & their little villages far more interesting, every House being separate with it's little garden & orchard. This answers to my notion of human nature; which distinguishes itself equally from the Tyger & the Sheep—& is neither solitary or gregarious, but *neighbourly.*—Add to this too, that the extreme misery and the earth & heaven-alarming wickedness & profanity of our English Villagers is a thing wholly unknown in Germany / The women too, who are working in the fields, always behave respectfully, modestly, & with courtesy.——Well—I must hasten on to Göttingen / we proceeded —but I ought to say that in the Church Yard at Catlenberg I was pleased with the following Epitaph. 'Johann Reimbold of Catlenburg.

Ach! sie haben	Ah! they have
Einen braven	Put a brave
Man begraben:	Man in Grave!
Vielen war er mehr.[']	He was more than Many!

This is word for word.

About a mile & a half from Catlenberg we came to a lovely scene, hillocks, & scattered Oaks, & Beeches, a sweet tho' very small Lake, a green meadow, & one white Cottage, & this spot exactly so filled was completely encircled by the grandest swell of woods, that I ever beheld—the hills were clothed as with grass / so rich was the verdure. So complete was the circle that I stood & looked around me, in what part the wood opened to admit our road—We entered the wood, and walked for two miles under a complete Bower, & as we emerged from it—O I shall never forget that glorious Prospect. Behind me the Hartz Mountains with the snow-spots shining on them / close around us Woods upon little Hills, little Hills of an hundred Shapes, a *dance* of Hills, whose variety of position supplied the *effect* of, & almost imitated, *motion*—two higher than the rest of a conical form were bare & stony; the rest were all hid with *Leafage* / I cannot say, trees— / for the Foliage concealed the Boughs that sustained [it.] And all these Hills in all their forms & *bearings*, which it were such a chaos to describe, were yet in all so pure a Harmony!—before us green corn-field[s] that fill'd the Plain & crept up the opposite Hills in the far-off distance, and closing our view in the angle at the left that high woody Hill on which stands the Monarch Ruin of the Plesse—& close by me in a deep dell was a sweet neighbourhood of houses with their Orchards in blossom.—O wherefore was there no water!—We were now only 7 miles from Gottingen / —I shall write one letter more from Germany / & in that letter I will conclude my Tour, with some minuteness, as it will give you at the same time the account of the Country near Gottingen.—/—I hope to leave this place in about a fortnight; but Sara must not be uneasy, if I should be home a week later than she expects—it may be a week earlier—/ but as I pass thro' Brunswick, Wolfenbüttel &c I may perhaps have opportunities of acquiring Information concerning Lessing which it were criminal in me to neglect—but I pine, languish, & waste away to be at home / for tho' in England only I have those that hate me, yet there only I have those whom I love!—

God bless my Friend!—

S. T. Coleridge

283. *To Josiah Wedgwood*

Address: Josiah Wedgewood Esq. | York Street | St James's Square | by favor of | Mr Hamilton
MS. Wedgwood Museum. Pub. Tom Wedgwood, *68.*

May 21st, 1799—Gottingen

My dear Sir

I have lying by my side six huge *Letters*,[1] with your name on each of them / & all excepting one have been written for these three months. About this time Mr Hamilton, by whom I send this & the little parcel for my wife, was as it were, setting off for England; & I seized the opportunity of sending them by him, as without any mock-modesty I really thought that the expence of the Postage to me & to you would be more than their Worth.—Day after day, & Week after week, was Hamilton going / & still delayed—and now that it is absolutely settled that he goes tomorrow, it is like-wise absolutely settled that I shall go this day three weeks / & I have therefore sent only this & the Picture by him / but the letters I will now take myself—/ for I should not like them to be lost, as they comprize the only subject, on which I have had any oppor-tunity of making myself thoroughly informed / & if I carry them myself, I can carry them without danger of their being seized at Yarmouth, as all *my* letters were, your's to the Von Axens, &c excepted which were luckily not sealed.——Before I left England, I had read the Book of which you speak[2]—I must confess, that it appeared to me exceedingly illogical. Godwin's & Condorcet's Extravagancies were not worth confuting; and yet I thought, that the Essay on Population had not confuted them.—Before Wallace,[3] Derham[4] & a number of German Statistic & Physiko-theological Writers had taken the same ground / namely, that Population increases in a geometrical but the accessional nutriment only in an arithmetical ratio—& that Vice & Misery, the natural conse-quences of this order of things, were intended by Providence as the Counterpoise. I have here no means of procuring so obscure a book, as Rudgard's; but to the best of my recollection, at the time that the Fifth Monarchy Enthusiasts created so great a sensation in England, under the Protectorates & the beginning of Charles the second's reign, Rudgard or Rutgard[5] (I am not positive even of

---

[1] See Letter 271.

[2] Wedgwood had asked Coleridge's opinion of Malthus's *Essay on Population.*

[3] Robert Wallace (1697–1771) published in 1761 *Various Prospects of Man-kind, Nature, and Providence,* a work which is said to have influenced Malthus.

[4] Coleridge probably refers to William Derham (1657–1735), who was a fre-quent contributor to the *Transactions* of the Royal Society.

[5] Cf. Thomas Tanner, *Primordia. . . . To which are added Two Letters of*

the name) wrote an Essay to the same purpose / in which he asserted, that if War, Pestilence, Vice, & Poverty were wholly removed, the World could not exist two hundred years &c. Süssmilch[1] in his great work concerning the divine Order & Regularity in the Destiny of the human Race has a chapter entitled a confutation of this idea / I read it with great Eagerness, & found therein, that this idea militated against the Glory & Goodness of God, & must therefore be false—but further confutation found I none!——This book of Süssmilch's has a prodigious character throughout Germany; & never methinks did a Work less deserve it.—It is in 3 huge Octavos, & wholly on the general Laws that regulate the Population of the human Species—but is throughout most unphilosophical, & the Tables, which he has collected with great Industry, proved nothing.—My objections to the Essay on Population you will find in my sixth Letter, at large—but do not, my dear Sir! suppose that because unconvinced by this Essay I am therefore convinced of the contrary.—No! God knows—I am sufficiently sceptical & in truth more than sceptical, concerning the possibility of universal Plenty & Wisdom / but my Doubts rest on other grounds.—I had some conversation with you before I left England on this subject; & from that time I had proposed to myself to examine as thoroughly as it was possible for me the important Question—Is the march of the Human Race progressive, or in Cycles?—But more of this when we meet.——/

What have I done in Germany?—I have learnt the language, both high & low German / I can read both, & speak the former so fluently, that it must be a *torture* for a German to be in my company—that is, I have words enough & phrases enough, & I arrange them tolerably; but my pronunciation is hideous.—2ndly, I can read the oldest German, the Frankish and the Swabian. 3dly—I have attended the lectures on Physiology, Anatomy, & Natural History with regularity, & have endeavoured to understand these subjects.—4th—I have read & made collections for an history of the Belles Lettres in Germany before the time of Lessing—& 5thly—very large collections for a Life of Lessing;—to which I was led by the miserably bald & unsatisf[act]ory Biographies that have been hitherto given, & by my personal acquaintance with two of Lessing's Friends.——Soon after I came into Germany, I made up my mind fully not to publish any thing concerning my *Travels*, as people call them / yet I soon perceived that with all possible

---

Mr. Rvdyerd's . . . One about the Multiplying of Mankind until the Floud. The Other concerning the Multiplying of the Children of Israel in Egypt, 1683.

[1] J. P. Süssmilch, *Die göttliche Ordnung in den Veränderungen des menschlichen Geschlechts*, 1761.

Economy my expences would be greater than I could justify,
unless I did something that would to a moral certainty repay
them.—I chose the Life of Lessing for the reasons above assigned,
& because it would give me an opportunity of conveying under a
better name, than my own ever will be, opinions, which I deem of
the highes[t] importance.—Accordingly my main Business at
Göttingen has been to read all the numerous Controversies in
which L. was engaged / & the works of all those German Poets
before the time of Lessing, which I *could not,* or could not *afford*
to buy—. For these last 4 months, with the exception of last week
in which I visited the Harz I have worked harder than, I trust in
God Almighty, I shall ever have occasion to work again—this
endless Transcription is such a body-and-soul-wearying Pur-
gatory!——I shall have bought 30 pounds worth of books (chiefly
metaphysics / & with a view to the one work, to which I hope to
dedicate in silence the prime of my life)—but I believe & indeed
doubt not, that before Christmas I shall have repayed myself; but
before that time I shall have been under the necessity of requesting
your permission, that I may during the year *anticipate* for 40 or
fifty pound.—I have hitherto drawn on you for 35 & 30 & 30 &
30 = 125£—of this sum I left about 32 or 33 pound in your hands,
of Mr Chester's, when I left England—& Chester has since desired
his Brother to transmit 25£, & again in his last letter 30£ / Words-
worth has promised me that he will pay into your hands 4£ for
me. 33 & 25 & 30 & 4 = 92£.—Hitherto therefore *I* have drawn
as it were about 33 or 34 pound / but this week, to pay both our
Gottingen Bills, and our Journey to England I must draw for 70£.
So that altogether I shall have in this year drawn for 103 Pound.——
.—I never to the best of my recollection felt the fear of Death but
once—that was, yesterday when I delivered the Picture to Hamil-
ton.—I felt & shivered as I felt it, that I should not like to die by
land or water before I see my wife & the little one that I hope yet
remains to me!—But it was an idle sort of feeling—& I should not
like to have it again.—/ Poole half mentioned in a hasty way a
circumstance that depressed my Spirits for many days—that you
& Thomas were on the point of settling near Stowey but had
abandoned it!—'God almighty! what a dream of happiness it held
it [out?] to me'! writes Poole.—*I* felt disappointment without
having had hope!——

—In about a month I hope to see you. Till then may Heaven
bless & preserve us!—Believe me, my dear Sir! with every feeling
of love, esteem, & gratitude

Your affectionate Friend
S. T. Coleridge

284. *To Charles Parry*

Transcript Ingpen and Company, Booksellers. Hitherto unpublished.

June 25—1799

My dear Fellow! my dear Parry! We are safe at Clausthal.[1] The
Coach horse near Clausthal fell down; but old Kutscher took a
walk up & down, mumbling a charm, then fell to, & up rose the
horse—Greenough & I lost our way and after much hallowing in
which we were mocked by some fine echoes we recovered our
Party—We were however amply repayed by the sight of a Wild
Boar with an immense Cluster of Glow-worms round his Tail &
Rump—Vale, φιλτάτη μοι κεφαλή! God bless you again & again,
my dear Fellow—& my kind Love to Frederic—& when I have
a Night Mair, I shall probably dream of him a top of me under that
charming Tree where we slept so warm & comfortable, some two
miles from a village called Mentfeld.

God bless you

S. T. Coleridge.

285. *To George Bellas Greenough*

Address: Den Herrn Greenough | Göttingen
Transcript Professor Edith J. Morley, Hitherto unpublished.

[Brunswick.]
July 6th, 1799. Saturday Morning ½ past 8—

My dear Greenough—God bless you! And eke Carlyon, and Charles
Parry, & little Fred.—Health & Happiness be with you all.—The
date of this Letter, at present in its Infancy, or rather in the very
act of Delivery (for Letters come into existence with their Heads
forward, in which respect, as in some others, they agree with young
Children) the date, I say, is July 6th, 1799, Saturday Morning
½ past 8.—On Wednesday Morning after quitting you we took
a melancholy Stroll on the Ramparts; then called on the Kaufmann
& begged him to take our Places in the Post auf Hamburg for
Saturday, & then walked forth for Helmstadt [Helmstedt].——
With coat on my arm, & hat in hand, I walked before & Chester
behind, & never stopped till we reached Helmstadt, which is

---

[1] On 24 June Coleridge and Chester set off on the first stage of their journey
to England. Following a circuitous route in the company of Greenough and
Carlyon, they went first to Clausthal, then over the Brocken to Elbingerode,
and from thence to Wolfenbüttel and Braunschweig. On 3 July the party
separated, Coleridge and Chester making an excursion to Helmstedt, and the
others returning to Göttingen.

23 miles from Brunswick—they called it 5 G.M. but it certainly is not, for we walked it exactly in 7 Hours.—Well—when we arrived there, we were *overdone* / behind my ears, all down the side of [my] neck, a longitudinal Bladder, the colours shifting prettily betwixt blue & Red—& such another on my Forehead—Chester had acquired a whitloe on his nose, with one dot of black & the Bile had occupied his Face / Red, White, black, & Yellow—poor Chester!—God bless him! He fell down on his bed at Helmstadt, and in the literal sense, *fell* asleep.——I drest myself (i.e. undrest myself & put on the same cloaths again) and delivered my letter to Hofrath Bruns—I saw his wife, a pretty affable Woman; but the Hofrath was at the Library. I left my letter & Card; but had scarcely arrived at my Inn, when Bruns came after me—welcomed me with great Kindness, took me in his arms to the Library, where we rummaged old Manuscripts, & looked at some Libri Rarissimi for about an Hour—(N.B. The Library resembles strikingly the Libraries of some of the little Colleges at Oxford and Cambridge.) After this he took me to his House, spoke to me of a little translation which Lowth[1] had made in his Presence of an Ode of Ramley [?]—talked of England, & Oxford, where he had resided some years, & I found, that he had been intimate with many of my Father's Friends—eat Butterbrot in his arbor with him & his Wife—a sweet Woman! / another Professor & Wife came—smoked a Pipe—all comfortable—all even affectionate to me / went away at past eleven / Bruns having promised to send the next morning to Beireis &c——

So passed Wednesday—i.e. Arsenic. Now for Verdegris—On Thursday morning received a note from Bruns that Beireis would see me & Chester at 10 o'clock. At ten Bruns came, introduced me to Beireis & left us there.—Beireis!—A short man, drest in black, with a very expressive Forehead—& small eyes—He went strait to work—asked no questions—offered no Civilities—but full of himself ever, & Retching began instantly—'You wish to see my Things—what do you wish to see—To see all, or half, or quarter is impossible in one or in two Days—name the collection— Pictures or Coins or Minerals, or Anatomical Preparations, or, or, or, or, or, &c. &c. &c.[']—Now I had heard that his Coins & Minerals were really admirable / so I would *not* see them / I was afraid of too much Truth, that Poisoner of Imagination! besides, for Coins, I don't care a dam! & minerals, have I not seen Professor Wiedermann's, & the Duke of Brunswick's, & Greenough's Collections? So I chose his Pictures—O Lord! it was a Treat!— His Eloquence which is natural & unaffected, really surprized

[1] Probably Robert Lowth (1710–87).

me— / in the space of half an hour, I counted on my fingers, at
least half a million sterling that he had given as purchase money—
The earliest attempts by Holbein, Michael Angelo, Raphael,
Correggio &c &c &c—& behind each a Distich, of Beireis's own
Composition—/——I wondered at all with broad eyes, hands up-
lifted!! like two Notes of Admiration & such a stupid Face of
Praise, that Beireis fell in raptures—Extacied as I was with each
& all, yet I never forgot to turn to the Back of each Picture, & read
aloud with admiring emphasis, the Latin Distich / still trying the
Experiment, whether I could not rise above Beireis's Self-Praises—
in Vain! My most extravagant compliments were as German
Mustard to Cayenne Pepper!—/—Some originals of Correggio he
certainly has—but of Rafael assuredly none / after all, his German
Pictures are—in my opinion, the most valuable—But hang his
Pictures—it was the *Man* that interested. I asked him once with
great earnestness whether he had not drawn on himself the envy
of all the European Sovereigns! O Ja! entsetzlich! was his answer.
But (rejoined I) it is lucky for you that the French Revolution has
happened—or beyond a Doubt you would have to fear an Inva-
sion!—On my Honour, even this was *not* too Extravagant——at
last, after three hours' Picture-seeing during which he spoke
constantly & always eloquently, I begged him, with trembling
voice & downcast eyes, to favor our thirsty Ears with only the
'Geschichte seines weltberühmten Demants [Diamanten],' to *see*
it would be too great a request—Immediately he gave us a narra-
tive quite as entertaining tho' not so probable as the story of the
Wonderful Lamp—then took me to see his Eating Duck of Brass,
which quacked like rusty Hinges / tho' Beireis asked me seriously,
if I could distinguish it from a real Duck's Quack!—I shut my
eyes——lifted up my hands,—listened—& cried—Herr Jesus!!!!
On our return from these Machineries into his Parlor, then, yes—
then he shook my hand friendlily—& out of his Pocket he pulled
the Diamond—apparently, a semi transparent Pebble almost as
large as my Fist!—I will write again from Celle—for now I must
interrupt my Narration to talk of piteous Cares. No Chest, no
Portmanteau!—the Kaufman has heard this Morning, that it
ought to have been here on the first of July——/—My Stars! What
shall I do!—Last night I sprinkled my shirt with [water?] hung it
up at the window, & slept naked—for my *one* clean shirt I *must*
keep till I get to Hamburg.—Heaven! I stink like an old Poultice!—
I should mislead any Pack of Foxhounds in Great Britain / Put a
Trail of Rusty Bacon at a Furlong Distance & me at a mile, and
they would follow *me*—I should hear a cry of Stop Thief close at
my ears with a safe Conscience—but if I caught only the Echo of

a Tally Ho! I should climb up into a Tree! You know me too well
to suspect Hyperbole—I stink damnably—& that's the Truth!
Lord a mercy on those poor Imps that are condemned to live
between the Toes of the Devil's Dam who wears black Worsted
Socks, & uses Turney Sarat for Corn Plaster—& those that live
under the Devil's Tail have a Heaven in comparison— / Marry—
& my Books—I shall be ruined—on the Debtor's Side in Newgate,
just 5 Yards distant from Sodomy, Murder, & House-breaking—
Soul of Lessing! hover over my Boxes! Ye Minnesänger! fly after
them!——Dear Greenough! Dear Parry! Carlyon, Fred—I go—
this Kaufmann had forgotten to take places so we go with the
Packages / Chester has got St Antony's Fire in his Legs—& his
Arse is sore—

Your affectionate
S. T. Coleridge.

286. *To Robert Southey*

Address: Mr Southey | Mr Holloway's | Minehead
MS. Lord Latymer. Pub. with omis. Letters, *i. 303.*
Stamped: Bridgewater.

July 29th, 1799
Nether Stowey

I am doubtful, Southey, whether the circumstances which impel
me to write to you, ought not to keep me silent— / & if it were only
a feeling of delicacy, I should remain silent—for it is good to do all
things in faith.—But I have been absent, Southey! ten months, &
little Hartley prattles about you / and if *you* knew, that domestic
affliction was hard upon me, and that my own health was de-
clining, would you not have shootings within you of an affection,
which ('tho' fall'n, tho' chang'd') has played too important a part
in the events of our lives & the formation of our characters, ever
to be *forgotten*? I am perplexed what to write, or how to state the
object of my writing— / Any participation in each other's moral
Being I do not *wish*, simply because I know enough of the mind of
man to know that is impossible. But, Southey, we have similar
Talents, Sentiments nearly similar, & kindred pursuits—we have
likewise in more than one instance common objects of our esteem
and love—I pray and intreat you, if we should meet at any time,
let us not withhold from each other the outward Expressions of
daily Kindliness; and if it not be no [any] longer in your power to
soften your opinions, make your feelings at least more tolerant
towards me— / a debt of humility which assuredly we all of us owe
to our most feeble, imperfect and self-deceiving Nature.—We are

few of us good enough to know our own Hearts—and as to the
Hearts of others, let us struggle to hope that they are better than
we think them / & resign the rest to our common maker.

God bless you & your's—

S. T. Coleridge

287. *To Robert Southey*

Address: Mr Southey
MS. Lord Latymer. Pub. E. L. G. i. 123.

[8 August 1799][1]

Southey—I had written a long letter to you & sent it to Mine-
head.—Therein I had descended into particulars / but I now think
that in the present state of your Feelings this was neither wise or
delicate— / I will therefore suppress it. Suffice it to aver, calmly
and on my honor as a man & gentleman, that I never charged you
with aught but your deep & implacable enmity towards me—&
that I founded this on the same Authorities, on which you founded
your belief of my supposed Hatred to you.—Southey!—for nearly
three years past Poole has been the Repository of my very
Thoughts—I have not written or received any letter of importance,

---

[1] On 8 Aug. 1799 a letter of self-justification and recrimination from Southey
arrived at Stowey. This letter from Coleridge was written immediately on
receipt of Southey's, and it was probably sent to Minehead, along with a letter
from Poole, dated 8 Aug., and reading in part 'I am satisfied that the motive
which induces me to write, you will consider a sufficient apology for the liberty
I take in addressing you. Coleridge and myself have long been in the habit of
confiding to each other those things which the most nearly and deeply interest
us—this being the case he naturally showed me your letter which he has just
now received—On perusing it I cannot help thinking but that my testimony
must in a great measure clear your mind from those doubts concerning Cole-
ridge's feelings and conduct towards you. . . . Without entering into particulars,
I will say generally that in the many conversations I have had with Coleridge
concerning yourself, he has never discovered the least personal enmity against,
but on the contrary the strongest affection for you; stifled only by the unto-
ward circumstances of your separation—such has been the general impression
I have received from him—and from him alone I have been acquainted with
your intellectual and moral character— . . . As for Chas. Lloyd, it would be
cruel to attribute his conduct to any thing but a diseased mind—be assured
from me, who have seen his contradictory letters, that his evidence amounts
to nothing. . . . I send this letter, with the knowledge of Coleridge by an
especial Messenger, thinking it probable that you may be induced to alter your
plan, and instead of going to the Valley of Stones, to accompany Mrs Southey
and Mrs Coleridge to Stowey— / I have written this because it appears to
me that the letter contains what Coleridge himself could not have written.'
(MS. in editor's possession.)

Poole's good offices were successful; Southey not only paid Coleridge a visit
at Stowey but the two families journeyed together into Devonshire.

which he has not seen——For more than one whole year I was with Wordsworth almost daily—& frequently for weeks together— Our conversations concerning you have been numberless—and during the affair with Lloyd under suppositions of a highly irritating kind— / If Wordsworth & Poole will not affirm to you solemnly that I have ever thought & spoken of you with respect & affection, never charging you with aught else than your restless enmity to me, & attributing even that to *Delusion,* I abandon myself for ever to the disesteem of every Man, whose Esteem is worth having.—You have received Evidence to the contrary— / and I could shew you written Testimonies contradictory to some sentences of your last Letter— / Yet on my soul I believe you—I do not require you to do at present the same with regard to me. But I pray you, let us be at least in the possibility of understanding each other's moral Being— / and with regard to what you have heard, to think a little on the state of mind in which those were *from* whom you heard it.—More I will not say ; but end by thanking you for your letter which under your Convictions was a wise & temperate one—

God bless you, & your's!

S. T. Coleridge

288. *To Richard Wordsworth*

Address : Mr Wordsworth | attorney at Law | Staple's Inn | Holborn | London
Post payed
MS. Dove Cottage. *Pub. Chambers,* Life, *335.*
Postmark : 12 September 1799. *Stamped* : Exeter.

Tuesday, Sept. 10, 1799   Exeter.

Dear Wordsworth

The letter by which I received the lottery Tickets gave me information that you had not received the Shirt &c / & this morning I received your letter to the express Purpose of the Same— / I am vexed, as you will easily suppose when I tell you that *within* a week of my arrival at Stowey I sent them directed to you, by Mr Stutfield,[1] a Wine & Brandy Merchant, who happened then to be at Stowey & offered to take the said parcel for me—promising me (with his own Mouth) to deliver the same——/—This Evening I will write to my Friend Poole who knows Stutfield's Address, requesting him immediately on receipt of mine to write to Stutfield—if I do not hear from Stutfield in the course of a decent time certifying that he has performed the promise, the performance of which he has so long & so unjustifiably neglected, Mrs Coleridge

---

[1] The father of Coleridge's later amanuensis, Charles Stutfield.

will not delay to do (what *she* now wishes)—i.e.—transmit a shirt
& cravat, trusting to your goodness for the acceptance of = for =,
it not being in my power to preserve absolute Identity——

I received this morning a letter from William & was agitated
to find that his Health is in a State which I should deem alarm-
ing——

Your's sincerely
S. T. Coleridge

P.S. Till I hear from Stutfield the very idea of your Shirt will stick
more burningly to my Memory than Deianira's Shirt did to
Hercules's Skin—altho' I entreat you to look into the Article of
domestic News in the London Papers to see whether or no a Mr
Stutfield was found on Hounslow Heath or elsewhere with his
throat cut from Ear to Ear—for he *ought* to be dead, as a Moral
Being / having promised me that if alive he would not delay to
deliver the parcel, the *great importance* of which I happened by a
sort of prophetic Presentiment to impress upon him with almost
a deathbed Energy & Solemnity.——

289. To Thomas Poole

Address: Mr T. Poole | Nether Stowey | near | Bridgewater.
MS. British Museum. Hitherto unpublished.
Stamped: Exeter.

Sept. 10 1799

My dearest Poole

We arrived safely, & were received with all love & attention—
Southey & his wife sojourned at Ottery a few Days & went to
Exeter from whence & from whose Room I now write—to morrow
I set off for a little Tour of 3 or 4 days with Southey——I now
write to you on the spur or rather the *Sting* of the moment—for I
have just received a letter from Wordsworth of Staple's Inn
bothering me with an ungentlemanlike Importunacy about that
damned old Shirt which I sent by Stutfield / & which he has not
received—Now I entreat you, my dear Poole, do not delay to write
immediately to Stutfield, telling him the same, that if by any
accident it be lost, I may transmit = for =. As to Stutfield, I
could almost wish that some Incubus would get into Bed with him,
& blow with a bellows the Wind of *cold* colic against *his* Posteriors—
& Wordsworth—nay—I will not dare to utter any thing vitu-
perative even of the Brother of my GREAT Friend / —Please Heaven
in the course of three days I will write you a letter that shall in
some measure pay postage / ——/—I am afraid that I shall hear
nothing from Cruckshanks about Alfoxden—I am very anxious to

have it—but expect nothing.—Poor Cruckshanks! it seems hard-
hearted for me to mingle any selfish Concern with his Distresses——
I have heard from W. Wordsworth—he is ill—& seems not happy—
Montague has played the fool, I suspect, with him in pecuniary
affairs—he renounces Alfoxden altogether / —

God bless you, my dear dear Poole! & now that you have come
to the End of my letter take up pen & paper & begin

Dear Stutfield

My Friend, the Bard, alias, S. T. Coleridge, has just received a
damn'd disagreeable dunning dirty dribbling Letter about a
beggarly Shirt &c &c &c——

Heaven bless you, my dear Poole! &
S. T. Coleridge

We are all well——
Wordsworth is an attorney at Law in Staple's Inn——

290. *To William Wordsworth*

Pub. Memoirs of Wordsworth, *i. 159.*

[*Circa* 10 September 1799][1]

I am anxiously eager to have you steadily employed on 'The
Recluse.' . . . My dear friend, I do entreat you go on with 'The
Recluse;' and I wish you would write a poem, in blank verse,
addressed to those, who, in consequence of the complete failure of
the French Revolution, have thrown up all hopes of the amelioration
of mankind, and are sinking into an almost epicurean selfishness,
disguising the same under the soft titles of domestic attachment
and contempt for visionary *philosophes*. It would do great good,
and might form a part of 'The Recluse,' for in my present mood
I am wholly against the publication of any small poems.

291. *To Thomas Poole*

Address: Mr T. Poole | Nether Stowey | Bridgewater | Somerset
MS. British Museum. Pub. with omis. Letters, *i. 305.*
Stamped: Exeter.

Exeter—Southey's Lodgings, Mr Tucker's, Forestreet Hill
Monday Night   Sep. 16 1799.

My dear Poole

Here I am, just returned from a little Tour of five days—
having seen rocks; and waterfalls; & a pretty River or two; some

[1] This fragment may be an answer to Wordsworth's letter, which Coleridge
received on 10 Sept. See Letter 288.

wide Landscapes; & a multitude of Ash-tree Dells; & the blue waters of the [']ROARING Sea!' as little Hartley says—who on Friday fell down stairs, & injured his arm—'tis swelled, & sprained; but God be praised, not broken.——The Views of Totness & Dartmouth are among the most impressive Things, I have ever seen / but in general, what of Devonshire I have lately traversed is tame to Quantock, Porlock, Culbone, & Linton.——So much for the Country—now as to the inhabitants thereof, they are Bigots; unalphabeted in the first Feelings of Liberality; of course, in all they speak and all they do not speak, they give good reasons for the opinions which they hold—viz. they hold the propriety of Slavery—an opinion which being generally assented to by Englishmen makes Pitt & Paul the first among the moral Fitnesses of Things.—I have three Brothers / that is to say, Relations by Gore—two are Parsons and one is a Colonel—George & the Colonel good men as times go—very good men; but alas! we have neither Tastes or Feelings in common. This I wisely learnt from their Conversation; & did not suffer them to learn it from *mine* / What occasion for it?—Hunger & Thirst— Roast Fowls, mealy Potatoes, Pies, & Clouted Cream—bless the Inventors thereof! An honest Philosoph may find therewith pre-occupation for his *mouth* / keeping his heart & brain, the latter in his Skull, the former in the Pericardium, some 5 or 6 Inches from the Roots of his Tongue!—Church & King!—Why, I drink Church & King—mere cutaneous Scabs of Loyalty which only ape the King's Evil, but affect not the Interior of one's Health— Mendicant Sores!—it requires some little Caution to keep them open, but they heal of their own accord.——Who such a friend as I am to the system of Fraternity could refuse such a Toast at the Table of a Clergyman and a Colonel—his Brothers?—/So, my dear Poole! I live in Peace—.——Of the other party, I have dined with a Mr Northmore,[1] a pupil of Wakefield's, who possesses a fine House half a mile from Exeter—in his Boyhood he was at my Father's School—& *my* Great-Grandfather was *his* Great great Grandfather's Bastard / but it was not this relationship however tender & interesting, which brought us acquainted / —But Southey & self called upon him, as Authors, he having edited a Tryphio-dorus & part of Plutarch & being a notorious Antiministerialist & Freethinker.—He welcomed us, as he ought to do / —and we met at dinner Hucks, at whose House I dine on Wednesday—the man who toured with me into Wales & afterwards published his Tour— / Kendall, a poet who really looks like a man of Genius, pale

---

[1] Thomas Northmore (1766–1851). Coleridge mentions his Τρυφιοδώρου 'Ιλίου "Αλωσις. *De plurimis mendis purgata, et notis illustrata,* 1791, and his *Plutarch's Treatise upon the Distinction between a Friend and Flatterer, with Remarks,* 1793.

& gnostic, has the merit of being a Jacobin or so / but is a shallowist/ and finally, a Mr Bamfield[1]—a man of sense, information, & various Literature—and most perfectly a Gentleman—in short, a pleasant man. At his House we dine to morrow— / Northmore himself is an honest vehement sort of Fellow, who splutters out all his opinions, like a Fizgig made of Gunpowder not thoroughly dry / sudden & explosive yet ever with an adhesive Blubberliness of Elocution—Shallow, shallow—a man who can read Greek well, but shallow— / yet honest, one who ardently wishes the well-being of his fellow men, & believes that without more Liberty & more Equality this Well being is not possible. He possesses a most noble Library.—

The Victory at Novi![2]—If I were a good Caricaturist, I would sketch off Suwarrow, in a Car of Conquest drawn by huge Crabs!! with what retrograde Majesty the Vehicle advances! He may truly say he came off with Eclat—i.e. A *claw*!—

I shall be back at Stowey in less than three weeks—in the mean time I intreat you, my dearest Poole! to send Ward to my House and on one of the Shelves in the Parlour he will [find] Green's Pamphlet on Godwin[3]—this he or you will not forget to take on Thursday to Bridgewater, & have it booked in the Exeter Coach, directed to / Mr Southey, at Mr Tucker's, Forestreet Hill, Exeter—& Southey will walk over with it to me / . This is of the utmost Importance/.—. Likewise, my dear Poole! be so kind as to let me have five guineas / which shall not be long on your Books against us.—This you will be so good as to transmit to Southey in a letter, from whom I have borrowed it, as soon as convenient—at all events, within a week or 8 days / as Southey leaves Exeter about that Time / — / .

We hope & trust, your dear Mother remains well.—Give my filial love to her.—God bless her!——I beg my kind Love to Ward.——

God bless you & S. T. Coleridge

Of course, I am uneasy about a House Business—. I am pretty certain, I could have a Pupil on very advantageous Terms. What do you think of this? Let me hear immediately from you—Of course, you wrote to Stutfield about the Shirt—.—Southey begs his kind remembrance to you.

---

[1] In Letter 298 Coleridge spells this name Banfyl; Southey refers to him as Banfill.

[2] At Novi Ligure, Italy, an army of Russians and Austrians under Suvaroff and Melas defeated the French on 15 Aug. 1799.

[3] Thomas Green, *An Examination of the leading Principles of the New System of Morals in Godwin's Political Justice*, 1798.

292. *To Robert Southey*

Address: Mr Southey | Mr Tucker's | Forestreet Hill | Exeter   Single
MS. Lord Latymer. Pub. E. L. G. i. 124.
Stamped: Bridgewater.

Wednesday Morning [25 September 1799]

My dear Southey—We arrived at Stowey last evening—& this morning poor Fanny left us.—As neither Sara or I have as yet any symptoms of infection, I hope & trust, that you & Edith, and Eliza, are safe.—Believe me, tho' obliged to bear up against the FRESH of my Wife's hypersuperlative Grief on the occasion, I have nevertheless suffered much anxiety lest poor Eliza or Mrs S. should have been colonized by these damn'd invisible Skin-moles— Moses [Hartley] received the Catholic Sacrament of Unction for the first time last night— / He was very merry during the performance, singing or chanting—I be a funny Fellow, And my name is Brimstonello.—I doubt not, that all will be well by tomorrow or at farthest next day—for he slept quiet & has never once scratched himself since his Embrimstonement.—/—

Have you seen Isaac Weld's Travels[1]—I find them interesting—/ he makes the American appear a most degraded & vile nation.——— In one of the ecclesiastical Historians I find that the Oak which Abraham planted at Mamre, was still existing in the time of Constantine & destroyed by his orders—a famous Mart being held there every summer, persons of all Religions, both Jews & Christians & Asiatic Gentiles in a general confluence doing honor thereto/—/— What a delightful subject this for an eclogue, or pastoral, or philosophical poem— / William Taylor[2] is the man to write it—his knowlege, his style, his all-half believing Doubtingness of all, his—in short, I wish that you would hint it to him.—

I wish, you would make my respects to Dyer, the Bookseller[3]— & beg to know the *lowest* price at which he will let *me have Bacon's Works*, & Milton's Prose Works— / If he mention the former at not above two guineas, I shall have it / Likewise, if he send them, to send his Catalogue—& should he have a Copy of Taylor's Sermons, by all means to let me have them / ——— / Any parcel for me to be addressed, Mr T. Poole, the old Angel, Bridgewater——/— (for Mr Coleridge.)—/—The money shall be payed him immediately

---

[1] Isaac Weld, *Travels through the States of North America and the Provinces of Upper and Lower Canada during the Years 1795, 1796, and 1797*, 1799.

[2] William Taylor of Norwich (1765–1836), translator and literary critic, was best known for his German studies.

[3] Gilbert Dyer (1743–1820), bookseller and antiquary of Exeter. He is **not** to be confused with the poet, George Dyer.

on my receipt of the Books, by some of my relations in Exeter.—
Tell him, that if he rides any where near Nether Stowey, I hope,
he will not forget my invitation, or consider it as a commonplace
Compliment.—

That Dyer, whom my Brother names a dark-hearted Jacobin,
is really an honest man—& I like him. The respect to men of
Genius which he payed in you in letting you have the Mambrinos
at your own price, pleased me——/—

This letter is not worth postage / but my Brain is dry, I having
been letter writing the whole morning— /

Sara's love—she hopes, that if Eliza was gone before Edith
received her letter, that Edith has written to caution her of what
has happened.

I shall go on with the Mohammed[1] / tho' something I must do
for pecuniary emolument / —I think of writing a School-book.—
Let me hear from you & of your proceedings——

Your's affectionately
S. T. Coleridge

293. *To George Coleridge*

Address: Revd G. Coleridge | Ottery St Mary | near | Honiton | Devon
MS. Lady Cave. Hitherto unpublished.
Stamped: Bridgewater.

Sunday, 29th Sept. 1799

Dear Brother

The little parcel may be put into the box of my books up at my
mother's, & go when they go.—At Mr Hart's are two folio volumes,
Sennerti opera,[2] standing by themselves on the chest in the back
part of his Book-golgotha— / say when you see him that he would
much oblige me by letting me have them at the price of their
Weight.—Be so kind as not to forget this—for there are facts in
Sennertus which I mean to cite in a future Work.—These too may
be packed with the others in the Box—there is ample room for
them / & I should be glad to borrow the four books which I have
not read, & which lie in our bedroom under the table (there are 5,

---

[1] As early as 1 Sept. Coleridge and Southey had planned a poem in hexa-
meters on Mahomet; and though only 14 lines by Coleridge (*Poems*, i. 329)
and 109 lines by Southey (*Oliver Newman*, 1845, p. 113) were actually written,
a rather ambitious plan was evolved. In the Mitchell Library, Sydney, Aus-
tralia, there is an unpublished manuscript, mainly in Coleridge's handwriting
but with corrections and additions by Southey; it gives a bare outline of this
proposed poem in eight books.

[2] Daniel Sennertus, *Opera omnia*, 2 vols., 1656.

but Morice's Coena quasi κοινη[1] I read, & of course do not want—)
I pledge myself to bring them back on my next visit.—If this can
be done, the Box will then be full & I will beg you, or rather Brother
Edward as having less to do, to have the said Box well corded, &
sent by the Carrier to Exeter to the place where the Taunton
Waggon or the Waggon which goes thro' Taunton sets off—Mr Hart
can tell him where it is / the Box, he sent, has arrived safely—Pray,
return my best Thanks to him for his Kindness & Trouble. The
address must be—

Mr T. Poole at the Old Angel | Bridgewater. | for Mr Coleridge

Oh—I left the Annual Anthology behind!—Save, O save it from
Edward's papyrologiophagous *Caco*daemony!—It can come with
the rest.—

As to the Commemoration Sermon I know but one person now
resident at Cambridge—he is not a Clergyman, and I have not
written these 5 years to him.—But if it would give you any
pleasure, I remember very well what Commemoration Sermons are,
& will write one with great willingness & without an hour's pro-
crastination—but I do not know Mr Sparrow's Address, or how
I am to convey it.[2]—

I rejoice that young Brimstonello has not proved himself a
member of the Propagandi Society / —he seems indeed totally
freed.—But alas! we have reason to suspect that in his fall down
the stairs at Exeter he seriously injured the bone—& poor little
Lamb! this morning as his Mother was pushing the door to, he put
his little arm in, & bruised it severely.—

We were talking of Hexameters while with you. I will for want
of something better fill up the paper with a translation of one of
my favourite Psalms into that metre, which allowing trochees for
Spondees as the nature of our Language demands, you will find
pretty accurate in Scansion.[3]

God is our Strength and our Refuge: therefore will we not tremble,
Tho' the Earth be removed; and tho' the perpetual Mountains
Sink in the Swell of the Ocean! God is our Strength & our Refuge.

---

[1] William Morice, *Coena quasi* κοινη, 1657.

[2] Using the Wisdom of Solomon iv. 16 as his text, Coleridge prepared a
Commemoration Sermon. He thus describes it: 'The original of a discourse
Written for whom I neither know or care as a College Commemoration Sermon
—Oct. 6th 1799. N.B. The one Side is all too hugely beangel'd, the other all
too desperately bedevil'd: yet spite of the Flattery, and spite of the Caricature
both are *Likenesses*. Sic de suo opere cogitabat S. T. Coleridge Oct. 8. 1799.
Stowey.' [MS. British Museum.]

[3] *Poems*, i. 326. The paraphrase is of Psalm xlvi.

There is a River, the Flowing whereof shall gladden the City, Hallelujah! the City of God! Jehova shall help her.

The Idolaters raged, the Kingdoms were moving in fury—
But He utter'd his Voice: Earth melted away from beneath them.
Halleluja! th' Eternal is with us, Almighty Jehova!

Fearful the works of the Lord, yea, fearful his Desolations—
But *He* maketh the Battle to cease, he burneth the Spear & the Chariot.
Halleluja! th' Eternal is with us, the God of our Fathers!—

God bless you—We desire love to all.—

Your affectionate
S. T. Coleridge

294. *To Robert Southey*

Address: Mr Southey | Mr Tucker's | Forestreet Hill | Exeter   *Single*
MS. Lord Latymer. *Pub. E. L. G. i. 126.*
Stamped: Bridgewater.

Monday Evening. Sept. 30 [, 1799]

My dear Southey

I am extremely interested with your account of Mr & Mrs Keenan. You have of course asked her whether Buonaparte is a man of Science / it is the mode & fashion to deny it.—Do not forget to procure from old Jackson a copy of poor Bamfield's Sonnets & Poems[1]—he will at least lend them you to copy out:—& let me know what you think of old Jackson.[2]—Male and Female Rhymes are neither more or less than single and double Rhymes—Right, Light, are Masculine Rhymes; Ocean, Motion, feminine.—At present, they are called Masculine & Feminine, not Male & Female— I should think that in Thalaba it would be better, on many accounts, if Allah were uniformly substituted for God—the so frequent Repetition of that last word gives somehow or other a sermonic Cast to a Poem / and perhaps too it might give a not altogether unfounded offence, that a name so connected with awful realities, is (so often, & so solemnly) blended with those bold Fictions which ask & gain only a transient Faith.—But I object now only from Recollection.

Our little Hovel is almost afloat—poor Sara tired off her legs

---

[1] John C. Bampfylde (1754–96) published *Sixteen Sonnets* in 1778.

[2] William Jackson (1730–1803), musical composer of Exeter. It was Jackson who befriended Bampfylde and who gave Southey details of that unfortunate poet's life. See *Life and Corres.* ii. 26–29.

with servanting—the young one fretful & noisy from confinement
exerts his activities on all forbidden Things—the house stinks of
Sulphur—I however, sunk in Spinoza, remain as undisturbed as
a Toad in a Rock / that is to say, when my rheumatic pains are
asleep. For you must know that our apothecary persuaded me &
Sara to wear Mercurial Girdles, as Preventives—accordingly Sara
arrayed herself with this Cest of the Caledonian Venus, and I eke/—
On the first day I walked myself into a perspiration, and O Christus
Jesus!—how I stunk!—Convinced as I was before of the necessity
of all parts of the human body, I now received double-damning
Nose-conviction, that all my pores were *Necessary Holes* with a
Vengeance—I walked, one Magnum Mercurii Excrementum, cursed
with the faculty of Self-sentience.—Well but the Nose is the most
placable of all the senses / and to one's own evil odours one can
reconcile oneself almost as easily as to one's own Vices. But whether
I caught cold or no, I cannot tell; but the next day a fit of the
Rheumatism laid hold of me from the small of my back down to the
Calves of my Legs, shooting thro' me like hot arrows headed with
adders' Teeth. Since my Rheumatic Fever at School I have
suffered nothing like it!—Of course, I threw off my girdle—for such
damned Twitches! I would rather have old Scratch himself, whom
all the Brimstone in Hell can't cure, than endure them!——I am
still however not free from them / tho' the latter attacks have
decreased in violence. You'd laugh to see how pale & haggard I
look——& by way of a Clincher, I am almost certain that Hartley
has not had the Itch—.

A great affliction has fallen on poor Daddy Rich & his Wife.
The old man's Son went away some two years ago for a Marine
leaving his Currying Business / to bring him up to which the good
old Creature had pinched his Belly & robbed his Back— / Ever
since he has been wishing & praying only to see him once more / and
about a fortnight ago he returned, discharged as an ideot.—The
day after I came back to Stowey, I heard a cry of Murder, & rushed
into the House, where I found the poor Wretch, whose physiog-
nomy is truly *hellish*, beating his Father most unmercifully with
a great stick— / I seized him & pinioned him to the wall, till the
peace-officer came—/—He vows vengeance on me; but what is
really shocking he never sees little Hartley but he grins with
hideous distortions of rage, & hints that he'll do him a mischief.—
And the poor old People, who just get enough to feed themselves,
are now absolutely pinched / & never fall to sleep without fear &
trembling, lest the Son should rise in a fit of insanity, & murder
them.—I shall not let Poole rest, till he has called the Parish, that
something may be done for them.—

The money shall be remitted to Dyer as soon as the Books are received / The Bacon is for Poole.——I suppose you have read Stedman's Narrative of an Expedition to Surinam.[1] Vol. 2nd, page 299 are these remarkable Words, 'Vultures are compared by some to the Eagle, though those of Surinam possess very opposite Qualities. They are indeed Birds of Prey, but instead of feeding on what they kill, like the other *noble* animal, their chief pursuit is Carrion—' Now this tickles me—the poor Vulture, the useful Scavenger in a Climate where Carrion would but for him breed the plague / the noble Eagle not only useless but a murderer, & probably tainting the air with his half devoured prey—! / There is indeed a sort of living Carrion, Sons of Corruption &c & eke some of the merciful Lady-Planters in Surinam, &c &c &c, on which the Vulture might, without departing from his utility as a Scavenger, exercise the Eagle attribute of first knocking on the head— / .— When you want a subject for Stewart, do prefix the Quotation from Stedman, & make some Verses underneath.—

As to what you say about the School book, I dissent— / I am decisive against ever publishing the Letters[2]—& were I not, it would take me more trouble to fit 'em up, than they are worth.— As to a Volume of Poems, I am not in a poetical Mood / & moreover am resolved to publish nothing with my name till my Great Work.—But the School book, which I am planning, will I think be a lucrative Speculation / & it will be an entertaining Job— When I have licked the plan enough for you to discern it's embryo Lineaments, I will send it you / —There are two works which I particularly want—& perhaps William Taylor has them—the one is, Herder's Ideas for the History of the Human Race[3]—I do not accurately remember the German Title / the second, Zimmerman's Geographie des Menschen[4]—It is not the Zimmerman who wrote the dull Thing about Solitude[5]——Would there be any impropriety in your asking W. Taylor to lend them me?—Probably, you know some one in London who would take the Trouble of receiving them, & booking them off in the Bridgewater Mail, directed to be

---

[1] J. G. Stedman, *Narrative of a Five Years' Expedition against the Revolted Negroes of Surinam, in Guiana, on the Wild Coast of South America, from the Year 1772 to 1777*, 2 vols., 1796.

[2] Presumably Coleridge refers to his German letters to Poole and to Mrs. Coleridge.

[3] Cf. J. G. von Herder, *Ideen zur Philosophie der Geschichte der Menschheit*, 1784–91.

[4] Cf. E. A. W. von Zimmermann, *Geographische Geschichte des Menschen*, 1778–83.

[5] J. G. Zimmermann, *Über die Einsamkeit*, 1756. The work ran to a number of English editions.

left at the old Angel, with my direction.—But if there be the least
Impropriety, I pray you, think no more of it——I would take care
that they should be safely redelivered within a month—.—

I have very serious Thoughts of trying to get a couple of Pupils /
very serious ones.——

Poole desires to be kindly remembered to you.—I wrote this
Epigram on Naso Rubicund, Esq. a dealer in Secrets.[1]—

> You're perfectly safe—for so ruddy your Nose,
> That talk what you will, 'tis all *under the Rose*.

I have found the long rigmarole Verses which I wrote about Pratt
&c / but there's nothing in 'em, save facility of Language & oddity
of Rhyme—. If however I go to Bristol, I will leave it with Cottle
to be sent with any parcel that may be moving towards you—

Sara is anxious to hear from Eliza—She desires her kind Love.
Young Brimstonello is fast asleep—he is a quaint Boy. When I told
him, you had sent your love to him in the Letter, he sat, & thought
& thought, and at last burst into a fit of Laughter—/.

God bless you & Edith—& all of us!—

Your's with affectionate Esteem
S. T. Coleridge

295. *To Thomas Ward*

Address: To Mr Ward | this *pen*tagonal | Letter | comes | as penn'd.—
MS. Miss Helen M. Cam. Pub. Thomas Poole, *i. 304.* 'Letter the first' thanks
Ward for some quill pens which he had commissioned the clerk, Govett, to
mend; 'Letter the second' is an acknowledgement of another batch of pens
which Ward, fearing Govett's might not be satisfactory, prepared himself.

Octob. 7. 1799   Stowey

Letter the first

My dear Ward
   Thank you!—

S. T. Coleridge

Letter the second

Most exquisite Benefactor!—I will speak dirt & daggers of the
Wretch who shall deny thee to be the most heaven-inspired,
munificent Penmaker that these latter Times, these superficial,
weak, and evirtuate ages, have produced—to redeem themselves
from ignominy!—And may he, great Calamist! who shall vilipend
or derogate from thy penmaking merits, do *pen*ance & suffer
*pen*itential *pen*ality, *penn'd* up in some *pen*urious *pen*insula of

[1] *Poems*, ii. 958.

*pen*al & *pen*etrant Fire, *pen*sive and *pen*dulous, *pen*ding a huge
slice of Eternity!—Were I to write till *Pen*tecost, filling whole
*Pen*tateuchs, my grateful Expressions would still remain merely a
*Pen*umbra of my Debt & Gratitude—

thine,

S. T. Coleridge

Your Messenger neither came or returns *pen*niless.

296. *To Thomas Ward*

Address: Mr Ward | at Mr T. Poole's | Nether Stowey | Somerset—
MS. Miss Helen M. Cam. Pub. Thomas Poole, *i. 305.*

1799—Oct. 8

Ward! I recant—I recant—solemnly recant and disannul all
praise, puff, and panegyric on you and your damn'd Pens—I have
this moment read the note which you had wrapped round your last
present[1]—and last night therefore wrote my Elogy on the assured
Belief that the first Batch were your's, and before I had tried the
second—.—The second! I'm sick on't—such execrable Blurrers of
innocent white paper, Villains with uneven Legs—Hexameter &
Pentameter Pens—Elogy—no—no—no—Elegies written with
elegiac Pens (whose L E Gees I wish in your Guts) elegies on my
poor Thoughts doing *pen*ance in white sheets, filthily illegible—My

---

[1] 'T Ward not having had time to mend the pens before tea delegated that
commission to Rd. Govett, but fearing their workmanship may not prove of
so superior a kind as his own, he now begs Mr Coleridge's acceptance of these
few pens which are his own manufacture, and which he hopes will suit Mr
C——'

On Ward's note Coleridge wrote the following fable:

The Fox, the Goose, and the Swan, a new Fable.

The Fox observing a white Bird on the lake thought it a Goose—leapt
in, & meant to have payed his respects, but met such a rebuff as had nearly
made his fate similar to that of his namesake, the celebrated *Guy.* However
he got off—with a most profound respect for the supposed Goose; but soon
received a Message from the Goose to this purport—Dear Frind! I have
sent this hopping—hir'd has ow u dun mee the onnur of a vissat—sorry u
dident hap to have meat with I— / That dowdy lanky neck'd Thing that
u saw is a distant relashon of I's, and I suffers r to swum about the Pond
when I is not at hum / but I is at hum now—& hop for the onnur of ure
cumpany—

Your luvving Frind
Guse.

The Fox came—&—you guess the Rest.— / / This Fable I address to the
Writer of the above notable instance of Incapacity self-detected thro'
Vanity!—

(537)

rage prevents me from writing sense—but o Govatt! dear Govatt! kick that spectacle-mongering Son of Pen-hatchet out of Creation— and remain alone, from the date hereof invested with the rank and office of Penmaker to my immortal Bardship, with all the dignities and emoluments thereunto annexed—

Given from Apollo's | Temple in the | odoriferous Lime-Grove— alias | Street——in what | olympiad our Inspiration | knows not, but of the | usurping Christian Æra | 1799—Oct. 8.

S. T. Coleridge

Govatt is expected to express his Gratitude by an immediate present of half a dozen pens—amended if indeed the reprobates be not incorrigible.—

297. *To William Wordsworth*

Pub. Memoirs of Wordsworth, *i. 159.*

Oct. 12. 1799

I long to see what you have been doing. O let it be the tail-piece of 'The Recluse!' for of nothing but 'The Recluse' can I hear patiently. That it is to be addressed to me makes me more desirous that it should not be a poem of itself. To be addressed, as a beloved man, by a thinker, at the close of such a poem as 'The Recluse,' a poem *non unius populi*, is the only event, I believe, capable of inciting in me an hour's vanity—vanity, nay, it is too good a feeling to be so called; it would indeed be a self-elevation produced *ab extra.*[1]

298. *To Robert Southey*

Address: Mr Southey | Burton | near | Ringwood | Hampshire   Single Sheet
MS. Lord Latymer. Pub. with omis. Letters, *i. 307.*
Stamped: Bridgewater.

Stowey, Tuesday Evening, Oct. 15, 1799

It is fashionable among our philosophizers to assert the existence of a surplus of misery in the world / which in my opinion is no proof, that either systematic Thinking or unaffected Self-observation is fashionable among them.—But Hume wrote—and the French imitated him—and we the French——and the French us—and so philosophisms fly to and fro—in serieses of imitated Imitations—Shadows of shadows of shadows of a farthing Candle placed between two Looking-glasses. I was meditating on this when I received your last letter—so I have begun with it. For in truth,

---

[1] The poem addressed to Coleridge became, of course, *The Prelude.*

my dear Southey!—I am *harrassed* with the Rheumatism in my head and shoulders not without arm-and-thigh-twitches— / but when the Pain intermits, it leaves my sensitive Frame *so* sensitive! My enjoyments are so deep, of the fire, of the Candle, of the Thought I am thinking, of the old Folio I am reading—and the silence of the silent House is so *most & very* delightful—that upon my soul! the Rheumatism is no such bad thing as *people make for*.—And yet I have & *do* suffer from it, in much pain, and sleep-lessness, & often sick at stomach thro' indigestion of the Food, which I eat from Compulsion—/—Since I received your former Letter, I have spent a few days at Upcott;[1] but was too unwell to be comfortable—so I returned yesterday.—Poor Tom! he has an adventurous Calling. I have so wholly forgotten my Geography, that I don't know where Ferrol[2] is, whether in France or Spain—. Your dear Mother must be very anxious indeed.—If he return safe, it will have been good—God grant, he may!——

MASSENA!—and what say you of the Resurrection & Glorification of the Saviour of the East after his Tryals in the Wilderness?[3]— I am afraid that this is a piece of Blasphemy— / but it was in simple verity such an Infusion of animal Spirits into me—/— Buonaparte—! Buonaparte! dear dear DEAR Buonaparte!—It would be no bad fun to hear the Clerk of the Privy Council read this paragraph before Pitt &c.—You ill-looking frog-voiced Reptile! mind you lay the proper emphasis on the third DEAR / or I'll split your Clerkship's Skull for you!—Poole has ordered a paper——he has *found out*, he says, why the *newspapers* had become so indiffer-ent to him.—*Inventive* Genius!——he begs his kind remembrances to you— / in consequence of *the* News he burns, like Greek Fire, under all the Wets and Waters of this health-and-harvest-destroy-ing Weather.—He flames while his Barley smokes——see! he says— how it *grows out again*, ruining the prospects of those, who had cut it down!—You are harvest man enough, I suppose, to understand the metaphor.—

Jackson is, I believe, out of all doubt a bad man. Why is it, if it be—and I fear, it is—why is it that the studies of Music & Painting are so unfavorable to the human Heart?—Painters have been commonly very clever men—which is not so generally the case with Musicians—but both alike are almost uniformly

---

[1] The temporary residence of Josiah Wedgwood.

[2] An erroneous report had reached England that the *Sylph*, on which Southey's brother Thomas was a midshipman, had been captured and brought to the port of Ferrol, a seaport in the province of Coruña, Spain.

[3] On 25–26 Sept. 1799 André Masséna won a battle over the Russians at Zürich, where he had been earlier defeated by the Austrians in June.

Debauchees.—It is superfluous to say how much your account of Bampfylde interested me—/—Predisposition to Madness gave him a cast of originality—and he had a species of *Taste* which only Genius could give; but his Genius does not appear a *powerful* or *ebullient* Faculty— / nearer to Lamb's than to the Gebir-man.[1] So I judge from the few specimens *I* have seen / if you think otherwise, you are right, I doubt not.—I shall be glad to give Mr & Mrs Keenan the right hand of welcome with looks & tones in fit accompaniment— / for the Wife of a man of Genius who sympathizes effectively with her Husband in his habits & feelings is a rara avis with me; tho' a vast majority of her own sex & too many of ours will scout her for a rara piscis.—If I am well enough, Sara & I go to Bristol in a few days—I hope, they will not come in the mean time. It is singularly unpleasant to me that I cannot renew our late acquaintance in Exeter without creating very serious uneasinesses at Ottery: Northmore is so preeminently an offensive character to the Aristocrats.—He sent Payne's Books as a present to a Clergyman of my Brother's Acquaintance / a Mr Markes—this was silly enough.—Either however I will not visit Exeter, or I will visit Banfyl / for I am much taken with him.—Did Hucks say aught of having received a letter from me, from Taunton, written on the same day on which we left Ottery?——Talking of Lane & Cosserat, do you know Baugh Allen, who was I believe in the same form with you—?—Your intelligence concerning George Dyer rejoices me.—I will set about Christabel with all speed; but I do not think it a fit opening Poem.—What I think would be a fit opener, and what I would humbly lay before you as the best plan of the next anthologia,[2] I will communicate shortly in another letter entirely on this Subject.—Mohammed I will not forsake; but my money-book I *must* write first.——In the last, or at least, in a late, monthly Magazine was an Essay on a Jesuitic Conspiracy & about the Russians. There was so much Genius in it, that I suspected William Taylor for the author—but the style was so nauseously affected, so absurdly pedantic, that I was half-angry with myself for the suspicion. Have you seen Bishop Prettyman's Book?[3]——I hear, it is a curiosity. You remember Scott, the Attorney—who held such a disquisition on my Simile of Property resembling Matter rather than Blood?—and eke of St John?

[1] Coleridge did not know that Walter Savage Landor was the author of *Gebir*, published anonymously in 1798.

[2] Coleridge refers to the *Annual Anthology*, edited by Southey in 1799 and 1800. *Christabel* was not published until 1816.

[3] George Pretyman, Bishop of Lincoln, published *Elements of Christian Theology* in 1799.

And you remember too that I shewed him in my Face that there was no Room for him in my heart?—Well, Sir! this man has taken a most deadly Hatred to me—& how do you think he revenges himself?—He imagines that I write for the Morning Post—and he goes regularly to the Coffee houses, calls for the Paper—& reading in it observes aloud—'What damn'd Stuff of Poetry is always crammed in this paper——! such damn'd silly Nonsense! I wonder what Coxcomb it is that writes it! I wish, the Paper was kicked out of the Coffee House!—' Now but for Cruckshanks I could play Scott a precious Trick by sending to Stuart—the Angry Attorney, a true Tale—and I know more than enough of Scott's most singular particoloured Rascalities to make a most humorous & biting Satire of it.

I have heard of a young Quaker who went to the Lobby, with a whore under his arm, a monstrous military cock'd Hat on his Head, with a scarlet coat, & up to his mouth in flower'd Muslin—swearing too most bloodily—all 'that he might not be unlike other people!' A Quaker's Son getting himself *christen'd* to avoid being remarkable is as *improbable* a Lie as ever Self-delusion permitted the heart to impose upon the understanding—or the understanding to invent without consent of the heart.—But so it is.[1]—Soon after Lloyd's arrival at Cambridge I understand Christopher Wordsworth wrote his Uncle Mr Cookson, that Lloyd was going to read Greek with him—Cookson wrote back recommending caution & whether or no an intimacy with so marked a character *might* not be prejudicial to his academical Interests—(this in his usual mild manner—) Christopher Wordsworth returned for answer that Lloyd was by no means a Democrat, & as a proof of it, transcribed the most favorable Passages from the Edmund Oliver—and here the affair ended.—You remember Lloyd's own account of this story of course more accurately than I—and can therefore best judge how far my suspicions of falsehood & exaggeration were well-founded.—My dear Southey! the having a bad Heart, and the not having a good one are different Things. That Charles Lloyd has a bad Heart, I do not even think; but I venture to say & that openly, that he has not a good one.—He is unfit to be any man's *Friend,* and to all but a very guarded man he is a perilous *acquaintance.*— *Your* conduct towards him, while it is wise, will, I doubt not, be

[1] In an unpublished letter to Coleridge Southey had written that Charles Lloyd's 'motive for being christened was that he might not be unlike other people, . . . and that he did not mean to budge an inch in matters of conscience. . . . With the conviction I feel that he has belied you and me to each other, I am somewhat irresolute how to act towards him.' MS. Bodleian Library.

gentle—of confidence he is not worthy; but social Kindness and communicativeness purely intellectual can do you no harm, and may be the means of benefiting his character essentially. Aut ama me quia sum Dei, aut ut sim Dei, said St Augustin—and in the *laxer* sense of the word 'Ama' there is wisdom in the expression notwithstanding it's wit.—Besides, it is the way of PEACE. I have great affection for Lamb / but I have likewise a perfect Lloyd-and-Lambophobia!—Independent of the irritation attending an epistolary Controversy with them, their *Prose* comes so damn'd dear!—Lloyd especially writes with a woman's fluency in a large rambling hand—most dull tho' profuse of Feeling— / I received from them in the last Quarter Letters so many, that with the Postage I might have bought Birch's Milton.———Sara will write soon—our Love to Edith & your Mother—from Bristol perhaps I go to London[1] / but I will write you where I am.

Your's affectionately
S. T. Coleridge

299. *To Dorothy Wordsworth*

Transcript Mary Wordsworth, Dove Cottage. Pub. with omis. Memoirs of Wordsworth, *i. 147.* Across the top of her transcript Mary Wordsworth wrote: 'Extract from a letter written . . . from Keswick to D. W. to Sockburn where they left her to make an Excursion among the Lakes—Coleridge's first visit

---

[1] Shortly after this letter was written, Coleridge left Stowey for Bristol, but instead of going to London he set off with Cottle on a trip to Sockburn, Durham, where the Wordsworths were visiting the Hutchinsons. That Coleridge rushed off to Sockburn without notifying Mrs. Coleridge is evident from her letter to her sister-in-law, Mrs. George Coleridge. The letter is dated 2 Nov. 1799 and was written from Old Cleeve Vicarage, a small hamlet near Watchet and twelve miles from Nether Stowey. 'You will perceive by the date of this that all my troubles respecting the Child are at an end. He is, I thank God! in all respects perfectly well. We have been at this place above a week, that is, myself and Hartley; for Samuel has been in Bristol nearly a fortnight. He left Stowey with an intention of proceeding to London in search of his travelling Chests if he did not find them in Bristol, but fortunately they arrived at Stowey two days after his departure. I am going to Stowey to-morrow and hope to find him safe at Mr Poole's, for our Cottage is shut up. . . . Samuel, too, . . . had the Rheumatism by getting wet through, and remaining unchanged. He went to Upcott in the midst of his pain, that I might have the house, sheets, blankets, and Cloaths washed, and the latter buried, but the scent still remains. . . . I expect when I return to Stowey, if Coleridge is not there, to find a letter inviting me and the Child to Bristol, for as I have no maid I cannot remain in the house alone.' (MS. letter.) In view of the affectionate letters Coleridge sent his wife from Germany, his abrupt and unannounced departure for the north is a little surprising. Apparently he did not write to her until December, for when he wrote to Cottle early in that month he did not even know where she was!

to the North—' Of this joint journal letter written by Coleridge and Words-
worth during their tour in 1799 only the excerpts made by Mrs. Wordsworth
survive. In order to give continuity to the account of Coleridge's activities
I have printed the whole of the transcript, including the Wordsworth extracts.

Coleridge left Bristol in the company of Cottle on 22 October, 'for my most
important journey to the North', and was at Sockburn by 26 October. The
next day he, Cottle, and Wordsworth set off for the Lake Country, but on
30 October Cottle returned to Bristol by way of London. Wordsworth and
Coleridge continued their excursion, lingering several days in Grasmere, and
arrived at Keswick, presumably on 10 November. John Wordsworth, the poet's
brother, was a member of the party from 30 October to 5 November. See
G. H. B. Coleridge, 'Samuel Taylor Coleridge discovers the Lake Country',
Wordsworth and Coleridge, ed. by E. L. Griggs, 1939, pp. 135–49, for an account
of the excursion drawn from Coleridge's notebooks.

[Keswick, *circa* 10 November 1799]

. . . William has received your 2 letters. At Temple Sowerby we
met your Br. John who accompanied us to Hawes Water, Winder-
mere, Ambleside & the divine Sisters, Rydal & Grasmere—here
we [he] stayed two days, & left on Tuesday [5 November]. We
accompanied John over the fork of Helvellyn on a day when light
& darkness coexisted in contiguous masses, & the earth & sky were
but *one*! Nature lived for us in all her grandest accidents—we
quitted him by a wild Tarn just as we caught a view of the gloomy
Ulswater. Your Br. John is one of you; a man who hath solitary
usings of his own Intellect, deep in feeling, with a subtle Tact, a
swift instinct of Truth & Beauty. He interests me much.

It was most lucky for us that poor dear Cottle returned. His
timidity is indeed not greater than is easily explicable from his
lameness & sedentary STATIONERY occupations; but it is extreme,
& poor dear fellow! his self-involution (for Alfred is *his* Self) *O me
that Alfred!*[1] William & I have atchieved one good Thing—he has
solemnly promised not to publish on his own account.

S. T. C.

[W.W. writes upon the same sheet.]

. . . We left Cottle as you know on Wed. Mg. [30 October] at
Greta Bridge. We were obliged to take the Mail over Stanemoor,
the road interesting with sun & mist. At Temple Sowerby I learned
from the address of a letter lying on the table with the Cambridge
post mark, the Letter from *Kit*[2] to Mrs C.[3] that he was gone to
Cambridge. I learned also from the Woman that John was at
New-biggin. I sent a note—he came, looks very well— . . . Your
Uncle has left you *£100, nobody else is named in his Will.* Having

---

[1] Coleridge refers to Cottle's *Alfred, an Epic Poem*, 2 vols., 1801.

[2] Wordsworth's youngest brother, Christopher (1774–1846).

[3] Mrs. Crackanthorpe, widow of Wordsworth's maternal uncle, Christopher
Crackanthorpe (Cookson).

learnt our plans said he would accompany us a few days. Next day, Thursday we set off, & dined at Mr Myers', thence to Bampton where we slept—on Friday proceeded along the Lake of Hawes water (a noble scene which pleased us much) the mists hung so low upon the mountains that we could not go directly over to Amble-side, so went round by Long Sleddale to Kentmere. Next to Troutbeck, & thence by Rayrigg & Bowness—a rainy & raw day, did not stop at Bowness but went on to the Ferry—a cold passage—were much disgusted with the New Erections & objects about Windermere—thence to Hawkshead—. . . No horses or lodgings at Hawkshead; great change among the People since we were last there. Next day Sunday [3 November] by Rydal & the Road by which we approached Grasmere to Robt. Newton's. Coleridge enchanted with Grasmere & Rydal. At Robt. Newton's we have remained till to day. John left us on Tuesday; we walked with him to the Tarn. . . .

This day was a fine one & we had some grand mountain scenery—the rest of the week has been bad weather.—Yesterday we set off with a view of going to Dungeon Ghyll—the day so bad forced to return. The evening before last we walked to the upper Water fall at Rydal & saw it through the gloom, & it was very magnificent. C. was much struck with Grasmere & its neighbour-hood & I have much to say to you, you will think my plan a mad one, but I have thought of building a house there by the Lake side. John would give me £40 to buy the ground, & for £250 I am sure I could build one as good as we can wish. I speak with tolerable certainty on this head as a Devonshire Gentleman has built a Cottage there which cost a £130 which would exactly suit us every way, but the size of the bed rooms; we shall talk of this. . . .

We shall go to Buttermere the day after tomorrow but I think it will be full ten days before we shall see you. There is a small house at Grasmere[1] empty which perhaps we may take, & purchase furniture but of this we will speak; but I shall write again when I know more on this subject.

W. W.

[Coleridge writes again.]

You can feel what I cannot express for myself—how deeply I have been impressed by a world of scenery absolutely new to me. At Rydal & Grasmere I recd I think the deepest delight, yet Hawes Water thro' many a varying view kept my eyes dim with tears, and this evening, approaching Derwentwater in diversity

---

[1] Wordsworth and Dorothy entered Dove Cottage on 20 Dec. 1799. See *Early Letters*, 234.

of harmonious features, in the majesty of its beauties & in the
Beauty of its majesty—O my God! & the Black Crags close under
the snowy mountains, whose snows were pinkish with the setting
sun & the reflections from the sandy rich Clouds that floated over
some & rested upon others! It was to me a vision of a fair Country.
Why were you not with us Dorothy? Why were not you Mary with
us?

300. *To Robert Southey*

MS. Lord Latymer. Pub. with omis. Letters, *i. 312.*

Keswick, Sunday Nov. 10 [1799]

My dear Southey

I am anxious lest so long silence should seem unaffectionate / or
I would not, having so little to say, write to you from such a
distant corner of the Kingdom. I was called up to the North by
alarming accounts of Wordsworth's Health / which, thank God!
are but little more than alarms—*Since*, I have visited the Lakes /
& in a pecuniary way have made the Trip answer to me.—From
hence I go to London / having had (by accident here) a sort of offer
made to me of a pleasant kind,[1] which, if it turn out well, will
enable me & Sara to reside in London for the next four or five
months—a thing I wish extremely on many & important accounts.
So much for myself.—In my last letter I said I would give you my
reasons for thinking Christabel, *were* it finished & finished as
spiritedly as it commences, yet still an improper opening Poem.
My reason is—it cannot be expected to please all / Those who
dislike it will deem it extravagant Ravings, & go on thro' the rest
of the Collection with the feeling of Disgust—& it is not impossible
that were it liked by any, it would still not harmonize with the
real-life Poems that follow.—It ought I think to be the last.—
The first ought, me judice, to be a poem in couplets, didactic or
satirical—such a one as the lovers of genuine poetry would call
sensible and entertaining, such as the Ignoramuses & Pope-
admirers would deem genuine Poetry.—I had planned such a one;
& but for the absolute necessity of scribbling prose I should have
written it.—The great & master fault of the last anthology was the
want of arrangement / it is called a Collection, & meant to be
continued annually; yet was distinguished in nothing from any
other single volume of poems, equally good.—Your's ought to have
been a cabinet with proper compartments, & papers in them.

[1] Daniel Stuart had offered Coleridge regular employment on the *Morning
Post.*

Whereas it was only the Papers.—Some such arrangement as this should have been adopted / First, Satirical & Didactic. 2. Lyrical. 3. Narrative. 4. Levities——Sic positi quoniam suaves miscetis odores.[1]—.—Neve inter vites corylum sere,[2] is, I am convinced, excellent advice of Master Virgil's.—N.B. A Good Motto—'tis from Virgil's seventh Eclogue, 61 Line—

> Populus Alcidae gratissima, vitis Iaccho,
> Formosae myrtus Veneri, sua laurea Phoebo;
> Phyllis amat corylos.——/

But still, my dear Southey! it goes grievously against the Grain with me, that *you* should be editing anthologies. I would to Heaven, that you could afford to write nothing, or at least, to publish nothing till the completion & publication of the Madoc.[3] I feel as certain, as my mind dare feel on any subject, that it would lift you with a spring into a reputation that would give immediate sale to your after Compositions, & a license of writing more at ease.—Whereas Thalaba[4] would gain you (for a time at least) more ridiculers than admirers—& the Madoc might in consequence be welcomed with an Ecce iterum.—Of course, I mean the verse & metres of Thalaba.——Do, do, my dear Southey! publish the Madoc quam citissime—not hastily, but yet speedily.—I will instantly publish an Essay on Epic Poetry in reference to it— / I have been reading the Æneid—& there you will be all victorious, excepting the importance of Æneas, & his connection with events existing in Virgil's Time.—This cannot be said of Madoc / there are other faults in the construction of your poem, but nothing compared to those in the Æneid— / Homer I shall read too—that is— if I can / for the good old . . . [remainder of manuscript missing.]

301. *To Joseph Cottle*

Pub. Early Rec. *i. 255.* To this letter Cottle added as a postscript a passage from Letter 195.

Leaving Keswick on 11 November, Wordsworth and Coleridge continued their tour of the Lake Country for another week or ten days; but by 24 November Coleridge had parted from Wordsworth and was back again with the Hutchinsons at Sockburn. A notebook entry for that date records a flirtation with Sara Hutchinson, for whom he was to harbour a hopeless passion for many years. See T. M. Raysor, 'Coleridge and "Asra"', *Studies in Philology*, July 1929, p. 307.

[1] Virgil, *Eclogue*, ii. 55.
[2] Id. *Georgics*, ii. 299.
[3] *Madoc*, published 1805.
[4] *Thalaba the Destroyer*, published 1801.

London, [*Circa* 1 December 1799][1]

Dear Cottle,

If Mrs. Coleridge be in Bristol, pray desire her to write to me immediately, and I beg you, the moment you receive this letter, to send to No. 17, Newfoundland Street, to know whether she be there. I have written to Stowey, but if she be in Bristol, beg her to write me of it by return of post, that I may immediately send down some cash for her travelling expenses, &c. We shall reside in London for the next four months.

God bless you, Cottle, I love you,
S. T. Coleridge.

302. *To William Wordsworth*

Pub. Memoirs of Wordsworth, *i. 160.*

London, Dec. 1799[2]

As to myself, I dedicate my nights and days to Stuart. . . . By all means let me have the tragedy and 'Peter Bell' as soon as possible.[3]

303. *To Robert Southey*

Address: Mr. Southey | Kingsdown Parade | Bristol   Single
MS. Lord Latymer. Pub. Letters, *i. 314.*
Postmark: 19 December 1799.

Thursday Evening. [19 December 1799][4]

My dear Southey

I pray you in your next give me the particulars of your Health. I hear accounts so contradictory that I know only enough to be a good deal frightened.—You will surely think it your duty to suspend all intellectual exertion—as to money, you will get it easily enough. You may easily make twice the money you receive from Stewart by the use of the Scissors / for your name is prodigiously high among the London Publishers. I would to God, your Health permitted you to come to London—You might have Lodgings in the same House with us, & this I am certain of, that

---

[1] Coleridge arrived in London 27 Nov. 1799; this letter must have been written shortly afterwards.

[2] This fragment is probably from one of the 'two Letters' Wordsworth mentions finding at Grasmere on his arrival there on 20 Dec. *Early Letters*, 234.

[3] On 24 Dec. Wordsworth wrote in answer to this letter: 'As to the Tragedy and Peter Bell, D will do all in her power to put them forward.' Ibid. 237.

[4] Misdated 'December 9, [1799]' by E. H. Coleridge.

not even Kingsdown is a more airy or healthful Place. I have
enough for us to do that would be mere Child's work to us, and
in which the Women might assist us essentially—by the doing of
which we might easily get 150£ each before the first of April. This
I speak not from Guess but from absolute Conditions with Book-
sellers. The principal work to which I allude would be likewise a
great source of amusement & profit to us in the Execution / &
assuredly we should be a mutual comfort to each other. This I
should *press* on you, were not *Davy*[1] at Bristol—but he is indeed an
admirable young man / not only must he be of comfort to you / but
on whom can you place such reliance as a medical man?—But for
Davy, I should advise your coming to London / the difference of
expence for three months could not be above 50£—I do not see
how it could be half as much. But I pray you write me all parti-
culars—how you have been, how you are—& what you think the
particular nature of your Disease.

Now for poor George.[2] Assuredly I am ready & willing to become
his Bondsman for 500£, if on the whole you think the Scheme a
good one—. I see enough of the Boy to be fully convinced of his
goodness & well-intentionedness—of his present or probable
Talents I know little. To remain all his Life an under Clerk as many
have done; and earn 50£ a year in his old age with a trembling
hand——alas! that were a dreary Prospect. No Creature under the
Sun is so helpless, so unfitted, I should think, for any other mode
of Life as a Clerk, a mere Clerk.—Yet still many have begun so—&
risen into wealth & importance—& it is not impossible that before
his term closed we might be able, if nought better offered, perhaps
to procure him a place in some public office.—We might between
us keep him neat in Cloaths from our own Wardrobes, I should
think—& I am ready to allow five guineas this year in addition to
Mr Savary's twelve £. More I am not justified to *promise*. Yet still
I think it matter of much reflection with you—The Commercial
Prospects of this Country are, in my opinion, gloomy—our present
Commerce is enormous—; that it must diminish after a peace is
certain / & should any accident injure the West India Trade, & give
to France a Paramountship in the American Affections, that
diminution would be vast indeed—& of course, great would be the
number of Clerks etc wholly out of employment. This is no visionary
speculation: for we are consulting concerning *a Life* for probably

---

[1] Humphry Davy (1778–1829). Davy, a native of Cornwall, arrived in
Bristol on 2 Oct. 1798 to join Dr. Beddoes's Pneumatic Institution. Coleridge
probably met him just before going from Bristol to Sockburn in Oct. 1799.

[2] George Fricker, Mrs. Coleridge's brother. Southey had written that 'Savary
will take George into his bank—if we each become security for £500.'

50 years. I should have given a more intense conviction to the goodness of the former Scheme of apprenticing him to a Printer / & would make every exertion to raise any share of the money wanting.—However, all this is talk at random / I leave it to you to decide.—What does Charles Danvers think? He has been very kind to George—but to whom is he not kind, that body-blood-bone-muscle-nerve-heart & head-good Man!—I lay final stress on his opinion in almost every thing except verses— / those I know more about than he does—'God bless him, to use a vulgar Phrase.'—This is a quotation from Godwin who used these words in conversation with me & Davy—the pedantry of atheism tickled me hugely.—Godwin is no great Things in Intellect; but in heart & manner he is all the better for having been the Husband of Mary Wolstonecroft—.[1]

Why did not George Dyer (who bye the bye has written a silly milk-&-water Life of you,[2] in which your Talents for *pastoral & rural* imagery are extolled, in which you are asserted to be a Republican) why did not George Dyer send to the Anthology that Poem in the last monthly Magazine?—It is so very far superior to any thing I have ever seen of his—& might have made some atonement for his former Transgressions.—God love him—he is a very good man; but he ought not to degrade himself by writing Lives of Living Characters for Phillips; & all his Friends make wry faces, peeping out of the Pillory of his advertisemental Notes.—I hold to my former opinion concerning the *arrangement* of the anthology / & the Booksellers, with whom *I* have talked, coincide with me.— On this I am decided, that all the *light* Pieces should be put together under one tit[le] with a motto thus—Nos haec novimus esse nihil[3]—Phillis amat corylos.—.—I am afraid that I have scarce poetic Enthusiasm enough to finish Christabel—but the poem, with which Davy is so much delighted, I probably may finish time enough.—I shall probably *not* publish my letters—& if I do, I shall most certainly *not* publish any verses in them. Of course, I expect to see them in the Anthology.—As to title, I

[1] Mary Wollstonecraft (1759–97), author of *Vindication of the Rights of Women*, 1792, had married Godwin in Mar. 1797.

[2] 'A gossiping account of the early history and writings of "Mr. Robert Southey" appeared in *Public Characters for 1799–1800*, a humble forerunner of *Men of the Time*, published by Richard Phillips, the founder of the *Monthly Magazine*, and afterwards knighted as a sheriff of the city of London. Possibly Coleridge was displeased at the mention of his name in connexion with Pantisocracy, and still more by the following sentence: "The three young poetical friends, Lovel, Southey, and Coleridge, married three sisters. Southey is attached to domestic life, and, fortunately, was very happy in his matrimonial connection."' *Letters*, i. 317 n.

[3] Southey used this motto in *The Minor Poems of Robert Southey*, 3 vols., 1815.

should wish a fictitious one or none / were I sure, that I could finish the poem, I spoke of.—I do not know how to get the conclusion of Mrs Robinson's Poem for you—perhaps, it were better omitted—& I mean to put the thoughts of that Concert Poem into smoother metre.[1]—Our 'Devil's Thoughts'[2] have been admired far & wide—most *enthusiastically* admired! I wish to have my name in the Collection at all events; but I should better like it to better poems than those I have been hitherto able to give you.—But I will write again on Saturday. Supposing that Johnson should mean to do nothing more with the Fears in Solitude & the two accompanying Poems, would they be excluded from the Plan of your Anthology?[3]—There were not above two hundred sold—and what is that to a newspaper Circulation? Collins's Odes were thus reprinted in Dodsley's Collection.

As to my future Residence I can say nothing—only this, that to be near you would be a strong motive with me, for my Wife's sake as well as myself.—I think it not impossible, that a number might be found to go with you & settle in a warmer Climate.—My kind Love to your Wife—Sara & Hartley arrived safe, and here they are—No / 21, Buckingham Street, Strand.—God bless you

& your affectionate
S. T. Coleridge

P.S. Mary Hayes[4] is writing the Lives of famous Women—& is now about your friend, *Joan.* She begs you to tell her what books to consult, or to communicate something to her.—This from Tobin who sends his Love.—

304. *To the Editor of the 'Morning Post'*

Pub. Morning Post, *21 December 1799.* Since the poem, Introduction to the Tale of the Dark Ladie, *is printed in* Poems, *ii. 1052, in the form in which it appeared in the* Morning Post, *it has been omitted here. See Letter 337 for the version of the poem published in* Lyrical Ballads, *1800, where it is entitled* Love.

December 21, 1799

Sir,

The following Poem is the Introduction to a somewhat longer one, for which I shall solicit insertion on your next open day. The use of the Old Ballad word, *Ladie,* for Lady, is the only piece of

---

[1] First published in the *Morning Post*, 24 Sept. 1799. *Poems*, i. 324.

[2] This joint production of Coleridge and Southey was published anonymously in the *Morning Post*, 6 Sept. 1799. *Poems*, i. 319.

[3] *Fears in Solitude*, and the accompanying poems, *France, an Ode*, and *Frost at Midnight*, published by Johnson in 1798, were not included in the *Annual Anthology*.

[4] Mary Hays published *Female Biography, or Memoirs of Illustrious and Celebrated Women*, 6 vols., 1803.

obsoleteness in it; and as it is professedly a tale of antient times, I trust, that 'the affectionate lovers of venerable antiquity' (as Cambden says) will grant me their pardon, and perhaps may be induced to admit a force and propriety in it. A heavier objection may be adduced against the Author, that in these times of fear and expectation, when novelties *explode* around us in all directions, he should presume to offer to the public a silly tale of old fashioned love: and, five years ago, I own, I should have allowed and felt the force of this objection. But, alas! explosion has succeeded explosion so rapidly, that novelty itself ceases to appear new; and it is possible that now, even a simple story, wholly unspired [unspiced?] with politics or personality, may find some attention amid the hubbub of Revolutions, as to those who have remained a long time by the falls of Niagara, the lowest whispering becomes distinctly audible.

S. T. Coleridge.

305. *To Robert Southey*

Address: Mr Southey | Kingsdown Parade | Bristol   *Single*
MS. Lord Latymer. Pub. Letters, *i. 319.*
Postmark: 25 December 1799.

Tuesday Night—12 o/clock. [24 December 1799]

My dear Southey

My Spinosism (if Spinosism it be and i' faith 'tis very like it) disposed me to consider this big City as that part of the Supreme *One*, which the prophet Moses was allowed to see.——I should be more disposed to pull off my shoes, beholding him in a *Bush*, than while I am forcing my reason to believe that even in Theatres he is, yea, even in the Opera House.—/——

Your Thalaba will beyond all doubt bring you 200£, if you will sell it at once—but do not print at a venture, under the notion of selling the Edition——I assure you, that Longman regretted the Bargain he made with Cottle concerning the 2nd Edition of the Joan of Arc—& is indisposed to similar negociations—; but most & very eager to have the property of your works at almost any price.—If you have not heard it from Cottle, why, you may hear it from me—that in the arrangement of Cottle's affairs in London the whole & total Copyright of your Joan & the first Volume of your poems (exclusive of what Longman had before given) was taken by him at 370£—You are a strong Swimmer & have borne up poor Joey with all his leaden weights about him, his own & other people's.—Nothing has answered to him but your works. By me he has lost somewhat—by Fox, Amos, & himself *very much*. I can

sell your Thalaba quite as well in your absence as in your presence.—
I am employed from I-rise to I-set—i.e. from 9 in the morning to
12 at night—a pure Scribbler. My Mornings to Booksellers' Com-
pilations[1]—after dinner to Stewart, who pays *all* my expences
here, let them be what they will—: the earnings of the Morning go
to make up an 150£ for my year's expenditure—: for supposing
all clear, my year's (1800) allowance is anticipated. But this I can
do by the first of April / at which time I leave London.—For
Stewart I write often his leading Paragraphs, on Secession, Peace,
Essay on the new French Constitution, Advice to Friends of
Freedom,[2] Critiques on Sir W. Anderson's nose,[3] Ode to Georgiana,
D. of D.[4] (horribly misprinted) christmas Carol,[5] &c &c—any thing
not bad in the Paper that is not your's is mine—so if any Verses
there strike you as worthy the Anthology, 'do me the honor,
Sir!'—However, in the course of a week I *do mean* to conduct a
series of Essays in that paper, which may be of public Utility. So
much for myself—except that I long to be out of London; & that
my Xstmas Carol is a quaint performance—& in as strict a sense
as is *possible*, an Impromptu. Had I done all I had planned, that
Ode to the Dutchess would have been a better thing than it is—it
being somewhat dullish/—I have bought the Beauties of the Anti-
jacobin—& Attorneys & Counsellors advise me to prosecute—
offer to undertake it, so as that I shall have neither trouble or
expence. They say, it is a clear Case.[6]—I will speak to Johnson
about the Fears in Solitude—if he give them up, they are your's.
That dull ode has been printed often enough; & may now be
allowed to 'sink with dead swoop, & to the bottom *go*'—to quote
an admired Author[7];—but the two others will do with a little
Trimming.——

My dear Southey! I have said nothing concerning that which
most oppresses me. Immediately on my leaving London, I fall to

[1] There is no evidence that Coleridge prepared any 'Compilations', but he
certainly entered into negotiations with Richard Phillips. See Letters 373 and
375, for Phillips's demand for the repayment of £25.

[2] For a list of Coleridge's forty prose contributions appearing in the *Morning
Post* from 7 Dec. 1799 to 21 Apr. 1800 see Wise, *Bibliography*, 257–64.

[3] *On Sir Rubicund Naso, Morning Post*, 7 Dec. 1799.

[4] Ibid., 24 Dec. 1799. [5] Ibid., 25 Dec. 1799.

[6] In 1799 *The New Morality*, a poem which had appeared in the *Anti-
Jacobin*, 9 July 1798, was reprinted in *The Beauties of the Anti-Jacobin*, with
an editorial note reading in part: 'He [Coleridge] has left his native country,
commenced citizen of the world, left his poor children fatherless and his wife
destitute. *Ex his disce* his friends Lamb and Southey!' Coleridge did not take
legal action for what Chambers calls a 'premature' charge. Chambers, *Life*,
92–93 and 120–1. See also *Biog. Lit.*, 1817, i. 70 n.

[7] See Coleridge's, *To the Author of Poems*, line 14.

the Life of Lessing—till that is done, till I have given the *Ws* some proof that I am *endeavoring* to do well for my fellow-creatures, I cannot stir. That being done—I would accompany you—& see no impossibility of forming a pleasant little Colony for a few years in Italy or the South of France. Peace will soon come. God love you, my dear Southey!—I would wr[ite] to Stewart & give up his paper *immediately.* You should [do] nothing that does not absolutely *please* you. Be idle—be very idle! The habits of your mind are such that you will necessarily do much—but be as idle as you can.

Our love to dear Edith—if you see Mary, tell her that we have received our Trunk. Hartley is quite well, & my talkativeness is his, without diminution on my side. 'Tis strange, but certainly many things go in the Blood, beside Gout & Scrophula.—Yesterday I dined at Longman's & met Pratt, & that honest piece of prolix Dullity & Nullity, young Towers who desired to be remembered to you. To morrow Sara & I dine at Mister Gobwin's as Hartley calls him—who gave the philosopher such a Rap on the shins with a ninepin that Gobwin in huge pain *lectured* Sara on his boisterous-ness. I was not at home. Est modus in rebus. Moshes is somewhat too rough & noisy / but the cadaverous Silence of Godwin's Children is to me quite catacomb-ish: & thinking of Mary Wolsten-croft I was oppressed by it the day Davy & I dined there. God love you, &

S. T. Coleridge

306. *To Robert Southey*

MS. Lord Latymer, Pub. with omis. Letters, *i. 328.*

No 21 Buckingham Street—Saturday. [28 December 1799][1]
My dear Southey

I will see Longman on Tuesday at the farthest; but I pray you, send me up what you have done, if you can, as I will read it to him; unless he will take my word for it. But we cannot expect that he will treat finally without seeing a considerable Specimen. Send it by the Coach; and be assured that it will be as safe as in your own Escritoire—& I will *r*emit it the very day Longman or any Bookseller has treated for it satisfactorily. Less than 200£ I would not take.—Have you tried warm Bathing in a high Tempera-ture?——As to your Travelling, your first Business must of course be to *settle.* The Greek Islands & Turkey in General are one con-tinued Hounslow Heath, only that the Highwaymen there have

[1] This letter was written in answer to one from Southey, dated 27 Dec. 1799 (see *Life and Corres.* ii. 35); and it was answered by Southey on 1 Jan. 1800. (See *National Review,* 1892, p. 704.)

an awkward Habit of murdering People. As to Poland and
Hungary—the detestable Roads & Inns of them both, & the
severity of the Climate in the former render travelling there little
suited to your state of Health.—O for Peace & the South of
France!—What a detestable Villainy is not this new Constitution?
I have written all that relates to it which has appeared in the
Morning Post—and not without strength or elegance. But the
French are Children.—'Tis an infirmity to hope or fear concerning
them—I wish they had a King again, if it were only that Sieyes
& Bonaparte might be *hung*. Guillotining is too a *republican* a
death for such Reptiles!——You'll write another Quarter for
Stewart? you will torture yourself for 12 or 13 guineas? I pray
you, do not do so!—You might get without the exertion and with
but little more expenditure of time from 50 to an 100£.—Thus,
for instance—Bring together on your table or skim over succes-
sively—Brucker, Lardner's History of Heretics, Russel's Modern
Europe, and Andrews' History of England[1]—& write a History of
Levellers and the Levelling Principle under some goodly Title,
neither praising or abusing them. Lacedaemon, Crete, and the
attempts at agrarian Laws in Rome—all these you have by
heart.——Plato & Zeno are I believe nearly all that relates to the
purpose in Brucker—Lardner's is a most amusing Book to read—
Write only a sheet of Letter Paper a day, which you can do easily
in an hour, and in 12 weeks you will have produced (without any
toil of Brains, observing none but chronological arrangement, &
giving your[self] little more than the trouble of Transcription)
24 Sheets Octavo—I will gladly write a philosophical Introduction
that shall enlighten without offending, & therein state the rise of
Property &c.—For this you might secure 60 or 70 guineas—and
receive half the money on producing the first 8 Sheets—in a
month from your first Commencement of the work.——Many
other works occur to me; but I mention this, because it might be
doing great good—in[asmuch] as Boys & Youths would read it
with far different Impressions from their Fathers & Godfathers—
& yet the latter find nothing alarming in the nature of the Work,
it being purely Historical.—If I am not deceived by the *recency*
of their date, my ode to the Dutchess, & my Xtmas Carol will *do*
for your Anthology.—I have therefore transcribed them for you.
But I need not ask you for God's sake to use your own Judgment
without spare.

[1] Nathaniel Lardner, *The History of the Heretics of the Two First Centuries
after Christ*, 1780; William Russell, *The History of Modern Europe*, 5 vols.,
1786; J. P. Andrews, *The History of Great Britain from the Death of Henry VIII
to the Accession of James VI of Scotland*, 1796.

Xtmas Carol[1]

1

The Shepherds went their hasty way
And found the lowly Stable shed,
Where the Virgin Mother lay.
And now they check'd their eager Tread,
For to the Babe, that at her Bosom clung,
A Mother's Song the Virgin Mother sung!

2

They told her, how a glorious Light
Streaming from an heavenly Throng
Around them shone, suspending Night!
While sweeter, than a Mother's Song,
Blest Angels heralded the Saviour's Birth,
Glory to God on high! and PEACE ON EARTH!

3

She listen'd to the Tale divine
And closer still the Babe she prest;
And while she cry'd, 'The Babe is mine![']
The Milk rush'd faster to her Breast.
Joy rose within her, like a Summer's Morn:
'PEACE, PEACE ON EARTH! The Prince of Peace is born![']

4

Thou Mother of the Prince of Peace,
Poor, simple, and of low estate!
That Strife should vanish, Battle cease,
O why does this thy soul elate?
Sweet music's loudest note, the Poet's Story,
Didst thou ne'er love to hear of Fame & Glory.

5

And is not WAR a youthful King,
A stately Hero clad in Mail?
Beneath his footsteps Laurels spring,
Him Earth's majestic Monarchs hail
Their Friend, their Playmate! And his bold bright Eye
Compels the Maiden's love-confessing Sigh!

[Remainder of manuscript is missing.]

[1] *Poems*, i. 338.

307. *To Thomas Poole*

Pub. Thomas Poole, *i. 1.*

December 31st, 1799

. . . I work from I-rise to I-set (that is, from 9 A.M. to 12 at night), almost without intermission. . . . I hope you receive the papers regularly. They are regularly sent, as I commonly put them in myself. . . .

Being so hurried for time I should have delayed writing till to-morrow; but to-day is the last day of the year, and a sort of superstitious feeling oppressed me that the year should not end without my writing, if it were only to subscribe myself with the old words of an old affection. . . .

God bless you, and him who is ever, ever yours—who, among all his friends, has ever called and ever felt you the Friend.

S. T. Coleridge.

308. *To Humphry Davy*

Address: Mr Davy | the Pneumatic Institution | Bristol   *Single*
MS. Royal Institution. Pub. E. L. G. i. 130. The holograph of this letter has a number of holes burned in it.
Postmark: 1 January 1800.

JAN. 1. 1800

My dear Davy

Longman deems it best for you to publish *a Volume*, & be determined by the Nature of the Sale at what interval you will publish a second—the Volume of what size you find convenient. And you may of course begin printing when you like. All the tradesman part of the Business Longman will settle with Biggs & Cottle.[1]——I expected to have heard from Southey—tell him, I have seen Longman, & find him all willingness. But I could only speak in generals; & am waiting anxiously for the arrival of the first Books.——

Davy! Davy! if the public Good did not iron and adamant you to England & Bristol, what a little colony might we [no]t make— / Tobin, I am sure, wo[uld] go—& Wordsworth—& I—& Southey.— Precious Stuff for Dreams—& God knows, I have no time for them!—

Questions.

On dipping my foot & leg into very hot water the first sensation

---

[1] Davy's *Researches, Chemical and Philosophical, chiefly concerning Nitrous Oxide, or Dephlogisticated Nitrous Air, and its Respiration,* published in 1800 by J. Johnson.

was identical with th[at] of having dipped it into very cold.—This identity recurred as often as I took my leg out in order to pour in the hot water from the Kettle, & put it in again. How is this explained in a philosophical Language divested of corpuscular Theories?

Define Disgust in philosophical Language—.—Is it not, speaking as a materialist, always a stomach-sensation conjoined with an idea?

What is the cause of that sense of cold, which accompanies inhalation, after having eat peppermint Drops?

If you don't answer me these, I'll send them to the Lady's Diary—where you may find fifty Questions of the same Depth & Kidney.—

A Private Query—On our system of Death does [it] not follow, that killing a bad man mi[ght do] him a great deal of Good? And that [Bon]aparte wants a gentle Dose of this kind, dagger or bullet ad libitum?——I wish in your Researches that you & Beddoes would give a compact compressed History of the Human Mind for the last Century—considered simply as to the acquisition of Ideas or new arrangement of them. Or if you won't do it there, do it for me—& I will print it with an Essay I am now writing on the principles of Population & Progressiveness.—

Godwin talks evermore of you with lively affection.—'What a pity that such a Man should degrade his vast Talents to Chemistry'—cried he to me.—Why, quoth I, how, Godwin! can you thus talk of a science, of which neither you nor I understand an iota? &c &c—& I defended Chemistry as knowingly at least as Godwin attacked it—affirmed that it united the opposite advantages of immaterializing [the] mind without destroying the definiteness of [the] Ideas—nay even while it gave clearness to them—And eke that being necessarily [per]formed with the passion of Hope, it was p[oetica]l—& we both agreed (for G. as we[ll as I] thinks himself a Poet) that *the Poet* is the Greatest possible character—&c &c. Modest Creatures!—Hurra, my dear Southey!—You, [& I,] & Godwin, & Shakespere, & Milton, with what an athanasiophagous Grin we shall march together—*we poets*: Down with all the rest of the World!—By the word athanasiophagous I mean devouring Immortality by anticipation—'Tis a sweet Word!—

God bless you, my dear Davy! Take my nonsense like a pinch of snuff—sneeze it off, it clears the head—& to Sense & yourself again——With most affectionate esteem

Your's ever
S. T. Coleridge

309. *To Thomas Wedgwood*

Address: Thomas Wedgewood Esq. | Cornwallis House | Clifton | Bristol
Single
MS. Wedgwood Museum. Pub. with omis. Tom Wedgwood, *74.*
Postmark: 2 January 1800.

No / 21, Buckingham Street, Strand.

My dear Sir

I am sitting by a fire in a rug great Coat. Your Room is doubtless
to a greater degree air-tight than mine; or your notion of Tartarus
would veer round to the Groenlanders' creed. It is most bar-
barously cold: and you, I fear, can shield yourself from it only by
perpetual imprisonment. If any place in the southern Climates
were in a state of real quiet & likely to continue so, should you feel
no inclination to migrate?—Poor Southey, from over great In-
dustry, as I suspect, the Industry too of solitary Composition, has
reduced himself to a terrible state of weakness—& is determined
to leave this Country as soon as he has finished the Poem on which
he is now employed. 'Tis a melancholy thing—so young a man &
one whose Life has ever been so simple and self-denying!—O for
Peace & the South of France.—I could almost too wish for a
Bourbon King if it were only that Sieyes & Buonaparte might
finish their career in the old orthodox way of Hanging.—Thank
God, I have *my Health perfectly* & I am working hard—yet the
present state of human affairs presses on me for days together, so
as to deprive me of all my chearfulness. It is probable, that a man's
private & personal connections & interests ought to be uppermost
in his daily & hourly Thoughts, & that the dedication of much
hope & fear to subjects which are perhaps disproportionate to our
faculties & powers, is a disease. But I have had this disease so long,
& my early Education was so undomestic, that I know not how to
get rid of it; or even to wish to get rid of it. Life were so flat a thing
without Enthusiasm—that if for a moment it leave me, I have a
sort of stomach-sensation attached to all my Thoughts, like those
which succeed to the pleasurable operation of a dose of Opium.
Now I make up my mind to a sort of heroism in believing the pro-
gressiveness of all nature, during the present melancholy state of
Humanity—& on this subject I am now writing / and no work, on
which I ever employed myself, makes me so happy while I am
writing.—

I shall remain in London till April—the expences of my last year
made it necessary for me to exert my industry; and many other
good ends are answered at the same time. Where I next settle, I

shall continue; & that must be in a state of retirement & rustica-
tion. It is therefore good for me to have a run of society—& that
various, & consisting of marked characters!—Likewise by being
obliged to write without much elaboration I shall greatly improve
myself in naturalness & facility of style / & the particular subjects
on which I write for money, are nearly connected with my future
schemes.—My mornings I give to compilations, which I am sure
cannot be wholly useless—& for which by the beginning of April
I shall have earned nearly an 150£—my evenings to the Theatres—
as I am to conduct a sort of Dramaturgy, a series of Essays on the
Drama, both it's general principles, and likewise in reference to
the present State of the English Theatres. This I shall publish in the
Morning Post[1]—the attendance on the Theatres costs me nothing,
& Stuart, the Editor, covers my expences in London. Two mornings
& one whole day I dedicate to the Essay on the possible Pro-
gressiveness of Man & on the principles of Population.—In April
I return to my greater work—the Life of Lessing.—My German
Chests are arrived; but I have them not yet—but expect them from
Stowey daily——when they come, I shall send a little pacquet
down to you—.

To pay my Wife's travelling expences & al[so] my first expences
in London I borrowed 25£ from my friend Purkis, for which I gave
him an order on your Brother, York Street, dating it Jan. 5,
1800.[2]—Will you be so kind as to mention this to him—He will
be kind enough to excuse my having done this without having
previously written; but I have every reason to believe, that I shall
have no occasion to draw again till the year 1801—& I believe, that
as I now [stand], I have not anticipated beyond the year; if I have
wholly anticipated that.—I shall write to Jos. tomorrow for
certain.—

I have seen a good deal of Godwin who has just published a
novel.[3] I like him for thinking so well of Davy. He talks of him
every where as the most extraordinary human Being, he had ever
met with. I cannot say that: for I know one whom I feel to be the
superior—; but I never met so extraordinary a young man.—I
have likewise dined with Horne Tooke. He is a clear-headed old
man, as every man needs must be who attends to the real import
of words; but there is a sort of charletannery [*sic*] in his manner
that did not please me. He makes such a mystery & difficulty out
of plain & palpable Things—and never tells you any thing without
first exciting & detaining your Curiosity. But it were a bad Heart

[1] For contributions recently identified see *P.M.L.A.*, June 1954, p. 681.
[2] See Letters 326 and 329.
[3] Godwin's *St. Leon, a Tale of the 16th Century*, was published in 1799.

that could not pardon worse faults than these in the Author of the Epea Pteroenta.——

Believe me, my dear Sir! with much affection your's S. T. C.

310. *To William Godwin*

Address: Mr Godwin | The Polygon | Sommers' Town
MS. Lord Abinger. Pub. William Godwin, *ii.* 1.
Postmark: 8 January 1800.

Wednesday Morning Jan. 8. 1800

My dear Sir

Tomorrow & Friday Business rises almost above smothering point with me, over chin & mouth—! but on Saturday Evening I shall be perfectly at leisure, and shall calender an Evening spent with you on so interesting a subject among my Noctes Atticae. If this do not suit your engagements, mention any other day, and I will make it suit mine—

Your's with esteem
S. T. Coleridge

P.S. How many Thousand Letter-writers will in the first fortnight of this month write a 7 first, & then transmogrify it into an 8—in the dates of their Letters! I like to catch myself doing that which involves any identity of the human Race. Hence I like to talk of the Weather—& in the Fall never omit observing—How short the Days grow! How the Days shorten! &c. Yet even that would fall, a melancholy phrase indeed on the heart of a Blind Man!—

311. *To the Editor of the 'Morning Post'*

Pub. Morning Post, *10 January 1800*.

January 10, 1800

Mr. Editor,

An unmetrical letter from Talleyrand[1] to Lord Grenville[2] has already appeared, and from an authority too high to be questioned: otherwise I could adduce some arguments for the exclusive authenticity of the following metrical epistle.[3] The very epithet which the wise ancients used, '*aurea carmina*,' might have been

---

[1] Charles Maurice de Talleyrand-Périgord (1754–1838) was appointed Minister of Foreign Affairs by Bonaparte in 1799.

[2] William Wyndham Grenville (1759–1834), Baron Grenville, was Secretary of State for Foreign Affairs from 1791 until 1801.

[3] Coleridge's lines, *Talleyrand to Lord Grenville*, were published in the *Morning Post* along with this letter. See *Poems*, i. 341.

supposed likely to have determined the choice of the French Minister in favour of verse; and the rather, when we recollect that this phrase of '*golden verses*' is applied emphatically to the works of that philosopher, who imposed *silence* on all with whom he had to deal. Besides, is it not somewhat improbable that Talleyrand should have preferred prose to rhyme, when the latter alone *has got the chink*? Is it not likewise curious, that in our official answer, no notice whatever is taken of the Chief Consul, Bonaparte, as if there had been no such person existing; notwithstanding that his existence is pretty generally admitted, nay, that some have been so rash as to believe, that he has created as great a sensation in the world as Lord Grenville, or even the Duke of Portland? But the Minister of Foreign Affairs, Talleyrand, *is* acknowledged, which, in our opinion, could not have happened, had he written only that insignificant prose-letter, which seems to precede Bonaparte's, as in old romances a dwarf always ran before to proclaim the advent or arrival of knight or giant. That Talleyrand's character and practices more resemble those of some *regular* Governments than Bonaparte's I admit; but this of itself does not appear a satisfactory explanation. However, let the letter speak for itself. The second line is supererogative in syllables, whether from the oscitancy of the transcriber, or from the trepidation which might have overpowered the modest Frenchman, on finding himself in the act of writing to so *great* a man, I shall not dare to determine. A few Notes are added by

Your servant,
GNOME.

P.S.—As mottoes are now fashionable, especially if taken from out of the way books, you may prefix, if you please, the following lines from Sidonius Apollinaris:

> Saxa, et robora, corneasque fibras
> Mollit dulciloquâ canorus arte!

312. *To Daniel Stuart*

Address: D. Stuart Esq. | Morning Post Office
MS. British Museum. Pub. Letters from the Lake Poets, *1889, p.* 3.

[January 1800][1]

Dear Stuart

I have a particular reason for begging you not to expect to see me till Sunday Evening. At that time you will see me—& I will

---

[1] This brief note is undated, but is endorsed by Stuart 'Supposed 1800 Jany.'

convince you that I am not trifling with your patience: & that
what I am now doing is to secure the regularity of my future
efforts with you.

Your's,

S. T. Coleridge.

313. *To Thomas Poole*

Pub. Thomas Poole, *ii. 1.*

[January 1800][1]

. . . the situation, is delicious; all I could wish. . . .[2] Sara being
Sara, and I being I, we must live in a town or else close to one, so
that she may have neighbours and acquaintances. For my friends
form not that society which is of itself sufficient to a woman. I
know nowhere else but Stowey (for to Bristol my objections are
insurmountable), but our old house in Stowey, and that situation
will not do for us. God knows where we can go; for that situation
which suits my wife does not suit me, and what suits me does not
suit my wife.[3] However, that which is, is,—a truth which always
remains equally clear, but not always equally pleasant. . . .

314. *To Robert Southey*

Addressed and franked: London Jan twenty-five 1800. | Mr Southey | Kings-
down Parade | Bristol   H. Wycombe
MS. Lord Latymer. Pub. with omis. Letters, *i. 322.*
Postmark: 25 ⟨January⟩ 1800.

Sat. 25. 1800—Jan.

My dear Southey

No day passes in which I do not as it were yearn after you / but
in truth my occupations have lately swoln above smothering
Point—I am over mouth & nostrils. I have inclosed a Poem which
Mrs Robinson gave me for your Anthology—She is a woman of
undoubted Genius. There was a poem of her's in this Morning's
paper which both in metre and matter pleased me much—She
overloads every thing; but I never knew a human Being with so
full a mind—bad, good, & indifferent, I grant you, but full, &
overflowing. This Poem I *asked* for you, because I thought the
metre stimulating—& some of the Stanzas really *good*—The first
line of the 12th would of itself redeem a worse Poem.—I think,

---

[1] This letter probably precedes Poole's letter to Coleridge of 21 Jan. 1800.
Thomas Poole, ii. 2.
[2] Coleridge refers to a house at Aisholt, some three miles from Stowey.
[3] Cf. the Latin passage in Letter 317.

you will agree with me; but should you not, yet still put it *in*, my
dear fellow! for my sake, & out of respect to a Woman-poet's
feelings.[1]—Miss Hays I have seen. Charles Lloyd's conduct has
been atrocious beyond what you stated—. Lamb himself confessed
to me, that during the time in which he kept up his ranting senti-
mental Correspondence with Miss Hays, he frequently read her
Letters in company, as a subject for *laughter*—& then sate down &
answered them quite a la Rosseau! Poor Lloyd! every Hour new-
creates him—he is his own Posterity in a perpetually flowing
Series—& his Body unfortunately retaining an external Identity,
THEIR mutual contradictions & disagreeings are united under one
name, & of course are called Lies, Treachery, & Rascality!—I
would not give him up; but that the same circumstances, which
have wrenched his Morals, prevent in him any salutary Exercise
of Genius—. / And therefore he is not worth to the World, that I
should embroil & embrangle myself in his Interests!

Of Miss Hay's intellect I do not think so highly, as you, or
rather, to speak sincerely, I think, not *contemptuously*, but
certainly very *despectively* thereof.—Yet I think you likely in this
case to have judged better than I—for to hear a Thing, ugly &
petticoated, ex-syllogize a God with cold-blooded Precision, &
attempt to run Religion thro' the body with an Icicle—an Icicle
from a Scotch Hog-trough—! *I* do not endure it!—my Eye
beholds phantoms—& 'nothing is, but what is not.'—

By your last I could not find, whether or no you still are willing
to execute the History of the Levelling Principle—Let me hear.—
Tom Wedgewood is going to the Isle of St Nevis.—As to myself,
Lessing out of the Question, I must stay in England / for I fear,
that a circumstance has taken place, which will render a Sea-
voyage utterly unfit for Sara.—Indeed, it is a pretty clear case.—
Dear Hartley is well, & in high force—he sported of his own accord
a theologico-astronomical Hypothesis—Having so perpetually
heard of good boys being put up into the Sky when they are dead,
& being now beyond measure enamoured of the Lamps in the
Streets, he said one night, coming thro' the Streets—'Stars are
dead Lamps—they *be'nt* naughty—they are put up in the Sky.'—
Two or three weeks ago he was talking to himself while I was
writing, & I took down his soliloquy—It would make a most
original Poem.—

You say, I illuminize—I think, that Property will some time

---

[1] *Jasper* by Mrs. Mary Robinson ('Perdita') appeared in the *Annual Antho-
logy*, 1800. The line with which Coleridge was so struck reads: 'Pale Moon!
thou Spectre of the Sky!' Coleridge included this line in his poem, *A Stranger
Minstrel*. See *Poems*, i. 352, line 58.

or other be modified by the predominance of Intellect, even as
Rank & Superstition are now modified by & subordinated to
Property, that much is to be hoped of the Future; but first those
particular modes of Property which more particularly stop the
diffusion must be done away, as injurious to Property itself—
these are, Priesthood & the too great Patronage of Government.
Therefore if to act on the belief that all things are a Process & that
inapplicable Truths are moral Falsehoods, be to illuminize—why
then I illuminize!—I know that I have been obliged to *illuminize*
so late at night, or rather mornings, that my eyes have smarted as
if I had *allum in eyes*! I believe I have mispelt the word—& ought
to have written Alum:——that aside, 'tis a *humorous Pun*!——

Tell Davy, that I will soon write.—God love him!—You & I,
Southey! know a good & great man or two in this World of ours!—

I have discovered so scoundrelly an act of Sheridan's & so
dastardly a one of Stuart's—that I am half-inclined to withdraw
myself from the Morning Post. A *Row* has happened at Norwich,
in which Tom Sheridan was concerned. Sheridan went himself to
Norwich—& on his re[turn] he gave in to Stuart, *himself*, an account
of the affair c[ontaining] the most *atrocious falsehoods*, all of which
he himself *knew* to be [falseh]oods—[for] Stuart had given me an
account of it from Sheridan's *own* mouth completely in contra-
diction— / & Stuart had the dastardly meanness to put it first in
the Courier, & afterwards in the Morning Post, under the lying
Title of 'an Extract of a Letter from Norwich!'[1]——This Sheri-
dan!—Is he not an *arch* Scoundrel?—This Extract breathed the
spirit of the most foul & sanguinary Aristocracy—& depend upon
it, Sheridan is a thorough-paced *bad man*!—

God love you, my dear Southey! & your affectionate
S. T. Coleridge

My kind Love to Edith. Let me hear from you—& do not be
angry with me, that I don't [ans]wer your Letters regularly.—

315. *To William Taylor*

Pub. Memoir of William Taylor of Norwich, *by J. W. Robberds, 2 vols., 1843,
i. 318.*

London, January 25th, 1800
My dear Sir,

I thank you for your kind attention to my letter. That 'extract
of a letter from Norwich' was given in to the Morning Post by
Sheridan himself, who *knew* the whole account to be a tissue of

——————
[1] Cf. *Morning Post*, 22 Jan. 1800.

atrocious falsehoods. Jacobinism evinces a gross and unthinking spirit; but the Jacobins as men are heroes in virtue, compared with Mr. Fox and his party. I know enough of them to know, that more profligate and unprincipled men never disgraced an honest cause. Robert Southey was mistaken—it was merely an account in a letter from Göttingen of a ridiculous statue. I will transcribe the passage. 'A statue has lately been put up in Ulric's garden in honour of Bürger the poet. It represents the Genius of Germany weeping over an urn. The Genius, instead of being eight faces high, is only five; nor is there anything superhuman about it, except perhaps its position, in which it is impossible for man, woman or child to stand. But notwithstanding all this, you must own, there is something very sylvanly romantic in seeing the monument of a great poet put up in the garden of an alehouse.' If I were in time to get a frank, here I should conclude; but I cannot endure to make you pay postage for half a sheet of almost vacant paper. I will transcribe therefore a passage or two from some letters which passed between me and Wordsworth in Germany (I should say from Wordsworth, for I have no copies of my own) respecting the merits of Bürger.

'We have read "Leonora" and a few little things of Bürger; but upon the whole we were disappointed, particularly in "Leonora," which we thought in several passages inferior to the English translation. "*Wie donnerten die Brücken*,"—how inferior to

"The bridges thunder as they pass,
But earthly sound was none, &c., &c."'

I admitted in my reply, that there are more passages of poetry in your translation, but affirmed that it wanted the *rapidity* and *oneness* of the original; and that in the beauty quoted the idea was so striking, that it made me *pause, stand still* and *look*, when I ought to have been driving on with the horse. Your choice of metre I thought unfortunate, and that you had lost the spirit of quotation from the Psalm-book, which gives such dramatic spirit and feeling to the dialogue between the mother and daughter, &c., &c.

Answer.—'As to Bürger, I am yet far from that admiration of him which he has excited in you; but I am by nature slow to admire; and I am not yet sufficiently master of the language to understand him perfectly. In one point I entirely coincide with you, in your feeling concerning his versification. In "Lenore" the concluding double rhymes of the stanza have both a delicious and *pathetic* effect—

"Ach! aber für Lenoren
War Gruss und Kuss verloren."

I accede too to your opinion that Bürger is always the poet; he is never the mobbist, one of those dim drivellers with which our island has teemed for so many years. Bürger is one of those authors whose book I like to have in my hand, but when I have laid the book down I do not think about him. I remember a hurry of pleasure, but I have few distinct forms that people my mind, nor any recollection of delicate or minute feelings which he has either communicated to me, or taught me to recognise. I do not perceive the presence of character in his personages. I see everywhere the character of Bürger himself; and even this, I agree with you, is no mean merit. But yet I wish him sometimes at least to make me forget himself in his creations. It seems to me, that in poems descriptive of human nature, however short they may be, character is absolutely necessary, &c.: incidents are among the lowest allurements of poetry. Take from Bürger's poems the *incidents*, which are seldom or ever of his own invention, and still much will remain; there will remain a manner of relating which is almost always spirited and lively, and stamped and peculiarized with genius. Still I do not find those higher beauties which can entitle him to the name of a *great* poet. I have read "Susan's Dream," and I agree with you that it is the most perfect and Shaksperian of his poems, &c., &c. Bürger is the poet of the animal spirits. I love his "*Tra ra la*" dearly; but less of the horn and more of the lute—and far, far more of the pencil.'

So much of my dear friend Wordsworth. Our controversy was continued, not that I thought Bürger a great poet, but that he really possessed some of the excellences which W. denied to him; and at last we ended in metaphysical disquisitions on the nature of character, &c., &c. My dear Sir, I feel a kind of conviction that one time or other we shall meet. Should choice or chance lead you to London, I have house-room for you, and, as far as loving some who dearly love you may entitle me to say so, heart-room too. I meet here a number of people who say, unconscious that they are lying, that they know you—for a regiment of whom neither you nor I care twopence.

Yours with unfeigned esteem,
S. T. Coleridge.

316. *To Josiah Wedgwood*

Address: Jos. Wedgewood Esq. | Cornwallis House | Clifton | Bristol   *Single*
MS. Wedgwood Museum. Pub. with omis. Tom Wedgwood, 77.
Postmark: 4 February 1800.

Tuesday Morning. [4 February 1800]
No / 21. Buckingham Street, Strand

My dear Sir

Your Brother's Health outweighs all other considerations; &
beyond doubt he has made himself well-acquainted with the
degree of Heat, which he is to experience there. The only objections
that I see are so obvious, that it is idle in me to mention them—
the total want of men, with whose Pursuits your Brother can have
a fellow-feeling; the length & difficulty of the return, in case of a
disappointment; and the necessity of Sea-voyages to almost every
change of Scenery. I will not think of the Yellow Fever: that, I
hope, is quite out of all probability.—Believe me, my dear Friend!
I have some difficulty in suppressing all that is within me of
affection & Grief—! God knows my heart, wherever your Brother
is, I shall follow him in spirit—follow him with my thoughts &
most affectionate Wishes!

I read your Letter, & did as you desired me. Montague is very
cool to me; whether I have still any of the leaven of the *citizen* &
visionary about me, too much for his present zeal; or whether M.
is incapable of attending to more than one man at a time; or
whether from his dislike of my pressing him to do something for
poor Wordsworth; or perhaps from all these causes combined—
certain it is, that he is shy of me. Of course, I can be supposed to
know but little of him directly from himself; this however in
Montague's case implies no loss of any authentic source of Informa-
tion. From his Friends I hear that the pressure of his immediate
circumstances increases, and that (as how could it be otherwise,
poor fellow!) he lives accumulating Debts & Obligations. He leaves
Wordsworth without his Principal or Interest,[1] which of course
he would not do, W.'s daily bread & Meat depending in great part
on him, if he were not painfully embarrassed—Embarrassed I
should have said: for Pinny tells me, that he suffers no pain from
it.—As to his views, he is now gone to Cambridge to canvass for
a fellow-ship in Trinity Hall; Mackintosh has kindly written to
Dr Lawrence, who is very intimate with the master; & he has other
interest.—He is likewise trying hard for & in expectation of, a
Commissionership of Bankruptcy, & means to pursue the Law with

---

[1] In 1795 Wordsworth loaned Basil Montagu most of the £900 legacy he
had recently received from Raisley Calvert.

all ardour & steadiness.—As to the state of his mind, it is that which it was & will be. God love him! he has a most incurable Forehead. John Pinny[1] called on him and looking on his Table saw by *accident* a Letter directed to himself—Why, Montague! that Letter is for me—& from Wordsworth!—'Yes! I have had it sometime.'—Why did you not give it me? 'Oh!—it wants some explanation first. You must not read it now—for I can't give you the explanation now.'—And Pinny, who you know is a right easy-natured man has not been able to get his own Letter from him to this Hour!—Of his Success at Cambridge Caldwell is doubtful, or more than doubtful. He says, that men at Cambridge don't trust overmuch these sudden changes of Principle. And most certainly, there is a zeal, an over acted fervor, a spirit of proselytism that distinguishes these men from the manners, & divides them from the sympathies, of the very persons, to whose party they have gone over. Smoking hot from the Oven of conversion they don't assort well with the old Loaves. So much of Montague; all that I know, & all, I suspect, that is to be known. A kind, gentlemanly, affectionate-hearted Man, possessed of an absolute *Talent* for Industry—would to God! he had never heard of Philosophy!—

I have been three times to the House of Commons, each time earlier then the former, & each time hideously crowded—the two first Day[s] the Debate was put off—yesterday I went at a quarter before 8, and remained till 3 this morning—& then sate writing, & correcting other men's writing till 8—a good 24 hours of un-pleasant activity![2] I have not felt myself sleepy yet— / Pitt & Fox completely answered my pre-formed Ideas of them. The elegance, & high-finish of Pitt's Periods even in the most sudden replies, is *curious*; but that is all. He *argues* but so so; & does not *reason* at all. Nothing is rememberable in what he says. Fox possesses all the full & overflowing Eloquence of a man of clear head, clean heart, & impetuous feelings. He is to my mind a great orator. All the rest that spoke were mere creatures. I could make a better speech myself than any that I heard, excepting Pitt's & Fox's. I reported that part of Pitt's which I have inclosed in crotchets—not that I report ex officio; but Curiosity having led me there, I did Stuart a service by taking a few Notes. I work from Morning to night; but in a few weeks I shall have accomplished my purpose—& then

---

[1] John Frederick Pinney had loaned Racedown to the Wordsworths in 1795.

[2] Coleridge's report of the debate on the continuation of the French war was published in the *Morning Post*, 6 Feb. 1800. See *Essays on His Own Times*, i. 285–92. Mrs. H. N. Coleridge attributes to Coleridge by internal evidence a commentary on this debate appearing in the *Morning Post* on 6 Feb. See *Essays on His Own Times*, ii. 367–71.

adieu to London for ever! We Newspaper scribes are true Galley-Slaves—when the high winds of Events blow loud & frequent, then the Sails are hoisted, or the Ship drives on of itself—when all is calm & Sunshine, then to our oars. Yet it is not unflattering to a man's Vanity to reflect that what he writes at 12 at night will before 12 hours is over have perhaps 5 or 6000 Readers! To trace a happy phrase, good image, or new argument running thro' the Town, & sliding into all the papers! Few Wine merchants can boast of creating more sensation. Then to hear a favorite & often urged argument repeated almost in your own particular phrases in the House of Commons—& quietly in the silent self-complacence of your own Heart chuckle over the plagiarism, as if you were grand Monopolist of all good Reasons!—But seriously, considering that I have Newspapered it merely as means of subsistence while I was doing other things, I have been very lucky—the New Constitution, the Proposals for Peace, the Irish Union—; &c &c—they are important in themselves, & excellent Vehicles for general Truths. I am not ashamed of what I have written.—I desired Poole to send you all the Papers antecedent to your own. I think you will like the different Analyses of the French Constitution.—I have attended Mackintosh regularly. He was so kind as to send me a Ticket, & I have not failed to profit by it. What I think of M. & all I think I will tell you in some future Letter.—My affectionate respects to Mrs W.—God love you, my dear Sir! I remain with grateful & most affectionate Esteem

Your faithful Friend—S. T. Coleridge

Uxor mea—&c. Sunt qui gemunt, quód sine sobole maneant; ast meo de pectore, spe, amore, religione nequaquam reclamantibus, suspiria aliquando eluctantur, anxia suspiria, ne mihi Juno et Dii maritales etiam plus optato faveant!——

317. *To Robert Southey*

Address: Mr Southey | Kingsdown Parade | Bristol   *Single*
MS. Lord Latymer. Pub. with omis. Letters, i. 324.
Postmark: 12 February 1800. *Stamped*: Strand.

My dear Southey

I shall give up this Newspaper Business—it is too, too fatiguing.— I have attended the Debates twice, & the first time I was 25 Hours in activity, & that of a very unpleasant kind—and the second Time from 10 in the Morning to 4 o/clock the next morning.—I am sure, that you will excuse my silence, tho' indeed after two such Letters from you I cannot scarcely excuse it myself. First of the book business—I find resistance which I did not expect to the *anony-mousness* of the Publication—Longman seems confident, that a work on such a Subject without a name would not do.——— Translations & perhaps Satires, are, he says, the only works that Book-sellers now venture on, *without a name.* He is very solicitous to have your Thalaba: & wonders (most wonderful!) that you do not write a *Novel.* That would be the Thing! And truly if by no more pains than a St Leon requires you could get 400£!!—or half the money, I say so too!——— / If we were together, we might easily *toss up* a novel, to be published in the name of one of us—or *two,* if that were all—& then christen 'em by lots. As sure as Ink flows in my Pen, by help of an amanuensis, I could write a volume a week—& Godwin got 400£!! for it—think of that, Master Brooks!—I hope, that some time or other you will write a novel on that subject of your's—I mean, the Rise & Progress of a *Laugher*—Legrice in your Eye——the effect of Laughing on Taste, Manners, morals, & happiness!—But as to the Jacobin Book, I must wait till I hear from you. Phillips would be very glad to engage you to write a School book for him, the History of Poetry in all nations—about 400 pages—but this too *must* have your name—He would give 60£—If poor dear Burnet were with you, he might do it under your eye & with your Instructions as well as you or I could do it—but it is *the name* / Longman remarked acutely enough—We Book-sellers scarcely pretend to judge the merits of the *Book,* but we know the *saleableness* of the name! & as they continue to buy most books on the calculation of a *first* Edition of a 1000 Copies, they are seldom much mistaken:———for the name gives them the excuse for sending it to all the Gemmen in Great Britain & the Colonies, from whom they have standing Orders for new books of reputation. This is the secret, why Books published by Country Booksellers, or by Authors on their own account, so seldom succeed.———

As to my schemes of residence, I am as unfixed as yourself—only that we are under the absolute necessity of fixing somewhere—& that somewhere will, I suppose, be Stowey—there are all my Books, & all our Furniture.—In May I am under a kind of engage-ment to go with Sara to Ottery—My family wish me to fix there, but *that* I must decline, in the names of public Liberty & individual Free-agency. Elder Brothers, not senior in Intellect, & not sympa-thizing in main opinions, are subjects of occasional Visits, not temptations to a Co-township. But if you go to Burton, Sara & I will waive the Ottery Plan, if possible, & spend May, & June with you—& perhaps July—but She must be settled in a house by the latter end of July, or the first week in August.—Till we are with you, Sara means to spend 5 weeks with the Roskillies, & a week or two at Bristol, where I shall join her. She will leave London in three weeks at least—perhaps, a fortnight: & I shall give up Lodgings, & billet myself free of expence at my friend, Purkis's at Brentford.—This is my present Plan——O my dear Southey! I would to God, that your Health did not enforce you to migrate— we might most assuredly contrive to fix a residence somewhere, which might possess a sort of centrality— / Alfoxden would make two Houses sufficiently divided for unimpinging Independence.—

Sara is shockingly uncomfortable—but that will be soon over— London does not suit either of us.—

My kindest Love to Edith—admodum verisimile est, quód paucis annis constitutio ejus revolutionem patietur (ipse multa istiusmodi exempla scio—) et cum valetu[do] ejus confirmata fuerit, tum et mater erit. Vacillante veró valetudine, minime optandum est; quippe non pote[rit] esse sine periculo *Consumptionis*. Interea, mi carissime, meum Parvulum ames!—Habes quod tibi gratuleris—habes maximum Dei optimi Donum, uxorem carissimam tuae indoli omnino conformatam et quasi constellatam. Mulier mea purissimae mentis est, probabili ingenio praedita, et quae *maternis* curis se totam dat, dicat, dedicat; Indoles veró quotidiana, et Sympathiae minutiores, meis studiis, temperamento, infirmitatibus eheu! minime consentiunt—non possumus omni ex parte felices esse.—In primis annis nuptialibus saepe vel miser fui—nunc vero (ut omnia mitescunt) tranquillus, imo, animo grato!——Mi Amice, mi Frater, Φίλτατόν μοι κάρα, non possumus omni ex parte felices esse.

Tell Davy that I have not forgotten him, because without an epilepsy I cannot forget him / & if I wrote to him as often as I think of him—Lord have mercy on his Pocket!—

God bless you again & again—S. T. Coleridge

I pass this Evening with Charlotte Smith[1] at her house—

318. *To Thomas Poole*

Address: Mr T. Poole | N. Stowey | Bridgewater | Somerset
MS. British Museum. Pub. with omis. Thomas Poole, *ii. 5.*
Postmark: 1⟨4⟩ February 1800.

Friday Feb. 14 1800

My dearest Friend

I am ashamed to address such a piece of Paper to you; but I am

---

[1] Charlotte Smith (1749–1806), poetess and novelist, was something of a literary celebrity. Coleridge had included two of her sonnets in his *Sonnets from Various Authors* in 1796.

weary of silence, & yet am so crowded with Business, that my very
soul is squeezed out.—How could you take such an absurd idea
in your head, that my Affections have weakened towards you?
Sometimes I have thought you rash in your Judgements of my
Conduct—but I perceived rather than felt it——But enough of
this—my affections are what they are, & in all human probability
ever will be.——I write now merely to desire you to be on the look
out for a House—I shall beyond all doubt settle at Stowey, if I can
get a suitable House—that is—a House with a Garden, & large
enough for me to have a Study out [of] the noise of Women &
children—this is absolutely necessary for me.—I have given up
the Morning Post; but the Editor is importunate against it—to
night I must go with him to the House of Commons. By Ham-
burgh Mails received to day it is made probable that there will be
a Peace on the Continent—& a Congress for that Purpose at
Prague. Ministers are the imbecil Dupes of all the other Powers of
Europe.—

Sara is shockingly uncomfortable, but it will be soon over I hope.
Give my kind Love to Ward—my love to Chester—& write to
me particulars of your dear Mother's Health—. If I can get a
House, I should wish to be settled [by] Midsummer—; but if no
House is to [be] got by that time, we shall take Lodgings at Mine-
head or Porlock.—

My health is pretty good, spite of bad hours—On the great
Debate I was in that terrible Crowd from 8 Monday Morning to
3 Tuesday Morning, & continued after that writing & correcting
till 9—25 hours!—

God bless you, my dear Friend! & your most sincere &
affectionate
S. T. Coleridge

Hartley is very well.

319. *To Robert Southey*

Address: Mr Southey | Kingsdown Parade | Bristol
MS. Lord Latymer. Pub. with omis. Letters, *i. 326.*
Postmark: 18 February 1800. *Stamped*: Strand.

Tuesday Feb. 18. [1800]

My dear Southey

What do you mean by the words—'it is induced by expecta-
tion?' speaking of your state of Health.—I can not bear to think
of your going to a strange country, without any one with you who
loves & understands you.—But we will talk of all this.—I have not

a moment's Time—& my head aches—I was up till 5 o clock this morning—My Brain so overworked, that I could doze troublously & with cold limbs, so affected was my circulation / I shall do no more for Stewart.—Read Pitt's Speech in the Morning Post of today (Tuesday Feb. 18.) I reported the whole with notes so scanty, that—Mr Pitt is much obliged to me.[1] For by heaven he never talked half as eloquently in his Life time. He is a *stupid insipid* Charlatan, that *Pitt*—Indeed, except Fox, I, you, or any Body might learn to speak better than any man in the House.— For the next fortnight I expect to be so busy, that I shall go out of London a mile or so to be wholly uninterrupted——I do not understand the Beguinages of Holland[2]——Phillips is a good for nothing fellow; but what of that?—He will give you 60£ and advance half the money now, for a Book which you can do in a Fortnight—or three weeks at farthest.—I would advise you not to give it up hastily.—Phillips eats no flesh—I observe wittily enough that whatever might be thought of innate Ideas, there could be no doubt to a man who had seen Phillips of the existence of innate Beef. Let my Mad Ox keep my name—Fire & Famine do just what you like with—I have no wish either way.— The fears in Solitude, I fear, is not my Property—& I have no encouragement to think, it will be given up— / but if I hear otherwise, I will let you know speedily—in the mean time do not rely on it—.

Your Review-Plan *cannot* answer for this reason—It could exist only as long [as] the Ononymous Anti-*a*nonymists remained in life, health, & the humor—& no Publisher would undertake a periodical Publication on so Gossamery a tie. Besides, it really would not be right for any man to make so many people have strange & uncomfortable feelings towards him—which must be the case, however kind the Reviews might be.—And what but Nonsense is published?—The Author of Gebir I cannot find out—There are none of his Books in Town—You have made a Sect of Gebirites by your Review[3]——but it was not a *fair*, tho' a very kind, Review.—I have sent a Letter to Mrs Fricker, which Sara directed to you—I hope, it has come safe.

Let me see, are there any other Questions. Sara.[4]

[1] William Pitt's speech on the continuance of the war with France was delivered on 17 Feb. 1800, and reported by Coleridge next day in the *Morning Post*. See *Essays on His Own Times*, ii. 293–306.

[2] John Rickman proposed to Southey the development in England of religious establishments for women, similar to the beguinages in the Netherlands.

[3] See *Critical Review*, Sept. 1799.

[4] Coleridge did not finish his sentence, but he apparently intended to say Sara will write, since Mrs. Coleridge added a note after his signature.

So, my dear Southey—God love you, & never, never cease to believe that I am

affectionately your's
S. T. Coleridge

Love to Edith.——Hartley well, save Cold—Sara still miserable.—

320. *To Thomas Poole*

Address: Mr T. Poole
MS. Lord Latymer. Hitherto unpublished.

Tuesday Evening. [25 February 1800][1]

My dear Poole

I have received both your letters——I should not write now, but, that Bathstone going to morrow, he must not go without a Letter—if only to let you know that I am alive, & Stowey-sick—Stewart won't let me go, but I don't do much for him—as you have seen / I am translating three manuscript Plays of Schiller[2]—& positively for the last week have worked with my pen in my hand 14 hours every day.—Hartley is quite well—Sara better—I middling.—I heard from Wordsworth—he is well & happy. Of your dear Mother I can *say* nothing—you know what I *feel*—Of Darwin's work[3] I have heard nothing——If I can get it given me by any Bookseller, I will send it you—. Poor Virgin!—My Love to Ward & tell him to write *me* all the Particulars—& of the Girl—directing to Lambe[4]—as usual. You have a little Deal Box in your little Room—you must unnail it—& there are my *loose Papers*, & letters——The Letters I don't want; but all the loose Papers I wish to [ha]ve—& Bathstone can [bri]ng 'em up for me.——Cruckshankum tantum vidi—but he has written me an affectionate Letter.—My report of Pitt's Speech made a great noise here—

----

[1] This letter was written in answer to one from Poole, dated 22 Feb. 1800.

[2] *The Piccolomini, or the First Part of Wallenstein. A Drama in Five Acts*, and *The Death of Wallenstein, A Tragedy in Five Acts*, both translated from the German of Frederick Schiller by S. T. Coleridge, 1800, for which Coleridge received £50 from Longman. See Letter 459. A third play, *Wallenstein's Camp*, and an *Essay on the Genius of Schiller*, promised in the advertisement to *The Piccolomini*, never appeared.

[3] Coleridge refers to Erasmus Darwin's *Phytologia; or the Philosophy of Agriculture and Gardening*, 1799.

[4] Coleridge had resumed his old intimacy with Lamb. Letters sent to London in care of Lamb but intended for Coleridge were addressed to Mr. *Lambe*, East India House, to identify them as Coleridge's. See Letter 592, and *Lamb Letters*, i. 313.

What a degraded Animal Man is to see any thing to admire in that wretched Rant—!——

I have a huge Hankering for Alfoxden / Sara's Love—'and my Lub—Hartley Cöidge's Lub.'—

Hartley said some time ago—that 'the Stars be dead Lamps—they be'nt naughty—they be put up in the Sky with my Brother Berkley.[']——

God love you, my dearest Poole—&
S. T. Coleridge

321. *To William Wordsworth*

Pub. Memoirs of Wordsworth, *i. 160.*

[February 1800]

I grieve that 'The Recluse' sleeps.

322. *To Robert Southey*

Address: Mr Southey | Kingsdown Parade | Bristol   *Single*
MS. Lord Latymer. Pub. with omis. Letters, *i. 331.*
Postmark: 28 February 1800. *Stamped*: Strand.

It goes to my Heart, my dear Southey! to sit down & write to you, knowing that I can scarcely fill half a side—the Postage lies on my Conscience—I am translating Manuscript Plays of Schiller—they are *Poems,* full of long Speeches—in very polish'd Blank Verse——. The Theatre! the Theatre! my dear Southey!—it will never, never, never do—!—If you go to Portugal, your History thereof *will* do—— / but for the present money Novels, or Translations——. I do not see, that a Book said by you in the Preface to have been written merely as a Book for young Persons could injure your reputation more than Milton's Accidence injured *his*—I *would do* it—because you can do it so easily——. It is not necessary that you should say much about French or German Literature—Do it so—Poetry of savage Nations.—Poetry of rudely civilized—Homer, & the Hebrew Poetry, &c—Poetry of civilized Nations, under Republics & Politheism— / State of Poetry under the Roman & Greek Empires——revival of it in Italy—in Spain—& England—then go steadily on with England to the end, except one Chapter about German Poetry to conclude with—which I can write for you—— /

In the Morning Post was a poem of fascinating Metre by Mary Robinson—'twas on Wednesday, Feb. 26.—& entitled the Haunted

Beach.[1] I was so struck with it that I sent to her to desire that [it] might be preserved in the Anthology—She was extremely flattered by the Idea of it's being there, as she idolizes you & your Doings. So if it be not too late, I pray you, let it be in——if you should not have received that Day's paper, write immediately that I may transcribe it—it falls off sadly to the last—wants Tale—& Interest; but the Images are new & very distinct—that 'silvery carpet' is so *just*, that it is unfortunate it should *seem* so bad—for it is *really* good—but the Metre—ay! that Woman has an Ear.[2]—William Taylor, from whom I have received a couple of Letters full of thought & information says, what astounded me—that Double Rhymes in our Language have always a *ludicrous* association— Mercy on the Man! Where are his Ears & Feelings?—His *taste* cannot be *quite* right, from this observation—but he is a famous Fellow, that is not to be denied.——

Sara is poorly still—Hartley rampant, & Emperorizes with your pictures—Harry is a fine Boy—Hartley told a Gentleman 'me tinks, you are *like Southey*.'—And he *was* not wholly unlike you— but the chick calling you simple—Southey—so pompously!—— God love you & your Edith—

                                                    S. T. Coleridge

    Love to Davy——

Your Simile of the Cucumbers & Dung tickled me hugely.

323. *To John Prior Estlin*

Address: Revd. J. P. Estlin | St Michael's Hill | Bristol   *Single*
MS. Bristol Central Lib. Pub. E. L. G. i. 135.
Postmark: 1 March 1800.

                                        Saturday, March 1st [1800]

My very dear Friend

    When I received your letter—some three minutes ago—I turned to my Guide des Voyageurs En Europe to know where Marburg was—I guess it to be Marburg in the Bishoprich of Padderbourn

---

[1] Published *Annual Anthology*, 1800.
[2]   The SPECTRE *band*, his MESSMATES bold,
                    Sunk in the yawning ocean!
            While to the mast, he lash'd him fast,
            And brav'd the storm's commotion!
            The *winter* MOON upon the sand
                    A silvery carpet made,
            And mark'd the sailor reach the land—
            And mark'd *his* MURDERER wash his hand,
                    Where the green billows play'd!
                            The Haunted Beach, stanza 6.

between Frankfort & Cassel—If so, I have not been within 40 miles
at least of it, having never been many miles below Cassel—At all
events, the name of the person, you mention, is wholly unknown
to me—I once knew a Miss Bouclerc in Devonshire.——As to
myself, I am *fagging*—& am delivering to the Press some plays of
Schiller's—— / I shall soon however slide away from this place, &
devote myself to works of more importance.—I have seen Mr &
Mrs Barbauld[1] two or three times—once at their own House—
admirable people!——Dr Disney's Sons, at all events, the younger,
with his Shirt collar half way up his cheek, gave me no high idea of
the propriety of Unitarian Dissenters sending their Sons to
Established & Idolatrous Universities— / It may be very true,
tha[t] at Hackney they learnt, too many of them, Infidelity—the
Tutors, the *whole* plan of Education, the place itself, were all
wrong—but many will return to the Good Cause, in which alone
plain practical Reason can find footing—at Cambridge & Oxford
they will not learn Infidelity perhaps, or perhaps they may—for
now 'tis common enough even there, to my certain knowlege—
but one thing they *will* learn—Indifference to all Religions but the
Religion of the *Gentleman—Gentlemanliness* will be the word— / &
bring with it a deep *Contempt* for those Dissenters among whom
they were born.—We Dissenters (for I am proud of the Distinction)
have somewhat of a simple & *scholarly* formality, perhaps: God
forbid, we should wholly lose it—! but with th[e] young men at
Oxford & Cambridge '*the Gentleman*[' is] the all-implying Word of
Honor—a thing more blasting to real Virtue, real Utility, real
Standing forth for the Truth in Christ, than all the Whoredoms &
Impurities which this Gentlemanliness does most generally bring
with it.——My dear Friend!—in the crowded heartless Party at
Dr Disney's O! how I did think of *your* Sunday Suppers—their
light uncumbrous Simplicity, the *heartiness* of manner, the literary
Christianness of Conversation——Dr Disney himself I *respect*,
highly respect—in the Pulpit he is an *Apostle* / but there—there it
stops.—

My best & overflowing Love to Mrs Estlin / kisses & love to your
Children—Sara is better—Hartley rampant—

Heaven bless you & your affectionate Friend

S. T. Coleridge

Mrs Coleridge begs to be remembered to you & dear Mrs Estlin
'with *all, all, all* my Heart'—There you have her own Words.—

P.S. Nothing is more common than for conscious Infidels to

---

[1] Mrs. Anna Letitia Barbauld (1743–1825), poet and miscellaneous writer
whom Coleridge had met in Bristol in the summer of 1797.

go into the *Church*—Conscious Arians or Socinians swarm in it—
So much for the *Morals* of Oxford & Cambridge.—With their too
early reasonings, and logic-cuttings, & reading Hume & such like
Trash, the young Dissenters are prone to Infidelity—but do you
know any Instance of such an Infidel accepting an office that
implied the belief of Christianity?—It cannot be said, that this is
owing to *our* Preferments being so much smaller: for the majority
are but Curates in the Established Church, or on small Livings—&
not so well off as George Burnet was, or Sam. Reed would have
been / but thus is it, my dear Friend!—The Education, which
Dissenters receive among Dissenters, generates Conscientiousness
& a scrupulous Turn / will this be gained at the Wine Parties at
Cambridge?—The truth is, Dr Disney himself sees only with too
much pleasure this Gentlemanliness—. I say thus much, my dear
Friend! because I once heard you speak in Commendation of that
which I am now deprecating.—
P.S. The more I see of Mrs Barbauld the more I admire her—that
wonderful *Propriety* of Mind!—She has great *acuteness*, very
great—yet how steadily she keeps it within the bounds of practical
Reason. This I almost envy as well as admire—My own Subtleties
too often lead me into strange (tho' God be praised) transient
Out-of-the-waynesses. Oft like a winged[1] Spider, I am entangled
in a new Spun web—but never fear for me, 'tis but the flutter of
my wings—& off I am again!——
   The little man so full of great affections—you cannot love him
better than I.—

324. *To Daniel Stuart*

Address: Mr Stuart
MS. British Museum. Pub. Letters from the Lake Poets, *4.*

                                   Eleven o/clock—[1 March 1800][2]
Dear Sir

I feel more uncomfortably respecting my conduct to *you* for
these last ten day[s,] than I have had occasion to feel on any
occasion for these last 20 months—Your last note has just reached
me / the former is here, but I have not read it, having been out of
London to avoid Interruptions—.—Whether we continue con-

---

[1] By the bye, there is no such Creature. But in similies if a Phoenix, why
not a winged spider? [Note by S. T. C.]

[2] This letter mentions that Mrs. Coleridge and Hartley 'leave London to
morrow'. They were in London on 1 Mar.; on 3 Mar. Coleridge was already
at Lamb's, and had been 'tipsy' the night before at Godwin's. Mrs. Coleridge
left London, therefore, on 2 Mar., to spend a month with the Roskillys at
Kempsford.

nected or no, I consider myself as two full weeks' Work in your
Debt for that which I have already received—.—These cursed
Plays play the Devil with me—I have been working from morning
to night, & almost half the night too, & yet get on too slowly for the
Printer—& Mr Longman is kept in constant [dread] that some rival
Translation may pop out before mine—and beside this, my wife
& child leave London to morrow, & I was particularly desirous to
have done enough to give me some *claim* to draw on him for the
few Pounds which I must draw on him, for their Journey.—These
Things I mention not as justifications of my breach of Promise,
but as palliations. So much for the Past—for the future thus
much.—In about four or five Days I shall have finish'd the first
Play—& that being finished, I may go on more leisurely with the
others.—I shall then be able to give you some assistance—probably
as much as you may want—a certain number of Essays I consider
myself bound to send you *as soon as possible*, in common honesty.
After these, if it be worth your while, I will do what I can—only
not for any regular *Stipend*.—That harrasses me—I know, that
hitherto I have received from you much more than I have earned—
& this must not be——I have no objection to be payed for what
I do, but a great objection to be paid for what I *ought* to do——.

This Translation Fag has almost knocked me up— / & I am so
confused that I scarcely know whether I have expressed myself
intelligibly—. My Wife goes to morrow Evening—& I shall be at
No 36, Chapel Street, Pentonville[1]—My Papers you will be so kind
as to have left at your Office, till they are called for—but Mr
Wedgewood's must be *sent* among your other papers—the Address

Jos. Wedgewood Esq. | Cornwallis House | Clifton, | Bristol—

I will certainly fill you out a good Paper on Sunday /

Mrs Coleridge desires me to send her respects, & to thank you
for your civilities to her——

Your's
S. T. Coleridge

325. *To William Godwin*

Address: Mr Godwin | Polygon | Sommers' Town
MS. Lord Abinger. Pub. with omis. William Godwin, *ii.* 2.
Postmark: 3 March 1800.

Mr Lamb's   No / 36 Chapel Street Pentonville—
8, Monday Morning [3 March 1800]

Dear Godwin

The Punch after the Wine made me tipsy last night—this I

---

[1] After Mrs. Coleridge's departure Coleridge stayed with Charles Lamb.

mention, not that my head aches, or that I felt after I quitted you, any unpleasantness, or titubancy—; but because tipsiness has, and has always, one unpleasant effect—that of making me talk *very* extravagantly / & as when sober, I talk extravagantly enough for any *common* Tipsiness, it becomes a matter of nicety in discrimination to know when I am or am not affected.—An idea starts up in my hand [head ?]—away I follow it thro' thick & thin, Wood & Marsh, Brake and Briar—with all the apparent Interest of a man who was defending one of his old and long-established Principles—Exactly of this kind was the Conversation, with which I quitted you / I do not believe it possible for a human Being to have a greater horror of the Feelings that usually accompany such principles as I then supported, or a deeper Conviction of their irrationality than myself—but the whole Thinking of my Life will not bear me up against the accidental Press & Crowd of my mind, when it is elevated beyond it's natural Pitch / .—

We shall talk wiselier with the Ladies on Tuesday—God bless you, & give your dear little ones a kiss a piece for me—

The Agnus Dei & the Virgin Mary desire their kind respects to *you*, you sad Atheist—!

Your's with affectionate | Esteem
S. T. Coleridge

326. *To Samuel Purkis*

Address: Samuel Purkis E[sqre] | Brentford
MS. New York Public Lib. Hitherto unpublished.
Postmark: 15 ⟨March⟩ 1800.

Saturday 2 o clock [15 March 1800]

My dear Purkis

Just before your [Draft arrived][1] I concluded a Bargain with Longman, who is to give me a 100£ for my Tour in the North of England[2]—to be advanced immediately.—Of course, I shall [return your Draft]—nay, to *talk big*, I can accomodate you with a Draft for 50£.[3]—Amazing, how a little Prosperity turns an Author's head!—I find, that I can with tolerable ease get 300£ a year by my pen—so that Authorship is really no such very bad speculation.—I will not quit Town without spending 2 or three Days with you, provided it be to you perfectly convenient——

---

[1] Words in brackets inked out in manuscript.

[2] Coleridge did not publish his tour of the north of England, but Letter 300 shows that he had such a plan in mind. His notebook entries for the tour were published by the Rev. G. H. B. Coleridge in 1939. See headnote to Letter 299.

[3] For Coleridge's complicated financial dealings with Purkis see Letters 309 and 329.

Don't come to town without calling——Affectionate Respects to Mrs Purkis—& love to your dear Children. Mrs Coleridge is rather better, I think—[1]

Your's affectionately, S. T. Coleridge

327. *To Daniel Stuart*

Address: Mr Stuart
MS. British Museum. Pub. Letters from the Lake Poets, *4.*]

[March 1800][2]

Dear Stuart

. I am very unwell—if you are pressed for the Paragraph to day, I will write it; but I cannot come out—but if it will do as well tomorrow, so much the better. For in truth my head is shockingly giddy—if you want matter, Lamb has got plenty of 'My Great Aunt's Manuscript'—I would advise you by all means to make it an Article in the Morning Post—please to send me the Pa[pers.]

Your's very sincerely—
S. T. Coleridge

P.S. I will send you by Lamb this Evening three or four paragraphs of 7 or 8 lines each—

328. *To Thomas Poole*

Address: Mr. T. Poole | N. Stowey | Bridgewater
MS. British Museum. Pub. with omis. Essays on His Own Times, *i, p. xci, and* Thomas Poole, *ii. 7.*

Friday Night [21 March 1800][3]

My dear Poole

I received your letter this night, left for me at Stuart's by I know not whom—Bastone I have not seen.—By my silence you will conclude, how much I have been occupied—indeed, I never worked so hard in my Life. In one day I wrote 500 blank Verse Lines, and that character of Pitt, in the same Evening, without previous meditation on it— / .

[1] 'I think' indicates that Mrs. Coleridge had left London.
[2] Coleridge made overtures to Stuart on behalf of Lamb in Mar. 1800— Coleridge, Lamb wrote to Manning on 17 Mar., 'has lugged me to the brink of engaging to a newspaper' (*Lamb Letters*, i. 178). This letter, as the post-script suggests, was written while Coleridge was staying with Lamb, after Mrs. Coleridge's departure.
[3] The reference to the famous 'character of Pitt', which appeared in the *Morning Post* on 19 Mar. 1800, dates this letter. See *Essays on His Own Times,* ii. 319–29.

Now for the Business—I like the Scheme very much, & shall write by the same post with this to my Wife, desiring her, if she thinks it will do, as well as I do, to write you immediately—the chief objection I see at present, is the *use* of the Garden—I suffered so much the last summer for want of Vegetables, that I am determined whatever it *cost* me in money, to have a Garden—not that I mean to work in it—that is out of the Question—but a Garden I will have——I shall not be down at Stowey for these two months; but Sara, I suppose, will—however, if the scheme suit her wishes, she will write you, concerning the Time, &c—As to money, I am not anxious—I am sure, if God give me health, to make all even before the End of this year—& I find that I can without any straining gain 500 guineas a year, if I give up poetry——i.e. original Poetry——. If I had the least love of money, I could make almost sure of 2000£ a year / for Stuart has offered me half shares in the two Papers, the M.P. & Courier, if I would devote myself with him to them—but I told him, that I would not give up the Country, & the lazy reading of Old Folios for two Thousand Times two thousand Pound—in short, that beyond 250£ a year, I considered money as a real Evil—at which he stared; for such Ideas are not animals indigenous in the Longitudes & Latitudes of a Scotchman's Soul. I shall continue to write for him, because three half Evenings in the week will suffice to earn four guineas a week— & I think there are but 2 good ways of writing—one for immediate, & wide impression, tho' transitory—the other for permanence— / Newspapers the first—the best one can do is the second——that middle class of translating Books &c is neither the one or the other—When I have settled myself *clear*, I shall write nothing for money but for the newspaper. You, of course, will not hint a word to any [one] of Stuart's offer to me.—He has behaved with th[e] most abundant honor & generosity.—

I would to God, I could get Wordsworth to re-take Alfoxden— the Society of so great a Being is of priceless Value—but he will never quit the North of England—his habits are more assimilated with the Inhabitants there—there he & his Sister are exceedingly beloved, enthusiastically. Such difference do small Sympathies make—such as Voice, Pronunciation, &c—for from what other Cause can I account for it—. Certainly, no one, neither you, or the Wedgewoods, altho' you far more than any one else, ever entered into the feeling due to a man like Wordsworth—of whom I do not hesitate in saying, that since Milton no man has *manifested* himself equal to him.

I am at Lamb's, No/ 36, Chapel Street, Pentonville—& never receive my papers, but when I go, or send for them—which is the

reason, you have them so irregularly—You must write—Mr
Lambe, East India House as usual.—I am very quiet here—but
wish, I were at Stowey—My kind Love to your Mother & to Ward.
Your's ever most affectionately,
S. T. Coleridge

329. *To Samuel Purkis*

Address: Samuel Purkis Esq. | Brentford
MS. McGill University. Hitherto unpublished. The top and the bottom of this
manuscript have been cut off. The words in brackets have been heavily inked
out, but through the courtesy of Mr. Richard Pennington of the Redpath
Library I have been able to examine the holograph and decipher the partially
obliterated passages.
Postmark: 27 March 1800.

. . . without some apology, for having neglected it so long, my next
& wiser way is to ask you—if there be not some *mistake*. I [drew
on you for 5£—] while at your house, [my Debt was augmented
to 20£] for which I gave you a [Draft on] Mr Wedgewood—[I
opened the Draft & altered it to 25£] for which you [payed me the
difference—] I afterwards wrote to you, [begging you to Lend me
10£ for 14 days]—you sent me [a Draft to that amount—] stating
that you should want it at the end of that time / I in the meantime
had concluded a Bargain with Longman, & did not [want the
Draft—] accordingly I destroyed it—& wrote you in answer that
I should not use it—.—Believe me my dear Fellow! it is so im-
probable that I should be more accurate [in money matters] than
you, that I cannot convey to you my *perplexity* . . . at your
Service— / I pray you, write to me immediately.

O this Translation is indeed a *Bore—never, never, never* will I
be so taken in again—Newspaper writing is comparative extacy—
I do not despair of making Bonaparte as good as *Pitt*—but there is
a 2nd Part of Pitt to come[1]—& a Review of a curious Pamphlet
connected with it[2]—That on Pitt has made sensation—

I am at present at Lamb's—Direct to me No/ 36 | Chapel Street, |
Pentonville.

Give my kind Love to Mrs P.—& believe me, my dear Purkis!
very affectionately
Your's
S. T. Coleridge

[1] Neither the character of Bonaparte nor the '2nd Part of Pitt' was ever
written.
[2] On 27 Mar. 1800 Coleridge printed in the *Morning Post* a brief review of
Arthur Young's pamphlet, *The Question of Scarcity Plainly Stated. Essays on
His Own Times*, ii. 395–403.

I have heard thrice from Sara—She & Hartley are both well— /
I have taken a House, or rather half a house, at Stowey——when
I go there, I cannot determine. Remember me kindly to Miss Fox—
and to Mary: my love & to John.

330. *To Thomas Poole*

Pub. Thomas Poole, *ii. 8–9.*

March 31, 1800

. . . You charge me with prostration in regard to Wordsworth.
Have I affirmed anything miraculous of W.? Is it impossible that
a greater poet than any since Milton may appear in our days?
Have there any *great* poets appeared since him? . . . Future great-
ness! Is it not an awful thing, my dearest Poole? What if you had
known Milton at the age of thirty, and believed all you now know
of him?——What if you should meet in the letters of any then
living man, expressions concerning the young Milton *totidem verbis*
the same as mine of Wordsworth, would it not convey to you a
most delicious sensation? Would it not be an assurance to you that
your admiration of the *Paradise Lost* was no superstition, no
shadow of flesh and bloodless abstraction, but that the *Man* was
even so, that the greatness was incarnate and personal? Wherein
blame I you, my best friend? Only in being borne down by other
men's rash opinions concerning W. You yourself, for yourself,
judged wisely. . . .

Do not,[1] my dearest Poole, deem me cold, or finical, or in-
different to Stowey, full and fretful in objection; but on so im-
portant an affair to a man who has, and is likely to have, a family,
and who *must* have silence and a *retired study*, as a house is, it were
folly not to consult one's own feelings, folly not to let them speak
audibly, and having heard them, hypocrisy not to utter them. . . .
My dearest friend, when I have written to you lately, I have
written with a mind and heart completely worn out with the fag
of the day. I trust in God you have not misinterpreted this into
a change of character. I was a little jealous at an expression in your
last letter——'I am happy you begin to feel your power.' Truly
and in simple verity, my dear Tom, I feel not an atom more power

---

[1] In introducing this paragraph Mrs. Sandford writes: 'In relation to the
question of lodgings Tom Poole seems to have mentioned some possibility of
renting part of a farmhouse, which would, however, involve the joint-use of
a kitchen. This Coleridge fears would lead to continual squabbles between their
servant and the farmer's wife, and "be worse than the old hovel fifty times
over".' (*Thomas Poole*, ii. 8.) Apparently Coleridge had first determined to
take the farm-house. See Letter 329.

than I have ever done, except the power of gaining a few more
paltry guineas than I had supposed. On the contrary, my faculties
appear to myself dwindling, and I do believe if I were to live in
London another half year, I should be dried up wholly. . . .

331. *To Robert Southey*

MS. Lord Latymer, Pub. Ill. London News, *27 May 1893, p. 634.*

Thursday, April [10,] 1800[1]
Amblesides, Westmoreland.

My dear Southey

If you stay longer, than the year on the Continent, *I and mine
will join you*—& if you return at that Time, you must join us.
Where we shall be, God knows! but in some interesting Country it
will be, in Heaven or Earth. I feel assurances & comfortable Hopes
of your full Recovery—Of all that you have written to me I need
not say I will be the Performer if needs be—and so help me God &
my Conscience, as all your's shall be to me as my very own. My
next I will direct to Lisbon—In a few days I move for Bristol—I
have been in excessive Perplexity of mind lately on sundry
subjects—and have besides over-worked myself—but all will be
calm again. Of your History of Portugal I anticipate great Things—
it is a noble Subject & of a certain Sale.—But still, Southey! be
ever a Poet in your higher moments.—I will find out some Lisbon
merchant in London or Liverpool, & manage to send you regularly,
what is interesting, without expence. Wordsworth publishes a
second Volume of Lyrical Ballads, & Pastorals. He meditates a
novel—& so do I—but first I shall re-write my Tragedy. If that
Reverend *Sir* continues his Insolence,[2] I will give him a scourging
that shall flea him / I *promise* you to exert myself to procure sub-
scribers for the Chatterton—I have ample materials for a most
interesting Historical & Metaphysical Essay on Literary Forgery
from the Hymns of Orpheus which deceived Aristotle to the
Vortigern of Shakespere that deceived Dr Parr—but Dr Parr was
the greater Booby.—

I cannot wholly approve of your Anthologizing; but you judge,
I will believe, wisely. My objections are various—& one of them
of a moral nature. But on all this I will write.—

Edith! my Love! May God in Heaven bless you!—

---

[1] This letter was written in answer to one from Southey, dated 1 Apr. 1800,
in which he announced his impending departure for Lisbon.

[2] Coleridge refers to a controversy between Southey and Sir Herbert Croft
concerning Chatterton. See *Monthly Magazine,* Nov. 1799, and the *Gentleman's
Magazine,* Feb., Mar., and Apr. 1800.

The time returns upon me, Southey! when we dreamt one Dream, & that a glorious one—when we eat together, & thought each other greater & better than all the World beside, and when we were bed fellows. Those days can never be forgotten, and till they are forgotten, we cannot, if we would, cease to love each other.——

S. T. Coleridge

332. *To Josiah Wedgwood*

Address: Josiah Wedgewood Esq. | No 39 | Gloucester Place | Portman Square | London
MS. British Museum. Hitherto unpublished.
Postmark: 25 April 1800. *Stamped*: Keswick.

Monday, April 21 1800

Mr Wordsworth's Grasmere near Ambleside, Westmoreland
My dear Sir

You may well suppose, what a pain at heart it is to me to have an explanation to make to *you* concerning money matters.—So far back as four years ago my Bill to Cottle for various articles, for cash among the rest, was 20£—Cottle was then in prosperous & promising circumstances, & gave me to understand that he should never consider me in his Debt, till I became a richer man than he— & refused to send me in his Bill. Lately, poor fellow! his affairs have fallen to rack & ruin / my debt stood on his Ledger—& he wrote me a very importunate Letter. He had suffered deeply from the very mean opinion, which I had frankly expressed to him of his Epic Poem—expressed wholly as an expedient to prevent him from publishing it at his own expence—& he made the application not without expressions of a wounded & angry mind. At the time I received his Letter I knew that within three weeks I should receive more than the 20£ from the Bookseller—& I sent him therefore a Draft on you—imagining of course that he would not present it till the expiration of the three weeks, before which time I should have not only advertised you of it, but included the 20£. This indeed was the sole reason of my not doing what, I am now sensible, I should have done—written to you immediately—but in truth, I was sore all over with the apprehension, that you might accuse me of irregularity & a presumption wholly unjustifiable, well knowing that I have already more than overdrawn myself. With an un-lucky, but I should hope, not very blameable Cowardice of feeling I felt a repugnance to acquaint you of it without at the same time sending the money. To morrow morning I send off the last sheet

of my irksome & soul-wearying Labor, the Translation of Schiller—
and as soon as I have received my stipend, I will remit to you.[1]—
My dear Sir—how much you have been harrassed by irregular men,
what disgust have you associated, of necessity, with them, & the
idea of meanness that attaches to the expedients of embarrass-
ment, I well know—and I am sure, the extreme pain & agitation,
which your letter gave me, did not seduce me into the slightest
censure of you, as unkind——but I anticipate a sort of comfort in
knowing that you can understand how much I suffered from pride
& far honester feelings than Pride.——

For these last six months I have worked incessantly——and
have lived with as much economy as is practicable by any man /
but many expences, not expected, & not immediately my own,
have still thrown me back. In this engagement of translating the
prolix Plays of Schiller I made too a very, very foolish bargain—
the Bookseller indeed has given me his word, that in case of their
success he will consider [me] as entitled to an additional Re-
muneration—but of their Success I have no hope— / for I can say
with truth, that I could have written a far better play myself in
half the time. But with all this I have learnt that I have Industry
& Perseverance—and before the end of the year, if God grant me
health, I shall have my wings wholly unbirdlim'd.—This is
Monday—and I shall be in London the beginning of next week—
I pray you, my dear Sir! be so kind as to write to me—for God
forbid that so sore an affliction should befall me, as that the con-
nection between us should ever be a source of Doubt to you, or
otherwise than honorable to me—.—Believe me

most affectionately | & | gratefully | Your's

S. T. Coleridge

333. *To William Godwin*

Address: Mr Godwin | Polygon | Sommers' Town | London   *Single*
MS. Lord Abinger. Pub. with omis. E. L. G. i. 137.
Postmark: May 23, 1800.

Mr T. Poole's N. Stowey Bridgewater.

Wednesday, May 21 1800

Dear Godwin

I received your letter this morning, & had I not, still I am almost
confident, that I should have written to you before the end of the
week. Hitherto the Translation of the Wallenstein has prevented
me; not that it so engrossed my time, but that it wasted and
depressed my spirits, & left a sense of wearisomeness & disgust
which unfitted me for any thing but sleeping or immediate society.

---

[1] See Letters 335 and 341.

I say this, because I ought to have written to you first; & as I am not behind you in affectionate esteem, so I would not be thought to lag in those outward & visible signs, that both shew & vivify the inward & spiritual grace.—Believe me, you recur to my thoughts frequently, & never without pleasure, never without my making out of the past a little day dream for the future. I left Wordsworth on the 4th of this month—if I cannot procure a suitable house at Stowey, I return to Cumberland & settle at Keswick—in a house of such prospect, that if, according to you & Hume, impressions & ideas *constitute* our Being, I shall have a tendency to become a God—so sublime & beautiful will be the series of my visual existence. But whether I continue here, or migrate thither, I shall be in a beautiful country—& have house-room and heart-room for you / and you must come & write your next work at my house.—My dear Godwin! I remember you with so much pleasure & our conversations so distinctly, that, I doubt not, we have been mutually benefited—but as to your poetic & physiopathic feelings, I more than suspect, that dear little Fanny & Mary[1] have had more to do in that business than I. Hartley sends his Love to Mary. 'What? & not to Fanny?' Yes—& to Fanny—but I'll *have* Mary.—He often talks about them.

My poor Lamb!—how cruelly afflictions crowd upon him![2] I am glad, that you think of him as I think—he has an affectionate heart, a mind sui generis, his taste acts so as to appear like the unmechanic simplicity of an Instinct—in brief, he is worth an hundred men of *mere* Talents. Conversation with the latter tribe is like the use of leaden Bells—one warms by *exercise*—Lamb every now & then *eradiates*, & the beam, tho' single & fine as a hair, yet is rich with colours, & I both see & feel it.——In Bristol I was much with Davy—almost all day. He always talks of you with great affection / & defends you with a friend's zeal against the Animalcula, who live on the dung of the great Dung-fly Mackintosh.—If I settle at Keswick, he will be with me in the fall of the year—& so must you——and let me tell you, Godwin! four such men as you, I, Davy, & Wordsworth, do not meet together in one house every day in the year—I mean, four men so distinct with so many sympathies.—

I received yesterday a letter from Southey—he arrived at Lisbon after a prosperous Voyage on the last day of April. His letter to me is dated May day. He girds up his loins for a great

---

[1] Fanny Imlay, natural daughter of Mary Wollstonecraft, and Mary Wollstonecraft Godwin (1797–1851), Shelley's second wife.
[2] Hetty, the Lambs' aged servant, had died, and Mary Lamb suffered her first serious mental attack since her father's death in Apr. 1799.

History of Portugal—which will be translated into the Portuguese, in the first year of the Lusitanian Republic.

Have you seen Mrs Robinson lately? How is she?—Remember me in the kindest & most respectful phrases to her.—I wish, I knew the particulars of her complaint. For Davy has discovered a perfectly new Acid, by which he has restored the use of limbs to persons who had lost them for many years, (one woman 9 years) in cases of supposed Rheumatism. At all events, Davy says, it *can* do no harm, in Mrs Robinson's case—& if she will try it, he will make up a little parcel & write her a letter of *instructions* &c.—— Tell her, & it is the truth, that Davy is exceedingly delighted with the two Poems in the Anthology.—N.B. Did you get my Attempt at a Tragedy from Mrs Robinson?—

To Mrs Smith I am about to write a letter, with a book—be so kind as to inform me of her direction.

Mrs Inchbald[1] I do not like at all—every time, I recollect her, I like her less. That segment of a *look* at the corner of her eye—O God in heaven! it is so cold & cunning—! thro' worlds of wildernesses I would run away from that look, that heart-*picking* look. 'Tis marvellous to me, that you can like that Woman.—

I shall remain here about ten days for certain. If you have leisure & inclination in that time, write—if not, I will write to you where I am going or at all events whither I am gone.

God bless you | & | Your sincerely affectionate
                                        S. T. Coleridge

Sara desires to be remembered kindly to you—and sends a kiss to Fanny & 'dear meek little Mary.'

334. *To Humphry Davy*

Address: Mr Davy | Pneumatic Institution | Hotwells | Bristol   *Single*
MS. Royal Institution. Pub. E. L. G. i. 139.
Stamped: Bridg⟨ewater⟩.

Saturday Morning [7 June 1800][2]
Mr T. Poole's Nether Stowey, Somerset.
My dear Davy

I sent you on Tuesday *last* a letter, inclosing 5£, being 5 shillings less than I owe you——in the same letter I craved a little of your acid, with a scrawl stating in what cases it might be used.——As my Letters go by cross post, I am anxious to know whether you have received it—because by the same post I sent a much larger

---

[1] Mrs. Elizabeth Inchbald (1753–1821), novelist, dramatist, and actress.

[2] Since Coleridge tells Davy that the acid must be sent 'before Thursday, if at all', and since he was in Bristol on Thursday, 12 June, this letter must have been written on 7 June.

sum up to the North.—If you can, send me a little tiny bottle of the acid, sending it to Mrs Fricker, No / 10, Stokes Croft, with a note to her—desiring her to have it delivered to Milton, the Stowey Carrier, for me. This must be done before Thursday, if at all. I have now finally determined on the North—so Much for Business.—

I received a very kind Letter from Godwin, in which he says, that he never thinks of you but with a brother's feelings of love & expectation.——Indeed, I am sure, he does not.—

I think of translating Blumenbach's manual of natural History[1]— it is very well written, & would, I think, be useful to Students as an admirable direction to their studies, & to others it would supply a *general* Knowlege of the subject—I will state the contents of the book—1 Of the Naturalia in general, and their division into three Kingdoms. 2 of organized Bodies in general. 3. of animals in general. 4 of the Mammalia. 5. Birds. 6.—Amphibions. 7 Fishes. 8. Insects. 9 Worms. 10. Plants. 11. of Minerals in general. 12. of Stones, and earthy Fossils. 13. of Mineral Salts. 14. combustible minerals. 15. of Metals. 16. Petrifactions—at the end there is an alphabetical Index—— / so that it is at once, a Natural History & a dictionary of Natural History. To each animal &c all the European names are given—with, of course, the scientific characteristics—.— I have the last Edition, i.e. that of April 1799.—Now I wish to know from you whether there is in English already any work, any work of one Volume (this would make 800 pages) that renders this useless.——In short, should I be right in advising Longman to undertake it?——Answer me as soon as you conveniently can.— Blumenbach has been no very great discoverer, tho' he has done some respectable things in that way; but he is a man of enormous knowlege, & has an *arranging* head.——Ask Beddoes, if you do not know.—

When you have leisure, you would do me a great service, if you would briefly state your metaphysical system of Impressions, Ideas, Pleasures, & Pains, the laws that govern them, & the reasons which induce you to consider them as essentially distinct from each other.—My motive for this request is the following— As soon as I settle, I shall read Spinoza & Leibnitz—and I particularly wish to know wherein they agree with, & wherein differ from, you. If you will do this, I promise you to send you the result—& with it my own creed.—

God bless you | &
S. T. Coleridge

---

[1] J. F. Blumenbach, *Beyträge zur Naturgeschichte*, 1790. Coleridge did not carry out his intention of translating the work.

Blumenbach's Book contains references to all the best writers on each subject.—My friend T. Poole begs me to ask what in your opinion are the parts or properties in the Oak bark which tan skins, and is cold water a complete menstruum for those parts or properties?—I understand from Poole, that nothing is so lit[tle] understood as the chemical Theory of Tan[ning], tho' nothing is of more importance, in the circle of Manufactures.—In other words, does Oak bark give out to cold water all those of it's parts which *tan*[?]—

335. *To Josiah Wedgwood*

Address: Josiah Wedgewood Esq. | 39 | Gloucester Place | Portman Square | London
MS. Wedgwood Museum. Pub. with omis. Tom Wedgwood, *93.*
Stamped: Bristol, 12 June 1800.

Bristol   Thursday June 12 1800
My dear Sir

Enclosed is 20£—I have had it by me these 4 weeks, in the purpose of seeing you in London; but have been prevented by my own affairs & other people's.—

I had heard such very pleasing accounts of your dear Brother, accounts exaggerated at second hand by the joy of the narrators, that T. Wedgewood's own statement came on me as a disappointment. Still however Bloxam must have seen a great difference, or he *could* not have written as he did. God in heaven bless him!——Your letter to me, that is, the account in your letter made the tears roll down Poole's face——.

I did not receive your letter till some time after it's arrival, having been down to Porlock a house hunting——but neither there, nor any where in the vicinity of Stowey can I get a suitable House— So I shall move Northward—but of this I shall write to you from Ambleside—At present the Bustle of the Office, in which I am writing, dings about me like Tavern Bells.—Old Mrs Poole is, I am afraid, dying.—I will write this day to Stuart to prevent the paper—.—

My respectful remembrances to Mrs Wedgewood—believe me with affectionate & grateful esteem

your sincere Friend
S. T. Coleridge

I leave Bristol to morrow—

To Biggs and Cottle

336. *To Biggs and Cottle*

Address: Messrs Biggs and Cottle | Printers | St Augustine's Back | Bristol[1]
Single

MS. *Yale University Lib. Hitherto unpublished.*

From the time of his return from Germany in May 1799, Wordsworth had been preoccupied with the sale and reception of *Lyrical Ballads,* and during Coleridge's visit to Grasmere in April 1800, he apparently determined to reissue the *Lyrical Ballads* of 1798 as volume 1, to prepare a second volume made up of new poems, and to publish the work in his own name. Accordingly, when Coleridge left for Bristol on 4 May, he took with him copies of several of Wordsworth's poems intended for the second volume. These poems he gave to Humphry Davy, who was to look over the proof sheets. He probably made arrangements with Biggs and Cottle to print the volumes; certainly, as an unpublished letter from Wordsworth shows, he made an agreement on Wordsworth's behalf for the publication of the two volumes by Longman. On his return to Grasmere on 29 June, he plunged whole-heartedly into the labour of preparing the work for the printers.

The manuscripts of the two volumes of *Lyrical Ballads,* except for one sheet containing the second instalment of the Preface and another containing three of Wordsworth's poems, are extant in the form in which they were transmitted to the printers. (See W. H. White, *A Description of the Wordsworth & Coleridge Manuscripts in the possession of T. N. Longman,* 1897, pp. 1–44.) Very little of this material is in Wordsworth's handwriting; instead, it was Dorothy and Coleridge who carried the burden of transcription. Indeed, an examination of the manuscript sheets sent to Biggs and Cottle and a review of Coleridge's activities during the latter half of 1800 reveal a devotion as disinterested as it was remarkable.

Coleridge was faced with several obligations when he arrived in Grasmere at the end of June: he had accepted an advance from Phillips, possibly for a 'bookseller's compilation'; he had agreed to prepare a volume of his German tour for Longman; and beyond all this, he was under a moral responsibility to write his life of Lessing, a work long promised to the Wedgwoods. Instead, however, of rescuing himself from a sea of embarrassments and paying heed to his own reputation, Coleridge gave his best efforts to Wordsworth's project. He unhesitatingly agreed to the inclusion of the four poems he had earlier contributed to the 1798 volume, and he rewrote his poem *Love,* which replaced Wordsworth's *The Convict.* He made far-reaching revisions of *The Ancient Mariner,* probably at the instigation of Wordsworth who was convinced that the poem had been 'an injury' to the *Lyrical Ballads* and that its 'strangeness' had 'deterred readers from going on' (*Early Letters,* 226–7). He agreed that *Christabel* should conclude the second volume, and, after a tremendous expenditure of creative energy, he succeeded in composing Part II of *Christabel,* before Wordsworth determined not to include it. Not only did he transcribe many of Wordsworth's poems and prepare directions to the printers; but once *Lyrical Ballads* was published, he did his utmost to win favourable reception for the volumes by writing long letters to several persons of eminence (see Letters 368 and 375). Poole had earlier cautioned against 'prostration in regard to Wordsworth'. Coleridge's utter disregard of anything but Wordsworth's reputation shows how rightly Poole had assessed the situation. (Letters 336, 337, 345,

[1] The following note appears on the address sheet: 'Begin the Printing immediately. W. W.—'

346, 347, 359, and 372 are drawn from the manuscripts of *Lyrical Ballads* and
contain Coleridge's instructions to the printers.)

This letter is the first communication to the printers and is drawn from
a sheet entirely in Coleridge's handwriting, except for two brief passages
written by Dorothy.
Stamped: Kendal.

[Mid-July 1800]

The first Volume of the Lyrical Ballads is to be printed in the
following order. The Advertisement is to be omitted—and the
Volume to begin with

1 Expostulation and Reply.
2 The Tables turned: an evening scene, on the same subject.
3 Old man travelling, &c
4 The Complaint of a forsaken Indian Woman
5 The last of the Flock
6 Lines left upon a seat in a Yew tree which stands near the Lake
   of Esthwaite, &c
7 The Foster mother's Tale, &c
8 Goody Blake & Harry Gill
9 The Thorn
10 We are seven.
11 Anecdote for Fathers, &c
12 Lines written at a small Distance from my House, and sent by
   my little Boy to the Person, to whom they are addressed
13 The Female Vagrant
14 The Dungeon
15 Simon Lee, the old Huntsman, &c
16 Lines written in early Spring
17 The Nightingale
18 Lines written when sailing in a Boat at Evening. ⎰Vide
19 Lines written near Richmond upon the Thames. ⎱Alterations
20 The ideot Boy
21 Love.—(Vide Alteration)
22 The Mad Mother
23 The ancient mariner, a Poet's Reverie.
24 Lines written a few Miles above Tintern Abbey, &c

N.B. The Convict is to be omitted—& in the rest the following
Alterations are to be made from the printed Copy. Mr Biggs will
be so good as to be careful that the printed Copy, which he uses,
shall be that which contains the Nightingale & not one of those first
Copies which contained Lewti, or the Circassian Love-chant.[1]——

---

[1] It was at first intended to include *Lewti* in the 1798 *Lyrical Ballads* and
a few copies containing that poem were printed. Later *Lewti* was cancelled
and *The Nightingale* substituted. See Wise, *Bibliography*, 211.

N.B. all the Titles are to be printed at full length from the printed Copy—except where an alteration is noticed in this & the following letter.—

Alterations to be made.[1]

The Foster mother's Tale, a Dramatic Fragment—to be printed The Foster mother's Tale a Narration in Dramatic blank Verse, & to begin at the words 'But that entrance Mother?' The first 15 lines to be omitted.—Likewise Page 56th line 14th—instead of 'hole' print 'cell.' Likewise line 18th for sung print sang. Likewise Page 57th Line 2nd instead of 'He always doted' Print 'Leoni doted.' In the same page omit the two lines

> 'Such as would lull a listening child to sleep
> His rosy face besoiled with unwiped tears'

The Dungeon. Line 2 & the comma after wisdom.

> Line 10 & the colon after 'plague-spot', & put a full
> stop instead.
> Line 14 ∧ a comma after the words 'clanking hour,'

The Nightingale. In the title omit the words 'a conversational Poem'. In p. 67 omit the following lines.

> On moonlight Bushes,
> Whose dewy leafits are but half disclos'd,
> You may perchance behold them on the Twigs,
> Their bright, bright eyes, their eyes both bright & full,
> Glist'ning, while many a Glow-worm in the shade
> Lights up her love-torch.

337. *To Biggs and Cottle*

Address: Messrs Biggs and Cottle | Printers | St Augustine's Back | Bristol
Single
MS. Yale University Lib. Hitherto unpublished.
This second communication to the printers is entirely in Coleridge's hand-writing and concludes the instructions for the first volume of *Lyrical Ballads*. It contains a new version of *Love*, earlier published in the *Morning Post*, 21 December 1799, under the title, *Introduction to the Tale of the Dark Ladie*; revisions for *The Ancient Mariner*; and slight corrections, not included here, for three of Wordsworth's poems.
Stamped: Kendal.

---

[1] In the manuscript Coleridge wrote out corrections for the first nineteen poems, Dorothy adding part of the directions for the *Yew Tree* and *The Foster-mother's Tale*. Only those changes affecting Coleridge's own poems are included here.

[Mid-July 1800]

[Poem] 21. In room of the Convict print the following Poem.

LOVE.[1]

All Thoughts, all Passions, all Delights,
Whatever stirs this mortal Frame,
All are but Ministers of Love
    And feed his sacred flame.

Oft in my waking dreams do I
Live o'er again that happy hour,[2]
When midway on the Mount I lay
    Beside the Ruin'd Tower.

The Moonshine stealing o'er the scene
Had blended with the Lights of Eve;
And she was there, my Hope, my Joy,
    My own dear Genevieve!

She lean'd against the armed Man,
The Statue of the armed Knight:
She stood and listen'd to my Harp
    Amid the ling'ring Light.

Few Sorrows hath she of her own,
My Hope, my Joy, my Genevieve!
She loves me best, whene'er I sing
    The Songs, that make her grieve.

I play'd a soft[3] and doleful Air,
I sang an old and moving Story[4]—
An old rude Song, that fitted well
    The Ruin wild and hoary.

She listen'd with a flitting Blush,
With downcast Eyes and modest Grace;
For well she knew, I could not choose
    But gaze upon her Face.

I told her of the Knight, that wore
Upon his Shield a burning Brand;
And that[5] for ten long Years he woo'd
    The Lady of the Land.

---

[1] *Poems*, i. 330.
[2] O ever in my waking dreams
  I dwell upon that happy hour, [Cancelled version of lines 5 and 6 above.]
[3] sad [Cancelled word in line above.]
[4] Ditty [Cancelled word in line above.]
[5] how [Cancelled word in line above.]

I told her, how he pin'd: and, ah!
The low, the deep, the pleading tone,
With which I sang another's Love,
    Interpreted my own.

She listen'd with a flitting Blush,
With downcast Eyes and modest Grace;
And she forgave me, that I gaz'd
    Too fondly on her Face!

But when I told the cruel scorn
Which craz'd this bold and lovely Knight,
And that[1] he cross'd the mountain woods
    Nor rested day nor night;

That[2] sometimes from the savage Den,
And sometimes from the darksome Shade,
And sometimes starting up at once
    In green and sunny Glade,

There came, and look'd him in the face,
An Angel beautiful and bright;
And that[3] he knew, it was a Fiend,
    This miserable Knight!

And that,[4] unknowing what he did,
He leapt amid a murd'rous Band,
And sav'd from outrage worse than Death
    The Lady of the Land;

And how she wept and clasp'd his knees,
And how she tended him in vain——
And ever[5] strove to expiate
    The Scorn, that craz'd his Brain.

And that[6] she nurs'd him in a Cave;
And how his Madness went away
When on the yellow forest leaves
    A dying Man he lay;

[1] how [Cancelled word in line above.]
[2] How [Cancelled word in line above.]
[3] how [Cancelled word in line above.]
[4] how [Cancelled word in line above.]
[5] For still she [Cancelled words in line above.]
[6] how [Cancelled word in line above.]

His dying Words——but when I reach'd
That tenderest strain of all the Ditty,
My falt'ring Voice and pausing Harp
    Disturb'd her soul with Pity!

All Impulses of Soul and Sense
Had thrill'd my guileless Genevieve,
The Music, and the doleful Tale,
    The rich and balmy Eve;

And Hopes, and Fears that kindle Hope,
An undistinguishable Throng!
And gentle Wishes long subdued,
    Subdued and cherish'd long!

She wept with pity and delight,
She blush'd with love and maiden shame;
And, like the murmur of a dream,
    I heard her breathe my name.[1]

Her Bosom heav'd[2]—she stepp'd aside;
As conscious of my Look, she stepp'd—
Then suddenly with timorous eye
    She fled to me and wept.

She half-inclos'd me with her Arms,
She press'd me with a meek embrace;
And bending back her head look'd up,
    And gaz'd upon my face.

'Twas partly Love, and partly Fear,
And partly 'twas a bashful Art
That I might rather feel than see
    The Swelling of her Heart.

I calm'd her fears; and she was calm,
And told her love with virgin[3] Pride;
And so I won my Genevieve,
    My bright and beauteous Bride.

[1] I saw her bosom heave and swell,
  Heave and swell with inward sighs;
  I could not choose but love to see
    Her gentle Bosom rise. [Cancelled stanza above.]
  [1 heave] rise
[2] Her wet cheek glow'd—[Cancelled words in line above.]
[3] Maiden [Cancelled word in line above.]

[Poem] 23 The Rime of the Ancyent Marinere in seven Parts.
Instead of this title print the Following—

The Ancient Mariner,
A Poet's Reverie.

Let the Argument be thus printed—

How a Ship, having first sailed to the Equator, was driven by
Storms to the cold Country towards the South Pole; how the
Ancient Mariner cruelly, and in contempt of the laws of hospitality,
killed a Sea-bird; and how he was followed by many and strange
Judgements;[1] till having finished this penance[1] and in what manner
he came back to his own Country.

p. 5.—alter the title, as before.

p. 5. First line of first stanza—for 'ancyent Marinere' print
'ancient Mariner.'

p. 6. line 4. for 'Marinere'! print 'Mariner'!

p. 6. line 12 for 'Marinere' print 'Mariner.'

p. 6. line 16 for 'Marinere' print 'Mariner[']

p. 8. line 3 for 'ancyent' print 'ancient'.

p. 8. line 4 for 'Marinere' read 'Mariner.'

p. 8. line 5 for 'Listen, Stranger! Storm & wind &c' print

'And now there came the stormy Wind'[2]

p. 8. line 9 for 'Listen, Stranger! Mist & snow' print 'And now
there came both Mist and Snow'.

p. 8. line 10. for 'cauld' print 'cold[']

p. 8. line 12 for 'Emerauld' print 'Emerald'——

p. 8. line 15. for Ne——ne print Nor—nor—

p. 9. line 4. for 'Like Noises of a swound' print

A wild and ceaseless Sound.

p. 9. line 7. for 'And an it were' print

'As if it had been'

p. 9. line 9. For 'Marineres' print 'Mariners.[']

p. 9. line 16. For 'Marinere's' print 'Mariner's'

p. 10. line 3. For 'fog smoke-white' print

'fog-smoke white'

[1-1] *Struck out in the MS.*

[2] Coleridge cancelled this direction to the printers and substituted:
p. 8. let the second stanza be thus printed

But now the Northwind came more fierce,
There came a tempest strong;
And southward still for days & weeks
Like Chaff we drove along.

(598)

p. 10. line 5 For 'ancyent Marinere!' print 'ancient Mariner![']
p. 11. print the first stanza thus

> The Sun now rose upon the Right;[1]
> Out of the Sea came he,
> Still hid in mist; and on the Left
> Went down into the Sea.

p. 11. line 8. for 'Marinere's' print 'Mariner's'
p. 12. line 1. for 'Ne dim ne red, like God's own head'
   print—   Nor dim nor red, like an Angel's Head.
p. 13. line 6. For 'ne—ne' print 'nor—nor'
p. 13. line 12 For 'Ne' print 'Nor'
p. 15. Omit the two lines 'I saw a something in the Sky
                          No bigger than my Fist'

and in their stead insert the following separate Stanza

> So pass'd a weary Time; each Throat
> Was parch'd, and glaz'd each eye,
> When, looking westward, I beheld
> A something in the Sky.

> At first it seem'd a little speck, &c

p. 15. line 9. For 'an' print 'as if'
p. 16. after the first stanza
   thus—

> With throat unslak'd, with black lips bak'd,
> We could nor laugh nor wail,
> Thro' utter Drouth all dumb we stood
> Till I bit my arm and suck'd the blood,
> and cry'd, A sail! a sail!

p. 16. last line but one   instead of
                'Withouten wind, withouten tide'

print 'without or wind or current tide[']—
in the same stanza instead of 'She doth not tack from side' print

> 'See! see! (I cry'd) she tacks no more![']'[2]

The last stanza of this page to be thus altered—

> 'See! see!' (I cry'd) 'she tacks no more!
> 'Hither to work us Weal
> 'Without a breeze, without a Tide
> 'She steddies with upright Keel![']

---

[1] Left [Cancelled word in line above.]
[2] *From* last line . . . no more— *is struck out in the MS.*

p. 18. Alter the first stanza of this page into the following:

> Are those *her* Ribs, thro' which the Sun
> Did peer, as thro' a Grate?
> And are those two all, all her crew,
> That Woman, and her Mate?

p. 18. line 9. For 'They're' print 'They were'

p. 18. last stanza alter the words 'are—are—are—is—is—makes'— into—'were—were—were—was—was—made'.

p. 19. line 10 For 'Oft' print 'Off'.

p. 19. line 13. For 'atween' print 'between[']

p. 21. line 1. For 'ancyent marinere' print 'ancient Mariner![']

p. 22. line 7. For 'eldritch' print 'ghastly'

p. 23. line 2. For 'Ne—ne' print 'Nor—nor.[']

p. 24. line 2. For 'Like morning Frosts yspread' print   'Like April Hoar-frost spread'

p. 26. line 3. For 'yeven' print 'given'.

p. 27. line 5. Instead of 'The roaring wind! it roar'd far off' print   'And soon I heard a roaring wind'

p. 27. line 9. For 'bursts' print 'burst.'

p. 27. line 11. For 'are' print 'were'

p. 27. line 13. For 'The Stars dance on between' print 'The wan Stars danc'd between.'

p. 27. Print the last stanza thus—

> And the coming wind did roar more loud;
> And the Sails did sigh, like sedge;
> And the Rain pour'd down from one black cloud—
> The Moon was at it's edge.

p. 28. Print the two first lines thus—

> The thick black Cloud was cleft, and still
> The Moon was at it's side:

p. 28. line 4. For 'falls' print 'fell'.

p. 28. Alter the two first lines of the second Stanza thus— /

> The loud[1] Wind never reach'd the Ship,
> Yet now the Ship mov'd on!

p. 28. line 11. For 'Ne—ne'—print 'Nor—nor'—

p. 28. line 16. For 'Marineres' print 'Mariners'

p. 29.—Omit the 7th & 8th lines, 'And I quak'd &c'[2]

p. 29. before the words 'The Day-light dawn'd' insert the following Stanza—

---

[1] strong [Cancelled word in line above.]
[2] For the omitted lines see *Poems*, ii. 1039, lines 337–8.

' I fear thee, ancient Mariner!'
Be calm,[1] thou Wedding-Guest!
'Twas not those[2] Souls, that fled in pain,
Which to their corses came again,
But a troop of Spirits blest:

and alter the words, 'The Day-light dawn'd'—
into 'For when it dawn'd,'

P. 30. line 2. For 'Lavrock' print 'Sky-lark'

P. 31.—Omit the whole of this page.[3]

P. 36. Line 6—For 'Withouten wave or wind?'
print 'Without or wave or wind?'

P. 36. Last line for 'Marinere's' print 'Mariner's'.

P. 37. line 11. For 'een' print 'eyes'

P. 37. line 12 For 'Ne' print 'Nor'

P. 37. Alter the last Stanza of this page into the following—

And[4] now this Spell was snapt: once more
I view'd the Ocean green,
And look'd far forth, yet little saw
Of what had else been seen.

P. 38. line 1. For 'lonely' print 'lonesome'

P. 38. line 8. For 'Ne—ne' print 'Nor—nor.'

P. 40. Omit five stanzas here—namely, the whole of this page, and
the first Stanza of p. 41.[5]

P. 42. line 13. For 'Eftsones' print 'But soon.'

P. 43. Omit the first Stanza of this page.[6]

P. 44. l. 4. For 'Marineres' print 'Mariners'.

P. 44. l. 5. For 'Contree' print 'countrée.[']

P. 45. line 1. for 'ne'rd' print 'ner'd'

P. 46. line 6. For 'Ne—ne' print 'Nor—nor'

P. 48.—Alter the last stanza into the following

Since then at an uncertain hour
That Agony returns,
And till my ghastly Tale is told,
This[7] Heart within me burns.

P. 50. line 12. Omit the comma after 'loveth well[']

P. 50. line 14. Omit the comma after 'loveth best'

[1] Fear not [Cancelled words in line above.]
[2] the [Cancelled word in line above.]
[3] For the omitted stanzas see *Poems*, ii. 1040, lines 362–77.
[4] But [Cancelled word in line above.]
[5] For the omitted stanzas see *Poems*, ii. 1043–4, lines 481–502.
[6] For the omitted stanza see *Poems*, ii. 1044, lines 531–6.
[7] My [Cancelled word in line above.]

P. 51. line 1. For 'Marinere' print 'Mariner'[1]

Directions will be sent by the next post for the second Volume—
in the meantime, Mr Biggs will be pleased to make all convenient
Dispatch with the first. He will probably find it advisable to take
a printed Copy of the Lyrical Ballads, & correct it himself through-
out, according to the directions in this & the preceding letter—

[1] Despite these careful revisions, Wordsworth seems to have retained his
objections to *The Ancient Mariner*; and in sending off to Biggs and Cottle the
last two paragraphs of the Preface and a long note defending *The Thorn*, he
added the following comment on Coleridge's poem, revealing thereby a critical
blindness and a disregard for the feelings of a fellow poet. The sheet containing
it must have been posted *circa* 1 Oct., since Dorothy Wordsworth says she
wrote out the manuscript on 30 Sept. and corrected it the next day (*Journals*,
i. 62). Coleridge was not at Grasmere from 26 Sept. to 4 Oct., this being the
time of his baby's serious illness, and I doubt that he saw Wordsworth's
ungracious note before it appeared in print.

I cannot refuse myself the gratification of informing such Readers as may
have been pleased with this poem, or with any part of it, that they owe
their pleasure in some sort to me; as the Author was himself very desirous
that it should be suppressed. This wish had arisen from a consciousness of
the defects of the poem, & from a knowledge that many persons had been
much displeased with it. The Poem of my Friend has indeed great defects;
first, that the principal person has no distinct character, either in his pro-
fession of Mariner, or as a human being who having been long under the
controul of supernatural impressions might be supposed himself to partake
of something supernatural: secondly, that he does not act, but is continually
acted upon: thirdly, that the events having no necessary connection do not
produce each other; and lastly, that the imagery is somewhat too laboriously
accumulated. Yet the poem contains many delicate touches of passion, and
indeed the passion is every where true to nature; a great number of the
stanzas present beautiful images & are expressed with unusual felicity of
language; and the versification, though the metre is itself unfit for long
poems, is harmonious and artfully varied, exhibiting the utmost powers of
that metre, & every variety of which it is capable. It therefore appeared to
me that these several merits (the first of which, namely that of the passion, is
of the highest kind,) gave to the poem a value which is not often possessed
by better poems. On this account I requested of my Friend to permit me
to republish it. (MS. Yale University Lib.)

Lamb's strictures on Wordsworth's note may account for its omission after
1800. 'I totally differ from your idea that the Marinere should have had a
character and profession. . . . The Ancient Marinere undergoes such Trials, as
overwhelm and bury all individuality or memory of what he was. . . . Your
other observation is I think as well a little unfounded: the Marinere from
being conversant in supernatural events *has* acquired a supernatural and
strange cast of *phrase*, eye, appearance, &c. which frighten the wedding guest.
. . . I am hurt and vexed that you should think it necessary, with a prose
apology, to open the eyes of dead men that cannot see.' *Lamb Letters*, i. 240.

338. *To Daniel Stuart*

Address: D. Stuart Esq. | No / 335 | Strand | London   Morning Post Office
MS. British Museum. Pub. with omis. Letters from the Lake Poets, 7.
Postmark: 19 July 1800. *Stamped*: Keswick.

Tuesday, July 15 1800

Dear Stuart

Since I quitted you, I have never been within 150 miles of London—I left Grasmere with the intention indeed, but at Kendal received letters which forced me Stowey-ward—. Since my re-arrival here, I have been confined part of the time to my bed by a sort of rheumatic fever—& till within this last brace of days, my eyelids have been swoln & inflamed to a degree which has made it imprudent even to write a common letter.—Why should I have wished to shun you?—Surely, we have always behaved kindly & honorably to each other——

Wordsworth's state of Health at this present time is such as to preclude all possibility of writing for a paper—as to myself, I will do what I promised the very first thing I do—this day & tomorrow I must write letters—. On Thursday I will set to, & will not leave off, on my word & honor, till I have done a second part of Pitt, & Buonaparte—. With these I will write you further, whether or no I shall be able to continue in any species of regular connection with your paper—. Whether I do or no, be assured that as a friend I shall be at your service, if you wish any thing particular at any particular time.

Wordsworth requests me to be very express in the communication of his sincere thanks to you, for the interest which you have been so kind as to take in his poems. We are convinced you have been of great service to the sale.—A second Edition is now printing, with a second Volume.

With regard to the play business, Wordsworth has a Tragedy by him, in my opinion, a most masterly one / this he would transmit by you to Mr Sheridan, for Mr Sheridan's opinion, provided *you* would engage that the *Copy* shall be returned to him—as he has but this one perfect Copy. Mr Sheridan will see by this of what kind Mr Wordsworth's dramatic Talents are; & if he should find the Tragedy unfit for representation, he might put Mr W. in the way of writing a play that *should* be fit for representation, by pointing out to him the defects that render the present one untheatrical. Mr Sheridan's conception of my obstinacy is a mistake—. When I sent my play to him, I gave at the same time expressly to him the whole & absolute power of alteration, addition, & omission—. I did indeed defend some parts of my play against Young Linley, but only as a *metaphysician*; never supposing myself to have any voice or suffrage, or even *opinion*, as to what was or was not suited for representation. After all, I never blamed Mr Sheridan for not bringing my play on the stage. God knows my inmost heart, & knows that I never for an hour together thought it likely to succeed —I blamed Mr Sheridan solely for taking no kind of notice even of the receipt of my play, for returning me no answer whatever, & for withholding from me the copy of my play after repeated applications; & those applications too made at a time when I had no copy in my possession, & wished to have disposed of it to the Booksellers—when the 30£, I might have had for it, would have been a draught of Nepenthe & heavenly restoration to me.—But this is all gone by!—I am convinced, I have no Talents for so arduous a species of composition as the Drama.—I should wish you however to state the foregoing account to Mr Sheridan.—My address henceforward will be

> Mr Coleridge, | Greta Hall, | Keswick | Cumberland.

I move thither on Tuesday next.—

N.B. The newspapers come very irregularly indeed.

> Your's sincerely
> S. T. Coleridge

We have never had the Newspaper with the Verses I sent you from Bristol.[1]

339. *To Humphry Davy*

Address: Mr Davy | Pneumatic Institution | Hotwells | Bristol
MS. Royal Institution. Pub. E. L. G. i. 141.
Postmark: 19 July 1800.   *Stamped*: Keswick.

Wed. July 15 [16], 1800

My dear Davy

Since my arrival at Grasmere I have been afflicted with continued illness, in consequence of a cold from wet—for days together I have been obliged to keep my bed; & when up, I have been prevented till within these few days from reading by a pair of swoln & inflamed Eyelids. I hope, that you have suffered no inconvenience from want of the money, which I borrowed of you— it has made me very uneasy; but in a few days I will take care, that it shall be remitted to you. We remove to our own House at Keswick on Tuesday week—my address is, Mr Coleridge, Greta

---

[1] No poetical contributions to the *Morning Post* between 24 Jan. and 13 Oct. 1800 have been identified.

Hall, Keswick, Cumberland. My dear fellow, I would that I could wrap up the view from my House in a pill of opium, & send it to you! I should then be sure of seeing you in the fall of the year. But you *will* come.—

As soon as I have disembrangled my affairs by a couple of months' Industry, I shall attack chemistry, like a Shark—. In the mean time do not forget to fulfil your promise of sending me a synopsis of your metaphysical opinions. I am even *anxious* about this.—I see your Researches on the nitrous oxyde regularly advertised—Be so kind as to order one to be left for me at Longman's, that it may be sent with my box. The difficulty of procuring Books is the greatest disadvantage, under which I shall labor. The carriage from London by the waggon is cross-roadish & insecure; that by the Mail attacks the Purse with 7 Hydra Mouths all open.—I read the day before yesterday in a German Book a fact which appeared to me analogous to those facts exhibited by the respiration of the nitrous Oxyde. The account of the sickness is circumstantially described by persons who attended the patient, 'a young, fiery, lively Youth in the 17th year of his age. At the commencement of the Summer of 1783 he was seized during dinner with a Cramp in his Chest, which was followed by a Fever that continued for four weeks; at the conclusion of which time symptoms of amelioration appeared; but one night he was attacked by the most frightful convulsions, which lasted in all their fury 24 hours without intermission. After these convulsions the Fever recommenced, & was accompanied by strong Delirium. The subject of Death, & his old occupations as a merchant's clerk formed the subjects of his Discourse—in which he discovered a power of mind, a regularity, a logic, an eloquence, wholly unknown in him in his state of health. These orations lasted always till they were intercepted by the cramp in his chest—and when the whole Paroxysm, all the Convulsions, delirious oration, & Cramp were over, instead of appearing exhausted he was to an extraordinary degree elevated, & in such extreme high spirits that whoever had seen him without knowing the previous circumstances would have concluded him to have been in rampant high health.—The Paroxysms returned, and ever with such impetuosity that five stout men could scarcely keep him down; yet ever they left him in the same high spirits & undiminished strength. During his paroxysms he exhibited a proud & fierce contempt for all around him; the color of black was intolerable to him—as were watch ribbons & watch chains & looking-glasses. If he saw one of these in the intervals, his Paroxysm returned instantly. After a Paroxysm, while he was in rampant high spirits, he was persuaded to have a vein opened—the Blood

was almost black, burst from the vein with violence, foam'd, and
was in every respect so remarkable' says the author ['] that it
[was] easily comprehensible how it should have produced this
strange revolution in the whole man. I asked him once how he *felt*
when the Paroxysm was coming on. He answered that at first he
had a sensation of heat from about the stomach spreading upwards
till it reached his head, & that then he began to be more & more
giddy & drunken, & objects grew more & more dim before his eyes,
till he lost all consciousness—and this was the moment in which
the Convulsions always began, which convulsions lasted in their
full fury never less than 8 minutes, but oftener for half an hour.—
In this way the Disease continued without any apparent abate-
ment ten weeks, at which time, after a violent Paroxysm, the
Patient said that *that* would be the last. And so it proved. From
this time the Convulsions ceased, and, to the astonishment of all,
the Patient had lost nothing either of his former Powers, or bodily
strength, or high animal spirits. He was ordered a medicinal Bath
(eine Badekur) that was to secure him from all future attacks—
but after three weeks the Paroxysms returned, tho' not so violently
—and without convulsions, except in [one] instance in which he
had been suddenly frightened. At the end of 14 days he was com-
pletely cured [by] a violent Dysenterie. From this moment to the
time in which the account was published (May 31, 1784) he enjoyed
the most perfect Health, had in no part of the Disease, & in no hour
after, lost any strength, and his animal spirits appear more im-
petuous than they were before. But he has not the least conscious-
ness of any one thing that past during his whole sickness—the whole
ten Weeks seem annihilated from his present Being.[']——This
account is in Moritz's Magazine for experimental Psychology,
p. 12. of the third number of the second Volume.—Does it not
seem here, as if Nature herself had elaborated the nitrous oxyde
out of the common Air?—

In Wordsworth's case, which I have sent to Beddoes, you will
see a curious instance of ideas, linked with feeling habitually, at
length forming blind associations with a particular pain, probably
in the right hypochondrium—so as immediately to excite that
pain.

I have read the little chemist's pocket-book twice over.—Do, do,
my dear Davy! come here in the fall of the year.—Sheridan has
sent to me again about my Tragedy—I do not know what will
come of it—he is an unprincipled Rogue.

Remember me to Mr Coates when you see [him]—and be sure
you do to Matthew Coates, & Mrs Coates. Will you be so kind as
just to look over the sheets of the lyrical Ballads?—What are you

now doing?—God love you! Believe me most affectionately, my
dear Davy, your friend

S. T. Coleridge

340. *To Thomas Poole*

Address: Mr T. Poole | N. Stowey | Bridgewater | Somerset
MS. British Museum. Pub. E. L. G. i. 144.
Postmark: 28 July 1800. *Stamped*: Keswick.

July 24, 1800

My dear Poole

Within a few days of my arrival at Grasmere I increased the
cold, which I had caught at Liverpool, to a rheumatic fever
almost, which confined me to my bed for some days, & left me so
weak, & listless, that writing was hateful to me——& my eye lids
were so swoln, that it was painful too. Had I written to you, I could
have written only as a Duty—and with that feeling never will I
write to you.—We met at Bristol a pleasant chaise companion
who did not leave us till we arrived at Liverpool—we travelled the
first day to Tewksbury, the next night we slept at Shrewsbury,
having passed thro' Worcester, Kidderminster, Bridgenorth &
Colebrook Dale—the next night at Chester, where we stayed a day
& a half. It is a walled city, a walk on the walls all around it—the
Air of the city is thick enough to be edible, & stinks. From Chester
we proceeded, crossing a ferry of 7 miles, to Liverpool.—At Liver-
pool we took up our quarters with Dr Crompton, who lives at Eton,
a noble seat four miles & a half from the town—he received us with
joyous hospitality, & Mrs Crompton, who is all I can conceive of
an angel, with most affectionate gladness. Here we stayed 8 or 9
days, during which I saw a great deal of Dr Currie, Roscoe, Rath-
bone (Colebrook Renyolds's Brother-in-law) & other literati.
Currie is a genuine philosopher; a man of mild & rather solemn
manners—if you had ever seen my Brother George, I would have
referred you to him for a striking resemblance of Currie.—I would
have you by all means order the late Edition in four Volumes of
Burns's Works—the Life is written by Currie, and a masterly
specimen of philosophical Biography it is.—Roscoe is a man of the
most delightful manners—natural, sweet, & cheerful—zealous in
kindness, and a republican with all the feelings of prudence & all
the manners of good sense—so that he is beloved by the Aristocrats
themselves. He has a nice matronly wife, & 9 fine children.—Rath-
bone is a quaker, as brimful of enthusiastic goodness as a vessel
of mortality can be. He is a man of immense fortune. The union
of all these men is most amiable—they truly love each other, a

band of Brothers! And yet by their wisdom in keeping back all
political trials of power in Liverpool they have stifled party spirit
in that city, & enabled themselves to be the founders of a most
magnificent Library—magnificent as a Building, respectable in it's
present stock of Books, & magnificent in what it is to be. They
have received last week an accession of 3000£, all to be laid out in
books of acknowleged reputation—& the yearly income of the
foundation is 1000£. The slave-merchants of Liverpool fly over the
heads of the slave-merchants of Bristol, as Vultures over carrion
crows.—This library is called the Athenaeum. In religion Currie,
I suppose, is a philosopher—Roscoe is a pious Deist—Rathbone, I
suppose, is the same; or more probably he cloathes his Deism even
to his own mind in the language of Scripture—a Christian, as
Taylor is a Platonist.—But this is all *guess.*

On this day I arrived at Keswick, & have entered on my habita-
tion. Wordsworth will stay at Grasmere for a year to come at
least—it is possible, he may not quit it at all.—He is well, unless
when he uses any effort of mind—then he feels a pain in his left
side, which threatens to interdict all species of composition to
him.——Our goods are all arrived—& now in house.—Of Keswick,
& [of] my house, heaven forbid that I shall begin to write at the
fag end of such a beggarly sheet of paper as this—. No! as soon as
the Stir & Hurry is over I shall open upon you in a sheet that might
serve for a sheet!—
My address is

Greta Hall, Keswick, Cumberland.

We are very anxious about your mother—I have said to myself,
that no news is good news.

My love to Ward.—My eyes still remain so weak that it is dis-
agreeable to me to read over my own letter.—I wish, that Ward
would immediately copy for me the third letter which I wrote,
descriptive of the Hartz Mountains.[1] I have got the two first; but
the last is lost—& I want it *immediately.*—Sheridan has sent me
a strange sort of a message about my Tragedy—wishing me to
write for the stage, making all his old offers over again, & charging
the non-representation of my play on my extreme obstinacy in
refusing to have it at all altered!—Did you ever hear of such a
damned impudent Dog?—God for ever bless you, my dear Poole—
& your most affectionate | Friend
S. T. Coleridge

[1] Cf. Letter 282. The copy made by Ward was sent to Coleridge and is now
in the New York Public Library.

341. *To Josiah Wedgwood*

Address: Josiah Wedgewood Esq. | Christ Church | Hampshire
MS. Wedgwood Museum. Pub. with omis. Tom Wedgwood, *102*.
Postmark: 28 July 1800.   *Stamped*: Keswick.

Thursday, July 24, 1800

My dear Sir

I found your letter on my arrival at Grasmere, namely, on the
29th of June—since which time to the present with the exception
of the last few days I have been more unwell, than I have ever
been since I left School—for many days I was forced to keep my
bed, & when released from that worst incarceration, I suffered most
grievously from a brace of swoln Eyelids, & a head into which on
the least agitation the blood felt as rushing in & flowing back
again like the raking of the Tide on a coast of loose stones.—
However, thank God! I am now coming about again. That Tom
receives such pleasure from natural scenery strikes me as it does
you—the total incapability, which I have found in myself to
associate any but the most languid feelings with the godlike
objects which have surrounded me lately, & the nauseous efforts
to *impress* my admiration into the service of nature, has given me
a sympathy with his former state of health which I never before
could have had.—I wish from the bottom of my soul that he may
be enjoying similar pleasures with those which I am now enjoying
with all that newness of sensation; that voluptuous correspondence
of the blood & flesh about me with breeze & sun-heat; which make
convalescence more than repay one for disease.

I parted from Poole with pain & dejection. For him & for myself
in him I should have given Stowey a decisive preference—it was
likewise so conveniently situated that I was in the *way* of almost
all whom I love & esteem. But there was no suitable house, & no
prospect of a suitable house—& the utter desolation, which a small
& inconvenient house spread thro' my literary efforts & hourly
comforts, & the contagious fretfulness of the weaker vessels in my
family, I had experienced to a degree which made it a *duty* for me
to live in no house, in which I could not command one quiet room.
Nor was Stowey without other objections—Mrs Coleridge had
scarcely any society there, and inter nos the nearness to Bristol
connected me too intimately with all the affairs of her family.
Likewise I will say to you what I should not say to another—the
antipathy of those of Poole's relations to whom he is most attached
(& by the most delicate ties) to me, to my wife, & even to my poor
little boy, was excessive—in more than one instance it led his
Brother's Widow into absolute insult to Mrs Coleridge, which

perhaps Poole should have noticed more than he did—perhaps, & more probably, he could not & ought not to have been otherwise than passive. However, it required no overstrained sensibility to make this at times very painful.—These things would have weighed as nothing, *could* I have remained at Stowey; but now they come upon me to diminish my regret.—Add to this Poole's determination to spend a year or two on the continent in case of a Peace & his Mother's Death—. God in heaven bless her! I am sure, she will not live long.—This is the first day of my arrival at Keswick—my house is roomy, situated on an eminence a furlong from the Town—before it an *enormous* Garden more than two thirds of which is rented as a Garden for sale articles, but the walks &c are our's most completely. Behind the house are shrubberies, & a declivity planted with flourishing trees of 15 years' growth or so, at the bottom of which is a most delightful shaded walk by the River Greta, a quarter of a mile in length. The room in which I sit, commands from one window the Basenthwaite Lake, Woods, & Mountains, from the opposite the Derwentwater & fantastic mountains of Borrowdale—straight before me is a wilderness of mountains, catching & streaming lights or shadows at all times— behind the house & entering into all our views is Skiddaw.—My acquaintance here are pleasant—& at some distance is Sir Guilfrid Lawson's[1] Seat with a very large & expensive Library to which I have every reason to hope that I shall have free access.—But when I have been settled here a few days longer, I will write you a minute account of my situation.—Wordsworth lives 12 miles distant—in about a year's time he will probably settle at Keswick likewise.—It is no small advantage here that for two thirds of the year we are in complete retirement—the other third is alive & swarms with Tourists of all shapes & sizes, & characters—it is the very place I would recommend to a novellist or farce writer.— Besides, at that time of the year there is always hope that a friend may be among the number, & miscellaneous crowd, whom this place attracts. So much for Keswick at present.

Have you seen my translation of the Wallenstein? It is a dull heavy play; but I entertain hopes, that you will think the language for the greater part, natural & good common-sense English—to which excellence if I can lay fair claim in any book of poetry or prose, I shall be a very *singular* writer at least.—I am now working at my introduction to the life of Lessing which I trust will be in the press before Christmas—that is, the Introduction which will be

---

[1] Coleridge at first confused the names of father and son. Sir Gilfrid Lawson died in 1794 and was succeeded by his son, Sir Wilfrid Lawson, who died in 1806. The family seat, Brayton Hall, is located near Aspatria in Cumberland.

published first I believe. I shall write again in a few days. Respects to Mrs W. God bless you &

S. T. Coleridge

I have had a sort of a message from Sheridan about my Tragedy.—

I thank you for your kind offer respecting the 20£; but if my health continue, I trust, I shall be able to sail smoothly, without availing myself of it.

342. *To Humphry Davy*

Address: Mr Davy | Pneumatic Institution | Hotwells | Bristol
MS. Royal Institution. Pub. E. L. G. i. 147.
Postmark: 28 July 1800. *Stamped*: Keswick.

Greta Hall, Keswick, Cumberland.
Friday Evening—July 25, 1800

My dear Davy

Work hard, and if Success do not dance up like the bubbles in the Salt (with the Spirit Lamp under it) may the Devil & his Dam take Success!—'Sdeath, my dear fellow! from the Window before me there is a great *Camp* of Mountains—Giants seem to have pitch'd their Tents there—each Mountain is a Giant's Tent—and how the light streams from them—& the Shadows that travel upon them!—Davy! I *ake* for you to be with us—.

W. Wordsworth is such a lazy fellow that I bemire myself by making promises for him—the moment, I received your letter, I wrote to him. He will, I hope, write immediately to Biggs & Cottle[1]——At all events those poems must not as yet be delivered up to them; because that beautiful Poem, the Brothers, which I read to you in Paul Street, I neglected to deliver to you—& that must begin the Volume.[2] I trust however that I have invoked the

[1] On Tuesday, 28 [29] July, Wordsworth wrote at Coleridge's instigation to Humphry Davy, with whom he was as yet unacquainted, his letter accompanying the first manuscript sheet of poems for the second volume of *Lyrical Ballads*: 'You would greatly oblige me by looking over the enclosed poems and correcting any thing you find amiss in the punctuation a business which I am ashamed to say I am no adept. . . . I write to request that you would have the goodness to look over the proof-sheets of the 2nd volume before they are finally struck off. In future I mean to send the Mss. to Biggs and Cottle with a request that along with the proof-sheets they may be sent to you. . . . Be so good as to put the enclosed Poems into Mr. Bigges hands as soon as you have looked them over in order that the printing may be commenced immediately.' *Early Letters*, 244-5. The 'enclosed Poems', in Dorothy's handwriting, were *Hart-leap Well, There was a Boy, Ellen Irwin*, and the first part of *The Brothers*.

[2] When *Lyrical Ballads* appeared, *The Brothers* was the third poem in the second volume.

sleeping Bard with a spell so potent, that he will awake & deliver up that Sword of Argantyr, which is to rive the Enchanter GAUDY-VERSE from his Crown to his Fork.——

What did you think of that case, I translated for you from the German/?—That I was a well meaning Sutor, who had ultra-crepidated[1] with more zeal than wisdom!!—I give myself credit for that word 'ultra-crepidated'—it started up in my Brain like a creation. I write to Tobin by this Post.

Godwin is gone Ireland-ward, on a visit to Curran, says the Morning Post—to Grattan, writes C. Lamb.——

We drank tea the night before I left Grasmere on the Island in that lovely lake, our kettle swung over the fire hanging from the branch of a Fir Tree, and I lay & saw the woods, & mountains, & lake all trembling, & as it were *idealized* thro' the subtle smoke which rose up from the clear red embers of the fir-apples which we had collected. Afterwards, we made a glorious Bonfire on the Margin, by some alder bushes, whose twigs heaved & sobbed in the uprushing column of smoke—& the Image of the Bonfire, & of us that danced round it—ruddy laughing faces in the twilight—the Image of this in a Lake smooth as that sea, to whose waves the Son of God had said, PEACE! May God & all his Sons love you as I do——

S. T. Coleridge

Sara desires her kind remembrances—Hartley is a spirit that dances on an aspin leaf—the air, which yonder sallow-faced & yawning Tourist is breathing, is to my Babe a perpetual Nitrous Oxyde. Never was more joyous creature born—Pain with him is so wholly trans-substantiated by the Joys that had rolled on before, & rushed in after, that oftentimes 5 minutes after his Mother has whipt him, he has gone up & asked her to whip him again.——

343. *To James Webbe Tobin*

Address: Mr. Tobin, Junr., | Berkeley Square, Bristol.
Pub. Atlantic Monthly, *July 1894, p. 97.*

Friday, July 25, 1800

From the leads on the housetop of Greta Hall, Keswick, Cumberland, at the present time in the occupancy and usufruct-possession of S. T. Coleridge, Esq., Gentleman-poet and Philosopher in a mist.

Yes, my dear Tobin, here I am, with Skiddaw behind my back;

---

[1] 'Ne Sutor ultra crepidam.' [Note by S. T. C.] See *Lamb Letters*, i. 193.

the Lake of Bassenthwaite, with its simple and majestic *case* of
mountains, on my right hand; on my left, and stretching far away
into the fantastic mountains of Borrowdale, the Lake of Derwent-
water; straight before me a whole camp of giants' tents,—or is it
an ocean rushing in, in billows that, even in the serene sky, reach
halfway to heaven? When I look at the feathery top of this
scoundrel pen, with which I am making desperate attempts to
write, I see (in that slant direction) the sun almost setting,—in ten
minutes it will touch the top of the crag; the vale of Keswick lies
between us. So much for the topography of the letter; as to the
chronology, it is half past seven in the evening.

I left Wordsworth yesterday; he was tolerably well, and medi-
tates more than his side permits him even to attempt. He has a bed
for you; but I absolutely stipulate that you shall be half the time
at Keswick. We have house-room enough, and I am sure I need say
nothing of anything else. What should prevent you from coming
and spending the next brace of months here? I will suppose you
to set off in the second week of August, and Davy will be here in
the first week of September at the farthest; and then, my dear
fellow, for physiopathy and phileleutherism—sympathy lemonaded
with a little argument—punning and green peas with bacon, or
very ham; rowing and sailing on the lake (there is a nice boat
obsequious to my purposes). Then, as to chemistry, there will be
Davy with us. We shall be as rich with reflected light as yon cloud
which the sun has taken to his very bosom!

When you come, I pray you do not forget to bring Bartram's
Travels[1] with you. Where is John Pinny? He talked of accom-
panying you. Wordsworth builds on his coming down this autumn;
if I knew his present address, I would write to him. Wordsworth
remains at Grasmere till next summer (perhaps longer). His
cottage is indeed in every respect so delightful a residence, the

---

[1] William Bartram, *Travels through North and South Carolina, Georgia, East
and West Florida, the Cherokee Country, the Extensive Territories of the Musco-
gulges, or Creek Confederacy, and the Country of the Chactaws; containing an
Account of the Soil and Natural Productions of those Regions, together with
Observations on the Manners of the Indians*, Philadelphia, 1791. A copy of
Bartram's *Travels*, with the following note from Coleridge to Sara Hutchinson
pasted in the volume, belongs to Mrs. Dickson of Stepping Stones, Grasmere:

Sara Hutchinson | from | S. T. C. | Dec. 19. 1801

This is not a Book of Travels properly speaking; but a series of poems, chiefly
descriptive, occasioned by the objects which the Traveller observed.—It is
a *delicious* Book; and like all *delicious* things, you must take but a *little* of it
at a time.—Was it not about this time of the year, that I read to you parts
of the 'Introduction' of this Book when William and Dorothy had gone out
to walk?—I remember the evening well, but not what time of the year it was.
[From a transcript kindly made by Mrs. E. F. Rawnsley of Allan Bank.]

walks so dry after the longest rains, the heath and a silky kind of fern so luxurious a bedding on every hilltop, and the whole vicinity so tossed about on those little hills at the feet of the majestic mountains, that he moves in an eddy; he cannot get out of it.

In the way of books, we are extraordinarily well off for a country place. My landlord has a respectable library, full of dictionaries and useful modern things; *ex. gr.*, the Scotch Encyclopaedia, the authors of which may the devil scotch, for toothless serpents that poison with dribble! But there is at some distance Sir Wilfred Lawson's magnificent library, and Sir Wilfred talks of calling upon me, and of course I keep the man in good humor with me, and gain the use of his books.

Hartley returns his love to you; he talks often about you. I hear his voice at this moment distinctly; he is below in the garden, shouting to some foxgloves and fern, which he has transplanted, and telling them what he will do for them if they grow like good boys! This afternoon I sent him naked into a shallow of the river Greta; he trembled with the novelty, yet you cannot conceive his raptures.

God bless you!

I remain, with affectionate esteem, | Yours sincerely,
S. T. Coleridge.

I open the letter, and make a new fold, to tell you that I have bit the wafer into the very shape of the young moon that is just above the opposite hill.

344. *To Samuel Purkis*

Address: Samuel Purkis Esq. | Brentford | near | London
MS. British Museum. Pub. E. L. G. i. 149.
Postmark: 1 August 1800. *Stamped*: Keswick.

Greta Hall, Keswick, Cumberland.
Tuesday, July 29. 1800

Dear Purkis

I write to you from the *Leads* of Greta Hall, a Tenement in the possession of S. T. Coleridge, Esq. Gentleman-Poet & Philosopher in a mist—this Greta Hall is a House on a Small eminence, a furlong from Keswick, in the county of Cumberland.—Yes—my dear Sir! here I am—with Skiddaw at my back—on my right hand the Bassenthwait Water with it's majestic *Case* of Mountains, all of simplest Outline—looking slant, direct over the feather of this infamous Pen, I see the Sun setting—my God! what a scene—! Right before me is a great *Camp* of single mountains—each in

shape resembles a Giant's Tent!—and to the left, but closer to it
far than the Bassenthwaite Water to my right, is the lake of
Keswick, with it's Islands & white sails, & glossy Lights of Even-
ing—*crowned* with green meadows, but the three remaining sides
are encircled by the most fantastic mountains, that ever Earth-
quakes made in sport; as fantastic, as if Nature had *laughed* herself
into the convulsion, in which they were made.—Close behind me
at the foot of Skiddaw flows the Greta, I hear it's murmuring
distinctly—then it curves round almost in a semicircle, & is now
catching the purple Lights of the scattered Clouds above it
directly before me—

           A. A. A. Is the river & B. my House.—

Till now I have been grievously indisposed—now I am enjoying
the Godlikeness of the Place, in which I am settled, with the
voluptuous & joy-trembling Nerves of Convalescence—. We
arrived here last week—I was confined a fortnight at Grasmere.—
At Liverpool I was very much with Roscoe, a man of the most
fascinating manners—if good sense, sweetness, simplicity, hilarity,
joining in a literary man who is a good Husband & the excellent
Father of nine children, can give any man's manners the claim to
that word.—

Sara Coleridge is well—she expects to be confined in the first
weeks of September. Hartley is all Health & extacy—He is a
Spirit dancing on an aspen Leaf—unwearied in Joy, from morning
to night indefatigably joyous.——

And how do you go on? and dear Mrs Purkis?—And your little
ones?—Surely 'tis but a needless *form* for me to say, with what
sincere exultation I should stretch out the right-hand of fellow-
ship to you, if chance or choice should lead you hither! I would,
I knew the spell that could force you.—We have pleasant acquain-
tance here—& I shall have free access to the magnificent Library
of Sir Wilfred Lawson—yet you may well suppose, I did not quit
Stowey without dejection, and that I cannot now think of my
separation from Poole without a Pang. Now, while I gaze, there is
one dark Slip of Cloud that lies across the bright Sun on the
Mountain Top!——And such, my dear Purkis! is that thought
to me.

I have greatly regretted, that my engagements in London pre-
vented me from *cultivating* the acquaintance of Mr Howard.[1] I was
exceedingly struck with him / & at that time & since have often
wished for an opportunity of experimenting concerning the benefit

---

[1] Probably Henry Howard (1769–1847), the painter.

which a Poet & Painter might be of to each other's minds, if they were long together. When you see him, remember me to him expressly—and add, that if wearied with town or permitted by his occupations to leave it for a while, he should feel any inclination to see how Nature [has been divers]ified at once to gratify & baff[le every responsive][1] Feeling, I have a plain table & a quiet room at his service, for any length of time he can stay with me. In short, I should be *very glad* to see him. Can't you come down together? Hang it—don't stand deliberating, but come. My wife will not let me stay on the Leads—I must go, & unpack a Trunk for her—she cannot *stoop* to it—thanks to my late Essay on Population!

God bless you &

[Signature cut off.]

345. *To Biggs and Cottle*

Address: Messrs Biggs & Cottle | Printers | St Augustine's Back | Bristol. *Single*

MS. Yale University Lib. Hitherto unpublished. This note appears in the second manuscript sheet of poems for vol. ii of *Lyrical Ballads.*
Stamped: Kendal.

[*Circa* 1 August 1800][2]

Memorandum. If the Printing of the second Volume have not commenced let 'The Brothers' *begin* the Volume[3]—and then the Hart-leap-well, etc, as stated in a former letter.

But if the Printing should have commenced, follow the old order. But if not, thus:

1. The Brothers. 2. Hart-leap-well. 3. There was a Boy, &c. 4. Ellen Irwin. 5. 6. 7. The Poems written overleaf.[4]

346. *To Biggs and Cottle*

Address: Messrs Biggs and Cottle | Printers | St Augustine's Back, | Bristol *Single* sheet.

MS. Yale University Lib. Hitherto unpublished. This note appears in the third manuscript sheet of poems for vol. ii of *Lyrical Ballads.* The sheet, which is entirely in Coleridge's handwriting, contains five poems, *The Waterfall and the Eglantine, The Oak and the Broom, The Fly, Lucy Gray*, and *The Idle Shepherd-Boys*, along with two notes. Coleridge prepared the sheet during Wordsworth's

[1] Manuscript cut off for signature.

[2] Coleridge was at Grasmere from 31 July to 2 Aug.; Dorothy copied *The Brothers* on 1 Aug. *Journals*, i. 53.

[3] See Letter 342.

[4] The poems in this sheet were the conclusion of *The Brothers* and *Strange fits of passion* in Dorothy's handwriting; *She dwelt among the untrodden ways* and *A slumber did my spirit seal* in Coleridge's.

stay at Keswick from 2 to 6 August, and the manuscript contains a few corrections by Wordsworth.
Postmark: 7 August 1800.   *Stamped*: Keswick.

Monday, August [4,] 1800

Memorandum—This is the second letter addressed to Messrs Biggs & Cottle—the first having been directed to Mr Davy.[1] W. Wordsworth particularly wishes, that the proof sheets may be sent to Mr Davy, with the copy—as Mr D. has kindly undertaken to correct them.

347. *To Biggs and Cottle*

[Addressed by D. W.] Messrs Biggs and Cottle | Printers | St Augustine's Back Bristol   Single sheet

MS. Yale University Lib. Pub. A Description of the Wordsworth & Coleridge Manuscripts, *by W. H. White, 1897, p. 13.* The fourth and fifth manuscript sheets for vol. ii of *Lyrical Ballads* contain sixteen poems in Dorothy's handwriting and must have been prepared during the Wordsworths' stay at Keswick from 8 to 17 August. The address page of the fifth sheet contains Coleridge's brief memorandum and the following note by Wordsworth:

The preface is not yet ready: I shall send it in a few days. I have written to Mr Longman requesting him to inform you whether he wishes to have the 1st Vol: sent up immediately before the preface is printed, which may with as much propriety be prefixed to the 2nd Vol:—The Title Page must stand thus

Lyrical Ballads
with other poems.
By W. Wordsworth
Quam nihil ad genium, Papiniane, tuum.
2nd Edition—

This Latin motto appears in John Selden's introductory letter to Drayton's *Poly-Olbion*. See *The Complete Works of Michael Drayton, 1876, i, p. xlv.*
Postmark: ⟨16?⟩ August 1800.   *Stamped*: Keswick.

[*Circa* 13 August, 1800]

Be careful to print the motto accurately—
Quam nihil ad genium, Papiniane, tuum!

348. *To Thomas Poole*

Address: Mr T. Poole | N. Stowey | Bridgewater | Somerset.
MS. British Museum. Pub. with omis. Letters, *i. 335.*
Postmark: 18 August 1800.   *Stamped*: Keswick.

Aug. 14. 1800

My dear Poole

Your two letters I received exactly four days ago—some days they must have been lying at Ambleside, before they were sent to

---

[1] Coleridge refers to Wordsworth's letter to Davy of 28 [29] July. See Letter 342.

Grasmere—and some days at Grasmere before they moved to Keswick. I read them / & liked them—and was writing them off in AGRICULTURAL LETTERS, with notes of my own,[1] when I received letters from Phillips so pressing that I was *obliged* to put the thing, I had engaged for, out of hand.—I meant to have sent the Letters to Stuart with orders to have them first in his paper, & then republished in the form of a Pamphlet.—A most important Question rises—has there been *any* Scarcity? The Newspapers are now running down the Monopolists &c—. Is it not a burning Shame, that the Government have not taken absolute means to decide a question so important? It grieved me, that you had felt so much from my silence—believe me, I have been *harrassed* with business, & shall remain so——for the remainder of this year—.

Our house is a delightful residence, something less than half a mile from the Lake of Keswick, & something more than a furlong from the town. It commands both that Lake, & the Lake Bassenthwaite—Skiddaw is behind us—to the left, the right, & in front, Mountains of all shapes & sizes—the waterfall of Lodore is distinctly visible—. In gardens, etc we are uncommonly well off, & our Landlord who resides next door in this twofold House, is already much attached to us—he is a quiet sensible man, with as large a Library as your's—& perhaps rather larger—well stored with Encyclopaedias, Dictionaries, & Histories &c—all modern.—The gentry of the Country, titled & untitled, have all called or are about to call on me—& I shall have free access to the magnificent Library of Sir Gilfred Lawson, a weak but good natured Man—. I wish, you could come here in October, after your harvesting—& stand Godfather at the christening of my child. Sara expects to lie in in the first week of September. In October the country is in all it's blaze of Beauty.—

We are well—& the Wordsworths are well— / The two Volumes of the Lyrical Ballads will appear in about a fortnight or three weeks[2]—. Sara sends her best kind love to your Mother—how much we rejoice in her health, I need not say. Love to Ward—& to Chester, to whom I shall write as soon as I am at Leisure.—I was standing on the very top of Skiddaw, by a little Shed of Slatestones on which I had scribbled with a bit of slate my name among the other names—a lean expressive-faced Man came up the Hill, stood beside me, a little while, then running over the names,

---

[1] These articles, 'Monopolists and Farmers', appeared in the *Morning Post* on 3, 4, 6, 8, and 9 Oct. 1800. Most of them are Poole's, but Coleridge wrote that of 3 Oct. and the introduction to the one of 6 Oct. See *Essays on His Own Times*, ii. 413–50.

[2] Actually the second edition of *Lyrical Ballads* did not come out until Jan. 1801, though 1800 appears on the title-page.

exclaim[ed,] *Coleridge*! I lay my life, that is the *Poet Coleridge.* | —
God bless you, & for God's sake never doubt that I am attached
to you beyond all other men.—

S. T. Coleridge

I will order the M. Posts to you that contain the Letters.—

349. *To William Godwin*

Address: Mr Godwin | Polygon | Sommers' Town | London   *Single*
MS. Lord Abinger. Pub. with omis. E. L. G. i. 151.
Postmark: 11 September 1800.   *Stamped*: Keswick.

Monday [8 September 1800]

Dear Godwin

There are vessels every week from Dublin to Workington, which
place is about 16 miles from my house thro' a divine Country—but
this is an idle regret. I know not the nature of your present pur-
suits, whether or no they are such as to require the vicinity of
large and curious Libraries— / if you were engaged in any work of
imagination, or reasoning, not biographical, not historical, I
should repeat & urge my invitation, after my wife's confine-
ment.—Our House is situated on a rising Ground, not two furlongs
from Keswick, about as much from the Lake, Derwentwater, &
about 2 miles or so from the Lake, Bassenthwaite—both lakes &
their mountains we command—the River Greta runs behind our
house, & before it too—& Skiddaw is behind us, not half a mile
distant—indeed just distant enough, to enable us to view it as a
Whole. The Garden, Orchard, Fields, & *immediate* country, all
delightful.—I have, or have the use of, no inconsiderable collection
of Books—in *my* Library you will find all the Poets & Philosophers,
& many of our best old Writers—below in our Parlor, belonging to
my Landlord, but in my possession, are almost all the usual Trash
of the Johnsons, Gibbons, Robertsons, &c with the Encyclopaedia
Britannica, &c &c. Sir Wilfrid Lawson's magnificent Library is at
some 8 or 9 miles distant—and he is liberal in the highest degree
in the management of it.—And now for your letter. I swell out my
chest, & place my hand on my heart, & swear aloud to all that you
have written, or shall write, against Lawyers & the Practice of the
Law. When you next write so eloquently & so well, against it or
against anything, be so good as to leave a larger space for your
wafer; as by neglect of this a part of your last was obliterated—
The character of Curran, which you have sketched most ably,[1] is

---

[1] For Godwin's description of John Philpot Curran (1750–1817), the Irish
judge, see *William Godwin*, ii. 5–6.

a frequent one in it's moral Essentials; tho', of course, among the
most rare, if we take it with all it's intellectual accompaniments.
Whatever I have read of Curran's has impressed me with a deep
conviction of his Genius. Are not the Irish in general a more
eloquent race, than we?—

Of North Wales my recollections are faint; and as to Wicklow,
I know only from the Newspapers, that it is a mountainous
Country. As far as my memory will permit me to decide on the
grander parts of Caernarvonshire, I may say, that the single
objects are superior to any, which I have seen elsewhere—but
there is a deficiency in combination. I know of no mountain in the
north altogether equal to Snowdon, but then we have an *encamp-
ment* of huge Mountains, in no harmony perhaps to the eye of a
mere painter, but always interesting, various, and, as it were,
nutritive. Height is assuredly an advantage, as it connects the
Earth with the Sky, by the clouds that are ever skimming the
summits, or climbing up, or creeping down the sides, or rising from
the chasms, like smokes from a Cauldron, or veiling or bridging the
higher parts or the lower parts of the water-falls. That you were
less impressed by N. Wales, I can easily believe—it is possible, that
the scenes of Wicklow may be superior, but it is certain, that you
were in a finer irritability of Spirit to enjoy them. The first pause &
silence after a return from a very interesting Visit is somewhat
connected with languor in all of us— / Besides, as you have ob-
served, Mountains & mountainous Scenery, taken *collectively* &
cursorily, must depend for their charms on their novelty— / they
put on their immortal interest then first, when we have resided
among them, & learnt to understand their language, their written
characters, & intelligible sounds, and all their eloquence so various,
so unwearied.—Then you will hear no 'twice-told tale.'—I question,
if there be a room in England which commands a view of Moun-
tains & Lakes & Woods & Vales superior to that, in which I am
now sitting. I say this, because it is destined for your Study, if you
come.—You are kind enough to say, that you feel yourself more
natural and unreserved with me, than with others. I suppose, that
this arises in great measure from my own ebullient Unreserved-
ness—something too, I will hope, may be attributed to the circum-
stance, that my affections are interested deeply in my opinions—.
But here you will meet too with Wordsworth 'the latch of whose
Shoe I am unworthy to unloose'—and four miles from Words-
worth Charles Lloyd has taken a house[1]—Wordsworth is publishing
a second Volume of the Lyrical Ballads—which title is to be dropt,

[1] The Lloyds settled at Old Brathay near Ambleside, where they remained
until 1815.

& his 'Poems' substituted[1] / Have you seen Sheridan since your return? How is it with your Tragedy?[2] Were you in town, when Miss Bayley's Tragedy was represented?[3] How was it, that it proved so uninteresting? Was the fault in the Theatre, the Audience, or the Play?—It must have excited a deeper feeling in you than that of mere curiosity: for doubtless, the Tragedy had great merit. I know not indeed, how far Kemble might have watered & thinned it's consistence—I speak of the printed Play.— Have you read the Wallenstein?—Prolix & crowded & dragging as it is, yet it is quite a model for it's judicious management of the *Sequence* of Scenes—and such it is held on the German Theatres. Our English Acting Plays are many of them wofully deficient in this part of the dramatic Trade & Mystery.

Hartley is well & all life, and action / I expect that Mrs Coleridge will lay down her burthen in 7 or 8 days—she desires to be remembered to you.—Let me hear from you when you have leisure & inclination—

Your's with | unfeigned Esteem
S. T. Coleridge

Kisses for Mary & Fanny—God love them! I wish, you would come & look out for a *house* for yourself here. You know 'I wish' is privileged to have something silly follow it——

350. *To William Godwin*

Address: Mr Godwin | Polygon | Sommers' Town | London
MS. Lord Abinger. Pub. Mary Shelley. A Biography, *by R. Glynn Grylls, 1938, p. 278.*
Postmark: 19 September 1800. *Stamped*: Keswick.

Tuesday, September 16. [1800]

Dear Godwin

Is it in your power to remit me 10£—You may depend on it's being redelivered to you on the first of next month.[4] This, I am

---

[1] Learning that Mrs. Robinson was publishing a volume entitled *Lyrical Tales*, Wordsworth planned to alter his title, but it was not changed. See *Early Letters*, 250 and note.

[2] Godwin's *Antonio* was produced by Kemble at Drury Lane on 13 Dec. 1800, and hopelessly damned. It was published in the same year.

[3] Joanna Baillie (1762–1851) published *A Series of Plays* in 1798. One of these, *De Montfort*, was produced in Apr. 1800 by Kemble, with himself and Mrs. Siddons in the leading roles, but despite the splendour of the production, the play was not a success.

[4] Coleridge kept his word. See Letter 354 to Stuart: 'You would oblige by inclosing to Mr Godwin, . . . 10£ in my name.'

afraid, will prove an untimely application / but the truth is, that by the first of October I shall have claim to as much money as I shall want——& the persons, to whom I could with more propriety have addressed myself in the mean time, than to you, opposed my settling in the North so strongly,[1] that I feel a great disinclination to write to them on any pecuniary Embarrassment, which they will attribute to my journey hither——& the consequent expences. This no doubt is the remote cause, but the immediate cause was the unexpected *necessity* of paying an old Cambridge Debt, which had pressed very little on my Conscience, and intruded very rarely into my memory. However, I was *forced* to part with eight pound at a very unseasonable time: / for, the day after, my wife presented Hartley with a little Brother.[2] She is as well as any woman in her situation, & in this climate, ever was or can be——the child is a very large one. She was brought to bed on Sunday Night ½ past 10. Will you come & stand Godfather?

If it be out of your power, I pray you, give yourself no concern about it—somehow or other I shall rub thro' the ensuing fortnight—and regard this letter only as a proof that I esteem you so much as not to be ashamed of suffering you to know any thing that befalls me—.

> Your's sincerely,
> S. T. Coleridge—

351. *To James Webbe Tobin*

Address: Mr J. W. [Tobin] | Berkley Square | Bristol   *Single*
MS. *Harvard College Lib. A few lines pub.* Christabel, *ed. by E. H. Coleridge, 1907, p. 39, and* Letters Hitherto Uncollected, *ed. W. F. Prideaux, 1913, 10.* Both E. H. Coleridge and Prideaux suggest that the letter was addressed to Humphry Davy, but J. W. Tobin was the addressee. The holograph bears evidence of tampering, the name Tobin in the salutation and address being pencilled in, probably over erasures.
Postmark: 20 September 1800. *Stamped*: Keswick.

Wednesday, Sept. 17. 1800. Grieta Hall, Keswick.—
My dear [Tobin]

Both Wordsworth and I shall be at home for these six months at least—& for aught I know to the contrary, for these six years. I need not say, how happy I shall be to see you & your friend—we

---

[1] The Wedgwoods and Poole, to whom Coleridge probably refers, strongly opposed his settling in the north. In 1813 Coleridge wrote to Poole of 'T. Wedgewood's farewell Prophecy to me respecting W., which he made me write down, and which no human Eye ever saw—but mine'. See also Letter 330.
[2] Derwent Coleridge was born 14 Sept. 1800.

have room for you—. The Miss Speddings are very good friends of
our's, and are not amiss in their exteriors, yet nothing remarkable,
in minds or bodies. They are chatty sensible women, republicans
in opinion, and just like other Ladies of their rank, in practice—.
You will no doubt see them. From Davy's long silence I augured
that he was doing something for me—I mean for me inclusive, as
a member of the Universe—God bless him! I feel more than I think
wise to express, from the disappointment in not seeing him—.
From the commencement of November next I give myself ex-
clusively to the Life of Lessing—till then I occupy myself with a
volume of Letters from Germany—to the publication of which my
Poverty but not my Will consents.——The delay in Copy has been
owing in part to me, as the writer of Christabel[1]—Every line has
been produced by me with labor-pangs. I abandon Poetry alto-
gether—I leave the higher & deeper Kinds to Wordsworth, the
delightful, popular & simply dignified to Southey; & reserve for
myself the honorable attempt to make others feel and understand
their writings, as they deserve to be felt & understood. There is no
thought of ever collecting my Morning Post Essays—they are not
worth it. Wordsworth, after these volumes have been published,
will set about adapting his Tragedy for the Stage—Sheridan has
sent to him about it. What W. & I have seen of the Farmer's Boy[2]
(only a few short extracts) pleased us very much.—

When you come, do not by any means *forget* to bring with you
a bottle of Davy's Acid for Wordsworth—. Does not Davy admire
Wordsworth's RUTH? I think it the finest poem in the collection.—
Excuse the brevity of this letter, for I am busied in writing out a
sheet for Biggs.—

Your's with unfeigned Esteem
S. T. Coleridge

P.S. My wife was safely & speedily delivered of a very fine boy on
last Sunday Night—both he & she are as well as it is possible that
Mother & new born Child can be. She dined & drank Tea *up*, in
the parlor with me, this day——and this is only Wednesday
Night!—There's for you.

Wordsworth's Health is but *so so*—Hartley is the same Animal
as ever—he moves & lives,

[1] Prior to 15 Sept., Coleridge sent to the printers all or a portion of Part I
of *Christabel*; for on that date Wordsworth wrote to Biggs informing him
that the printing of *Christabel*, if it had begun, must be delayed so that three
of his poems, which were to precede Coleridge's poem, could be inserted. See
Early Letters, 255, Letter 111.

[2] Robert Bloomfield's *Farmer's Boy* was published in a sumptuous quarto
in Mar. 1800 and sold an estimated 26,000 copies within three years.

As if his Heritage were Joy
And Pleasure were his Trade.

I heard from Godwin a few days hence—he is delighted with
Ireland & Curran——

352. *To William Godwin*

Address: Mr Godwin | Polygon | Sommers' Town | London
MS. Lord Abinger. Pub. with omis. E. L. G. i. 154.
Postmark: 25 September 1800. *Stamped*: Keswick.

Monday, Sept. 22. 1800
Dear Godwin

I received your letter, and with it the inclosed Note, which shall
be punctually redelivered to you on the first of October.—
Your Tragedy to be exhibited at Christmas!—I have indeed
merely read thro' your letter; so it is not strange, that my heart
still continues beating out of time. Indeed, indeed, Godwin! such
a stream of hope & fear rushed in on me, when I read the sentence,
as you would not permit yourself to feel. If there be any thing yet
undreamt of in our philosophy; if it be, or if it be possible, that
thought can impel thought out of the visual limit of a man's own
scull & heart; if the clusters of ideas, which constitute our identity,
do ever connect & unite into a greater Whole; if feelings could ever
propagate themselves without the servile ministrations of un-
dulating air or reflected light; I seem to feel within myself a
strength & a power of desire, that might dart a modifying, com-
manding impulse on a whole Theatre. What does all this mean?
Alas! that sober sense should know no other way to construe all
this except by the tame phrase—I wish you success.—
That which Lamb informed you, is founded in truth. Mr Sheridan
sent thro' the medium of Stewart a request to Wordsworth to
present a Tragedy to his stage, & to me a declaration that the
failure of my piece was owing to my obstinacy in refusing any
alteration. I laughed & Wordsworth smiled; but my Tragedy will
remain at Keswick, and Wordsworth's is not likely to emigrate
from Grasmere. Wordsworth's Drama is in it's present state not
fit for the stage, and he is not well enough to submit to the drudgery
of making it so. Mine is fit for nothing except to excite in the minds
of good men the hope, that 'the young man is likely to do better.'
In the first moments I thought of re-writing it, & sent to Lamb for
the copy with this intent—I read an act, & altered my opinion, &
with it my wish.—Your feelings respecting Baptism are, I suppose,
much like mine! At times I dwell on Man with such reverence,

resolve all his follies & superstitions into such grand primary laws
of intellect, & in such wise so contemplate them as ever-varying
incarnations of the eternal Life, that the Lama's Dung-pellet, or
the Cow-tail which the dying Brahman clutches convulsively,
become sanctified & sublime by the feelings which cluster round
them. In that mood I exclaim, My boys shall be christened!—But
then another fit of moody philosophy attacks me—I look at my
doted-on Hartley—he moves, he lives, he finds impulses from
within & from without—he is the darling of the Sun and of the
Breeze! Nature seems to bless him as a thing of her own! He looks
at the clouds, the mountains, the living Beings of the Earth, &
vaults & jubilates! Solemn Looks & solemn Words have been
hitherto connected in his mind with great & magnificent objects
only—with lightning, with thunder, with the waterfall blazing in
the Sunset—/—then I say, Shall I suffer the Toad of Priesthood
to spurt out his foul juice in this Babe's Face? Shall I suffer him
to see grave countenances & hear grave accents, while his face is
sprinkled, & while the fat paw of a Parson crosses his Forehead?—
Shall I be grave myself, & tell a lie to him? Or shall I laugh, and
teach him to insult the feelings of his fellow-men? Besides, are we
not all in this present hour fainting beneath the duty of *Hope*?
From such thoughts I start up, & vow a book of severe analysis,
in which I will tell *all* I believe to be Truth in the nakedest Language
in which it can be told.—

My wife is now quite comfortable—Surely, you might come, &
spend the very next four weeks not without advantage to both of
us. The very Glory of the place is coming on—the local Genius is
just arraying himself in his higher Attributes. But above all, I
press it, because my mind has been busied with speculations, that
are closely connected with those pursuits which have hitherto
constituted your utility & importance; and ardently as I wish you
success on the stage, I yet cannot frame myself to the thought,
that you should cease to appear as a *bold* moral thinker. I wish you
to write a book on the power of words, and the processes by which
human feelings form affinities with them—in short, I wish you to
philosophize Horn Tooke's System, and to solve the great
Questions—whether there be reason to hold, that an action bearing
all the *semblance* of pre-designing Consciousness may yet be simply
organic, & whether a *series* of such actions are possible—and close
on the heels of this question would follow the old 'Is Logic the
Essence of Thinking?' in other words—Is *thinking* impossible
without arbitrary signs? &—how far is the word 'arbitrary' a
misnomer? Are not words &c parts & germinations of the Plant?
And what is the Law of their Growth?—In something of this order

I would endeavor to destroy the old antithesis of *Words & Things*, elevating, as it were, words into Things, & living Things too. All the nonsense of vibrations etc you would of course dismiss.

If what I have here written appear nonsense to you, or commonplace thoughts in a harlequinade of outré expressions, suspend your judgement till we see each other.

Your's sincerely,
S. T. Coleridge

I was in the Country when Wallenstein was published. Longman sent me down half a dozen—the carriage back the book was not worth—

353. *To Daniel Stuart*

Address: Daniel St[uart] | No /   *Double Sheet.*
MS. British Museum. Pub. Letters from the Lake Poets, *11.*

[28 September 1800][1]

Dear Stuart

I have written five more Essays of the same length on this subject——namely, two on the War as respecting Agriculture, one on the Raising of Rents in consequence of high Prices of Provisions, one on the Riots—and one on the countenance which Government have given to the calumnies, &c of foolish people, on the King's Proclamation, and the probable Views of the Minister.——To morrow I shall transmit you two—two on Tuesday, and the last on Wednesday or Thursday[2]——immediately after these I will send you without fail a second Part of Pitt, & Bonaparte—better late than never.—

My wife has given me another Son—but alas! I fear, he will not live.[3] She is now sobbing & crying by the side of me.——Be so good as to have my Paper directed to me, Mr Coleridge, Greta Hall, | Keswick, Cumberland—

As it is, I never see them, till too late. . . . [Remainder of manuscript missing.]

[1] This letter, written on Sunday, obviously antedates Letter 354 by two or three days.

[2] In addition to the essays on 'Monopolists and Farmers' referred to in Letter 348, only one further prose contribution to the *Morning Post* during this period has been identified, that of 14 Oct. 1800. See *Essays on His Own Times*, ii. 451.

[3] 'September 27, 1800. The child being very ill was baptized by the name of Derwent. The child, hour after hour, made a noise exactly like the creaking of a door which is being shut very slowly to prevent its creaking.' MS. note S. T. C. See *Letters*, i. 338 n.

354. *To Daniel Stuart*

Address: Daniel Stuart Esq. | No / 335 | (Morning Post Office.) | Strand |
London   Double Sheet
MS. British Museum. Pub. Letters from the Lake Poets, *12.*
Postmark: ⟨3?⟩ October 1800. *Stamped*: Keswick.

Greta Hall, Keswick, Cumberland.
[*Circa* 30 September 1800]

Dear Stuart

I am prevented by Mrs Coleridge's distress concerning our
Infant from transcribing the fifth Essay, on this blank Paper.—
I have sent you the third and fourth. I am fearful the third is too
long, especially if you print it (as I confess, I think it well deserves)
leaded.—/ In the fifth & sixth Essays I return to the monopolists
& the Riots—and advert on the conduct & probable motives of
ministry. In [the] 7th I take a survey of what is called the Pros-
perity of the Kingdom.—You may [th]en republish PITT, to which
I shall lead— / then you shall have a second part of Pitt, &
Bonaparte.—When these are finished, I should [wis]h the whole to
be published together in the form of a Pamphlet / but of this [y]ou
will be the best Judge.—I shall send you the fifth Essay to
morrow. / —I have by me, tho' in a rough state, a very long Letter
to Sir Francis Burdett Jones,[1] on the subject of solitary imprison-
ment; concerning which I am in doubt, whether I shall publish it
just before the meeting of Parliament, in the form of a Pamphlet,
or whether I shall split [it] into a series of Letters, & send it forth
in your paper. If I were convinced, that it would be serviceable to
your paper, I should not hesitate a moment; but altho' it will not,
I trust, be found deficient in eloquence indignant & pathetic, nor
in examples various, apt, and entertaining, yet a large part of it is
devoted to the austerest metaphysical [re]asoning / and this I
suspect would ill harmonize with the tastes of [Lond]on Coffee
house men & breakfast-table People of Quality, on whom [poss]ibly
your paper depends in a great degree. But if it would [do yo]ur
paper no *good*, no positive good, I mean, I should be [reluc]tant
that a work on which I had exerted so much thought, should [be]
inserted at all. I would far rather send it to the Baronet, in manu-
script, & never publish it.—

Wordsworth's health declines constantly—in a few days his
Poems will be published, with a long poem of mine. Of course, you
will procure them. The Preface contains our joint opinions on
Poetry.[2]

[1] Sir Francis Burdett (1770–1844), the politician, whose mother was the
heiress, Eleanor Jones.
[2] Within two years Coleridge was to disavow complete agreement with

You will be so good as not to forget to have the Newspaper addressed to me, at Keswick—If these Essays should please you, & suit your purpose, and if you are not deterred by my long Silence from entering into any engagement with me, I am willing to recommence my old occupation, binding myself down to send you six columns a week / any week in which I do not send at least five Columns I should consent to be counted as nothing.—At all events, whether you enter on any engagement or no, you would oblige by inclosing to Mr Godwin, the Polygon, Sommers' Town, 10£ in my name.[1]—Before this week has passed I trust I shall have gone a good way towards earning it.—

Your's sincerely
S. T. Coleridge

355. *To Daniel Stuart*

MS. British Museum. Pub. with omis. Letters from the Lake Poets, *15.* The bottom of pages 1 and 2 of the holograph is cut off and the remainder of the manuscript is missing. Apparently Stuart crossed out the letter and turned over to the printer Coleridge's draft of *Alcaeus to Sappho.* The missing part of the manuscript may have contained *The Two Round Spaces; A Skeltoniad,* a blatant satire on James Mackintosh, Stuart's brother-in-law. (Coleridge sent the poem to Davy two days later. See Letter 356.) Writing in the *Gentleman's Magazine* in May 1838, Stuart said: 'Coleridge sent one [poem] attacking Mackintosh, too obviously for me not to understand it, and of course it was not published.' Stuart was in error. The poem appeared in the *Morning Post,* 4 December 1800, with the omission of seven offensive lines on Mackintosh.

Greta Hall, Keswick—Tuesday Night, Octr. 7—1800

Dear Stuart

The illness of my dear friend, Wordsworth, called me peremptorily to Grasmere; I have this moment returned—& found your letter.—To be known to Schiller was a thought, that passed across my brain & vanished—I would not stir 20 yards out of my way to *know* him. To *see* Bonaparte I would doubtless stir many a score miles—; but as I freely believe you, so I trust you will believe *me* when I say, that his praise or admiration or notice, were it ever in my power to attain it, might amuse me but would gratify no higher feeling.—If I know my own heart, or rather if I be not profoundly ignorant of it, I have not a spark of *ambition* / and tho' my *vanity* is flattered, more than it ought to be, by what Dr John-

Wordsworth (see Letters 444 and 449), and later, in the *Biographia Literaria,* he dealt at length with the Preface. Many years afterwards Wordsworth asserted that he 'was put upon to write' the Preface by Coleridge's 'urgent entreaties'. See *The Later Years,* i. 537, ii. 910, iii. 1248–9.

[1] See Letter 350.

son calls 'colloquial prowess', yet it leaves me in my study. This is no virtue in me, but depends on the accidental constitution of my intellect—in which my taste in judging is far, far more perfect than my power to execute—& I do nothing, but almost instantly it's defects & sillinesses come upon my mind, and haunt me, till I am completely disgusted with my performance, & wish myself a Tanner, or a Printer, or any thing but an Author.—To morrow you may *depend* on my sending you two other Numbers—and Bonaparte shall not loiter.—I should like to see Mr Street's Character.—I shall fill up these Blanks with a few Poems—. It grieves me to hear of poor Mrs Robinson's illness.[1]—Pray, who was the Author of the Imitation of Modern Poetry?[2]—It was very droll—the only fault . . . [an]d mingled the vices of other kinds of poetry . . . &

A[LC]AEUS to SAPPHO.[3]

How sweet, when crimson colors dart
  Across a breast of snow,
To see, that you are in the heart
  That beats and throbs below!

All Heaven is in a Maiden's Blush
  In which the Soul doth speak,
That it was you who sent the Flush
  Into the Maiden's cheek!

Large stedfast Eyes, Eyes gently roll'd
  In shades of changing Blue,
How sweet are they, if they behold
  No dearer Sight than you!

And can a Lip more richly glow
  Or be more fair than this?
The World will surely answer, No!
  I, SAPPHO! answer, Yes!

Then grant one smile, tho' it should mean
  A Thing of doubtful Birth,
That I may say, these Eyes have seen
  The fairest Face on Earth!

[1] Mary Robinson died 26 Dec. 1800.
[2] Cf. *Morning Post*, 2 Oct. 1800. The *Imitation* is signed merely H.
[3] First published *Morning Post*, 24 Nov. 1800. Although this poem is printed in *Poems*, i. 353, as Coleridge's, it was written by Wordsworth. See *Early Letters*, 222 and note. In sending the poem to Stuart, Coleridge did not claim it as his own, but merely said: 'I shall fill up these Blanks with a few Poems.'

356. *To Humphry Davy*

Address: Mr Davy | Pneumatic | Institution | Hot Wells | Bristol   *Single*
Sheet
MS. Royal Institution. Pub. with omis. Letters, *i. 336.*
Postmark: 13 October 1800.   *Stamped*: Keswick.

Thursday Night—Oct. 9. 1800

My dear Davy

I was right glad, glad with a *Stagger* of the Heart, to see your
writing again— / Many a moment have I had all my France-&
England-Curiosity suspended & lost, looking in the advertisement
front-columns of the Morning Post Gazetteer on *Mr Davy's*
Galvanic Habitudes of Charcoal—Upon my soul, I believe there is
not a Letter in those words, round which a world of imagery does
not circumvolve—your room, the Garden, the cold bath, the
Moonlight Rocks, Barrister Moore & simple-looking Frere /[1] and
dreams of wonderful Things attached to your name—and
Skiddaw, & Glaramára, and Eagle Crag, and you, and Words-
worth, & me on the top of them!—I pray you, do write to me
immediately, & tell me what you mean by the possibility of your
assuming a new occupation / have you been successful to the extent
of your expectations in your late chemical Inquiries ?—

In your Poem[2] 'impressive' is used for impres*sible* or passive,
is it not?—If so, it is not English—life-diffus*ive* likewise is not
English— / The last Stanza introduces *confusion* into my mind,
and despondency—& has besides been so often said by the
Materialists &c, that it is not worth repeating—. If the Poem had
ended more originally, in short, but for the last Stanza, I will
venture to affirm that there were never so many lines which so
uninterruptedly combined natural & beautiful words with strict
philosophic Truths, i.e. *scientifically* philosophic.—Of the 2, 3, 4, 5,
6th, & 7th Stanzas I am doubtful which is the most beautiful.—
Do not imagine, that I cling to a fond love of future identity—but
the thought, which you have expressed in the last Stanza, might
be more grandly, & therefore more consolingly, exemplified——I
had forgot to say—that 'sameness & identity' are words too
etymologically the same to be placed so close to each other.—

[1] Probably John Hookham Frere (1769–1846), diplomatist and translator,
afterwards one of Coleridge's intimate friends.
[2] This poem was entitled, *Written after Recovery from a Dangerous Illness.*
For the text see John Davy, *Memoirs of the Life of Sir Humphry Davy*, 2 vols.,
1836, i. 390. 'Coleridge's critical remarks apply to it as it was first written;
the words objected to are not to be found in it in its corrected printed state.'
John Davy, *Fragmentary Remains of Sir Humphry Davy*, 1858, p. 81 n.

As to myself, I am doing little worthy the relation—I write for Stuart in the Morning Post—& I am compelled by the God Pecunia, which was one name of the supreme Jupiter, to give a Volume of Letters from Germany / which will be a decent *Lounge-book*—& not an atom more.—The Christabel was running up to 1300 lines[1]—and was so much admired by Wordsworth, that he thought it indelicate to print two Volumes with *his name* in which so much of another man's was included—& which was of more consequence—the poem was in direct opposition to the very purpose for which the Lyrical Ballads were published—viz—an experiment to see how far those passions, which alone give any value to extraordinary Incidents, were capable of interesting, in & for themselves, in the incidents of common Life.[2]——We mean to publish the Christabel therefore with a long Blank Verse Poem of Wordsworth's entitled the Pedlar—I assure you, I think very

[1] A puzzling statement. *Christabel*, including the conclusion to Part II, has 677 lines. Chambers's suggestion is as good as any: 'conceivably part remained only in Coleridge's head'. *Life*, 136.

[2] On 4 Oct. Coleridge came to Grasmere, and the Wordsworths were 'exceedingly delighted with the second part of *Christabel*'. The next day 'Coleridge read a 2nd time *Christabel*; we had increasing pleasure'. But on 6 Oct. Dorothy Wordsworth's *Journal* remarks laconically, 'Determined not to print *Christabel* with the L.B.'. (*Journals*, i. 64.) Coleridge accepted this decision with apparent equanimity, but subsequent letters show that the exclusion of *Christabel* increased in him a sense of his shortcomings as a poet. (See Letters 369, 371, and 390.) In 1818 he spoke of the Wordsworths' 'cold praise and effective discouragement of every attempt of mine to roll onward in a distinct current of my own—who *admitted* that the Ancient Mariner [and] the Christabel... were not without merit, but were abundantly anxious to acquit their judgements of any blindness to the very numerous defects'. (MS. New York Public Lib.)

The determination to abandon *Christabel* involved Wordsworth in some difficulty. The first sheet of the Preface, which has a Bristol postmark of 30 September, contained the following comment: 'For the sake of variety and from a consciousness of my own weakness I have again requested the assistance of a Friend who contributed largely to the first volume, and who has now furnished me with the long and beautiful [long and beautiful *struck out in MS*.] Poem of Christabel, without which I should not yet have ventured to present a second volume to the public.' When Wordsworth decided on 6 Oct. to exclude *Christabel*, however, the Preface and all the copy, except that of Coleridge's poem, were in the printers' hands, and he was now faced with the necessity of adding more poems. Accordingly, he wrote a letter, postmarked 10 Oct., ordering the printers to cancel the sheets of *Christabel* already printed, and altering the passage from the Preface cited above to read: 'It is proper to inform the Reader that the Poems entitled The Ancient Mariner, The Foster-mother's Tale, The Nightingale, The Dungeon, and Love are written by a friend, who has also furnished me with a few of those Poems in the second volume, which are classed under the title of "Poems on the Naming of Places".' *Early Letters*, 255–6. Finally, when Coleridge did not compose any such poems (see Letter 359), Wordsworth again amended the passage in the Preface to the form in which it appeared in the 1800 edition.

differently of CHRISTABEL.—I would rather have written Ruth, and Nature's Lady[1] than a million such poems / but why do I calumniate my own spirit by saying, *I* would rather——God knows—it is as delightful to me that they *are* written—I *know*, that at present (& I *hope*, that it *will* be so,) my mind has disciplined itself into a willing exertion of it's powers, without any reference to their *comparative* value.—I cannot speak favorably of W's health—but indeed he has not done common justice to Dr Beddoes's kind Prescription. I saw his countenance darken, and all his Hopes vanish, when he saw the *Prescriptions*—his *scepticism* concerning medicines—nay, it is not enough *scepticism*!—Yet now that Peas & Beans are over, I have hopes that he will in good earnest make a fair & full Trial. I rejoice with sincere joy at Beddoes's recovery.——

Wordsworth is fearful, you have been much teized by the Printers on his account—but you can sympathize with him—. The works which I gird myself up to attack as soon as money-concerns will permit me, are the Life of Lessing—& the Essay on Poetry. The latter is still more at my heart than the former—it's Title would be an Essay on the Elements of Poetry / it would in reality be a *disguised* System of Morals & Politics—.

When you write (& *do* write soon) tell me how I can get your Essay on the nitrous oxyd—if you desired Johnson to have one sent to Lackington's to be placed in Mr Crosthwaite's Monthly parcel for Keswick, I should receive it. Are your Galvanic discoveries important? What do they lead to?—All this is *ultra-crepidation* / but would to Heaven, I had as much knowlege as I have sympathy—!——My Wife & Children are well—the Baby was dying some week ago—so the good People would have it baptized—his name is Derwent Coleridge—so called from the River: for fronting our House the Greta runs into the Derwent— / had it been a Girl, the name should have been Greta——. By the bye, Greta, or rather Grieta, is exactly the Cocytus of the Greeks—the word litterally rendered in modern English is 'The loud Lamenter'—to Griet in the Cumbrian Dialect signifying to roar aloud for grief or pain—: and it does *roar* with a vengeance!—By way of an oddity I fill up the blank space with the following

Skeltoniad[2]

(to be read in the Recitative *Lilt*)

The Devil believes, that the Lord will come
Stealing a March without beat of Drum

---

[1] Presumably *Three years she grew in sun and shower.*
[2] *Poems*, i. 353. See also headnote to Letter 355.

About the same Hour, that he came last,
On an old Christmas Day in a snowy Blast.
Till he bids the Trump sound, nor Body nor Soul stirs,
For the Dead Men's Heads have slipp'd under their Bolsters.

Ho! Ho! Brother Bard!—In *our* Church Yard
Both Beds and Bolsters are soft and green;
Save one alone, and that's of Stone
And under it lies a Counsellor Keen.
'Twould be a *square* Tomb if it were not too long,
And 'tis rail'd round with Irons tall, spear like, and strong.
From Aberdeen hither this Fellow did skip[1]
With a waxy Face and a blabber Lip,
And a black Tooth in front to shew in part[2]
What was the Colour of his whole Heart!
This Counsellor sweet! This Scotchman compleat!
Apollyon *scotch* him for a Snake—
I trust, he lies in his Grave awake!*

On the 6th of January
When all is white, both high & low,
As a Cheshire Yeoman's Dairy,
Brother Bard, ho! ho!—believe it or no,
On that tall Tomb to you I'll shew
After Sun sèt and before Cock Cròw
Two round Spaces clear of snow.
I swear by our Knight and his Forefathers' Souls,
Both in Shape and in size they are just like the Holes
    In the House of Privity
    Of that ancient Family.

On these round spaces clear of snow
There have sate in the night for an hour or so
(He kicking his Heels, she cursing her Corns
All to the tune of the Wind in their Horns)
    The Dev'l and his Grannam
    With a snow-drift to fan 'em,
Expecting and hoping the Trumpet to blow:
For they are cock-sure of the Fellow below!
    * (a *humane* Wish) *inserted by S. T. C. in the margin.*

I will say nothing about *Spring*——a thirsty man tries to think

[1] This and the six lines following were not printed in the *Morning Post*.
[2] 'Mackintosh had had one of his front teeth broken and the stump was black.' Note by Daniel Stuart, *Gentleman's Magazine*, May 1838.

of any thing, but the Stream when he knows it to be 10 miles
off!—God bless you &

Your most affectionate
S. T. Coleridge

P.S.—Love to Tobin—tell him to set off——

357. *To Thomas Poole*

Address: Mr T. Poole | Stowey | Bridgewater | Somerset
MS. British Museum. Pub. E. L. G. i. 156.
Postmark: 14 October 1800.   *Stamped*: Keswick.

[Circa 11 October 1800]

For this last fortnight, my dear Poole, I have been *about* to
write you—but jolts & ruts, and flings have constantly unhorsed
my Resolves. The truth is, the endeavor to finish Christabel,
(which has swelled into a Poem of 1400 lines[1]) for the second Volume
of the Lyrical Ballads threw my business terribly back—& now I
am sweating for it— / Dunning Letters &c &c—all the hell of an
Author. I wish, I had been a Tanner.—However to come to
business—The Essays have been published in the Morning Post /
and have (to use the cant phrase) made great *sensation*. In *one*
place only I ventured to make a slight *alteration* / and I prefixed
one Essay, *chiefly* of my own Writing, & made two or three *addi-
tions* in the enumeration of the effects of War—Now I wish all to
be republished in a small pamphlet; but should like to have one
more Essay, of considerable length, detailing the effect & operations
of paper currency on the price of the articles of Life.[2] You have
Sir Frederic Eden's Book[3] which would furnish important Docu-
ments—. In the meantime, I wish you could contrive between you
& Chester or Macky to take in the Morning Post——You will see
therein all I am able to say & reason, and your arguments will come
up in the Rear like the Roman Triarii, on whom alone, you know,
depended the Stress of the Battle, and the Hope of the Victory.—
Those hitherto published I shall cut out, & inclose in a letter (paying
the postage, that you may not lose your temper.) I shall write for
Stuart till Christmas; and intend to carry on a periodical Work,
in numbers, to be afterwards republished in a Volume. Mrs
Coleridge & Child are well—I am tolerable, only my eyes are bad—
Indeed this complaint in my poor eyes & eye lids recurs with alarm-

---

[1] See Letter 356, p. 631, note 1.
[2] For Poole's reply of 14 Nov. 1800, see *Thomas Poole*, ii. 17–20. No such
'small pamphlet' as Coleridge mentions was issued.
[3] Frederick Eden, *The State of the Poor*, 3 vols., 1797. The work has taken
a permanent place in economic literature.

ing frequency. Wordsworth's Health is very indifferent—I see him upon an average about once a month, or perhaps three weeks. Love to Ward & your Mother—

God love you, & your affectionate

S. T. Coleridge

358. *To William Godwin*

Address: Mr Godwin | Polygon | Sommers' Town | London
MS. Lord Abinger. Pub. with omis. William Godwin, ii. 11.
Postmark: 16 October 1800. *Stamped*: Keswick.

Monday, Oct. 13, 1800

Dear Godwin

I have been myself too frequently a grievous Delinquent in the article of Letter-writing to feel any inclination to reproach my friends when peradventure they have been long silent. But, this out of the question, I did not expect a speedier answer: for I had anticipated the circumstances which you assign as the causes of your delay.—

An attempt to finish a poem of mine for insertion in the second Volume of the Lyrical Ballads has thrown me so fearfully back in my *bread-and-beef* occupations, that I shall scarcely be able to justify myself in putting you to the expence of the few lines, which I may be able to scrawl in the present paper—but some points in your letter interested me deeply—& I wished to tell you so.—First then, you know Kemble, & I do not. But my conjectural Judgements concerning his character lead me to persuade an absolute passive obedience to his opinions—and this too, because I would leave to every man his own Trade. *Your* Trade has been in the present Instance, 1st to furnish a wise pleasure to your fellow-beings in general, & 2ndly to give to Mr Kemble and his associates the means of themselves delighting that part of your fellow-beings assembled in a Theatre. As to what relates to the first point, I should be sorry indeed if greater Men than Mr Kemble could induce you to alter a 'but' to a 'yet', contrary to your own convictions— above all things, an Author ought to be *sincere* to the public, and when William Godwin stands in the title page, it is implied, that W. G. approves that which follows. Besides, the mind & finer feelings are blunted by such obsequiousness.—But in the Theatre it is Godwin & Co ex professo.—I should regard it in almost the same light as if I had written a song for Haydn to compose, & Mara[1] to sing—I know indeed what is poetry, but I do not know so

[1] Franz Joseph Haydn (1732–1809), the Austrian composer, and Mrs. Gertrude Elizabeth Mara (1749–1833), the singer.

well as he & she, what will suit his notes & her voice. That actors &
managers are often wrong, is true ; but still their Trade is their Trade,
& the presumption is in favor of their being right——For the Press,
I should wish you to be solicitously nice ; because you are to exhibit
before a larger & more respectable Multitude, than a Theatre
presents to you, & in a new part—that of a Poet employing his
philosophic knowlege practically. If it be possible, come therefore,
and let us discuss every page & every line. The Time depends, of
course, on the day fixed for the representation of the Piece.—

Now for something which I would fain believe, is still more
important, namely, the propriety of your future philosophical
Speculations. Your second objection derived from the present
Ebb of opinion will be best answered by the fact, that Mackintosh
& his Followers have the *Flow*. This is greatly in your favor—for
mankind are at present *gross* reasoners—they reason in a perpetual
antithesis. Mackintosh is an oracle, & Godwin therefore a Fool.—
Now it is morally impossible that Mackintosh & the Sophists of
his School can retain this opinion—you may well exclaim with Job,
O that my Adversary would write a Book——when he publishes,
depend on it, it will be all over with him & then the minds of men
will incline strongly in favor of those who would point out in
intellectual perceptions a source of moral progressiveness. Every
man in his heart is in favor of your general principles——A party
of dough-baked Democrats of Fortune were weary of being dis-
severed from their Fellow Rich men—they want to say something
in defence of turning round—: Mackintosh puts that something in
their mouths—and for a while they will admire & bepraise him.
In a little while these men will have fallen back into the ranks from
which they had stepped out / and life is too melancholy a thing to
men in general for the doctrine of improgressiveness to remain
popular. Men cannot long retain their Faith in the Heaven *above*
the blue sky—but a Heaven they will have—& he who reasons
best on the side of that universal Wish will be [the] most popular
philosopher.—As to your first objection, that you are no logician,
let me say, that your habits are analytic ; but that you have not
read enough of Travels, Voyages, & Biography—especially, of
Men's Lives of themselves—& you have too soon submitted your
notions to other men's censures in conversation. A man should
nurse his opinions in privacy & self-fondness for a long time—and
seek for sympathy & love, not for detection or censure—. Dismiss,
my dear fellow! your theory of Collision of Ideas, & take up that of
mutual Propulsions.—I wish to write more—to state to you a
lucrative Job, which would I think be eminently serviceable to
your own mind, & which you would have every opportunity of

doing here—I now express a serious wish that you would come & look out for a house. Did Stuart remit you 10£ on my account?

S. T. Coleridge

I would gladly write any Verses, but to a Prologue or Epilogue I am absolutely incompetent. What did you mean by—Alfred?

359. *To Biggs and Cottle*

[Addressed by D. W.] Messrs Biggs & Cottle, Printers | St Augustine's Back | Bristol   Single sheet
MS. Yale University Lib. Pub. with omis. Wordsworth's Poet. Works, *ii. 111.*
Coleridge's memorandum appears on a manuscript sheet containing copies of several of Wordsworth's poems in Dorothy's handwriting.
Stamped: Keswick.

[*Circa* 17 October 1800][1]

To the Printer. The poems beginning at 'It was an April Morning:'—are to have a separate Title page & advertisement. The Title Page to be Poems on the Naming of Places.[2] The Advertisement as follows: Advertisement. By Persons resident in the country & attached to rural Objects, many places will be found unnamed or of unknown names, where little Incidents will have occurred, or feelings been experienced, which will have given to such places a private & peculiar Interest. From a wish to give some sort of record to such Incidents or renew the gratification of such Feelings Names have been given to Places by the Author & some of his Friends—& the following Poems written in consequence.——

360. *To Humphry Davy*

Address: Mr Davy | Pneumatic Institution | Hot Wells | Bristol
MS. Royal Institution. Pub. Letters, *i. 339.*
Postmark: 21 October 1800.   *Stamped:* Keswick.

October 18, 1800

My dear Davy

Our Mountains Northward end in the Mountain Carrock—one huge steep enormous Bulk of Stones, desolately variegated with the heath-plant—at it's foot runs the river Caldew, & a narrow vale

---

[1] Since this sheet begins with the concluding part of *A Poet's Epitaph*, of which the first instalment was sent to Bristol on 10 Oct. in a sheet now lost, Coleridge's note was probably written during Wordsworth's visit to Keswick of 15–17 Oct. *Journals,* i. 65–67.

[2] It would appear that Wordsworth came to Keswick with the purpose of obtaining Coleridge's contributions to *Poems on the Naming of Places.* See Letter 356, p. 631, note 2. His disappointment is reflected in an entry made in Dorothy's journal: 'Coleridge had done nothing for the L.B.' *Journals,* i. 67.

between it & the Mountain Bowscale—so narrow, that in it's
greatest width it is not more than a Furlong. But that narrow vale
is *so* green, *so* beautiful! there are moods, in which a man would
weep to look at it. On this mountain Carrock, at the summit of
which are the remains of a vast Druid Circle of Stones, I was
wandering—; when a thick cloud came on, and wrapped me in
such Darkness that I could not see ten yards before me—and with
the cloud a storm of Wind & Hail, the like of which I had never
before seen & felt. At the very summit is a cone of Stones, built by
the Shepherds, & called the Carrock *Man*—Such Cones are on the
Tops of almost all our Mountains, and they are all called *Men*. At
the bottom of this Carrock Man I seated myself for shelter; but
the wind became so fearful & tyrannous that I was apprehensive,
some of the stones might topple down upon me. So I groped my way

further down, and came to 3 Rocks, placed in this wise —

each supported by the other like a Child's House of Cards, & in the
Hollow & Screen which they made I sate for a long while sheltered
as if I had been in my own Study, in which I am now writing—
Here I sate, with a total feeling worshipping the power & 'eternal
Link' of Energy. The Darkness vanished, as by enchantment—:
far off, far far off, to the South the mountains of Glaramára &
Great Gavel, and their Family, appeared distinct, in deepest
sablest *Blue*—I rose, & behind me was a Rainbow bright as the
brightest.—I descended by the side of a Torrent, & passed or
rather crawled (for I was forced to descend on all fours) by many
a naked Waterfall, till fatigued & hungry (& with one finger almost
broken, & which remains swelled to the size of two Fingers) I
reached the narrow vale, & the single House nested in Ashes &
Sycamores—. I entered to claim the universal hospitality of this
County; but instead of the life & comfort usual in these lonely
Houses I saw dirt & every appearance of misery—a pale Wo[man]
sitting by a peat Fire—I asked her [for] Bread & Milk, & she sent
a small Child to fetch it, but did not rise herself—. I eat very
heartily of the black sour bread, & drank a bowl of milk—& asked
her to permit me to pay her. Nay, says she—we are not so scant as
that—you are right welcome—but do you know any Help for the
Rheumatics; for I have been so long ailing that I am almost fain
to die.—So I advised her to eat a great deal of Mustard, having
seen in an advertisement something about Essence of Mustard
curing the most obstinate cases of Rheumatism—but do write me,
& tell me some cure for the Rheumatism—it is in her Shoulders &
the small of her back, chiefly—I wish much to go off with some

bottles of Stuff to the poor Creature—I should walk the 10 miles, as ten yards.—With love & honor, my dear Davy, your's

S. T. Coleridge

361. *To the Editor of the 'Morning Post'*

MS. New York Public Lib. Pub. Poems, *i. 356.* E. H. Coleridge says, 'The "Lines" were never sent or never appeared in the *Morning Post.*' The poem and the letter were first published by J. D. Campbell (*Poetical Works*, 158), but he called the poem a fragment, printed the first six stanzas, and added the following comment: 'There are five stanzas more, but they are too imperfect for print' (ibid. 625). The holograph, however, contains only eight stanzas. In printing the poem I have given Coleridge's alterations, because E. H. Coleridge's recording of them varies from the original. Stanzas cancelled by Coleridge have been placed in footnotes.

[Late October 1800]

Sir

I am one among your many readers, who have been highly gratified by your extracts from Mrs Robinson's Walsingham; you will oblige me by inserting the following lines [written] immediately on the perusal of her beautiful poem, the Snow Drop.

ZAGRI.

To the Snow Drop

1

Fear no more, thou timid Flower!
Fear thou no more the winter's might;
The whelming thaw, the ponderous shower,
The silence of the freezing night!
Since Laura murmur'd o'er thy leaves
The potent sorceries of song,
To thee, meek Flowret! gentler gales
And cloudless skies belong.[1]

3 whelming thaw] *first* tempest storm, *second* howling Blast   7 meek] *originally* sweet

[1] Coleridge first wrote and then cancelled the following stanza:

1

Fear thou no more the wintry storm,
Sweet Flowret, blest by LAURA'S song!
She gaz'd upon thy slender form,
The mild Enchantress gaz'd so long;
That trembling as she saw thee droop,
Poor Trembler! o'er thy snowy bed,
With imitative sympathy
    She too inclin'd her head.

2

~~pity~~

eager ~~feelings~~ unreprov'd

~~With steady eye & brooding thought~~

Her eye with tearful meanings fraught

~~My Fancy saw her gaze at thee~~

She gaz'd, till all the body mov'd

~~Till all the moving body caught~~

Interpreting the Spirit's thought—

The Spirit's eager sympathy.

Now

~~She~~ trembled with thy trembling stem,

And while thou drooped'st o'er thy bed

      sweet

    ~~fair~~ unconscious sympathy

With ~~sweet unconscious portraiture~~

      I   the drooping

    ~~She too~~ inclin'd ~~her~~ head[1]

3

She droop'd her head, she stretch'd her arm,

She whisper'd low her witching rhymes:

Fame unreluctant heard the charm,

And bore thee to Pierian climes!

Fear thou no more the matin frost

That sparkled on thy bed of snow:

For there mid laurels evergreen

    Immortal thou shalt blow.

3 Fame unreluctant] *originally* A gentle Sylphid   6 sparkled] *originally* glitter'd

[1] Coleridge first wrote and then cancelled the following stanza, incorporating most of the lines into stanza 3.

2

She droop'd her head, she stretch'd her arm,

She whisper'd low her witching rhymes:

A gentle Sylphid heard the charm,

And bore thee to Pierian climes!

Fear thou no more the sparkling Frost,

The Tempest's howl, the Fog-damp's gloom:

For there mid laurels ever-green

    Immortal thou shalt bloom!

5 sparkling Frost] *originally* Tempest's Howl

4

Thy petals boast a White more soft,
The spell hath so perfumed thee,
That careless LOVE shall deem thee oft
A Blossom from his myrtle tree.
Then laughing at the fair deceit
Shall race with some Etesian wind
To seek the woven arboret
    Where LAURA lies reclin'd.

1 White more soft] *originally* richer white   3 That careless LOVE]
originally LOVE'S careless eye   5 Then] *originally* Now   6 Shall race]
originally He races   6 some Etesian] *originally* the western

5

All them, whom Love and Fancy grace,
When grosser eyes are clos'd in sleep,
The gentle Spirits of the place
Waft up th' insuperable steep
On whose vast summit broad & smooth
Her nest the Phoenix Bird conceals;
And where by cypresses o'erhung
    The heavenly Lethe steals.

1 All] *originally* For   4 insuperable] *originally* unvoyageable   5 vast]
originally strange   7 where] *originally* there   8 The] *originally* A

6

A sea-like sound the branches breathe
Stirr'd by the Breeze that loiters there:
And, all that stretch their limbs beneath
Forget the coil of mortal care—
Such mists along the margin rise
As heal the guests who thither come,
And fit the soul to re-endure
    It's earthly martyrdom.

3 that] *originally* who   5 Such] *first* Such *second* Strange   5 along
the margin] *originally* of magic odour   6 As] *originally* To

7

The margin dear to moonlight elves
Where Zephyr-trembling Lilies grow
And bend to kiss their softer Selves
That tremble in the stream below—

    1 moonlight] *originally* midnight

There, nightly born, does Laura lie
A magic slumber heaves her breast:
Her arm, white wanderer of the Harp,
Beneath her cheek is prest.

5 There, nightly born,] *originally* Along that marge   6 A magic] *originally* Full oft, when

8

The Harp, uphung by golden chains,
Of that low Wind which whispers round
With coy reproachfulness complains
In snatches of reluctant sound.
The music hovers half-perceiv'd
And only moulds the slumberer's dreams:
Remember'd LOVES illume her cheek
With Youth's returning gleams.

2 Which] *originally* that   7 illume] *originally* relume   8 Youth's returning] *originally* Beauty's morning

362. *To Josiah Wedgwood*

Address: Josiah Wedgewood Esq. | Gunville | near | Blandford | Dorset Single
MS. Wedgwood Museum. Pub. E. L. G. i. 157.
Postmark: 4 November 1800.   *Stamped*: Keswick.

Nov. 1. 1800.—Keswick

My dear Sir

I would fain believe, that the experiment which your Brother has made in the W. Indies, is not wholly a discouraging one. If a warm climate did nothing but only prevented him from growing worse, it surely evidenced *some* power—and perhaps a climate equally favorable in a country of more various interest, Italy or the South of France, may tempt your Brother to make a longer trial. If (disciplining myself into *silent* cheerfulness) I could be of any comfort to him by being his companion & attendant for two or three months, on the supposition that he should wish to travel & was at a loss for a companion more fit, I would go with him with a willing affection. You will easily see, my dear friend, that I say this, only to increase the *Range* of your Brother's choice—for even in *chusing* there is some pleasure.—

There happen frequently little odd coincidences in time, that recall a momentary faith in the notion of sympathies acting in absence. I heard of your Brother's Return for the first time on

Monday last (the day on which your Letter is dated) from Stod-
dart.[1]—Had it rained on my naked Skin, I could not have felt
more strangely. The three or 4 hundred miles that are between us,
seemed converted into a moral distance; & I knew that the whole
of this Silence I was myself accountable for, for I ended my last
letter by promising to follow it with a second & longer one before
you could answer the first.—But immediately on my arrival in
this country I undertook to finish a poem which I had begun,
entitled Christabel, for a second volume of the Lyrical Ballads.
I tried to perform my promise; but the deep unutterable Disgust,
which I had suffered in the translation of that accursed Wallen-
stein, seemed to have stricken me with barrenness—for I tried &
tried, & nothing would come of it. I desisted with a deeper dejection
than I am willing to remember. The wind from Skiddaw & Borro-
dale was often as loud as wind need be—& many a walk in the
clouds on the mountains did I take; but all would not do—till one
day I dined out at the house of a neighbouring clergyman, & some
how or other drank so much wine, that I found some effort &
dexterity requisite to balance myself on the hither Edge of
Sobriety. The next day, my verse making faculties returned to me,
and I proceeded successfully—till my poem grew so long & in
Wordsworth's opinion so impressive, that he rejected it from his
volume as disproportionate both in size & merit, & as discordant in
it's character.[2]—In the meantime, I had gotten myself entangled
in the old Sorites of the old Sophist, Procrastination—I had suffered
my necessary businesses to accumulate so terribly, that I neglected
to write to any one—till the Pain, I suffered from not writing,
made me waste as many hours in dreaming about it, as would have
sufficed for the Letter-writing of half a Life. But there is something
beside Time requisite for the writing of a Letter—at least with me.
My situation here is indeed a delightful situation; but I feel what
I have lost—feel it deeply—it recurs more often & more painfully,
than I had anticipated—indeed, so much so that I scarcely ever
feel myself impelled, that is to say, *pleasurably* impelled to write
to Poole. I used to feel myself more at home in his great windy
Parlour, than in my own cottage. We were well suited for each
other—my animal Spirits corrected his inclinations to melancholy;

[1] Sir John Stoddart (1773–1856), the King's and the Admiralty Advocate
at Malta, 1803–7. His sister, Sarah, married William Hazlitt. It was mainly
because of Stoddart that Coleridge went to Malta in 1804. See Letter 513.

[2] In an unpublished letter to Longman Wordsworth explains his reason for
not including *Christabel*: 'A Poem of Mr Coleridge's was to have concluded
the Volumes; but upon mature deliberation, I found that the Style of this
Poem was so discordant from my own that it could not be printed along with
my poems with any propriety.' MS. New York Public Lib.

and there was some thing both in his understanding & in his affection so healthy & manly, that my mind freshened in his company, and my ideas & habits of thinking acquired day after day more of substance & reality.—Indeed, indeed, my dear Sir, with tears in my eyes, and with all my heart & soul I wish it were as easy for us all to meet, as it was when you lived at Upcott.— Yet when I revise the step, I have taken, I know not how I could have acted otherwise than I did act. Every thing, I promised myself in this country, has answered far beyond my expectation. The room in which I write commands six distinct Landscapes—the two Lakes, the Vale, River, & mountains, & mists, & Clouds, & Sunshine make endless combinations, as if heaven & Earth were for ever talking to each other.—Often when in a deep Study I have walked to the window & remained there *looking without seeing*, all at once the Lake of Keswic[k] & the fantastic Mountains of Borrodale at the head of it have entered into my mind with a suddenness, as if I had been snatched out of Cheapside & placed for the first time on the spot where I stood.—And that is a delightful Feeling—these Fits & Trances of *Novelty* received from a long known Object. The river Greta flows behind our house, roaring like an untamed Son of the Hills, then winds round, & *glides* away in the front—so that we live in a penins[ula.]—But besides this etherial Eye-feeding, we have very substantial Conveniences. We are close to the town, where we have a respectable & neighbourly acquainta[nce] and a sensible & truly excellent medical man.— Our Garden is part of a large nursery Garden / which is the same to us & as private as if the whole had been our own, & thus too we have delightful walks without passing our garden gate. My Landlord,[1] who lives in the Sister House (for the two Houses are built so as to look like one great one) is a modest & kind man, & a singular character. By the severest economy he raised himself from a Carrier into the possession of a comfortable Independence— he was always very fond of reading, and has collected nearly 500 volumes of our most esteemed modern Writers, such as Gibbon, Hume, Johnson, &c &c.— / His habits of economy & simplicity remain with him—& yet so very disinterested a man I scarcely ever knew. Lately when I wished to settle with him about the Rent of our House he appeared much affected, told me that my living near him & the having so much of Hartley's company were great comforts to him & his housekeeper[2]—that he had no children to provide for, & did not mean to marry—& in short, that he did not want any rent at all from me.—This of course I laughed him

---

[1] William Jackson was the owner of Greta Hall.
[2] Mrs. Wilson, the children's beloved 'Wilsy'.

out of; but he absolutely refused to receive any rent for the first
half year under the Pretext, that the house was not completely
finished.——Hartley quite *lives* at the house—& it [is] as you may
suppose no small joy to my wife to have a good affectionate
motherly woman divided from her only by a Wall. Eighteen miles
from our House lives Sir Guilfred Lawson, who has a princely
Library, chiefly of natural History—a kind, & generous, but weak
& ostentatious sort of man, who has been abundantly civil to me.—
Among other raree shews he keeps a wild beast or two, with some
eagles &c——The Master of the Beasts at the Exeter change sent
him down a large Bear—with it a long letter [of] directions con-
cerning the food &c of the animal, & many solicitations respecting
other agreeable Quadrupeds which he was *desirous* to send to the
Baronet at a moderate Price, concluding in this manner—'and
remain your Honor's most devoted humble Servant, J.P.—
P.S.—*Permit* me, Sir Guilfred, to send you a Buffalo and a Rhino-
ceros.'—!——As neat a Postscript as I ever heard—! the trades-
manlike coolness with which those pretty little animals occurred
to him just at the finishing of his Letter——!!—

You will in the course of three weeks see the Letters on the rise
& condition of the German Boors.[1] I found it convenient to make
up a volume out of my Journeys &c in North Germany—& the
Letters (your name of course erased) are in the Printers' Hands—/.
I was so weary of transcribing & *composing*, that when I found
those more carefully written than the rest, I even sent them off as
they were.—

Poor Alfred! I have not seen it in print—Charles Lamb wrote
me the following account of it—I have just received from Cottle
a magnificent Copy of his Guinea Alfred! Four & 20 books to read
in the Dog Days. I got as far as the mad Monk the first day, &
fainted. Mr Cottle's Genius strongly points him to the very simple
Pastoral, but his inclinations divert him perpetually from his
calling. He imitates Southey as Row did Shakespeare with his
Good morrow to you, good Master Lieutenant!—Instead of *a* man,
a woman, *a* daughter he constantly writes 'one, a man,' 'one, a
woman,' 'one, his daughter'—instead of *the* King, *the* Hero, he
constantly writes 'He, the King'—[']He, the Hero'—two flowers
of Rhetoric palpably from the Joan. But Mr Cottle soars a higher
pitch, and when he *is* original, it is in a most original way indeed.
His terrific Scenes are indefatigable. Serpents, Asps, Spiders,
Ghosts, Dead Bodies, & Stair-cases made of NOTHING with
Adders' Tongues for Bannisters—my God! what a Brain he must
have! he puts as many Plums in his Pudding as my Grandmother

---

[1] See Letter 271 headnote.

used to do—& then his Emerging from Hell's Horrors into *Light*, & treading on pure Flats of this Earth for 23 Books together!— C.L.[1]——

My *littlest* One is a very Stout Boy indeed—he is christened by the name of 'DERWENT'—a sort of sneaking affection, you see, for the *poetical* & the *novellish* which I disguised to myself under the Shew, that my Brothers had so many children, Johns, James, Georges, &c &c—that a handsome Christian-like name was not to be had, except by incroaching on the names of my little Nephews.

If you are at Gunville at Christmas, I hold out Hopes to myself that I shall be able to pass a week with you then.—I mentioned to you at Upcott a kind of a Comedy that I had *committed*—to writing, in part.—This is in the *wind*.

Wordsworth's second Volume of the Ly. Ball. will, I hope & almost believe, afford you as unmingled pleasure as is in the nature of a collection of very various poems to afford to one individual mind. Sheridan has sent to *him* too, requesting him to write a Tragedy for Drury Lane. But W. will not be diverted by any thing from the prosecution of his Great Work.

I shall request permission to draw upon you shortly for 20£— but if it be in the least inconvenient to you, I pray you, tell me so—for I *can* draw on Longman, who in less than a month will owe me 60£, tho' I would rather not do it.

Southey's Thalaba in 12 books is going to the Press. I hear—his Madoc is to be *nonum-in-annum'd*.[2]—Besides these, I have heard of four other Epic Poems—all in Quarto! a happy age this for tossing off an *Epic* or two!——

Remember me with great affection to your Brother—& present my kindest respects to Mrs Wedgwood.—Your late Governess wanted one thing which, where there is Health, is I think indispensable in the moral character of a young person—a light & chearful Heart—. She interested me a good deal; she appears to me to have been injured by going out of the common way without any of that Imagination, which if it be a Jack o'Lanthorn to lead us out of that way is however at the same time a Torch to light us whither we are going. A whole Essay might be written on the Danger of *thinking* without Images.—

God bless you, my dear Sir, & him who is with grateful and affectionate Esteem

Your's ever

S. T. Coleridge

---

[1] Cf. *Lamb Letters*, i. 211–12. For Lamb's kindly words to Cottle on the subject of the epic, ibid. i. 216–17.

[2] Cf. Horace, *Ars Poetica*, 388. The publication of *Madoc* was delayed until 1805.

363. *To Josiah Wedgwood*

Address: Josiah Wedgewood Esq. | Gunville | near | Blandford | Dorset.
MS. Wedgwood Museum. Pub. Tom Wedgwood, *110.*
Postmark: 15 November 1800.   *Stamped*: Keswick.

Wednesday, Nov. 12 1800

My dear Sir

I received your kind letter with the 20£—My eyes are in such a state of inflammation that I might as well write blindfold—they are so blood-red, that I should make a very good Personification of Murder. I have had Leaches twice, & have now a blister behind my right Ear. How I caught this Cold, in the first instance, I can scarcely guess; but I improved it to it's present glorious state by taking long walks all the mornings, spite of the wind, & writing late at night, while my eyes were weak. I have made some rather curious observations on the rising up of Spectra in the eye in it's inflamed state, & their influence on Ideas &c—but I cannot *see* to make myself intelligible to you. Present my kindest remembrances to Mrs W. & your Brother. Pray, did you ever pay any particular attention to the first time of your little One's smiling & laughing[?] Both I & Mrs Coleridge have carefully watched our little one and noted down all the circumstances &c, under which he smiled & under which he laughed for the first six times—nor have we remitted our attention—but I have not been able to derive the least confirmation of Hartley's or Darwin's Theory.

You say most truly, my dear Sir! that a *Pursuit* is necessary—*Pursuit*, I say—for even praise-worthy Employment, merely for good, or general good, is not sufficient for happiness, is not fit for Man—

God bless you, my dear Sir! and Your sincerely affectionate
Friend,   S. T. Coleridge

P.S. I cannot at present make out how I stand in [a] pecuniary way—but I believe that I have anticipated on the next year to the amount of 30 or 40 pound probably more—

364. *To the Editor of the 'Monthly Review'*

Pub. Monthly Review, *November 1800, p. 336.* Coleridge's letter was answered by the editor as follows: 'As Mr. Coleridge has thought it worth his while to transmit the above letter, we readily insert it: but we do not see that the matter to which it relates is of much importance. We used the words "partizan of the German theatre" solely with reference to the occasion on which they were written: but perhaps the expression was too comprehensive.'

Greta Hall, Keswick   Nov. 18, 1800.

Sir,

In the review of my Translation of Schiller's *Wallenstein* (*Rev.* for October) I am numbered among the Partizans of the German Theatre. As I am confident that there is no passage in my Preface or Notes from which such an opinion can be legitimately formed; and, as the truth would not have been exceeded, if the direct contrary had been affirmed, I claim it of your justice that in your answers to Correspondents you would remove this misrepresentation. The mere circumstance of translating a manuscript play is not even evidence that I admired that one play, much less that I am a general admirer of the plays in that language.

I remain, Sir, with respect etc.
S. T. Coleridge.

365. *To Humphry Davy*

Address: Mr Davy | Pneumatic Institution | Hot Wells | Bristol
MS. Royal Institution. Pub. Letters, *i. 341.*
Postmark: 5 December 1800.   *Stamped*: Keswick.

Greta Hall, Tuesday Night, Decemb. 2, 1800

My dear Davy

By an accident I did not receive your Letter till this Evening. I would, that you had added to the account of your indisposition the probable causes of it. It has left me anxious, whether or no you have not exposed yourself to unwholesome influences in your chemical pursuits. There are *few* Beings both of Hope & Performance, but few who combine the 'Are' & the 'will be'—For God's sake therefore, my dear fellow, do not rip open the Bird, that lays the golden Eggs. I have not received your Book—I read yesterday a sort of a Medical Review about it. I suppose, Longman will send it to me when he sends down the Lyrical Ballads to Wordsworth. I am solicitous to read the latter part—did there appear to you any remote analogy between the case, I translated from the German Magazine, & the effects produced by your gas?—Did Carlisle[1] ever communicate to you, or has he in any way published, his facts concerning *Pain*, which he mentioned when we were with him? It is a subject which *exceedingly interests* me—I want to read something by somebody expressly on *Pain*, if only to give an *arrangement* to my own thoughts, though if it were well treated, I have little doubt it would revolutionize them.—For the last month I have been tumbling on through sands and swamps of Evil, & bodily

[1] Sir Anthony Carlisle (1768–1840), the surgeon.

grievance. My eyes have been inflamed to a degree, that rendered reading & writing scarcely possible; and strange as it seems, the act of poetic composition, as I lay in bed, perceptibly affected them, and my voluntary ideas were every minute passing, more or less transformed into vivid spectra. I had leaches repeatedly applied to my Temples, & a Blister behind my ear—and my eyes are now my own, but in the place, where the Blister was, six small but excruciating Boils have appeared, & harrass me almost beyond endurance. In the mean time, my darling Hartley has been taken with a stomach Illness, which has ended in the yellow Jaundice; & this greatly alarms me.—So much for the doleful! Amid all these changes & humiliations & fears, the sense of the Eternal abides in me, and preserves unsubdued

> My chearful Faith that all which I endure
> Is full of Blessings![1]

At times indeed I would fain be somewhat of a more tangible utility than I am, but so, I suppose, it is with all of us—one while cheerful, stirring, feeling in resistance nothing but a joy & a stimulus; another while drowsy, self-distrusting, prone to rest, loathing our own Self-promises, withering our own Hopes, our Hopes, the vitality & cohesion of our Being!—

I purpose to have Christabel published by itself—this I publish with confidence—but my Travels in Germany come from me with mortal Pangs. Nothing but the most pressing necessity for the money could have induced me—& even now I hesitate & tremble. Be so good as to have a copy of all that is printed of Christabel sent to me per post.[2]

Wordsworth has nearly finished the concluding Poem.[3] It is of a mild unimposing character; but full of beauties to those short-necked men who have their hearts sufficiently near their heads—the relative distance of which (according to Citizen Tourdes, the French Translator of Spallanzani)[4] determines the sagacity or stupidity of all Bipeds & Quadrupeds.—

There is a deep Blue Cloud over the Heavens; the Lakes, & the vale, & the Mountains are in darkness;—only the *summits* of all the mountains in long ridges, covered with snow, are bright to a dazzling excess. A glorious Scene!—Hartley was in my arms the other evening looking at the Sky—he saw the moon glide into a

---

[1] *Tintern Abbey*, lines 133–4.

[2] No such printed sheets have survived.

[3] *Michael*.

[4] J. Tourdes, author of *Lettre sur les Médicaments administrés à l'Extérieur de la Peau dans les Maladies*, 1797 ?, and translator of Spallanzani's *Expériences sur la Circulation*.

large Cloud—Shortly after, at another part of the Cloud several Stars sailed in. Says he—'Pretty Creatures! they are going in to s[ee] after their mother Moon.'

Remember me kindly to King. Write as often as you can; but above all things, my loved & honored dear fellow, do not give up the idea of letting me & Skiddaw see you.

God love you &
S. T. Coleridge

Tobin writes me that Thompson has made some lucrative Discovery—do you know aught about it?—

Have you seen T. Wedgewood since his return?

366. *To Thomas Poole*

Address: Mr T. Poole | N. Stowey | Bridgewater | Somerset
MS. British Museum. Pub. with omis. Letters, *i. 343.*
Postmark: 9 December 1800.   *Stamped*: Keswick.

Saturday Night—Dec. 6 1800
Greta Hall, Keswick.

My dearest Friend

I have been prevented from answering your last letter entirely by the state of my eyes, & my wish to write more fully to you than their weakness would permit. For the last month & more I have indeed been a very crazy machine, & I write at this present with 6 Boils behind my ear, the discharges from which have however both relieved the inflammation in my eyes & the rheumatic pains in the back of my head. THAT consequence of this long continued ill-health, which I most regret is that it has thrown me so sadly behindhand in the performance of my engagements with the Booksellers that I almost fear I shall not be able to raise money enough by Christmas to make it prudent for me to journey Southward. I shall however try hard for it. My plan was to go to London, & make a faint Trial whether or no I could get a sort of dramatic Romance which I had more than half finished upon the stage[1]—& from London to visit Stowey & Gunville. Dear little Hartley has been ill in a stomach complaint which ended in the yellow Jaundice & frightened me sorely as you may well believe. But praise be to God, he is recovered & begins to look like himself.—He is a very extraordinary creature, & if he live, will I doubt not prove a great Genius. Derwent is a fat pretty child, healthy & hungry. I de-

---

[1] Coleridge may refer to *The Triumph of Loyalty*, of which a fragment exists. *Poems*, ii. 1060–73.

liberated long whether I should not call him Thomas Poole Coleridge, & at least [*sic*] gave up the idea only because your Nephew is called Thomas Poole, & because if ever it should be my destiny once again to live near you, I believed that such a name would give pain to some branches of your Family—

You will scarcely exact a very severe account of what a man has been doing who has been obliged for days & days together to keep his Bed. Yet I have not been altogether idle, having in my own conceit gained great light into several parts of the human mind which have hitherto remained either wholly unexplained or most falsely explained. / To one resolution I am wholly made up—to wit, that as soon as I am a Free Man in the World of Money I will never write a line for the express purpose of money / but only as believing it good & useful, in some way or other. Altho' I am certain, that I have been greatly improving both in knowlege & power in these last twelve months, yet still at times it presses upon me with a painful Weight, that I have not evidenced a more tangible utility. I have too much trifled with my reputation.—You have conversed much with Davy—he is delighted with you. What do you think of him? Is he not a great Man, think you?—Wordsworth's second Vol. is on the point of publication—of a mild unimposing character, but full of beauties to those short-necked Men who have their heads sufficiently near to their hearts—the distance between which (according to Citizen Tourdes, the Fr. Translator of Spallanzani) determines the sagacity or stupidity of all Bipeds & Quadrupeds.

I and my Wife were beyond measure delighted by your account of your Mother's health—give our best & kindest Loves to her. Charles Lloyd has settled at Ambleside, 16 miles from Keswick. I shall not see him. If I cannot come, I will write you a very, very long Letter—containing the most important of the many thoughts & feelings, which I want to communicate to you but hope to do it face to face. Give my Love to Ward—& to J. Chester—. How is poor Old Mr Rich & his Wife?—God have you ever in his keeping, making Life tranquil to you. Believe me to be what I have been ever & am, attached to you *one* degree more at least than to any other living man.

S. T. Coleridge.

367. *To William Godwin*

Address: Mr Godwin | Polygon | Sommers' Town | London
MS. Lord Abinger. Pub. William Godwin, *ii. 13.*
Postmark: 9 December 1800.   *Stamped*: Keswick.

Saturday Night. [6 December 1800]

Dear Godwin

The cause of my not giving you that immediate explanation which you requested was merely your own intimation that you could attend to nothing until the fate of your Melpomenie was decided. The plan was this—a System of Geography taught by a re-writing of the most celebrated Travels into the different climates of the world, chusing for each climate one Traveller, but interspersing among his adventures all that was interesting in incident or observation from all former or after travellers or voyagers—annexing to each Travel a short Essay, pointing out what facts in it illustrate what laws of mind, &c &c.—If a Bookseller of Spirit would undertake this work, I have no doubt of it's becoming a standard School Book—It should be as large as the last Editions of Guthrie[1]—12 or 1400 pages. I mentioned it to you, because I thought that sort of Reading would be serviceable to your own mind—but if you reject the idea, mention it to no one, for in that case I will myself undertake it. The Life of Bolin[g]broke will never *do*, in *my* opinion—unless you have many original unpublished papers &c. The *Good* People will cry it down as a Satan's Hell-broth warmed up anew by Beelzebub. Besides, entre nous, my Lord Bolingbroke was but a very shallow Gentleman—he had great, indeed amazing *living* Talents—but there is absolutely nothing in his Writings, his philosophical Writings to wit, which had not been more accurately developed before him. All this, you will understand, goes on the supposition of your being possessed of no number of original Letters. If you are, & if they enable you to explain the junction of intellectual power & depraved Appetites, for heaven's sake, go on boldly—& dedicate the work to your Friend Sheridan. For myself, I would rather have written the Mad Mother,[2] than all the works of all the Bolingbrokes & Sheridans, & their Brother Meteors, that have been *exhaled* from the Morasses of human depravity since the loss of Paradise.—But this, my contempt of their intellectual powers as *worthless*, does not prevent me from feeling an interest & a curiosity in their moral Temperament: and I am not weak enough to hope or wish, that you should think or feel as I think & feel.

[1] William Guthrie's *A New System of Modern Geography, or a Geographical, Historical, and Commercial Grammar*, 1770, was frequently reprinted.
[2] Later entitled *Her Eyes are Wild*.

One phrase in your letter distressed me. You say, much of your *tranquillity* depends on the coming hour. I hope that this does not allude to any immediate embarrassment.—If not, I should cry out against you loudly—the motto which I prefixed to *my* Tragedy when I sent it to the manager I *felt* & have continued to feel—

Valeat res scenica, si me
Palma negata macrum, donata reducit opimum![1]

The success of a Tragedy in the present size of the Theatres (Pizarro[2] is a Pantomime) the success of a TRAGEDY is in my humble opinion rather improbable than probable—. What *Tragedy* has succeeded for the last 15 years? You will probably answer the Question by another—What Tragedy has *deserved* to succeed? and to that I can give no answer.—Be my Thoughts therefore sacred to Hope—! If EVERY *Wish* of mine had but a pair of Hands, your Play should be *clapped* thro' 160 successive nights—and I would reconcile it to my conscience (in part) by two thoughts, first that *you* are a good man; & secondly that the divinity of Shakespere would remain all that while unblasphemed by the applauses of a Rabble, who if he were now for the first time to present his pieces would hiss them into infamy. Κοῦφον ἦτορ ἔχει τὸ πλεῖστον ἀνθρώπων. The mass of Mankind are blind in heart, & I have been almost blind in my *eyes*.

For the last 5 weeks I have been tormented by a series of bodily grievances and for great part of the time deprived of the use of my poor Eyes by inflammation / and at present I have six excruciating Boils behind my right Ear, the largest of which I have christened *Captain Robert*, in honor of Defoe's Capt. Robert Boyle[3]— / Eke I have the Rheumatism in my hand—If therefore there be any thing fretful & splenetic in this Letter, you know where to lay the fault—only do not cease to believe that I am interested in all that relates to you & your Comforts. God grant, I may receive your Tragedy, with the Πότνια Νίκη in the Title page.

My darling Hartley has been ill; but is now better. My youngest is a fat little creature not unlike little Mary. God love you & S. T. Coleridge.

P.S.—Do you continue to see dear Charles Lamb often?— Talking of Tragedies, at every perusal my love & admiration of *his*

[1] Horace, *Ep.* II, i. 180–1; for *scenica* read *ludicra*.
[2] Sheridan's 'patriotic melodrama', *Pizarro*, was produced at Drury Lane on 24 May 1799.
[3] *The Voyages of Captain R. Boyle*, 1728, was not written by Defoe, but W. R. Chetwood.

Play[1] rises a peg. C. Lloyd is settled at Ambleside—but I have not seen him. I have no wish to see him, & likewise no wish not to see him.

368. *To Thomas N. Longman*

Transcript Coleridge family. Pub. E. L. G. i. 163.
Stamped: Keswick.

Monday Dec. 15 1800

Dear Sir

It gives me great pleasure that I am able to inform you, that the last sheet of the Lyrical Ballads is sent off[2]—I have already commenced negociations for securing them a fair & honest Review—I should advise that 3 or 4 Copies should be sent to different people of eminence: one to Mrs Jordan[3] (who intended to sing stanzas of the Mad Mother in Pizarro if she acted Cora again—) one to Mrs Barbauld and one to Mr Wilberforce[4]—if you agree with me Mr Wordsworth will write appropriate complimentary Letters with each / With neither of these has Mr W. any acquaintance. I propose it only as likely to push the sale—of their ultimate & permanent success I have no doubt—I am especially pleased that I have contributed nothing to the second volume, as I can now exert myself loudly and everywhere in their favor without suspicion of vanity or self-interest. I have written Letters to all my acquaintance whose voices I think likely to have any Influence. In all this I am guided, if I know my own heart, wholly & exclusively by my almost unbounded admiration of the poems—The second volume is indeed greatly superior to the first.—Now for myself. In Christmas week I shall be in London, & I will explain to you the delay in my manuscript / tho' indeed the explanation is short enough. After I had finished the work & written you, I was convinced by a friend that a long account which I had given of the Illuminati would raise a violent clamour against me & my publisher—yet I have said nothing but what I am afraid was the truth / at the same time Mr Wordsworth who had been in a different part of Germany offered me the use of his Journal tho' not of his name—I immediately resolved to throw my work into Chapters instead of Letters, & substitute my friend's account of Germany farther south than I

[1] *John Woodvil*, published 1802.

[2] Actually, the last of the material for the *Lyrical Ballads* did not arrive in Bristol until 23 Dec.

[3] Mrs. Dorothea Jordan (1762–1816), the actress.

[4] William Wilberforce (1759–1833), the parliamentary leader of the abolitionists. For Wordsworth's letter to Wilberforce, which was composed by Coleridge, see Letter 375.

had been instead of the obnoxious Letters. This however would have taken so little time that you would have had the copy, within a week or ten days at most later than the day appointed— but at that time a complaint seized my head & eyes, which made it impracticable for me even to read, and after a six weeks' continuance, during which time I had in vain used Leaches, Blisters, & God knows what, it was carried off by six large Boils which appeared behind my ear down to my shoulder & which are not yet quite healed—I leave this place the day after Christmas Day, & you may depend on it that from the first of January to the printing of the last page your Printer shall not have to complain of an hour's delay.[1]

Mrs Coleridge & my two children are well. You will present my best respects to Mrs Longman & believe me, dear Sir, with a great sense of your constant civility

Your obliged humble Servant,
S. T. Coleridge.

369. *To John Thelwall*

Address: Mr Thelwall | Llynswen | (by the three cocks) | near the | Hay | Brecknockshire   [Readdressed in another hand] Widemarsh Street | Hereford
MS. Pierpont Morgan Lib. Hitherto unpublished.
Stamped: Keswick.

Keswick, Cumberland   Dec. 17th, 1800.

Dear Thelwall

I should have ruined a richer man than you or myself, if I had written to you as often as I have thought of you with tender recollections, or as often as I have felt for your afflictions with dim eyes.—But, in truth, my old aversion from letter-writing has become tenfold—I am *hardened* in the sin, and enjoy that deep calm of a seared Conscience, which precedes the Devil's Whirlwinds in Reprobate Spirits.—I write now to know certainly whether you are still at Lyswin Farm—& whether I have directed the present Letter so as to find you in the best & speediest way. A young man (I am not permitted to mention his name) whose principles are not over democratic, but who honours your talents & purity of intention, desired me in my own person, and as from myself, to assume the privilege of friendship & send you 10£—this of course I would not do, both because it would give you a most inaccurate idea of the state of my pecuniary circumstances, & because it is right for you to know that you are honored where you have never been seen,

---

[1] It is worth remarking once for all that Coleridge did not publish a German tour.

and by others than of your own political sentiments, & because, I cannot but believe, that it will gratify you to be assured, that to all, who know me intimately, I labor to communicate my own affectionate Esteem for you. I shall receive the money to a certainty at the latter end of this week—a trifle in itself, but probably it may be useful to you, and it should contribute to your pleasure in receiving it, that it was *no* trifle in the pocket from which it came, inasmuch as the most honorable situation an ill-used Man can occupy, is to be considered by good men as the object of a public *Duty*.—Write to me all particulars of yourself, I mean, your present Self—& whether in the higher excitements of mind, ratiocinating or imaginative, you have been able to conjure up *religious* Faith in your Heart, and whether if only as a Ventriloquist unconscious of his own agency you have in any mood or moment thrown the voice of your human wishes into the space without you, & listened to it as to a Reality.—For even that is something. I am settled in this delightful county comfortably—Wordsworth lives 13 miles from me. My literary pursuits are, 1 the Northern Languages, the Sclavonic, Gothic, & Celtic, in their most ancient forms, as an amusing study, & 2. as a serious object, a metaphysical Investigation of the Laws, by which our Feelings form affinities with each other, with Ideas, & with words. As to Poetry, I have altogether abandoned it, being convinced that I never had the essentials of poetic Genius, & that I mistook a strong desire for original power.—My Wife, and Hartley are well—little Berkley is gone from us—but we have another little one, christen'd Derwent, who was born Sept. 14. 1800.—I would you had sympathy enough with my Christian Hope to receive comfort from my Wish, that our little ones may have met & talk'd of their Fathers in a happier Place.—My kindest Love to your Wife. If you are writing any poems, & want a lively Idea of Murder personified, it is a pity you can not see *me*—: for I have two blood-red Eyes that would do credit to Massacre itself!

God bless You & S. T. Coleridge

370. *To William Godwin*

Address: Mr Godwin | Polygon | Sommers' Town | London
MS. Lord Abinger. Pub. with omis. William Godwin, *ii. 15.*
Postmark: 20 December 1800.   *Stamped*: Keswick.

Greta Hall, Keswick.   Wednesday Night, Dec. 17. 1800
Dear Godwin

I received the Newspaper with a beating heart & laid it down with a heavy one. But cheerily, Friend! it is worth something to have learnt what will not please. Kemble, like Saul, is among the Prophets——The account in the Morning Post was so unusually well written & so unfeelingly harsh, that it induced suspicions in my mind of the Author—Stuart assuredly, nor any of his regular workmen, wrote it.

If your Interest in the Theatre is not ruined by the fate of this, your first piece, take heart, set instantly about a new one, and if you want a glowing Subject, take the Death of Myrza, as related in the Holstein Ambassador's Travels into Pe[r]sia, in p. 93. Vol. II of Harris's Collections.[1] There is Crowd, Character, Passion, Incident, & Pageantry in it—& the History is so little known, that you may take what Liberties you like without Danger. It is my present purpose to spend the two or three weeks after the Christmas Week in London / then we can discuss all & every thing. Your last play wanted one thing, which I believe is almost indispensable in a play—a *proper Rogue*, in the cutting of whose throat the Audience may take an unmingled pleasure. I go to Grasmere at the end of the week——if you should wish to write to me, direct thus

> Mr Wordsworth, | Grasmere, | near | Ambleside, | Westmore-
> land.   For | Mr Coleridge

We are all tolerably well.—God love you, and

S. T. Coleridge

P.S. There is a Paint, the first coating of which, put on paper, becomes a dingy black, but the second turns to a bright *gold* Color.—So I say—Put on a second Coating, Friend!—

371. *To Francis Wrangham*

Address: Revd F. Wrangham | Hunmanby | near | Burlington [Bridlington]
MS. New York Public Lib. Pub. E. L. G. i. 165.
Stamped: Keswick.

Greta Hall Keswick.   Dec. 19, 1800

My dear Wrangham

Rather than not answer your kind letter immediately, I have made up my mind to write but half a dozen Lines, as a sort of promissory Note. Wordsworth received your letter, & meant to have answered it immediately. I'll write to him *to day*, quoth he. For you must understand, that *W.* has innovated very vilely the good old *Common-Law* of Procrastination—instead of Tomorrow,

---

[1] John Harris, *Navigantium atque Itinerantium Bibliotheca*, 2 vols., 1705.

& To Morrow, & To Morrow, it is To Day, To Day, and To Day, which I the more disapprove of, as it appears to me a tame Plagiarism from the Lie of the Taverns & Coffee Houses—'Coming *this instant*, your Honor!'—But seriously, he is a hardened offender in these sins of Omission—& has so many claims of an elder Date to satisfy, that verily I believe he had a scruple of conscience against writing to *you*, lest he should give that to Pleasure which he had in so many instances refused to Duty——Wordsworth & I have never resided together—he lives at Grasmere, a place worthy of him, & of which he is worthy—and neither to Man nor Place can higher praise be given. His address is,

Grasmere, near Ambleside, | Westmoreland.

As to our literary occupations they are still more distant than our residences—He is a great, a true Poet—I am only a kind of a Metaphysician.—He has even now sent off the last sheet of a second Volume of his Lyrical Ballads—.

I have ample House-room for you, and you shall have whenever you come a good bed, a good dinner, a kind welcome, & as Alcaeus say[s] ἡδὺν οἶνον ἡδυτέρας τε Μώσας—to which I may add, diviner Prospects than his Lesbos could boast. In truth, my Glass being opposite to the Window, I seldom shave without cutting myself. Some Mountain or Peak is rising out of the Mist, or some slanting Column of misty Sunlight is sailing cross me / so that I offer up soap & blood daily, as an Eye-servant of the Goddess Nature.—I shall be glad to see a Poem from you on so interesting a subject—Poor Godwin!—I am told, it was a dull Tragedy damn'd—from whence you may conclude that it was a damn'd dull Tragedy—yet I liked it in it's unfinished state when I saw it in Manuscript——I have two fine little boys—God bless you,

& S. T. Coleridge

P.S. My House stands on the River Grieta, which is a literal Translation of the Word Cocytus—

Nam'd from lamentation loud
Heard on the rueful stream.[1]

To griet is to lament aloud, and a is the masculine termination of the substantive—

---

[1] *Paradise Lost*, ii. 579–80.

372. *To Biggs and Cottle*

[Addressed by D. W.] Messrs Biggs and Cottle | Printers | St Augustine's
Back | Bristol   Single Sheet
MS. Yale University Lib. Hitherto unpublished. This memorandum precedes
a copy made by Coleridge of the first 216 lines of *Michael* as it appeared in
1800; the remainder of the poem, probably transcribed by Sara Hutchinson,
is in a separate sheet.
Postmark: 23 December 1800.   *Stamped*: Keswick.

Michael, a pastoral Poem.

(N.B. This poem with a separate title-page; & be so good as to put
a very large Capital letter where there is one in the MS., with
more than an ordinary interspace between the Paragraphs.)

PRINTED IN
GREAT BRITAIN
AT THE
UNIVERSITY PRESS
OXFORD
BY
CHARLES BATEY
PRINTER
TO THE
UNIVERSITY